A Financial History of Western Europe

By the same author

International Short-Term Capital Movements (1937)
The Dollar Shortage (1950)
International Economics (1953)
The Terms of Trade: A European Case Study (1956)
Economic Development (1958)
Foreign Trade and the National Economy (1962)
Economic Growth in France and Britain, 1851–1950 (1964)
Europe and the Dollar (1966)
Europe's Post-war Growth: The Role of the Labor Supply (1967)
American Business Abroad: Six Lectures on Direct Investment (1969)
Power and Money: The Politics of International Economics and the Economics of International Politics (1970)
The World in Depression, 1929–1939 (1973; rev. ed., 1986)
Economic Response: Comparative Studies in Trade, Finance and Growth (1978)
Manias, Panics and Crashes: A History of Financial Crises (1978; rev. ed., 1989)
International Money: A Collection of Essays (1981)
Multinational Excursions (1984)
Keynesianism vs Monetarism and Other Essays in Financial History (1985)
Marshall Plan Days (1987)
International Capital Movements: The Marshall Lectures (1987)
The International Economic Order: Essays on Financial Crisis and International Public Goods (1988)
The Germany Economy, 1945–1947: Charles P. Kindleberger's Letters from the Field (1989)
Economic Laws and Economic History: The 1980 Mattioli Lectures (1990)
Historical Economics: Art or Science? (1990)
The Life of an Economist: An Autobiography (1991)
Mariners and Markets (1992)

A Financial History
of Western Europe

SECOND EDITION

Charles P. Kindleberger

New York   Oxford
OXFORD UNIVERSITY PRESS
1993

Oxford University Press

Oxford New York Toronto
Delhi Bombay Calcutta Madras Karachi
Kuala Lumpur Singapore Hong Kong Tokyo
Nairobi Dar es Salaam Cape Town
Melbourne Auckland Madrid

and associated companies in
Berlin Ibadan

Copyright © 1993 by Oxford University Press, Inc.

Published by Oxford University Press, Inc.,
200 Madison Avenue, New York, New York 10016

Library of Congress Cataloging-in-Publication Data
Kindleberger, Charles Poor, 1910-
A financial history of western Europe / Charles P. Kindleberger. -
- 2nd ed.
p.   cm. Includes bibliographical references and index.
ISBN 0-19-507737-7   —   ISBN 0-19-507738-5 (pbk.)
1. Finance—Europe—History. I. Title.
HG186.A2K56 1993
332′.094—dc20   92-24425

9 8 7 6 5 4 3 2 1

Printed in the United States of America
on acid-free paper

A Financial History
of Western Europe

SECOND EDITION

Charles P. Kindleberger

New York   Oxford
OXFORD UNIVERSITY PRESS
1993

Oxford University Press

Oxford   New York   Toronto
Delhi   Bombay   Calcutta   Madras   Karachi
Kuala Lumpur   Singapore   Hong Kong   Tokyo
Nairobi   Dar es Salaam   Cape Town
Melbourne   Auckland   Madrid

and associated companies in
Berlin   Ibadan

Published by Oxford University Press, Inc.,
200 Madison Avenue, New York, New York 10016

Oxford is a registered trademark of Oxford University Press

Library of Congress Cataloging-in-Publication Data
Kindleberger, Charles Poor, 1910-
A financial history of western Europe / Charles P. Kindleberger. -
- 2nd ed.
p.   cm. Includes bibliographical references and index.
ISBN 0-19-507737-7   —   ISBN 0-19-507738-5 (pbk.)
1. Finance—Europe—History.   I. Title.
HG186.A2K56   1993
332′.094—dc20   92-24425

9 8 7 6 5 4 3 2 1

Printed in the United States of America
on acid-free paper

To S. M. K.
Still again, after fifty-five years,
with feeling.

Preface

The primary reason to revise a work like this is to incorporate in it what the author has learned since the initial writing and to correct mistakes, often pointed out by reviewers. Revising a textbook is perhaps different, bringing the work up to date but also incorporating a touch of planned obsolescence. It is not clear to me whether this is a textbook or more nearly a work of reference. It was initially written from notes for a course I gave twice, but I am unaware that similar courses are given elsewhere. In any event, I have learned a bit more about the subject since completing the draft written in 1982, particularly going back in time to the sixteenth and seventeenth centuries, and at the nearer end, watching European monetary integration unfold in the daily issues of the *New York Times*.

The research on the centuries from 1492 came about more or less by accident. Based on a slight acquaintance with Thomas Mun's *England's Treasure by Forraign Trade* (1664, but written in the 1620s), I was asked to write an introduction for a German publisher's facsimile edition of the book; it required substantially deeper knowledge than I possessed of mercantilism, especially in currency questions. And at an international economic history congress, a young scholar, Mark Steele, wondered why I had not included in Chapter 13, on transfer cases, the story of how the Spanish kings supplied money to their generals in Flanders fighting in the Counter-Reformation (1572–1652), money needed to pay their mercenary troops, by means of *asientos*. The answer was ignorance, which, however, proved to be correctible within limits. These investigations led to a more ambitious study of the worldwide distribution of Spanish silver produced in Peru after 1560, and later Mexico, largely through Europe to the Far East, but some directly. In due course I was caught up in the so-called *Kipper- und Wipperzeit*, a rampant inflation of 1619–23, starting before the Thirty Years' War of 1618–48 in the Holy Roman Empire (largely German principalities, city-states, and the like), different from but with some similarities to the monetary chaos in Germany after World Wars I and II. Further gaps in the coverage of Chapter 15 on financial crises, and in the monograph on which it is based, were plugged to an extent in papers commissioned, one for a conference, another for a Festschrift.

As I start the revision, the press records the retirement of Karl Otto Pöhl, president of the German Bundesbank, and his sharp criticism of the West German government for the way it went about incorporating East Germany in the financial institutions of the West. There are further exciting issues about monetary institutions in the dissolved Soviet Union. Happily for the completion of the revision, I leave these questions to others. The book remains focused on Western Europe, although some issues touch on Austria in Central, Scandinavia in the North, and Italy and Spain in the South.

In the papers on financial history written since 1984, I acknowledged with thanks the generous assistance of a number of scholars. I forbear from repeating their names here, except for Professor Wolfram Fischer of the Free University of Berlin, who went well beyond the limits of collegial friendliness in supplying me with copies of hard-to-locate articles in German provincial historical quarterlies, and Mark Steele for overcoming his shyness toward one more than twice his age and pointing to the gaping hole in my coverage. Leonard Miall, who provided the epigraph for Chapter 4 in the first edition from G. K. Chesterton's *The Flying Inn,* which could not then be verified, has, with the help of the agony column of the magazine *Quote ...Unquote,* put me deeper in his debt by providing the precise quotation from Chesterton's *Napoleon of Notting Hill* for this revised edition.

A revision is not a complete rewriting. When the original version referred to a scholar's thought as I knew it then, I do not feel obliged to find out whether he or she has had a change of mind. Apologies may thus be due to some whose more mature views are misrepresented.

Lexington, Mass.   C. P. K.
June 1992

Apologies and Acknowledgments
from the First Edition

An obvious criticism of this book is that it relies almost entirely on secondary sources. But this, I think, is inevitable with any work of synthesis having a wide scope; and such works are surely of value, not only to the general reader but also to the scholar who, working on original sources, while investigating in detail a narrow field, is always in danger of seeing no further than the hedges around his own field.
(D. P. Walker in the *New York Review of Books,* 29 October 1979, reviewing Elizabeth I. Eisenstein, *The Printing Press as an Agent of Change*)

When a widower friend of ours married another friend, a widow, my wife said, "Goody: I love to use up leftovers." So do I, and this book is the writing out of lecture notes of a course given first at the University of Texas at Austin in the spring of 1979 and again at MIT in the fall of 1980. If I were to pursue the rather disagreeable metaphor, I might add that most of the ingredients come from the store, rather than being homemade.

Some years ago I reviewed a book with a broad overview of economic history and concluded that the author was superficial on everything I knew well but very good on what I did not. This finally struck me as a compliment, and I hope to do as well.

The organization of the book will confuse some and irritate others, but it represents a somewhat arbitrary choice among the inevitable compromises between a functional and a chronological arrangement. More than half of the book—fifteen of twenty-four chapters—is devoted to roughly four centuries to 1914, and the last half to the seventy years since then. The first section is divided into "parts" dealing with money, banking, and finance, with the last consisting in an *omnium gatherum* for governmental and private finance, together with foreign lending and a chapter on national and international financial crises, sandwiched in more or less arbitrarily. The rest of the book consists of two parts. Part IV deals with the interwar period from 1914 to 1939, again organized partly as a functional discussion of the problems of various European currencies as they recovered from the financial strain of war, and partly chronologically. Part V brings the story down almost to the present with wartime and postwar financial reconstruction after World War II and a chapter on the unfinished process of European financial integration.

The book is not statistical for two reasons: it is not my style, and statistics do not go back far on most aspects of the subject.

While there is some danger to them of implicating people in this work, I have taken advantage of my position as teacher to extend my reach through term papers of students not only in the courses mentioned but also in earlier courses on European economic history generally. I may omit some names because I have not always taken full notes, but the record shows that I have been helped by Stuart Glosser, William Pierson, Joseph Ricciardi and Ross van Wassenhove at the University of Texas, and by Dean Amel, Scott Bales, Axel Börsch-Supan, Riccardo Faini, David Johnson, Stephen Kanner, Arnold Kling, Adam Lerrick, Stephen Lewis, Alan Marcus, Robert MacCauley, Ian McKenzie, Angelo Melino, Anthony Pappas, Matthew Shapiro, Martin Ramsler, Christophe Riboud, John Rust, George Thaler, Jean Tirole, and José Vinals-Iniquez in my MIT classes, some students attending from Harvard. At a somewhat more senior level, I have benefited from communications in the form of reprints, elusive references, answers to specific questions, and the like from Knut Borchardt, Jean Bouvier, Michel Brugière, Gordon Craig, Scott Eddie, Gershon Feder, David Good, Raymond Goldsmith, Earl J. Hamilton, David Lewis, Maurice Lévy-Leboyer, Bernard Malamud, Larry Neal, Sidney Pollard, Barry Supple, Herman Van der Wee, Karen Vaughn, and H.R.C. Wright. Peter Bernholz and I had a series of useful discussions. Edward Shaw and Walter J. Levy read Chapters 5 and 7, respectively. Peter Bernstein, Carlos Diaz-Alejandro, and Peter Temin read a number of chapers and offered useful comments. My greatest debts, however, are to Rondo Cameron and Philip Cottrell, who went through the entire work with great care and wide knowledge and gave me the benefit of their detailed and frank criticism. Since I did not always accept their suggestions for improvement, neither is to be blamed for its remaining shortcomings.

First drafts of Chapters 2 to 20 were written in the spring of 1981 at the Center for Advanced Study in Behavioral Science at Stanford, California, under a grant from the National Science Foundation, no. BNS 76 22943. The center is the nearest thing to a scholar's heaven that I can imagine. I am enormously grateful to it, to its leadership and staff, and especially to the enthusiastic word processors, Anna Tower and Barbara Witt, and to Dorothy Brothers, who added the foreign accents that the culture-bound machine, a Xerox 360 word processor, was unable to provide. The remaining typing was performed partly at MIT by Meg LeClair and partly at Middlebury, Vermont, with a grant from Middlebury College, by Helen Reiff. Virginia Van Vranken checked the references against the text.

Lincoln, Mass.   C. P. K.
June 1982

Contents

III   *Finance, 153*

V   After World War II, 391

A Financial History of Western Europe

1

Introduction

> The nations with which economic historians are chiefly concerned organize their economic activities under the form of making and spending money. . . . Cannot economic history be organized most effectively around the evolution of pecuniary institutions?
> (Mitchell, 1944 [1953], "The role of money in economic history," p. 67)

It is not clear that there is need to justify a financial history of western Europe. The fact that no such modern history exists is not enough, for none may be needed. There are monetary histories of the world (Vilar, 1969 [1976]; Groseclose, 1934 [1976]; perhaps Galbraith, 1975) and several financial histories of separate countries. The latter miss out on comparison; the former are perhaps too diffuse. Europe, and more particularly western Europe, appeals to me as the ideal subject for specialized history because it constitutes a unit, made up of somewhat but not entirely disparate elements, because it was the breeding ground of modern world economic history, and because it enables us to trace financial evolution as financial preeminence moves after the Middle Ages from the Italian city-states to Spain, southern Germany, the Low Countries, France, and Britain. Western European connections with the rest of the world—the Levant, Far East, Russia, Africa, after 1492 North and South America, and ultimately the Antipodes—cannot be ignored. But western Europe is a unit that can be disaggregated. Its elements are alike in broad terms, different in detail. As such, it constitutes a good background for ranging economic theories against the facts of history and, if possible, deriving theories from accumulated fact.

COMPARATIVE FINANCIAL HISTORY

My interest is in comparative financial history, or perhaps it would be more accurate to say in comparative historical money, banking, and finance. Most of economics today is deductive in character, the construction of mathematical models of beauty and elegance, without in all cases a close approximation to human behavior. History can serve as a laboratory to test whether such theories are useful to political economists, with their interest in policy, and comparative economic history can test for generality, to set aside the theories that fit only the single case. There is a considerable difference between the purposes of social scientists and historians in all this. The former are looking for generality, as they seek to uncover the laws of human society, the latter for an explanation of an individual case. I may make too much of this (see, for example, J. G. Williamson, 1978, p. 788), but comparative historical economics, I contend, is a necessary adjunct of economic theory. In a strong view, moreover, an economic historian contends that economic history develops more facts, better facts, better economic theory, better economic policy, and better economists (McCloskey, 1976). Three types of comparative history have been distinguished (Cantor, 1971): the impressionist or romantic that searches for parallels; the quantitative of the sort undertaken by Bairoch, Chenery, Goldsmith, Kuznets, or Maddison; and the sociological or model building that provides criteria for looking from one country to another for general explanations. I aspire to the third but may fall into the trap of the first.

FINANCE

So much for history. Why finance? General economic history runs the risk of being unfocused. Economists have a lot to say about partial equilibrium problems—changing one variable while the rest of the system is assumed to be unchanged or enclosed in the protection of *ceteris paribus,* other things equal. General equilibrium analysis in which anything else can be affected by the initial shock or disturbance and reverberate through the system, setting up repercussions and feedbacks, is a much harder task—some think close to impossible. Economic histories are usually organized around some theme, thread, or thesis, whether economic growth, the level of living, technical change, distribution of income, or something else. Financial history has a particular interest for those of us who were raised on the subject, and it poses some deep, even imponderable, questions of its own.

In the first place, one may ask whether monetary and financial events and institutions matter. In the Keynesian revolution of the 1930s, it was concluded (briefly) that money did not matter. Antithesis in the monetary counter-revolution took the form that money alone mattered. Synthesis: money matters along with other things. In this context, debate runs between changes in money supply and changes in spending—in technical jargon between shifts in the L-M curve (representing the relationship of the money supply to interest rates) and the I-S curve (setting out equilibrium positions at which savings equals investment at various interest rates)—as to which dominates changes in national income and prices in such an episode as the Great Depression that began in 1929. In *Did Monetary Forces Cause the Great Depression?* (1976), Peter Temin has argued against the monetarist views of Milton Friedman and Anna Schwartz (1963), contending that a sharp reduction of spending produced the depression and brought about the decline in money supply, rather than that an independent reduction in the money supply gave rise to the decline in spending. The debate has continued (Brunner, ed., 1981). In his *Lessons from the Great Depression,* Temin argues that the gold standard mentality produced deflationary policies in the leading countries—Britain, France, Germany, and the United States—and that peoples' expectations of further deflation in turn produced the depression (1989, p. 58). My own view is that the causes of the 1929 depression were considerably more complex and involved than most of the parties to the debate allow (Kindleberger, 1973 [1986], 1979 [1985], 1981*b*). In a historical context, W. W. Rostow in *The World Economy* (1978, pp. xlii–xliii) sets out an ultra-Keynesian view:

> For some, at least, monetary affairs will appear to have been slighted. In the analysis of the pre-1914 era monetary affairs appear only when I believe they left a significant impact on the course of events, e.g. transmitting the effects of bad harvests in the eighteenth and nineteenth centuries; in helping create the settings for cyclical crises and then (in Britain at least), cushioning their impact; in stimulating, under the gold standard, the inflationary diversion of resources to gold mining. In the post-1918 world of more conscious monetary policies, they emerge on stage in the 1920s with the French devaluation and the British return at the old rate, as well as the failure of the United States to accept its responsibilities for the trade and monetary structure of the world economy. After 1945, the rise and fall of Bretton Woods forms, of course, a part of the narrative.
>
> Nevertheless it should be underlined that the view taken here of the course of production and prices—in cycles, trend periods, and in the process of growth itself, would regard non-monetary factors as paramount. . . . Men and societies have devised and evolved monetary systems which more or less met their deeper needs and purposes as they conceived them. Different monetary policies, at different times and places, might have yielded somewhat different results than history now records. The same could be said with equal or greater strength about fiscal policies. But down to 1914 modern concepts of monetary and fiscal policy did not exist, except perhaps in a few unorthodox minds: and prevailing notions ordered the monetary system substantially passive and responsive.

In a subsequent essay, Rostow (1980) defends this position, insisting that pre-1914 monetary systems were passive and flexible and that price changes emanated from the supply side through changes in output and costs rather than from demand through the money supply. This view has not gone unchallenged, however (Bordo and Schwartz, 1980; Sylla, 1980).

The quotation from Rostow is given at length because it neatly poses the central issue of this book. The sharp discontinuity that Rostow sees at the time of World War I is doubtful on the face of it—although a glance at the Contents will show that I give a disproportionate share of attention to the almost eighty years after 1914, as compared with the four centuries before it. Equally dubious in my judgment is the view that finance is almost always accommodating and flexible, rather than—fairly often—an independent force for good or ill. One can easily exaggerate the importance of finance, both when it is skillfully conducted and when it is not, but the suggestion that it usually falls into line and accommodates real forces—discoveries, inventions, population change, and the like—stretches belief. Indeed, we shall encounter the view that discoveries themselves on occasion have been induced by the need for more money.

That institutions do not matter is the essence of the so-called Coase theorem (1937, 1960), which maintains that demand and supply call the tune and that institutions dance to it. Institutionalists, of course, take exactly the contrary position, asserting that relationships among the actors in the economy encrusted in habitual or customary attitudes and ways of doing things are often (usually?) critical to how an economy behaves. Along with institutionalists, many other groups have thought that financial events and decisions have had a major influence on economic outcomes, namely, mercantilists, bullionists, monetarists, Keynesians, historians of the British national debt (Dickson, 1967), of the French Revolution (Bosher, 1970), or French postwar foreign policy in the 1920s (Schuker, 1976), and so on. Schumpeter explicitly contrasts monetary analysis with real analysis, doubting that money can *ever* (his emphasis) be "neutral" in any meaningful sense (1954, pp. 277–78). A distinguished group of economic historians—Hoselitz (1956), Gerschenkron (1962), and Cameron (1961)—have ascribed primary importance in the economic growth of France in the middle of the nineteenth century to the establishment of a particular kind of bank, the Crédit Mobilier, although, as often happens, opinion has backed off a few steps from the original bold assertion that this sort of bank was a substitute for missing entrepreneurship not only in French industry but throughout continental western Europe. In a subsequent statement, Cameron (with a colleague, Hugh Patrick) adopted the more eclectic position that banking may operate in any one of a number of ways in particular circumstances. It may stimulate, inhibit, or accommodate economic growth (1967, p. 2).

Raymond Goldsmith (1969) has shown that economic development involves a gradual but steady increase in the ratio of financial assets in a community to its money income, starting from a small fraction and leveling off at somewhere less than a doubling. If such a generalization is universally valid, discussion of the history of banking and finance should throw light on questions such as the comparative growth of Britain and France, an issue that was regarded as settled thirty years ago but one that has lately been reopened by a number of scholars, some of whom contend that France had a level of living per capita as high as Britain's in 1789 and grew as fast as Britain from 1815 to about 1870 (O'Brien and Keyder, 1978). Financial history shows, however, that France lagged about a hundred years behind Britain in the development of modern institutions—a central bank, reform of national finances, use of bank notes and deposits, insurance, and so on. The possibility exists that financial institutions were irrelevant to economic growth and that France was able to produce a higher level of living and grow faster with an archaic financial system. It seems unlikely. A sizable group claims that Britain's ability to mobilize resources—both its own and those of other countries—after 1688 enabled it, with one-third the manpower of France, to defeat the French, unable because of dug-in interests to reform its system of taxation and borrowing (Dickson, 1967; Bosher, 1970). Can finance be relevant to military outcomes, as widely insisted on, but not to the course of economic development?

WAR FINANCE

Pecunia nervus belli (Tacitus). Money is the sinew of war (Ehrenberg, 1896 [1928], p. 22). When asked in 1499 by Louis XII what was needed to take Milan, Condotierre Gian Ciacomo de Trivulzio said "three things: money, money, money" (ibid., p. 24). "It has been said that war is a 'sensible thing'—which, we suppose, means that it likes hard cash. According to Louis XIV, the last guinea will always win" (Bagehot, 1856 [1978], vol. 9, p. 297). J. A. Hobson thought finance so important to war that the Rothschilds could have prevented World War I by refusing to finance it (1927 [1938], p. 57). The same remark was made by a German in 1914 (Kaufmann, 1914,p.9). Baron James de Rothschild insisted to Gerson Bleichröder in the 1860s that this was not so: "It is a principle of our houses not to advance money for war even if it is not in our power to prevent war, then our minds at least can be easy that we have not contributed to it" (Stern, 1977*a*, p. 73). ("Our houses" refers to other Rothschild firms as well as to the French house.) Bleichröder may have subscribed to the principle. Under pressure from Bismarck in 1864, 1866, and 1870, however, his and other leading banks in Germany failed to abide by it as they financed the Prussian war machine by loans when Bismarck was unable to get the necessary funds voted by the Landestag (ibid., pp. 84–85).

The pages that follow are filled with war finance. Modern historiography as exemplified by the *Annales* school in France has moved away from recounting the stories of dynasties and wars in favor of the history of everyday life—of the family, disease, death, housing, the role of women, and the like. (It may be noted, however, that the Shelby Cullom Davis Center for Historical Studies at Princeton University chose "War and Society" as the topic for its seminar in 1982–83 and 1983–84.) Financial history cannot escape dealing with war. War is a hothouse and places enormous strain on resources, which finance is used to mobilize. Financial innovation occurs in wartime. It is no accident, for example, that the Bank of England was established in the midst of the Nine Years' War, called on the Continent the War of the League of Augsburg, or that the Bank of France was established by Napoleon in 1800 to help finance his wars. In the Middle Ages bankers were brought to ruin less by the collapse of commodity and security markets, as in modern times, than by failure of kings to meet debts incurred to raise mercenary armies and to subsidize allies. The investment of Antwerp by Spanish troops in 1585 destroyed the waning financial power of that city, while French occupation of Amsterdam in 1792 delivered the coup de grâce to its financial leadership, taken over from Antwerp two centuries earlier. Dynasties are less important for us than wars, although the financial capacities, pretensions, and irresponsibility of some rulers deserve attention.

ISSUES OF RELEVANCE

Any history is intermingled with the history of thought, although courses in departments of economics try to keep them distinct. History, like Everest, is worth exploring for its own sake, because the past is there. One who comes to it from contemporary economics, however, finds it irresistible to note similarities, parallels, precedents that bear on current problems and issues. An earlier historical examination on the development of European financial centers, for example, threw some light on the current issue of the economic processes entering into the probable emergence of a single financial center in Europe to focus the forces of financial integration (Kindleberger, 1974*a* [1978]). A gallop through the financial crises of the last 250 years in Europe illustrated indirectly the potentialities for crisis in foreign exchange speculation that brought down the German Herstatt Bank and the American Franklin National in 1974, not to mention the spurt in bank lending to developing countries that started in 1972 and was spurred by increases in oil prices by the Organization of Petroleum Exporting Countries (OPEC) in 1973 and 1979 (Kindleberger, 1978*b* [1989]).

The more general as well as more ambitious financial history of half a millennium in Europe is also intended to illuminate modern problems and controversies. One such is the debate between Keynesians and monetarists, referred to earlier— an issue that did not have its origin in the 1920s or 1930s, as many students of the subject think, but can be traced back to the seventeenth century and earlier.

A subset of the controversy between Keynesianism and monetarism is found in balance-of-payments theory and whether deficits are caused by real factors, such as bad harvests, subsidies to allies, the need to pay reparations, an OPEC oil price rise, and the like, or have their origin mainly in overissue of money. The debate arises in every country and every century.

A theme running through all monetary theory and history is embodied in the so-called Gresham's law: bad money drives good into hoarding or export. This is relevant not only to good and bad coins of the same precious metal but to bimetallism that uses silver and copper or, more widely, gold and silver; to paper money and coin; to the gold exchange standard that permits switches in central bank reserves from gold to national money and back again; or to a pure exchange standard with two reserve currencies. The problem is virtually insoluble: two or more monies are necessary because different monies are needed to perform different tasks, but two or more monies are unstable.

It is perhaps tedious to discuss each modern monetary controversy on which history can provide some evidence, but a list may be helpful in alerting the reader:

1. Flexible versus fixed exchange rates.
2. Monetary reform after wartime inflation.
3. The character of money as a public good that must be provided by a monopoly government or central bank, or whether there is merit in free competition in the issuing of money as Hayek (1972), Vaubel (1977), and many others have recommended.
4. The interpretation of economic history as a process of establishing property rights in private hands to provide incentive (North and Thomas, 1973) and the compelling counterexample that private control of governmental revenue and expenditure in the system of tax farming and venal paymasters strongly inhibited governmental finance in seventeenth-century England and especially eighteenth-century France.
5. The desirability of explicit and complete rules for monetary authorities or whether they should be called upon to exercise judgment and discretion.
6. The transfer of large sums of wealth across national boundaries and foreign exchanges and whether this is done by income changes, the shift of price levels, or, in the first instance at least, by recycling.
7. The geography of money and finance and particularly whether financial centers are best arranged in a hierarchical structure for efficiency or whether concentration of financial power leads to exploitation of the periphery by the center.

8. The basis for shifts in the dominant financial center in Europe, whether in military power, economic capacity, or adaptability to economic change.
9. The growth of financial markets in size and capacity to deal with new problems and the integration of local markets into regional, national, and international ones. Such markets required intermediaries that bridge time by lending long and borrowing short and bridge risk by their greater capacity than the individual small lender to collect from defaulting borrowers.
10. The capacity of financial markets to deal with risk not only through intermediating between lender and borrower but also through insurance and portfolio diversification.
11. Whether the instability implicit in Gresham's law from having two or more monies in the world can be eliminated by moving to only one or whether more than one money is needed because of the existence of different kinds of work for money to do—in size of transactions, in distance of payments, and in different countries.
12. The capacity of societies—economies, nations, governments—to adapt to change, imitate new financial institutions developed elsewhere, and create new financial institutions of their own to meet new problems.

This last issue is one that goes to the root of social science as it asks whether sociology and politics can best be explained by economic analysis, as Gary Becker and the Chicago school think, or whether, on the contrary, economic and financial behavior is grounded in the sociopolitical matrix at any given time, leaving little, if any, room for the free will exercise of economic policy choices by kings, finance ministers, and central bank governors. The question arises in any discussion of inflation, which in some views is always the consequence of an overissue of money that a correct policy could have avoided and in others is regarded as an ineluctable response of the monetary authorities to the pressures of groups in society that, in the aggregate, demand more than 100 percent of the national income or are unwilling to bear their share of some sizable burden—wartime expenditure, reparations, reconstruction costs, correction of a balance-of-payments deficit, and the like. The question is also posed by the success of England in reforming its finances after the Glorious Revolution of 1688; the inability of France to do likewise until the bloody revolution of 1789 in which twenty-eight *financiers* were guillotined; the fact that the three leading financial reformers in Catholic France in the eighteenth century (apart from Turgot) were foreigners and Protestants—John Law, Isaac Panchaud, and Jacques Necker—outside the establishment and not locked in to its values. Bankers' quarrels form a theme running through the history of European finance. They can be judged at two levels: as petty rivalry coming from personality and interest clashes or as part of a process of innovation. New men, new ways of doing things threatened the old. The Bank of England and the Bank of France were started by outsiders. The quarrels are most conspicuous where the old men are deeply resistant and unwilling to accommodate to innovation.

In all this, the time frame is important. In the long run, the quantity theory of money is valid. It is often a poor approximation of reality in the short run. On some very long showing, moreover, the quantity of money may be responding to the demands of the real system. The general view is that the price revolution of the sixteenth century was the result of the discovery of the New World with its gold and especially silver. A profound student of money goes further and argues that the discoveries themselves were a response to the need for money in Europe in the fifteenth century (Vilar, 1969 [1976]).

OLD CONTROVERSIES

At the same time that light may be thrown on current questions, there is no escape from old controversies: What is the nature of money? Is money what the state decrees, as G. F. Knapp held in Germany in 1905 (Ellis, 1934, ch. 2), or is the final decision in the choice of what is money made by the market? How much can one rely on financial planning, and to what extent is it necessary to accept the outcome of Darwinian processes of natural selection and survival of those institutions that are fittest? Does the bank of issue require a monopoly? Is the credit system inherently unstable? Is inflation—or the premium on gold in terms of local currency— caused mainly by an excess of issue of domestic currency, or does it come from the balance of payments by way of outpayments, which lead to currency depreciation and thus to inflation? And, as a branch of the perennial debate between expansionists (called Keynesians) and contractionists (monetarists), there is the issue whether bimetallism is good because it increases the money supply or bad because of the instability of Gresham's law.

CHRONOLOGIES, GLOSSARY, RATES OF EXCHANGE

To help readers not specialized in European history to thread their way, I offer here four chronologies on major wars, monetary, banking, and other financial events, and, at the back of the book, a glossary of terms and abbreviations and a set of tables of order-of-magnitude exchange rates for prominent currencies at particular times to assist in converting specified amounts in a rough way. "Billion" in this book follows American usage and means "one thousand million." A number of the chapters provide outline maps. Each chapter beginning with Chapter 2 is completed by a list of suggested supplementary reading. A complete list of works referred to is contained at the end.

CHRONOLOGY I: WARS

1453	End of Hundred Years' War between France and Britain
1508	War of the League of Cambrai against Venice
1521–59	Six wars between France and Spain-Austria
1562–98	Wars of religion in France

1568–1648	Dutch War of Independence from Spain with truce from 1609–21
1618–48	Thirty Years' War on Continent
1642–49	Civil War and Revolution in England
1652–54 1665–67 } 1672–74	Three Anglo-Dutch Wars
1660	Restoration of the Stuarts
1689–97	Nine Years' War (War of the League of Augsburg)
1702–13	Queen Anne's War (War of the Spanish Succession)
1739–48	War of Jenkins's Ear
1740–48	War of the Austrian Succession
1756–63	Seven Years' War (French and Indian War)
1775–83	American War of Independence
1780–84	Fourth Anglo-Dutch War
1788–89	War of the Bavarian Succession
1789	French Revolution
1793	Reign of Terror, War of the First Coalition
1795–1815	Directory, Consulate, and Empire in France under Napoleon
1802	Treaty of Amiens, interrupting Napoleonic Wars
1803	War resumed
1815	Waterloo, Treaty of Vienna
1848	Revolutions in France, Germany, and Austria
1854–56	Crimean War
1859	Austro-Sardinian war, Unification of Italy
1864	Prusso-Danish War
1866	Prusso-Austrian War
1870–71	Franco-Prussian War
1877–78	Russo-Turkish War
1899–1902	Boer War
1914–18	World War I
1939–45	World War II
1950	Korean War
1989	End of cold war

CHRONOLOGY II: MONETARY EVENTS

1252	First gold coin minted in western Europe since Roman times, Genoa and Florence
1448	Portugal sails to the Gold Coast
1492	Columbus discovers America
1540	Great Tudor debasement of silver under Henry VIII
1545	Discovery of Potosi silver mountain in Peru
1560	Specie flow from America shifts from gold to silver
1596	Spain blackens its coinage with copper
1602	Return to the livre tournois in France

1619–23	*Kipper- und Wipperzeit* (debasement of subsidiary coinage in Holy Roman Empire, leading to hyperinflation)
1666	Free coinage and end of seignorage in England
1680	Discovery of gold in Minas Gerais, Brazil
1696	British silver recoinage
1717	Newton fixed price of gold at £3 17*s* 10½*d* per troy ounce .9 fine
1726	French monetary reform
1774	Silver demonetized in England
1789–95	French issue of *assignats*
1797	British suspension of convertibility of pound
1803	French adopt the franc germinal in place of the livre
1816	England adopts the gold standard de jure
1819	Britain resumes pound convertibility
1838	Dresden Convention settling exchange rate between north and south Germany
1848	France briefly suspends convertibility
1849	Discovery of gold in California
1851	Discovery of gold in Australia
1857	Munzverein (Union of Coinage) among German states and Austria
1859	Discovery of Comstock silver lode in Nevada
1860	Unification of Italian lira
1860s	Cyanide process for recovering silver
1865	Latin Monetary Union
1866–81	*Corso forsozo* (forced circulation) of Italian lira
1867	International Monetary Conference—Universal Money
1870	Temporary suspension of franc convertibility
1871	German monetary unification
1873	Germany adopts the gold standard
1878	International Monetary Conference—bimetallism ends on Continent
1886	Discovery of gold in Witwatersrand
1914	Suspension of convertibility of all currencies on outbreak of war
1919	Supports for pound sterling and French franc abandoned—depreciation
1923	Hyperinflation in Germany, followed by Rentenmark
1924	Reichsmark
1924	Squeeze in French francs punished speculators
1925	Restoration of pound to par
1926	De facto stabilization of French franc at devalued level
1931	German Standstill Agreement
1931	Britain abandons the gold standard
1934	United States after abandoning gold standard 1933, raises gold price from $20.67 an ounce to $35
1936	Gold bloc collapses; Tripartite Monetary Agreement
1940	Devaluation of the pound to $4.40
1944	Bretton Woods Agreements to establish Fund and World Bank

1946	Anglo-American Financial Agreement
1947	Pound made convertible; lasted only six weeks.
1949	British pound devalued; other currency exchange rates adjusted
1958	French franc devalued, pound made convertible
1960	Gold pool established in London
1960	General Arrangements to Borrow extended the International Monetary Fund agreement
1961	Basle Agreement instituted central bank swaps
1967	Devaluation of the pound
1968	Dissolution of gold pool, adoption of two-tier price system
1969	Devaluation of the French franc
1970	European Economic Community (EEC) adopts Werner Plan for Economic and Monetary Union by stages
1971	Connolly shock imposing 10 percent import surtax and Smithsonian Monetary Agreement; dollar devalued
1973	Dollar floated
1979	EEC adopts European Monetary System
1985	Plaza Agreement among leading countries to stabilize exchange rates
1987	Louvre Agreement to same end
1991	Maastrict Agreement among EC members to reach a single currency and a European central bank in stages by 1999.

CHRONOLOGY III: BANKING LANDMARKS

12th and 13th c.	Fairs of Champagne
1397–1494	Medici bank established 1397, failed 1494
1407	Bank of St. George, Genoa, established
1442	Beginning of decline of Bruges
1445	French forbidden to attend fair at Geneva; beginning of fair at Lyons
1487	Fugger Bank established
1534	Genoans expelled from Geneva fair, started another at Besancon
1557, 1597, 1607, 1627, 1647 }	Stops of the Spanish Exchequer
1571	Interest permitted in England at 10 percent (1624, 8 percent; 1660, 6 percent; 1713, 5 percent)
1585	Closing of the river Scheldt and decline of Antwerp
1586	Bank of St. George opens accounts in gold
1587	Bank of Venice established—public, with private forerunners
1609	Bank of Amsterdam (Wisselbank) established
1616	Bank of Middelburg established
1619	Bank of Hamburg; Bank of Venice (Giro) established
1621	Bank of Delft; Bank of Nuremberg established

1635	Bank of Rotterdam established
1668	Swedish Riksbank established—first central bank in Europe
1672	Stop of the English Exchequer
1694	Bank of England established
1715	Banque Générale formed by John Law
1716	Banque Royale formed by John Law
1750	Early formation of British country banks
1776	Caisse d'Escompte formed by Isaac Panchaud
1782	Bank of St. Charles (Madrid) established
1800	Bank of France established
1800s	Wave of British country banks
1810	Savings bank movement starts in Britain
1818	First savings bank formed in Paris
1822	Société Générale pour Favoriser l'Industrie Nationale des Pays-Bas
1826	Joint stock banking permitted in England sixty-five miles from London
1833	Joint stock banks without note issue permitted in London
1844	Bank Act divided Bank of England into issue and banking departments
1848	Collapse of French regional banks, establishment of *comptoirs d'escompte*
1852	Crédit Mobilier and Crédit Foncier established
1853	Bank of Darmstadt established
1850s	Wave of new banks established in England, France, and Germany
1850s	Penetration of French banks into Italy, Spain, and Austria
1854	Joint stock banks admitted to London clearing
1863	Crédit Lyonnais established
1864	Société Générale pour Favoriser le Développement du Commerce et de l'Industrie en France established
1866	Crédit Agricole established
1867	*Enquête* (Inquiry) into French monetary and credit conditions
1870	Deutsche Bank established
1875	Reichsbank established
1880s–1914	Mergers of English joint stock banks
1882	Failure of the Union Générale
1893	Bank of Italy formed from various note-issuing banks
1893–94	Wave of banks formed in Italy by German banks
1924	Rentenbank and Golddiskontobank established
1930	Bank for International Settlements (BIS) established
1931	Collapse of Creditanstalt in Austria, Danatbank in Germany
1933	Istituto per la Ricostruzione Industriale (IRI) established
1950	European Payments Union (EPU) established
1957	European Investment Bank established
1973	EC Directive on Abolition of Restrictions
1977	EC First Banking Coordination Directive
1988	Second EC Banking Directive

| 1988 | BIS Agreement on capital standards for banks |
| 1990 | Liberalization of EC capital market |

CHRONOLOGY IV: FINANCIAL EVENTS

1492	Expulsion of Jews from Spain
1502	Expulsion of Moors from Spain
1519	Election of Charles V as emperor of Holy Roman Empire
1522	Financial crisis
1557	Financial crisis
1600	Formation of English East India Company
1602	Formation of Dutch East India Company
1620–23	Financial crisis
1636	Tulip mania
1649	Financial crisis following execution of Charles I
1661	Chamber of Justice set up by Colbert, minister to Louis XIV
1667	English financial crisis
1672	Stop of the Exchequer—English financial crisis
1680	Formation of Sun Assurance Company
1685	Revocation of the Edict of Nantes, removing Huguenots from official toleration
1696	Financial crisis, innovation of Exchequer bill
1715	Visa I in France after death of Louis XIV
1719	Mississippi Bubble
1719	South Sea Bubble
1720	Both bubbles burst. Bubble Act in England, formation of the Royal Exchange and London Assurance companies.
1721–22	Visa II in France
1745	Jacobite invasion threat, financial crisis in England
1749	Sir Henry Pelham's debt conversion, including consolidated (irredeemable) debts or consols
1763	International financial crisis at end of Seven Years' War
1772	Anglo-Dutch financial crisis
1770	One-fifth of French government debt repudiated by abbé Terray
1776	Turgot's fiscal reforms abort
1781	Dutch lending switches from Britain to Necker's (multiple) life annuities
1782	Financial crisis
1789–93	Financial reforms by French government
1795–1816	Napoleon levying indemnities, the British providing subsidies
1799	London-Hamburg crisis
1806	Blockade crisis
1813	Financial crisis in London
1817–19	French indemnity recycled by Baring loans
1824	War loan conversion in England

1825	Country banks, insurance companies, and South American loans— financial crisis
1828	1 billion French franc indemnity to émigrés
1832	British indemnity to slave owners
1836–37	Anglo-American financial crisis
1847	Railway mania and wheat crisis
1850s	British government guarantees Indian colonial issues
1856	French government guarantees interest on railroad bonds
1857	Anglo-American, Scandinavian, and Hamburg financial crises
1856, 1863	Incorporation generalized in Britain
1863, 1867	Incorporation adopted in France
1866	Overend, Gurney & Company crisis in England; financial crises in Italy, Spain, and Germany
1869	Incorporation adopted Germany (North German Confederation)
1871–72	Franco-Prussian indemnity, recycled by Thiers *rentes*
1873	Financial crisis involving Germany, Austria, and the United States
1878	Collapse of the Egyptian debt
1882	Financial crisis in France
1887	*Lombardverbot* issued; financial war between Germany and Russia; France recycles Russian borrowings from Germany
1888	Collapse of the Comptoir d'Escompte and the copper ring
1890	Baring crisis over Argentine land bonds
1893	Panama scandal in France
1904	J. P. Morgan & Company transfers payment of $40 million for Panama Canal to Paris
1907	New York–Turin financial crisis
1914	Closing of stock exchanges on outbreak of war
1920	Stock market collapse in London and New York
1924	Dawes loan to recycle German reparations
1929	New York stock market crash
1930	Young loan
1931	Hoover moratorium on war debts and reparations; German standstill agreement and beginning of foreign exchange control
1932	Exchange Equalization Account (EEA) established to hold down sterling
1942	Adoption by the United States of lend-lease to its allies
1946	Anglo-American Financial Agreement
1948	Adoption of Marshall Plan to aid European reconstruction
1957	The Rome Treaty establishes the European Economic Community (EEC)
1974	Fringe bank financial crisis in London
1985	EC White Paper on the Completion of the Internal Market by end of 1992
1986	London deregulates financial markets in Big Bang
1987	Black Monday on New York Stock Exchange

I
MONEY

Chapter 2 deals with the early development of money in Europe, money initially in the form of coins, later of bank notes and bank deposits. The story is one of continuous innovation in order better to discharge the functions for which money was required—a standard by which to measure values and a mechanism for conducting trade without the cumbersome and inefficient device of barter. Evolution proceeded along several lines at the same time: devices to make money recognizable in quality and quantity without the need for elaborate testing and counting, to economize on its use where that was expensive because of the cost of guarding and transporting it. There was continuous worry that there would not be enough money in circulation to facilitate trade and to enable producers to dispose of their output. These worries arose partly because the mining of silver and gold was limited in Europe but to a great extent because of the unbalanced trade with the East—the Baltic, the eastern Mediterranean, and the Far East—which meant that silver was continuously drained from Europe to pay for spices, silks, furs, timber, and the like. The periodic shortages of money led to both the cultivation of substitutes and the policy of mercantilism, which sought to limit exports of specie and encourage imports.

Other monetary problems arose from the continuous warfare of the period and its finance on frequent occasions by debasement, both adulterating silver with copper and using less precious metal for given coins. With the discovery of America—which some believe was a response to the bullion famine of the fifteenth century—new gold and, especially, silver poured into Europe and gave rise to, or at least supported, a substantial rise in prices called the price revolution. The association of the silver from Peru and Mexico with these price increases led to the early formulation of the quantity theory of money.

The inefficiency associated with payments in specie, especially payments at a distance, led to the substitution for it of bills of exchange that could be cleared in various directions and of bank money, discussed in Chapter 3. Italians were the first European bankers, as money changers, dealers in bills of exchange at fairs and in distant trade, and lenders to kings, nobles, and the Church. In particular, they transmitted money from place to place. In the sixteenth century, the Italians were displaced by Germans from Augsburg and Nuremberg who dominated the fairs of Lyons and Frankfurt, the bourse of Bruges, and later Antwerp and, with Genoa, helped distribute the silver pouring into and through Europe by way of Seville and

Cadiz. After Bruges and Antwerp, financial supremacy shifted to Amsterdam where the Bank of Amsterdam, created at the beginning of the seventeenth century, was the first deposit bank outside Italy and Spain, whose bank money went to a premium over coin because of its assured high quality and ease of handling.

Chapter 4 addresses the development of international monetary standards, and especially bimetallism, including both its necessity and the problem to which it gave rise. The necessity for more than one money lay in the fact that monetary transactions range from the very small to the very large and a money that would serve adequately at one end of the scale would not do for the other. Copper was needed for small retail transactions, gold for large-scale commerce, and silver for the bulk of payments between. The problem with using two monies—say, gold and silver— was that if the market price should differ from the mint price, the undervalued money would be hoarded or exported as metal, whereas the overvalued metal would be brought to the mint or spent. Gresham's law was formulated (though not by Sir Thomas Gresham) that bad money drove out good. In theory, the mint price might stabilize the market price by establishing a very large demand of one metal and supply of the other when the market price tended to diverge; in practice, the market price, destabilized by arbitrary discoveries of new mines in disproportionate amounts, destabilized the mint price. Britain demonetized silver in stages beginning in 1774, thereby shifting from bimetallism to the gold standard. After an unsuccessful attempt to sustain bimetallism, the rest of Europe followed a century later.

Gold went to a premium over bank notes in England during the Napoleonic Wars, arousing a debate over the cause of the agio on gold, depreciation of the pound, between the banking and currency schools—a debate that has its echoes in the twentieth century over the causes of German inflation in the 1920s and in Europe as a whole in the 1970s and 1980s. The triumph of the currency school in Britain led to the Bank Act of 1844, which established the British monetary system down to 1914. As the gold standard evolved in Europe as a whole from 1870, the question was raised whether world monetary conditions reflected the quantity of gold in the system or whether the gold standard was a managed system effectively run by the Bank of England from London.

2

The Evolution of Money in Western Europe

"Papa, what's money?"

The abrupt question had such immediate reference to the subject of Mr. Dombey's thoughts, that Mr. Dombey was quite disconcerted.

"What is money, Paul?" he answered. "Money?"

"Yes," said the child, laying his hands on the elbows of his little chair, and turning the old face up toward Mr. Dombey's. "What is money?"

Mr. Dombey was in a difficulty. He would have liked to give him some explanation involving the terms circulating-medium, currency, depreciation of currency, paper, bullion, rates of exchange, value of precious metals in the market, and so forth; but looking down at the little chair, and seeing what a long way down it was, he answered: "Gold, and silver, and copper. Guineas, shillings, half-pence. You know what they are?"

"Oh yes, I know what they are," said Paul. "I don't mean that, Papa. I mean what's money after all" . . . "I mean, what can it do?"

(Dickens, *Dombey and Son,* 1848 [1864], p. 92)

THE FUNCTIONS OF MONEY

Standard textbooks ascribe two functions to money: to serve as a means of payment and as a unit of account. Each function has two dimensions in time. In the short run, as medium of exchange, money eliminates the necessity of barter, which is inefficient. It rarely happens that the seller of one good wants exactly the good the buyer offers for it in the appropriate amount—a so-called double coincidence of wants. Through time, money is a store of value that enables production and consumption to be temporally independent, another gain in efficiency as one does not have to spend simultaneously with earning or earn at a given moment in order to spend. The medium-of-exchange function has a spatial as well as a time dimension. Payments are made locally and at a distance, within a country and to foreign countries with different currencies. If this is to be done efficiently without large gross movements of money back and forth, there must be clearing. Debts owed in one direction are offset against those in the other. The clearing need not be bilateral but may involve three or more countries and currencies. Merchants, exchangers, banks, and money markets have continuously experimented to increase the efficiency and reduce the costs (increase the profitability) of domestic and international money payments.

As unit of account, money simplifies comparison of values. It is a *numéraire,* or standard of measurement as economists use the word, perhaps wrongly (to economic historians it means merely cash).[1] If there are N commodities and no common yardstick, each commodity must be priced in terms of every other, which gives $N\left(\frac{N-1}{2}\right)$ prices (one divides by two because measuring A in terms of B makes it unnecessary to measure B in terms of A). With one commodity chosen as money—silver, gold, copper, pieces of paper with numbers written on them, even pepper, or cigarettes—there are simply $N-1$ prices. Every commodity is priced in terms of the *numéraire;* any two commodities can then easily be compared. $N-1$ is a much smaller number than $N\left(\frac{N-1}{2}\right)$ when N is anything larger than a very small integer.

Over time, the unit of account functions as a standard of deferred payment—used in contracts involving payments or debt.

Two monies may be less efficient than one. No problem arises in the short run from the existence of more than one money as medium of exchange or if two or more monies are related to one another in value at a fixed price. Sir John Hicks has produced a theorem that states that when two goods have a fixed price, they can be regarded as one. This applies especially to money, although changing from one currency to another at the fixed price may involve some transaction cost. When the relative value of the two monies changes from time to time, however, difficulties arise. A household, firm, government, or other entity seeking to maintain the value of its money holding has to choose among monies and may want to switch back and forth from one to another as the relative values change. The function of money as unit of account becomes especially difficult when the relative values of two or more monies alter. How should distance be measured if the yard and the meter keep altering in relation to each other?

Money in exchange is a private good, although efficient use of money in effecting payments and availability of money to households and firms have the public good quality of assisting efficient operation of markets for goods and services. A private good is one consumption of which by one person or firm precludes use by others. A public good, on the contrary, is defined as something that can be used by any economic actor without subtracting from amounts available to others. As a public good, money has been compared with language that assists in national and international intercourse. Italian was the commercial language of the Mediterranean in the late Middle Ages and Renaissance (Braudel, 1949 [1972] Vol. 1, p. 131) and Dutch the language of Baltic trade in the seventeenth and eighteenth centuries (deJong-Keesing, 1939, p. 220), just as English (or American) is the commercial language today. By the same token, the Venetian ducat and the Florentine florin were the dollars of the late Middle Ages and Dutch currency (or currencies) the dollar of the seventeenth century (Vilar, 1969 [1976], p. 205).[2]

---

1. My *Nouveau petit Larousse* (French dictionary) gives both meanings: (1) the legal value of coins, which implies the unit of account, and (2) an amount of money in circulation. As an economist more than economic historian, I incline to the unit-of-account meaning.

2. What is said to have been the currency that outstripped the dollar in stability and intrinsic value, lasting from the fourth century to the fall of Constantinople in the crusades of 1204, was the bezant of the Byzantine Empire, called by Lopez the dollar of the Middle Ages: "More than a lump of gold, it was a symbol and a faith" (1951, p. 214). But its history lies outside our frame of time and space.

MONETARY EVOLUTION

Economic historians have occasionally maintained that evolution in economic intercourse has proceeded from a natural or barter economy to a money economy and ultimately to a credit economy. This view was put forward, for example, in 1864 by Bruno Hildebrand of the German historical school of economics; it happens to be wrong. Postan has shown that credit was widely used, if perhaps not highly developed, in medieval times (1928 [1973], p. 5), and Braudel observed that the three stages coexisted well into modern times. As late as the nineteenth century, the rural economy used a great deal of barter in such a country as France, the national economy organized along the roads used silver, and the international economy operating in ports and major financial centers used bills of exchange—a credit instrument—and settled balances that could not be cleared by bills in gold and silver payments (Braudel, 1977).

COIN

For the medium-of-exchange function, money early took the form of coins. Many were named after the person or object represented on them: the ducat was named after the doge of Venice, the louis d'or after King Louis of France (sometimes spelled in English "lewidor"), and self-evidently the Napoleon, English noble, and angel, coins that were minted only briefly, and later the sovereign, crown, and half-crown. The unit-of-account function was emphasized by designating some denominations of money by weight—the pound, shilling, and penny, derived from the Roman pound, solidus, and denier, and paralleled by the French livre and Italian lira, along with the mark and peso. Penny as a measure of weight survives in English primarily in grading nails.

It is not necessary to have actual coins in order to reckon in money of account, just as one does not need a yardstick to calculate distance. In early times, the pound and shilling were used for pricing goods when only the silver penny was coined. The monetary unit of account was needed additionally, and most importantly, to compare the values of different coins, as a money *numéraire,* a sort of money's money. In Milan in the eighteenth century, as many as fifty different coins were in circulation, which could be handled only by equating them to an abstract, even imaginary unit, the livre or lira (Einaudi, 1936 [1953], pp. 242–44).

Of the many notable features in the financial history of France, none is more remarkable than the complete distinction between the money of account and the money in actual circulation. The distinction was neither unique nor original . . . but in no country was it so sharply drawn as in France from the 10th to the 18th century. . . .

What is more remarkable is that the money of account became localized as well as the circulating coins. Thus we hear of *livres, sous,* and *deniers* with local designations, e.g. Parisis, Tournois, Manceaux, Poitevin, Toulousain, Angevin, etc. During the process of centralization one of the local monies came to be adopted by the crown. The *livre tournois* had come into general use in southern France, and when Languedoc was annexed to the royal domain, its method of reckoning was adopted and retained side by side until the reign of Louis XIV, who abolished the *livre parisis* and retained only the *livre tournois* which had long been the money of account in ordinary use. (Higgs, 1925–26 [1963], Vol. 2, pp. 617–18)

The example bears on a critical point of monetary theory that has gone out of text-books as of little modern relevance (mistakenly in my judgment)—the difference between the Knapp state theory of money (that money is what the state declares it to be and designates as legal tender for debts public and private) and nominalism (that money is what the market uses to fulfill the purposes of money). States may propose, but markets dispose. The quotation from *Palgrave's Dictionary* omits a passage to the effect that the Capet kings, originally dukes of Paris, sought to decree the use of the livre parisis as unit of account for France. In the end they had to follow the market. (The passage is also of interest in pointing to the use of a single money over a wider and wider area to take advantage of economies of scale.) But let us return to circulating money.

Not all coins derived their names from an image or a measure of weight. The florin was named after Florence; the thaler, which evolved into the dollar, after Joachims*tal* in Bohemia where it was minted near the silver mines; the guinea after the African source of the gold from which it was first made; the cruzeiro for the Crusades for which it was coined.

The public good character of money was early recognized by rulers who laid down standards for mints within their jurisdictions and tried to see that they were maintained. The Holy Roman Empire, for example, decreed ordinances for regulating the number of mints within its constituent elements and the weight and fineness of the coins struck, and it sent imperial assayers on visits to see that its standards were adhered to. The lesser governments had their own interests in raising funds—for consumption, for building palaces, and, when war broke out, for hiring mercenaries—and these often clashed with the overall public interest. The principalities, duchies, bishoprics, imperial cities, and the like were tempted from time to time to debase the currency issued by their mints, to earn income by minting more coins for a given amount of metal, and then to encourage the taking of debased coins across the border and exchanging them for good coins. If a coin were not too badly worn, sweated (i.e., rubbed), clipped, or adulterated, it could pass at its nominal value, especially if it were a subsidiary coin used in retail trade and the payment of wages. If, on the other hand, it was badly deteriorated or was a large silver or a gold coin, it had to be weighed and tested before the recipient would be willing to accept it. The 12 million escudos paid by Francis I of France in 1529 to ransom his two sons, who had been substituted for him as hostages when he was captured in the war between France and Spain, took four months to count and test, and 40,000 coins were rejected by the Spanish as below standard (Vilar, 1969 [1976], p. 174).

While officially sanctioned mints might debase coins, clipping was undertaken by a wider public until milled edges were adopted to make the mutilation of a coin more recognizable. This was a response to a wave of clipping in Britain in 1660 at the time of the Restoration of the Stuarts (Macaulay, 1848 [1906], Vol. 4, p. 186).

Another device to overcome the disability of coins that could not be accepted at face value was for bankers or money changers to sew assayed and weighed coins into sacks or purses with the true amount designated on the outside (Udovitch, 1979, p. 267). False representation was severely punished by the state. Governments tried to enforce maintenance of prescribed standards by penalties—confiscation of goods, years in the galleys, death—that seem excessive by modern standards of white-collar crime (Hamilton, 1934 [1965], pp. 15n, 31n, 48, 49, 80, 99, etc.). In *The Merchant of Venice* Shylock laments that Jessica has stolen "two sealed bags of ducats / Of double ducats" (Act II, sc. viii). As late as the nineteenth century, the practice was still followed in the eastern Mediterranean, where one denomination of money in use was the "purse" (Marlowe, 1975, p. 153). The practice of sacking coins after counting and testing continued to be used by central banks, but the development of bank money, discussed in the following chapter, reduced the need for elaborate devices to safeguard the standard money in large amounts.

While silver was the standard money throughout most of the medieval period to early modern times, other metals also served. Copper was adopted as the basis of money in Sweden in 1625, a country in which the government was part-owner of the largest copper mine in Europe, Stora Kopperberg. Worth only one-hundredth the value of silver, it was unsatisfactory for ordinary payments because of the great weight. Burglars could not steal the money because they could not carry it, and wagons were needed for ordinary payments (Heckscher, 1954, pp. 88–90). Copper was also used for adulterating silver money, as in Spain at the end of the sixteenth century, in alloys of varying proportions of copper and silver called billon or vellon. The process of adulteration was sometimes known as "blackening" money. Copper was produced in Hungary as well as Sweden in substantial amounts, and elsewhere on a smaller scale, sometimes in connection with other metals, as with tin in Cornwall in England. Its problems as money included not only its weight and bulk for fairly large payments but also the difficulties it posed for institutions that handled a large volume of transactions of low unit value. The Régie des Postes in the Napoleonic era, for example, used to receive 9 million to 10 million livres in copper annually and paid for its wages and supplies in silver. The French government tried to make copper legal tender in settlement of debts up to one-fortieth of the amounts involved. It failed to help (Mollien, 1845, Vol. 3, pp. 165n, 171). In August 1800, the Bank of France was instructed to pay no more than one-twentieth of the service on *rentes* in copper (Menias, 1969, p. 98).

Gold coins had been used in Roman times, but the first gold coin produced in western Europe in the medieval period was the genoin of Genoa, minted in 1252 (Lopez, 1956). Before that, considerable use had been made of the bezant, a gold coin minted in the Levant, or Byzantium. The genoin and other gold coins minted in Italy, such as the florin of Florence, were a response to the commercial revolution of the thirteenth century that called for larger payments to satisfy debts arising in larger and more numerous transactions. But silver was the principal money in use in ordinary transactions within countries until late in the eighteenth century. A balanced export of silver against the import of gold from England in the early seventeenth century provoked a scarcity of effective money (Supple, 1959, p. 173). When Isaac Newton set the mint price of gold at £3 17*s* 10½*d* an ounce in 1717—a price that was to last with wartime interruptions for 200 years—money to the ordinary man in Britain was silver (Carswell, 1960, p. 16). In similar fashion, the French set the price of the livre in terms of gold and silver in 1726. While the price of silver changed, that of gold lasted, again with interruptions, the livre tournois being equal to the gold franc, until 1928 (Lüthy, 1961, Vol. 2, p. 27). But until the 1870s, metallic money in use was silver, not gold.

Parenthetically, it may be noted for later elaboration that Marcel Bloch, the great French economic historian who was killed by a German firing squad for his role in the Resistance, regarded these monetary stabilizations of the early eighteenth century—fixing the price of gold in England and France for what proved to be 200 years—as "a major turning point in the economic history of Europe" (quoted in Day, 1986, p. 22). Bloch was a monetarist who believed that money is a permanent, indeed, a dominant factor in economic life, because it serves as an instrument and measure of exchange (ibid., p. 15).

OUTPUT AND USE OF PRECIOUS METALS BEFORE COLUMBUS

Before 1492, or more accurately before the substantial flow of silver from America beginning about 1560, silver was available mainly from central Europe, from the mines in what are now Germany, Austria, and Czechoslovakia. Much of it was drained south to Venice, and thence shipped to the Levant in exchange for spices, silks, other luxury products such as cotton, and some gold. Gold from the eastern Mediterranean originated largely in Africa, especially the West Sudan and the Gold Coast, now Ghana. It initially moved by caravan to Cairo and Alexandria. Later gold was exchanged by the Ashanti, who panned it in alluvial rivers, against salt furnished by the Moors, crossing the Sahara from north to south. The trade was risky; caravans of as many as 2,000 men and 1,800 camels on one occasion could be lost. The rewards were great: at one time the terms of trade between gold and salt—the latter desperately needed in Africa to preserve meat—reached one pound for one pound (Bovill, 1958, p. 236).

Although some scholars regard the sale of silver from Europe against gold as balanced (Bautier, 1971, p. 168), most take the view that there were net exports of money on balance that produced a "bullion famine" in the fifteenth century. Domestic production of gold in Europe was small—one metric ton a year in the thirteenth and early fourteenth centuries, rising to three or four tons between 1325 and 1385 (Day, 1978 [1987]). The Black Death set back silver mining after 1348. In the fifteenth century, population was rising again, and expanding economies needed enlarged means of payment.

Against new production of silver and a small amount of gold, there was, in addition to exports, a continuous drain of as much as 5 percent per year of the quantity of coin in circulation, representing losses from ordinary wear (that varied with velocity) and fluctuating losses from the melting pot, hoarding, shipwreck, and movements into especially silver plate, utensils, and other tableware and ornaments. In periods of acute shortage, plate was melted down and coined, but as Adam Smith pointed out (1776 [1937], p. 186), increases in income led to higher demands for silver, both for increased circulation and from "vanity and ostentation." Chance findings of buried gold and silver coin secreted intentionally or accidentally lost, representing christening and wedding presents in the case of single or a few coins, ecclesiastical treasures, tax collections, working capital of merchants, or Gresham's law hoards have been analyzed by numismatists to afford insight into the circulation of money in particular areas. In a 1984 find of 395 gold and 23,600 silver coins buried in the basement of a Lübeck merchant's warehouse between 1533 and 1537, only 26 percent of the gold and larger silver coins had been minted in north Germany, including the Wendish Monetary Union of Lübeck, Hamburg, Lünenberg, and Wismar, plus Mecklenburg to the east, as contrasted with 94 percent of the small silver (subsidiary) coins. Comparison of the Lübeck find with fifteenth-century coins found over the years in the south Baltic region showed the growing internationalization of circulation of the larger-denominated coins (North, 1990, Tables 5, 14, pp. 34, 63).

Net exports, losses in use, and wider circulation led to pressures to acquire more money. Barter expanded, especially in local payments. Commodities were used as media of exchange, especially salt produced in the west (Meuvret, 1947 [1970], pp. 141–45), pepper brought from the East Indies to the Mediterranean by caravan, and then to Italy and Spain (Van der Wee, 1977, p. 306), and even cochineal, a red dye, treated like bullion with a conventional price of £1 a pound avoirdupois (Day, 1978 [1987], p. 4). Pepper was so identified with money that German princes called their bankers "peppermen" (Stone, 1956, p. 99). The point to be emphasized is that when a market lacks money sufficient for its needs, it takes steps to correct the deficiency.

The net loss of precious metals to the East runs counter to the modern theory of balance-of-payments adjustment, developed by Thomas Mun and William Petty in the early seventeenth century and more fully in 1756 by David Hume. According to that theory, loss of specie in western Europe should have lowered commodity prices, resulting in an increase in exports, reduction in imports, and an improved balance of trade, with the opposite process taking place in the Far East. Such exchange of silver for gold as took place occurred because the ratio of gold to silver was as low as 5:1 in China and India, as against 11 or 12:1 in Europe at the time. This spread provided incentive to arbitrage even in the face of heavy transport costs. The imbalance, however, was caused by the fact that the East then, and until the late nineteenth century, like a number of the members of the Organization of Petroleum Exporting Countries (OPEC) today, was what we call a "low absorber," that is, an economy in which increases in income from rising exports do not spill readily back into imports. In the low absorbers among the OPEC countries, notably Kuwait, Saudi Arabia, Abu Dhabi, and Taiwan in the Far East, the reason lies in the rapidity of the rise in income and the lag in raising levels of living and investment. In the East in the fifteenth and sixteenth centuries and continuing to the present day, especially in India, the "failure to adjust" was ascribable to the tendency to hoard specie. Hoarding was a form of insurance against crop failure; it was rational in a region close to the subsistence level with wide variability in the yield of the harvest and primitive institutions for consumption loans.

Silver moved east by way of the Mediterranean, principally through Venice but to some extent from Genoa. Some went through the Baltic as Russia sought to acquire specie in the West to enable it to import luxury goods for its own aristocratic consumption—jewelry, richly ornamented arms, and rugs and fabrics woven with gold and silver (Bogucka, 1980, p. 15). Hanseatic traders from northern Germany even traded directly with the Middle East by sailing up the Neva to Lake Ladoga and Novgorod, then overland and down the Dnieper to the Black Sea (Dollinger, 1964 [1970], p. 27). A number of these left Arab gold coins buried at Visby on the island of Gotland because of the absence of banks in the twelfth century, coins whose owners failed to return or to find them again, now turned up by metal detectors. For purchases in the Levant, they took silver. Later, after the passage to India around the Cape of Good Hope, various East India companies of England, Holland, and France were a steady drain on the silver supplies arriving from Spanish America as they took coin with them to compensate for the unbalanced trade in merchandise. The Far East had little interest in European goods—woolens unsuitable for hot climates or grain and drink that might spoil on a long voyage—whereas rising incomes in Europe increased the demand for Eastern luxuries.

THE AGE OF DISCOVERY

The first step in compensation for the bullion famine came about the middle of the fifteenth century when the spread of the lateen (fore-and-aft) sail to supplement the square-rigged caravel, together with the development of the stern rudderpost and the compass, made possible larger ships and extended the range of Portuguese sailors. Penetration far south along the African coast had faced the disability of a difficult return to the north against prevailing trade winds. With lateen sails, the sailors of Henry the Navigator were able to sail around Cape Bojador and to approach the gold country of the Upper Volta from the coast (Vilar, 1969 [1976], ch. 5). Genoans observed the success of the Portuguese and copied it. By the end of the century, Columbus had set off on his voyage into the unknown Atlantic. That it was motivated by the search for gold is attested by the fact that his diary of the voyage lasting less than a hundred days mentions gold sixty-five times (ibid., p. 63). Small deposits of gold were found in the Caribbean and, on later voyages, in Brazil. The more impressive result was the discovery of rich silver deposits, first in Peru and then in Mexico. From about 1560, silver took the spotlight away from gold.

The major mine in Peru, Potosi, was discovered in 1545, 4,000 meters high in the Andes, remote from both oceans. The trip to Lima on the Pacific took two and a half months; Buenos Aires on the Atlantic "South Sea" was 2,400 kilometers away. Full exploitation of Potosi awaited the 1563 discovery at Huancavelica in Peru of mercury needed to refine silver. This produced more than half the mercury needed at Potosi, the rest being brought from Almaden in Spain, mines pledged to the Fuggers in the sixteenth century as a gauge against loans, and worked by the Rothschilds in the nineteenth century (Ehrenberg, 1896 [1928], p. 337). Rounding up the labor for Potosi was a formidable task, calling even for enslavement of local Indians. Population around the mines rose from 45,000 in 1555 to 120,000 in 1585 and 160,000 in 1610. At the peak, production of silver in all the Americas, including the major Mexican mines of Guanajuato and Zacatecas, which expanded after output at Potosi had started to wane, reached 300 tons a year. Some was used locally, some shipped directly to the Far East to take advantage of high prices there, and, on the average, 170 tons a year were sent to Europe (Vilar, 1969 [1976], ch. 14). This torrent of silver, distributed in complex ways, drove the gold/silver price from such figures as 11.3 to 1 in 1519 and 10.6 to 1 in 1553–63, when gold was in the ascendancy (Spooner, 1972, p. 15), to 12.2 in 1566–1608, 13.3 in 1609–42, and 15.45 in 1643–50 (Hamilton, 1934 [1965], p. 71).

The Spanish Crown tried to monopolize the flow of silver to Europe. One-fifth of it was taxed away, and the rest was required to be brought to the mint at Seville. Romance has it that Dutch, French, and English fleets and privateers captured the Spanish annual *flota* from time to time, but Hamilton is impressed how little slipped out of Spanish hands en route to the Peninsula (ibid., p. 19). The Dutch captured the fleet in 1628 under Admiral Piet Hein—the sailors rioted on return to Amsterdam because their bonus amounted only to sixteen months' pay instead of the promised seventeen (van Loon, 1930, p. 34); the English diverted most of the Terra Ferma flotilla in 1658. But gold and silver did not stay long in Spain.

The Spanish were at war during most of the sixteenth and first half of the seventeenth century until the Treaty of Westphalia, which brought an end to the Thirty Years' War in 1648. They were encouraged in warlike pursuits and discouraged in the more humdrum pursuits of agriculture, commerce, and industry by the rich treasure uncovered in the New World. The treasure was spent as fast as, and frequently even faster than, it was acquired. Ferdinand and Isabella borrowed from the Fuggers, other German bankers, and the Genoans, first to equip their fleets, then to make war, and had to pay them back when their arrears did not mount to such heights that default was a reasonable option. Treasure, especially silver, poured into Seville and out again by a variety of routes, by water successively to Antwerp, Amsterdam, London, and at the last Hamburg; southward via Barcelona to Genoa and its fairs at such places as Piacenza; and by land in a less extensive trickle to France by way of Biarritz. Despite all the silver that went through its hands, Spain was forced at the end of the sixteenth century to debase its money with copper bought in Europe, issuing money made of vellon, which by the reign of Philip III in 1599 was virtually pure copper. The Iberian Peninsula suffered another bullion famine, which was not alleviated until the Portuguese discovered gold in 1680 in Minas Gerais in Brazil. This brought a new flow of specie to Europe, this time to Portugal and through it to London, which formed an alliance with Portugal in the 1703 Treaty of Methuen in order to help divert the flow from Amsterdam. In one view, this monetary stimulus helped pave the way for the industrial revolution almost a hundred years later (Spooner, 1972, p. 40). The claim seems excessive, but such an economic historian as Werner Sombart lent his reputation to it.

THE QUANTITY THEORY OF MONEY

The first statement of the quantity theory of money in any complete form was made in 1568 by Jean Bodin, a Frenchman, writing a reply to the paradoxes of Malestroit concerning the price rise of the period. Malestroit had been fully aware that prices had risen but ascribed that fact primarily to debasement of the coinage. Debasement had occurred in most countries, especially in England under Henry VIII and in France. But prices calculated in silver had risen as well as prices in monetary units, as Bodin pointed out (Vilar, 1969 [1976], pp. 90–91). Hamilton's classic study provides a diagram tracking the movement of prices in Spain against the arrivals of specie from 1501 to 1650. Except at the beginning, when an increase in German silver output raised prices, and at the end when an epidemic and overissue of vellon again distorted the relationship, the two curves conform well. They are claimed by Hamilton (1934 [1965], p. 301) to demonstrate convincingly the truth of Irving Fisher's twentieth-century formulation of the quantity theory of money (Figure 2.1).

There are problems here, however. Hamilton's figures rely on the records of the Casa de la Contratacion (House of Trade) in Seville, which have been shown to be incomplete. Larger ships and the formation of a bar in the Guadalquivir River made it necessary after about 1630 to unload downstream at Cadiz. Specie was required to be brought up to Seville so that the 5 percent tax could be levied, but not all was. Some was illegally sold in Cadiz to Dutch and English East India companies en route to the East. Some was offloaded in Lisbon. Using Dutch newspapers, M. Morineau concludes, and a Swedish scholar concurs, that the Hamilton estimates of a substantial decline after 1630 are mistaken. There was some decline in the 1640s and 1650s from the range of 9 million rixdollars a year, somewhat below the peak level of 11.3 million a year from 1591 to 1600, but 9 million held until 1640. Then followed a substantial increase to the level of 14 million after 1660 as Mexico took over from the fading production of Peru, and this was sustained until the end of the century (Attman, 1986, Tables 1.1 and 1.3, pp. 14, 15). But Morineau is said to overstate the net addition to silver in Europe in neglecting to take full note of the stream of silver moving east by way of the Baltic (ibid., p. 75, note 2).

DEBASEMENT

Some allowance for debasement must be made in the price revolution of the sixteenth century. It took two forms. The first was a deliberate attempt by sovereigns to acquire resources, generally for war, by issuing more units of money for the same amount of metal brought to the mint. This happened once in English history, under Henry VIII during the French-Spanish Wars. The plunder of the monasteries was insufficient for the satisfaction of the Tudor appetite, and between 1526 and 1546 Henry raised the prices of gold and silver in a series of uneven steps from £24 per troy pound for gold to £30 and from £2 to £2 8*s* for silver (Gould, 1970, pp. 9–11). Some adjustment was made in the opposite direction on a number of occasions in British financial history: in 1561 under Elizabeth I, in 1696 during the "great recoinage" of the Nine Years' War (Li, 1963), and in the two postwar revaluations of the pound sterling about a hundred years apart, in 1819 and 1925. All involved deflation. That of the "calling down" of the testoon (old shilling) from 12*d* to 9*d* and further to 6*d* in 1551 and to 4½*d* for the better base testoons in 1561 was deflationary in the long run but inflationary in the short as people tried to spend existing

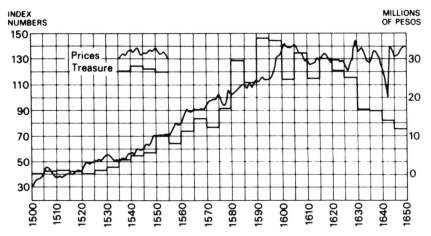

Figure 2.1 Total quinquennial treasure imports and composite index numbers of commodity prices. *Source:* Hamilton (1934 [1965] p. 301).

coins before their value fell. We return to the deflationary aspects of 1696, 1819, and 1925 below.

A steady form of debasement came about from using two precious metals as money, with a changing market price between them. A change in the demand or supply for either metal would lead to a change in the market price of one or the other and the need to make an adjustment of mint prices to make them conform to the market. One could keep existing coins and adjust the tariff or tale (nominal value) of one of them, enhancing a coin, or crying up its nominal value, or calling the other down; or one could keep existing denominations of the coins and adjust metallic weight of one set. Whether the tale was adjusted or the weight, there was a choice between raising the tale (calling up) or lowering the weight of the undervalued coin, or lowering the tale (or raising the weight) of the overvalued. Raising the weight or lowering the tale was expensive for the sovereign, and hence generally avoided. The easy course was to "call up" undervalued coin, that is, raise their nominal value, or to lower their weight. As silver fell in price in the market, existing coins were called up or their weight lowered. On the few occasions it became gold's turn, the same procedure was followed. The result was a ratchet, with continuous depreciation of metallic coins. A troy pound of silver that originally was worth a pound sterling ended up in 1816 at a price of £3 6s. (The word *troy* comes from the system of weights used at the fairs of Troyes in France and amounts to 12 ounces avoirdupois.)

Debasement could also come in a spurt, as the *Kipper- und Wipperzeit* of the Thirty Years' War in the Holy Roman Empire demonstrates. This involved: (1) needs for funds of governments in anticipation of and during war, at a time when the elementary state of tax systems and capital markets meant that profits from the minting of coins were the most convenient source of revenue; (2) a breakdown in limits on the numbers of mints and of their surveillance to ensure that their output conformed to established standards; (3) use of bad coins to pay mercenary soldiers and to exchange against the good coins of a neighboring territory, with unsophisticated people being hoodwinked into giving up goods or good coins for debased coin; and (4) the authorities of the cheated area defending their territory by debasing their money in turn. The process is described in van Klavaren (1969, pp. 105–10) and the hyperinflation graphed in Kindleberger (1991a, p. 164). Inflation started slowly before the outbreak of war in 1618 and escalated rapidly from 1619 to 1622, at different rates in different parts of the Holy Roman Empire—more slowly in the north than in the south. Unlike subsequent German hyperinflations, this began before war had gone far and was over in a short time, long before the war's end. The halt came when everyone, including simple folk, understood that the newly minted monies were worthless—mostly copper whitened to look like silver. When no one would accept the debased money, the emperor and the rulers of the separate entities were forced to reinstate the Augsburg Ordinance of 1559 setting standards for coinage and start again.

THE PRICE REVOLUTION?

Since Hamilton's book came out in 1934, something of a question has arisen whether the discovery of Spanish America produced a price revolution de novo or whether it merely supported one already underway. The argument is a familiar one that we shall encounter a number of times—in the debate between the banking and the currency school in nineteenth-century England; between those who blame the first great depression represented by the fall in prices between 1873 and 1896 on slowdown in the rate of increase in gold stocks and demonetization of silver, and those who ascribe it to real factors; and again in the explanation of the German inflation after World War I, held by monetarists to be due to simple overproduction of money and by their opponents to a complex set of real factors, including reparations, restocking, and speculation.

Malestroit ascribed the rise of prices in the first half of the sixteenth century not only to debasement but also to real factors, notably civil unrest and the loss of labor following famines. Bodin's development of the quantity theory was a reply to these paradoxes, and for a long time it carried the day, especially with the help of Hamilton's data. Lately, however, something of antithesis or synthesis has developed. It is noted, for example, that the price revolution began well before Spanish silver reached its full flood, which was not until 1560 or 1570, whereas prices had risen to 400 by 1560 (1411–75 as 100); that food prices rose more than luxuries, suggesting a slower rise in supply rather than an increase in demand; that prices rose fairly uniformly everywhere, three and a half to five times in Spain, three to four times in England, two and a half to three and a half times in Poland, which was off the main track of Spanish suppliers (C. Wilson, 1976, pp. 27—29). It is noted that the demand for money was not fully satisfied by Spanish silver, so that gold and silver plate was brought to mints to be coined.

There is some objection, too, to Hamilton's price data. He used the most abundant and available source—records for municipal hospitals—in which prices may reflect long-term contracts with actual price fluctuations absorbed by changes in quality (Outhwaite, 1969, p. 32). Hamilton's faith in this source is not particularly convincing; he concludes from it that the level of living in early eighteenth-century France was high. If patients in charity hospitals were served beef, mutton, chicken, butter, eggs, fish, and cheese, he asserts hospital administrators must believe that this is what they were accustomed to at home, rather than the bread and water on which most scholars thought they subsisted (Hamilton, 1969, p. 136).

A strong movement of population took place in the second half of the fifteenth century, when money was scarce and grain cheap, from the countryside to the cities. When food became scarce in the sixteenth century because of crop failures, prices rose, but unevenly. On a base of 1511–20 as 100, grain rose to 274 over 1561–70, other foodstuffs to 161, and industrial goods to 118, while wages fell to 81, all this well before the flood of silver had had time to work (North, 1990, p. 225). One odd feature of the price movement that fails to square with the monetary explanation is that prices of lamb and geese actually fell because the price of fodder rose so high that the animals had to be slaughtered (ibid., p. 186). By and large the view that the price rises of the sixteenth century were a purely monetary phenomenon based on Spanish-American silver has lost out to the belief that it had real roots in population growth and crop failure.

The main a priori attack on the price revolution rests on the belief that, apart from the short run when money may be inelastic and halt a boom, money adjusts to trade rather than trade to money as the quantity theory would have it (Maynard, 1962, p. 69, n.1, quoted by Outhwaite, 1969, p. 43). If a clear-cut choice must be made between real factors and the quantity theory of money, this goes to the heart of the issue. But both explanations can be right and leapfrog one another: the bullion famine of the fifteenth century led to frantic search for money; in the early stages there was likely dishoarding and the coinage of plate; then came the arrival of considerable supplies of silver from America, an uncertain amount of which remained in Europe after normal losses and shipments to the East (Table 2.1). Population growth, harvest failures, war, and net accretions of money interacted. Monetarists such as Hamilton and Bloch blamed the silver for the price revolution. The general economic historian Postan, supported by the agricultural economists Wilhelm Abel (1966) and B. H. Slicher van Bath (1960 [1963]), favor the "real" explanation.

SEIGNORAGE

Seignorage is the profit on minting of coins, earned by the mint, usually owned or farmed out by the sovereign, who has a certain *droit de seigneur* or monopoly on

Table 2.1 The Circulation of Precious Metals, 1550–1800 (in millions of rixdollars per year)

Supplies from America	1550	1600	1650	1700	1750	1780	1800
To Spain	3	10	8–9	10–12	10–15	15–20	20–25
To Portugal				0.5	8–10	3	2
Bullion flow to the East	(2–3)	4.4	6	8.5	12.2	14.7	18

Source: Attman (1986, Table 1.15, p. 33).

such profits. The issue of whether money should be monopolized or open to competition is one of the oldest conundrums in the sensitive question of money that will occupy us in later chapters. Friederich A. Hayek and Roland Vaubel have urged a return to competition in the issuance of money on the widely accepted ground that monopoly breeds inefficiency and exploitation (Hayek, 1972; Vaubel, 1977). The issue arose in modern context largely over the best method of arriving at European monetary union, with Vaubel, for example, arguing for a system of parallel currencies that compete for acceptance rather than attempt to construct a single European monetary unit. Possible concern for Gresham's law instability that may enter when there are two or more monies is dismissed with the observation that this cannot arise if the several currencies are free to move in value against one another. It is even claimed that Gresham's law—a subject reserved for Chapter 4— can work the other way as good money drives out bad. Theoretically this could happen in sellers' markets when the sellers insist on being paid in good money; history reveals few such episodes. What history does reveal is that when bad money becomes so bad that nobody, even the innocent and unsophisticated, will accept it, good money is drawn into the vacuum. But this is not so much good money driving out bad as good, or perhaps only better, money being drawn into situations where money has ceased to exist. And short of that eventuality, which occurs infrequently in hyperinflations, history records a steady and hardly misguided series of monetary reforms, consisting of reducing the number of mints or note-issuing banks and seeking, not always successfully, to get better control of the money supply.

Debasing the coinage to raise seignorage for governments has been briefly noted in the discussion of the *Kipper- und Wipperzeit* of 1619–23. The practice was by no means new then. In France, Aragon, and Catalonia between approximately 1000 and 1125, businessmen were so disturbed by debasement of the coinage that they entered into contracts with the ruling authorities to maintain the currency in exchange for voluntary payments. Kings and lords were not only urged to "conserve" the coinage; they were paid to do so. A bishop of Catalonia excommunicated those who debased, counterfeited, or clipped the episcopal money. Agreements to buy and sell goods were written specifying good coin, or money of legitimate weight, or coin of the best gold (Bisson, 1979, passim, esp. pp. 1, 55, 63–64). The payments were gradually transformed into a money tax or tallage. And before long, the seigneurs went back to exacting seignorage as well as the taxes.

As debasement spread over the turn from the sixteenth to the seventeenth century, attempts were made to limit the number of mints in the Holy Roman Empire. In 1603 and 1604, it was ordained that there should be no more than three or four mints to a *Kreis* (or circle), a district administering monetary standards, usually comprising a considerable number of smaller governmental units, except for those circles that contained silver mines. This ordinance was opposed by a number of cities in the Lower Saxon Circle, each with a mint—Bremen, Brunswick, Lübeck, Magdeburg, and Rostock. When this opposition succeeded, other towns started mints—those with traditional privileges establishing more mints and others starting up new. Rulers established or leased mints to others, who added their profit to the rental payment, acclerating the debasement. Even the Holy Roman emperor himself, Ferdinand II, leased a mint to a consortium of rich merchants and nobles against a payment of 6 million guilders. Brunswick had seventeen mints in 1620 and forty by 1623, including among the latter one installed in a convent with 300 to 400 workers.

The extraction of seignorage was more draconian in south Germany than in the mercantile cities along the Baltic and North Sea coasts. Confusion equally abounded in Holland about this time, when each province had its own mint—one had two—and six cities had municipal mints, making fourteen in all, each operating to maximize seignorage as revenue for governmental purposes. An attempt to standardize the coins issued and restrict the systems of coins to four failed. It was not until 1681 that the number of mints was reduced to eight and regulations governing standards were adequately enforced (Vilar, 1969 [1976], p. 205). But the path the Dutch chose out of the monetary chaos of the period led through the creation of banks and the issuance of deposits against coin that was assayed and weighed, a topic reserved for the next chapter.

A ruler has a choice between his private short-run interest and the public long-run one. In the short run, profits can be maximized by adulteration; in the long run, by producing to quality standards. There is no a priori basis for determining that a given society will conform to one standard of performance or the other.

When the Crown has a monopoly and charges seignorage, there is still a dilemma. If seignorage is too high, coins may not be accepted, and little, if any, bullion will be brought to the mint. If it is too low, nonexistent, or negative, existing or newly minted coins are in danger of being melted down or exported whenever the market price for metal rises even slightly above the mint price.

MERCANTILISM

The drain of specie from Europe in the Middle Ages and the resulting shortages of money led to a doctrine favoring measures to safeguard the national money supply that came to be known loosely as mercantilism. A comparable doctrine existed in the field of food—the "policy of abundance," or "policy of supply," that induced city- and nation-states to restrict exports of food from the countryside as a whole, or from certain regions, until there was adequate assurance that cities could be fed during the year. Many cities imported grain for government account and, as in Venice, established a "grain office" to hold stocks against a bad harvest. Physiocratic doctrine developed in opposition to the policy of supply, producing the slogan, "Laissez faire, laissez passer," to permit the export of grain so that higher demand would raise prices and agricultural income. This recommendation was adopted in the seventeenth and eighteenth centuries, possibly because of the force of the argument, but probably because of an increase in agricultural production, on the one hand, and, on the other, the extension of international trade that made it possible, beginning in the 1590s, to import grains from East Prussia and Poland to the Italian city-states to make up for shortages.

The mercantilist school was attacked as bitterly as were proponents of the policy of supply, and yet there was some basis for their fears of depression in commerce and agriculture, resulting from losses of specie and inadequate substitutes. Keynes's defense of mercantilism (1936, ch. 23) has been dismissed as full of inaccuracies and misinterpretations (deRoover, 1949, p. 287n), but a new defense has been put forward by Robert Mundell, who in a recent paper has a section on "The Alleged Mercantilist Fallacy," suggesting considerable merit to the notion in a period of economic growth (1989, pp. 399–403). Mercantilist fears began to lessen from the middle of the sixteenth century with the gain of silver from Latin America, which, together with money substitutes, reduced the danger of monetary famine. Money substitutes lagged in such a country as France because, according to Hume, it had great quantities of bullion in coin and plate (1752 [1898], p. 338). But while the alarm felt earlier was not completely unreasonable, most measures that were proposed, and even adopted, to counteract exports of bullion and coin revealed unthinking prejudice and limited understanding of the mechanics of international trade.

The devices used were many and varied: prohibition against the export of specie and efforts to enforce it against rampant smuggling; the requirement that exporters bring back gold or silver in payment for part of their foreign sales; statutes of employment that demanded that importers pay for some part of their foreign purchases with goods produced in the country (that of 1390 forced merchants who imported foreign goods to spend half their value on wool, tin, lambfells, and other native commodities—(Ehrenberg, 1896 [1928], p. 39); concentration of all transactions in bills of exchange in a royal exchanger, an office actually established in 1576, quickly abandoned, but frequently proposed anew thereafter, with the sole right to buy and sell bills of exchange, coin, and bullion in foreign transactions, and the mission of achieving the appropriate balance. Some wanted the exchange rate depreciated through debasing the coinage in order to expand exports, reduce imports, and halt the loss of specie. Thus John Gilbert, a goldsmith who favored debasement in the depression of 1620 to relieve the tightness of the money market, bring bullion to the mint, and lower the rate of interest ("decrease the price of usury"), is called a Lord Keynes by de Roover (1949, p. 90). Gresham himself wanted to manipulate the exchange rate to appreciate sterling so as to repay loans contracted in Antwerp more cheaply in English money; he was a strong deflationist, ready to accept lower prices and unemployment for the sake of the queen's financial interest (ibid., p. 92). Among his interesting recommendations was one for the establishment of a "bank" or stabilization fund to intervene in the exchange market and achieve the desired appreciation. Gerald Malynes, the quintessential mercantilist, argued in favor of the royal exchanger with the mission of holding the exchange rate at par against the conspiracies of foreign dealers. (The theme that the exchange rate is manipulated by foreign speculators is one that crops up continuously, and especially in France in the 1920s.)

A considerable part of the disputes of the period had their origin in the strong xenophobia of the English, especially against Italian exchange dealers, disliked by the City of London and thought to connive to drain England of bullion. Antwerp bankers, too, were suspected of Catholic plots on behalf of the king of Spain, Charles V, who was also the Holy Roman Emperor (ibid., p. 107).

Controversy over the foreign exchanges in England occupied leading bankers and merchants over a number of years. Royal commissions were established on the occasion of each setback or depression (in 1564, 1576, 1600, and 1622), after the

English government took the extreme steps of suspending all exchange dealings in 1551 and establishing a royal exchanger in 1576. The various proposals listed earlier were put forward at one time and another, sometimes tried, including a small adjustment of the silver price in the direction of debasement—from 60*s* per troy pound to 62*s,* in 1600.

Thomas Mun was a member of the 1622 Royal Commission, a strong opponent of conspiracy theories and an advocate of leaving the exchanges alone. He thought, in fact, that it was impossible to affect the exchange rate. Merchant, director of the East India Company, grandson of a master of the mint, he opposed especially the school led by Malynes that wanted to manipulate the exchange rate. In 1630 he wrote *England's Treasure by Forraign Trade, or the Ballance of Trade is the Rule of our Treasure,* published by his son in 1664, and attacked the notion that the exchange rate could be diverted from levels set by the market, or that it should be, given the mechanism by which foreign trade adjusted itself:

. . . in Italy where the greatest Banks and Bankers of Christendom do trade, yet I could never see nor hear, that they did, or were able to rule the price of Exchange by confederacie, but still the plenty or scarcity of money in the course of trade did always overrule them. . . .

Any attempt to maintain our store of money in the realm . . . will only make our native commodities dearer and cause their forraign consumption to fall, while causing us to consume more forraign wares . . . lest when we have gained some store of money by trade, we lose it again by not trading with our money. (Mun, 1664 [1965], p. 20)

For completeness of the record, it should be noted that mercantilism in France under Colbert had a strong positive element of creating a nation with national markets, centralized direction of foreign trade, and national money, out of a collection of loosely joined provinces.

Was mercantilism in the English version always a misguided doctrine, or, while it was poorly based intellectually because its proponents inadequately understood foreign trade and payments, had the underlying anxiety that prompted the worries been real? A clear-cut answer is difficult to provide since the complexities of the payments mechanism interact with the real difficulties of balancing trade with a country or area that we would call today a low absorber. In one discussion, for example, Heckscher criticizes the mercantilists for worrying over silver losses in the Baltic and refers to the possibility that trade with Poland and Russia could have been settled through bills of exchange on a triangular basis. The issue anticipates the discussion of bills of exchange in the next chapter, but Heckscher's position has been criticized in pointing out that there was little possibility for triangular balancing for English trade with the Baltic when Dutch ships, which did the bulk of the business, were also going eastward with silver coin and a great deal of ballast (C. Wilson, 1949 [1953]; Heckscher, 1950; Supple, 1959, p. 85). Even Mun conceded that the English needed specie for purchases in the Baltic and the Far East, but by his time it was becoming easy to attract silver from Spain.

BULLIONISM

A lineal descendant of mercantilism is bullionism, which flourished especially in the nineteenth century but is also alive today in the thought of such men as the late

Jacques Rueff of Paris and Robert Mundell of Columbia University. To the bullionist, the only real money is gold (or silver). Money substitutes are money only to the extent that they are limited in quantity to a volume of specie that is set aside. The most famous bullionist of the nineteenth century was Lord Overstone, taken by Dickens as the model for Mr. Dombey—most unfairly, insofar as Mr. Dombey is an unsympathetic figure who had no friends and who failed in business, whereas Lord Overstone had a wide circle of intimates and was inordinately successful as banker and as pundit on financial questions.

The thread of bullionism will run through the chapters below. But the next task is to discuss the rise of bank money as a substitute for coin.

SUGGESTED SUPPLEMENTARY READING

Feaveryear (1931 [1963]), *The Pound Sterling.*
Hamilton (1934 [1965]), *American Treasure and the Price Revolution in Spain, 1501–1650.*
Heckscher (1935) [1985]), *Mercantilism.*
Shaw, W. A. (1895), *The History of Currency, 1252 to 1894.*
Van der Wee (1977), Money, credit and banking systems.
Vilar (1969 [1976]), *A History of Gold and Money, 1450–1920.*

In French
Sédillot (1953), *Le Franc.*

3
Bank Money

Alterations in the traffique, hath forced them of Genoa to change their course of trading with wares, into the exchanging of their money: which for gain they spread not only into diverse Countreys where the trade is performed with Merchandise, but more especially do therewith serve the wants of the Spanish in Flanders and other places for their wars. Whereas they find no means in their own Countrey to employ and trade their great wealth to profit, they content themselves to do it in Spain and other places . . . by exchanging their monies for grain to those Merchants who trade therewith in wares. And thus wheresoever they (the monies) live abroad for a time, circuiting the world for gain; yet in the end the Center of this profit is in their own Native countrey.

(Mun, *England's Treasure by Forraign Trade,* 1664 [1965], pp. 52–53)

TRADE AND FINANCE

The usual textbook view is that banking developed from goldsmiths who issued receipts for gold left with them, which later circulated from hand to hand, and that observation of this circulation ultimately induced goldsmiths to issue receipts without previous deposit. The story is well told but inaccurate. Goldsmiths evolved into bankers only in the middle of the seventeenth century in England. Banking developed much earlier and was connected especially with foreign trade. Even in the eighteenth century more banks in England developed from merchants than from goldsmiths. At that stage, moreover, many other paths led to banking—industry issuing tokens to pay wages, tax farmers handling public funds, notaries (scriveners) recommending investments and then making them for others, and so on. But the merchant connection remained paramount.

Early merchants conducted trade in a sort of barter. They would sell goods in a town for local money and use the proceeds to buy goods in the same market. As the bill of exchange developed, it became possible for the individual merchant to sell or buy in one direction only, against bills of exchange. Before long, trade in goods became less interesting for some, and a number of merchants developed into dealers in bills of exchange or into bankers.

By "merchant" in this connection I mean "great merchant," and by "great merchant" one who deals in international trade, not a domestic wholesaler or jobber, and assuredly not a retailer. In France the term is *négociant,* distinct from the *marchand,* and in German the *Kaufmann,* not the *Händler.* In Holland, distinction was made among the First Hand who brought goods to, and took them from, Amsterdam, from and to abroad; the Second Hand who did sorting, packing, grading, finishing; and the Third Hand who distributed locally—but the English language has no such distinction.

Adam Smith claimed that the only difference between a competent retailer and a great merchant was the quantity of his capital (1776 [1937], pp. 113–14). It is perhaps heretical to take issue with the founder of economics, but the opinion calls for rejection. The great merchant had to deal with foreign exchange rates and bills of exchange, frequently speculated in commodities, and to a great extent needed competence in foreign languages.

In many cases, and for a long time, trade and banking went along together. Hope & Company, great Dutch bankers of the eighteenth century, operated in commodities and regarded themselves as commodity speculators, long after the bulk of their business shifted to billbroking, "from which foreign loans emerged as a natural consequence" (Buist, 1974, esp. ch. 10; C. Wilson, 1941, ch. 3, esp. p. 66). In particular, bankers were happy to operate a monopoly in a commodity, as Sir Horatio Palavicino, exchange dealer for Queen Elizabeth after Sir Thomas Gresham, did in alum or the Fuggers in Spanish mercury. But the strong contributor to the transition from trade to finance was desire for less risk, less trouble, and higher status. Dealing in money instead of goods was safer and easier (Ehrenberg, 1896 [1928], p. 243). And everywhere the change from sea to land led to enrollment of the most successful merchants in the gentry, sometimes in the aristocracy (Burke, 1974).

STATE VERSUS PRIVATE MONEY

An issue that runs through the history of money is its intrinsic nature. Is money what the state says is money—legal tender in some formulations that must be accepted in payment of debts, if offered—or is it what people use as money? The question is connected with the differences between coin, discussed in the previous chapter, and bank money, which is the subject here. It goes wider and deeper, however. As a unit of account, money is a creature of the state; as a medium of exchange, despite the legal tender question, it is what markets use. Three French economists have produced a book, *Monnaie privée et le pouvoir des princes,* tracing out the two types of money with their different but overlapping functions in Latin Christianity—Italy, Spain, and France—during the Renaissance, and especially the sixteenth century. They emphasize the development and spread of the network of bills of exchange as private money, extending the use of coin produced in mints under the authority of rulers, who frequently insisted that the coins be struck marked with royal symbols (Boyer-Xambeu, Deleplace, and Gillard, 1986). Metallic money, of course, goes back to ancient times. Private money developed only during the present millennium. It required a network of traders and financiers who knew and trusted one another. The bill of exchange could not be used in trade with or in the Hanseatic League, with eastern Europe, or with the Middle or Far East, which is why the silver (and to a lesser extent the gold) of western Europe flowed eastward. Latin Christianity, and especially Italy, pioneered the way. Northern and eastern Europe for the most part followed at the end of the sixteenth century and in the seventeenth. The start went back to medieval times and to the fairs on the routes between Italy and Flanders in eastern France.

FAIRS

In medieval times local trade was handled in markets, international trade in fairs. Among the earliest fairs were those of Champagne in France, which dealt importantly in Flemish cloth and flourished particularly in the twelfth and thirteenth centuries. Fairs were highly organized, coming at regular intervals, twice or four times a year, at regular places, and evolving a set procedure, such as nine days for trading cloth (six for showing and three for sales), eleven for leather, two weeks for goods sold by weight (*avoirs du poids*), and then fixed days for settlement (Usher, 1943, pp. 118–19). During the time of fairs, foreigners were given the protection of the seigneur—the count of Champagne, the duke of Burgundy, or the king of France—rights to which they were not entitled at other times.

Settlement involved a species of clearing. Each merchant kept a book in which he entered what he owed (the *vostro*) and what was owed him (*nostro*). When the date for settlement came, an official of the fair would validate the claims and liabilities in the merchant's book and effect cancellations to reduce the need for payment in coin (Ehrenberg, 1896 [1928], p. 284). Uncanceled balances might be paid in currency, in bills of exchange brought to the fair, or in new bills drawn to carry the claim or debt over to the next fair. Gradually tax collectors came to fairs to buy bills on other fairs or towns to which they needed to transmit payments or to sell bills to collect funds held elsewhere. Agents of royal borrowers would attend the settlement to raise cash against bills or other evidence of debt, normally secured by a city, the pledge of taxes, valuable possessions, or some sort of concession to manage mines, or escape restrictions. Cancellation or clearing provided part of the settlement, but much of it was handled through bills of exchange. Merchants brought and took away some specie. It also inevitably helped settlement for the fair to receive a shipment of silver or gold, coin or bullion, brought by some merchant or banker to exchange for commodities or bills of exchange on a place to which he wanted the money transferred. In due course, all kinds of financial transactions came to be handled at fairs, not only foreign exchange but real estate, banking, early forms of insurance, and lotteries. In 1600, the turnover at the Piacenza fair came to as much as 3 million or 4 million crowns (Braudel, 1949 [1972], Vol. 1, p. 439).

Fairs flourished at various times and places. When the Champagne fairs began to decline in the fourteenth century, a move was made to Geneva on the western route between northern Europe and Italy (Usher, 1943, p. 120). In 1445 French merchants were forbidden by the king to attend the Geneva fair; in due course a French fair was established at Lyons. Later in 1534 the Genoans were excluded from Lyons for political reasons and started a rival fair in Besançon. This gradually moved to the south, stopping at various places such as Beaucaire in southern France, and finally to Italy, mostly to Piacenza, where it developed into a Genoan fair purely for trading in foreign exchange. It continued to be called the Besançon fair, or in Italian *Bisenzone* (da Silva, 1969, Vol. 1, ch. 1).

First at Bruges and then, after its decline starting in the second half of the fifteenth century, in Antwerp, trade became permanent, year round. Antwerp started with two fairs a year, acquired the payments portion of the two fairs at Bergen-op-Zoom,

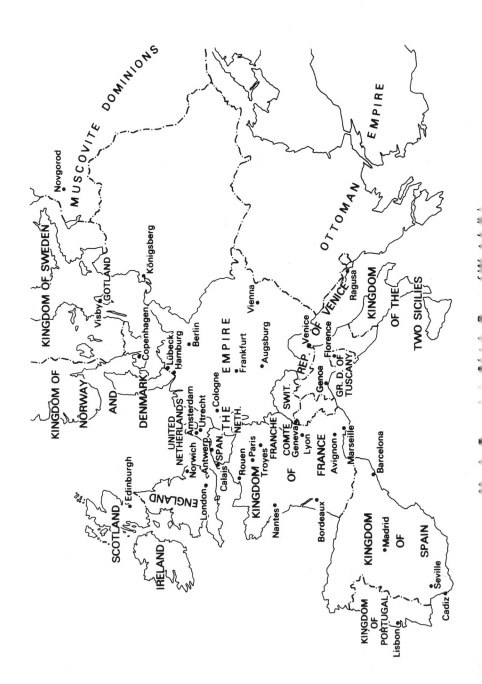

NORWAY AND

KINGDOM OF NORWAY

KINGDOM OF SWEDEN

MUSCOVITE DOMINIONS

Novgorod

Visby

GOTLAND

Königsberg

Copenhagen

DENMARK

Lübeck

Hamburg

Berlin

Vienna

Frankfurt

Augsburg

THE EMPIRE

Cologne

Utrecht

Amsterdam

UNITED NETHERLANDS

SPAN. NETH.

Norwich

Antwerp

London

Calais

Rouen

Paris

Troyes

FRANCHE

KINGDOM OF

Nantes

Edinburgh

SCOTLAND

IRELAND

ENGLAND

SWIT.

Geneva

Lyon

COMTE OF

FRANCE

Avignon

Marseille

Genoa

GR. D. OF TUSCANY

Florence

REP. OF VENICE

Venice

Ragusa

OTTOMAN

EMPIRE

KINGDOM OF THE TWO SICILIES

Barcelona

KINGDOM OF SPAIN

Madrid

Seville

Cadiz

KINGDOM OF PORTUGAL

Lisbon

Bordeaux

which made it four fairs a year, and then settled down as a permanent international market for goods and money. A bourse was built in 1531, patterned after the square in Bruges, called Burse, where the Italians had done their trading (Ehrenberg, 1896 [1928], pp. 55, 237). Sir Thomas Gresham, Queen Elizabeth's royal exchanger, was stationed in Antwerp from 1551 or 1552 and later built the Royal Exchange in London as a bourse for trade in international paper.

Foreign merchants and dealers were sometimes organized into "nations," within which they had rights as in the German Fondaco dei Tedeschi in Venice, the Hanseatic Steelyard in London, or the Swiss "nation" in Lyons. In Bruges there was a "house of all nations," an expression taken as the title for a novel on twentieth-century banking by Christina Stead (1938). Italian bankers in London remained closely tied to their native land, returning there to marry and to be buried (Bratchel, 1980).

Antwerp came under siege at the end of the sixteenth century, being blockaded by the Dutch at the mouth of the river Scheldt in 1572 and by Spanish troops in 1585. These actions cut off grain from the Baltic, copper from Hungary, silver from Spain. The foreign community moved off to Amsterdam and with it a number of Flemish merchants and bankers. In a very short space of time Amsterdam became the relay for European trade and payments for the next 150 years until it was overtaken by London in trade about 1730 and in money dealings during the Napoleonic Wars. Like financial centers before it, it innovated in trade and finance.

THE BILL OF EXCHANGE

The bill of exchange was a powerful innovation of the Italians in the thirteenth century that economized on the need to barter, clear books face to face, or to make payments in bulky coin, plate, or bullion, which were vulnerable to theft, by clearing or canceling a debt owed in one direction by one owed in the other or, more accurately, by one owed in another. To illustrate the bilateral case, if *A* in Florence bought goods from *B* in Bruges, he would often pay for them by buying a bill of exchange drawn by *C* in Florence, or perhaps another Tuscan town, who had sold goods to *D* in Flanders. *C* draws a bill on *D* and collects his money by selling it for local currency to *A,* usually indirectly through an exchange dealer. *A* sends the bill to *B* in payment for his goods, and *B* collects from *D* when the bill matures. Goods move from *B* to *A* and *C* to *D;* payment runs from *A* to *C* and *D* to *B*. If *D* were unable to pay, the bill would be "protested" and the transaction undone. In a broad market, the amounts and places need not be the same.

Bills were originally assignable, or salable, but not actually negotiable because the bearer did not have the right of recourse against previous holders until negotiability became general in the early seventeenth century. Like cancellation on the books of a merchant at a fair, it was nonetheless a money substitute.

The bill had to be sold in the Middle Ages, not discounted, since discounting implied charging interest, forbidden by the Church in Rome as usury. The equivalent of interest was realized, and credit provided, by the buyer of the bill, paying as a rule at an exchange rate below that at which the drawee ultimately paid the bearer. The rate was determined currently in the exchange market, however, and hence was not certain; uncertainty justified the "profit" of the exchange dealer and converted it from interest, which was proscribed.

Credit was involved in dealing in bills even when the request for payment was ostensibly at sight. Mails of the day took time. Bills were payable at sight, at "usance," or sometimes half-usance or double-usance. Usance was the standard credit period for a given trade. From Genoa at the beginning of the sixteenth century, it ran five days for Pisa, six for Milan, fifteen for Ancona, twenty for Barcelona, thirty for Valencia and Montpellier, two months for Bruges, and three for London (Braudel, 1949 [1972], Vol. 1, p. 375). From London usance was one month to Antwerp, two to Hamburg, and three to the northern Italian cities. It was seldom changed: the one month between London and Antwerp lasted from the fourteenth century to 1789 (de Roover, 1949, p. 109).

Along with bills of exchange arising from trade were finance bills, essentially promissory notes, in which A drew on B, who might be his branch or affiliate, and sold the bill to a dealer, undertaking to provide foreign money to make good his debt to B when time was up. "Dry exchange" was a local borrowing disguised as a bill of exchange in order to hide payment of interest; the drawee of the bill would charge for transfer of the credit abroad but agree to accept repayment later at the site of the original transaction (Lopez, 1979, p. 15). A debit balance remaining at the end of a fair might be met by selling a bill drawn on oneself payable at the next fair. This failed to involve an exchange rate and hence was usurious. Fair-to-fair discount might run 2 or 3 percent, which with four fairs a year constituted 8 to 12 percent a year.

Finance bills were sometimes carried out in a series of steps, especially late in the period under discussion, and notoriously by the Ayr Bank of Scotland, which went bankrupt in 1772. Adam Smith called the practice so well known to men of business that there was no need to give an account of it, and then proceeded to do so. A in Edinburgh draws on B in London at two months. B accepts A's bill, that is, agrees that he owes A the money, on condition that he can discharge the debt by selling a bill drawn on A when the draft comes due (1776 [1937], pp. 292–300). If the process is repeated, A discounts now with one banker, now with another to prevent the banks from seeing what is going on. In the 1930s finance bills were sometimes disguised as trade bills by drawing them for odd rather than round amounts. In chains, B would draw on C, rather than back on A, in due course C on D, and so on. Adam Smith called the system pernicious and ruinous, because charges for interest and renewal commissions were heavy. The practice became universal in booms in seventeenth-century Amsterdam, and a Dutch name came into existence for it—*Wisselruiterij* (in German *Wechselreiterei*), meaning "chains of bills of exchange"; firms in trouble would pay off a maturing draft with a new one on another house (Buist, 1974, p. 13).

The prejudice against finance bills, sometimes called accommodation paper, extended into the twentieth century, although a moderate view would distinguish between a straight finance bill and chains of bills, which have on occasion raised credit of individuals or firms far beyond the ordinary capacity of the borrower. There is no magic in a trade bill that ensures its final liquidation: the commodities involved in the underlying transaction may fall in price and leave the paper worthless, whereas finance paper on a good name constitutes a valuable asset (Hawtrey, 1919 [1927], p. 224). It is sometimes difficult to distinguish the two: the firm of Carlos & Claes Grill in Stockholm in the eighteenth century would export consistently to its London correspondent, Lindegren, and draw bills on him consistently. After a time, particular bills stopped being associated with particular consignments of goods; the Grills drew on Lindegren when they needed money and sent remittances when bills were available for that purpose (Samuelsson, 1955, p. 188).

Payments cleared by bills need not be bilaterally balanced. When the office of royal exchanger was set up in 1576 in England, Italian exchange dealers objected, pointing out that bilateral trade was wasteful in requiring specie movements: with their help English importers of wine from Bordeaux remitted bills on Lyons that were sold by the exporters to pay for Bordeaux purchases from Lyons (Tawney, 1925, p. 68; de Roover, 1949, pp. 212–13). Until 1763 at the end of the Seven Years' War when direct exchange was carried out, London purchases and sales from and to Russia were carried out in Dutch bills, Amsterdam serving as a clearing center for much of British trade with the Continent. The mark of an expert exchange dealer—a Gresham, Palavicino, or Rothschild—was to find new ways around and through the bill markets, especially in time of war. Mistakes were costly: in the time of Henry VIII, £20,000 was sent abroad in specie by the government to pay Swiss mercenaries, when it would have saved £2,000 to have bought bills (Tawney, 1925, p. 69).

USURY

The usury laws of the Church did not so much cut down the amount of lending and borrowing as complicate them by the necessity to disguise the state of affairs. The basis for the prohibition against charging interest is found in the ethical prescription in a primitive society, close to the subsistence level, against taking advantage of the misfortunes of others. When a crop fails and a family goes hungry, brotherhood exacts a charitable response, not an exploitive one. As capital starts to become productive, however, there is no ethical requirement for the owner to share its fruit and to lend to others for their positive advantage. Moreover, investments for profit do not require a communal relationship between lender and borrower. Benjamin Nelson sums up these considerations neatly in the title of a book, *The Idea of Usury: From Tribal Brotherhood to Universal Otherhood* (1949). In many societies moneylenders belong to a different religion, and hence are not bound by the ethical standards of the community. Part of the reason for Jewish participation in trade and moneylending in Europe, however, was that, in most states, they were forbidden to own land.

Lending at interest became acceptable in England when Henry VIII broke away from the Church of Rome. The usury laws of 1487 and 1495 were relaxed in 1545, and a limit set to interest that could be charged at 10 percent. Edward VI restored the prohibition against charging interest, but in 1571 Elizabeth I removed it again. Thereafter the limit to interest that was not usurious was gradually lowered to 8 percent under James I in 1624, 6 percent under Charles II in 1660, and 5 percent under Queen Anne in 1713. In 1668 Sir Josiah Child, the East India Company director and a merchant and goldsmith, argued for reducing the permitted level from 6 to 4 percent in order to have capital as cheaply as the Dutch (Letwin, 1969, p. 44).

Usury—whether charging interest at all or setting a limit above which it is illegal to charge it—belongs less to economic history than to the history of ideas, since it neither stopped usurers nor shackled economic advance (LeGoff, 1979, p. 25). There was much hair-splitting. One device was deathbed repentance and instruction to one's heirs to turn over the fortune to charity. It was said to be legitimate to lend borrowed money but not one's own (Ehrenberg, 1896 [1928], p. 42). Or distinction was made between pawnbrokers, regarded as no better than prostitutes—sinners but necessary to society—and money changers and deposit bankers (Lopez, 1979, p. 7). Uncertainty that removed the taint of usury was found not only in bill dealings but also in the purchase of annuities as an outlet for investment. By one device or another—commissions for contracting and renewing loans, *douceurs* or sweeteners to be paid for entering commitments—the ban on usury could be circumvented. The restriction did not apply to princes, but they were not loath to invoke it as a defense when they were on the point of default (Ehrenberg, 1896 [1928], p. 42).

Outside of business and finance, widespread support existed for usury laws, especially on the part of borrowers for consumption from avaricious moneylenders, when the only hope of repayment depended on lowering one's standard of living or selling off possessions. In his introduction to Sir Thomas Wilson's book on usury (1572), Tawney writes of two usurers in a single hundred (subdivision of a county, with its own court) of wealthy Norfolk worth £100,000 each, a third worth £40,000, and another who maintained a gang of bullies to intimidate witnesses in the thirty suits that had arisen against his usurious dealings (1925, p. 89). Among moneylenders of the Tudor and Stuart period, Sir Horatio Palavicino and Sir Arthur Ingram were regarded as unduly grasping, welcoming default on mortgage lending so that they could foreclose (Stone, 1956, pp. 272–73; Upton, 1961, pp. 177–79). There was more to the Church's rule than cultural lag; consumption loans weighed heavily on all classes of society. The rules seem never to have been sufficiently stringent or binding to inhibit commerce or industry, or borrowing for consumption for that matter.

ITALIAN BANKING

There is a confusing welter of types of banks to be encountered in the financial history of western Europe, some with different names for broadly the same sort of institution, some with similar names but distinct forms and functions. Consider merchant, private, exchange, deposit, discount, public, court, joint stock, mixed, industrial, investment, universal, crédit-mobilier-type banks, *banques d'affaires,* and so on. In Italy, as noted, there were principally three types: pawnbrokers, money changers, and deposit banks. While money changers had a bench, or *banca* (from which the word *bank* derives and meaning "bank" in Italian), or sometimes a *tavola* or table, they conducted business largely in exchange of currencies, with no element of credit. Over time, money changers evolved into exchange bankers who remitted funds, or deposit bankers who transferred them locally and sometimes made loans, but such a firm as M. M. Warburg, formed in 1798 in Hamburg, changed its name from money changer (*Geldwechsler*) to banker only in 1863 (Rosenbaum, 1962, p. 124).

Banks sprang up particularly in the Tuscan towns—Florence, Siena, Lucca—later spreading to Venice and Genoa. The city-states involved recognized the public good aspect of the business, requiring banks to keep records, and on occasion to obtain guarantors of loans. In the beginning, lending was highly local, especially to finance the harvest, which could be seen in the fields and appraised. Quickly, Italians became skilled in transferring monies in international trade and handling the substantial payments received and dispensed by the Church in Rome. Italian bankers spread through Europe, establishing nations of their countrymen as correspondents in Avignon, Barcelona, Bruges, the Champagne fairs, and later Lyons, Besançon, Antwerp, Amsterdam, London, and Hamburg. The designation of Lombard Street in the City of London derives from all north Italians, called Lombards, and not especially citizens of Lombardy such as the Milanese. Lending to English kings proved disastrous to the Ricciardi of Lucca, who lent £400,000 between 1272 and 1310 and then failed when they could not collect their due. The Bardi and the Peruzzi of Florence helped finance the English side of the Hundred Years' War. They were bankrupted when Edward III defaulted to them in 1348 (Prestwich, 1979, p. 78; de Roover, 1966, p. 2).

Where possible, loans to sovereigns were secured by pledges of jewels or plate or by assignment of revenues, such as customs receipts or an excise tax, though on occasion a king would assign the same source of income to more than one banker. The debts of a sovereign might be guaranteed by a city—the City of London for the English or the Hôtel de Ville of Paris for French kings. Unlike kings, cities could be sued and goods of their merchants seized. Or an individual might guarantee the king's debt. In 1626 Philip Burlamachi, an English royal exchanger and his brother-in-law, Philip Calandrini, offered to stand security for a loan of £58,400 raised by Charles I in Amsterdam when jewels deposited proved insufficient and Dutch lenders demanded the guarantee of some merchants (R. Ashton, 1960, p. 58). Some intermediary was needed to stand between the sovereign and the ultimate lender. The risk of lending to princes was high and known, but the benefit might also be substantial. Italians in England paid only nominal rent on some manors, might be exempted from taxes and jury duty, and were allowed to nominate candidates for ecclesiastical office. In addition, they could obtain permission to export wool to Italy and trade at favorable exchange rates (Prestwich, 1979, pp. 87–93). They did not contribute greatly to the development of industry or agriculture, though their mercantile insistence on wool's being properly graded and packed constituted a form of value added through bringing producers up to the standards of international trade, an important aspect of trade that is often overlooked.

In the fifteenth century Italian banking was dominated by the Medici Bank, small by comparison with the Bardi and the Peruzzi of the previous century but nonetheless impressive. It had branches in Venice, Genoa, Milan, and Rome, as well as a head office in Florence in Italy, and outside representation in London, Bruges, Geneva, later Lyons, plus a correspondent in Lübeck (de Roover, 1966, pp. 37–38).

In due course, the Italians lost their stellar role in European banking. Not all Italian cities rose and fell at the same pace. Florence went down in the 1520s, when Francis I seized Florentine property in Paris, Lyons, and Bordeaux in 1521, for having betrayed his war preparations against the Spanish in Flanders, and when he again defaulted to Florentine bankers in 1529 after the ransom of his sons following the Treaty of Cambrai left him too little to pay his debts (Ehrenberg, 1896 [1928], pp. 206, 209). Genoa became the central focus of trade and money after 1557, succeeding Venice, but succumbed, in turn, about 1620 to the ascendant Amsterdam (Braudel, 1949 [1972], Vol. 1, pp. 387, 394). There were strong links between particular centers: Venice (and the Hanseatic League) to Bruges; Florence to Lyons (and Bruges); south Germany (and Genoa) to Antwerp.

THE HANSEATIC LEAGUE

The Hansa represents something of a puzzle in this period, since it resisted the intrusion of Italian bankers and at the same time failed to develop adequate banking facilities of its own. Its merchants relied heavily on bilaterally balanced trade, buying goods in such markets as Bruges and London to match the value of those sold but, of course, also used coin (Dollinger, 1964 [1970], pp. 203–4). In trade with Russia, goods were sold also against marten fur, which served almost as a monetary unit (ibid., pp. 205, 235). An Italian evaded the rules against residence by foreigners by marrying the daughter of the burgomaster of Lübeck. He set up a bank in 1410, but it was liquidated on his death. The resistance of Hansa towns to banking and credit provides a curious counterexample to the Coase theorem that institutions develop readily to meet economic needs.

Hanseatic merchants were prepared to make loans in specie to the kings of England to preserve their privileges in the Steelyard and their exemption from taxation. The more backward English of the fifteenth century were beginning to innovate in finance when the Hansa was not, except in the attempt at currency unification represented by the monetary union of Wendish towns led by Lübeck, Hamburg, Wismar, and Lüneburg (ibid., pp. 207–8). This attempt to spread the medium of exchange and unit of account to achieve scale related only to coins. In credit, the Hansa was especially backward. In contrast the Staple of Calais of the English Merchant Adventurers in wool was issuing three sorts of obligations in the fifteenth century that "almost deserved the name of currency": debentures, bills of the mint, and warrants of partition, all this, says Postan, well before the goldsmiths and the negotiable bill of exchange of the seventeenth century (1930 [1973], p. 49).

SOUTH GERMANY

The focus of banking shifted in the sixteenth century away from north Italy to southern Germany and to the towns of Augsburg, Nuremburg, and Regensburg, lying athwart the eastern north-south route to Italy. The Fuggers of Augsburg got their start in trading woolens and silver against silks and spices, especially pepper, to Venice, spread into lending locally to the archduke of the Tyrol against the security of a mortgage on local silver mines, then to the House of Hapsburg to ensure the election of Charles V as Holy Roman Emperor, and gradually expanded over Europe to Leipzig, Rome, Naples, Lyons, Antwerp, Denmark, and so on. In all, at their height, they had eighteen "factories" or branches, consisting of a house, barn, garden, stabling, counting house, and especially a warehouse for goods. During the wars between Spain and Austria, on the one hand, and France on the other, the Fuggers backed Charles V, the Genoan banks Francis I. By the 1540s the Fuggers were borrowing in Antwerp to relend to Spain on *asientos* repayable in Castile in silver with the right to export it. German banker loans to the Spanish Crown in Antwerp reached manic proportions in the 1550s as the Counter-Reformation war of Spain against Dutch Protestants and their allies boiled up. The loans were interrupted in 1557 when Philip II, son of Charles V, ordered payments to his creditors stopped, two shipments of silver due them confiscated, and the obligations, drafts drawn in Spain on Antwerp and backed by arriving silver, converted forcibly into long-term loans. Spanish finances staggered from crisis to crisis, on the average every twenty years—1557, 1575, 1596, 1607, 1627, and 1647 (Ehrenberg, 1896 [1928], p. 334). On the third occasion in 1596, the crisis brought the Fuggers still further down and the Genoese up. The brief age of the Fuggers was followed by that of Genoa (Braudel, 1949 [1972], Vol. 1, p. 500). During the age of the Fuggers, however, they and other south German bankers had changed not only the locus of banking in Europe but also its character. They developed the system of financial intermediation, borrowing from wealth owners everywhere and lending to a king (Bergier, 1979).

The economic role of intermediary was partly borrowing at retail and lending at wholesale, with a return based on the saving in transaction cost for the borrowing government, the fiscal apparatus of which was typically rudimentary. To a considerable extent, however, the small lender needed the security of the intermediary's bargaining power since the latter was much better placed as a rule to collect repayment in the event of difficulty. Few people had such status. One might be a courtier, such as Sir Stephen Fox in the reign of Charles II in England, who proved his worth by collecting on his Treasury orders after the 1672 Stop of the Exchequer, which ruined many others (C. Clay, 1978, pp. 76–78). Or kings might hesitate to default to enormously rich bankers from whom they hoped to borrow in the future.

Notice that intermediation is of various kinds: in simple marketmaking, like the exchange dealer; in credit, as in lending long and borrowing short, which intermediates between the borrower who wants an extended period in which to repay and the lender who wants liquidity; and in risk, with the intermediary standing between the risky borrower and the risk-averse lender. The three aspects of intermediation may be theoretically distinct; they are usually thoroughly mixed up in practice. Banks and bankers, in particular, act as middlemen, making the market, and as institutions recycling risky long-term debts into liquid secure claims. Marketmaking, credit stretching, and risk minimization are threads that run throughout financial history.

Though the most famous, the Fuggers were not the only German bankers. The

Welsers had factories in Genoa, Venice, Aquila (in southern Italy), Milan, Antwerp, Lyons, Vienna, and Schackenwald in Bohemia—the first four illustrating the traditional ties to Italy; the Hochstetters were involved in the spice trade between Lisbon and Antwerp; there were the Seilers, and so on. Some were partly banker and partly fiscal agent for a prince, among these Hans Kleberg, the "good German" of Lyons who funneled the money of south German merchants to Francis I of France and gave handsomely to local charity; Lazarus Tucher, who built a fortune speculating in pepper and lending to the English Crown on the ruins of the House of Hochstetter. Tucher was modern in the sense that he was said to have been restless and to eat only ten meals at home à year (Ehrenberg, 1896 [1928], p. 179). This is an order of magnitude ahead of, or behind, Samuel H. Armcost, elected to be president of the Bank of America at the end of 1980, who was away from home 162 days during his last year in the bank's London branch (*New York Times,* 7 December 1980, Business Section, p. 6). Bagehot stated that "bankers have great leisure. If they are busy something is wrong" (1873 [1978], Vol. 9, p. 156, echoed in pp. 159, 177, and 184).[1] The dictum may apply in a constitutional era instead of to absolute monarchy and to a time of fewer wars. Records of the Middle Ages and Renaissance speak of "great anxiety and impatience," for example, when shipments of gold and silver were awaited from Spain (da Silva, 1969, p. 4). Confiscation of the fleet in Seville in 1552 caused widespread panic in Antwerp. Merchants asked that fair payments be postponed, and Hapsburg credit suffered a brutal collapse (Van der Wee, 1963, Vol. 2, p. 205). I am told by a colleague in a private communication that there is no record of such a confiscation in the standard Spanish monograph on Spanish trade in the sixteenth century (Sanza, 1980).

PUBLIC BANKS

The currency of a great state, such as France or England, generally consists almost entirely of its own coin. Should this currency, therefore, be at any time worn, clipt, or otherwise degraded below its standard value, the state by the reformation of its coin can effectively reestablish its currency. But the currency of a small state, such as Genoa or Hamburgh, can seldom consist altogether in its own coin, but must be made up, in great measure, of the coins of all the neighboring states with which its inhabitants have a continual intercourse. (Smith, 1776 [1937], p. 446)

1. But note that John Parish's clerk in Hamburg wrote 200 letters a day at the end of the eighteenth century, and that when the ice broke up in 1795 and thirteen English posts came in at once, it took John Parish three days just to read his portion (Ehrenberg, 1925, pp. 46, 69). An earlier workaholic in trade and finance was Francesco di Marco Datini, the merchant of Prato, who left 150,000 letters, 500 account books and ledgers, 500 deeds of partnership, 400 insurance policies, and several thousand bills of lading and checks in the Datini archives. When he was over 60 he said he was "not well today on account of all the writing I have done in these two days without sleeping, either by night or by day, and in these two days eating only one loaf" (Origo, 1957, p. xiv). Again: "It is the ninth hour and I have neither eaten nor drunk and tomorrow I will do the same" (ibid., p. 97).

In contrast, and to support Bagehot's contention, Kenneth Grahame, secretary of the Bank of England for ten years at the turn of the nineteenth century, had time on the job to write *The Wind and the Willows,* a classic story for children (Sayers, 1976, Vol. 1, pp. 5–6).

Thus Adam Smith begins his famous digression on banks of deposit, particularly concerning that of Amsterdam, with emphasis on the need to develop bank money in which bills of exchange can be paid.

The Bank of Amsterdam, sometimes called the Wisselbank or Bank of Exchange, was begun in 1609. The first state deposit bank, the Casa di San Giorgio (Bank of St. George) in Genoa, had been established, however, two centuries earlier, in 1407. The same century saw the development of deposit banks in Spain and, in 1555, one in Palermo, Sicily. The purpose of each was that described by Adam Smith: to provide the public good of a validated money in place of motley assortments of coins of uncertain worth.

The need had long been recognized. Sealed purses and sacks of weighed and assayed coins marked with their value were mentioned in Chapter 2. The fairs of Champagne of the twelfth and thirteenth centuries issued tokens to assist the clearing, representing deposits of coin, plate, and bullion that had been tested. At one stage the fair of Lyons found it useful to exclude specie from its clearing, presumably because the need to calculate disparate values slowed the cancellation process (Usher, 1943, p. 12).

Perhaps by accident, the Bank of Venice was not the earliest public bank, having been established by the authorities as Il Banco della Piazza del Rialto only in 1587, but its antecedents went back to the fourteenth century when the public function of transferring valid money was undertaken privately. Venice maintained what amounted to a permanent fair as early as the thirteenth century. In due course, some bankers undertook to clear mercantile payments, in addition to their commerce, shipping, and moneychanging. In 1374 a committee of scholars proposed creation of a public bank, but the task continued to be carried out in the old way for another 200 years (Luzzatto, 1934, pp. 39–45). The Banco della Piazza del Rialto was replaced by a Banco del Giro (clearing bank) in the seventeenth century, but by this time Venice had lost its commercial and financial élan.

Early banks of deposit were fairly primitive because of the necessity to effect transfers on their books in person, first the payer and the payee appearing together at the bank, but later meeting elsewhere with a notary. Starting from the state's requirement that they pay out only good coin, the deposit banks were unwilling to accept bad at nominal value. In the course of time they formed close connections with state mints, where bad coins were melted down and restruck. Other functions were acquired, including holding funds in escrow to await disposition in legal proceedings; in 1433 at the Taula de Canvi (Bank of Deposit) in Barcelona, 28 percent of total liabilities were of this character. From 1525 forward Valencian institutions "habitually" kept funds on deposit with the Taula de Valencia and made substantial payments through transfers on its books (Hamilton, 1934 [1965], p. 133).

In theory at least, early banks of deposit were not discount or lending banks. They did not create money but served a system of 100 percent reserves, such as some monetarists today would like to see established. Overdrafts were forbidden. In practice, the standards proved difficult to maintain, especially in face of public emergency. The Taula de Valencia was on the verge of using its deposited treasure to buy wheat for the city in 1567. Illegal advances were made to city officials in 1590 and illegal loans to the city itself on a number of occasions. Hamilton indicates that when the bank failed and had to be reorganized in 1613 at the height of the currency disruption in Spain, the news came as no surprise (ibid., pp. 133–34). A century and a half later the Bank of Amsterdam failed for the same reason, having advanced funds in the emergency of the Fourth Anglo-Dutch War to the city of Amsterdam, which had gone to the rescue of the Dutch East India Company. The company had lost many ships and cargos to the British navy (van Dillen, 1934, pp. 113–14).

In 1609 when the Bank of Amsterdam was founded, the Dutch Republic was young, having been formed in 1579 by the Union of Utrecht. Amsterdam had had a thriving sixteenth-century trade with the Baltic and west as far as the Bay of Biscay in France. It was not until the last fifteen years of the century, however, with the inflow of merchants and bankers from Antwerp and the southern Netherlands, that Amsterdam trade expanded explosively and extended to encompass trade with the Mediterranean (Barbour, 1950 [1966], p. 15).

The immediate foundation of the Bank of Amsterdam was in response to a petition of cloth importers. Not only was there confusion from foreign coin, as observed by Adam Smith, but also disorder of local origin. Fourteen mints competed for seignorage in the United Provinces, one for each province (two in one province), plus six municipal mints. The republic had tried unsuccessfully in 1585 to limit the number of mints to one for each of the seven provinces (two in one of them) plus six municipal mints, and it prescribed uniformity of coinage in ordinances of 1603 and 1609. Standardization was sought to prevent money changers from selecting out good coin and exporting or melting it down. The ordinances failed to achieve standardization, however. In a loose federal system, the higher level—the States-General of the United Provinces—could not impose its will on the lower.

With the establishment of the bank, the City of Amsterdam decreed that all bills of exchange of 600 florins or more be paid at the Bank of Amsterdam in bank money rather than elsewhere in current coin. This is said to have been a provision of the Bank of Venice (van Dillen, 1934, p. 84), without specifying whether it was the Banco della Piazza di Rialto of 1587, known as the Banco di Rialto, or the Banco de Giro (bank of circulation), set up in 1619, ten years after the foundation of the Bank of Amsterdam. The Banco di Rialto was created primarily to correct the overissue of bank money by private banks and may or may not have had a monopoly on the payment of bills of exchange. The idea was not new; the public bank of Barcelona, which went back to 1401, did have such a monopoly (Usher, 1943, pp. 313–16). So did the Banco del Giro. It is possible that in the second case, the monopoly may have been copied from the Bank of Amsterdam. The fact that exporters and importers were required to transact sizable bills of exchange meant that they had to keep accounts there. (Transfers of less than 300 florins were allowed, but the bank tried to discourage them by charging higher transfer fees.)

Profits of the bank came from fees for opening an account and effecting transfers, from penalties for infractions of rules against overdrafts, failure to balance accounts annually, and the like, and from trading in "bank money." The convenience of a deposit at the bank—safety of the money and assurance that one received money of satisfactory quality—meant that bank money went to a premium over currency, which varied from zero, or even small negative amounts when the safety of the bank was in question, to 9 or 10 percent at the height of the *Kipper- und Wipperzeit*. For the most part it ran at about 5 percent. If it went higher, the bank would typically buy coin with bank money; if lower, sell. Some of the bank's profit was derived from this arbitrage.

What led Adam Smith into his digression on the Bank of Amsterdam was that the exchange rate between London and Amsterdam differed, depending upon whether one was quoted money or bank money. The difference was the premium on bank money.

An instant success, the Bank of Amsterdam was followed by further public banks: the Banco del Giro, as noted, the Bank of Hamburg, also in 1619, and the Bank of Nuremberg in 1621. Three more Dutch banks—at Middelburg, Delft, and Rotterdam—were started in 1616, 1621, and 1635, respectively, at the instigation of importers of English cloth—a clear connection with assisting payments in foreign trade (van Dillen, 1934, p. 84). In addition, the Bank of Rotterdam was probably a response to the rapidly growing English colony in that city—22,000 in 1622 and 50,000 at the end of the century (Klein, 1984, pp. 117–18)—since it was established well after the peak of the currency disorders of the 1620s. The three lesser Dutch public banks at Middelburg, Delft, and Rotterdam all failed in the crisis of 1672, when French armies invaded Holland in the Third Anglo-Dutch War. Having advanced credit on securities—more probably discounts—they were unable to make good on the flood of withdrawals. The Bank of Amsterdam was able to meet the demands on it, for it had not made loans at that stage, contemporary Swedish opinion to the contrary notwithstanding (Heckscher, 1934, p. 162). In financial questions, sturdiness in the face of adversity when others fail constitutes an important earning asset for the future; it is claimed, for example, that the success of Hartford, Connecticut, as an insurance center is owed to its companies' success in paying off policyholders after the Chicago fire of 1871 when New York insurance companies closed their doors.

Outside Holland, the Bank of Hamburg established in 1619 as the *Kipper- und Wipperzeit* approached a climax was copied from the ten-years-older Bank of Amsterdam (Sieveking, 1934, p. 125). Some traders who dealt with Holland and Friesland had objected to the founding of such a bank as early as 1614, but its establishment in 1619 enlisted the support of the English mercantile colony, some Dutchmen (ibid.), and a group of Portuguese Jews (Kellenbenz, 1958, pp. 253–54). It was connected with a lending bank for small loans and pledged personal articles (Sieveking, 1934, pp. 128–30). The main pressure, one would judge, came from the accelerating debasement of the German currency. The bank survived, and even flourished, until 1875, when it was absorbed, most reluctantly, into the newly founded German Reichsbank (ibid., p. 125).

The Bank of Nuremberg was founded in 1621 for the same reason as the Bank of Hamburg two years earlier: to stabilize the currency. It failed in this, however, possibly as a result of having to contend with much more in the way of bad monies from its thirteen mints, as well as that seeping across the city's boundaries. As a result, the benefits of good money had to wait two more years until 1623 when the return to the Augsburg Imperial Ordinance of 1559 was finally achieved. It ultimately failed in the 1630s for the same reasons that undid most of the primitive banks of deposit in Spain, having been pressured into lending money to the city at the height of the Thirty Years' War and ultimately being unable to make good its deposits in coin (ibid., p. 133).

In the seventeenth century, the Bank of Amsterdam made an important contribution to Dutch trade in coin. Silver arriving from Mexico by way of Seville was minted, as well as for local use, into various coins for export, for the Levant and Asia Minor, Asia and the Far East, and the Baltic and Poland (Vilar, 1969 [1976], p. 205). In 1683 the bank undertook the establishment of a system of six-month advances of bank money against bullion or coin together with a transferable receipt. Acceptance of gold deposits had been instituted by the Casa di San Giorgio as early as 1582 (Spooner, 1972, p. 32). On payment in of bank money and presenting the receipt, a claimant could have the exact specie back, less a small fee. The receipt could be renewed if the specie was not withdrawn; if not renewed, the specie would accrue to the bank. The system was designed to capture and hold trade in specie for the Dutch over claimant rivals in Spain, Genoa, and London through providing better financing.

The Bank of Amsterdam was not a lending or discounting bank, apart from its occasional aberrations in dealings with the City of Amsterdam and the East India Company in the middle of the seventeenth century and its fatal one in the 1780s. Adam Smith asserted categorically that for every guilder circulated as bank money, there was a guilder deposited in the bank (1776 [1937], p. 453). Van Dillen, who studied the books of the bank, confirms that Smith was broadly right: in 1760 the metallic stock was 16.3 million florins against total liabilities of 18.7 million florins (1934, p. 109). The Fourth Anglo-Dutch War of 1780–84 changed the position. During the Napoleonic Wars, moreover, the precious metals trade moved to Hamburg, and the Bank of Hamburg took up where the Bank of Amsterdam had left off. Toward the end of the war, in 1814, the remnants of the latter were converted into the Netherlands Bank, a very different kind of institution.

THE RIKSBANK (BANK OF SWEDEN)

The Bank of Amsterdam was a public bank, a deposit bank, and an exchange bank; it was not a credit bank. One of the last was founded in Holland shortly after the Bank of Amsterdam when the so-called Huys van Leening, or Bank of Lending, was established by the municipality in 1614, which authorized it to make lombard loans (on securities). It failed to flourish. It served, however, as a precedent for the Riksbank (Bank of Sweden), which was organized in 1656 and divided from the beginning into two departments: one an exchange, or Wechselbank, patterned after the Bank of Amsterdam, and the other a Lanebank, or Bank of Lending. The two were presumed to operate separately, but Heckscher states that the separation was only on paper (1934, p. 169). To the modern mind, the division evokes the English Bank Act of 1844, which divided the Bank of England into two departments that some contemporary observers—for example, Lord Overstone (Overstone, 1856 [1971], Vol. 2, p. 655)—thought should have been two separate banks: the Issue Department, a deposit bank with 100 percent reserves of gold (and silver) against its liabilities above a small fiduciary issue consisting of government securities acquired over the years, and a Banking Department, which discounted bank acceptances (bills of exchange) against notes and deposits. There is nothing to indicate that Peel and his cabinet were conscious of the two-century-old precedent of the Swedish Riksbank. The contrasting modes of operating are inherent in ways of thinking about money and credit.

The Riksbank was taken over by the state in 1668, which makes it the oldest central bank in the world. Its tercentenary celebration in 1968 was the occasion for creating a fund for the award of a Nobel prize in economics. The bank has one more claim to pioneering distinction. In 1661 before the state takeover, it issued the first bank notes in Europe. As a substitute for coin, bank notes were third, not first, after bills of exchange and deposits. Sweden was first to issue them but for an odd reason. Its monetary reserves at this time were copper, enormously cumbersome not only in international trade as a substitute for silver or gold but in domestic transactions as well. Accordingly, copper companies substituted payment in "copper notes" for coin in wages paid to miners, and these proved to be sufficiently popular to go to a premium over coin. Goldsmith receipts were circulating as money in England in the seventeenth century as well, but the Swedish copper notes of 1661 were the first to be issued by a bank, and hence the first bank notes. The Riksbank played only a small role in clearing payments in commerce. Swedish bills of exchange were drawn on Hamburg and Amsterdam, even though the bulk of exports went to England, and the Swedish rixdollar was quoted for Hamburg or Dutch currency, not bank money.

GOLDSMITHS

Silversmithing was a widely practiced trade in Europe in the Renaissance and early modern times, especially after 1560 in Seville, where the silver fleet arrived in Spain from Hispaniola. Wealth was held to an extent in the semiliquid form of silver plate and jewelry, which could be brought to the mint when the occasion demanded it for conversion into coin. The silversmiths in Seville belonged to the highest class of artisans. Many were rich and members of the upper classes (Pike, 1972, pp. 132–47, where they are mentioned fifteen times), but no mention is made of their serving as bankers.

The development of goldsmiths into banks in England in the seventeenth century is a story well known to beginning students of economics. Starting out as jewelers and lapidaries, makers and sellers of goldware and silverware, some of them gradually developed in the Tudor and Stuart periods into bankers, along with merchants, brokers, scriveners, tax farmers, and so on. In the reign of Henry VIII goldsmiths had received a boost from the need to dispose of the treasure of the monasteries that Henry had taken over and again from the Act of 1545 permitting interest. The scrivener, however, seems to have preceded the goldsmith as one who accepted deposits. Needed to write out letters and contracts in a time of illiteracy, the scrivener became a skilled adviser, middleman, broker, and then lender who accepted deposits (Tawney, 1925, p. 98). At the end of the reign of Elizabeth I, a country gentleman was as likely to write to his draper for a loan of £200 as to a goldsmith, even when he had dealt with a goldsmith before (ibid., p. 94). While lending to the king proved fatal to some goldsmiths, they and scriveners were unimportant as lenders to James I and Charles I as compared with tax farmers (R. Ashton, 1960, p. 14). Tawney is determined to qualify the simplistic theory that banking evolved from goldsmithery, a myth that developed largely, he implies, from the fact that certain English banks today trace their origins back to one or more goldsmiths, facts that bulk large in their anniversary histories (1925, p. 102). In this revisionist view, he is supported by de Roover (1949, p. 102).

Goldsmiths nonetheless existed (anonymous pamphlet [1676] in Anderson and Cottrell, eds., 1974, ch. 17). Two acted as bankers for other goldsmiths, anticipating the role of the Bank of England as a bankers' bank. The general run of goldsmiths paid interest, supplied loans, and bought and sold tallies (discussed in Chapter 9) and various other types of Treasury and Exchequer obligations issued to suppliers of goods and services. Especially, they discounted payment orders, promissory notes, and bills of exchange. In addition, of course, they dealt in gold and silver coin, melting down heavy coin for export. And in lending, where possible, they inscribed deposits on their books rather than pay out coin. Sir Dudley North said that "merchants kept their money with Goldsmiths and Scriveners, whose accounts show Ten thousand cash, but they seldom have a thousand in specie" (Richards, 1965, p. 18).

The goldsmith road into banking was not a smooth one. In 1640 Charles I confiscated the gold and plate that had been deposited for safekeeping in the Tower of London, destroying the reputation of the mint as a safe place of custody. The treasure was returned only after merchants and goldsmiths had agreed to lend the king £40,000 on the security of the Customs Farm. Richards comments that this helped pave the way for the spread of private banking in England (ibid., pp. 35–36). Again in January 1672, Charles II defaulted on his obligations in the Stop of the Exchequer. Financiers with access to court favorites managed to escape intact, whereas five goldsmiths were bankrupted. Among the assets the goldsmiths had were repayment orders issued by the Treasury with tallies, which were made assignable by Parliament in 1667 and circulated between that date and the Stop. Their purpose was to indicate the order in which tallies would be paid, and like draft choices in the professional football selection of college players, the repayment orders became a tradable asset in their own right. William Shaw, the monetary historian of the last century, calls this the origin of paper money in England (ibid., p. 60). For paper money that lasted without interruption, we shall have to wait a few years to 1694 and the establishment of the Bank of England.

EARLY BANKS IN ENGLAND

The second half of the seventeenth century was a period of great trade expansion in England, if disorder in the finances of the Crown. For a long time, and largely inspired by the Bank of Amsterdam, which itself drew on examples of the Bank of Venice and the Casa di San Giorgio in Genoa, proposals had been made for the establishment of banks in England. The English were ambivalent about the Dutch. They fought them in three wars in the seventeenth century and introduced a number of pejorative expressions into the language to make clear their disdain—*Dutch treat, Dutch uncle, Dutch courage,* and so on. Holland was "a counting house, protected by a navy." They nonetheless envied Dutch success in shipping, trade, and finance and resolved to divert as much of all three to themselves, especially through the Navigation Acts of 1661 and 1666. Many proposals were made for the establishment of banks on the Dutch model. England was slow; toward the end of the century, there were thirty public banks on the Continent.

An early proposal was made in a Bill of 1571 for seven banks in London, York, Norwich, Coventry, West Chester, Bristol, and Exeter, but these were intended to lend to needy persons for consumption, like the Italian Monte di Pietà, rather than to finance commerce and industry (Richards, 1965, p. 93). The same thought was part of a wider set of proposals by one Hugh Peters, a Puritan, who had spent seven years in exile in the Netherlands. During the Commonwealth (1649–60), he advocated a municipal bank for every town to lend to reliable persons at reliable rates on pawn, a great commercial bank, a clearinghouse, and a bank of deposit that would lend to the state. Profits from these operations were to be used for the public purpose of rebuilding London in stone or brick instead of wood—this before the fire of 1666 (Brailsford, 1961, p. 647).

Various purposes were implied by these several proposals directed against usury, in favor of efficient payments, toward public improvements, to spread credit through England and away from the City of London. In addition there were signs of Keynesianism, the establishment of banks to expand economic activity and employment. A man named Potter wanted banks of money created in a number of towns "to issue negotiable bills for deposits" and thus quicken the revolution of money and credit (Richards, 1965, p. 97). Dr. Chamberlen, an Anabaptist, suggested the formation of a syndicate to employ the poor at improving and cultivating land, take over inventions and run them, operate a national bank on the security of public land, and capture the business of "all nations." It would also operate the herring fleet and use the profits to run the navy (Brailsford, 1961, p. 435). There were numerous, less complex proposals patterned more closely after the Bank of Amsterdam, with the narrower objective of improving the transfer of payments in trade.

When it was founded in 1694, however, the Bank of England departed sharply from these models, to serve the different purpose of assisting the marketing of national debt in time of war—the Nine Years' War with the French that lasted from 1688 to 1697, and for the private purpose of making a profit through lending newly issued bank notes. As we shall see, tension between the private and public purposes of the Bank of England persisted through the nineteenth century. The Bank of England did not improve the money supply; on the contrary, it worsened it, its note issue exacerbating wartime inflation and accelerating the debated decision to undertake the silver recoinage. The bank was quickly pressed into service at home as fiscal agent of the government in debt transactions, and abroad, remitting funds to the Continent via Amsterdam to support English troops and their allies in the field. But the men who started the bank, led by William Patterson, were interested in profit, not public service. By way of contrast, officials of deposit banks on the Continent were frequently city employees.

The founders of the bank provided the state with £1.2 million in exchange for a perpetual annual payment of £100,000. The bank got the money from its stock-holders, who consisted of a wide range of City financial people, plus Amsterdam investors, among whom were Huguenots, recently expelled from France, Jews, and English residents abroad, with real Dutch investing in English securities mostly after 1713 (Dickson, 1967, p. 306). The war is thought by one scholar to have provided capital for the bank by cutting England off from wine imports. Stocks of wine ran down in England, with no opportunity of replacing them. Wine merchants built up cash that sought suitable opportunities for investment (D. W. Jones, 1972). It is clear, in any event, that it was neither the goldsmiths' goldsmiths that evolved into a bankers' bank nor a merchant elite serving its private interest in achieving a more efficient payments mechanism. State financial machinery had collapsed in the Third Anglo-Dutch War and was reconstructed after the Glorious Revolution of 1688 with an entirely different division of authority. Parliament took back the power to spend from the Crown, and with it the power to borrow. In combination with the need to triple expenditure during the Nine Years' War from £2 million a year to £5 million or £6 million, this offered an opportunity to merchant outsiders that they were quick to seize. It was this same group that was petitioning against the East India Company's monopoly and by whom the New East India Company (later merged with the old) was briefly formed in 1698.

The proximate causes of the establishment of the Bank of England as a major innovation in the history of finance are perhaps of less interest than the deep-seated evolutionary forces in banking, on the one hand, and the sociopolitical position on the other. Some sort of banking in England was well-nigh certain: trade was exploding, and the economic community was infused with large numbers of foreign merchants, bankers, and investors with a knowledge of continental institutions—very much like the infusion that the United Provinces had received after the fall of Antwerp a century earlier. Equally, or perhaps more, important, the newly limited monarchy reduced the risk of arbitrary seizures of concentrated assets such as occurred in 1640 and 1672. It is not an accident that banking was most advanced in the Netherlands and England where absolutist government had been overcome (R. Davis, 1973, p. 249).

SUGGESTED SUPPLEMENTARY READING

Center for Medieval and Renaissance Studies (1979), *The Dawn of Modern Banking*.
deRoover (1966), *The Rise and Fall of the Medici Bank, 1397–1494*.
Ehrenberg (1896) [1928]), *Capital and Finance in the Age of the Renaissance*.
Smith (1776 [1937]), *The Wealth of Nations*, esp. bk. 1, ch. 4; ch. 11, pt. 3, Digression; bk. 2, ch. 2; bk. 4, ch. 3, pt. 1, Digression.
van Dillen (ed.) (1934), *History of the Principal Public Banks*.

In French
Boyer-Xambeu, Deleplace, and Gillard (1986), *Monnaie privée et pouvoir des princes*.

4

Bimetallism and the Emergence of the Gold Standard

Dr. Polycarp was, as you all know, an unusually sallow bimetallist. "There," people of wide experience would say, "There goes the sallowist bimetallist in Cheshire." Once this was said so that he overheard it; it was said by an actuary, under a sunset of mauve and grey. Polycarp turned upon him. "Sallow!" he cried fiercely, "Sallow! *Quis tulerit Gracchos de seditione querentes.*" It was said that no actuary ever made game of Dr. Polycarp again.

(Chesterton, 1904 [1950], pp. 35–36)

MORE THAN ONE MONEY

The medium-of-exchange function can tolerate more than one money without too much trouble; the unit-of-account function cannot. It is tolerable to measure length in feet and/or meters when the length of a meter in feet is unalterable or the price of a good in either gold or silver when the price of silver in terms of gold is fixed. But when there are two monies and their relation, one to the other, changes from day to day, a problem arises. Should the price be measured in gold or silver, and if it is unchanged in gold between period t and $t + 1$, has the price changed if the price of silver had moved against gold?

For efficient discharge of the unit-of-account function, one money is needed. If this is imaginary money, one needs to take money in use and convert it to money of account, calling for another calculation. For efficiency in measurement, it is desirable to have the medium of exchange serve as the unit of account. But this runs into the difficulty that, with metallic money, no single metal serves well over the entire range of transactions required in an economy: the amount of gold needed to buy a glass of beer is so small as to be impossible to handle, of copper to buy a house too big. To a considerable extent, as we saw in Chapter 2, articles of different value were traded with different sorts of money—but only to a considerable extent. At the margins, various monies can be used to buy the same goods, whether national currencies in the case of foreign trade goods, or gold and silver, silver and copper, coin and paper money. To make a system with two or more monies work well, the relations between, or among, the monies must be fixed.

But fixed relations among several monies are difficult—some say impossible—to sustain. Alfred Marshall, the great nineteenth-century English economist, advocated symmetallism, a device for ensuring that gold and silver kept the same price relationship to one another by melting them into an alloy to be used in balancing international accounts as bullion and in domestic use as coin (1924, pp. 64–67). The device has two drawbacks: the convenience of separate monies for separate sizes of transactions is lost, and with a little trouble the two metals can be separated again. But similar devices of telescoping two monies into one have been tried before and proposed later. In 1541 Charles V, troubled by the disappearance of gold coins from circulation, ordered all bills of exchange to be paid two-thirds in gold, one-third in silver. A month later Burgos merchants petitioned for the cancellation of the measure, which was destroying trade rather than bringing undervalued gold back into circulation (Spooner, 1972, p. 133). On the contemporary scene, a Dutch economist responded to the instability of the gold exchange standard of two monies—gold and foreign exchange—with a proposal to require settlement of international payment imbalances in fixed proportions of gold and foreign exchange (Posthuma, 1963). The idea never got to first base.

THEORY OF BIMETALLISM

Bimetallism is usually discussed in terms of gold and silver, although Sweden abandoned the silver-copper standard only in 1772, and Russia was still on it in 1793 (Buist, 1974, pp. 77–78, 126). Its intellectual defense is that the mint price stabilizes the market prices of, say, gold and silver. If the price of gold falls in the market, more gold will be brought to the mint, and less silver, which will raise the market gold price and lower the silver to reestablish the market price at the mint level. Something of the sort happened in 1252. The commercial revolution of the thirteenth century needed a coin of greater value than the silver denier, and the price of gold in terms of silver was at its lowest level in centuries. Minting of the gold genoin in Genoa in 1252, followed by new gold coins produced in Florence the same year, in Venice in 1282, and Siena in 1333 raised the market price of gold (Lopez, 1979, p. 19; 1956, p. 219). There have been few, if any, cases since. Instead of the mint price stabilizing the market price, the market price, responding to changes largely in supplies of precious metals, has destabilized the mint price through the workings of Gresham's law.

GRESHAM'S LAW

Sir Thomas Gresham was a skillful exchange dealer, a loyal servant of Elizabeth I, a philanthropist, and a rich man, but he did not discover the instability inherent in having two or more monies. The false attribution, with the survival value inherent in myth, was made by Henry D. McLeod, a nineteenth-century economist, who misinterpreted a statement by Gresham to the effect that Henry VIII's debasement of the pound had depreciated the English exchange on Antwerp—a statement not about two monies but about the law of one price, that a given money will have the same price in all markets that are joined (de Roover, 1949, p. 91). While it is perhaps antiquarian weakness to take interest in origins of ideas and echo the cliché,

"No, that's at least a hundred years older," the law has been traced by a French economist of the nineteenth century, somewhat more careful than McLeod, to Nicholas Oresme, bishop of Lisieux, who in 1360 described it accurately in his *De moneta* (Wolowski, 1869, p. 15). The bishop maintained that the king had no right to debase the coinage—a different problem—and added "or to change the bimetallic ratio." In 1368 he explained his conclusions personally to the 30-year-old Charles (Tuchman, 1978, p. 238). Venice, too, understood about bad and good money in 1472, almost a hundred years before Gresham (Braudel, 1949 [1972], Vol. 1, p. 388). The principle was known to Copernicus in 1525; in 1551 an obscure Englishman named Humphrey Holt complained that debased coins were driving good coins abroad and serving to raise prices (in nominal money) in England (de Roover, 1949, p. 92). Association of the principle with Gresham may also come from this statement in the year Sir Thomas went to Antwerp to serve as exchange dealer and fiscal agent for the queen.

French partisans of bimetallism in the nineteenth century sought to attack the instability argument with metaphors. Wolowski quotes Molière's *La Malade imaginaire:* "Me, cut off an arm, pluck out an eye in order to get along better?" (1869, p. 91n). Implicit in the comparison is that gold and silver are complements, not alternatives. Or another bimetallist, Cernuschi: "The world offers two fuels; is it necessary to proscribe wood because one burns coal?" (ibid., p. 217). Here are alternatives; what is missing is an attempt to fix the price between them or to use them as money.

Stability or instability was one issue. Another was the quantity of money. Until the nineteenth century when the world started a stampede from bimetallism to the gold standard, bimetallism was thought to reduce the money supply as good money was hoarded, melted down, or exported. It was only when silver was in process of demonetization that agrarians and populists, enlisted in the cause of higher prices to combat the great depression from 1873 to 1896, thought of monometallism as lowering the money supply and depressing prices.

The price ratio sought by the populists in the United States in the nineteenth century was 16 to 1 (1 ounce of gold worth 16 ounces of silver). The ratio for silver had been much higher earlier in Europe (fewer ounces of silver per ounce of gold) and a great deal higher in the Far East (Table 4.1). The wide difference between western Europe and the Far East is explained by the difficulties of transport, which inhibited arbitrage, and the fascination of the Chinese and Indians with hoarding, primarily as insurance against bad harvests. Note that the gap narrows sharply and even threatens to open up in the other direction in the 1640s when the Dutch and English East India companies were carrying large quantities of silver to the east, with more, both Peruvian and Mexican, going directly from Acapulco on the Pacific coast of Mexico to Manila, where Chinese junks would trade silk for it. Table 4.2 shows much narrower but still significant divergences in Europe in the sixteenth century. It is not clear what, if any, significance attaches to the facts that the British ratio was the highest for silver in the early part of the century and almost the lowest in the second half. The impact of arrivals from the New World after mid-century, however, is clearly, if unevenly, seen.

Table 4.1 Silver/Gold Ratio at Various Centers, Selected Periods

Flanders		Egypt		India		China	
Date	Ratio	Date	Ratio	Date	Ratio	Date	Ratio
						1000	6.3
	.					1126	13.3
						1134	13.0
		1194–1199	9.3			1198	12.1
1373	10.57					1375	4.0
1384	9.89	1382–1403	9.3			1385	5.0
1416	8.81	1415	8.9			1415	10.0*
1433	10.87	1433	11.1			1436	5.0
1482	10.89	1483	10.3			1481	7.0
1503	11.14	1503	8.5			1502	9.0
						1572	8.0
Amsterdam				1583	9		
1600–04	11.21						
1620–24	12.17			1621	10	1620	8.0
1635–39	12.25			1633	12.5	1635	10.0
1640–44	13.35			1640	13	1637–40	13.0
1645–49	13.93			1644–45	14		
				1658	16.40		
1660–64	13			1664	14.94/15		

*Author unable to explain departure from trend.
Source: Kindleberger (1990, p. 76).

BEGINNINGS OF THE GOLD STANDARD IN BRITAIN

Like so much of monetary history, fixing the pound sterling in 1717 at a gold price that lasted, with lapses from 1797 to 1819 and from 1914 to 1925, until 1931, was largely inadvertent, rather than the outcome of design. The problem at the time was silver. Following the Great Recoinage of 1696, silver was undervalued at the mint and disappearing from circulation. Since its introduction in 1662, milling had reduced the amount of clipping, sweating, and rubbing, but milled coins were still being hoarded and melted down for export. Recoinage had constituted a victory for John Locke over Secretary of the Treasury William Lowndes. To keep coins in circulation, Lowndes wanted to raise the mint price of silver to the market price. Action was needed to counteract the shortage of money that had resulted in circulation of paper money in the country and had even led to the establishment of offices in London and the countryside for bartering goods. Locke opposed changing the mint price, proposing instead to increase the weight of light coins through recoinage. He argued that to devalue silver would raise silver prices of goods and services, that scarcity of silver was due to war and interruption of the arrival of the Spanish *flota* (or fleet), that silver not gold was the monetary standard, and that if relative prices of the two metals were wrong, the correct course was to lower that of gold (Li, 1963, chs. 5, 6). In May 1695 Parliament had tried to prohibit the export of silver; that failed. At the year end, recoinage was enacted with provision of a short period during which light coins would be accepted for payment in taxes and repay-

Table 4.2 Silver/Gold Ratio, Various Centers in Europe, Sixteenth Century

	1500	1515	1540	1550	1560	1575	1600
Flanders	11	11	11.2	11.6	11.9	12.8	13
Austria	11.1	11	11	11.2	11.2	10.2	10.9
France	11.2	10.1	10.5	10.9	11.9	11.5	11.4
Spain	10.1	10.1	10.6	10.6	10.6	12.1	12.1
England	10	10	10	11.1	13.5	13.5	13.5
Portugal			10	11	12		
Germany				10.8	12.1		
Venice	11.7	9.6	11		11.9	10.6	14
Rome			10.6	10.6	10.8	11	
Sicily		13					
Milan				10.8	10.8	11.4	11.9
Florence	10.7	10.7	10.8	11.2			
Genoa	10.4				11.1		

Source: Boyer-Xambu, Deleplace, and Gillard (1986, p. 230).

ment of Exchequer loans but not thereafter. New taxes were levied to meet the expense of recoinage. Five and a half million pound sterling in nominal value of old coins were turned in and reminted into £2.7 million of full-weight coins. But the heavy coins failed to stay in circulation. In 1698 four commissioners, including Locke, were appointed to consider the matter further. They determined that the price of gold was 6 percent higher in England than in Holland and recommended that it be reduced.

The guinea had been as high as 30*s* during the depreciation of silver. In 1699 it was high at 22*s,* and the mint reduced it to 21*s* 6*d.* This proved to be still too high. Gold was brought to the mint but very little silver. At 22*s* per guinea, the gold/silver ratio was 15.93 to 1; at 21*s* 6*d,* 15.58 to 1, and at 21*s,* 15.21 to 1, compared with a ratio close to 15 to 1 in Hamburg (ibid., p. 168). In 1717 Sir Isaac Newton, master of the mint, observed that a lewidor (louis d'or) was worth 17*s* and 3*f* (*f* = farthings) in France but 17*s* 6*d* in England, which brought a large inflow of gold to London (U.S. Senate, 1879 [1978], p. 319).

In the same year, carrying out the recommendations of the commission, the price of the guinea was lowered, first to 20*s* 8*d,* and then raised partway back to 21*s.* The mint stopped coining guineas, shifting to the sovereign, a gold coin of 20*s* or £1 sterling. There was no thought that this put England on the gold standard; gold was not standard monetary metal. Newton, writing to Cantillon, asserted that silver was the true and only monetary standard. But gold kept coming to Britain; the only silver that remained in circulation was clipped and worn. Shortages of shillings and sixpences became serious, and the crown, worth 5*s,* disappeared altogether about 1760.

While many date the gold standard from 1717 when Newton set the price of gold at £3 17*s* 10½ *d,* demonetization of silver did not occur until 1774. That was the date of a gold recoinage, of recognition that silver was a subsidiary coinage, and of setting a limit on use of silver coin by prohibiting imports of light coin and eliminating silver as legal tender for sums in excess of £25, except on the basis of weight. An Act of 1798 restricted free coinage of silver as the market price had fallen below

He: "THAT'S MRS. GRIMSHAW, WHO LECTURES ON BIMETALLISM. I'VE HEARD HER. HOW EXASPERATINGLY CLEVER SHE SEEMS TO BE!"

She: "YES—BUT HOW CONSOLINGLY UGLY!"

Cartoon by George du Maurier (1895), from R. E. Williams (ed.), *A Century of Punch Cartoons* (New York: Simon & Schuster, 1955), p. 16.

the mint price. After the defeat of Napoleon, Lord Liverpool's Coinage Act of 1816 provided for coining 66 shillings out of a troy pound of silver instead of the previous 62 shillings, introducing an element of seignorage to help hold silver coin in circulation. In another generation, the Bank Act of 1844 would specify the gold reserve to be held in the Issue Department but allow silver to make up one-fifth of the total (Vilar, 1969 [1976], p. 314).

BIMETALLISM IN FRANCE

While Britain was backing into the gold standard, other countries on the Continent, notably France, were backing into official bimetallism. The importance of gold and gold coins was thoroughly recognized, but money was mainly silver. Continuous adjustments of the sort made in Britain were required from time to time, almost entirely, after 1726, in the price of silver. A traumatic experience with paper money under John Law set back the evolution of bank notes for a century. The bimetallic nature of French money was settled in legislation shortly before the second unhappy bank note experience, this time with the *assignats* over 1793–95. A controller-general of French finances, de Calonne in 1785, a commission of 1790 under Desoutours, and after the *assignats,* with the establishment of the Bank of France under the Consulat, French monetary officials pushed for, and achieved, bimetallism at the ratio of 15½ to 1 instead of the 14⅚ to 1 that had been established in 1726. There were advocates of monometallism, but their favored alternative was the silver standard. Gaudin, finance minister in 1803, defended bimetallism on the ground that gold coins, which constituted one-third of the French circulation of the time, were needed to effect large payments to purchase supplies for the army, for which sacks of silver coin were too bulky and unwieldy (U.S. Senate, 1879 [1978], pp. 249–306). No thought, however, was given to adoption of the gold standard.

SUSPENSION OF CONVERTIBILITY IN BRITAIN, 1797

The Reign of Terror in early 1793 produced a sharp outflow of capital from France, which took the form of a movement of both gold and silver to Britain. This increased liquidity in the British banking system and helped finance the peak of the "canal mania," which had started a couple of years earlier. When the *assignats* collapsed in France in 1795, money for use in ordinary payments was desperately short, and those with claims on Britain, or credit there, drew on them to fill the gap. This reflow of hot money put deflationary pressure on Britain. When a French military detachment appeared on the Welsh coast at Fishguard, a panic ensued and a run to convert bank notes into specie. The Bank of England somewhat lost its head and was given permission to suspend convertibility of bank notes into coin, well before its reserves had run out. There developed what came to be called an agio (premium) on gold, but since the exchange rate on Hamburg had also risen, it was clearly a depreciation of the pound. For the early years of suspension the agio was relatively mild but still sufficient to induce the government to appoint a committee to investigate it. The resulting Bullion Report, which became one of the classic documents of British monetary history, appeared in 1810 just as the agio picked up from 110 (10 percent above the base of 100) to 136 at the peak in 1813.

THE BULLION REPORT, 1810

In testifying before the Bullion Committee, the Bank of England denied that its action in expanding the note issue during the war had been responsible for the agio. It was safe to expand the note issue, the bank asserted, with subsequent support from the so-called banking school, so long as the notes were needed to meet requirements of trade. Provided that the transactions financed represented trade bills and not finance bills, expansion of bank notes parallel with rising trade requirements was a legitimate policy. The agio on gold or the depreciation of sterling, the banking school explained as the consequence of special problems in the balance of payments: subsidies to British allies that had to be transmitted through the foreign exchanges, bad harvests that enlarged the demand for imports of grain from the Baltic, tight money in Hamburg that raised interest rates there and attracted British capital.

The majority of the Bullion Committee did not accept this reasoning, blaming the agio on the expansion of the bank's note issue resulting from extended discounting. It argued that the "real bills" doctrine—that it was safe to enlarge discounts so long as underlying transactions represented goods moving in trade from seller to buyer—was fallacious: rising prices in these circumstances could lead to expansion of the note issue and to further rise of prices in a positive feedback mechanism. The same difference in view will be met in the debate over German inflation after World War I. It is related to, although not completely congruent with, the debate between monetarists and Keynesians today. The Bullion Committee and the currency school that emerged from its conclusions were monetarists, believing that independent or exogenous increases in the note issue led to depreciation of the exchange rate, rather than that depreciation caused higher prices, which induced expansion of the money supply. Its classic statement is found in the Bullion Report and in David Ricardo's *The High Price of Bullion* (1811).

In the very short run, the banking school had some forceful arguments. Thomas Tooke, Russian merchant (in the sense of a merchant dealing with Russia) and head of an insurance company, was its leader and wrote a five-volume history of prices in England with William Newmarch. They showed that in short periods, the bank's circulation could contract while the agio rose, or expand while the agio fell (1838 [1928], pp. 80–81, 96–97). A century later, Gayer, Rostow, and Schwartz adopted a point of view sympathetic to the banking school. They broke the period 1797 to 1819 down into six short sections and found that within periods, depreciation tracked with balance-of-payments difficulties better than with short-run changes in notes in circulation (1953, Vol. 1). If the years of suspension are divided merely in two, however—expansion from 1797 to 1814, followed by deflation to 1822—as Viner does (1937, chs. 3, 4), a different picture emerges. Bank of England credit represented by discounts of commercial paper and advances to the government rose from a low of £14.1 million in 1798 to £41.4 million in 1815. During this time the agio rose. Thereafter, total advances of the Bank of England (a slightly different concept) declined from £42.9 million in 1814 to £14.8 million in 1824, as the agio on gold fell away to zero. Here we encounter the basic economic truth that reasoning appropriate to the short run may not apply in the long, and vice versa.

RESUMPTION, 1819

Debate over the Bullion Report continued and intensified after the Napoleonic Wars as the time came to decide what to do about the monetary standard. The Bank Restriction Act of 1797 had provided that it would lapse six months after the end of the war. It was necessary to extend the limit a number of times. A small group in Parliament opposed going back to gold at the old price, and some opposed going back to convertibility at all. A few, like Lord Lauderdale and Alexander Baring (later Lord Ashburton), of the banking firm, supported a return to silver, not gold, although Baring finally voted for gold because of an unwillingness to support lost causes. Most of whom Fetter calls the "economists" in Parliament favored bimetallism but voted for resumption at par as a means of defeating the supporters of continued inconvertibility (1980, p. 95). There were many nuanced positions: in a letter to Trower, Ricardo stated that he would never advise a government to restore a currency that had been depreciated 30 below par (the point was made again with the same number in a letter to Wheatley in September 1821—Foxwell in Andréadès, 1909, p. xx); an earlier speech of Thornton, the banker, maintained that resumption was appropriate if depreciation lasted only two or three years, but the standard should be changed after a long depreciation of fifteen or twenty years (Acworth, 1925, p. 113; Thornton, 1811 [1962], p. 345). In his *Principles of Political Economy and Taxation* (1817 [1933]), Ricardo proposed a capital levy and in Parliament said that such a tax was the best, in fact the only, way of handling the burden of accumulated wartime debt. He also advocated that resumption be undertaken only for large amounts of sterling, in gold ingots and not in coin, the so-called gold bullion standard finally adopted more than a hundred years later. This proposal was unacceptable to the Bank of England, which had undertaken in 1817 to pay out gold coin for £1 and £2 notes, issued for the first time under the Suspension Act, as an experiment to see whether resumption was ultimately feasible. The bank opposed the issue of small notes again for a different reason: its fear of forgery (Acworth, 1925, pp. 92–94).

As would happen later in 1925, discussion of resumption helped it along. The Bank of England assisted as well by contracting the note issue. But foreign speculation in sterling, based on anticipation of resumption, drove the exchange rate up and the gold agio down, leaving a "trifling distance" to go to resume convertibility at £3 17s 10½d. The word is used twice by Tooke more or less contemporaneously (1838 [1928], Vol. 2, pp. 66, 76) and again by Hawtrey a century later (1919 [1927], p. 351).

The Birmingham school had been interested in a lower level for the pound and a higher price for gold, primarily for the sake of the unemployment, which was sufficiently serious in that manufacturing city to produce a petition of the "Distressed Mechanics of Birmingham" in 1817. It was not particularly interested in the burden of debt, though Thomas Attwood, Birmingham banker and the most articulate spokesman for the group, conceded the classic case for resumption, provided all debts and obligations would be adjusted. Attwood introduced a series of proposals in Parliament, first to abandon gold altogether, then to delay setting a parity. When these failed, he proposed raising the gold price to £8, a figure later modified to £6 and still later to £5 (Checkland, 1948, pp. 5, 15). A less radical proposal was that of Lord Folkstone, who urged a price of £4 0s 6d, corresponding to the market price of gold in 1819 and producing a "trifling" depreciation.

Whether one approves or disapproves of resumption in 1819 probably turns on choice between the long and the short run. In the short run, from about 1817 to 1823, preparations for resumption and the closing of the distance left after speculation drove the pound up were deflationary. The deflation was far from that predicted by the radical and monetary crank, William Cobbett, who predicted universal ruin of all who held stocks of goods, owed large sums, or had heavy mortgages, with a million people dying of hunger (Doubleday, 1847, pp. 248–49).

In the long run, after recovery in 1824, resumption at the 1717 price of gold rooted the gold standard deeply in the British economic habit system, defeating supporters of silver, bimetallism, and inconvertibility, and rejecting any, and all, adjustments proposed to ease the transition. It probably also misled the British about the difficulties of resumption in 1925. The parallel maintenance of the 1726 price of gold in France after the Napoleonic Wars with, however, bimetallism, made for two centuries of more or less monetary stability (with interruptions) of which Lüthy has said it is "impossible to exaggerate the political, economic, and even the spiritual effect" (1961, Vol. 2, p. 27).

CENTRAL BANK COOPERATION

Britain on the gold standard and the Continent, mainly France, with bimetallic money were called upon to cooperate on a number of occasions in the next half-century. In the crisis of 1825 when the Bank of England was faced with a run, the Bank of France came to the rescue with a shipment of gold sovereigns, sought by the public, exchanged against silver. The £400,000 arriving on Monday, 19 December, with the help of the Rothschilds and what Clapham calls "the smooth-working French bimetallic system," prevented the bank from having to shut its doors (1945, Vol. 2, p. 101). The disparate systems cooperated through more straightforward advances from France (and the Bank of Hamburg) to England in 1836 and 1839 and from the Bank of England to France in 1847, in all cases to help cope with financial crises.

A more interesting case from the viewpoint of bimetallism arose in November 1860 at the outbreak of the Civil War in the United States. The continued drain of specie to the east and enormous demands for liquidity in New York, which drew capital and specie from both London and Paris, put pressure on reserves in both capitals. Paris was reluctant to raise its discount rate, which tended to sustain the loss of reserves. With silver undervalued at the mint after the gold discoveries of California and Australia, the Bank of France was anxious to pay out only gold. Its silver reserves were £13 million, gold only £4 million (Bagehot, 1876 [1978], Vol. 10, p. 150). To have run through the gold portion and to have had to pay out silver would have extended the run since there was an assured profit for market *arbitrageurs* in exchanging francs for silver, presumably to sell in foreign markets. To get more gold, the Bank of France swapped £2 million of silver against gold coin with the Bank of England and was enabled to continue paying out gold for a time. The run continued into 1861, leading the Bank of France next to buy gold in London, even though the exchange rate was above the gold import point. It also exchanged 31 million francs of silver against gold with the Russian State Bank, which wanted silver to coin, and 9 million francs in Italy, presumably in the open market; and it bought 15 million francs worth of gold (with silver) in October 1861 from the Bank of Amsterdam (Plessis, 1985b, pp. 240–46). Negotiations with the Bank of England (called in Paris at the time the "Bank of London") had been started in November 1860 and were completed in May 1861, ending "the war of the banks," which I judge to have been some coolness and lack of cooperation between the Bank of France and the Bank of England (ibid., p. 245). Still more gold coin was needed, and the Bank of France drew £2 million in bills on London, through Rothschild and Baring, until a flight of capital from New York to Europe finally cut off the westward movement of specie (Morgan, 1943, pp. 175–77).

CALIFORNIA, 1849; AUSTRALIA, 1851

Prior to the conscious cooperation between the French bimetallic and the British gold standard in 1860, the two systems meshed smoothly and automatically in response to the large increase in gold production that followed the discoveries in California and Australia. Some estimates suggest that world gold production rose tenfold. Gold poured into London as Britain fulfilled the Spanish role of principal source of supplies needed in the mining communities. As earlier in Spain, it did not stay. Gold was shipped in large measure to France, which used it to replace silver dispatched, in turn, to the Far East (Martin, 1977). Michel Chevalier called silver the parachute that retarded the fall in the price of gold (1859, p. vii).

The increase in gold output did bring the market ratio of the prices of gold and silver down in London, from 15.70 in 1850 to 15.21, from which it recovered to 15.40 in the mid-1860s. It also gave rise to an intense debate on bimetallism in France. The government appointed four commissions in quick succession to study the issue, largely with the same cast of experts. The first sat in 1857, its successors in 1861, 1867, and 1868. The majority typically voted to retain bimetallism. One monetary expert, Michel Chevalier, voted for a silver standard in the first two commissions, but after the silver discoveries in the American West in the late 1850s and the 1860s, particularly the Comstock lode of 1859 in Nevada that brought the ratio back up to 15.58, Chevalier's championship of silver gave way, and he switched to the gold standard. Another monetary expert whose voluminous writings of the period lie unread today, Esquirou de Parieu, stayed with the gold standard throughout (Wolowski, 1869, pp. 183–96). Interest in the issue was widespread. Wolowski reports the opinions of chambers of commerce and receivers-general, even though they slightly favored the gold standard when he was a staunch bimetallist. Bordeaux and Strasbourg came out for bimetallism; Lyons and Rouen for gold, and so on.

Bimetallism went down to defeat in Britain in 1816, on the Continent in the 1870s, and in the United States two decades later. Nonetheless, at all times it retained, and even today retains, its adherents. The virulence of the debate was so strong that one leading German bimetallist, under attack in print from what Schumpeter is said to have called a "monometallic maniac," the monetary economists, Karl Helfferich, sued for slander. The case was thrown out of court, but Helfferich's biographer states that he was "too shrill" (Williamson, 1971, pp. 26–35). Most bimetallists came from the agricultural interests that wanted more money to achieve higher prices for foodstuffs, but there were bankers in the ranks, including one ex-governor of the Bank of England who was a strong advocate of bimetallism in the 1890s (Cassis, 1984, pp. 346–47). Today, a century later, one distinguished economist, Milton Friedman, admits to having been converted to bimetallism as a standard superior to gold alone. He offers the counterfactual suggestion that if the "hasty decision" to adopt gold as the currency standard after the Napoleonic Wars had been replaced by the adoption of bimetallism, the monetary history of the century to 1914 would have been very different (1992, esp. ch. vi).

THE LATIN MONETARY UNION

In 1865 a Latin Monetary Union was formed among France, Belgium, Switzerland, and Italy, acceded to in the same year by the Papal States and in 1867 by Greece and Rumania. It took effect on 1 August 1866. The immediate cause of the union was decision by France, Italy, and Switzerland to reduce the fineness of their 5-franc pieces (sometimes called dollars) to limit their disappearance because of mint undervaluation. France and Italy chose to move from a standard of 0.9 fine to 0.835. Switzerland happened to choose 0.800. This threatened to lead to displacement of French and Italian silver coins by Swiss ones. At this stage Belgium saw the wisdom of making its fineness conform to that of the neighboring states using the franc (including Italy, where the lira was equal to 1 franc). The instinct or reasoning that prompted the decision would be known in the 1960s as the theory of "optimum currency areas" (Mundell, 1961; McKinnon, 1963). Belgium was too small to have an independent currency.

A meeting was held to discuss the issue of fineness of silver. At the meeting the Swiss, Belgians, and Italians were in favor of shifting from bimetallism to the gold standard, but French resistance dominated. A treaty was concluded fixing the 5-franc (lira) silver coin at 0.9 fine but lesser coins at 0.835. A limit was set on the minting of lesser coins because of their substantial seignorage; without such a limit, fixed at 6 francs of lesser coin per inhabitant of each country, one state might earn revenue from overminting and introducing the excess coinage into neighboring markets.

Then came a series of blows to silver. The Comstock lode was one. Development of an electrolytic process for refining made it possible to work low-grade ores and even the tailings of old mines economically. An exchange crisis in Italy in 1866 led to an outflow of specie, largely silver. Still later, after victory in the Franco-Prussian War, the formation of the Reich, and the founding of the Reichsbank, Germany shifted from bimetallism to the gold standard. By 1877 it had sold 579 million francs of silver on the world market and still held an unknown amount, estimated at £17 to £20 million worth, or perhaps another 500 million francs, that hung over the market (U.S. Senate, 1879 [1978], p. 59).

From 1865 to 1867, however, the Latin Monetary Union worked reasonably well, and its success suggested the desirability of expanding it to arrive at a "universal money."

UNIVERSAL MONEY

The term *universal money* was perhaps first used in 1588 by one Davanzati in his "Discourse on Coin" to the Academy at Florence. He maintained that while the prince could make money out of "iron, leather, wood, cork, lead, paper, salt or the like, as sometimes happen'd" such money could not circulate outside the realm and therefore could not be universal money (Vilar, 1969 [1976], p. 190). François Nicholas Mollien, Napoleon's minister of finance, approached the same idea, without the identical term, in writing that it was desirable for all people to adopt a uniform system of measures and that, of these, the uniformity that contributes most to the convenience of nations is uncontestably that of money (1845, Vol. 3, p. 498). Interest in enlarging the optimum currency area, that is, in adopting universal money, came principally from France, and especially from de Parieu, vice-president of the Conseil d'Etat, the economist who had supported the gold standard against bimetallism. He had been the leading spirit in the Latin Monetary Union; he was instrumental in calling the International Monetary Conference of 1867, held in Paris in connection with the Universal Exhibition of that year, bringing together Treasury and mint officials, with a few national representatives from among the commissioners to the exposition.

The idea behind universal money was partly to assist travellers in having coins interchangeable but primarily to simplify the calculation of exchange rates to facilitate foreign trade (U.S. Senate, 1879 [1978], p. 817). Bagehot is not impressed with these reasons. The advantage in a universal money is not as medium of exchange, he claimed, but as unit of account, in enabling foreigners to understand English *price language* (1868 [1978], Vol. 11, p. 71, his italics) and to enable British bankers to know how much bullion there is in the Bank of France: "Of course all English bankers *can* turn francs into pounds, and some think they *will;* but few ever do" (ibid., Vol. 11, p. 73).

The conference opened by adopting the evolutionary method of making adjustments in existing monies rather than starting afresh with a new set of coins to be adopted by all countries. One scheme was to coin a 25-franc gold piece, equal to the English pound and to 5 American dollars after adjustment of the sovereign to change its fineness from eleven-twelfths (0.917) to 0.90, and the dollar to an equivalent of 5 to the pound instead of 4.866. The U.S. commissioner to the Exposition thought that the 3½ percent appreciation of the dollar would be acceptable. Back in London, Lord Overstone and his intimate correspondent, G. W. Norman of the Court of the Bank of England, regarded tampering with the weight of the sovereign as "fraud in disguise" (O'Brien, 1869 [1971], Vol. 3, p. 1187).

Minting a 25-franc coin was not completely satisfactory to the French since it failed to fit into the metric system by which they set store as another universal standard. They sought to build around the Napoleon of 20 francs, or a 10-franc piece, once known as a ducat, which fitted the metric system still more neatly. The Dutch wanted a 15-franc standard, equal to 4 thalers, and were supported by south Germany and Wurtemberg, although Austria objected. The Prussian delegate had no instructions.

The conference ended on 6 July 1867, settling on the 5-franc gold piece (dollar) as the pivot of the system but with recommendations for the coinage of a 25-franc piece equal to the sovereign and the American half-eagle ($5.00), and to a coin adopted by the Vienna Conference of 1857 on German monetary unification to represent 10 florins. It concluded in favor of the gold standard but with a gradual transition from bimetallism.

INTERNATIONAL MONETARY CONFERENCE, 1878

The recommendations of the Conference of 1867 were almost universally pigeon-holed. The only actions taken were by Austria which gave the Hôtel des Monnaies (mint) in Paris the right to mint a 25-franc piece with the label "10 florins," and by Hungary, which minted an 8-florin coin identical to the 20-franc piece. Then the Franco-Prussian War supervened, with subsequent disruption of European exchanges in 1871 and 1872 as the 5 billion franc idemnity was paid. Next came the boom of 1872–73, the transformation of the Prussian National Bank into the Reichsbank, and of the four currencies of mosaic Germany after the 1857 agreement into the mark. The Germans adopted the gold standard and sold silver. The gold/silver ratio tumbled from 15.92 in 1873 to a low (for silver) of 20.17 in London in July 1876 before recovering to 17 to 1 in 1877. By this time, however, the Latin Monetary Union had had to stop minting overvalued silver. Europe, as a whole, went over to the gold standard.

In calling an International Monetary Conference in 1878, the United States, with silver interests, hoped to obtain agreement to reinstitute the bimetallic standard. In theory, the more countries that adhered to bimetallism, the more likely was the mint ratio to dominate the market ratio and hold up the silver price. There was never a chance. Poor countries like Mexico and China remained on the silver standard; Europe and, shortly afterward, the United States shifted to gold. True believers such as the Junkers in Germany and the Populists in the United States blamed the great depression from 1873 to 1896 on the abandonment of silver and agitated for its readoption to raise agricultural prices. Bimetallism in Europe was dead. The spurt in gold production in the Witwatersrand of South Africa in the 1890s, and in

Alaska in the 1900s, evoked no discussion of the issue similar to that following the discoveries of California and Australia.

THE GOLD STANDARD FROM 1880 TO 1914

While the gold standard in England goes back to 1717 or to 1774, its universalization in Europe dates from 1875 or 1880. Two opposing views have developed about it. One can be called world monetarism and maintains that world production of precious metals—from 1875 gold—determined the world money supply and world prices. The view has strong affinities with the bullionists (currency school) in England, who were unwilling to regard bank deposits as money, much less bills of exchange or utilized credit lines. Bank notes counted because they were backed by gold. In its extreme form today, as espoused in the United States by Robert Mundell and Arthur Laffer, this view tends to regard central banking as having been futile, since interest rates, money supplies, prices—virtually all significant monetary variables—were determined by mining costs rather than by central bank policy. At the other extreme is the view that the gold standard was, in effect, a sterling standard, managed and operated worldwide by the Bank of England at the center.

The second of these views was, on the whole, the earlier to develop in the twentieth century. Ralph Hawtrey (1919 [1927]), W. Edwards Beach (1935), William Adams Brown, Jr. (1940), Arthur I. Bloomfield (1959, 1963), and a host of others have described in detail the working of the system and how the discount rate of the Bank of England affected prices (through affecting the cost of holding stocks) and attracted or repelled short-term capital flows from the rest of the world, and hence gold movements. The price-specie-flow mechanism developed by David Hume in the eighteenth century must be modified since gold movements respond more readily and more frequently to capital flows induced directly by discount rate changes than to changes in price levels and trade balances. Relationships were asymmetric. Britain financed exports and imports in sterling bills, other countries their third-country trade also in sterling bills. Other countries thus had to hold balances in sterling (Lindert, 1969). Britain drew no bills on other countries, and held no balances in other currencies. Its task was to manage its gold reserve.

The Bank of England learned how to manage its international reserves during a long period of experiment in the first half of the nineteenth century, culminating in the Bank Act of 1844. This had to be suspended in crises in 1847, 1857, and 1866, until the bank mastered the technique of discount rate manipulation. Countries such as France, which held its discount rate fixed except for a short period between 1856 and 1865, would employ other devices to manage their exchanges, such as paying out overvalued metal, as we have seen, or lightweight coin, or changing their effective specie prices and thus the gold (and silver) export and import points, offering dealers interest-free advances, and so on (Morgenstern, 1959). The system was a managed one; the central focus of that management was the Bank of England.

Implicit in all this is that management was required because the market will respond to market restriction, if it gets the bit between its teeth, by creating more money. The boom of the 1850s, for example, was by no means solely the result of the discoveries of 1849 and 1851. These were dampened by the flow of silver to the Far East. The market responded to the euphoria created by investment in railroads and the suppression of the Revolution of 1848 on the Continent by a wave of money creation. The Bank Act of 1844 had restricted bank notes but not bills of exchange or bank deposits, and these expanded in England by large amounts (Hughes, 1960, ch. x). The Crédit Mobilier, first established in France in 1852, and later the action of the Bank of France in admitting railroad securities to discount in 1856, were of greater importance than the discoveries (although the expansion of the Crédit Mobilier was stimulated by the new bullion). A wave of bank formation in Germany, Italy, Austria, and Spain—to be discussed in subsequent chapters— was only tangentially connected with gold and silver, if at all.

The great depression of 1873 to 1896, in this view, was the result of real factors, importantly the reduction of costs of production of many products—for example, the substitution of long-lived steel for iron—and especially the decline in transport costs through railroads and steamships. Trade in grain that had been confined to the Mediterranean and the Baltic–North Sea waters before the sixteenth century, and then Europe as a whole, now became worldwide. The Ukraine, Canada, United States, and Australia poured wheat into Europe and drove down prices there. Wheat prices rose in producing areas.

The contrary view of world monetarism starts with the price revolution of the six-teenth century that resulted from Spanish treasure and blames the reduced economic activity of the seventeenth and eighteenth centuries, but especially the post-Napo-leonic depression, on the failure of gold and silver supplies to expand continuously. The boom of the 1850s is ascribed to California and Australia, and, when this ran its course, the great depression was the consequence of decline in the rate of growth of the money stock. Little notice is taken by monetarists of demonetization of silver. Total gold production remained virtually unchanged from the 1850s to the late 1880s, but the rate of growth of the stock declined from about 4 percent per year in 1852 to 2 percent in 1870, and below 2 percent until 1890 when the Rand discoveries were made (Marjolin, 1941, p. 185). It was not the fall in the stock of gold that drove the price level down from 142 in 1872 in France, for example, to 82 in 1896. The gold stock actually rose. Its rate of growth declined, and this received blame for the price decline. Skeptics observe that monetarists shift easily from the absolute level to the rate of change without always explaining the basis for switching models.

In the latest version, combining the new economic history with world monetarism, central banks and central bank policy are asserted to have had no control over interest rates, prices, or incomes, which were set by the world stock of money. Unless one or another central bank sterilized gold inflows and outflows, gain or loss of gold by one country was offset by loss or gain of another. World markets for traded goods are assumed to be unified, so that one price, and only one price, prevails for traded goods everywhere. Within a country, prices of traded and nontraded goods move together. Hence the world price level is determined by the world money supply, or, more pre-cisely, by the world stock of gold (McCloskey and Zecher, 1976).

One could take issue with this picture by pointing to the assumptions of no trans-port costs, no sterilization, and independent central-bank actions so that central banks in different countries do not happen to expand or to contract simultaneously. But confrontation between the managed view of the gold standard and world monetarism can be softened along lines of the distinction already made between short- and long-run views of economic processes. In the short run, money broadly defined to include coin in circulation, bank notes, bank deposits, bills of exchange, and perhaps other credit instruments is highly variable, or if money is defined more narrowly, such as only coin and bank notes or a stock of high-powered money that changes slowly, monetary velocity moves through a wide range. In the medium term, average velocity varies less sharply, and the quantity of money is undoubtedly a powerful motor of the economic system. In the long run, however, innovation may take place in a youthful and dynamic society, to create new monies when they seem required to increase efficiency in the use of existing media of exchange. How long a run this is depends on the country and, for a given country, how responsive it is at a given time to opportunities and to the necessity to surmount obstacles.

The monetary view that central banks are helpless because rates of interest, prices, and nominal money income are determined on a world basis by the gold stock fails to allow for asymmetries in the system. It can happen that most central banks had a limited ability to affect either their own or world conditions, but that the Bank of England, despite operating on a small gold base, did. On this showing, the Bank of England set the level of world interest rates, which accounts for the fact that national interest rates moved up and down together, while other countries had power only over a narrow differential between the domestic level and the world rate. With sterling bills traded worldwide, serving as a close substitute for money in foreign countries, and their interest rate manipulated in London, the gold standard was a sterling system.

But all this presupposes an understanding of the history of banking in Europe, to which we now turn.

SUGGESTED SUPPLEMENTARY READING

Acworth (1925), *Financial Reconstruction in England, 1815–1822.*
Bordo and Schwartz (eds.) (1984), *A Retrospective on the Classical Gold Standard, 1821–1931,* which, however, lacks an essay on the French experience.
Brown (1940), *The International Gold Standard Reinterpreted, 1914–1934.*
deRoover (1949), *Gresham on Foreign Exchange.*
Friedman (1992), *Monetary Mischief.*
Hawtrey (1919 [1927]), *Currency and Credit.*
McCloskey and Zecher (1976), How the gold standard worked, 1880–1913.
Thornton (1802 [1962]), *An Enquiry into the Nature and Effect of the Paper Credit of Great Britain.*
U.S. Senate (1879 [1978]), *International Monetary Conference of 1878.*

In French
Bouvier (1973), *Une siècle de banque française,* chap. ii.

II

BANKING

Part II deals with the development of banking in Europe to 1914, with chapters divided among the four main western countries—Britain, France, Germany, and Italy—and rather sketchy treatments of Scotland, Austria, Sweden, Switzerland, and Spain woven among them. A series of functional issues arises in the course of the historical description, with emphasis that varies depending on the country:

1. The evolution of money from coins alone to coins and bank notes, to coins, bank notes, and bank deposits, and the evolution of banks from deposit banks that merely validate receipts of coin on a one-for-one basis to lending banks, which actually create deposits or money.
2. The many paths to banking from not only, or even mainly, goldsmiths but also merchants, scriveners (notaries), industrialists, and tax farmers.
3. The rise of single financial centers, such as London and Paris, which dominate national finance, and the process of the formation of such centers as seen in countries like Germany and Italy where political unification came late and was followed by the pull of regional banks to a newly formed center.
4. The spread of banks from the center in national networks covering the entire country.
5. The rise of central banks as the government banker and a bankers' bank with responsibility for monetary policy. As part of this process, central banks seek to take over the issue of bank notes as a monopoly.
6. The development of the role of a lender of last resort in financial crisis to prevent bank runs and the spread of crises.
7. The elaboration of the doctrine that banks are needed to stimulate trade and industry through money creation, and especially the formulation of the doctrine by Saint-Simonism in France and its implementation in the establishment of the Crédit Mobilier in 1852 and the spread of its example to much of the rest of continental Europe.
8. The relationships of banking with commerce, with which it had close links in all countries, and industry where such relations differed from country to country. In Britain banks financed mainly trade, although on occasion there occurred forays into industrial lending. The Continent saw much closer relations, beginning with Belgium in the second quarter of the nineteenth century. The Crédit Mobilier has been widely regarded as the prototype of

industrial lending, but its investments were largely in public works, rail-roads, ports, utilities, and the like and in speculation in bonds and mort-gages. The closest connections between banks and industry were in Ger-many, Austria, Sweden, and, until the 1930s, Italy.

9. A comparison of British and French history in money and banking indicates that Britain was a century ahead of France in evolving most of its financial institutions. In these circumstances, it is doubtful that the French level of income per capita was ahead of, or equal to, that in Britain. A suggestion that Sweden was an "impoverished sophisticate" with banks and money, and capital markets developed far in advance of its general economic growth, which is of some considerable interest to the application of the Coase theo-rem that institutions adapt to the underlying real situation, does not seem to bear close examination.

10. In Gerschenkron's theory of backwardness, banking serves as a substitute for entrepreneurship in moderately backward countries (and government in more backward). The theory does not seem to apply well to Italy where French banks failed to achieve an industrial breakthrough in the 1860s, and the German banks, which are given credit for leading the growth process in the 1890s, were quickly converted to Italian institutions, and remained Ger-man only briefly.

11. Banking failed to sustain economic development in Spain. Both Italy and Spain are seen as "colonized" by foreign banking by the time of the nine-teenth century, as contrasted with institutions that grew up out of local ini-tiatives.

5

English and Scottish Banking

> The gold and silver money which circulates in any country, and by which the produce of its land and labour is annually circulated and distributed to the proper consumers, is . . . all dead stock. It is a very valuable part of the capital of the country, which produces nothing to the country. The judicious operation of banking, by substituting paper in the room of a great part of this gold and silver, enables the country to convert a great part of this dead stock into active and productive stock; into stock which produces something to the country. The gold and silver which circulates in any country may properly be compared to a highway . . . The judicious operation of banking . . . provides, if I may be allowed so violent a metaphor, a sort of waggon-way through the air.
>
> (Smith, *The Wealth of Nations,* 1776 [1937], p. 305)

THE EIGHTEENTH CENTURY

The early days of the Bank of England were associated largely with operations in government debt, to transform the chaotic assortment of obligations issued by the English government during its almost continuous wars into funded obligations, widely distributed. Its success has been called a financial revolution that enabled England with a population one-third that of France to defeat it time and again in battle throughout the eighteenth century (Dickson, 1967).

The road was rough. The inflation created by initial note issues led to runs in the 1690s. In 1707 the East India Company's insiders, opposed by the new men who had organized the Bank of England and the New East India Company, tried to organize a run on the bank, first draining the City of specie and then presenting £ 300,000 in bank notes for payment. A panic and run ensued, but thanks to the help of Queen Anne, the dukes of Somerset, Newcastle, and Marlborough, and other nobles who advanced considerable sums, they were allayed (Andréadès, 1909, p. 120; T. S. Ashton, 1959, p. 114). The next test came from a different quarter. The bank's development was threatened by aspirations of the South Sea Company, which sought to take over the role of major intermediary in English government debt. Moreover, the bank's original charter had been written for a limited period. As the end of each period approached, it was necessary to renew the charter, usually at the price of lending the government more money on a permanent basis and at an interest rate below the market, although a new charter also gave opportunity for adding to the Bank's powers and prerogatives.

The South Sea Company was intimately associated with the Sword Blade Bank. This latter had started out as a manufacturing company using Huguenot swordsmith techniques, failed, and then had been converted by a scrivener, John Blunt, into a land bank granting mortgages, accepting deposits, and issuing notes. When the Bank of England undertook to negotiate its charter renewal in 1707, three years in advance of the expiry of the old, the Sword Blade Company bid against it and forced the bank to increase the amount of its loan to the government and lower the rate of interest (Carswell, 1960, ch. 2). Renewal in 1708, however, did give the Bank of England a monopoly of joint stock banking in England (Joslin, 1954 [1962], p. 343). Nonetheless, its troubles were not over. In 1711 the Sword Blade syndicate took away from the bank a lottery to raise £2 million. The same group then formed the South Sea Company to undertake trade in the South (Atlantic) Sea, once the Spanish government had granted permission in the form of an *asiento,* as its ostensible purpose, but more seriously to fund a further portion of the government debt. Holders of this debt, especially of life and perpetual annuities, were to exchange them for stock in the South Sea Company, with the English Treasury then paying the interest to the new intermediary. The founders were attracted mainly to stock promotion. They proposed to sell stock in the company for cash, as well as debt exchange, and to run the value of the stock up to make fortunes on the amounts sold to themselves at low prices early in the game. The Bank of England made a rival offer, which was rejected after the South Sea Company raised its bid (Carswell, 1960, pp. 111–13). Bank stock fell, and some City opinion thought it was finished.

This is not the place to recount the rise and collapse of the South Sea Bubble. Two points must be made, however. First, the Bubble Act of June 1720 that halted formation of unincorporated joint stock companies and was a device to serve the South Sea Company by halting diversion of cash subscriptions to rival promotions, not an attack on it, constituted a barrier to company formation for a hundred years. Second, the Bank of England moved to the rescue of the battered South Sea Company, late in the day and after considerable hesitation, which enabled the latter to continue as a financial company intermediating government debt but on a more sedate basis. It refused to help the Sword Blade Bank, the failure of which, in September 1720, marked the last challenge to the dominance of the Bank of England (ibid., p. 184). The position of the bank was further strengthened in the charter renewal of 1742 when, after the usual additional advance to the government, it was granted a monopoly of the note issue in England, except for private banks, partnerships of six persons or less (Andréadès, 1909, p. 147). These private banks were divided into two groups: those in London and "country banks."

For the early part of its life, the Bank of England was actually the "Bank of London." Few of its notes circulated outside the capital, even as late as 1802 (Thornton, 1802 [1962], p. 113). The notes, moreover, were not intended for hand-to-hand circulation but as a substitute for gold in large transactions. No note below £20 was issued before 1759 when the £10 denomination was introduced. The £5 note was first put out in 1794 to satisfy the demand for liquidity arising from the 1793 panic resulting from the canal mania and the French Reign of Terror. With suspension of convertibility of bank notes into specie during the Napoleonic Wars, £2 and £1 notes were issued in 1797 for the first time but were withdrawn, as noted in the previous chapter, beginning in 1817.

Profitability of the bank rested on acceptance and circulation of its notes. In 1745 when the bank's notes were turned in for coin in a crisis started by the southward march of the Pretender, who crossed the border from Scotland, took Carlisle, and marched as far as Derby without resistance, the run was slowed by paying out six-pences—a device used in an earlier episode in 1720, either by the Bank of England (Andréadès, 1909, p. 137) or by the Sword Blade Bank (Carswell, 1960, p. 184) but presumably not both. The bank used the time gained to get the merchants of London to sign a statement of willingness to accept Bank of England notes in lieu of coin. The same sort of manifesto was signed by 1,140 merchants and investors in a single day in 1797 at the time of suspension of convertibility (Andréadès, 1909, p. 151), organized by Lewis Loyd, the father of Lord Overstone (D. P. O'Brien, ed., 1971, p. 13). The eighteenth century thus saw the spread of bank notes for coin. Their convenience was indubitable. Confidence in those of the Bank of England, as distinct from those of the country banks, grew slowly, unevenly, surely.

LONDON BANKS

The eighteenth century also saw the expansion of private banking in London and its gradual specialization. In the early years, banking was intermingled with gold-smithing, dealing in precious stones, and speculating in commodities and ships, with many new firms entering and dying down again in the ferment of the South Sea Bubble. By the 1720s specialization had gone some distance as private banks more and more gave up goldsmith activity. Numbers rose from twenty-four in 1725 to fifty-two in 1785.

These private bankers were divided into two distinct groups: those of the "City" of London, the downtown financial district, and those of the West End, near the Houses of Parliament but more especially near the homes of the gentry and nobil-ity. The former dealt in some degree in bills of exchange but mainly in government "stock" (in American parlance "bonds") and the shares of the Bank of England, East India Company, and South Sea Company. They undertook financial com-missions for Dutch investors and for country banks for which they served as main correspondents. West End banks did most of their business with the gentry and aris-tocracy, lending on mortgages or overdrafts, transmitting rents from the country-side to Mayfair in seasonal surges in November and May, providing travelers' checks for the upper classes touring Europe. Some landowners borrowed to finance town houses, new or extended country seats, enclosures, drainage projects, turn-pikes, and canals; many did so for consumption, including dowries to be settled on children about to marry.

New banks came from all sorts of sources, including, in addition to the usual merchants, scriveners, tax farmers and goldsmiths, brewers and distillers, who had learned to finance substantial stocks of grain, on the one hand, and output, on the other (Joslin, 1954 [1962]).

CLEARING

Just as Amsterdam, and later London, was an international clearing center for trade, so London early became a clearing center for national payments. London banks issued few bank notes of their own and settled balances with each other, on their own account and for accounts of their correspondents, in Bank of England notes. In the seventeenth century, banks had kept running accounts with each other, which enabled them to cancel offsetting claims (Sheppard, 1971, p. 72). The activity was transferred first to a public house and, in 1773, to a newly established "clearinghouse," rented in Lombard street. Only thirty-one of thirty-six City banks joined the clearinghouse, and none of those in the West End (Joslin, 1954 [1962], p. 357). Private banks dominated London clearing even after joint stock banks were formed after the Acts of 1826 and 1833. The joint stock banks were not admitted to the London clearing until 1854, then grudgingly, and did not receive a voice in policy for another twenty years (Leighton-Boyce, 1958, p. 286).

A system of exchanging one another's bank notes on a friendly basis was developed by Scottish banks as early as 1752. Before 1788 it had become customary for English country banks in Newcastle to exchange notes at regular intervals. In 1826 bankers in the north of England came together at weekly or biweekly intervals to exchange sight claims, including notes, settling remaining balances in Bank of England notes then circulating outside London. By 1837 settlement took place in Bank of England branches, which spread over the country after 1826. Most of the principal cities of England had clearinghouses by 1872 when a clearinghouse was established in Newcastle with settlements made by checks on the Bank of England (Bisschop, 1896 [1968], pp. 237–40).

Local clearing was one problem, readily solved with exchange of notes and later clearinghouses, using first Bank of England notes, and then checks. For interregional settlement, there was, in addition, the inland bill of exchange. This went back to the end of the fourteenth or the fifteenth century (Postan, 1930 [1973], p. 58) and started to die down in the third quarter of the nineteenth century when improvements in transport and communications—the telegraph, railroad, steamship, Suez Canal, and so on—reduced the need to finance inventories on the previous massive scale. Finance then shifted to overdrafts and advances and payment to checks (Nishimura, 1971). In the seventeenth century, army pay was transmitted to garrison towns by inland bills. The year was divided into seven musters, occasions when the commissary general of the muster would visit a regiment, check that all on the rolls were present, properly equipped, and eligible for pay. Agents of the regiments near London then obtained the cash for troop pay from London bankers; those at a distance either bought bills in London on a town near the garrison station or from a distance drew on the paymaster-general or his bank, and sold the bills locally to raise cash. Only if all else failed would coin be physically transported (C. Clay, 1978, pp. 147, 157–60). Later, to be sure, Bank of England notes and ultimately bank deposits would be used.

A separate clearing for country banks was established in London in 1857 but was not successful. The rise of branch banking began to make it possible for joint stock banks to clear payments from one branch to another within the system and for payments due to, or from, other banks in the general London clearing. In 1858 the National Provincial Bank thought it preposterous for a bank in Manchester to collect a check on Newcastle-upon-Tyne by way of London. The system of country clearing, it held, would only encourage the use of checks instead of country banker drafts (inland bills of exchange) and notes (Taylor, 1964, app. 5, esp. pp. 225, 229). By 1866, however, it was ready to give up the note issue privilege, start a London banking office, and settle for its system through the regular London clearing. Special country clearing was already superfluous (Bisschop, 1896 [1968], p. 240).

COUNTRY BANKS

Outside London, there were few banks in 1750, perhaps a dozen; after that date, their number rose exponentially. Agreement on exact numbers is difficult, and estimates for separate dates, based on different series, may not be comparable. An old estimate suggests that the twelve banks in 1750 doubled by 1772 and reached almost 400 by 1800, despite the fact that 100 banks disappeared in the aftermath of the canal mania of the early 1790s (ibid., pp. 150, 164, 173n). A later and more systematic estimate runs from 119 in 1784 to 280 in 1793, although the figures may not be entirely comparable, with a decline to 230 in 1797. By 1809 an official series shows 755 country banks that shrink to 521 in 1821, rise to 547 in 1824, and then enter a long decline to 311 in 1842 when the series ends (Pressnell, 1956, p. 11).

Three main types of activities led into early country banking: industrialists who needed to make local payments; scriveners and remitters of funds between the country and London, especially traders; and collectors of government revenue (ibid., p. 13). A member of the first group set back formal banking in Lancashire. T. S. Ashton explained that Lancashire used bills of exchange as a circulating medium, even in small and odd amounts, with long strings of endorsements, because of antagonism to local note issues, probably arising from the bankruptcy in 1788 of a well-known firm of Blackburn calico printers that failed for £1.5 million and defaulted on a large volume of small notes issued in wage payments. The bankruptcy led to others, including that of a bank, plus a run on the Manchester banking house, Jones & Company, from which Jones, Loyd & Company, Lord Overstone's bank, descended. In commenting on the use of bills of exchange as money, Thomas Ashton stated, "When the state fails in the elementary function of providing a proper supply of legal tender, the community seeks to create a currency of its own," and added, apropos of the failure, that generations later men's minds turned back to 1788 (1953a, pp. 37–49). This is an indication of the impact of financial disaster on collective memory and sometimes future behavior that we shall encounter again, more than once.

There was a need for a money intermediate between that used for local payments, often tokens issued by manufacturers, and the bill of exchange that served in distant payments. For the most part, until after 1826 the notes of country banks filled this gap, providing an effective illustration of institutions rising to serve economic needs (Jeffrys, 1938 [1977], p. 15).

Scriveners have been discussed. Remitters to London are exemplified by Thomas Smith who started as a mercer in Nottingham and in 1671 was appointed a subcommissioner for the excise, along with others, largely for his financial connections with leading London goldsmith bankers. The firm retained the excise business until 1841 (Leighton-Boyce, 1958, pp. 13–15). His grandson, Abel Smith II, like ten London and three other country bankers, was a contractor to the British government in the American Revolutionary War, providing rations delivered to 60,000 troops in America, a lucrative, if not at the outset a highly efficient, undertaking (Baker, 1971, pp. 218, 225–26). At this time Smith was well connected, two of his sons being members of Parliament.

Members of the family started a London affiliate, Smith & Payne, later Smith, Payne & Smith, in 1758 and subsequently unit banks in Lincoln (1775) and Hull (1784). The London bank gradually took over the principal management of the firm's resources and served as agent for fourteen other provincial banks as well. It had many clients among the hosiery trade of Nottingham, a few aristocratic depositors, though most did their banking in London with other bankers. It survived the crisis of the 1790s through holding down loans and overdrafts as a percentage of total assets—never more than 39 percent before 1792 and reduced to 14 percent at the peak of difficult times. Leighton-Boyce calls Smith's the first branch bank in England—though not in Great Britain because of earlier branching in Scotland (1958, p. 74).

After Mowbray, Hollingsworth & Company of Durham opened a London house in 1814, the ambition of many country banks was to form or acquire a London office of their own (Bisschop, 1896 [1968], p. 191). Pole, Thornton & Company, of which Henry Thornton, Jr., son of the author of *Paper Currency,* was a partner, had thirty-eight country correspondents when it stopped payment in the crisis of 1825 (T. S. Ashton, 1953*b*, p. 100). With the coming of the joint stock banks in 1826, however, a gradual shift took place to networks of banks, ultimately headed in London, which effected a considerable amount of remitting and clearing within a given bank.

Country banks used London either to obtain funds or to get rid of them. Some counties, mainly the agrarian, had surplus savings; some, usually the industrial, needed to borrow to satisfy their clients. In 1873 Walter Bagehot quoted a bill broker, one Mr. Richardson, testifying before the Bullion Committee in 1810:

In some parts of the country there is little circulation of bills drawn on London, as in Norfolk, Essex, Sussex, etc. . . . I receive bills to a considerable extent from Lancashire in particular, and remit them to Norfolk, Suffolk, etc., where the bankers have large lodgements, and much surplus money to advance on bills for discount. (Bagehot, 1873 [1978], Vol. 9, p. 192)

Accurate in Richardson's time, the practice was out of date when Bagehot referred to it, for joint stock banks had begun to replace the physical movement of bills drawn on London from the north and west to be discounted in the south and east (Sayers, 1978, p. 35).

MERCHANT BANKING

The development of banking from commerce frequently encountered a prolonged intermediate stage known in England originally as merchant banking. The merchant banker was a merchant who loaned his credit to others (Hidy, 1939 [1978],

p. 139). This was done in various ways: by making advances to producers before the goods were sold, either goods entrusted to the merchant on commission for sale abroad or those received on consignment from abroad; by issuing letters of credit under which merchants could draw bills of exchange; or by buying and selling outright bills of exchange created by trade (Perkins, 1975, p. 2). Most merchant bankers gradually drifted from generalized commerce into specialized commerce and from specialized commerce into finance. The evolution was a means of reducing the risks and stresses of overseas trade. The transition could be short or long. John Hope & Company of Amsterdam were bankers in the eighteenth century and, at the same time, engaged in trade at first and second hand, trading all articles: "money, grain, colonial produce, ships' articles, gold, silver, dry saltery, ordinance, textiles, tobacco, tea, wine, flower bulbs, in short anything that could be sold at a profit" (Buist, 1974, p. 33). Hope was also an avid speculator, buying flax and hemp in St. Petersburg, Russia, during the Napoleonic Wars and storing them for shipment and sale at the end of the hostilities (ibid., ch. 7). At about the same time in Frankfurt, Meyer Amschel Rothschild traded in coffee, sugar, and tobacco, along with British manufactures, all smuggled through the Continental blockade, as well as in bills of exchange. His son, Nathan, taking £20,000 to England to make his fortune, went first to Manchester where he bought (and later sold) mainly fibers and dyestuffs for cloth, and cloth itself, but also "anything, everywhere, where it was good and cheap" (Corti, 1928, pp. 52, 91).

In the flourishing Anglo-American trade of the nineteenth century, Alexander Brown started out in Baltimore importing Irish linen into the United States and, with his sons, spread into importing mainly cotton dry goods into the country and exporting cotton to Liverpool. Brown's dabbled in tobacco, shipping, government, and railroad securities, before settling down to cotton and dry goods (Perkins, 1975, ch. 4). The firm would sometimes buy cotton for its own account to fill out a cargo on one of its own ships. Its arch-rival in the transatlantic trade, Baring & Company, on the other hand, dealt after 1840 mainly for its own account (ibid., pp. 82, 107). Brown's tended to be conservative in making advances on cotton for export or goods consigned for sale in the United States. Advances were normally two-thirds to four-fifths of the anticipated proceeds of a shipment, and the proportion was lowered when prices rose, as Brown's was suspicious of speculation. Despite this conservative attitude, the British end of the firm, Brown, Shipley, then of Liverpool (after 1857 of London), had to be rescued by the Bank of England in 1837 since it held £400,000 of acceptances of the three "W" banks of Liverpool, American houses in the Anglo-American trade—Wiggins, Wildes, and Wilson—which had recklessly advanced money on cotton textiles shipped to the United States in the 1836 boom when prices were rising and were in trouble when prices fell (Hidy, 1939 [1978], p. 85).

Merchants entered finance not only to reduce the risk and stress of commerce but also to increase the supply of goods they needed for export or import. Swedish exports of timber, oats, and iron to England after the middle of the nineteenth century were largely financed by credits extended by London importing houses to Swedish exporting merchants and by the latter in turn to local producers. Capital requirements were large in agriculture with a short growing season: farmers borrowed in winter, largely in January and February, and during the planting season; they paid their debts off after the harvest. A somewhat different seasonal requirement for credit applied to Swedish timber and iron where production took place rather more regularly throughout the year, but output could be moved by land to the ports only during winter when the soft roads were frozen (Fridlizius, 1957, ch. 9; Söderlund, 1952, ch. 6).

Despite the retention of mercantile activities by some banks, the general transition was from commerce, where successful, to banking. This transition took place in Holland in the eighteenth century (C. Wilson, 1941, ch. 3) and in England more fully in the nineteenth. The term *merchant banker* was retained long after buying and selling for the firm's own account had ceased, so that a merchant banker in the twentieth century is, in effect, a private bank with partners, whereas in the eighteenth century it was more nearly a merchant who undertook lending.

London bankers have been attacked as a closed society, politically dominant, and, in some instances, responsible for having started World War I. A sociological study by a scholar of foreign origin exonerates them from such accusations. The author is interested in genealogies, intermarriage, education, fortunes, residences, clubs, and directorships, the last of which run to insurance, shipping, and railroads, but little to industry. The group, or rather the collectivity of three subgroups—Quakers, Anglicans, and foreign, the last divided between old foreign and new foreign, many of them Jewish—was closed, with few self-made men among them. Merchant bankers developed from trade and differed in attitude from bankers in the provinces and the London great banks, which did lend to industry. Those elected to Parliament limited their participation to questions of trade and finance, such as the budget, the gold standard, and free trade, but on the last two issues their opinions were not unanimous, as, for example, in the question of bimetallism versus the gold standard (Cassis, 1984).[1]

SCOTTISH BANKS

The slaughter of country banks in the 1825 crisis gave rise to a demand for joint stock banks such as then existed in Scotland. Before 1695 Scotland had been financially primitive. Bills of exchange were limited, as well as goldsmiths and money changers. In 1695, a year after the formation of the Bank of England, the Scottish Parliament incorporated the Bank of Scotland with limited liability and a twenty-one-year monopoly of joint stock banking in the country. After the monopoly had run out, a second joint stock bank was chartered in 1727, the Royal Bank of Scotland. The two waged war on one another, collecting and presenting quantities of each other's notes for payment in specie. In 1746 a joint stock company in linen was formed, the British Linen Company, but with a wide charter that permitted banking into which the company directly proceeded. The three were known as public banks.

1. The Cassis book is in French; those who lack ease in that language can read a summary article (Cassis, 1985), but they would miss an agreeable typographical error: *méchant* bankers for *merchant* bankers (Cassis, 1984, p. 74). *Méchant* in French means "naughty."

In addition to Scottish public banks, there were private banking companies and provincial banks with joint stock form. Among the banking companies were the upstart Ayr Bank, disliked by the establishment, which collapsed in 1772 when its London agent failed. A private bank was Messrs. Coutts, which started out in Edinburgh, dealing in grain, wine, lead, salmon, and ultimately bills of exchange before opening a branch in London that became the head office and the quintessence of West End respectability (Forbes, 1803 [1969], pp. 154–65). A provincial bank established in 1810 had 673 "partners", smaller ones sprang up in the 1820s and 1830s. Before 1810, most joint stock companies had fewer than thirty partners but more than the six to which English banks were restricted (Checkland, 1975, pp. 170–75). Thereafter they grew by absorbing smaller banks and branching. Scottish banks retained existing note-issue privileges under the British Bank Act of 1845 that followed the Bank Act of 1844 but were not allowed to issue more bank notes except on a one-for-one basis, note against gold.

A number of other innovations ascribed to Scottish banks have been held up, or downplayed, as a model for banking, for example in the French inquiry of 1867 (Ministère des Finances et al., 1867, Vol. 1, p. 460; Vol. 2, pp. 386–98; Vol. 6, p. 124): branches, bank notes as small as £1, and, before 1767, even 10*s,* 1*s,* or 6*d,* cash credit/overdraft facilities, perhaps mergers. One could work up debates on each of these issues, and perhaps the differences between Scottish and English banks were not as great as they had appeared in the 1820s to such an Englishman as Thomas Joplin, Newcastle timber merchant with strong views on the desirability of joint stock banking, which may have derived from the spotty record of the banks of his city. Chevalier in France was interested in the Scotland/France, not the Scotland/England comparison, and the fact that his country had but one-twelfth the number of banks per inhabitant of Scotland (ibid., Vol. 6, pp. 124–25).

Scottish banking continues to be debated. In today's discussion of bank regulation in Europe and the United States, the Scottish experience from the failure of the Ayr bank in 1772 to the Bank Act of 1845 plays something of a role since banking in Scotland proceeded without a central bank, regulation, or bank failure. Proponents of so-called free banking who advocate complete absence of supervision, cite this experience as proof that, if left to themselves, markets function efficiently (see esp. L. H. White, 1984, and inter alios, Selgin, 1988). The case that regulation can be dispensed with is that any bank that makes excessive loans, issuing notes or adding to deposits, will find itself losing reserves in interbank clearing. In Scotland, and in the case of the the First Bank of the United States after the War of 1812, some bank or banks collected the notes of the bank pushing its circulation, and presented them for conversion into coin. In so doing, it or they acted to a certain extent as a central bank. In addition, Scottish banks maintained secondary reserves in London and could discount their paper there when clearings became adverse; when this occurred, the Bank of England acted in part and indirectly as a central bank for Scotland. The literature on free banking is enormous, and the several positions adopted by economists today, as in the nineteenth century, are subtly differentiated one from another. Milton Friedman, for example, is opposed to central banks but wants strict control of the money supply. On the other hand, writing on the evolution of central banks, in theory and with concise case histories, Charles

Goodhart insists that central banking represents an evolutionary response to real needs. While the value of investments traded in open markets can be tracked in a mutual fund, loans and advances of banks lack similar objective means of judging their quality. In addition, the great mass of depositors is unable to tell when a bank raises the interest it pays on deposits, whether this is because of its greater efficiency or because of the need to attract deposits because of bad loans (1989).

As it happened, the failure of 73 of 770 banks in England in 1825 was not a very different ratio from 3 of 36 in Scotland (as of 1830), but the large absolute number made a lasting impression, as did the intensity of the panic. The country came within forty-eight hours of "putting stop to all dealings between man and man except by barter," if one is to believe William Huskisson (quoted in Joplin, 1832, p. 35), and the panic was remembered for fifty years (Bagehot, 1873 [1978], Vol. 9, p. 138).

BANK OF ENGLAND BRANCHES

On recovery from the panic, Parliament adopted joint stock banking. Under the Act of 1826, the Bank of England was designated the sole joint stock bank with privilege of note issue within sixty-five miles of London. Outside that limit, it was now possible to have more than six partners in a bank, though, unlike Scotland, no limited liability until 1858. The Bank of England was further enjoined at the behest of Lord Liverpool to establish branches beyond the sixty-five-mile limit in order to manage provincial credit by gradually taking over the note issue from, and serving as a lender of last resort to, the country banks (Moss, 1981, p. 540). The first was opened in Gloucester with instructions to discount nothing that had the appearance of accommodation paper (finance bills). Eight more were in being by the end of 1827, and by 1830 eleven branches discounted £3.5 million for 1,000 clients— more than the head office in Threadneedle Street (Clapham, 1945, Vol. 2, pp. 111–15). The network of remittances throughout the country by bills of exchange, on the one hand, and the branch banks slowly gathering speed in formation, on the other, was supported by a pattern of central banking that undergirded the whole structure and not merely its apex in London.

JOINT STOCK BANKING

The Act of 1826 led to considerable activity in forming joint stock banks outside London. The first opened that same year in Lancaster. By 1833 there were nearly 50, and by 1841–42, while private banks were shrinking from 554 in 1825 to 331 (largely through conversion or merger), joint stock banks in the provinces numbered 118 (Crick and Wadsworth, 1936, pp. 17–21). Several of these quickly took up local branching, often putting the word *county* or *district* in their names. Among the few started as early as 1836 was the Birmingham & Midland, which survives today among the three major British banks as the Midland Bank.

A cousin of Thomas Joplin, George Fife Angus, started the National Provincial Bank, based on the ingenious idea of forming a network of bank branches, de novo, with a board of directors in London but no banking office there, and hence full rights to issue bank notes at its provincial branches. The scheme was concocted in 1828, authorized in 1833, and got underway in 1834 with the establishment of the first branch, again at Gloucester. By the second annual meeting, it had twelve branches. Existing banks were taken over, and some new branches were created; the geographical spread was extensive, including Gloucester, Stockton, Darlington, Kingsbridge, Manchester, Ramsgate, Newcastle, and Emlyn. By 1866 when it renounced the note-issue privilege amounting to £450,000 (Emden, 1938, p. 65) in order to be able to undertake banking in London, it had 122 offices and 2,000 share-holders (Withers, 1933, pp. 38–39).

In the early 1830s the time for renewal of the Bank of England's charter approached once more, and this was done in the Act of 1833, which extended it for twenty-one years, with the right to raise the question of further extension after ten, and further relieved the bank of the 5 percent limit on its discount rate under the usury laws. The wording of the act, however, led Joplin to contend that while no joint stock bank with note-issuing privileges could be formed in London, a bank willing to operate without the privilege could do so on a joint stock basis. The Court of the Bank of England (its board of directors) objected that this was not the meaning of the new charter and that its monopoly extended to joint stock banking altogether and not merely the right of note issue, but it was overridden by a declaration inserted in the new charter (Clapham, 1945, Vol. 2, p. 128). In 1833 the London & Westminster Bank was organized, as its name implies, both in the City and in Pall Mall in the West End. It signaled the beginning of the decline of the bank note as contrasted with the bank deposit. The point remained obscure to contemporary opinion, and the Bank Act of 1844, a decade later, intended to regulate the supply of money, dealt with bank notes alone and not with bank deposits. Then, in Dickens's time, as noted in the epigraph to Chapter 2, and even now, people were, and are, unclear about what constitutes money. Colonel Robert Torrens wrote to Lord Overstone in January 1857: "I have ventured on what may be regarded as heresy; inasmuch as I have placed in the category of Money, Deposits not actually represented by bullion." Lord Overstone replied with the assurance that characterizes many monetarists:

If you publish this you let loose upon us the Floodgates of Confusion. It will be the Deluge of Monetary science. Tooke will be in third Heaven. . . . You give an abstract Definition of the Term Money, which shall include Deposits. But in so doing you attribute to the Term Money a meaning to which all doctrines hitherto applied to Money are inapplicable . . . Precious Metals alone are money. Paper notes are money because they are representations of Metallic Money. Unless so, they are false and spurious pretenders. One depositor can get metal, but all cannot, therefore deposits are not money.

Torrens was properly chastened: "I have no confidence unless you approve. I throw deposits to the dogs" (Overstone, 1857 [1971], Vol. 2, pp. 707, 713–17).

BUILDING A NETWORK

Whether individual banks started in London or in the provinces, centripetal forces led fairly quickly to the formation of national networks in England and Wales, all ultimately headquartered in London. Scottish and Irish banks stayed within their own systems. The process was Darwinian—failure of banks, often poorly located, that lacked support of a system of branches, and success of those located well or helped by a broad network. Apart from the National Provincial, which started as a system, bank branches grew by accretion. Provincial branches that needed a London correspondent—as all did—sought to internalize the benefits of access to outlets for, or sources of, funds that London afforded by merging with a London bank rather than by paying correspondents for the services. A belated entry, the Bank of Liverpool, had five correspondents in London in 1918; its head, Sir James Hope Simpson, was convinced of the advantages of a bank's securing a seat on the London Clearing House; it was obviously an economy to centralize the work of its five correspondents. It therefore merged with Martins Bank, calling itself for some years the Bank of Liverpool & Martins Ltd., with a head office in Liverpool, shortening the name to Martins Bank after a few years and, after the death of Simpson, ultimately transferring the head office to London (G. Chandler, 1964 [1968], Vol. 1, pp. 420–22).

The Bank of Liverpool was slow. Lloyds Bank and the Midland Bank had been through the identical process before. Members of the Lloyd family centered in Birmingham joined private banks in London as partners as early as 1763, and while the last Lloyd partner in the best known of these—Hanbury, Taylor, Lloyd & Bowman, formed in 1770—died in 1807, the firm, which time had metamorphosed by 1864 into Barnett, Hoares, Hanbury & Lloyd, merged with the Birmingham Bank in 1884. The new combination absorbed another important London bank, Bosanquet, Salt, the same year and gradually shifted its center of gravity from Birmingham to London (Sayers, 1957, ch. 1). The Midland followed suit in 1891 when the Birmingham & Midland Bank, with its localized branches, absorbed the Central Bank of London, the ninth of its amalgamations to that point but the first outside its fairly restricted initial area (Crick and Wadsworth, 1936, p. 312). One writer with a weakness for biological and physical metaphor calls the process in separate passages one of "natural selection" of banks, with a gravitational movement of deposits to London, and the money market patterned after the solar system (Powell, 1915 [1966], pp. 301, 370, 372, ch. xv).

The last of the Big Five, later reduced to three, was Barclays, which started in 1896 as an amalgamation of twenty private banks, including eight in which the Gurney (Quaker) family was interested. The three largest were Barclays of London, Gurney & Company of Norwich, and Jonathan Backhouse of Darlington. Barclays itself was a fusion of a number of private banks, some with origins as goldsmiths in the seventeenth century; its full name was Barclay, Bevan, Tritton, Ransom, Bouverie & Company. The bank started with strength in London, the east, southwest, and northwest but not the industrial Midlands, Lancashire, or the northeast (Matthews and Tuke, 1926, chs. 1, 2). One by one these various combinations spread through amalgamation to cover the country. Those strong in the south sought out banks in the north, those east in the west, and vice-versa in all cases. London was critical to provincial banks, and the provinces to those strong in London. "Our country business is out of all proportion to our Metropolitan business," said officials of the Midland Bank in 1898 before absorbing the London Joint Stock Bank,

Map 2 England, Scotland, and Wales

also formed, like it, in 1836 (Crick and Wadsworth, 1936, p. 316). Students of industrial economics may recognize the same tendency in oil companies in the 1950s and 1960s. Companies with an excess of crude petroleum looked to expand in marketing; those with big marketing networks stepped up the intensity of their search for crude. Fear of being cut off from outlets for product or sources of input is a general phenomenon leading to vertical integration (Niehans, 1977).

New joint stock banks were still being formed on balance in the second third of the nineteenth century, and the merger movement achieved pace only in the last decade, as Table 5.1 suggests. In 1865, Walter Bagehot testified before a French inquiry into the principles that govern monetary circulation to the effect that the banking system of England was superior to that of France in transferring savings from households to industry since each village in England had at least two banks, "thanks to which no shilling of savings was lost" (Ministère des Finances et al., 1867, Vol. 1, p. 24). In that year there were 1,582 banking offices in England and Wales, a number that doubled by 1892 and quadrupled by 1913 (Nishimura, 1971, pp. 80–81).

For the individual branch bank, the network internalized profits that would otherwise have been earned by correspondents, reduced the danger of being cut off from outlets with excess funds, or from sources of funds when demands for them were exigent, and gained access to London clearing for provincial banks. The benefits in crisis were ambiguous and depended upon whether the source of trouble was at home or abroad. If trouble came from overgenerous lending at home, as in the continuous difficulties of the banks of Newcastle, it was helped by access to resources available in the rest of the system. Local banks specialized: Bradford in wool, Oldham in cotton, Sheffield in steel, Lincolnshire in agriculture, Newcastle in coal mining, London in international trade and investment. In times of difficulties in the specialty, a local bank was trapped (Crick and Wadsworth, 1936, p. 345). On the other hand, if the trouble developed elsewhere, it was desirable not to be too intimately integrated into the network, since tight links were a means of communicating inward difficulties originating outside. The North and South Wales Bank, which later formed an integral part of the Midland Bank, easily weathered the crises of 1847, 1857, and 1866 because its business was largely in Liverpool and then backwater Wales. It also had excellent management. Later when it was integrated

Table 5.1 Numbers of Banks and Branches in England and Wales, 1855–1913 (by fifteen-year intervals)

Year	Joint Stock Banks		Country Private Banks		London Private Banks		Total		Offices per Bank
	Banks	Offices	Banks	Offices	Banks	Offices	Banks	Offices	
1855	100	631	252	492	57	62	409	1,185	2.9
1870	117	1,063	206	518	42	47	365	1,628	4.5
1885	120	1,814	160	598	39	48	319	2,460	7.7
1900	83	4,212	59	329	22	29	164	4,570	27.9
1913	41	6,476	17	133	12	14	70	6,573	93.9

Source: Abridged from Nishimura (1971, pp. 80–81).

into the national system, the bank found itself strained because of loans in Liverpool and Manchester (ibid., pp. 180–92).

In 1850 banking in England was still divided between London and the country. Such a bank as the Midland still had a deposit rate of 1½ percent on accounts in Birmingham and one in London that varied with bank rate. When the latter rose above 4 percent, depositors in the country were tempted to transfer their accounts to London—even before Lloyds Bank had the firm London base acquired in 1884. With amalgamation, the tendency grew stronger. It was not until long afterward, in the 1920s, however, that a single deposit rate was established for town and country. A 7 percent bank rate in 1920 had forced the bank to extend the town rate far into the country; it finally went all the way (Sayers, 1957, pp. 165, 270–71). The test of integration is the prevalence of one price such as prevails in one (integrated) market. On this showing, complete financial integration was not achieved in Britain until the twentieth century.

BANK OF ENGLAND DISCOUNT POLICY

The banking and the currency schools disagreed in the first half of the nineteenth century on both the cause of the gold agio during Suspension from 1797 to 1819, and the proper basis for issuing bank notes in relation to gold reserves of the Bank of England. They were united in believing that the bank should keep its notes convertible into specie, despite diverging on the appropriate rule to achieve that end. And they further agreed that the Bank of England did not behave responsibly in the crises of 1836 and 1839 in raising discount rates belatedly after the boom had broken of its own weight, with the result that the market was subject to the discomfort of both falling prices and tight money. Palmer's rule, set out in a memorandum by G. W. Norman of the Bank Court, with marginal notes by J. Horsley Palmer, the bank governor, held that the bank's reserve should consist of two-thirds securities and one-third coin and bullion but a fixed amount of securities, presumably for the sake of earnings, while letting the reserve move passively (Overstone, 1840 [1971], Vol. 1, pp. 251–74). Criticism of the bank in this period was that it was too interested in its own profits, as contrasted with the public good of stable money market conditions; that Palmer's rule made it respond too slowly to an external drain of reserves, so that when it had to move, it did so too stringently (ibid., p. 269).

The banking school would have been content with the Bank of England's being required to keep a reserve equal to some proportion of its note liabilities, such as one-third, the de facto but not legally imposed ratio practiced by the Bank of France. The currency school wanted to fix the supply of money by limiting the issue of bank notes to a ratio of one to one, above a limited fiduciary issue, to reserves of coin and bullion in the Issue Department. It also sought ultimate monopolization of the issue of bank notes by the Bank of England for the sake of enforcing control of the supply.

In later years Walter Bagehot explained that this system, which concentrated the gold reserves of the country in the central bank rather than in separate commercial banks, was not a "natural" one, but that since it had developed over time, it was, like the British monarchy and however irrational, impossible to alter. In at least eight passages Bagehot makes the point, adding that if one were to start to construct the banking system de novo, one would not have a centralized reserve. Under a natural system, each bank would have its own (1978, Vol. 9, pp. 81, 214, 338, 377, 428, 444, 451, 453); but the system existed and could not be changed for essentially traditional reasons. There is reason to doubt that the theory would argue against centralized reserves. The insurance principle makes it clear that it is desirable to pool reserves, so as to require fewer, provided, of course, that the banks in the system act relatively independently of one another.

The Bank Act of 1844 left discretion in setting discount rates to the merchant bankers making up the Court—officials of joint stock banks were excluded from the group—although the clear implication was that it was desirable to raise the discount rate early when the country was threatened by an external drain. If one waited, the bank's reserves might be exhausted in the period it took to reverse capital flows. The rule propounded in the 1860s by Viscount Goschen, later chancellor of the exchequer, called for increases of a full percentage point but decreases in smaller steps of a half percentage point. In due course, after the troubles of the later 1830s and the lessons of crises in 1847, 1857, and 1866, the bank went in for fine-tuning of the discount rate to the extent that in the tense year 1873, with crisis rampant on the Continent, it changed its rediscount rate twenty-four times (Hawtrey, 1938, p. 92).

No discretion was allowed in the issuance of bank notes, however. The currency school wanted the bank run by rules, not by intuitive decisions of mere men. Sir Robert Peel, the prime minister, first contemplated allowing a relaxing power in the 1844 legislation but ultimately decided against it, to the relief of Charles Wood (later Lord Halifax), chancellor of the exchequer, a member of the currency school, and friend of Lord Overstone, the school's leader (D. P. O'Brien, ed., 1978, Vol. 1, p. 355n). Peel protected himself, however, in a letter from Windsor Castle, written on 4 June 1844.

My Confidence is unshaken, that we have taken all the Precautions which Legislation can prudently take against a Recurrence of a pecuniary Crisis. It may occur in spite of our Precautions; and if it does, and if it be necessary to assume a grave Responsibility, I dare say men will be found willing to assume such a Responsibility. (British Parliamentary Papers, 1847 [1969], Vol. 2, p. xxix)

The difficulty in making the note issue inelastic, as the currency school sought to do and succeeded in doing, is that it became inelastic at all times, when the requirement in an internal financial crisis is that money be freely available. The subject arises again in Chapter 15.

THE LENDER OF LAST RESORT

The Bank of England came to the rescue of the South Sea Company belatedly, and at a punishing price, in order to dispose finally of a dangerous rival. Its recognition of its responsibilities in preventing, or at least mitigating, financial crisis in the public interest took more time. There was a lag in understanding the need to have the money supply inelastic in the long run but elastic in the short. A further question was whose task it was to serve as lender of last resort.

T. S. Ashton has stated that the remedy for panics—an emergency issue of some paper that bankers, merchants, and the general public would accept—was well known long before economists rationalized it into general rules and that the Bank of England was already the lender of last resort in the eighteenth century (T. S. Ashton, 1959, pp. 111, 114). It is true that the bank was pressured to discount bills and notes in crisis, and sometimes less liquid assets, but its response was, on the whole, reluctant and defensive, far from Bagehot's dictum that "a panic is a species of neuralgia, and you must not starve it" (1873 [1978], Vol. 9, p. 73). The bank occasionally took steps that increased the public's fear, slowing down payment of its notes, as in the 6*d* episode of 1745, applying selective limitations on discounts in 1772, refusing to make advances on scrip issued in advance of a government loan in 1782 (Clapham, 1945, Vol. 1, ch. 7, esp. pp. 234, 245, 256, 261). In 1793 it precipitated the rush for liquidity by refusing the paper of Lane, Son & Frazer (Andréadès, 1909, p. 187). In the panic of 1793, moreover, the bank stepped aside and let the public's fears of inability to get liquidity be assuaged by the issue of Exchequer bills, short-term obligations of the Treasury that were available to merchants against security of inventories and that they could discount at banks. Exchequer bills were used again in limited amount in a financial crisis when prices fell sharply in 1799 and were proposed for another, caused by the Continental blockade in 1811. The latter occasion provoked a spirited debate in the House of Commons between those who were sympathetic to the distress of the merchants with excess stocks, cut off from normal markets, and those concerned with overissue of money (Smart, 1911 [1964], Vol. 1, pp. 267–71). In the end a £5 million pound issue was reluctantly voted, but no more than £2 million was actually drawn upon.

Critical debate over who should act as lender of last resort, between government issuing Exchequer bills or the Bank of England, took place behind closed doors in December 1825. The bank was eager to have the government take the lead, but Lord Liverpool, having warned the market in the spring of 1825 that the speculators were going too far and that the government would not save them, felt committed not to come to the rescue. He threatened to resign if Exchequer bills were provided (Brock, 1941, pp. 209–10, cited by Clapham, 1945, Vol. 2, p. 108). The emergency required action by someone, however, as recognized even by Lord Liverpool, who applied enormous pressure on the bank to force it to issue special advances to merchants against inventories, along with its specie swap with the Bank of France and regular discounts.

The lender-of-last-resort function reached full flower under the Bank Act of 1844. "Overtrading," which Adam Smith held to be the cause of financial crises—which were in his lexicon "revulsion" and "discredit"—produced incidents in 1847, 1857, and 1866. As the bank's gold reserves declined and approached the limit to its capacity to provide bank notes against discounted paper, the rush for liquidity intensified. Rather than suspend convertibility, as in 1797, men of responsibility, foreseen by Sir Robert Peel, figured out a way to suspend the Bank Act. The law was not changed; rather, the chancellor of the exchequer issued a letter to the

Bank of England promising to indemnify it for any loss it might suffer from having violated the provisions of the act. This made the bank's reserves available to the market and quieted its fears. In 1847 and 1866 suspension was sufficient to reduce the demand for cash, and the legal limit of the note issue was not exceeded. The limit was exceeded in 1857 but only by a small amount.

In his rationalization of the way the London money market worked, *Lombard Street,* Bagehot called on the Bank of England to lend freely in a panic although at a high discount rate in order to impose a penalty on borrowers and discourage those whose liquidity was manageable. Various quarters suggested that the act itself be amended to allow its automatic suspension in time of difficulty, with rules, for example, that the discount rate must be 10 percent before suspension could be resorted to (E. Wood, 1939, p. 147, and ch. 15, sec. 2). A former governor of the Bank of England, Hankey, called the notion of a lender of last resort "the most mischievous doctrine ever breathed in the monetary or banking world" (Bagehot, 1873 [1978], Vol. 9, p. 133). Neither view understood the nature of the dilemma and the resultant need for ambiguity. Knowledge that a bank or firm will be saved from its folly does, in fact, increase its temptation to relax high standards and indulge in folly. On this score, one must swear not to rescue it. On the other hand, once the folly has been perpetrated, it is in the nature of bankruptcy and failure to spread, like fire, avalanche, runaway horses, and panic in a crowd. At such times it is incumbent on responsible authorities to take steps to arrest collapse.

By 1890 the Bank of England was beginning to act like Lord Liverpool in 1825. When Baring Brothers had to suspend payments because of frozen investments in Argentine land bonds, the chancellor, Lord Goschen, offered the Bank of England a letter of indemnity. It was refused. Instead the governor, Lord Lidderdale, arranged for leading banks in London, including the Bank of England, to guarantee the liabilities of Barings. A fund of £7.5 million was raised during the morning of 15 November 1890, £10 million by 4 P.M., and ultimately £17 million. Some banks that were in trouble joined the guarantee fund to symbolize strength (Chandler, 1964 [1968], Vol. 1, p. 330); others, like Lloyds, which was still a country bank with its head office in Birmingham, insisted on being included to demonstrate their rising strength and importance (Sayers, 1957, pp. 213–15).

LOANS TO INDUSTRY

Tradition has it that British banks discounted commercial acceptances freely but abstained from making loans to industry. Like most other generalizations, the statement is simplification of complex truth. In the early years of the industrial revolution, industrial long-term capital needs were very small in relation to total investment and were provided largely by the entrepreneur, a small local circle of family, friends, and neighbors; and if the enterprise proved successful, reinvested profits. Need was small since buildings could be rented, inputs bought with credit, outputs sold for cash or drafts, which were then discounted, and machinery was simple (Crouzet, ed., 1972; Mathias, 1979, ch. 5). A bank like Smith's restricted loans and overdrafts (advances) to 39 percent of total assets at the peak and normally held them nearer to 20 percent. A liquidity ratio of cash and discounts to liabilities, which might run perhaps 35 percent for a clearing bank in this century, would be more nearly 60 or 70 percent for Smith's in the nineteenth (Leighton-Boyce, 1958, pp. 59–60, 164). The London & Westminster Bank made no advances for factories, mines, or ships though some for railways (Gregory, 1936, Vol. 1, p. 267). Opinion was held worldwide that British banks engaged in short-term financing only.

The truth was rather more varied. Industrialists were especially dependent on banks in the north in the nineteenth century and paid for that association with a high rate of failure (Jeffrys, 1938 [1977], pp. 15–18). Cotton banks in Lancashire, restricted to a local area and under heavy pressure from industry, tended to become overlent, especially in periods of seasonal tightness, undertaking advances that might be short term in form but long term in reality (Crick and Wadsworth, 1936, p. 165). Banks claimed to lend only for working capital and not for fixed assets, but continuous renewals of overdrafts amounted practically to providing long-term loans. Banks maintained close relations with business in the same provincial locality in the nineteenth century, with the Midland Bank deeply involved in cotton textiles, Lloyds in coal, and the National Provincial in iron and steel (Ross, 1990, pp. 52–55). Neither the stock exchange nor the London and provincial banks that financed stock exchange speculators supported investment in new industries from 1870 to 1913 (Kennedy, 1990). Country banks speculated in foreign bonds even in the 1820s and 1830s (Sayers, 1957, p. 186), and, at the end of the century, such a bank as Gilletts had as much as one-quarter of its assets, though generally one-sixth, in foreign bonds (Sayers, 1968, p. 49).

General incorporation in 1856 and 1862, discussed in Chapter 11, and the precedent of the Crédit Mobilier in France led to a burst of forming of investment banks, known in England as finance companies. Most of them disappeared in the crisis of 1866 precipitated by the collapse of Overend, Gurney & Company. There were the so-called Crédit Foncier and Mobilier of England, the International Land Company (Emden, 1938, p. 141), an International Financial Society,[2] a General Credit & Finance Company, and a European Bank with branches in London, Birmingham, Dublin, Paris, Marseilles, Amsterdam, and Rotterdam, among many others, but pride of place was assumed by Overend, Gurney itself. This firm had incorporated under the new legislation, the original partners had retired, and the new team extended the firm's activities beyond its earlier discount and bill broker business into grain trading and speculation, iron, shipbuilding, shipowning, railroad finance, and "into every sort of speculative and lock-up business" (Crick and Wadsworth, 1936, pp. 69–70; King, 1936, pp. 232, 247). Much of the business of so-called discount houses at this time consisted of discounting accommodation bills

2. For those who like triple puns, it may be noted that a quartet of amateur musicians at the Bank for International Settlements in 1940 was termed by their leader and the bank's president, J. W. Beyen, "the International Financial Society for the issuance of false notes." Mr. Beyen was later Dutch director to the IMF and was said to have lost the opportunity to become successor to Camille Gutt and Ivar Rooth, the first two managing directors, by saying, "The trouble with the IMF is that Gutt had no roots, and Rooth had no guts."

for railroad contractors against the security of vendors' shares—stock issued by railroad companies under construction to their suppliers in lieu of cash payment (Cottrell, 1972).

Another wave of bank lending to industry, with similarly awkward and close to disastrous results, occurred during and after World War I. But that gets us ahead of our historical account.

SUGGESTED SUPPLEMENTARY READING

Anderson and Cottrell (eds.) (1974), *Money and Banking in England* (documents).
Bagehot (1873 [1978]), *Lombard Street, Collected Works*, Vol. 9.
Carswell (1960), *The South Sea Bubble*.
Checkland (1975), *Scottish Banking*.
Clapham (1945), *The Bank of England*, 2 vols.
Collins (1988), *Money and Banking in the United Kingdom: A History*.
Goodhart (1989), *The Evolution of Central Banks*.
Joslin (1954 [1962]), London private bankers, 1720–1785.
Morgan (1943), *The Theory and Practice of Central Banking, 1797–1913*.
Powell (1915 [1966]), *The Evolution of the Money Market (1385–1915)*.
Pressnell (1956), *Country Banking in the Industrial Revolution*.
Richards (1965), *The Early History of Banking in England*.
White, L. H. (1984), *Free Banking in Britain*.

More generally on the history of banking, see:

Cameron et al. (1967), *Banking in the Early Stages of Industrialization,* with individual
    essays on banking in England, Scotland, France, Belgium and Germany.
Cameron (ed.) (1972), *Banking and Economic Development,* with studies on Austria, Italy
    and Spain.
Cassis, ed. (1992), *Finance and Financiers in European History, 1880–1960*.

In French

Cassis (1984), *Les Banquiers de la City à Londres à l'époque Edouardienne (1890–1914)*.
Van der Wee (ed.) (1991), *La Banque en Occident* (profusely illustrated).

In German

Born, K. (1977), *Geld und Banken im 19. und 20. Jahrhundert,* translated into English (1983)
    as *International Banking in the 19th and 20th Centuries*.

Largely in Italian

(Felloni, G. ed.) (1991), *Banchi pubblici, banchi privati et monti di pietà nell' Europa preindustriale* (2 vols.).

6

French Banking

It has been suggested that we look into industrial affairs. There are certainly some excellent ones, but industrial enterprises, even the best conceived and the most wisely administered, carry risks which we consider incompatible with the indispensable security with which the funds of deposit banks should be employed. The Crédit Lyonnais can find no better example for the employment of its funds than the Bank of France.

(Henri Germain, president of the Crédit Lyonnais, at a stockholders' meeting, quoted in Pose, *La Monnaie et ses institutions,* 1942, Vol. 1, p. 212)

THE SWITCH FROM LYONS TO PARIS

The fair at Lyons made it the financial center of France from the transfer of the fair from Geneva in 1461 to the failure of Samuel Bernard in 1709. An effort to shift to Paris took place at the end of the sixteenth century; Florentine bankers moved there in such numbers that few were said to be left in Lyons in 1575 (Ehrenberg, 1896 [1928], p. 218). There is some doubt on this score, however; a later study shows the number of Florentine merchants declining only from thirty-three in 1571 to twenty-two in 1575, and in the latter year they still constituted the largest body of exiles in the city (Gascon, 1971, pp. 908–15).

The Italians made a brave start in Paris but succumbed to a wave of xenophobia early in the seventeenth century. Italian *financiers* and *officiers,* fiscal agents of the Crown in farming taxes and dispensing expenditure, were replaced by successful French merchants and nobles, and Italian bankers, after the Edict of Nantes, by Protestants. The last group was concentrated in Languedoc, an economically marginal part of France, which repelled its successful merchants and bankers (Chaussinand-Nogaret, 1970, p. 22), perhaps as the rocky farms of Connecticut pushed the more restless and energetic of their youth to New York (Albion, 1939, pp. 241–52). Lyons was a halfway station between Languedoc and northern France, and after the 1685 Revocation of the Edict of Nantes that drove the Huguenots abroad, between France as a whole and the diaspora of Huguenots in Geneva (and Amsterdam, Frankfurt-am-Main, Hamburg, and London).

The failure of Samuel Bernard in 1709 was of the usual sort: he had loaned Louis XIV 15 million livres by 1703, 20 million by 1704, and 30 million by 1708, when he refused further advances, needed to fight the War of the Spanish Succession, was cut off from payments on the outstanding debt, and unable to repay his drafts (*Dictionnaire,* 1954, Vol. 6, p. 74). Inspiration for withholding payments to him, an abjured Calvinist, may have come from the *financiers,* largely Catholic, for whom a project of Bernard for a public bank that would issue notes was anathema, as it would have reduced the profits reaped by them in handling royal finances (Bosher,

1970, p. 16). Bernard recovered to such an extent that he volunteered to pay a fine of 6 million livres in the Visa of 1715 run by the Paris brothers of the *financier* set. The theme of quarrels between financial groups continues throughout French history at least to World War II. However temporary Bernard's 1709 eclipse, moreover, it marked the shift of the French financial center of gravity from Lyons to Paris (Braudel, 1977, p. 101).

JOHN LAW

The financial history of France in the *ancien régime* is dominated by foreigners, or members of such minorities as Protestants. Beyond the Italians were Isaac Panchaud, who founded the Caisse d'Escompte (Discount Bank) in 1776 and was a Swiss, as was Jacques Necker, who tried to reform French finances before and even during the Revolution. The most provocative of these foreigners, however, was the Scotsman John Law, founder of the Banque Générale, and its successor, the Banque Royale, monetary theorist of the Keynesian stripe, promoter of the Mississippi Bubble, reformer of government finances, who, in combination with the *assignats* of the French Revolution, set back the cause of banking and bank notes in France more than a century.

In Scotland John Law had insisted that society needed more money and active banks to combat unemployment. Following Harvey's discovery of the circulation of blood in 1621, he, with many others, argued that credit was the blood of society. In *Money and Trade Considered: With a Proposal for Supplying the Nation with Money* (1705), he asserted: "When blood does not circulate throughout the body, the body languishes; the same when money does not circulate" (Harsin, 1928, p. 146):

As Money encreas'd, the Disadvantages and Inconveniences of Barter were remov'd; the Poor and Idle were employ'd, more of the Land was labour'd, the Product encreas'd, Manufactures and Trade improv'd, the Landed-men lived better, and the People with less dependence on them. (Law, 1705, p. 11)

He was a firm believer in the real-bills doctrine and gave twenty-four examples to show that if the money supply were increased by bank notes issued for productive loans, employment and output would rise proportionately and the value of money would remain stable (Hamilton, 1968, p. 79).

Exiled from Britain for having killed a man in a duel, Law went to Amsterdam, then to France from which he was banished in 1706 for having asserted that paper money was superior to gold and silver. He returned in 1713 after the War of the Spanish Succession. Following the death of Louis XIV in 1715, he bombarded the new government of the regent with proposals for using a bank to tidy up the debt remaining after the Visa. (This last was a secret Chamber of Justice held in 1715, which subtracted excess winnings from profiteers, munitioneers, bankers, and tax farmers, including the 6 million livres volunteered by Samuel Bernard, in accordance with a French practice following the end of a war or a regime.) Law's arguments convinced the regent, and after Demarets had undertaken a brutal appreciation of the livre, which led to serious deflation (Lüthy, 1959, Vol. 1, p. 281), finally persuaded the duc de Noailles and the Council of Finance. "No other 'Keynesian' ever had such a golden opportunity" (Hamilton, 1968, p. 81). Whereas in October 1715 the Conseil Extraordinaire had voted four in favor of Law's bank, eight against, with various other members saying not now but possibly later, by May 1716, the project won (Levasseur, 1854 [1970], pp. 40–41). The Banque Générale opened its doors in June 1716, the first real bank in France according to Hamilton (1969, p. 79), though this, of course, ignores a large number of private banks.

The course of Law's career—from Banque Générale to Banque Royale, Compagnie d'Occident (Louisiana or Mississippi Company), tobacco monopoly, mint, tax farm, and ultimately minister of finance until the Mississippi Bubble burst in April 1720—is too labyrinthine to be set forth in detail here. A few points may be made, however. The Banque Générale, to a considerable extent a deposit bank rather than a lending bank, was a success with a limited note issue, branches in the provinces, which spread means of payment away from Paris and Lyons, and a gentle stimulant to trade and industry. This was in strong contrast to the successor Banque Royale, as the Banque Générale was reorganized in 1718 with no limit to its right to issue notes beyond permission of the regent, later merged with the Compagnie d'Occident, which had acquired the right to trade with Mississippi, and the stock of which became the object of frenzied speculation in the rue Quincampoix. The stock rose to giddy heights, with profits available to anyone, especially insiders, who bought early and sold in time—the same sort of chain letter operation that characterized the South Sea Bubble by which it was infected—but no possibility for all to win. When new speculators ceased to be drawn in and old ones wanted to liquidate their profits and get out, the party was over and collapse was inevitable.

Second, Law tried to reform French finances. The issue is reserved for later discussion. Hamilton believes he succeeded in effecting lasting improvement (ibid., p. 81); others do not (Levasseur, 1854 [1970], p. 152; Lüthy, 1959, Vol. 1, p. 423). Lüthy observes that the Atlantic ports, especially Nantes and Lorient, were expanded as a result of the abortive attempt to settle large numbers of Frenchmen in Louisiana and to trade there but that this was Law's only benefit (ibid.).

Third, a few merchant bankers made solid gains by taking profits out of France in gold or bills of exchange on Geneva or Amsterdam; other insiders who kept their winnings in France were for the most part forced to submit to a second Visa, in 1721–2, when the Paris brothers, *financiers* as contrasted with merchant bankers, and monetarists as opposed to expansionists (Keynesians), led the effort at tidying up. Many chose not to report their winnings in now virtually worthless notes of the Banque Royale, shares of the Compagnie d'Occident or *billets d'état* (state sight debt). Fifteen hundred to 2,000 clerks in fifty-four offices examined the accounts turned in, with 550,000 claimants for 2.2 billion in notes and 125,000 shares with a nominal value of 250 million, worth five times that amount at the market's peak (Marion, 1926, p. 39). The claims were written down to one-twentieth of their stated value.

One economist who did well in the Mississippi Bubble, Richard Cantillon, was, like Law, an outsider—an Irishman, not a Scot—and a monetarist, as opposed to the Keynesian that Law was. Cantillon sold most of his stock in the Compagnie d'Occident in 1719, cleared a profit of 6.5 million livres tournois, and managed to get the bulk of it to Amsterdam and London by the summer of 1720. Cantillon's *Essai sur la nature du commerce en général* (1755) does not mention Law and is not dogmatic in opposition to the *Système,* believing that increases in the money supply can, on occasion, produce short-run increases in output and employment rather than simply and immediately higher prices (Murphy, 1983).

French experience with John Law was such that there was hesitation in even pronouncing the word *bank* for 150 years thereafter—a classic case of collective financial memory. The Bank of France created in 1800 was an exception. Apart from it, however, banking institutions were typically called *caisse, crédit, société,* or *comptoir,* and not *bank,* until the *banques d'affaires* (industrial banks) of the last quarter of the nineteenth century, following the relaxation of the French company law.

CAISSE D'ESCOMPTE

The general view is that there was no public banking in France in the eighteenth century after Law (Juglar, 1860 [1967]; Bosher, 1970, p. 92). This is not entirely accurate. Isaac Panchaud, a Swiss banker, formed the Caisse d'Escompte in 1776 that lasted until the French Revolution and was followed by a successor, created in 1798, that was quickly assimilated into the new Bank of France two years later. The Caisse discounted bills of exchange and issued notes. Panchaud quarreled with some of the directors who wanted to deal only with private banks. He favored lending to the public. Note circulation reached 70 million livres by 1783 and 100 million by 1787 when the Caisse was forcibly reorganized by the government and required to lend 100 million to the king in exchange for a thirty-year extension of its charter. The change led its notes to lose public confidence. Reserves fell away, and convertibility was suspended in 1788, a year before the Revolution that led to the Caisse's liquidation (Harsin, 1933, ch. 2).

The fact that public banking was so limited, however, did not imply that there was no paper money. The system of venal *financiers, officiers,* accountants, tax farmers, receivers-general, and treasurers-general (disbursing agents) is to be discussed later. These bodies and individuals, however, borrowed as well as loaned, and much of their gross borrowing outside the circle of government on notes (*billets*) and "rescriptions" passed from hand to hand in France as a sort of paper money (Bosher, 1970, pp. 14, 94–95). Officers of the Crown who had official duties of collecting, receiving, and paying out royal revenues were not in business as bankers. Nonetheless, they borrowed from the public at, say, 5 percent, loaned especially to the king or state at 7 percent, and on a credit amounting to 15 million livres could earn 300,000 livres a year (ibid., p. 99). There were, moreover, private banks, and quasi-bankers, notaries, merchants, and rich individuals—who undertook to take care of money for those with surpluses and then loaned it out to those in need of borrowing.

ASSIGNATS

The financial crisis of 1788 led Louis XVI to proclaim an issue of new interest-bearing paper money. Because of strenuous general disapproval, the measure was withdrawn. To Mirabeau, paper money was theft. With the Revolution in 1789, however, such disdain became a luxury. In considerable part the Revolution had been about regressive taxation. When it succeeded, the tax receipts of the government fell drastically, and some of the most productive imposts—the *dîme,* taking a tenth of the income of land from non-nobles, and the *gabelle,* a heavy tax on salt—were abandoned altogether in response to public demand. Reform of royal finances, moreover, made it necessary to pay off tax farmers who had advanced funds to the king. Later, when war came in 1795, expenditure rose. Without a central bank it was necessary to find some new source of funds, whether taxes or printing money. New taxes were assigned for collection to the provinces, which lacked enthusiasm for the task. The ratio of taxes to expenditure plummeted from 48 percent in December 1789 to 8 percent in November 1795 (S. E. Harris, 1930, chs 1, 2).

In the circumstances, the idea presented itself of using Church lands confiscated in the Revolution as security for the issue of paper money. Notes would be "assigned" to given land; for a time it was thought that particular *assignats* would represent particular land parcels, and the related *assignats* would be destroyed when the land involved was sold. In 1705 John Law had thought it safe to issue money against land; in 1716 and 1718 he turned to government debt and shares in the Compagnie d'Occident as a substitute. Lüthy suggests that he thought he was getting away from land as security for money, but the Compagnie d'Occident really represented the abundant lands of Louisiana (1959, Vol. 1, p. 189) or perhaps, as the duc de la Rochefoucauld put it, "undiscovered gold mines" (S. E. Harris, 1930, p. 14). A later precedent was Catherine II of Russia's formation of an *assignat* bank in 1768 to finance a war with Turkey (Buist, 1974, p. 93).

Assignment did not last long. Early issues were for 1,000, 500, and 200 livres, but it soon became necessary to provide small denominations. By May 1791 the lower limit had reached 5 livres, but denominations of 50 to 10 sous were needed. For a time this was accomplished by issuing *assignats* to a special Caisse Patriotique (Patriotic Bank), which, in turn, put out small *billets de confiance.* These lost public confidence in December 1791 and had to be followed by issues of small-denomination *assignats,* which lost all touch with given land. In due course, the initial 800 million of *assignats* had reached 7 billion, and the system exploded in 1795. Prior to that time, Harris claims, *assignats* kept fourteen armies in the field, with the help of requisitions and price controls, destroyed class and privilege, destroyed the monarchy, and established the First Republic (1930, p. 53). They also embedded paranoia about paper money and banks more deeply in the French subconscious and helped establish Napoleon successively as consul and emperor.

The inflations of the 1980s have renewed interest in the *assignats* as well as in other inflationary experience of the past, with special attention to the ends of inflationary episodes. One study lays less blame on the issuance of the *assignats* as such than on the general financial turmoil, with French inability to raise taxes, and with the price controls imposed to contain the "inflationary tax" needed to fight the war (Brezis and Crouzet, 1990). In any event the French fought the war without being able to borrow, as the British could, and with hard money rather than paper, to the extent that they used money to pay their troops at all, coin largely collected in indemnities levied on the countries Napoleon conquered (Bordo and White, 1991).

THE BANK OF FRANCE

Napoleonic finances are badly understood. Records were poor, and a systematic attempt to assemble what information does exist has not been undertaken. As a financial thinker, Napoleon was idiosyncratic. He had strong objections to paper money and to government debt, to speculation and to free markets. In 1799, for example, his armies had not been paid for ten months; they lived for several years, in fact, on *assignats* and victories (Thiers, 1894, Vol. 1, p. 6). Victories helped because a defeated country could be made to pay an indemnity. Initially bills were paid with *bons d'arréarage* and *bons de requisition,* which went to large discounts but could be bought to pay taxes. Napoleon then shifted to a system of cash or nothing, leaving no residue of paper to go to a discount (ibid., Vol. 1, p. 357). To help with the cash in 1800 he created the Bank of France, with a capital of 30 million livres, reexpressed three years later as 30 million francs, to discount rescriptions.

In 1802 Napoleon entered into correspondence with his minister of the public treasury, François Nicholas Mollien. Mollien was the son of a Rouen manufacturer, an admirer of the works of Adam Smith whom the French on the whole disdained because he had been critical of Colbert. Mollien had started out as a *commis* (clerk) in the General Farm of Taxes, where he devised new methods of forecasting general revenues and later introduced double-entry bookkeeping into French finances. While he admired British banking and debt management, he was deeply impressed by the 1797 crisis in England that led to Suspension. This probably generated his aversion for bank lending and his strong monetarist ideas (Liesse, 1908, p. 69).

In correspondence with Napoleon, who had asked about banks, Mollien replied that there were two sorts of banks: those of deposit like the Bank of Amsterdam and those of circulation. There was no question of the first in France. Perhaps it was a matter of "topography"—a comment that may refer to the fact that France was large compared with the United Provinces,—and it was therefore difficult to maintain communication between capital and provinces (1845, p. 447). The following year Napoleon established the new unit of account called the "franc germinal" equal to the livre tournois in precious metal, the phrase coming from the peculiar metric calendar system adopted for a time in the Revolution—and extended the bank's monopoly for thirteen years. Its capital was increased from 30 million to 50 million and then to 90 million francs.

Like the Bank of England, the Bank of France was established by outsiders, by merchant bankers who differed from the *financiers* and *officiers* who had served the court but were wiped out by the French Revolution. The bankers were cosmopolitan, interested in all sorts of enterprise, including insurance and especially international trade; the *officiers* had been far more parochial, to some extent interested in industry, but for the most part happy to lend for consumption and government deficits (Bouvier, 1973, p. 78).

The Bank of France acted more like a "Bank of Paris" than one of the entire country. Its extension to the provinces was an issue that occupied it and the experts for the rest of the century. In 1810 Napoleon wrote to Mollien from Antwerp, insisting that the country would emerge from the crisis caused by the Continental blockade in which the French tried to prevent the British from trading with the Continent and the British cut France off from North and South America—if only cheaper credit were available outside Paris. He wanted the Bank of France to extend its system of *comptoirs*—subsidiary offices that had already been established at his insistence in commercial centers at Rouen and Lyons—to manufacturing places such as Amiens, St. Quentin, Lille, Valenciennes, and Cambrai. He objected to the fact that the regents had bought up 15 million francs of the bank's capital, reducing it to 75 million francs, to protect the dividend, and wanted it doubled instead to 180 million or 200 million. The regents waited for demand for credit; Napoleon wanted a vigorous supply to take the lead. In a second letter from Le Havre at the end of May 1810, Napoleon asked a series of questions: What is a deposit at the Bank of France? Who issues the notes? Who makes the profits? Who furnishes the funds? According to Mollien, Napoleon regarded the Bank of France as his creation, and everywhere he traveled in the country he wanted to leave a *comptoir d'escompte* (discount office) as a monument of his visit.

Mollien's answer to these requests was several-fold. As a monetarist, he insisted that bank notes were a substitute for specie and that the most important objective in banking was to maintain convertibility of notes into specie. To have local branches of the bank would create difficulties since for every 1,000-franc note in circulation, one would have to have 1,000 francs in specie in several locations to ensure convertibility on demand (Mollien, 1845, Vol. 1, p. 455). Second, he told Napoleon that when he was pressed by delegations seeking a local branch of the bank to ask them for lists both of individuals who could subscribe the capital of the local office and of merchants prepared to discount several millions of good bills of exchange a year with the branch, so that the new branch could earn its way (ibid., Vol. 3, p. 157). Implicit in his view was that "every tub should stand on its own bottom" and there was no question of central banking as a public good such as is sometimes evoked for branch lines of railroads or feeders for airlines that cannot cover average cost but are needed to keep a community, town, or region going. Finally, he insisted that spreading the Bank of France into the countryside would lead to local paper being discounted in Paris, as smaller communities sought to borrow from the financial center, when discounting should always be undertaken locally as only local bankers knew the values of different paper, and the credit standing of various merchants and industrialists in their community (Liesse, 1908, p. 114; Mollien, 1845, Vol. 3, p. 158).

Napoleon was opposed by Mollien on another issue—the government or the Bank of France acting as a lender of last resort. He asked Mollien to investigate the bankruptcies of communal banking offices, promised loans to manufacturers in trouble because of the Continental blockade, and directed Mollien to make advances of 1.2 million francs in one case, 600,000 francs in a second, and 1.5 million in a third to houses facing bankruptcy in Amsterdam. Whether his rationale was sympathy for the individual case or fear of spreading collapse is not indicated. To all this, Mollien objected strenuously, arguing that the task was too great even for the government of France (1845, Vol. 3, pp. 274–79).

SAINT-SIMONISM

Claude-Henri de Rouvroy, count of Saint-Simon (1760–1825), great-nephew of the duke of Saint-Simon, the great memoirist of Louis XIV's day, was ruined by the Revolution, made and lost a new fortune speculating in *biens nationaux* (national goods or assets, that is, land confiscated by the Revolution from the Church and the king), and devoted himself thereafter to social reform. In 1788 he traveled in Spain and visited a banker of French origin, Francesco Cabarrus, founder of the Bank of St. Charles in Madrid, who wanted to correct Spanish economic decadence through programs of bank expansion and public works, the latter carried out in large part by the army. To these themes of vigorous bank expansion and public works, Saint-Simon added education, the "spirit of association," and work for all citizens. The emphasis on banks, public works, and work for all were thoroughly Keynesian ideas, like those of John Law. Saint-Simon (and Keynes, too, for that matter) was not, in theory, devoted to pure expansionism. Bank credit should work in both directions, as motor and brake, stimulus and regulator, impellor and director, exciter and coordinator (Vergeot, 1918).

Saint-Simonien ideas formed the basis of a school that was taken over by Prosper Enfantin after Saint-Simon's death and converted into a cult that drove away many people previously attracted by the force of the ideas. Among those who remained faithful to the thought were Jacques Laffitte, Michel Chevalier, and Emile and Isaac Pereire.

Laffitte started out as a *commis* in the private bank of Perrégaux; in due course, he took it over and became head of the Bank of France from 1814 to 1819. In 1825, as a private banker again, he tried to start a Bank of Commerce and Industry but was refused permission from the Conseil d'Etat, which acted in such matters on advice of the Bank of France. Finally in 1837 after a change of government (the July monarchy of 1830) and his recovery from bankruptcy, he started a Caisse Générale du Commerce et de l'Industrie as a *société en commandite* to make loans to industry, including those at long term.

Michel Chevalier stayed with the cult long enough to go to jail with Enfantin for publishing articles on sexual freedom for women—Enfantin's ideas—but Chevalier was editor of the *Globe* and wrote the articles in which the ideas appeared. He broke with Enfantin in jail and was released in 1833 to travel to America to study banking, public works, and life in general. Keynesian, in the sense of wanting bank expansion and low interest rates in Europe, he was more of a monetarist in the United States, reacting to the influence of wildcat banking, on the one hand, and Andrew Jackson's veto of the Second Bank of the United States on the other. In 1840 he became professor of economics at the Collège de France, the first and for a long time the only such post, later adviser to Louis-Napoleon during the Second Empire, and the French negotiator of the low-tariff Anglo-French Treaty of Commerce of 1860, the so-called Cobden-Chevalier Treaty. He was a strong supporter of bank expansion, the silver standard, and the Pereire point of view (discussed below), in the 1867 Inquiry into money and banking in France on the examining commission for which he sat.

The Pereire brothers were of Portuguese-Jewish origin from Bordeaux. The older brother, Emile, had worked for Rothschild in the 1840s on the Chemin de Fer du Nord (North Railroad) and had been successful. Thereafter, he split from the Rothschild concern and, with his brother Isaac, took off on his own, helping with the formation of the Paris Comptoir d'Escompte in the 1848 crisis, starting the Crédit Mobilier in 1852, and taking the refunding of government debt away from the Rothschild syndicate in 1854. Enmity between the Rothschilds and the Pereires went deep, because Baron James de Rothschild could not forgive Emile's independence—the Rothschilds were said to bear "implacable hatred toward all former employees turned rivals" (Stern, 1977, p. 41)—or because of the later challenge in banking and debt funding, or because Emile bought an estate adjoining Rothschild property that the latter wanted to acquire (Bouvier, 1967, ch. 8, esp. p. 179).

JACQUES LAFFITTE

Laffitte's name is associated with the Anglo-French Baring loan of 1817 to finance the French post-Napoleonic indemnity and with the abortive government debt conversion of the 1820s. I discuss both issues in Chapter 12. Relevant here is his interest in last-resort lending, in spreading banking through France, and in industrial lending as exemplified in the Caisse Générale.

Laffitte was a lender of last resort in a private capacity: he spent 2 million francs from his own purse to set up the new government after Napoleon's departure, loaned Louis XVIII 5.7 million from the Bank of France in 1815, and had the Bank of France come to the rescue of the bourse in 1818 (Laffitte, 1840 [1932], p. xvi; Lévy-Leboyer, 1964, p. 483n). Michel Chevalier stated that the Bank of France was quick to help out in crises up to 1826 but did not show the same courage in 1831–32 (1834 [1838], Vol. 1, p. 37n).

Branches of the Bank of France had been opened in Lyons, Rouen, and Lille at the insistence of Napoleon but were folded up by the bank after 1815. On becoming governor of the Bank of France, Laffitte withdrew the bank's previous objections to independent local banks with the right of note issue in the provinces, and such were established in Rouen (1817), Nantes (1818), and Bordeaux (1818), all ports to be sure, as contrasted with the manufacturing towns that Napoleon had wanted to help. Laffitte welcomed these banks, previously perceived as both rivals and a danger, because he wanted to transform the Bank of France into a simple commercial bank, free of government control, and without a monopoly of the note issue (Cameron, in Cameron et al., 1967, p. 103). During his term as governor, however, he failed to persuade the regents to give up a monopoly of the note issue in Paris.

CAISSE GÉNÉRALE DU COMMERCE ET DE L'INDUSTRIE

Laffitte has been called the first investment banker (Redlich, 1948). This may be so conceptually, because of his rejected application of 1825, but the first actual investment bank was the Société Générale de Belgique, formed in Brussels in 1822, and spearheading a speculative boom in the formation of Belgian industrial joint stock banks that later died away after a crisis in 1838 led the Banque de Belgique to close its doors (Morrison, 1967; Lévy-Leboyer, 1964, ch. 9). It was later reorganized (Cameron, in Cameron et al., 1967, p. 134). This was the year in which Laffitte, at the age of 70, founded his Caisse Générale du Commerce et de l'Industrie with a nominal capital of 35 million, 15 million paid up. The bank was allowed to issue only interest-bearing obligations, not bank notes, of five, fifteen, and thirty days yielding 3, 3½, and 4 percent interest, respectively (Liesse, 1908, p. 293), a device that preserved the Bank of France's monopoly of the note issue. Even in the 1820s as private banker, Laffitte was involved in investing in insurance, canals, Paris real estate, stonecutting and glass, newspapers, a cotton-spinning mill, and although there is some debate about it, coal mines and iron works (Cameron, in Cameron et al., 1967, p. 114; Gille, 1959, pp. 193–94; Lévy-Leboyer, 1964, p. 505n). Rothschild was a member of the group that supported the proposed bank in 1825. By 1837 he had changed his mind, saying, "Laffitte acquired his popularity by the extreme facility by which he advanced money to industry. Other bankers say that his greatest fault is to interest himself in all these enterprises . . . instead of limiting himself to being a simple lender and getting good guarantees" (Gille, 1965, Vol. 1, p. 193). The Caisse failed in 1848 shortly after Lafitte's death. It had been saved once by the Bank of France, as perhaps befits a former governor. Its founding was followed by a crop of other *caisses.* All failed in 1847 (Liesse, 1909, p. 75).

REGIONAL BANKS OF ISSUE

After Laffitte's term as governor, the Bank of France became hostile both to independent regional banks of issue and to having its own *comptoirs* or branches. No progress was made in spreading banking to the countryside until the July monarchy of 1830, which began with Laffitte as prime minister for a short period. Six new regional banks were formed: Marseilles and Lyons (1835), Lille (1836), Le Havre (1837), and Toulouse and Orléans (1838) (Pose, 1942, Vol. 1, p. 149). Further banks were planned for Chartres, Foix, Nîmes, Avignon, Bourges, Nevers, Limoges, and Angoulême, but these were successfully killed by the Bank of France, which also vetoed a second bank at Rouen (Cameron, in Cameron et al., 1967, p. 125). The Bank of France also strove to prevent regional banks from redeeming their notes in Paris and issuing bank notes in denominations smaller than 250 francs. In 1846 the mercantile community put pressure on the government to force the bank to issue notes of 100 francs, but this was turned down by the bank in favor of notes of 200 francs, an uninteresting number given the existence of 250-franc notes (Gille, 1970, p. 56). There was pressure for the bank to issue notes of 50 and

25 francs in the 1847 crisis, but, bearing in mind that the memory of the *assignats* was only 50 years old, the government lowered the limit only to the 100-franc denomination. In the 1867 Inquiry, Thiers said that bank notes constituted roughly 20 percent of the total circulation and largely took the form of 1,000-franc notes. The 50-franc note, which had been authorized by that time, amounted to only 30 million out of 1 billion francs in bank notes and hardly penetrated the countryside. Paper was reserved for large payments. Metal, Thiers said, was better than paper for the use of a great country (Ministère des Finances et al., 1867, Vol. 3, p. 419). The loss of silver to the East under the bimetallic system was creating a vacuum, however, that could be filled most readily by bank notes.

Regional banks had problems beyond the antipathy of the Bank of France, particularly the ebb and flow of funds to and from Paris. There was a marked seasonal movement, with funds flowing to the countryside with the harvest and back to Paris in the winter and spring. A center such as Lyons had a particular problem of financing the seasonal purchase of silk cocoons from Italy. On top of these movements were less regular and predictable flows, such as those associated with financial tension. Le Havre merchants preferred a regional bank to a *comptoir* of the Bank of France because they felt that the latter in a crisis would order the provinces to restrict credit in ways that took no account of the local situation (Gille, 1970, p. 24). On the contrary, the Bank of France had the regional situation very much in mind in the crisis of 1846–48. It allowed all regional banks to fail, refusing to come to

Map 3 France

their rescue as a lender of last resort, and replaced them with newly created *comptoirs d'escompte,* without the right of note issue, in order to add a third signature to commercial acceptances to make them eligible for discount at the Bank of France. The requirement that discountable paper should have three names was debated throughout the nineteenth century, including the debate of 1840 when the bank's charter was renewed to run from 1843 to 1867 (Bigo, 1947, p. 103). The reason behind the requirement was later explained by Thiers. Two-name paper may often be accommodation paper. If a third man, firm, or bank adds its signature, it is because it knows the validity of the underlying transaction (Ministère des Finances et al., 1867, Vol. 3, p. 396). Sixty *comptoirs* in all were formed. After the crisis, many were converted into banks, such as the Caisse d'Escompte in Paris, which became a great national bank (Bouvier, 1973, p. 84), and the Crédit du Nord in Lille (Pose, 1942, Vol. 2, p. 493).

The question of regional banks with note-issue privileges persisted and was still intently discussed in the 1867 Inquiry. In his testimony, Emile Pereire held fast to his 1834 views on the reform of the Bank of France when he had demanded:

1. Two signatures on discountable paper in place of three.
2. The issue of 100-franc notes instead of the 250-franc minimum.
3. New *comptoirs d'escompte* in a long list of towns.

He wanted no place in France to be without a bank within 20 or 30 leagues (80 to 120 kilometers), with the Bank of France to triple its note circulation, popularize its credit throughout France, and bring redundant capital from Paris to the provinces. He also wanted to destroy the note-issue monopoly of the Bank of France, starting by retaining and expanding the note-issue privilege of the Bank of Savoy, which he and his brother Isaac had bought. The Bank of Savoy had had the right of note issue when Savoy was part of Italy. After the province's transfer to France as part of the price for Napoleon's help with Italian unification in 1860, the Bank of France was anxious to repress the privilege so as not to lose its monopoly through the back door.

Still another issue on which the Keynesians, Chevalier and the Pereires, differed from the monetarist Bank of France, the House of Rothschild, and such academic theorists as Wolowski and Cernuschi was on the expansion of the branches of the bank itself. The expansionists had won a victory in inserting in the bank charter renewal of 1857 a requirement that the bank should proceed to establish branches in each of the ninety *départements* of France. It moved slowly. At the time of the Inquiry ten years later, there were only fifty-four in existence. Chevalier urged that there be 200, or 300, or as many as 1,000 (Ministère des Finances et al., 1867, Vol. 6, pp. 125–26, 165–68). It was not until the charter renewal of 1894 and the expansionist governor, Georges Pallain, took office in 1897 that a policy of more extensive branching was undertaken (Dauphin-Meunier, 1936, p. 129). Dauphin-Meunier calls Pallain, who also abandoned the three-signature requirement, the most eminent governor of the Bank of France in the nineteenth century after Laffitte. This view was not universally shared.

THE BANK OF FRANCE AT MID-CENTURY

The Bank of France took the occasion of the crisis of 1847 to suppress the competition of the regional banks, a campaign said to have begun in 1840 when a law was passed at its instigation calling a halt to the formation of more regional banks of note issue (ibid., p. 70). How the bank behaved in the political crisis is open to some dispute. In one strongly pro-bank view it became the sole bank of issue more as a result of unforeseen circumstances than of any consistent policy or design. The regents responded to the situation posed by the revolutionary government and showed "decision and daring" (Liesse, 1909, p. 64). In the bourse panic of March 1848, it discounted bills of exchange, but let the 5 percent *rente* fall from 116 on 23 February to 89 on 7 March, the 3 percent from 73 to 47, "not because of animosity to the new government but because it thought its first duty was to industry and commerce" (Ramon, 1929, pp. 218–19). "It passed the test of fire and never again was concerned for its notes" (Liesse, 1909, pp. 84–85).

According to this same partisan, in the next phase of the crisis the bank's rescue operations were skillful: lending 50 million to the state without interest, 30 million to the Caisse des Dépôts et Consignations (Fund for Deposits and Consignments), making loans to Paris, to Lyons, and to the Department of the Seine, plus 34 million to a metal works to execute railroad company orders. Convertibility was suspended in February 1848 and resumed at the end of the year de facto, de jure in August 1850. The bank was helped with a loan of £1 million in 1847 from the London market and by an offer from Russia to buy 50 million of *rentes* the same year that enabled France to continue the import of grain from that country during the acute shortage without the necessity to ship specie (Juglar, 1860 [1967], p. 417). This was in marked contrast with Britain, which decided to leave the provisioning of Ireland in the potato famine of 1846 entirely to the market (Woodham-Smith, 1962).

A minority opinion to the contrary exists. In the view of Dauphin-Meunier, a partner in the Banque de Paris et des Pays-Bas but antiestablishment, the Bank of France originally assisted the revolutionary government in return for its help in closing the regional banks under a decree of April 1848 and then refused to renew the loan in June of the same year, thus forcing the closure on 21 June of the *ateliers nationaux* (national workshops) that employed the poor of Paris. Only when the government had given way to a "dictatorial" one did the Bank of France provide the loan it had refused the Republic. A final portion of the indictment states that the bank secretly advanced monies through Fould to finance Louis-Napoleon's coup d'état (Dauphin-Meunier, 1936, pp. 72–75).

The claim that the Bank of France was never concerned for its notes after 1848 is wrong. It came within an ace of inconvertibility on at least two occasions in the next two decades. But the statement suggests that mid-century was a turning point in the use of bank notes. According to one estimate, payments in France before 1850 were effected 3 percent in gold, 90 percent in silver, and 7 percent in bank notes. The California and Australian discoveries, plus the sale of silver to the East, changed the proportions of specie, but the use of bank notes expanded as well. In 1856 payments were effected 50 percent in gold, 30 percent in silver, and 20 percent in bank notes (Bigo, 1947, p. 41). A decade later, testifying before the Inquiry in 1865, James Rothschild said that it had been impossible to travel in France with bank notes twenty years earlier (Ministère des Finances et al., 1867, Vol. 1, p. 461). The Inquiry went on to ask bankers and economists what they thought of paper money and drew some dubious and ambiguous responses. A banker, J. Bischoffsheim, when asked about the utility of bank notes, could not make up his mind: they were not without utility, but they produced some sad results. They enabled the Bank of France to earn 9 million to 12 million francs a year—the private good of the stockholders—but he wonders whether they were worth it. He would not dream of repressing the Bank of France's note-issue privilege, and he observed that money that rang on the counter (*écus sonnants*) was unfashionable in such countries as Holland, etc. (ibid., Vol. 2, pp. 110–11). Emile Pereire made the point that bank notes did not circulate in small towns and ascribed the financial crisis of 1864, usually attributed to the fall in cotton prices when the end of the Civil War was clearly in sight, to a drain of specie from Paris to the countryside to pay for goods suddenly made available to the cities by the railroad, a drain required because small towns would not accept notes (ibid., Vol. 1, pp. 622–23).

The gradual spread of bank notes in France in the 1850s and 1860s was contemporaneous with the shift in Britain from bank notes to bank deposits and checks. Accessibility to banking was still limited in France, far behind the Pereire requirement of 1834 that no town should be more than thirty leagues from a bank. In 1863 three-quarters of French territory lacked access to banking, although the standard of "access" may have been considerably less than 30 leagues (Bigo, 1947, p. 42). Bankable places—again not defined—were beginning to multiply. They rose from 115 in 1881 to 205 in 1885, 479 in 1908, and 583 in 1913 (ibid., p. 116).

A detailed social and financial history of the Bank of France from 1851 to 1870 in three volumes covers, first, the stockholders, largely members of the 200 noble families descended from the *officiers* and *financiers* of pre-Revolutionary France; second, the regents and governors who ran the bank, drawn from merchant but not deposit banking,—men like James de Rothschild, Hottinguer, Mallet, and Pillet-Will,—many of Swiss origin, and industrialists in iron and steel, like Schneider of Creusot and de Wendel from Lorraine; and third, the policy of the bank (Plessis, 1982, 1985*a,* 1985*b*). Plessis maintains that the bank was transformed in these years but never really rid itself of its obsession with John Law and the *assignats,* concerned more with order and stability than with dividends or expansion (ibid., 1985*a,* pp. 281, 390). In the early 1850s it was pushed by Louis-Napoleon and experimented with varying the discount rate, reducing it after it had been steady at 4 percent for twenty-seven years (ibid., 1985*b,* pp. 89ff.) but returning to fixity in 1865 (ibid., pp. 215–38).

THE PEREIRES AND THE CRÉDIT MOBILIER

The failure of the Laffitte Caisse and its imitators did not discourage the Pereire brothers. In exile, Louis-Napoleon had dabbled in Saint-Simonien doctrine, and when he became successively president of the Second Republic and, after the coup, emperor of the Second Empire, the Pereire brothers advanced their old idea of the need for more banks, more bank lending, and especially more bank lending to industry. In December 1852, a year after the coup d'état, the Crédit Mobilier opened its doors with a capital of 60 million francs—a large sum for the day—and the right to issue interest-bearing obligations to the public. While it was not without precedent, as we have seen, modern economic historians—Bert Hoselitz (1956), Alexander Gerschenkron (1962) and Rondo Cameron (1961)—have hailed it as a major innovation and discontinuity in the finance of not only France but of Europe as a whole. Gerschenkron built around it his theory of economic backwardness—that the slower its start in industrialization, the more a country depends on first banks and then, in the most backward countries, on government to substitute for the private entrepreneurs who produced the industrial revolution in England. Cameron has emphasized the point that the Crédit Mobilier not only greatly stimulated economic growth in France but that it also served as a prototype for industrial banks in Germany, Austria, Italy, Spain, and Sweden, thus contributing to the economic development of continental Europe, including Russia, as a whole.

Within "industry" a distinction should be made between manufacturing and public works so far as the Crédit Mobilier and its immediate imitators and foreign subsidiaries were concerned. The Crédit Mobilier played no great role in manufacturing investment, despite the claims of Gerschenkron and Cameron, as industry continued its normal financing with private banks for working capital and autofinancing (reinvested profits) for fixed. For the most part the Crédit Mobilier put its money into public works, although what brought the Pereire brothers to grief after Louis Napoleon had turned away from them to favor their arch-rival the Rothschilds was a large investment in mortgages. Initial investments were made in railroads, banks, and then ports, waterworks, and gas works but not notably in manufacturing. Strongly antipathetic to the Pereires, the Rothschilds were ready to imitate them, especially in foreign investment, by creating banks, constructing railroads, and supporting utilities in rivalry with the Pereires, especially in Austria, Italy, and Spain.

THE BANK OF FRANCE AS STIMULATOR OF FRENCH GROWTH IN THE 1850s

In official pronouncements, the Bank of France held strictly to the requirement that it loaned only on three-name paper. Like the Bank of England, however, it made frequent exceptions in practice. In the crisis of 1830 it admitted short-term paper to its discount facilities and guaranteed some canal bonds, though it rejected others (Gille, 1959, p. 88). Its debated rescue of the government in 1848 has been mentioned. In the 1850s it became much more active. In 1852 it acquired the right to lend on both railroad securities and the obligations of the City of Paris, which was being rebuilt by Baron Haussmann (Ramon, 1929, p. 255). Its activity may have been in imitation of the Crédit Mobilier (Plessis, 1985*b*, p. 87). The expansive force of the Crédit Mobilier and the Bank of France together, however, pushed so hard that the regents of the bank came almost to the point in 1856 of resigning themselves to abandoning convertibility of the franc, as they had done in 1848 (ibid., pp. 176–78). The finance minister, Magne, later the chairman of the Conseil Supérieur that conducted the 1867 Inquiry, stated that inconvertibility was avoided only by the categorical statement of the government that it wanted to escape it at any price (Ministère des Finances et al., 1867, Vol. 6, p. 113). The bank strove to maintain convertibility by buying 250 million francs of gold at 1½ percent premium in 1856 and 560 million at 1⅓ percent premium in 1857. In addition, it obtained a charter renewal in 1857, ten years in advance of expiry of the old charter and, having freed itself from the application of old usury laws, undertook to manipulate its discount rate, which had hitherto been held at 4 percent since the bank's founding (Liesse, 1909, pp. 86–8a).

The bank had another brush with *cours forcé* (forced circulation or inconvertibility of its bank notes) in 1864, and again, as in 1856, the government resisted strongly the bank's attempt to lay down its burden. Finance Minister Magne explained it three years later in terms of the public good dominating over the private good:

The Bank of France has an enormous monopoly. It is not like this or that branch of commerce. It is almost absolute in the affairs of the country. To be sure it is interested in the affairs of its stockholders, but the Government cannot yield to the arbitrary will of a financial society. . . . It was entirely legitimate for the government to intervene and say "It's you who are wrong; you have inspired fear in others." If the Government had shared the opinion of the bank, what ruin for the business of the country, what a bad example, and I say even, what dishonor. (Ministère des Finances et al., 1867, Vol. 6, pp. 155–57).

CRÉDIT FONCIER AND CRÉDIT AGRICOLE

The 1850s produced another change in French banking with the establishment by government of specialized agencies for lending for building and to agriculture to fill gaps in the credit structure. These outlets had been served to some extent by private banks, and especially by the informal capital market operated at the local level by notaries who, like the scriveners of Britain, served as intermediaries between borrowers and lenders. The Crédit Foncier in the mortgage field was started in 1852 with a capital of 60 million francs. In 1858 it was instructed to lend 100 million for draining swamps as part of Napoleon III's Saint-Simonien program of public works. It managed, however, to allocate only 1.7 million for this purpose. In 1860 its authority was extended to Algeria, it was instructed to lend within France to departments, communes, and agricultural associations, and it formed the Société de Crédit Agricole (Josseau, 1860 [1884], pp. xlix, lx).

Both the Crédit Foncier and Crédit Agricole came in for criticism but for rather different reasons. The former was attacked for concentrating its lending in Paris instead of the provinces, the latter for diverting its attention and funds altogether from French agriculture to speculation in Egyptian bonds. These securities enjoyed a flurry of speculative interest during the cotton famine that resulted from the American Civil War. The deputy governor of the Crédit Agricole was even accused of dumping depreciated securities of his own on the public institution (Robert-Coutelle, n.d., but after 1876). Moreover, the Crédit Agricole had a poor way of providing credit, when it did, to its intended clientele. Rather than raise money centrally in a wholesale market and dole it out to farmers against mortgages, it issued needy borrowers its own obligations, which they had to sell in order to get cash, in fragmented rural markets in which unsophisticated farmers were likely to be exploited.

DEPOSIT BANKS

The late 1850s and early 1860s produced still another innovation—the so-called deposit bank—not a deposit bank in the sense of the Bank of Amsterdam that issued bank money with 100 percent reserves of specie behind it but more like British joint stock banks that dealt in deposits. The first three were the Crédit Industriel et Commercial, founded in 1859, the Crédit Lyonnais of 1863, and the Société Générale pour Favoriser le Développement du Commerce et l'Industrie en France of 1864 (Bouvier, 1955 [1970], p. 341). Napoleon III, still a Saint-Simonien, though he had broken with the Pereires, insisted on the last phrase in the title of the Société Générale (Bigo, 1947, p. 179). The innovation was not in the foundation of the banks but rather that after an initial period of investment in industry, including manufacturing, they moved away in a policy of disengagement (Bouvier, 1955 [1970], p. 358).

The early years of the Crédit Lyonnais to 1882 have been written up by Jean Bouvier in a magisterial thesis that makes four points that apply more or less to other deposit banks:

1. After initial interest, the bank turned from loans to manufacturing to short-term loans to commerce and especially to speculation in foreign bonds.
2. Within France, the bank was more interested in acquiring deposits than in making loans, looking to establish branches in communities with excess savings, rather than in those with a vigorous demand for credit, in order to accumulate pools of money—the French word for the process is *drainage*—for investment abroad.
3. The bank started in Lyons, closely associated with the silk trade, but quickly built a network of branches, starting in the south and finally spreading throughout the nation; this aspect of the bank's experience has also been studied by a geographer, who produced one of the few monographs in the geography of finance (Labasse, 1955).
4. In the course of time, the bank shifted headquarters from Lyons to Paris. There were personal reasons that Henri Germain, founder and president, would want to move—his remarriage to a Parisienne, election to the Chamber of Deputies, and others. The deeper and more fundamental reason was that Paris, the principal financial center, dominated Lyons. Lyons was "a gold mine of savings" (Bouvier, 1961, Vol. 1, p. 274), but Paris was a wholesale market for the demand as well as supply of the nation.

Diversion of the Crédit Lyonnais to speculation in bonds was connected with the spectacular success of the Thiers *rentes,* issued in 1871 and 1872 to finance the

Franco-Prussian indemnity (see Chapter 13). Banks made enormous profits, and many turned from industry to securities, and, later, when domestic interest rates fell in the great depression, to foreign securities. There are episodes in Bouvier's account of the Crédit Lyonnais when domestic loans are called to amass resources for investment abroad (Bouvier, 1961, Vol. 1, pp. 106–10) and refusals of loans to men with excellent credit. "It does not suit us to be attached by a simple advance to the success of an industrial affair" (ibid., Vol. 1, p. 306). As between *enterprises* and *affaires*—industrial concerns and security dealing—the Crédit Lyonnais came down squarely on the side of *affaires,* often justifying itself by comparison with English banks that were leery of industrial advances but also, as a rule, shy of speculative foreign bonds.

BANQUES D'AFFAIRES

Along with deposit banks, the French developed in the last third of the nineteenth century a kind of investment bank. One generation of them was started from 1870 and another from 1878 to 1882, a time that also saw the mushrooming and collapse of the Union Générale patterned after the Crédit Mobilier. Those that survived did so on profits made and squirreled away from the Thiers *rente.* Ostensibly formed primarily for investment in industry—*affaires* in the title meaning "business" rather than, as earlier, "security operations"—it took them some time to find their stride. By the 1890s, the Banque de Paris et des Pays-Bas (nicknamed Paribas), the Banque de l'Union Parisienne, Banque de l'Indo-Chine, and others were making loans and buying securities in electricity, iron and steel, transport, gas, and the like, along with the perennial foreign bonds (Baldy, 1922, passim). The Banque de Paris et des Pays-Bas was formed in 1872 by a merger of the Banque de Paris with the Banque de Pays-Bas, the latter started in 1864 by Ludwig Bamberger, exiled from Mainz for his participation in the 1848 Revolution in Germany. The Banque de Pays-Bas had its main branch in Paris but its nominal head office in Amsterdam to avoid French control (Helfferich, ed., 1900, p. 10)—a prototype of the Eurocurrency market of a century later. One striking specialty of Belgian *banques d'affaires* was teaming up with manufacturers of tramways and trolley cars to finance urban transit systems throughout Europe (McKay, 1976, passim).

UNION GÉNÉRALE

The brief and eventful career of the Union Générale, which was formed in 1878 but collapsed in 1882, has also been studied by Bouvier (1960). It contains echoes of the South Sea and Mississippi Bubbles, along with the clash between the outsider Catholic and aristocratic group that organized the bank and the Protestant-Jewish establishment of the *hautes banques* (leading private banks) and the Bank of France. The Union Générale rode a stock market and bond market boom upward but was unable to get clear in time. Paris came to the rescue in a highly circumscribed way, to save the brokers of Lyons where the bank was located, but not the bank itself or its stockholders. Some banks antithetical to the Union Générale abstained altogether. In all, a syndicate of 18 million francs was formed (ibid., p. 152). When the establishment-connected Comptoir d'Escompte was saved six years later after Denfert-Rocherau had lost enormous sums trying to corner the world copper market—along much the same lines that the Hunt brothers tried to corner the world silver market in 1979—the Bank of France put together a syndicate and 140 million francs to rescue it. Rouvier, the French finance minister, explained the difference: if the Comptoir d'Escompte had collapsed after the Union Générale, the entire French banking system might have been destroyed (Pose, 1942, Vol. 1, p. 215). As it was, little savers in the villages of France received renewed confirmation of their suspicion of banks and even lost confidence in the notary who had invested their money in the Union Générale (Bouvier, 1960, p. 231).

MONEY AND BANKING IN FRANCE

The theme of such scholars as Hoselitz, Gerschenkron, and Cameron is that French economic development had been held back by inadequate financial facilities until the innovation of the Crédit Mobilier. Maurice Lévy-Leboyer's monumental thesis on banking in Europe in the first half of the nineteenth century takes exception to this verdict (1964, p. 699). In summarizing his conclusions later, Cameron argued that French banking held back economic development because of (1) an inadequate number and distribution of banking offices; (2) an insufficient variety of specialized financial institutions; (3) artificial and unnecessary restrictions on the volume of credit; and (4) an inelastic and unnecessarily expensive stock of money (in Cameron et al., 1967, p. 167). Lévy-Leboyer returned to the negative emphatically. According to his calculations, there was no French retardation as compared with Britain. Britain grew during the first half of the nineteenth century at ¼ percent a year, whereas France grew at almost triple that rate (1968). A recent study of comparative growth in Britain and France offers conclusions, not undisputed, in support. France, it is claimed, grew faster than Britain in the eighteenth century and again after an interval for the Napoleonic Wars, from 1815 to about 1870. Moreover, the French had reached a higher standard of living in 1786 than the British (O'Brien and Keyder, 1978, passim). If this were true, financial institutions are either deceptive in outward appearance, as Lévy-Leboyer would contend, or do not count at all, to reflect the Rostow view of Chapter 1.

This issue goes to the root of the problem of the relationship between financial institutions and economic growth. As I see it, France lagged behind Britain in financial institutions and experience by a hundred years or so in a wide variety of dimensions, some to be sure of no particular importance. I have great difficulty, moreover, in accepting the O'Brien and Keyder econometric conclusions, based on the manipulation of a great many statistics, often of uncertain provenance, as compared with the historian's picture, painfully built from archival material by Eugen Weber, in *From Peasants into Frenchmen* (1976). This shows the peasant, who made up more than half the French population in 1850, to be illiterate, backward, immobile, and hungry. On backwardness, observe that the metric system was introduced in France during the Revolution and the franc in 1803; in 1870 the French peasant was still reckoning in feet, inches, pounds, livres, and écus. So immobile was he, moreover, that the few members of a village who had been to Paris were called Parisians (ibid., ch. 2, p. 198).

It is true that elaborate financial machinery will not create economic growth by itself. Sweden, discussed in the next chapter, has been called an "impoverished sophisticate," a country with good finances and good government that did not experience much economic development before the middle of the nineteenth century (Sandberg, 1978, 1979), though this conclusion does not go undisputed (Kindleberger, 1982). Holland's delicately refined financial apparatus was not sufficient to get it to transform from commercial success at its peak in 1730 to an industrial structure, achieved only a century and a half later (Krantz and Hohenberg, eds., 1975, ch. 3). Financial machinery is surely not sufficient; the question is whether it is necessary and, if not, whether a country like France can be economically ahead of a country like Britain when it is a hundred years behind it in financial institutions.

Consider the following:

1. The Bank of England was formed in 1694, the Bank of France in 1800.
2. The British fiscal revolution, to be discussed in Chapter 8, took place between 1688 and 1740 (Dickson, 1967), the French only after the French Revolution of 1789.
3. The bank note came into widespread use in Britain in the eighteenth century, in France only after the middle of the nineteenth.
4. The bank deposit spread through Britain beginning about 1826 and quickly after 1850, slowly in France after 1875.
5. In 1855 England and Wales had 409 banks with 1,185 banking offices; the comparison is far from exact, but in 1863 three-quarters of France lacked access to banking, and in 1913 there were 583 bankable places in France compared with 115 in 1881.
6. The London clearinghouse was established in 1772, the Paris one in 1872.
7. French use of the bill of exchange went back to a limited extent before 1700 and came into its own in the eighteenth century; the bill of exchange was stereotyped all over England by the end of the fifteenth century (Postan, 1930 [1973], p. 54).
8. There were four securities quoted on the Paris bourse in 1815 (Freedeman, 1979, p. 75). There were fourteen securities quoted in the London *Daily Post* in 1725, and twenty in 1740 (Cope, 1978, p. 19).
9. The first insurance company in England was started in 1680 with the big expansion taking place in 1720 (Dickson, 1960; Supple, 1970); as noted in Chapter 10, fire and life insurance in France got underway on a sustained basis only after the Napoleonic Wars, although marine insurance, largely confined to underwriting at the ports, began early in the eighteenth century.

France was not a hundred years behind England in all respects, to be sure. The uprising of the *Fronde* in the 1640s was contemporaneous with the Civil War between Cavaliers and Roundheads, and, on the financial level, incorporation with limited liability arrived everywhere in Europe simultaneously in the 1850s and 1860s as the railroad required the amassing of large amounts of capital. In foreign lending, too, France was behind England but by nothing like so much as a century.

O'Brien and Keyder explicitly dismiss the testimony of contemporaries—Arthur Young, Alexis de Tocqueville, Michel Chevalier, John Bowring, Joseph Marshall, Johann Conrad Fischer, J. G. Bodmer, and the like—who uniformly testify to the superiority of the British in production and, *pace* Engels on *The Condition of the Working Class in England,* level of living, this despite the admonition of econometricians not to reject a priori views except on the basis of strong evidence. Contemporaries in France admired and strove to emulate British financial institutions. Panchaud wanted to create his Caisse d'Escompte on the model of the Bank of England so that it would eventually become strong like it (R. D. Harris, 1979, p. 27). Necker admired British public credit, one reason for the strength of which was the annual submission of a budget, which was published (ibid., p. 87). Mollien was impressed by the Bank of England and by British debt management (1845, Vol. 1, pp. 186–87, 454–55, 460). A theme running through the 1867 Inquiry in France was that Britain was in advance of France in financial institutions; Baron James de Rothschild added that there was a need to let new habits develop and that Rome was not built in a day (Ministère des Finances et al., Vol. 1, p. 461).

This chapter can hardly resolve the issue, but I cannot forebear expressing the opinion that institutions both count and reflect economic conditions, that France lagged a hundred years behind Britain in money, banking and finance, and that this was both a reflection and a cause of its economic retardation.

SUGGESTED SUPPLEMENTARY READING

Cameron (1961), *France and the Economic Development of Europe (1800–1914).*
S. E. Harris (1930), *The Assignats.*
Liesse (1909), *Evolution of Credit and Banks in France.*

In French

Bouvier (1973), *Un Siècle de banque française.*
Levasseur (1854 [1970]), *Recherches historiques sur le système le Law.*
Lévy-Leboyer (1964), *Les Banques européennes et l'industrialisation internationale dans la première moitié du XIXe siècle.*
Lüthy (1959), *La Banque protestante en France de la révocation de l'édit de Nantes*
Plessis (1982), *La Banque de France et ses deux cents actionnaires.*
Plessis (1985), *Les Régents et gouveneurs de la Banque de France sous le Second Empire.*
Plessis (1985), *La Politique de la Banque de France de 1851 à 1870.*
Pose (1942), *La Monnaie et ses institutions.*

7

German Banking

There was no Isaac Pereire, but hundreds of Mevissens on top of more Crédit Mobiliers than Germany had princes.
(Marx, as quoted by Blumberg, "Die Finanzierung der Neugründungen und Erweiterungen von Industriebetrieben," 1960, p. 172)

MOSAIC GERMANY

Countries typically experience slow and sometimes painful integration of monetary and banking institutions by regions. In Germany the process is particularly evident because the country was unified so late—in 1871 after the Prussian victory over France. In 1790 there were 300 rulers in Germany. The process of integrating these into one government took eighty more years and was one in which money and banking brought up the rear rather than serving in the van. Trade unification through customs union was a spearhead of the process; banking might have moved much faster had it been permitted to do so. Monetary unification, however, seems to follow rather than precede political integration, as so many functional integrationists think is desirable or appropriate in the European Community today.

Germany was backward in mercantile and financial development. The Hanseatic League had been fairly primitive in credit institutions—about two centuries behind the Italian ones in 1500 (de Roover, 1942 [1953], p. 82)—although it anticipated the European Monetary Union by more that half a millennium by forming the Wendish Monetary Union in the fourteenth century. Other monetary unions were put together in the Rhineland, the Upper Rhineland, and Swabia, and there were a number of them in Franconia (North, 1990, p. 29). Hamburg established a bourse to trade in commodities and bonds in 1558 and the Bank of Hamburg in 1619, but it lagged far behind Amsterdam and London in the development of bills of exchange (Pohl, 1986, ch. 1). Strongly influenced by Italian bankers, south Germany achieved an advanced state of financial sophistication, for its time, in promoting silver mining, trade with the Levant through Venice, and lending to princes through Lyons, and especially Antwerp, in the sixteenth century before sinking back into financial obscurity in the seventeenth. The history of different states and principalities, regions, and cities diverged. Ports were different, and so were Frankfurt, Breslau, Baden, Saxony, and Prussia. Generally, however, the banks of Germany remained primitive until well into the nineteenth century.

PRUSSIA

Prussian financial history is closely associated with financing armies, on the one hand, and providing mortgage credit to the Junker nobility, on the other. During the Seven Years' War, Frederick the Great several times debased the currency, which had been new in 1750, in order to get funds to continue fighting. With peace in 1763, he had to help the prince of Saxony, a territory acquired as a result of victory, especially to aid weakened Leipzig banks. He also sought to reconstitute his silver coinage and bought silver in Amsterdam and Hamburg on credit. His total borrowing on bills in Amsterdam was fifteen times greater than the cash available in that city, so that when he started to draw specie, the liquidity crisis was acute. Arend, Joseph & Company failed at the beginning of 1763, Gebrüder de Neufville at the end of July, and fifty more houses by the end of August (Bloom, 1937, p. 198; Wirth, 1893, pp. 88–93). The crisis boomeranged back to Hamburg and Berlin and spread deflation. As one measure to counteract this, Frederick started a Königliche Giro- und Lehnbanco (Royal Clearing and Loan Bank) in 1765 that evolved into the Prussian Bank. Little use could be made of it, however, because its reserves of specie were so small. The Prussian state had a sizable treasure—23.6 million thalers in 1775 and 55.2 million in 1786—but this was a war chest, acquired in accordance with cameralist theory, and deposited in the royal palace and the Fortress Spandau, rather than in the bank (Born, 1977, p. 29). The Prussian Bank dealt in loans on bills of exchange and securities (Lombard loans) and in mortgages on Junker estates. In the same year that the Prussian Bank was formed, another province established the Fürstliches Leyhaus (princely Leyhaus) that evolved into the Braunschweigische Staatsbank (Brunswick State Bank) (ibid., p. 61).

Of greater interest than the Leyhaus or similar banks in other mini-states that made loans out of capital but did not issue notes was the founding by Frederick the Great in 1772 of the Königliche (Royal) Seehandlung, a corporation in the mercantilist spirit designed to stimulate overseas trade and shipping. The king originally provided seven-eighths of the capital, although in the next ten years the division became half private, half royal. The Seehandlung was granted monopolies over export of wax and import of salt and by 1790 evolved to the point of a bank dealing in exchange credits and underwriting state loans (ibid., p. 61). The bank had a rocky start in trade due to the interruption of the Napoleonic Wars and suspended payments when the Prussian state, after defeat by Napoleon and the levying of an indemnity, defaulted on its debt service. Reorganized as a pure state bank in 1809, it gathered strength and widened its range of activities during the remainder of the half-century before its conversion into a note-issuing bank in 1846.

The first note-issuing banks in the German states were the Bayerische Hypotheken und Wechselbank (Bavarian Mortgage and Exchange Bank) established in 1835 and the Bank of Leipzig in Saxony in 1838 (Tilly, 1967, p. 157). Before that time, however, the Prussian government had issued paper in 1806 to finance the war against Napoleon (Tilly, 1966, p. 32). These notes were regarded as debt of the government rather than money. Other states issued their own obligations for use as money, and by 1853 there were note-issuing banks (Zettelbanken after Zettel, a slip of paper) only in Berlin, Stettin, Munich, and Leipzig (Blumberg, 1960, p. 168).

Means of payment remained in short supply. In 1846, in the crisis, Christian Rother received permission to convert the Prussian Bank to one that issued notes. By the time of the Reichsbank in 1875, twenty different *Länder* in Germany had issued paper notes and thirty-three banks bank notes. As everywhere, if government or banks did not fill the need, others did. In Silesia merchants and manufacturers were creative in developing money substitutes (Tilly, 1966, p. 136).

INTEGRATING THE COINAGE

The German mini-states' experience illustrates precisely Adam Smith's statement that small countries are obliged to use foreign monies. The Rhineland, for example, had at least seventy types of foreign coins in circulation in 1816 (ibid., p. 20). The economic condition of the Rhineland had been altered by French occupation during the Napoleonic Wars. Feudal obligations had been removed, Jews were free to move from town to town, commerce was stimulated, and manufacturing had begun to shift from guilds and cottage industry into factories. The western part of Prussia differed sharply from east Prussia even before the liberating influence of the French: farming was conducted by peasants on small plots rather than by Junkers using serfs on *latifundia*. Aristocracy was weak, not dominant (they even paid taxes, which was not true of the east); peasants were free; and the position of merchants and banks was higher than in Berlin where bureaucracy held all power. Prussia tried to enforce uniform domestic standards throughout its sprawling state but with incomplete success. Gold was undervalued at the mint and disappeared from circulation; seignorage on Prussian silver coins was excessive, which led the Rhineland to acquire coin or notes elsewhere. By the 1830s the thaler had become the regions' unit of account, but French coins dominated the circulation.

The Zollverein or customs union had its start in 1818 with the unification of the Prussian tariff and among the German states in 1828 with the formation of northern, central, and southern groups, which were joined into one in 1833. The initial treaty made provision for the payment of customs duties in the gold or silver coins of any of the members, thus preserving monetary sovereignty, but contemplated an ultimate uniform system of weights, measures, and coinage. The first step in coinage was a partial one. A group of southern members entered into a treaty in Munich in 1837, establishing the gulden, or florin, minted 24½ out of a Cologne mark of fine silver (233.855 grams) as the common monetary unit. The northern tier responded with a monetary agreement of July 1838 fixing on the existing Prussian thaler, 14 to the Cologne mark of silver, followed by the Dresden convention between the north and the south settling the exchange rate at 4 Prussian thalers to 7 gulden. It also provided for the minting of a common new silver coin, the Vereinsmünze, equal to two thalers or 3½ gulden.

The Dresden convention continued in force for the next twenty years or so, until Austria entered the picture. Austria was contending with Prussia for leadership of the German states and first sought to enter the Zollverein for which, with its weak industrial position, it needed high tariffs. When this was turned aside, it shifted to currency. Its need in this area was genuine. The Austrian National Bank had suspended convertibility in the revolutionary troubles of 1848. With the gold discoveries in California and Australia, it suggested in 1854 that it and the Zollverein states move to a new monetary system based on gold. This was rejected. In 1856 Austria yielded to Prussian insistence that currency negotiations be limited to improvement of the Dresden Agreement of 1838. A year of negotiation produced the Münzverein, or Union of Coinage, abandoning the Cologne mark of silver for a Zollpfund (customs union pound) of 500 grams, divided metrically (as part of the general movement to the metric system in mid-century). Thirty thalers, 52½ south German florins, and 45 Austrian florins were to be coined from a Zollpfund of silver, producing a simplified exchange rate structure of 1 thaler equal to 1¾ south German florins equal to 1½ Austrian florins. A new gold coin, the crown, was to be minted but only for international use. As part of the agreement, Austria agreed to return to bank note convertibility into silver and did so in September 1858, only to suspend again in April 1859 when war broke out with Italy. War between Austria and Prussia in 1866 led Austria to withdraw from the Münzverein, with its bank notes still inconvertible.

German commercial interests were less than satisfied with the Dresden arrangements for a fixed-rate system within the Zollverein and preferred a single currency. They were unable, however, to agree whether it should be the thaler or the gulden. After debating the issue for some years, they suddenly, following the lead of the International Monetary Conference held in Paris in 1867, came out for "universal money." The fourth German Commercial Convention (Handelstag) held in October 1868 passed a resolution favoring speedy monetary unity in Germany, abandonment of the gulden and the mark (one-third of a thaler), and abandonment of the silver standard, in favor of a gold coin of 5 francs, with decimal multiples, and division into 100 shillings, plus a 25-franc piece divided into 100 kreutzers (U.S. Senate, 1879 [1978], pp. 727–28). This proposal stemmed from the international group of German merchants, led by Dr. Adolf Soetbeer of Hamburg, a strong advocate of the gold standard. It evoked no response. The North German Bund with its thaler won not only over French hegemony, rejecting the 25-franc gold coin of the Latin Monetary Union, but over the south's silver gulden (Zucker, 1975, pp. 66, 69). Monetary reform in October 1871 adopted the mark, divided into 100 pfennigs as its unit of account, with the principal coin the gold 10-mark piece (Borchardt, 1976, pp. 6–7). The gold standard was adopted; silver was sold off, as noted in Chapter 4. Although many Junkers would have preferred to retain bimetallism in the belief that monometallism was deflationary and that they, as debtors, would suffer from it, Bamberger and the internationalists carried the day on this issue. The Prussian currency standard prevailed, even though the name of the unit of account was discarded in favor of Hamburg, which had kept its books in mark banco.

The nineteenth-century history of German monetary unification as a pattern for the monetary integration of Europe today (discussed in Chapter 24) is a matter of some debate. It can be argued that full monetary unification required preliminary political unification, achieved after Prussia's defeat of France in 1870, much as monetary unification in Italy waited until after political union—by some decades, in fact. One authority, however, reciting the history above in greater detail, concludes that the German case was one of monetary unification preceding political union. It was true that there was no central bank until after the establishment of the Reich and no paper money, but most trade was conducted with coin (Holtfrerich, 1989). The issue remains debatable. History suggests that the monetary unification before 1870, without a central government, much like that in the late Middle Ages with a weak Holy Roman Empire, was likely to come unstuck as various interests pulled this way and that. Steps toward monetary union may precede political unification, but without effective government, their chances of holding are not assured.

PRIVATE BANKS

The German states had numerous banking centers in the eighteenth and in the early nineteenth centuries—notably Hamburg, effecting payments in international trade; Cologne a one-time Hanseatic city left behind in international commerce by the increase in the size of ships that could not now mount the Rhine but nonetheless with a strong international trading tradition; Frankfurt lying athwart the north-south and east-west routes of Europe on the ford (*furt*) used by the Franks to cross the Main; Berlin with its court and court bankers; and many more.

Hamburg was the leader of the independent neutral cities during the Napoleonic Wars—Lübeck, Bremen, Nuremberg, Augsburg, and Frankfurt-am-Main—though that did not save it from French invasion (Wiskemann, 1929, p. 137). Its trading interests with London, especially after the weakening of the Navigation Acts in 1823, led it to be called the "all-English" city (Böhme, 1968); Bremen, in contrast, concentrated on transatlantic trade in coffee and cotton (Wiskemann, 1929, p. 143). Hamburg was full of foreign (and Jewish) merchants and bankers. Preeminent was John Parish of England who had the greatest banking house in Germany in 1800, having grown rich in transmitting subsidies to British allies on the Continent, selling *assignats,* and speculating in commodities (Emden, 1938, p. 20). He was the banker who testified before the Bullion Committee in London in 1810 on the Hamburg-London exchange rate (Rosenbaum and Sherman, 1976 [1979], p. 6). There were Huguenots such as Chapeaurouge and Goddefroy, Jewish houses like Salomon Heine and Moritz Warburg, and banks of native Hamburg families such as Berenberg, Gossler, Martin Donner, and so on. Similar heterogeneous groups were found in the other principal cities. Among the prominent Jewish houses were Rothschild of Frankfurt, which later spread to London, Paris, Amsterdam, and Vienna, plus Gebrüder Bethmann of the same city, Abraham Oppenheim of Cologne, and the Mendelssohn and Bleichröder houses of Berlin. Frankfurt had its share of Huguenot families—de Neufvilles, de Barys, and d'Orvilles. Cologne and the Rhineland were a prodigious hotbed of bankers of bourgeois origin, including Gustav Mevissen, David Hansemann, August von der Heydt, and Ludolf and Otto Camphausen, the last three of whom served the Prussian government as minister of either finance or commerce.

The prodigious wealth and power of the Rothschild banking house have led to many histories, most recently in connection with the French branch (Bouvier, 1967; Gille, 1965, 1967). The origin of the firm is found in the Napoleonic Wars when Prince William of Hanau, elector of Hesse-Kassel, sought to bring back from

England some of the money amassed by his father, Landgrave Frederick, and himself providing soldiers to Britain. The elector had a hard time investing his capital and started by entrusting the task to an Amsterdam house. When the French occupied the Netherlands, he was forced back to Frankfurt. Meyer Amschel Rothschild took on the tasks both of transmitting the elector's fortune from place to place and keeping it profitably invested, whether in London, Denmark, or Austria or in goods smuggled through the Continental blockade to Frankfurt. Son Nathan was sent to England to help at that end and, after a short stretch speculating in commodities, settled down in London to lend to peers and royalty. James went to France in 1811 at the age of 19 to maintain the lines of communication between Nathan in London and the Frankfurt house. In due course, the London, Paris, and Vienna houses established themselves as independent concerns. With the death of Meyer Amschel, the fountainhead of the firm declined and was eclipsed by the tributaries (Corti, 1928, chs. 1, 2).

Rhineland bankers were exposed to strong French influences, both during the Napoleonic occupation and later as they undertook their training abroad. Mevissen had been in Paris in 1838 and absorbed the views of the Saint-Simonien bankers with whom he consorted. Abraham Oppenheim was a brother-in-law of the Paris banker, Benoit Fould, and knew well Emile and Isaac Pereire. David Hansemann, somewhat older, had flourished in selling cloth during the occupation, traveled widely in the course of seven years, and fashioned an insurance company in 1824 on the current French model. Camphausen served his banking apprenticeship in Belgium and France (Benaerts, 1933, pp. 339–42). Somewhat later, Ludwig Bamberger of Mainz sought work and study out of Germany under different circumstances: he was condemned to death for his role in the Revolution of 1848, escaping only by going abroad. A nephew of the Bischoffsheims, bankers in Paris and London, he got jobs in Holland, Paris, and Brussels before returning to Germany, a rich man, under an amnesty of 1866, to contribute ultimately to starting the Deutsche Bank in 1870 and the Reichsbank in 1875 (Zucker, 1975). Max Warburg of Hamburg worked his apprenticeship in Frankfurt, Amsterdam, Paris, and London as a matter of course (Rosenbaum, 1962, p. 136).

GREAT BANKS

A. Schaffhausen was a private bank that started to collapse in the financial crisis that accompanied the disturbances of 1848. The founder's grandfather had made a great deal of money in dealing in church and royal lands sold off during the French occupation and possibly from swindling while dealing in French *assignats* (Krüger, 1925, p. 46). The merchant-banking house traded in (Rhine) wine for export and (South American) hides and leather for import, as did many Cologne firms, but it ended up as a typical bank, lending to textile houses on the left bank of the Rhine and to nascent industry, such as Harcourt and Krupp in steel and Felten & Guillaume in rubber. In 1848, however, its troubles arose from speculation in real estate in the city. It sought help from the Prussian Bank branch in Cologne, then from the branch in Münster, from the Royal Seehandlung, and finally from the Prussian state lottery. Each came through with a limited amount, though insufficient in the aggregate to save the bank. It appealed to the Prussian government for the right to reorganize as a joint stock bank. In a temporary wave of liberalism induced by the Revolution of 1848, the bureaucracy granted permission, and the Schaffhausen's-chen Bank was created with wide powers (Tilly, 1966, p. 112).

Prussian Junker bureaucrats intended to permit no more large banks. They were anticommerce, anticities, anti-industry, and antibanking but pro-military and pro-large-scale agriculture. In 1848 the Prussian government rejected an application by Sal. Oppenheim & Company to form a Rheinische Hypothekenbank (mortgage bank), leading it to turn to Paris at the beginning of the 1850s to work with Achille Fould and the Pereires. The government also turned down an application by Mevissen to establish a Crédit Mobilier in Cologne, which was in Prussia, and one of the Schaffhausen'schen Bank to move from Cologne to Berlin (Riesser, 1911, p. 509).

The Mevissen answer was to try to start a Crédit Mobilier with Oppenheim money in Frankfurt, if not in Cologne, and, when this too was rejected, to turn to Darmstadt in Hesse, on the outskirts of Prussia and of the city of Frankfurt. The Bank für Handel und Industrie, usually called the Darmstädter Bank, was established there in 1853. Its statutes were patterned somewhat after those of the Crédit Mobilier of Paris but more especially after the Schaffhausen'schen Bank with which Mevissen was associated, often word for word. They went beyond the latter, however, in permitting investment banking—the holding of shares in companies, underwriting company shares, and arranging for mergers (ibid., pp. 57–58; Cameron, 1956). Another major bank, the Diskontogesellschaft, found a place outside Prussia in the mini-principality of Dessau. David Hansemann served briefly as minister of finance of Prussia and then as president of the Prussian Bank when it was reorganized in 1846 and endowed with the right to issue bank notes. When he lost his personal fortune in the financial crisis that accompanied the Revolution of 1848, he resigned from the Prussian Bank to reorganize the Diskontogesellschaft as a Crédit-Mobilier-type bank (Seidenzahl, 1960 [1966], pp. 215–19). Mevissen and Oppenheim teamed up to start another bank in Darmstadt, the Bank für Süd-deutschland. On 29 February 1856, which complicates counting birthdays, the Mit-teldeutsche Creditbank was formed in Meiningen in Saxony because it could not get permission to start another bank in Frankfurt (*Hundert Jahre,* 1956, p. 13).

Then came a discovery of a loophole in the Prussian bureaucracy's regulations, rather akin to that found by lawyers in England in 1833 that permitted joint stock banks to be established within sixty-five miles of London so long as they went without the note-issue privilege. While the state would not give permission to organize further joint stock banks, it lacked power to prevent the formation of *Kommandit-gesellschaft auf Aktien* (limited partnerships with transferable shares). Immediately new banks were formed and old ones reorganized. The Berliner Handelsgesellschaft was founded in the capital city. The fever spread. A Schlesische Bankverein was begun in Silesia in Breslau and the Allgemeiner Deutscher Credit-Anstalt at Leipzig in Saxony (Helfferich, 1921–23 [1956], p. 25). Even Hamburg, the commercial "English" city, was unable to resist and started the Vereinsbank in July 1856 and the Norddeutschebank in October of the same year, although the city turned out, over the long haul, to have close relations with the Berliner Handelsgesellschaft.

Banks outside Hamburg, a city dedicated to financing commerce, looked immediately to their relations with industry and primarily manufacturing and mining as well as railroads and public utilities, which had been so central to the Crédit Mobilier of Paris. The Darmstädter took part in seven industrial companies in 1856 that it founded as, or transformed into, stock companies, retaining about one-third of the new shares for its own account (Riesser, 1911, pp. 81, 498). Even earlier, the Schaffhausen'schen Bank had participated in the foundation of the Hoerder Bergwerk- & Hüttenverein in 1851 (mine and foundry), the Kölner Bergwerkverein in 1852, along with the establishment of the Kölnische Baumwollspinnerei (cottonspinning mill), the Kölnische Maschinenbau Aktiengesellschaft, the Köln-Müsener Bergwerks-Aktiengesellschaft, and the Kölnische Rückversicherung-Gesellschaft (reinsurance), as well as helping with the founding of other banks and the amalgamation of railroads (ibid., pp. 71–72). One could recite lists of individual participations for other banks outside Hamburg.

Not every banker in Germany was enthusiastic for industrial participations at this stage. In a memorandum written for the president of the Baden Finance Ministry in 1856, David Hansemann, founder of the revamped Diskontogesellschaft, made distinctions among (1) industrial banks of the Crédit Mobilier type, (2) note-issuing banks, and (3) banks that combined both functions. He regarded the last category as dangerous, seeking to hold long-term assets against short-term liabilities. Baden sought his views because it had lacked all banks since the failure of the prominent private house of Haber & Sons, which had gone bankrupt in Karlsruhe in the financial crisis of 1848 (Seidenzahl, 1960 [1966], p. 216). When David Hansemann turned the direction of the Diskontogesellschaft over to his son Adolph, the bank moved more strongly into industrial lending, finding itself in close relationships with the electrotechnical industry, especially the Allgemeine Elektrizitäts Gesellschaft (AEG or general electric company), heavy industry such as mining and smelting, and street railways plus minor steam railroads (Riesser, 1911, pp. 518–21). Association with AEG proved highly profitable.

Like the Crédit Mobilier in France, the new industrial banks also made a start in issuing foreign loans—for Austria, Sweden, Italy, Russia on an important scale, and even Peru—sometimes opposing and sometimes cooperating with foreign banks such as the Rothschilds in Austria or France (Helfferich, 1921–23 [1956], p. 27).

Bank formation of the 1850s was halted by the financial crisis of 1857 but was followed after a fifteen-year interval by another wave of banks in the boom associated with the successful war against France, the founding of the Reich, and the institution of the mark. The Dresdener Bank had the same purposes as the industrial banks of the Crédit Mobilier type. The Commerz Bank was established in Hamburg ostensibly to discount foreign bills in support of foreign trade. The Deutsche Bank founded in Berlin by Adalbert Delbrück, a private banker, Ludwig Bamberger, and Hermann Wallich, the last two with extensive foreign experience, was organized explicitly for the purpose of challenging British banking domination of foreign finance. Speculative excitement in the 1871–73 *Gründungsjahre* (foundation years) boom quickly diverted them to domestic industrial finance. The central figure in the formative years of the bank's history was Georg von Siemens, a cousin of Werner Siemens of the electrical company, who joined the bank in 1877.

The Deutsche Bank annual report for 1871 made clear that it was difficult to establish direct relations with overseas financial markets, other than by continuing to deal with, and through, London. It placed part of the blame on the fragmentation of German money and the need for a single German money and exchange rate instead of separate quotations for the mark banco, louis d'or, thaler, and gulden. While the German navy bought its foreign exchange through the Deutsche Bank instead of through London, it did so at some extra cost (ibid., pp. 51–52). The bank set up a few foreign branches or affiliates. Mainly, however, it turned inward, like the others, to busy itself with state loans, loans to communities, railroad securities, and ultimately, industrial, insurance, and construction participation. By the late 1870s and early 1880s, it was issuing securities for Krupp, the chemical companies, and finally Siemens & Halske.

A decade later, with the mark replacing the four German currencies, the problem of developing a German exchange market was still unsolved. Of a sale of £100,000 in Hamburg in 1884, only £2,000 could be placed in Germany (Wiskemann, 1929, p. 235). Berlin kept urging the development of a German exchange market for trade with such a country as Brazil, for example, rather than buying and selling reis in London. The Hamburg Chamber of Commerce regarded Berlin as inlandish and bureaucratic, given to underestimating the overpowering place of London as a gold, exchange, and capital market and unaware of the need for German trade to grow substantially if any German city were going to rival London (ibid., pp. 236–38).

THE CONSTRUCTION BOOM

The excitement of victory and unification let loose not only a new wave of great banks but also a building boom, especially in Berlin (and Vienna), that gave rise to a mushroom crop of companies converted to banks, called either *Maklerbanken* (real estate brokers' banks) or *Baubanken* (construction banks). In two and a half years, 40 billion marks was invested in these institutions, which started out dealing in building sites and undertaking construction but failed after merely having speculated in urban real estate. Branches were set up in some instances in Breslau, Frankfurt, Leipzig, Posen, and other German and Austrian cities. Wirth estimated that only one-fifth of 1 percent was actually spent on construction. Much of this was sold at a loss when real estate prices tumbled in the summer of 1873 (1893, pp. 472–84). All sorts of quasi- and actual swindles occurred, involving some prominent notables on the boards of newly formed companies to lend respectability when they could furnish no money—firms speculating in their own stock, insiders milking corporations at the expense of little stockholders, and the like. Like England in Dickens's *Little Dorrit* and France in Balzac's *César Birotteau* and Zola's *L'Argent,* Germany had a classic popular novel celebrating booms, swindles, and collapse, Spielhagen's *Stormflut* (Storm Flood) (1877). This compared the wave of speculation to an inundation caused by an 1874 tidal wave on the Baltic Coast. Both catastrophes were the consequence of ignoring clear warnings.

Possibly worse than the misuse of funds in urban real estate were the swindles in railroad securities. Before the May 1873 crash, Edmund Lasker, a Landestag delegate, detested by Bismarck, called unwanted attention to these scandals and the involvement in them of prominent political figures, newspaper editors, and high nobility close to the Hohenzollern court (Wirth, 1858 [1890], p. 484; Stern, 1977a, pp. 168, 242). One particularly unsavory character was Bethel Henry Strousberg, who used money realized in selling shares in a Rumanian railroad project to bail out other of his investment projects that were running short. He ran into trouble early in the boom and appealed to Bismarck for help in December 1870. Bismarck turned to Bleichröder, his private banker, and to Adolph Hansemann of the Diskontogesellschaft. They rescued Strousberg but had to wait twelve years before they got their money back, without interest. Bleichröder's reward was ennoblement for having kept a potential scandal far from the court (Stern, 1977a, ch. 14). Strousberg has been compared with a French tout-swindler of a couple of decades earlier, Jules Mirès, who used to sell unpaid-up railroad shares as if they were fully paid, despite stringent laws against the practice (Redlich, 1967). A minority view, based on the opinions of Ludwig Bamberger and one Max von Schinkel, maintains that Strousberg was unjustly maligned as a swindler (Rosenbaum and Sherman, 1976 [1979], p. 78n).

REICHSBANK

With unification of German money, it was time to establish a central bank to regulate it. This was largely done by the Reichstag and within that legislative body by the leadership of Ludwig Bamberger. Bamberger was interested in centralizing financial authority—"shared responsibility is no responsibility" was a remark of his—and, in this, he was opposed by Ludolf Camphausen, the Prussian finance secretary who wanted to retain states' rights.

The solution, reached after a three-cornered struggle also involving Rudolf von Delbrück, president of the Imperial Chancellery, was conversion of the Prussian State Bank to a Reichsbank and tolerance for the other thirty-two note-issuing banks, though with a limit on their right of note issue and a restriction of their operations to their state territory. This latter was found to be so confining that fifteen of these *Zettelbanken* gave up immediately and sixteen more by 1905.

The Reichsbank was required to maintain a reserve amounting to one-third of its note liabilities but permitted to exceed that amount on payment of a fine equal to 5 percent of the excess. This requirement was conceived as a less traumatic device for handling crises than the British suspension of the Bank Act of 1844, which legislation was taken explicitly into account. In all these technical questions, Bamberger for the Reichstag dominated the proceedings.

CONSTRUCTION OF THE BANKING NETWORK

Following the unification of Germany, another process got under way: converting the network of banks in scattered locations into a hierarchical structure with its apex at Berlin. The first banks to move their head offices were the Darmstädter from

Hesse and the Mitteldeutsche Creditbank, which by this time had established itself in Frankfurt. The crash of 1873 produced a lull in the flow. Thereafter came the Dresdener Bank in 1882 and the Commerz & Diskonto Bank, the result of a merger, from Hamburg but in stages. The Commerz Bank arrived in Berlin by way of Frankfurt, embarrassed as any republican Hamburger would be, to defer openly to the aristocratic Junker capital. In 1897 it decided to follow the fashion of the times and found a subsidiary in Berlin. To do this it merged with a Frankfurt private bank, J. Dreyfus & Company, which had been started in Frankfurt in 1868 and acquired a Berlin subsidiary in 1891. The main interest of the Commerz Bank was in the Berlin subsidiary, not the Frankfurt head office. After an interval it turned the Frankfurt office loose as a private bank again and went on developing the offices in both Berlin and Hamburg until, by 1914, it had eighteen branches in Hamburg and forty-four in Berlin, together with the head office. The move was dictated by a shift of interest from trade finance to state loans, railroads, and such industrial participations as the Schukert group (*Hundert Jahre*, 1956, pp. 16, 44–46).

It is not evident from the secondary sources whether banks were pulled to Berlin by the establishment of the clearinghouse there in 1882. The Deutsche Bank was among the first to develop a deposit business, patterned on what Georg von Siemens had observed in London in 1867. Not much success was achieved, it would appear, since a check law was not enacted until 1908 (Helfferich, 1921–23 [1956], pp. 63–64). One factor in the movement was the rise to ascendancy of the Berlin stock exchange over that in Frankfurt, ascribed by Helfferich, somewhat opaquely, as "thanks to the nimbleness and skill (*Rührigkeit und Geschicklichkeit*) of Berlin bankers" (ibid., p. 27). A more persuasive explanation would argue the presence of the government and economies of scale.

The presence of the national government in a city is not a sufficient condition for the location of a financial market there, as Rome versus Milan, Berne versus Zurich, Washington versus New York, and others demonstrate. Where the governmental capital and the major commercial center coincide, however, as in London, Paris, Brussels, Stockholm, Copenhagen, and to a lesser extent Berlin, banks are attracted to it. The economies of scale are those of agglomeration, widely observed in location theory, where firms selling the same service, and sometimes their customers buying it, tend to cluster together. Cities will typically have whole districts devoted to theatre, music, and superior retail shopping, not to mention insurance and finance. As indicated in the discussion of London, some banks will stretch out to the main financial center of the country to find outlets for surplus funds and others to gain access to the surpluses of others. This centripetal tendency thus provides economies of scale for both buyers of financial services, who can shop with convenience, and sellers who find the customers gathered into one place (Kindleberger, 1974*a* [1978]).

"D" BANKS

The process of concentration in banking went, if anything, a little further in Germany than in Britain and France before World War I because of the German propensity for bigness. Six banks had capital of over 100 million marks by 1910; the Deutsche Bank with 200 million, the Dresdener with 180 million, the Diskontogesellschaft with 170 million, the Bank für Handel und Industrie (Darmstädter) with 154 million, the Schaffhausen'schen Bank with 145 million, and the Berliner Handelsgesellschaft with 110 million. All had head offices in Berlin by this time, as did the Commerz Bank with a capital of 85 million and the Nationalbank für Deutschland, later to merge with the Darmstädter to form the Danatbank, with 80 million. These were the eight great Berlin banks (Riesser, 1911, p. 642). The first four were the famous Berlin "D" banks. Three of them, minus the Danat, which closed its doors in July 1931, remain today.

RELATIONS WITH INDUSTRY

French private banks often had close ties with industry: the Perier Bank to the Anzin Coal Company; or Gouin, the locomotive builder, to Gouin the banker; Schneider of Schneider-Creuzot, the steel company, came from the Seillières Bank to take his industrial post. In Germany, intimate ties ran between industry and the large banks—for example, between Siemens & Halske and the Deutsche Bank; AEG and the Berliner Handelsgesellschaft; the Gelsenkirchen Bergwerkgesellschaft and the Diskontogesellschaft. Industrialists were represented on the boards of banks and banks on the boards of companies (Riesser, 1911, pp. 617, 865 n. 63). Banks cultivated the business of holding the securities of investor-depositors and voting the stock along with that owned by the bank itself. A few firms, like Thyssen and Stinnes in iron and steel, and a few industries, such as chemicals, stayed clear of deep involvement with banks (ibid., pp. 721, 741). For the most part, the relations were intimate and reciprocal and formed part of the evidence for Gerschenkron's generalization that the more backward the country, compared to Britain, the more banks (and government) substituted for the private initiative of independent entrepreneurs.

Tilly takes exception to Gerschenkron's views on backwardness, holding rather that the mainsprings of German economic development in the second half of the nineteenth century lay neither in banks nor in planning by an efficient state bureaucracy but in thousands of profit-oriented decisions by capitalist entrepreneurs operating throughout Prussia and especially in the Rhineland (1966, p. 138). As the epigraph of this chapter indicates, Marx focused on the hundreds of Mevissens. But not many Mevissens were needed. Gustav Mevissen sat on the boards of six mines (including the executive committees of two) and two industrial companies (of which he was board chairman), was president of the Darmstädter Bank and of the Luxemburger Internationale Bank, and sat on the boards of the Schaffhausen'schen Bank, the Bank für Süddeutschland, the Kölner Privatbank, and the Berliner Handelsgesellschaft, not to mention the Rheinische Eisenbahngesellschaft (railroad). His friend Vierson, a textile merchant and manufacturer, had eight directorships (Blumberg, 1960, pp. 199–200). There may have been thousands of decisions, but they were made by relatively few people.

The close connections running between the large "mixed banks" and big German firms have given rise to a claim that German banking slowed economic growth in the country by favoring heavy industry over light. Such a bias would have meant that some other industries with faster growth potential than the favored heavy industries were charged higher rates for credit and did not obtain all the loans they could have used (Neuberger and Stokes, 1974). The argument has been conducted in terms of the "new economic history" and econometric testing and led to a sharp debate over both the quality of the data and the techniques employed (Fremdling and Tilly, 1976; Neuberger and Stokes, 1976, 1978; Komlos, 1978). While the charge may not have been proved conclusively, all participants in the discussion are agreed on the particularly close relationships that ran between the great banks and large-scale industry in Germany—a relationship that was quite distinct from that existing in Britain and in France.

OTHER BANKS

Great banks dominated the German scene, along with the private banks that gradually shrank in importance over the nineteenth century. A number of other kinds deserve mention. In the first decades of the nineteenth century, so-called *Landschaften* (land companies) collected Prussian savings by issuing *Pfandbriefen* or mortgage bonds that passed from hand to hand as money in addition to assisting the Junker landowners (Tilly, 1966, p. 136). Another category consisted in the Raiffeisen banks, started by Frederick Wilhelm Raiffeisen with his own fortune, after the troubles of 1846–48, to build a series of rural credit cooperatives for peasants. Another series of cooperative banks were the result of the initiative of Hermann Schultze-Delitsch, who was concerned to assist small shopkeepers and tradesmen with cooperative credit. These were formed under the Prussian law of 1867. In terms of total assets, local savings banks with 21 billion marks in 1913, regional banks of issue with 13.7 billion, and private mortgage banks with 13.6 billion made up more than half of the total assets of all financial institutions in Germany in that year and far outweighed the assets of the large nationwide banks with assets of 8 billion (Goldsmith, 1969, table D-9). But size and decision power are far different. The great banks constituted less than a tenth of the total assets of financial institutions of the country but were found at the critical margin affecting economic growth.

NOTES ON NEIGHBORING COUNTRIES

Austria

Austria participated in the upswing of the 1870s and in the collapse of 1873. Before that time, however, it had created a state bank, the Wiener Bank (Bank of Vienna), as early as 1703, charging it, like the Hôtel de Ville in Paris, mainly with the task of paying interest on the state debt (Riley, 1980, p. 127). From 1762 the Bank of Vienna issued notes that were, in effect, state debt. With the deep and painful Austrian involvement in the Napoleonic Wars, the state deficit led the bank into excessive issues and hyperinflation as measured by an agio of 775 percent on silver in 1811, and eventually into bankruptcy (Sieveking, 1934, pp. 153–54).

A new bank of issue was created in 1816 as Austria emerged from the Napoleonic Wars after the Congress of Vienna. By the middle of the century it was serving both Austria and Hungary. It was organized like the Bank of England, after the Bank Act of 1844, with a fiduciary circulation of 200 million florins and 100 percent reserves of specie on note issues above that. Unlike the Bank of England in mid-century, however, it suspended convertibility requirements, not just briefly but for long periods of time. The crisis of 1869 required the government to count foreign bills of exchange as equivalent to specie—a hint of the gold exchange standard to come; the reserve requirement was suspended altogether in the crisis of 1873. With charter renewal in 1887, the Austrian-Hungarian National Bank shifted over to the German fractional reserve system of a 40 percent reserve note liabilities, with the elastic provision that the bank could hold a lower proportion of legal reserves provided that it paid a 5 percent tax on the deficiency (Komlos, 1979, pp. 5–9).

When convertibility was suspended in the financial crisis of 1873, a high agio on silver built up until 1879, when it started to decline—not because the Austrian florin was improving but rather due to the falling price of silver. Austria remained with forced circulation, that is, suspended convertibility of paper money into silver, during the 1880s, but the decline in the price of silver led the market to try to convert silver into paper (März, 1968, pp. 220, 257). In August 1892 Austria finally gave up the flexible exchange (off-silver) standard and went on the gold standard. It was assisted by a stabilization loan of 60 million gulden raised in the German, Dutch, and Belgian markets by a syndicate headed by the Creditanstalt and the Rothschilds. Exporters, farmers, speculators, and industries competing with imports resisted the return to a fixed exchange rate but were overruled by the monarchy in the interest of orthodoxy (ibid., pp. 259–62). Schumpeter regarded the movement to gold at this time by Germany, Austria, Italy, and Russia as largely ideological. All interests that really counted were opposed to the move, which was taken because of the prestige of the gold standard, "the symbol of sound practice and badge of honor and decency" (1954, p. 770).

The boom in banking in Austria paralleled that in Germany in various respects, down to the formation of great banks in the 1850s and 1860s, though with foreign capital, whereas German sources of bank capital, except for the Darmstädter with French funds as well as a French model, were almost entirely domestic. There was also the rash of small speculative banks to fuel the building and railroad boom in the early 1870s and the spread of a banking network that integrated the provinces with the central city of Vienna late in the nineteenth century (Good, 1977). Rudolph claims that Austrian bankers were not prepared to take risks to spur economic development, preferring to back established firms that had already accumulated fat profits (1976). The Creditanstalt, founded in 1855 by prominent Viennese financiers led by Baron Anselm von Rothschild who had taken over from his father Salomon the year before, was, however, partly a response to the initiative of one-time Finance Minister Carl Bruck, who wanted to push Austria further down the path from a barter to a money economy. It was followed two years later by the

Niederösterreichische Escomptegesellschaft (Lower Austria Discount Bank) started by David Hansemann of the Diskontogesellschaft in Germany and was, in turn, followed in the 1860s by the Bodenkreditanstalt, founded in 1863 with French money, and by the Anglo-Austrian Bank founded in 1864. A clearinghouse was started in 1864 on the initiative of the Creditanstalt; in the first month, payments of 27.75 million gulden were cleared with the help of 12.75 million in bank notes, suggesting a primitive stage of development of the payments mechanism (März, 1968, p. 126).

Bleichröder, the Berlin banker, thought in 1866 that Austrian military preparations were hampered by inadequate finance (Stern, 1977*a*, p. 79). He was entirely correct. Austria lost the war to Germany (and Italy) in barely a month of fighting. The war loan and the 30 million silver gulden indemnity paid to Germany afterward slowed bank formation. The revelation of a major defalcation (400,000 gulden) in the Creditanstalt produced panic. Thereafter things looked up sharply. A major contributor to the improvement was a bumper harvest in 1867, which kept the railroads inordinately busy, gave them high profits, helped exports, and converted the wartime shortage of *numéraire,* accentuated by the indemnity, into a plethora (ibid., p. 139). The boom led to more bank formation. At the beginning of 1869 there had been four big banks. Thirty-six more banks were formed that year, though the so-called little crisis of 1869 knocked out eight of them. This setback was followed by a new burst of speculative activity—in railroads, building and building sites in Vienna, American railroad shares, and so forth—spilling over from the German *Gründungsfieber* (speculative fever of the year of the founding of the German Reich), and ultimately by the collapse of May 1873.

The Austrian banks were at the height of their power just before World War I after the currency disorders left over from the 1873 stock market crash had settled down. The Credit Anstalt, which had controlled two industrial companies in 1890, had fifty-seven in 1914. In 1908 its managers sat on the boards of directors of 121 other enterprises (Stiefel, 1986, pp. 81–82).

The difference from English banking may be more apparent than real to an extent, but universal banking with strong connections running back and forth between industry differs at basis from a system based ostensibly on financing trade rather than industry.

Sweden

Space permits singling out only two aspects of Swedish monetary and banking history prior to the twentieth century, in addition to the earlier mentions of the Riksbank and the first issues of bank notes in Europe. The first is the bullionist controversy of the 1760s, half a century before the more widely known debate of similar character in Britain; the second touches the debate whether Swedish financial institutions in 1850 were well in advance of its general economic development.

Between 1739 and 1772, Sweden enjoyed a constitutional monarchy, with two parties contesting for political power—the Hats representing large business and export industry supported by France, and the Caps who stood for small merchants, manufacturing, and importing merchants and who were favored by Russia. The

Hats held power from 1738 to 1765 and undertook strong expansionary policies of what might be regarded today as a Keynesian type, which put pressure on the balance of payments. For a time they sought to stabilize the rixdollar with the help of French subsidies, but a severe crop failure in 1756, plus Swedish entry into the Seven Years' War, overwhelmed stabilization efforts, and the exchange rate (the price of the Hamburg mark banco) went from 112 of parity in 1756 to 247 in 1765. Like the bullionists in England later, the Caps contended that depreciation of the exchange rate was due to expansion of the money supply. In rebuttal, the Hats insisted that depreciation had started with the balance of payments; causation had run from balance of payments to depreciation to rising prices, not from money supply to rising prices to balance of payments and depreciation. The Hats believed in restricting imports to improve the exchange rate and increasing loans to business, even if it meant an enlargement of the money supply, for the sake of expanding production for exports—an early example of supply-side economics. Inflation resulted in the Hats' losing political power in 1765. In 1766 the Caps applied their medicine, which was serious deflationary pressure, believing that this would merely take profits away from the beneficiaries of the depreciation and not hurt employment. When this proved wrong and widespread unemployment was realized, the Hats were returned to power in 1771 but were cut off by a coup d'état of Gustav III in 1772 (Eagly, 1971, pp. 1–21).

A perceptive contemporary lecturer in moral philosophy, the branch of learning that encompassed economics in the period, sorted out the arguments in 1761. Per Niclas Christtiernin, whose lectures read very much like Henry Thornton on *Paper Credit* in 1802 in synthesizing what is valid on both sides, blamed depreciation on the excessive bank note issue but recommended going back to convertibility not at the old par but at existing prices of gold and silver. This was in fact done by Gustav in 1772 (ibid., pp. 22, 36).

The second point about Sweden relates to its proliferation of banking institutions in the 1850s and 1860s, considerably ahead of the rapid economic growth that transformed the country from one of the poorest in Europe to one of the richest in the short period 1870 to 1914. In the middle of the century, Sweden was said to be an "impoverished sophisticate," to use Sandberg's expression. It was, he claimed, far in advance of France, for example, in the use of paper money and bank deposits and not far behind in commercial and other banking, with a well-functioning capital market. In the two decades after 1850, the system was strengthened with the Stockholm Enskilda Bank, an industrial bank, founded in 1856, and by the spread of a network of branch banking throughout Sweden after the removal of some restrictions in 1863 when banks were offered a choice between limited liability and the right to issue bank notes (Sandberg, 1978, p. 663). The Stockholm Enskilda Bank went one step further than earlier banks of the same sort in pushing the deposit business, which proved more profitable than bank notes (Flux, 1910, p. 53).

There is some controversy over this characterization, however—over both whether Sweden, in fact, had a highly developed financial system at mid-century and, if it did, whether this made a difference to Swedish rates of growth. On the latter score, the view has been expressed that financial institutions made no difference to Sweden's economic take-off (Gardlund, cited by Stolper, 1966, p. 233n).

The major cause of that rapid growth beginning in 1850, but especially from 1870, was the British repeal of the Corn Laws, the timber duties, Navigation Acts, and other tariffs in the 1840s and 1850s. Swedish farmers sold oats for the horses of London, timber for the British building boom (once the Canadian preference was lifted), and iron to feed the rise of British steel.

Moreover, the evidence that Swedish banking institutions were sophisticated is not conclusive. The leading Swedish economic historian insists that merchant trading houses provided credit to producers of grain, timber, and iron, rather than banks' doing so, and that when the banks did appear, largely after 1856, they were assisted by trading houses, rather than vice versa (Heckscher, 1954, p. 245). There was no capital market (ibid., p. 247) and no credit market (ibid., p. 249). At mid-century the country belonged to the underdeveloped areas of Europe with "a weak money market" (Fridlizius, 1957, p. 266). Banking was "underdeveloped" (ibid., pp. 205–7). The money market had only "a very primitive form of organization" (Söderlund, 1952, p. 198). One observer asks why it took so long for a modern banking system to reach Sweden (Samuelsson, 1968, p. 198), and a general historian characterizes all the national banks in Scandinavia in this period as "limited in their functions and obsolete in their techniques" (Hovde, 1943 [1972], pp. 241–22). Innovations in banking got under way only in the 1860s, and the banking and credit system grew rapidly in importance primarily after 1870 (Dahmén, 1970, p. 64).

Sandberg is surely right on the sophistication of Sweden in literacy and education, compared to other parts of Europe (1979). It is further true that, on occasion, the borrowing of institutions may put them ahead of society's capacity to use them effectively. This is said to occur frequently in political science, with newly independent countries adopting complex constitutions in use in older states and setting up bicameral legislatures before they have learned to practice democratic methods. Demonstration effect occurs in consumption as well—that is, the adoption of items of consumption from high standards of living before an economy has acquired the capacity to earn the income with which such items are usually associated. Developing countries have even adopted the statutes of modern central banks at the behest of advisers such as Kemmerer, Niemeyer, or Triffin. In Swedish finance, however, the weight of the evidence seems to be against singling out the nineteenth-century experience as an exception to the Coase theorem that institutions respond to need. Institutions may lag, as in the case of Hanseatic banking and insurance, which were nonexistent, or in France, if the revisionists are right who claim that French economic development was up to, or ahead of, that of Britain—when its financial institutions lagged by roughly a century. At first glance, it seemed that Sweden might be a case where institutions led. A second look makes this doubtful (Kindleberger, 1982).

One distinctive feature of Swedish industrial banking, as it developed before the war, was the predominance of long-term deposits, as opposed to current accounts used for making payments. In 1913 approximately 66 percent of total deposits, or 87 percent if savings deposits are included, were long term in nature. Competition among banks raised the rates offered to savers, who financed industry through the banks rather than through purchases of shares, as compared, for example, with the practice in Britain (Montgomery, 1939, pp. 126–27)

Switzerland

The Swiss case also cannot occupy us long. Interest in its historical development turns on the slowness with which a federal state built a unified banking structure with a central banking place. The country was long divided into independent cantons with a variety of political structures—democracies in the poor Alpine districts, patrician aristocracies in the plains, corporative oligarchies in commercial cities, and an assortment of monarchies and aristocracies, secular and ecclesiastical, absolute and qualified, in mixed cases (Rappard, 1914, ch. 1). The cantons, moreover, perceived an independent currency standard as a sign of state sovereignty (Ernst, 1905, p. 16) and yielded it to the federal state only slowly and reluctantly.

Geneva was the first major banking center in Switzerland. Together with Amsterdam, it financed Louis XIV in the War of the Spanish Succession. Its bankers, many of them ejected from France by the Revocation of the Edict of Nantes in 1685, grew in numbers from one in 1698 to a dozen by 1709 and were deeply engaged in the South Sea and Mississippi Bubbles of 1718–20 (Lüthy, 1959, Vol. 1, ch. 3). During the eighteenth century, they formed close relations with the Swiss nation in Lyons, the ports from Marseilles to the Atlantic and the Channel, and with Paris. During the French Revolution, Swiss bankers retreated from the French ports to Geneva, until French occupation in 1798 drove them farther inland. With the return of peace, fifteen out of twenty-two of the *hautes banques* of Paris were of Geneva origin (Lévy-Leboyer, 1964, p. 432n). A Swiss echo of the Crédit Mobilier, entitled the Banque Générale Suisse de Crédit Internationale Mobilier et Foncier, was started in 1853 and liquidated in 1865 (Iklé, 1972, p. 15).

A second early Swiss financial center aimed in a different direction, toward the Rhine valley to the north, and to both France and Germany, as far as Karlsruhe and Stuttgart on the German side, and to Mulhouse, Strasbourg, Besançon, and Nancy on the French. The Alsatian textile center, Mulhouse, was even called the daughter of Basle finance (Gille, 1970, p. 88). Basle became the site of the Schweizerischer Bankverein (Swiss Bank Corporation), formed in 1895 out of the Basler Bankverein and the Zurich Bankverein. It was also chosen in 1930 as the location of the Bank for International Settlements, to be encountered later, because of its pivotal railroad connections—this a few years before the shift of bankers to air travel—with Germany, France, Switzerland, and, through the Simplon and Gotthard tunnels, to Italy.

These older financial centers were ultimately dominated by Zurich, which rose to power partly as the result of the efforts of one man, Alfred Escher, "the strongest personality in economic and political life at the time" (Iklé, 1972, p. 18). Escher was president of the Swiss Creditanstalt, formed in 1856 with half its capital from Germany, of the Northeastern Railroad, and promoter of the Gotthard tunnel to Italy. He repulsed a threat to the dominance of his city, bank, and railroad by Winterthur and gradually built Zurich into an international banking center connected with all parts of Europe and the world, in contrast to the more regional-oriented Geneva and Basle. The big Zurich banks all developed in the twentieth century. The Swiss National Bank was formed in 1907 by merging four note-issue banks.

The federal organization of Switzerland, rooted in history and consolidated in the national constitution of 1848, is reflected in the banking structure also through a strong system of cantonal banks. Unlike the discount banks, the big three of which ended up operating in all three major cities—Zurich, Geneva, and Basle—the cantonal banks must stay put, in their native cantons. The discount banks lend on domestic and international bills of exchange. Roughly 30 percent and 7 percent of their assets, respectively, were devoted to these sorts of obligations before World War I. The cantonal banks, on the other hand, loaned largely on mortgages, which constituted about half their assets in 1910 (Jöhr, 1915, p. 456). The cantonal banks dominated Swiss finance by size until neutrality in World War I and dealing with both sides gave the discount (deposit) banks their opportunity really to expand.

The cantonal banks belong to the Swiss confederation; the larger banks of Basle, Geneva, and Zurich to Europe or the world. Like the Banque de Pays-Bas, formed in Amsterdam to operate in France, the major Swiss banks and Swiss private banks have always been more or less Euro-currency banks, operating perhaps mainly in France but in significant part in Germany and from Lugano in Italy. With the rise of the Euro-currency market in the 1960s on a far wider scale, Switzerland came into its own as an international banking and financial center, to use the title of Iklé's book (1972).

SUGGESTED SUPPLEMENTARY READING

Riesser (1911), *The Great German Banks and their Concentration.*
Tilly (1966), *Financial Institutions and Industrialization in the Rhineland, 1815–1870.*
Whale (1930 [1968]), *Joint-Stock Banking in Germany.*

In German

Blumberg (1960), Die Finanzierung der Neugründungen und Erweiterungen von Industriebetrieben.
Born (1977), *Geld und Banken im 19. und 20. Jahrhundert.*
Helfferich (1921–23 [1956]), *Georg von Siemens.*
März (1968), *Österreichische Industrie- und Bankpolitik in der Zeit Franz Josephs I, am Beispiel der k.k. priv. Österreichischen Creditanstalt für Handel und Gewerbe.*

8

Italian and Spanish Banking

> Here is a truly vicious circle because great savings are possible only with intense productive activity and this is not possible without an abundance of capital.
>
> (Ellena, *La statistica di alcune industrie italiane*, 1880)

ITALY

Italy Before Unification

Like Germany, Italy was badly fragmented politically until the *Risorgimento* (national revival) of the nineteenth century. There were city-states like Genoa whose star had started setting in 1620, mini-states, divided kingdoms, and especially foreign domination of large portions of its territory—by Austria in Venetia and Lombardy, Spain in Naples. The pope had spiritual power everywhere but temporal authority in the Papal or Pontifical States. Metternich summed it up in the view that Italy was not so much a country as a geographical expression.

As in Germany, too, political unification began with tariffs. In 1847, largely as a response to the Zollverein, the Kingdom of Sardinia, consisting of Piedmont and the island of Sardinia, joined with Tuscany and the Pontifical States to form a single tariff unit. Austria refused to let Lombardy or Venetia take part, and the Kingdom of the Two Sicilies, represented largely by Naples, abstained. The Tuscan city of Leghorn played the role of Hamburg in insisting on retaining its status as a free city. It was far behind Hamburg in financial development. There was a variety of weights and measures and, in the absence of a discount bank like the Bank of Hamburg, transactions were denominated in a variety of currencies—pesos, ducats, escudos, francs, lire, and pecchini. No attempt was made to provide a deposit bank. Proposals for a discount bank went back to the eighteenth century, became serious in 1815, and were finally realized in 1836. Even then, it had no great success; commission agents diverted bills of exchange to private discounters who paid higher commissions (Lo Romer, 1987, pp. 137–41).

The monetary position in Leghorn was duplicated throughout Italy. By the time of unification, there were hundreds of old currencies that had to be replaced and converted into the new lira, as not only provinces but also towns had their own coins with different weights, different metals, different systems of division. The province of Tuscany, which included Leghorn, had twenty-four such currencies. Unification of the currency, like that of the country, came in stages with four currencies circulating initially—the Napoleonic lira of Piedmont, the new lira of Parma, the Austrian florin of Lombardy and the Roman escudo. Ultimately in

Map 4 Italy at the time of Unification

August 1862, following unification of the country in 1861, the lira of the Kingdom
of Sardinia, which had played the leading role in unification under Count Cavour,
took over the country just as the thaler of Prussia, or the fraction of it called the
mark, did in Germany. (The Kingdom of Sardinia was formed at the Congress of
Vienna in 1815 from that island, Piedmont and Liguria, which includes Genoa). A
new coin, the silver escudo, was minted, equal to 5 lire (as opposed to the old
Roman escudo equal to 5.32 lire—Luzzatto, 1963, Vol. 1, pp. 60–61). The lira was
made equal to the franc because of French influence in Piedmont. The decimal
system, which already existed in Lombardy, Sardinia, Rome, Tuscany, and
Naples, was adopted. The gold/silver ratio was fixed at the French rate of
15½ to 1.

Central banking proceeded in Italy with even more of a lag than in Germany. The Banca Nazionale degli Stati Sardi (National Bank of the Sardinian States) was formed in 1850 from the Banks of Genoa and Turin. With Italian unification in 1861, this was converted into the Banca Nazionale del Regno d'Italia, which then absorbed the Banca degli Stati Parmensi (State Bank of Parma) and the Banca per le 4 Legazioni (Bank of the Four Legations). In 1867, after Venezia had been taken from Austria in the Austro-Prussian War of 1866, the Banca del Regno took over the Stabilimento Mercantile di Venezia (Venetian State Bank) (De Mattia, ed., 1977, Vol. 3, pt. 1, p. 37).

During this time, banks of issue were being built in other Italian states. The Cassa di Sconto di Livorno (Discount Bank of Leghorn) had had a stormy history in the Revolution of 1848 and later defeat of the city by the Austrian army. In the emergencies, it made substantial loans to the municipality, then to the state government in Florence, and strained its financial capacity to the limit. The years from 1853 to 1856 were active in trade, partly as a consequence of the Crimean War, and the bank had to be helped out by the government. It was closed for a month and infused with government funds in exchange for trade bills. In 1857 it and the Cassa di Sconto di Firenze (Discount Bank of Florence) were forcibly merged into a new Banca Nazionale Toscana, to the disgruntlement of many of the Leghorn stockholders who felt their city had been humiliated (Lo Romer, 1987, pp. 138, 249). A second smaller bank of issue was started in Florence in 1860, the Banca Toscana di Credito per le Industrie e il Commercio. In the early years of unification, the Banca Nazionale Toscana proceeded to absorb small discount banks in other cities of the province, some with ancient banking tradition—Siena, Arezzo, Pisa, and Lucca. When unification extended to the Pontifical States in 1870, the Banca degli Stati Pontifici (Bank of the Pontifical States), founded in 1850, was converted into the Banca Romana. Other banks of issue were the substantial Banco di Napoli and the much smaller Banco di Sicilia.

The Banca Nazionale del Regno was interested in establishing branches in all principal towns, while other banks of issue stayed within provincial limits. A problem arose during the period of forced circulation from 1866 to 1881; when they appeared in other provindes, local bank notes had to be exchanged on a barter basis, one for one, because no remainder could be converted into coin. The Banca Nazionale del Regno absorbed the two Tuscan banks of issue and the ailing Banca Romana into a newly created Bank of Italy in 1893, some thirty years after the process of unification had begun and twenty-three years after its completion. The Banco di Napoli and the Banco di Sicilia retained note-issue privileges all the way to 1926.

The First Wave of Foreign Banks

Unification gave impetus to a new wave of imports of foreign capital, both direct borrowing abroad by the new government and via foreign banks. There were three banks of ordinary credit (equivalent to joint stock banks) in 1862. Thirteen new ones were created between 1863 and 1866. Among them were the Anglo-Italian Bank, formed by the Ricasoli family and the British ambassador, the Società Generale di Credito Mobiliare created by the Crédit Mobilier of Paris, and the Banca di Credito Italiano, formed by the French Crédit Industriel et Commercial with Rothschild money. The most notorious was the Banco di Sconto e Sete (Bank of Discount and Silk). All were formed in Turin, capital of Piedmont, which had been the leader of Italian unification, on the one hand, and had close ties with France, on the other. The Credito Mobiliare moved to Florence in 1865 when the capital of Italy was briefly shifted there, but it later returned.

Unification and the invasion of foreign banks started a boom in Italy, based on railroad construction. It was short-lived. The Italian government had assumed a substantial debt, largely arising from Piedmont's ambitious program of public works in the 1850s and, along with the debt, Piedmont's low tariff schedule, which reduced state income. Commitment to build a unified country required railroad construction, and foreign contractors had to be enticed with privileges and subsidies. The government tried to raise monies by selling off ecclesiastical and Crown lands acquired in the course of unification. The original intention had been to use these lands to improve the highly skewed distribution of agricultural land. Under pressure of fiscal necessity, they were sold originally to middle-class buyers and then, to speed up the receipt of revenue, in a lump to a syndicate supplied with foreign capital, the Società Anonima per la Vendita dei Beni del Regno d'Italia, with the deal sweetened by a grant of a monopoly in matches.

At the time of unification, government debt amounted to 2.4 billion lire, 1 billion inherited from the Kingdom of Sardinia alone. The deficit during the first year was 500 million lire. By the end of 1866, the national debt had risen to 5 billion lire, with 2 billion held abroad, without counting that indirectly owned by foreign banks in Italy. With the supervention of financial crises in Paris in 1864 and 1866, the flow of foreign credit was abruptly cut off, and the country, on 1 May 1866, found itself unable to continue the conversion of lira bank notes into specie. The date coincided with the mobilization of the Prussian army against Austria and preceded by ten days the crash of the Overend Gurney Corner House in London on 11 May. Local historians regard each of these as separate and independent events. Clapham, for example, says that panic and strain in London were strictly British and cites as evidence that the Paris discount rate was only 4 percent, whereas the Bank of England rediscount rate rose to 8 percent on 10 May (1945, Vol. 2, p. 268). By this time, however, the Bank of France had returned to its 1800–56 policy of an unchanged discount rate. What counted was not the price of credit but whether, and how, it was rationed. A sharper crisis had occurred in France in 1864 when the prospect of an end to the Civil War produced a precipitous drop in the price of cotton. Investment in Italy started downward then, recovered in 1865, and fell away completely in the less acute crisis of 1866 in Paris but one in which credit tension was felt throughout Europe.

In return for its freedom from obligation to convert its notes into specie, the Banca Nazionale del Regno in May 1866 lent the government 250 million lire. Or perhaps this is better stated the other way: the government lacked both money and credit. Forced to borrow from the central bank, itself low on reserves, it chose to push the bank into inconvertibility to get cash.

Il Corso Forzoso *(Forced Circulation)*

Forced circulation of the paper lira, that is, abandonment of convertibility into specie and depreciation of the currency, was a traumatic event in a country so little accustomed to paper money and impressed by its dangers by consciousness of French experience under John Law. In 1865 only one-tenth of the money in circulation consisted of bank notes. Such notes were said to stay in circulation no longer than ten weeks on the average before they were presented at a bank window for conversion into silver or gold. With inconvertibility, the agio on gold went immediately to 20 percent, which proved to be the highest level reached during the entire period. Recovery was followed by wide variability, and a second high of 17.65 percent was reached in 1881. Despite uncertainty of the value of Italian money at home and abroad, forced circulation helped Italian financial development in several respects. It spread acceptance of bank notes. It provided protection to Italian industry, which had suddenly been exposed to foreign competition when the low Piedmont tariff took effect throughout Italy. It helped correct the balance of payments. Above all, it gained time for the Italian government while it completed the infrastructure of Italy in railroads and balanced its budget. Heavy governmental deficits of the 1860s absorbed virtually all of the nation's savings outside of agriculture, plus borrowing capacity from abroad, and crowded out demands for capital arising from industry other than railroads and public works.

The capital outflow that led to the *corso forzoso* was largely financed by sales of silver, which, in their turn, helped to depress the price of silver abroad and contributed to the problems of bimetallism in the rest of the Latin Monetary Union.

Evaluating the Success of Franco-Italian Banks

Why did not Franco-Italian banks of the 1860s succeed in producing rapid economic growth as the German banking invasion of the 1890s is said to have done? The Gerschenkron thesis, it will be remembered, is that banks substitute for entrepreneurship in backward countries and he points, as a prime example, to Italy and the German banks—the Banca Commerciale Italiana of 1893 and the Credito Italiano of 1894. But the Credito Mobiliare and the Banca di Credito Italiano of the 1860s were banks, and, according to Gerschenkron, their efforts should have resulted in rapid economic growth. The Credito Mobiliare did not lend much to industry (Luzzatto, 1963, p. 67). It had power to do so; its charter permitted it to participate in subscriptions to public loans, lend to state and local entities, Italian and foreign; trade in securities, public and private, excluding, however, speculation in secret; create all sorts of enterprises—ordinary roads and railroads, canals, clearing and improvement of land, factories, mines, docks, illumination; undertake the merger and transformation of corporations, and the issuance of their securities; collect taxes; make advances on stocks of goods and follow the ordinary operations of banks (ibid., p. 66). In actuality, it made investments mostly in railroads, canals, and purchases of state land, which last failed altogether to stimulate industrial development directly and represented an investment more akin to an annuity.

Was it the nationality of the banks that accounted for the difference between French lack of success in the 1860s and German accomplishment in the 1890s? There were German banks before the 1890s. A Banca Italo-Germanica was founded in Florence in 1871 during the *Gründungsfieber,* moved to Rome, and constructed branches in Naples, Milan, Trieste, and Leghorn, but it speculated unwisely and collapsed in 1874. A Banca Austro-Italiana of 1872 had a similar brief and undistinguished career. Somewhat less specifically Teutonic and longer lived was the Banca Generale founded in 1871 with Milanese and foreign capital (Clough, 1964, p. 125). While the Deutsche Bank had a major role in forming the Banca Commerciale Italiana in 1893, its connection with Italian affairs had begun a decade earlier without spectacular result. In 1883 Georg von Siemens journeyed to Rome to make a loan to that city for 170 million lire, and later in the decade the Deutsche Bank undertook loans for Italian railroads (Helfferich, 1921–23 [1956], pp. 125–26). These efforts produced no industrial spurt. Moreover, it will be noted that the new banks of the 1890s did not long remain uniquely German. The case that nationality was decisive is hard to make.

The Crisis of 1885–93

Return to convertibility in 1881 was made possible by three important changes: (1) near balancing of the government budget, which showed an actual surplus in one year, 1875; (2) consolidation and transfer of 1 billion lire of government debt from the Banca Nazionale del Regno to a consortium of all banks of issue; and (3) a 644 million lire stabilization loan, originally planned to be issued in Paris but shifted to London because of lack of demand in Paris (Lévy-Leboyer, 1977*a*, p. 129). This stabilization loan transferred in specie was available for conversion of bank notes into coin but, like all successful stabilization loans, was not needed because of its availability. On the contrary, it produced a return flow of Italian capital and renewal of foreign lending to Italy, together amounting to 500 million lire in the next four years. Government bonds rose from 88.32 in 1883 to 101.6 in 1886; market rates of interest fell to 4 percent in 1884 and as low as 3 percent on occasion.

New availability of capital seeking investment after the end of governmental crowding out led to some formation of industrial companies and some lending to steel, chemical, and electrical companies. Its major impact, however, was to start a housing boom of the sort that had occurred in Berlin and Vienna more than a decade earlier, and with the same dolorous result. The Banca Tiberina moved its head office from Rome to Turin to get better access to funds there for funneling to Roman building. In 1884 the Banca Napoletana acquired new capital from the Banca Nazionale del Regno and from Genoa, Turin, and Swiss investors, to convert itself into the Banca di Credito Meridionale (Bank of Southern Credit) to take advantage of a new law enabling it to invest in Neapolitan real estate. The Roman bank of issue, the Banca Romana, became deeply involved in real estate speculation in the capital city, as did the Banco di Roma, which had been founded in 1880. The Credito Mobiliare's president, Domenico Balduino, died in 1885, and change in leadership led it into real estate speculation in Rome and Naples. As long as Balduino was alive, the bank's speculations were happy; his successor tried to turn it into a bank of discount, with sad results (Pareto, 1895 [1965], p. 94). Some of the trouble is ascribed to the fact that a substantial inflow of capital from London, which financed the boom, was suddenly cut off in 1887 when Italian loans were seen in the City as risky (Toniolo, 1989, p. 287) and perhaps because of the British boom in brewery and other shares.

The financial crisis climaxing this speculative bubble was precipitated by two events: tariff war between Italy and France that broke out in 1887 and led to a new cut in the flow of French capital into Italy and a sharp drop in the price of Italian bonds in Paris; and the revelation that the Banca Romana had violated limits on its right of note issue with some connivance of government officials. In the crisis, the Banca Tiberina collapsed—its stock going from 600 lire in March 1887 to 35 lire four years later, along with the Società dell' Esquilino, the stock of which went from 294 to 2 over the same period (Pareto, 1895 [1965], p. 8). The Banco di Sconto e Sete approached bankruptcy but was saved by a massive transfusion from the banks of issue as a group. The Banca Nazionale del Regno required government permission to raise the ceiling on its note issue by 50 million lire.

German Banking in Italy

Troubled by low prices of Italian securities on the Paris bourse, Premier Crispi sought help from Germany via Prince Bismarck, who turned to his bankers. An approach was made in April 1889, and help was initially provided by German buying of Italian securities in Paris, with major roles played by Bleichröder, Bismarck's private banker, based on political initiative rather than profit making. This was a prelude to the 1893 formation of new banks—the Banca Commerciale Italian by a syndicate consisting of German and Swiss banks plus the Austrian Creditanstalt, and the reorganization of the Banca Generale as the Credito Italiano by Milanese, along with German, Belgian, and Swiss, investors.

In the initial consortium the Creditanstalt and five German banks—the Darmstädter, Berliner Handelsgesellschaft, Deutsche Bank, Diskontogesellschaft, and Bleichröder—had 10.3 to 12.3 percent each, the three Swiss banks had 2.5 percent, and a scattering of other German banks had 1, 1.5, or 2 percent. Italian investment was limited to two shares owned by Sanseverino Vimercati, the bank's president, to allow him to qualify for a seat on the board. But the bank did not stay largely German for long. Italian shareholdings rose to 17 percent in 1894 and still higher in 1897 when the capital was raised from the initial 20 million lire to 30 million, and the bank absorbed the Credito Industriale of Turin. An increase in capital from 30 million to 40 million lire in 1899 was provided largely by the Banque de Paris et des Pays-Bas (Paribas), giving the French 28.3 percent of the capital and three members of the board. In the first phase of the bank's life there were two committees,—one Italian, meeting in Milan, and a foreign committee with its seat in Berlin. In 1900 the capital was raised by another 20 million lire to 60 million with Paribas taking three-fifths of the new issue and Bleichröder two-fifths. The top ("central") committee of directors was altered to consist of two Italians, two Germans, two French, one Austrian, and one Swiss and presumably moved from Berlin (Confalonieri, 1976, Vol. 3, pp. 3–17).

The new interest of French capital was a result of the commercial treaty of 1898 bringing the tariff war to a close. German readiness to sell is attributed by Gille not to "defiance" but to more productive uses for the capital at home in electricity and mechanical engineering (1968, pp. 71–72, 371).

The crisis of 1893 also saw the end of the Credito Mobiliare, which closed its doors that year, and the founding of the Bank of Italy, produced by enforced amalgamation of the ailing Banca Romana with the two Tuscan banks of issue and the dominant Banca Nazionale del Regno. Just as the Cassa di Sconto di Livorno had resented being forced into the Banca Nazionale Toscana, so the stockholders of the latter resented having their identity submerged in the Banca d'Italia (De Mattia, ed., 1977, p. 37).

One result of the crisis was the shift of financial power in Italy from Turin to Milan. Rome had long been unimportant except as a sinkhole for funds absorbed in building. The Banco di Roma, which remained as one of the big three of the twentieth century, along with the Banca Commerciale Italiana and the Credito Italiano, started out in real estate, went into foreign lending, especially in North Africa, and contributed to industrial financing only in 1900 after the major spurt in Italian growth had gotten under way (Cohen, 1967, p. 368). In the early days it stayed clear of intense competition in northern Italian banking.

1907

One more Italian banking crisis occurred before World War I—in 1907. From 1896 to 1907 Italian industrial growth was rapid, especially in electricity and chemicals in which the Banca Commerciale Italiana and the Credito Italiano were interested. But 1907 saw all banks troubled because they were deep in lending to industrial companies that were not strong enough to earn sufficient profits to expand on their own through autofinancing. Some banks of ordinary credit, moreover, had loaned to companies that chose to speculate rather than use the funds for production. Security prices were bid up from 1901 to 1905. Many new corporations were formed, some fictitious. Twenty-eight of 240 securities listed on Italian stock exchanges at the end of 1906 belonged to companies that had not issued their first statement. They nonetheless had a market value of 215 million lire, with a par value of 149 million, a premium of 44 percent before operations had begun (Bonelli, 1971, p. 21). The stock market stumbled in 1905, recovered, rose again, fell once more in October 1906, and finally plummeted in the spring of 1907, bringing down the Società Bancaria Italiana (SBI).

The SBI was a weak and speculative bank that started in 1898 as the Società Bancaria Milanese, was transformed into Weill-Schott, and finally picked up the husks of the Banco di Sconto e Sete, then in liquidation, in 1904. It raised its capital continuously from 4 million to 5 million lire in January 1899, to 9 million in 1900, 20 million in 1904, 30 million in May 1905, and 50 million in March 1906. Most was done by merger. At each stage new bankers joined the firm. The SBI was supported by the Bank of Italy, which was interested in building up another bank in Lombardy, in Liguria, and, above all, in Genoa. The bank lacked central direction. The Milan office did not know the risks being taken in Genoa (ibid., p. 36).

The precipitant was again a cut-off of external credit, again from France. During the 1880s that culminated in the tariff war, French investors had sold off their old portfolio of securities issued by Italy, Spain, and Portugal and started to buy Russian, southeastern European, and Latin American securities (Lévy-Leboyer, 1977*a*, p. 139). The Italian share of total foreign debt service paid in France fell from 90 percent in 1880 to 54 percent in 1899. With rapprochement in 1898 came new bank penetration. A Banque Générale Italienne was formed in Paris in 1899. Paribas purchases of equity in the Banca Commerciale Italiana have been detailed already. By 1913 the proportion of total Italian debt service paid in France had climbed back to 79 percent, although some of this now reflected income on Belgian, Dutch, and Austro-Hungarian holdings channeled through the Rothschild house in Paris (Milza, 1977, p. 244). By 1907 Franco-Italian financial connections were again strong and critical to Italian financial stability.

The stock market crisis in New York tightened interest rates in London and Paris. Paris stopped lending to Italy. Bonelli states that "colonial countries found themselves suddenly deprived of capital" and had to halt investment projects and reduce industrial output (1971, p. 43). The use of the word *colonial* is evocative, indicating Italian incapacity to provide its own capital needs and dependence on a steady flow of funds from abroad. Industrial banks that provide equity capital to private firms are called "mixed banks" in Italy. They were required because of the underdeveloped state of the domestic capital market, with savings both limited— hence the heavy dependence on foreign capital—and held in highly liquid form as deposits in banks of ordinary credit or mixed banks, rather than in ownership of shares in enterprises or directly in bonds. After World War I this basic weakness of the private capital market led to the transformation of the ad hoc Istituto per la Ricostruzione Industriale (IRI, or Italian Reconstruction Finance Corporation) into a permanent body to make good the weakness of the domestic capital market in the absence of the availability of foreign capital. In 1907 security markets in Italy were thin, with prices moving widely in response to small transactions (ibid., p. 24). The Bank of Italy helped out the SBI in the fall of 1905, held back in October 1906, and finally withdrew in 1907 to allow it to collapse.

Gerschenkron (1962, pp. 87–89) and Cohen (1967, pp. 366–69) point to the success of the Banca Commerciale Italiana and the Credito Italiano in achieving a spurt in Italian economic development at the turn of the century, and Gerschenkron believed that these banks substituted for missing entrepreneurship. It seems more likely that they were a replacement for an ineffective capital market. True, effective entrepreneurs could have made profits, which could have been plowed back into autofinancing; profits in Italy were held down by inappropriate tariff policies—effective rates of protection being negative in many lines as tariffs on raw materials exceeded those on finished goods—and by governmental misallocation of resources through heavy subsidies to railroad construction and operation.

What differentiated French from German banks or the banks of the 1860s from those of the 1890s? For a time I thought that the difference lay in the fact that Italy from 1860 to 1880 was still fragmented by barriers to communication and that instead of having one capital market in this earlier period there were several small and inefficient ones. This presumably was corrected in the 1870s and 1880s by the development of the railroad network for northern Italy. But it is hard to make the case that the national capital market was unified by 1900, if the Bank of Italy could find a necessity for supporting a new bank in Genoa, and two branches of the same bank behaved in different ways. There may also be a difference between "capital deepening" and "capital repression" that has a bearing on the behavior of the Ital- ian capital market in these two periods.

Capital deepening and capital repression are concepts produced in two books relating financial institutions, and well-functioning capital markets in particular, to economic development (Shaw, 1973; McKinnon, 1973). Shaw is interested in financial deepening that increases the ratio of financial assets to gross national prod- uct through additional layers of financial intermediaries. This has the benefit of decreasing lender uncertainty and risk, releasing capital from inferior uses, improv- ing liquidity in the system for lenders, while lengthening loan maturities for bor- rowers. McKinnon's focus is somewhat different—on repression in capital markets representing distortions or preferences imposed by government, or investor failure to maximize because of inadequate information and weakness in communications. It results in preference for large-scale operations such as mining, railroads, and espe- cially investment in government bonds, and it limits access of medium and small entrepreneurs to external finance as opposed to the entrepreneurs' own money and profits earned. Unhappily there is insufficient information to make a choice between repression and shallowness as the explanation of the weakness of the Ital- ian capital market. Goldsmith's data on financial intermediaries do not extend to the period before 1880 (1969, table D-14). On the basis of qualitative impressions, one could say that the Italian capital market suffered from 1860 to at least 1913 from both repression and shallowness.

One major difference in the economic position in the 1890s as contrasted with the 1860s was the flow of immigrant remittances into Italy from abroad, and espe- cially from the United States and Argentina. Bonelli calls it a *deus ex machina* that greatly eased the financial position (1971, p. 51). Instead of having to worry about gold, silver, and foreign exchange, as in 1866 to 1881, the Bank of Italy could focus on domestic banking problems alone; reserves of specie and foreign exchange never declined. Emigration of Italian workers abroad started about 1880 as a response to worldwide decline in the price of wheat and accelerated rapidly in a positive feed- back process. Remittances continued to mount steadily—not, however, without frauds and violations of trust (de Rosa, 1980)—and by 1913 amounted to $500 million (2.5 billion lire) annually, enabling Italy to cut down on foreign borrowing. The steady growth of remittances reduced the vulnerability of the economy to vaga- ries of capital flow.

Were Italian financial institutions inadequate? The difficulty would seem to lie deeper in the sociopolitical fabric—in the weakness of the middle classes who nor- mally respond to economic stimuli, in the weight of the economically parasitical Church, and the continued dominance of feudal values. Government lacked the innovative bureaucracy provided by the Junkers in Germany. When business and banking opportunities presented themselves, they were seized for the most part by foreigners.

SPAIN

Bank of St. Charles

For present purposes, Spanish financial history may be said to begin with the American War of Independence when Spain joined France on the side of the colonies against Britain. It was an expensive decision. British ships cut Spain off from the flow of silver from Vera Cruz in Mexico, and the Spanish government turned to printing vales reales, royal notes, the first paper money in Spanish history. These quickly went to a discount; it was to remedy the problem created by this discount that Francesco Cabarrus, of French origin, developed the idea of forming the Bank of St. Charles, much as John Law at the beginning of the century had urged the creation of the Banque Générale in France to deal with *billets d'état*. The Banco Nacional de San Carlos (Bank of St. Charles) was popularly known from the start as the Bank of Spain, although a successor did not acquire that name formally until seventy-five years later.

The Bank of St. Charles had some features unique to central banks. It was required to supply the army and navy with provisions, for a 10 percent commission, though no interest was paid on arrears, which stretched out longer and longer. It was encouraged to trade in its own stock to widen its appeal to investors. All earnings were required to be paid out as dividends, so that the bank was unable to build a reserve. Stockholders were allowed to borrow the par value of their stock from the bank at a 4 percent interest rate (Hamilton, 1945, pp. 101–5).

The bank got off to a slow start during the war, having a hard time selling its stock despite the favorable terms for stockholders. It nevertheless managed to work the vales reales back to par where they stayed for ten years until war broke out with France in 1793–95, followed by war with England over 1796–1802. These periods were again hard on the Spanish Treasury because of the loss of revenue from the West Indies, cut off from Spain by blockade, and led to fresh issues of vales reales (Barbier and Klein, 1981). In further imitation of John Law, the bank was given the right to form a Compagnie des Philippines for trade with that colony, as the Banque Générale had teamed up with the Compagnie d'Occident in France for trade with Louisiana.

Occupation of Spain by, first, Napoleon and then the duke of Wellington compounded the monetary chaos. Spanish, French, English, and Portuguese coins circulated on the peninsula, but for the most part bad coin, of copper. The vales reales, which had been profitable and reliable for the Treasury, were issued in increasing amounts and ultimately depreciated to 4 percent of their par value. When the government stopped printing them after the end of the Napoleonic Wars, the price level dropped sharply. There was a tremendous shortage of specie. Silver was undervalued at the mint and not offered for minting during the brief period between the end of the war and the loss of Spanish colonies that followed, especially Peru in 1821 and Mexico in 1822. The Bank of St. Charles hesitated to fill the void. Its note issue had never amounted to more than 14 percent of its capital, averaging close to 3 percent. In consequence the bank was reorganized in 1829 as the Banco Español de San Fernando—still popularly known as the Bank of Spain.

The Bank of San Fernando

The Bank of San Fernando had a capital of 60 million reales, 40 million taken over from the Bank of St. Charles. Like its predecessor, it moved cautiously because of memory of failures. Eighty percent of its lending was to the government. The mint tried to cope with the shortage of money by raising the prices paid for gold and silver. Change in the ratio from 15½ to 16 to 1 further undervalued silver, and Spanish silver coins disappeared from circulation. By 1848 half the money in circulation consisted in foreign coins (Vicens Vives, 1969, p. 713). Some help to the balance of payments, to the money supply, and to domestic investment came from repatriated savings of émigrés returning from the former colonies and from personal fortunes made in the still Spanish Cuba (ibid., pp. 724, 727).

Despite selling off aristocratic, civil, and Church land, government depended heavily on the banks. The sale of land was begun not for fiscal purposes but as a progressive reform designed to accommodate growing numbers of landless peasants. It was proposed in the eighteenth century and undertaken spasmodically in the second decade of the nineteenth. Progressive governments pushed forward; reactionary ones pulled back. The pace speeded up in the 1830s and 1840s and came to a climax with the passage of the Disentailment Law of 1855 when Progressives won power for two years. The program achieved certain successes in Catalonia in raising production and incomes among poorer farmers. Most observers hold that the program was a failure, not merely because it increased the holdings of aristocrats who acquired the bulk of the civil and Church land but also because it slowed economic growth by diverting savings away from infrastructure and industry to landholding by technically unprogressive absentee landlords. By themselves, of course, sales of existing assets do not absorb savings unless the seller uses the proceeds for consumption. This the Spanish government did.

A couple of banks were started in Catalonia in the first half of the nineteenth century—the private banking firm of the Marqués de Remisa, founded in 1827 and dealing in bills of exchange largely with the capital of its owner, plus a small volume of deposits, and the Bank of Barcelona, founded in 1844, a note-issuing bank that proved to be well managed and long-lived. The same year saw the founding of the Bank of Isabella II, patterned after the Caisse Générale of Jacques Laffitte of Paris, by the aggressive financier and cabinet minister José de Salamanca. It sought to compete with the Bank of San Fernando by aggressively discounting, lending, promoting industrial ventures, and issuing small-denomination notes. An upsurge of speculation occurred in 1847, followed by a crash, the merger of the two banks into the New Bank of San Fernando, and the passage of legislation, much like the Bubble Act of 1720 in England, restricting the formation of joint stock companies (Harrison, 1978, pp. 44–46). The boom of the 1840s attracted money of former colonists in Spanish America, as well as some European funds, and stimulated railroad building and some industry. The crash seems to be unrelated to the crisis of that year in Britain, or, if connection existed, it was obscured by ties running from England to France, Holland, and German cities (Evans, 1849 [1969]).

The reorganized Bank of San Fernando took over the capital of its two predecessors amounting to 200 million reales and tried to add a like sum in new money.

The public did not respond. In 1851 the bank was reorganized and its capital reduced to 120 million. The bank was split into an issue and a banking department in 1848, after the new pattern of the Bank of England, but these proved to interfere with one another and were telescoped in 1852. As the bank's capital was reduced, questionable loans and assets were collected or written off. From 1852 to 1855 it managed to get its note circulation up to 120 million reales in the boom spilling over from Europe as a whole and resulting particularly from demand for Spanish grain and minerals stimulated by the Crimean War. A change of government from Moderates to Progressives occurred in 1854. While the Progressives lasted in power for only two years, they changed the direction of the economy drastically.

The Boom of 1856–66

Spain adopted the decimal system in 1849, following a worldwide movement that had extended by 1847 to France, Lombardy, Sardinia, Rome, Tuscany, Naples, Holland, Switzerland, Russia, Greece, Portugal, the United States, Mexico, China, Egypt, and Persia (report of John Bowring, 1847, quoted by O'Brien, ed. (1971), Vol. 3, p. 1, 384) but included neither Sweden nor England. A further measure of reform, related to the discoveries of gold in California and Australia, was a law of 1854, allowing coinage of gold—in effect, a shift from silver to bimetallism. The New Bank of San Fernando changed its name officially to the Bank of Spain and was granted the right to increase its circulation. Under the Bank of Issue Act of 1856, provision was made for a bank of issue in every city in Spain, whether a branch of the Bank of Spain or a local bank with the right to issue bank notes up to one-third of its paid-up capital or the bank's reserves of gold and silver, whichever was smaller. New banks were, in fact, established all over Spain—in Málaga, Seville, Valladolid, Zaragoza, La Coruña, Santander, Bilbao, and so on. Most collapsed within a decade, although the banks at Santander and Bilbao still flourish today (Tortella, 1972, p. 111). In 1855 a General Railway Act was passed offering free entry of capital goods, rolling stock and fuel, and eliminating the idiosyncratic restrictions of a 1844 act that limited concessions to ten years, required fares to be revised periodically downward to prevent excessive profits, and set a standard of 6 Castilian feet for the track gauge. And in 1856, a Credit Company Act opened the door to investment companies or banks modeled on the pattern of the French Crédit Mobilier.

The new law produced immediate French response. The Pereire brothers, the Rothschild firm, and one Alfred Prost rushed to form "mercantile societies" and to carve out railroad concessions. The Pereires formed a Credito Mobiliario, with a paid-in capital of 114 million pesetas, which was nearly four times the Bank of Spain's 30 million (at 4 reales to the peseta), the Rothschilds set up a Sociedad Española Mercantile Industrial, and Prost (of the Compagnie Général des Caisses d'Escompte) the Compañia General de Crédito en España. Neither the Rothschilds nor the Prost bank—with authorized capital of 75 million and 100 million pesetas, respectively, set high to enlist Spanish capital to supplement that brought from France—ever had their capital paid up. In addition to these three French firms, thirty-one Spanish credit companies were formed under the law.

The Pereires concentrated on the northern railroad, el Norte, connecting Madrid with Bayonne on the Bay of Biscay and then, via the Chemin de Fer du Midi, with Paris. They would have liked a concession from Madrid to Cadiz, but this was owned by Salamanca, who made it available to the Rothschilds whose other line ran from Madrid to France on the Mediterranean coast via Zaragoza (the MZA). Both railroad companies were financed partly in Spain but primarily in France, with the participation of a number of Belgian banks. The boom raised total kilometers of track in Spain from 332 in 1854 to 5,145 in 1866, absorbing 1.55 billion pesetas in investment, as contrasted with 98 million invested in all Spanish manufacturing in the period (Harrison, 1978, p. 48). Substantial profits in construction were returned abroad. There were no linkages into rail, rolling stock, or equipment manufacture because of the concession to imports in the law. The design of the railroads, favoring interconnections with France rather than optimum interconnections among Spanish population centers, had overtones of colonialism (ibid., pp. 52–53). Close to 90 percent of all investment (presumably infrastructure and industry) from 1854 to 1866 was made in railroads. When the boom collapsed, the railroads were all dressed up but with no place to go—that is, little passenger or freight traffic to haul.

The collapse started in 1864 when the Spanish government stopped paying railroad subsidies. The Pereire Credito Mobiliario pulled out of Spain for a time, partly as a consequence of the French crisis of 1864. It was followed in 1866 by withdrawal of the Prost interest and in 1868 by the retreat of the Rothschilds. The Bank of Spain not only failed to act as a lender of last resort in the crisis touched off by this reversal of capital flow; it withdrew liquidity from the market. Monetary circulation had peaked in 1864 and went sharply down thereafter. The number of banks fell from fifty-seven in 1864 to thirty-three in 1869 and thirty in 1870. When the Rothschilds withdrew, not one mercantile company of the thirty-four at the peak was left. On top of domestic deflation, the balance of payments turned adverse. Between capital withdrawals and domestic deflation, the interest rate went from 6 to 12 percent between 1864 and 1866.

Modernizing the Monetary System

As the peak of the crisis passed, the Spanish government sought to bring the country into line with the Latin Monetary Union, changing from the real to the peseta as unit of account, and to official bimetallism. This latter failed to endure, however. The fall in silver prices in the market was interpreted in Spain as a rise in the price of gold, and in 1873 the country stopped coining gold, going de facto on the pure silver standard in 1876. Reform of the banking law in 1874 gave the Bank of Spain a monopoly of the note issue and increased its legal limit. Many of the small note-issuing banks were absorbed into the national bank. From 1874 to 1889, the note issue of the Bank of Spain increased tenfold, from 72 million to 735 million pesetas. Only a small portion of the increase was the result of absorption of smaller banks. For the most part, the notes were a substitute for gold and silver coin in circulation, which decreased drastically (Sardá Dexeus, 1948, p. 202).

LESSONS OF THE ITALIAN AND SPANISH CASES

In their first book on banking and economic development (1967), Cameron, Patrick, and their teammates studying the banking histories of England, Scotland, Belgium, France, Germany, Russia, and Japan concluded that appropriate financial institutions, and such energizing institutions as the Crédit Mobilier, were of great help in the process of development. In a second book (1972), when the cases of Austria, Italy, and Spain were added, the earlier conclusion was modified. Gerschenkron's thesis that banks could substitute for entrepreneurship had to be watered down. Banks might be necessary; they were not sufficient to achieve economic development. In Italy and Spain they produced big railroad networks, but these were fiascos, resulting in no development in the first instance, though later some progress was made with German banks (Cameron, ed., 1972, p. 14). In Spain, and to some extent in Italy, economic development was in fact set back a generation. Banks were needed, but so was an adequate sociopolitical matrix of laws, regulation, and custom in which they operated and appropriate government policies. Like France in the eighteenth century, Spain was a dual economy with a fringe of commercial cities and Madrid, plus the solidly agricultural interior. Italy's duality divided on north-south lines. In Italy, it can be argued that the railroad network produced by French banks permitted northern goods to move south more readily and increased the disparity in the country, rather than working to close the gap. A weaker case of the same sort applies in Spain.

Unasked in the Cameron studies was whether it makes a difference whether the banks are run by foreigners or by local financiers. Cameron's earlier study of the Crédit Mobilier (1961) led him to the conclusion that that French bank helped speed development in Germany, Sweden, and Austria and presumably in Italy and Spain. Later studies from the perspective of the host country reveal less certainty because of the Italian and Spanish cases.

Having discussed money and banking in western Europe up to World War I, we now turn back some distance to deal with finance more generally, and especially with government and private finance, plus foreign lending and financial crises.

SUGGESTED SUPPLEMENTARY READING

Cohen (1966 [1977]), *Finance and Industrialization in Italy, 1894–1914.*
Hamilton (1945), The foundation of the Bank of Spain.
Harrison (1978), *An Economic History of Modern Spain.*
Luzzato (1957 [1969]), The Italian economy in the first decade after unification.

In Italian

Bonelli (1971), *La crisi del 1907.*
Confalonieri (1976), *Banca e industria in Italia, 1894–1906,* 3 vols.
De Mattia (ed.) (1977), *Storia del capitale della Banca d'Italia e degli istituti predecessori,* 3 vols.

III
FINANCE

Part III follows up the history of money and banking in Europe to 1914 with a rather inchoate batch of subjects on finance: one chapter on government finance, two on private finance, three on foreign lending, and one dealing with financial crises.

The discussion of government finance in Chapter 9 goes back to early modern times—the seventeenth century—and treats the development of efficient systems for collecting and spending taxes out of the rudimentary devices previously in effect and the development of a market for government debt. Prior to the change on the first score, the king raised revenue partly by selling offices and honors and relied on individuals working for their private gain to undertake the government's expenditure and tax collection. The experience of major countries differed. The "financial revolution" in England not only changed the mechanics of governmental receipts and payments but took the final decision from the king and gave it to Parliament. It was achieved peacefully after the Glorious Revolution of 1688 that replaced the Stuarts with William and Mary of Orange. In France a series of attempts at reform in the eighteenth century all failed, and the changes were not completed until after the French Revolution and the Reign of Terror in which twenty-eight *financiers* were guillotined. Strong government in Prussia with a strong bureaucracy manned by working nobles—the Junkers—obviated the necessity for convulsive change in governmental finance and missed out on an opportunity for democratic political evolution. The contrast of the three experiences suggests that institutions are not entirely responsive to real economic forces but are shaped to a considerable degree by the cultural-political makeup of a society.

Private finance's two chapters deal first with individuals, families, their wealth, and the single proprietorship in Chapter 10 and incorporation in Chapter 11. In the former, central themes are the diminishing appetite for risk as income and wealth grow, the shift from commercial success to either finance or the life of ease, and growing preoccupation with protecting the economic well-being of widows and orphans and with what that meant for the character of investments. A long digression on insurance arises out of the discussion of risk, with some attention to the efficiency of financial, as opposed to "real," spreading of risk. The point is further made that the early stages of the industrial revolution did not require much capital formation through banks, except for some working capital. The aristocratic predilection for conspicuous consumption, including flamboyant risk taking in gambling, meant that a considerable amount of capital accumulated by those mounting the socioeconomic ladder was consumed by those on the way down.

Chapter 11 deals with the rise of the corporation, which became general virtually simultaneously all over western Europe after the middle of the nineteenth century as the factory, railroads, and larger ships, iron-clad and powered by steam, outstripped the capacity of local capital markets to provide finance. Between the large amounts raised in the central capital market and the small brought forward by local enterprise and individuals, there may have been a gap not filled by the spontaneous creation of innovative institutions. A connection running from Chapter 10 on individuals and risk through the corporation and capital market to foreign lending is whether the central capital markets of London and Paris, but not Berlin, starved local industry of capital in their fascination with foreign loans, partly based on the mistaken belief that government securities—the obligations of practically any government—were safer than industrial investments and therefore suitable for inclusion in trusts.

The three chapters on international transactions again present organizational difficulties. Chapter 12 is largely historical in dealing with foreign lending successively by Amsterdam, London, Paris, and Berlin. Chapter 13 treats the transfer across national boundaries, and from one money to another, of indemnities, subsidies, and, in one case, enormous profits, leading up from earlier, relatively small, but complex instances to the Franco-Prussian indemnity of 1871–72, the largest single financial operation in the world to its time. Chapter 14 addresses a series of analytical points that are necessary to an understanding of the history of foreign lending. It concludes with a comparison between London and Paris, which, from the Napoleonic Wars to 1914, were rivals for preeminence as the leading international financial center.

The final segment of Part III, Chapter 15 on "Financial Crises", is related to the Banking of Part II, the private finance of Chapters 10 and 11, and to several of the striking financial successes in transferring monies internationally. A model is adduced of an exogenous shock to the system, followed by overoptimistic calculation of the newly opened profit possibilities, excessive speculation based on expanded credit, and a rush out of money into real or long-term financial assets, supported by debt. The initial stimulus may be economic or political; the objects of speculation may be commodities, innovations such as canals or railroads, land, buildings, domestic or foreign securities, and the like. At some stage, credit is seen to be stretched too tightly. When, and if, the crisis breaks, the danger is that a rush out of real or long-term financial assets back into money and debt repayment may turn into a panic if the money supply is limited. It then behooves a lender of last resort to make money available, under conditions. It is of interest that in much modern monetary theory, based for example on rational expectations, financial crises are impossible, and there is no need for a lender of last resort. The historical record shows abundantly, in contradiction of such theories, that financial crises are a persistent phenomenon and that they are generally, but not always, alleviated by a lender of last resort, often one that insisted in advance that it would not come to the rescue.

9

Government Finance

> Indeed, if we fix our attention on the immense credit which is enjoyed by England, and which constitutes at this day her principal force in the war, we shall not be hasty in attributing it entirely to the nature of her government. . . .
>
> But another cause of the great credit of England is, indubitably, the public notoriety to which the state of her finances is submitted. . . The Money-lenders, being thus regularly made acquainted with the proportion maintained between the receipts and disbursements are not rendered uneasy by those chimerical suspicions and fears which are the inseparable concomitants of a more dignified conduct.
>
> In France the state of the Finances has constantly been made a matter of mystery.
>
> (Necker, *State of the Finances of France Laid before the King,* 1781, pp. 2–3)

FINANCIAL REVOLUTION

In the economic history of western Europe the center of attention is usually the industrial revolution of the eighteenth and nineteenth centuries. There is occasional reference to an earlier industrial revolution from 1540 to 1640 (Nef, 1945), and the inference from the title of Phyllis Deane's book, *The First Industrial Revolution* (1965 [1979]), is that others have followed. Deane's chapter headings make clear, moreover, that the industrial revolution was preceded, or accompanied, by other revolutions—in commerce (not the first, however, which went back to the Middle Ages), transport, agriculture, and demography. Like most other economic historians, she ignores the existence of, or need for, a financial revolution.

The term *financial revolution* might refer to major change in banking, as with the rise of the London and country banks in eighteenth-century England. One offhand assertion by a historian of French finances states, in fact, that the industrial revolution in Britain was based on an earlier revolution in banking (Dent, 1973, p. 21). For the most part, however, *financial revolution* refers to a large structural change in public finance, whether in the locus of power to tax and the kinds of taxes used, in institutions for collecting and spending government revenue, or in handling of government debt. The focus of this chapter is largely on the last two subjects, and especially on public credit in England, and the system of treating governmental income and outgo in France as the private domain of *officiers* and *financiers,* who bought the right to collect or disburse royal funds and treated it as a private enterprise, operated for profit. In particular, we shall deal with two books, P.G.M. Dickson's *The Financial Revolution in England: A Study in the Development of Public Credit, 1688–1756* (1967), which relates the change not to the industrial revolution but to Britain's ability to defeat France, a country with three times its population, in war after war in the eighteenth century; and to J. F. Bosher's *French Finances,*

1770–1795: From Business to Bureaucracy (1970), where the thesis that the French Revolution was necessary to convert a venal system of government finance to one more efficient and less corrupt is implied in the dates and the subtitle. Note well that the financial revolution of England preceded that of France by a century and that the view that British military success was owed to its financial capacity is matched by the statement that financial incompetence of the French monarchy was the main reason for its ultimate collapse (Dickson, 1967, p. 11). Note, too, that the necessity to alter a system of private business in the king's finances provides a possible counterexample to the North and Thomas thesis (1973) that progress in economic development is achieved only when property rights become clearly defined in private ownership.

DUTCH FINANCE

There was no financial revolution in Holland. Frequent wars made taxes heavy, and domination of society by the commercial oligarchy ensured that taxes were levied not on trade but on consumption. In the usual view, this raised wages and inhibited industrial development (Mokyr, 1977; Wright, 1955). The Dutch were far ahead of the British in funding debt and spreading it widely among savers. There were annuities—for life or thirty or thirty-two years—bonds, lottery loans, and the like but no splitting up of debt to assign it to particular revenues as contrasted with the corpus (full faith and credit) of the state's income. Confidence, especially confidence in the honesty of financial administration, seldom slipped and was always quickly restored. Sir William Temple, the English ambassador, noted that 65,500 Dutch *rentiers* invested in governmental annuities (C. Wilson, 1968, p. 34). The principal deficiency was secrecy, and lenders did not have a clear view of the government budget (Ehrenberg, 1986 [1928], pp. 350–52). Without any revolution Dutch finances evolved toward those of a modern state, insofar as management of debt was concerned, as early as the seventeenth century.

Nor was there significant traffic in offices. The basic reason was that with land in short supply and nobility weak, the Dutch bourgeoisie did not seek advancement into the nobility through purchase of offices, a fact noted as early as 1675 by the literary French merchant Jacques Savary. Instead, successful merchants stayed in commerce, as did their children (Barbour, 1950 [1966], p. 141). Tax farming gradually died out in the middle of the eighteenth century, but it had not been scandalous before that time (Ehrenberg, 1896 [1928], p. 351).

THE POWER TO TAX IN ENGLAND

England had two revolutions in the seventeenth century: the Civil War, led by Oliver Cromwell from 1642, and the Glorious Revolution of 1688, when William of Orange was invited to succeed the deposed James II. Both were connected with the division of financial power between monarch and Parliament and with such arbitrary and irresponsible acts as Charles I's seizure of the treasure deposited in the mint in 1640, and Charles II's Stop of the Exchequer in January 1672 (see p. 47). Together they produced a drastic reduction in the power of the king to spend monies raised by taxation or borrowing and a shift of control to Parliament. Neither revolution by itself produced significant immediate change in handling of royal revenues or funding of debt.

OFFICES AND HONORS IN ENGLAND

It was a commonplace that Tudors and early Stuarts had to administer a modern state with medieval methods of finance (R. Ashton, 1960, p. 15). Ordinary expenditure of the Crown was that for the royal household, guards and garrisons, and regular expense. This was met by regular taxation. Extraordinary revenues were expected to be voted by Parliament to pay for such charges as costs of royal funerals, weddings, coronations, and especially war (ibid., p. 38). Adam Smith explained why states need to borrow for war. Expenditure begins immediately, and even if new taxes are levied, their receipt will be so slow that deficits are inevitable (1776 [1937], pp. 861–62, 871). But taxation and borrowing are not the only expedients available to meet royal extravagance or the cost of war. The sovereign can leave bills unpaid—for a time—although high rates of interest quickly find their way into prices paid by the royal household; he or she can sell off existing assets, whether those already in the royal domain, like Louisiana for Napoleon, those precipitously acquired, as in the case of Henry VIII and the monasteries and their treasure, or assets newly created, such as offices and honors.

Offices and honors were sold not only by the Crown, as in England and France, but also, and on a large scale early, by such a republic as Venice. An inflation of offices had taken place in Venice in 1510 to help finance the troops during the War of the League of Cambrai (F. Gilbert, 1980, p. 30). In the seventeenth century, Venice undertook an inflation of honors that enabled anyone to buy his way into the nobility for 100,000 ducats (Burke, 1974, p. 19).

England went in less for offices, as compared with France, but perhaps more for honors. Lawrence Stone's *The Crisis of the Aristocracy, 1558–1641* (1967) observes that Elizabeth I starved the bourgeoisie of honors, such as knighthoods, and was equally parsimonious in handing out cash gifts and pensions to courtiers. James I reversed both policies. Titles of knight and baronet were first sold against a cash payment of £1,095 and the maintenance of thirty soldiers in Ireland for a year, then granted to courtiers to be sold by them to the highest bidder, or handed out to friends. An enlarged supply brought the going price quickly down to £700 in 1619 and £220 in 1622; the gentry turned its interest elsewhere. Power to distribute titles acquired a cash value; Lionel Cranfield bought the right to create six knights from his unattractive friend, Sir Arthur Ingram, for £373 1s 8d—a curiously odd amount. The estimated yield of the sale of all honors between 1603 and 1629 was £620,000 (ibid., ch. 2). In addition, James I awarded insiders at the court, especially the Scottish peers who had supported his claim to the throne, some £4 million in gifts and pensions.

Sales of offices, as opposed to honors, produced roughly the same total yield over the same years—some £650,000, of which £100,000 went into the pockets of peers and courtiers who had obtained the right of appointment. Official fees for such offices as lord treasurer, cofferer of the household, treasurer of the chamber, mastership of the courts of the wards and the like were a few hundred pounds a year only, but several thousand pounds additional could be obtained from moneylending, sale of lesser offices, New Year's gifts, and bribes (ibid., pp. 192, 206).

TAX FARMING

Among offices there were especially the rights to collect taxes, both customs and excise, to regulate monopolies, and to serve as disbursing agent of the armed forces and the royal household. In England there were special farms to tax sweet wine, currants, alum, and the like, as well as general farms for customs, on the one hand, and excise on the other. A tax farmer bought the right to collect the tax for a stipulated amount, kept what he extracted above that, and had use of the money between its collection and payment to the Lords of Treasury. He often borrowed to buy a particular farm, as an individual or in a syndicate. Or he might be awarded the office in return for a loan rather than an outright purchase. Sir Stephen Fox bought the appointment of his nephew as cashier of customs against a loan to the king of £30,000 (C. Clay, 1978, p. 211).

Justification for tax farming was that the state was relieved of the necessity to create its own machinery, revenues were stabilized, and tax farming created a source from which the state could borrow (ibid., p. 93). Accountants working for private profit were considered to be more energetic, efficient, and economical than salaried administrators (Bosher, 1970, p. 174). In the sixteenth century Sir Thomas Gresham urged a shift from collecting customs through government officials to tax farming, on the ground that young merchants who had engaged in smuggling and knew how to get goods ashore without payment of customs would be more efficient as collectors than government officials, if given the proper incentive (de Roover, 1949, p. 191). In addition there was the agency problem: it was foolish to let poorly paid, venal officials collect small sums (Ehrenberg, 1896 [1928], p. 37). There were ancillary arguments: in a period of rising costs or sticky or declining revenues, government was particularly tempted to sell the collection of its taxes in order to stabilize revenue (Tawney, 1958, p. 93). With tax farming, short-term credit of the state depended less on the credit standing of the sovereign, who was notoriously unreliable, than upon the personal credit of individual financiers (Dent, 1973, p. 63). Tax farming by a central administration, moreover, could be regarded as an improvement on a system under which each province of France kept, for local expenditure, what it needed, or thought it needed, of the taxes it raised, and sent the surplus to the central government (Lodge, 1931 [1970], p. 87). It was also believed that tax monies in process of collection were dead funds and should be circulated to stimulate the kingdom (Bosher, 1970, pp. 93, 109).

There were various ways to improve the efficiency of tax farming. In France the usual method was audit of the farmer's accounts, though the process was slow, taking ten years in the best conditions, and results were often obtained only after the *officier's* death (ibid., p. 250). In England the more usual way was to auction the right to collect the general farm for a limited period, after which it could be auctioned again and sold to the same or a different syndicate. The five-year lease was reduced to three years and in 1628 to one year without, however, producing much change. A Jones-Salter-Garaway syndicate held the customs farm in England from 1604 to 1621, lost it to an Abbot-Garaway-Wolstenholme-Jacob group from 1621 to 1625, which lost it, in turn, to a Pindar group in which Wolstenholme and Jacob joined, and kept it until 1641 (R. Ashton, 1960, ch. 4). The state was often far from maximizing its yield, however, as is clear from the fact that James I would award particular revenues to seven peers, who would immediately turn around and sell the taxes to merchant contractors for a net return to the peers of £27,500 a year. Stone maintains that the system did little harm except for the incentive it provided to the king to levy more customs duties (1967, p. 202). This effect of a tax exists, however, no matter how it is collected.

The reputation of tax farming in England was not as bad as that in France (Tawney, 1958, p. 92), but continuous objection was raised to the system. Many contemporaries pointed out that the profits of the Great Farm (on customs) could have gone to the Crown if it had been able to produce an efficient system of administration (R. Ashton, 1960, p. 79). Sir Arthur Ingram, a customs officer whose interests had turned to selling land from the royal domain and to the court, urged an end to tax farming or keeping leases very short. His biographer observes that he was not being practical, as the strength of the vested interest was too powerful to permit even the most determined and enlightened of reformers to make headway (Upton, 1961, p. 68). Sir John Harrison, a customs expert dismissed by the Long Parliament in 1641, put forward elaborate schemes for direct administration of the customs farm, including management by a commission (R. Ashton, 1960, p. 80; Tawney, 1958, p. 93). Robert Ashton claims that the royal finances were never in sufficiently good shape to make the transition, that the remedy was expensive, and that while customs farming piled up long-run difficulties by vesting public powers in private hands, it partially solved the short-run problem of providing revenue (ibid.).

The Long Parliament started the process of reform; the Civil War advanced it. Charles I had rejected Sir John Harrison's proposals for reform. The Long Parliament prepared a bill to confiscate the estates of the tax farmers but ultimately levied a fine of £150,000, a substantial sum considering that the amounts advanced by the farmers were estimated, perhaps overestimated, at £250,000. Repayment of these advances was delayed until the Restoration in 1661 (ibid., pp. 111–12). This fine and the penalties voted by the House of Commons in 1720 against the culprits responsible for the South Sea swindle (Carswell, 1960, ch. 13) were the nearest that the English came to a Chamber of Justice on the French model.

While the farming system was restored in 1661 with the Stuarts, a financier such as Sir Stephen Fox proved, like Lionel Cranfield in the earlier reign, to be a poacher turned gamekeeper. Fox started out as a courtier, not a merchant, and slowly built his fortune in various offices in the king's household, and ultimately as paymaster of the army. In these capacities, he drew on the receiver-general of the excise and about 1674 came to see the wisdom of combining these offices into a single "Undertaking." When tax collection was slow, he would advance his own money, and monies borrowed by him, to meet the Crown's expenditure, for example in the Third Anglo-Dutch War. Christopher Clay states that the system developed by Fox in the 1660s and 1670s constitutes a neglected chapter in the history of government finance and, while abortive, paved the way for the innovations in tax administration of the eighteenth century (1978, pp. 108–9).

Another vital part of this reform was the subtle shift at the end of the eighteenth century of taxation from goods to direct taxation of land, as the power of the landowning aristocracy declined after 1688. One successful merchant, insurer, financier, and landowner, Sir John Banks, saw his taxes, which prior to 1689 he had not segregated, rise from £789 in 1692 to £1,370 in 1699, and to something like 20 percent of his income from rental property, largely farms, in the last years of his life. Despite his roots in finance rather than the gentry, he did not pass the increase on to his tenants (Coleman, 1963, pp. 179–80).

FUNDING ENGLISH DEBT

Financial revolution in England, according to Dickson, was not the change in the locus of the power to tax or in the structure of taxation, or the shift from farming to central collection, but funding of the national debt. Such funding had taken place earlier in Holland and France. It was required in England because of the shambles of unfunded debt resulting from three Anglo-Dutch wars, the Nine Years' War, and the War of the Spanish Succession. Centralization of tax and expenditure functions in the Treasury followed, rather than preceded, funding even though attempts at reform of the systems of tax farming and separate disbursing agents had taken place earlier. The beneficial effects of the revolution were not only centralization of taxes and expenditure, which followed quasi-automatically and greatly enlarged the capacity of the government to collect the nation's savings. In addition, with growth of a capital market that made government debt liquid, investors became readier to turn away from debilitating investment in land as the only safe asset (R. Davis, 1973, ch. 14).

As earlier explained, establishment of the Bank of England, the South Sea Bubble, and even charter renewals of the East India Company were aspects of this process. One year before the founding of the bank, an attempt was made to raise £1 million by a tontine lottery. (A *tontine,* named after the clerk of Cardinal Mazarin of France, an Italian named Lorenzo Tonti, was an annuity paid to a group of investors who divided it equally among the survivors until the last was dead.) This was a failure, yielding only £108,000. The full million was reached by selling single-life annuities in 1693 and early 1694. In 1694 came a lottery loan of £1 million, in which the rate of interest of investors over the course of the ensuing sixteen years depended upon luck of the draw, with £1 per annum for blanks, and £1,000 a year for the highest prize. This Million Loan was followed in April by the £1.2 million subscribed by founders of the Bank of England (Dickson, 1967, p. 48). In 1696 a new form of short-term debt was introduced, the Exchequer bill, carrying $3d$ interest per day on a subscription of £100, or 4.6 percent a year. This innovation lasted almost 200 years to 1877 when it was replaced by the Treasury bill, invented by

Walter Bagehot, in which interest represented the discount between the price at which the bill was sold and the face amount at which it was paid off (ibid., ch. 14; Sayers, intro. to Bagehot, 1856 [1978], Vol. 9, p. 27).

These funded loans replaced a variety of government obligations that differed from one spending agency to another—seamen's tickets, army debentures (from the Latin for "what is owed"), and especially tallies. These were hazel faggots, notched in a code expressing amount paid into or owed by the Treasury, and then split, with the divided foil given to the depositor or purveyor, and the counterfoil kept by the Exchequer. When the tally was presented for payment, the two were matched and together destroyed (Carswell, 1960, p. 25n). Until the Bank of England started to lend on tallies, discounts on foils in circulation ran from 10 to 36 percent of the face value. Goldsmiths bankrupted by the Stop of the Exchequer in 1672 had improvidently bought large quantities of tallies (at a discount) from purveyors to the government. At the Restoration in 1661, the tally was authorized to bear interest and was accompanied by a payment order, which indicated the priority of payment by the Treasury (Richards, 1965, p. 59), and, as already noted, functioned as money. There were other annuities, both lifetime and for ninety-nine years. But the total picture prior to 1700 was best described as chaotic.

With funding for long-term debt and introduction of the Exchequer bill, markets for government debt broadened and deepened. Government stock, along with the shares of the South Sea Company, the Bank of England, and the East India Company, all three of which were intermediaries between government and their shareholders, created a capital market that could gather national savings and make them available to government. A series of new loans was issued during the War of the Austrian Succession, and in 1749 Parliament accepted a plan of Sir Henry Pelham to convert 4 percent government stock to 3½ percent immediately and to 3 percent by 1757 while making it irredeemable. A first step in the process had been to get Samson Gideon, a leading financier of the period, to undertake conversion of East India Company bonds to 3 percent (Sutherland, 1952, p. 23). The irredeemable issue was the so-called consolidated debt, or "consols" with £57.7 million of various issues called and £50.75 million in consols issued (Dickson, 1967, p. 239). The Glorious Revolution of 1688, in which William and Mary of Holland took over from the Stuarts as king and queen of England, led the Dutch, after the financial revolution, to invest in British government obligations. A further link in the chain was Dutch and British investing in other securities, culminating in 1719–20 in the South Sea Bubble (E. Schubert, 1988).

THE TOTAL FUNDED DEBT

British success in amassing resources for war can be seen in a glance at Table 9.1. The figures differ from those given (up to 1776) by Adam Smith (1776 [1937], pp. 874–75) because his include unfunded debt. The slight rises in some figures between wars, moreover, are caused by funding of previously unfunded obligations.

The British government borrowed 31 percent of expenditure in the War of the Spanish Succession, 37 percent in the Seven Years' War, and 40 percent in the

Table 9.1 British National Debt, 1697–1920

Year	Debt	Annual Interest Charge (£000,000s)	Extraordinary Expenditure
1697	14.5	1.2	End of Nine Years' War
1702	12.8	1.2	
1714	36.2	3.1	War of the Spanish Succession
1739	46.4	2.0	
1748	75.4	3.1	War of the Austrian Succession
1757	77.8	2.7	
1763	132.1	5.0	Seven Years' War
1776	130.5	4.8	
1781	187.8	7.3	American War of Independence
1786	243.2	9.5	Fourth Anglo-Dutch War
1793	244.7	9.5	
1802	523.3	19.5	Napoleonic War
1815	834.3	31.4	Napoleonic War
1828	800.0	29.2	
1853	812.2	27.6	
1860	821.7	26.0	Crimean War
1880	769.9	29.6	
1902	745.0	27.3	
1914	649.8	22.7	
1920	7,831.7	349.6	World War I

Source: Hargreaves (1930 [1966], p. 291).

American Revolution, during the chaotic tenure of Lord North. Thereafter, William Pitt reduced the level to 26.6 percent after 1797 by enacting a 10 percent income tax to supplement the land tax, malt tax, and so on (Binney, 1958, ch. 3). François Crouzet contends that 1797 was one of the most lugubrious years in history: the British invented income tax and the French military conscription.

SINKING FUND

Annuities were self-liquidating after a period of time since the lender got a portion of his capital back with his interest in the annual payment. Adam Smith commented that the *officiers* and *financiers* in France were generally people of mean birth, great wealth, and great pride, too proud to marry their social equals and disdained in marriage by women of quality. They remained bachelors, content to eat up their capital in annuities, in contrast with the wealthy in Britain who saved for posterity (1776 [1937], pp. 871–72). Both facts and social analysis are open to doubt.

For permanent debt, the British have from time to time sought to institute a sinking fund. Lord North retired the debt with budget surpluses and canceled the bonds bought. Pitt made the sinking fund invariable but did not cancel. He thought his sinking fund would constitute his greatest claim to fame (Fetter, 1980, p. 111). Bonds held in the fund earned interest, and if the government were short of revenue, it could resell them to obtain monies outside of parliamentary control (Binney, 1958, p. 118). During and after the Napoleonic Wars, the sinking fund became troublesome and even, on occasion, farcical. In 1810 the government borrowed from the Bank of England to get monies to buy bonds for the sinking fund, in effect monetizing the bonds bought in a fashion akin to open-market operations. It was sometimes thought that the sinking fund worked in peacetime when government ran surpluses but not in war when it had deficits. Acworth insists that it never worked. Proposals were made for its abandonment as early as 1821, and by 1827 it was abandoned (Acworth, 1925, ch. 4).

DEBT CONVERSION

National debt has long been regarded as a burden on society, and some economic analysts take that view today, although most regard its effects as only second order. One way to reduce the debt after a war was a capital levy, and many such proposals were advanced after the Napoleonic Wars, including among the proposers David Ricardo (ibid., ch. 5). None was acted upon. Instead, the technique was adopted of converting the interest rate on bonds issued in wartime to a lower coupon rate after the war. This can be done only if savings have recovered and old bonds have been bid up above par. A heavy weight of high-coupon wartime bonds, however, holds short-term interest rates high as the wartime bonds approach maturity, because investors are irrationally reluctant to buy short-term obligations at substantial premiums over par and to experience nominal capital losses. If the bond is callable, as it usually is, there is thus a benefit to the Treasury in formal conversion to a lower coupon rate before maturity.

One such conversion took place in 1717, another under Pelham from 1748 to 1757, still another from 1823 to 1834. But while the annual cost to the Treasury is reduced, there may well be side effects. In particular, holders of retired debt may not be prepared quietly to accept a lower level of income and, in an effort to prevent this, may switch from government stock into higher-yield and riskier investments. "John Bull can stand many things, but he can't stand 2 percent."[1] Capitalists, no less than ignorant labor in primitive countries, may be "target workers," insistent on achieving a certain level of income.

In 1717, the Walpole conversion contributed to the speculative excitement that led to the South Sea Bubble. No side effects were evident in the middle of the eighteenth century, but again in 1823 and 1824 debt conversion touched off a speculative boom in insurance and, with the success of the Baring indemnity loan to France and the liberation of the American colonies from Spain, a bubble in foreign lending that collapsed in December 1825. Another peacetime conversion under Goschen in 1887 fed the boom in securities that culminated in the Baring crisis of 1890.

1. This nineteenth-century financial cliché is used at least three times by Bagehot (1852, 1856, and 1873 [1978], Vol. 9, pp. 118, 273, 300).

FRENCH *RENTES*

The French *rente* goes back to the sixteenth century. It was not regarded as borrowing but as the sale of a stream of income, a view that enabled it to escape the Church's ban on lending at interest, or usury. The buyer entered into a contract with the seller of the *rente* to pay an immediate capital sum for a series of annual payments stretching out in time. There were perpetual *rentes,* like the consols of Britain, and *rentes viagères* for the lifetime of the buyer, and hence an annuity. Most were callable and were, if not repaid, refunded at a different interest rate for a different period of time. In the seventeenth century, fear of the average investor was not that their *rentes* would not be repaid but that they would be. *Rentes* of private individuals adequately secured were steadier and safer than trade in goods or slaves and equally profitable in the long run, being exceeded in profitability only by tax farming (Forster, 1980, pp. 72–73).

Lending to the Crown, on the other hand, or rather buying one of its *rentes,* was notoriously insecure. As a result, the buyer of a royal *rente* wanted the intermediation of a responsible body that would be accessible and solvent in the event of the Crown defaulting. An early important debt operation was the *Grand Parti* of Henry II in Lyons in 1555 to consolidate the floating debt of France and to raise new money. The plan provided for amortization of capital and payment of interest at forty-one successive fairs at Lyons, that is, over ten years, and assigned repayments to the receivers-general of Lyons, Toulouse, and Montpellier (Van der Wee, 1978, p. 16). An innovative aspect was that it was open to all lenders, large and small, rather than negotiated with a few bankers. It was hence called a *monte,* after the Italian word for *pawnshop.* It was also called the "Bank of Lyons," though it was not a bank in any significant sense, with only one asset—the claim on the king—if many creditors (Ehrenberg, 1896 [1928], pp. 290–304).

In the light of these innovations, the reign of Henry II was regarded briefly as the golden age of French finance, but matters proceeded downhill rapidly after 1558. Payment on the *Grand Parti* stopped that year. The *Petit Parti* followed to consolidate three-quarters of the floating debt by *rentes* issued on the corpus of the city of Lyons. The Crown equally failed to make these good. French kings next sold *rentes* on the Hôtel de Ville (city hall) of Paris, as the center of finance switched briefly from Lyons to that city, until these *rentes* became valueless about 1630 because of overissue. At this stage the state encouraged private *financiers* to intermediate between the public and the Crown.

Parenthetically, public finance in Spain at the time was little or no better. Philip II used to finance his wars by bills drawn in Medina del Campo on bankers in Antwerp, Genoa, or Lyons, to be paid for by delivery of silver from New Spain. Overwhelmed by debt in 1557, he confiscated two silver fleets and consolidated the drafts forcibly, that is, without negotiation, into perpetual *rentes* called *juros* guaranteed by a newly created Casa de Contratación de Sevilla on the basis of its revenues from America. This has sometimes been called the first central bank in Europe. Its only central banking function, however, was to service government debt, and this it did in very staccato fashion. *Juros* were sold throughout Europe between 1561 and

1575, when they were followed by a relentless cycle of Spanish excessive borrowing, default, and forcible consolidation (Van der Wee, 1978, p. 17).

OFFICES AND TAX FARMING IN FRANCE

The kings of France raised money by selling offices to men who either had wealth or could borrow it. As a rule, they were neither aristocrats—nobles of the sword or of the robe—nor practicing merchants. Frequently they were successful merchants *en route* to retirement or sons of merchants who bought an office and hoped with success to make progress through the ranks and end up as a noble of the robe, on the one hand, and rich on the other (Durand, 1971, pp. 187–94). Success might be achieved in administration, as in the case of Turgot who spent seventeen years as an *intendant* (administrative officer) in Limoges, before moving up to the role of a comptroller-general of Louis XVI; or in borrowing, collecting, or spending the king's funds and lending them out; or even investing them in private business, while they were in the *financier's* possession.

There were stages of progression, from straw man, who lent his name to a *financier* lending to the state to conceal the latter's identity, *traitant,* who held a lower office, *munitionnaire* contracting for the armed services, *officier* in one of many sorts of office, farmer-general (raising taxes), and receiver-general (holding and dispensing them) (Dent, 1973, p. 132). A *traite* was a contract between the king and the *traitant.*

Prices for offices ran from 25,000 livres (£1,000 at that time, perhaps $25,000 today) to be a secretary of the king, a somewhat empty honor with no financial duties; 150,000 to 200,000 livres for a *maître des requêtes,* who judged petitions from individuals and corporations for royal letters patent; 200,000 for *intendant des finances;* 450,000 for controller-general in 1657; the same amount for superintendent of finances of the queen in 1659; to 850,000 to 900,000 as secretary to the councils, and 1 million as secretary of savings (ibid., pp. 144, 165–66).

Every French city had an assortment of twenty to twenty-five treasurers or receivers who kept government funds divided into many separate *caisses* or cash accounts. The price for a receivership was 100,000 livres and for the post of receiver-general five times that amount (Bosher, 1970, pp. 79, 140). There were 418 receivers who collected taxes on people and land—the capitation, *taille* (on land), and the *vingtième* (one-twentieth of the income of land)—divided into forty-eight generalities. The General Farm collected taxes on production and movement of goods, including the salt and tobacco tax and tolls. The office of treasurer of France at the local level with as many as thirty-five in Montauban or Toulouse, or as few as six in Nantes, administered property of the king, supervised public highways, assessed the tax on land (the *taille*), and received formal declarations of seigneurial rights and patents of nobility. In 1721 it cost 50,000 livres. Paul-Charles, the son of Paul-François Depont, merchant and shipowner at Nantes, stayed in Nantes as treasurer. His son went to Paris, first as *conseiller de Parlement,* an office costing 48,000 livres in 1748, and then *maître de requêtes* for 100,000 livres, before becoming *intendant,* first at Moulin, then Metz (Forster, 1980, pp. 15, 51, 118).

Munitionnaires took on separate contracts to supply the army. The *commissionaire des vivres* (foodstuffs) might engage in contracts running up to 10 million livres. Cardinal Mazarin was the leading such contractor in the 1640s. A certain Fargues, who served defective food to the army, was hanged (Dent, 1973, pp. 140, 161).

The theory was that one could take the government, break down its functions into separate operations, and establish each one as a profit-making operation in charge of a profit-maximizing entrepreneur, who paid a capital sum for the opportunity. The trouble with the system was that it ignored the greed and corruption of some ambitious men and the fact that there were linkages among the various functions of government. *Officiers* and *financiers* were for the most part rich, the king continuously short of funds through overspending. When the king borrowed for one pocket, he often did it from another at great expense for interest that went to the *financier,* not to him. Some *financiers* were corrupt; others were careless and would go bankrupt in some enterprise that wasted monies owed the Crown (Bosher, 1970, pp. 183, 191, 314, etc.).

Many tried to reform the system: Colbert in 1661, John Law in 1718–20, Turgot in 1776, Necker in two attempts, from 1777 to 1781 and again in 1788–92. All failed. It was left to the guillotine and the *assignats* to change it. Thirty-five farmers-general were arrested, and on 8 May 1794, twenty-eight were executed, including among them the scientist Lavoisier (Chaussinand-Nogaret, 1970, p. 315). Lavoisier had started out in 1768 buying one-third of the investment of François Baudon, one of the sixty farmers-general, for 520,000 livres—340,000 in cash and the rest in bills endorsed by his father. In 1774 he took a larger share and, active in management as well as participating financially, specialized in administering the excise on goods coming into Paris. His scientific work was limited to early morning and evening, plus one full day a week. For the rest, he was deeply engaged as a *financier* and administrator, including the administration of gunpowder, and under sentence of the guillotine, assembled the accounts of the farmers-general to defend them against corruption (Gillespie, 1980, pp. 60–66).

CHAMBERS OF JUSTICE

In theory the system might have worked. Prices for offices might have captured for the Crown excess profits of *officiers,* including the loss to the king from borrowing his own money. A Chamber of Accounts checked over the books and charged the *officiers* and *financiers* for deficiencies. The difficulty was that this chamber was typically twenty years behind. To take up the slack, the French developed a Chamber of Justice, which met on occasion, after a war or death of a king, to make a concerted attack on previous corruption. We have already discussed two such chambers, called Visa (see p. 98), after the death of Louis XIV and the War of the Spanish Succession, and following the collapse of the Mississippi Bubble. In the seventeenth century Chambers of Justice were held frequently. Sully abandoned one in 1607 when thirty-three *financiers* agreed to pay the Crown 1 million livres.

A Chamber of Justice of 1624 was similarly abruptly terminated when 10.8 million livres were paid in.

The most famous Chamber of Justice, that of 1661–65, ended in the imprisonment of Nicholas Fouquet and six others excluded from a general amnesty. It was an attempt by Colbert, minister to Louis XIV, to reform the royal finances. In that purpose it failed completely, and the length of the chamber discouraged those who normally loaned to the Crown. Four hundred ninety-four people were fined 156 million livres. Of the total, ninety-seven are identified by Dent as belonging to the financial elite. These were fined an average of 1 million livres each, whereas lesser fry paid an average of only a tenth that amount (1973, cf. 4, p. 61).

The Chamber of Justice has been cynically regarded as a deal between those who needed protection because of financial transgression and those who had protection for sale—agents of the Crown (Chaussinand-Nogaret, 1970, p. 79). It was also one way the king would raise money, or perhaps one could say, take back the money that had been taken from him or his predecessor. In France, though significantly not in England or Venice, the nobility was excused from taxes on the ground that it defended the state with its lives. That this happened is exemplified by the fact that the three sons of Jean-Baptist Colbert died on the field of battle or from wounds (Dent, 1973, p. 236). Squeezing taxes out of peasants had long approached levels that were close to intolerable in years of bad harvest. The rich could be made to pay by Chambers of Justice, by sale of new offices, by demanding new payments for offices already paid for, or withholding the promised payments of salary or pension due on offices. These salaries were normally fixed at one-eighth a year of the capital cost of the office, plus an additional pension. In 1664, however, during the Chamber of Justice, *officiers* were paid only one-quarter of what was owed them (ibid.).

REFORMING THE SYSTEM

Sully succeeded in correcting major abuses and checking waste in his ministry under Henry IV that began in 1598. He was unable to make headway in correcting the system of offices or to eliminate the exemption of the nobility of the sword from taxation (Lodge, 1931 [1970], ch. 6). His progress was lost because of the Thirty Years' War from 1618 to 1648. Under Louis XIII and Richelieu taxation increased. With their deaths in the early 1640s, Mazarin became the chief adviser of Louis XIII's widow, Anne, as regent for Louis XIV, and while amassing his own fortune he tightened the screws on lesser *officiers* while leaving the exalted tax farmers and receivers-general alone. The office-holders resisted and erupted in revolt in what is called the *Fronde,* or "slingshot," from the stone metaphorically slung at Mazarin by the *parlementaires* and *officiers.* The bourgeoisie were partly inspired by the success of the Roundheads under Cromwell in England. After Anne and Mazarin had been driven from Paris in October 1648, the duc d'Orléans, called Monsieur, granted a number of reforms in taxes, providing for control over Crown lands, over extraordinary expenditure, and over creation of offices—the last being particularly of concern. The *Fronde* was interested less in overall reform than in the distribution of power within the system. The beheading of Charles I in February 1649 shocked the French, as the Reign of Terror in 1793 was later to shock the British. Mazarin came back in triumph in 1653, and with Louis XIV's series of new wars, reform was again dead.

Subsequent attempts at reform were also frustrated. Colbert was defeated by the ambitions of Louis XIV, John Law by the *financiers,* led by the Paris brothers (Chaussinand-Nogaret, 1970, p. 129), Turgot by the nobility he tried to tax to lighten the crushing load on the peasants (and by his attempt to destroy the guild system at the same time) (Lodge, 1931 [1970], p. 241). Necker came the closest and was subject to a campaign of vilification and abuse from which Robert Harris has tried to rescue him (1979). Many of the rumors and stories spread about Necker have been taken seriously by historians—concerning his speculation in Canadian notes in 1763 and his insider operations in a revived Compagnie des Indes after 1764 (ibid, chs. 1, 2). Harris may succeed in exonerating him from these charges and from the disdain of those like Arthur Young who thought his talents merely those of a bank clerk (Lodge, 1931 [1970], p. 254). He is less successful in defending him from overgenerous borrowing (see pp. 212–13), or from the charge that he failed to understand that he borrowed too much for war.

Necker undertook many reforms. He insisted that *financiers* should keep records up to date; wanted paying *caisses* reduced in number, concentrated in a few hands, and made responsible to the keepers of the royal treasury; wanted particularly to shift from farming taxes to *régies* (administrations) in which the *régisseur* was a salaried official rather than an independent entrepreneur; and gingerly explored the idea, as John Law before him, that the work of many offices could be performed adequately by a *commis* or clerk and did not require the presence of a noble magistrate (Bosher, 1970, p. 120, chs. 7, 8; R. D. Harris, 1979, ch. 8, p. 139). But his ideas on macroeconomic fiscal policy harbored a fatal confusion.

There was no doubt that French expenses for the War of Independence on top of the Seven Years' War were heavy and that the burden of taxation in the countryside was crushing. Turgot had advised against intervention in the American war on the ground that finances would not permit it (R. D. Harris, 1979, p. 119). Necker was not troubled. He felt that so long as the ordinary budget was balanced, including on the expenditure side interest and amortization on new as well as old debt, it was safe to borrow for war. He insisted on getting by without new taxes, *sans douleur* (without pain), and is mocked for it by Lodge, who suggests he sounds like a dentist advertising painless treatment (1931 [1970], p. 254). Robert Harris has recorded Necker's savings in normal expenditure, called *améliorations,* amounting to 84.5 million livres, which served the same purpose in balancing the ordinary budget as new taxes, and insists that he balanced the ordinary budget on a current basis, even though the course of actual receipts and expenditure, the record of which is available only two or more years later, showed deficits (1979, pp. 155–59, 224).

The major point, not noted by Harris, is that Necker's implicit fiscal model is what economists call partial equilibrium rather than general equilibrium. Partial equilibrium analysis assumes other things equal, as if there were no repercussions or feedbacks. In general equilibrium one has to take into account repercussions throughout the system. The difference illustrates the fallacy of, say, President Eisenhower, who suggested more than once that the state was like a family and like a family could not spend more than it took in as revenue for long without running out of liquid assets and access to credit. The analogy is faulty on one score: families cannot levy taxes at will or create money. But it is further true that the spending of the individual family by itself has no impact on national income, employment, prices, or the balance of payments, so that the family has no responsibility for these macroeconomic variables, whereas the state can affect them and has responsibility. The fact that Necker had "funded" war expenditure by providing for interest and amortization on the debt is irrelevant to the question as to whether the country could, or could not, pay for the war. (The same critical issue will arise again in German finance in World War I, in Chapter 16.)

To round off the reform question, reform was achieved through bloody revolution and the inflation of the *assignats*. *Officiers* and *financiers* were dug in so deeply in France, as opposed to Holland and England, that they could not be dislodged without the complex social convulsion of the French Revolution (Lefebre, 1939 [1967], ch. 2).

PRUSSIA

No financial revolution was required in Prussia or, if one was, only revolution from above (E. N. Williams, 1970, p. 303). The Great Elector, Frederick I, his son, Frederick William I, and his son, Frederick the Great, all understood the importance of a competent bureaucracy for financing an army: "Always think highly of a good army and money, out of which the glory and security of a prince are made," said the father to Frederick the Great (ibid., p. 310). It was a lesson not learned by Richelieu, Mazarin, or Louis XIV (Dent, 1973, p. 19), and one could add many another significant figure in political history—Metternich, Bismarck, de Gaulle—who did not think such things important.

In the seventeenth century, the Great Elector had two sources of income: taxes and the yield of the royal domain. The House of Hollenzollern owned land containing somewhere between a quarter and a third of the peasantry of the country and collected income in various ways—rents, profits on production for the market, miscellaneous tolls, taxes, and monopolies. The main tax was the Contribution, paid on land and polls, which fell on peasants and townspeople but from which nobles were exempt. The Great Elector borrowed the idea of excise taxes on consumption from the Dutch to shift some of the burden to the nobles (Williams, 1970, pp. 299–300).

Frederick William I built the bureaucracy. Exasperated by a quarrel over whether Excise or Domain officials should have jurisdiction over breweries, he clapped them together in a General Directory. By careful management, he amassed a war treasure of 8 million thalers, an army of 80,000 soldiers, and a budget that rose from 3.7 million thalers in 1714 to 7 million in 1740 (ibid., pp. 315, 320).

The upper class dominated both army and bureaucracy. If private enterprise existed anywhere in government, it was in the army where an officer bought his commission from a predecessor, and farmed it, receiving a fixed allowance from the state, which gave him permission to let the soldiers work as peasants or artisans in time of peace while he kept their pay. Some became rich in this way. The *Steuerrat* (tax commissioner) in a town, on the other hand, was likely to be a noble ex-officer on salary. The fundamental difference between the Prussian and the British or French social system that deeply affected financial institutions was that in the *ancien régime,* nobility could be acquired in Prussia only through the sword, not through purchase.

THE NINETEENTH CENTURY

Space is available for only a few points about nineteenth-century ideas on finance:

1. *Financial Reform,* the title of a book by Henry Parnell in the 1830s, meant streamlining taxes so as to improve yield and reduce administrative (transactions) costs (including the cost of conducting the perennial war on smuggling to escape customs duties). Lower duties on tobacco, for example, were advocated on the ground that the supply of smuggling was highly elastic. Beyond that, the task was to reduce numbers of duties, eliminate those that produced little or no revenue, and find the right level for major producers. The protective effect was secondary to the revenue effect, except perhaps in the Corn Laws and timber duties. The process started with William Huskisson, chancellor of the exchequer in the 1820s. In the early 1840s, prior to the repeal of the Corn Laws, timber duties, and Navigation Acts, Peel streamlined duties on 4,000 items. Removal of the tariff on corn (actually grain of all kinds but mainly wheat) made such a dent in government revenue that it was necessary for a time to reinstate the income tax, which had been removed after the Napoleonic Wars. The process of simplification went forward under William Gladstone as chancellor of the exchequer in the 1850s, prior to the Cobden-Chevalier Treaty of 1860, until the bulk of tariff revenue came from a handful of goods not produced in Britain—tea, coffee, sugar, tobacco, wine, brandy—making the schedule qualify as a "tariff for revenue only."

2. Napoleon took over as consul and in 1804 as emperor when the national debt had been virtually wiped out by the *assignats.* What there was was selling at a deep discount. An immediate announcement that the *rente* would be paid in specie brought the market price up from a low of 11.38 francs two days before the takeover of power to 42 afterward, then 50 and 60 francs. Menias, bearing in mind the recovery of the franc under Poincaré in 1926, said that there had never been such a recovery of confidence (1969, pp. 23–25). Napoleon was opposed to state borrowing and relied mainly on indemnities and treasure obtained from conquest. His treasurer, Mollien, had been strongly impressed by Pitt's sinking fund and believed in paying debt down. In consequence a Caisse d'Amortissement was established immediately upon Napoleon's accession to the throne, but amortizing debt was the least of its functions in Napoleon's view. He used it to support the market price of the *rente,* receive occasional indemnity payments from defeated adversaries, make

loans to manufacturers, give advances to the Treasury—in other words, as another bank. With the restoration of the monarchy, a parallel Caisse des Dépôts et Consignations (Fund for Deposits and Consignments) was established in 1816. Its ultimate use was to amass funds of savings banks throughout France and invest them centrally (ibid., pt. 2, ch. 1).

3. The Saint-Simonien school had rather odd views on debt management. It regarded public debt as an asset, especially British public debt. Existence of a national debt built credit and investor confidence. Jacques Laffitte went further: he favored borrowing rather than taxes in government finance because of his Keynesian predilections. Taxes were harmful because they hurt "active" money, whereas borrowing was useful because it galvanized into action "dead" money. At the same time he favored amortization of existing debt, which was contrary to orthodox Saint-Simonien doctrine, and was criticized for this heresy in the Saint Simonien newspaper, the *Globe,* by Prosper Enfantin and Adolphe d'Eichtal (Liesse, 1908, p. 287).

   An illustration of the kernel of truth in this view is that payment of the Napoleonic indemnity by Prussia after the defeat at Jena helped Prussia develop its capital market (Brockhage, 1910, p. 42).

4. As an introduction to private finance taken up in the next two chapters, note that whereas in the early part of our period, with offices and tax farming, private wealth holders intermediated between others and the Crown, in the nineteenth century the Crown intermediated between various sets of private investors and wealth holders. The issuance of Exchequer bills in 1793, 1797, and 1810 in Britain to help merchants render unsold stocks of merchandise liquid has been mentioned. In 1833 the British government borrowed £12 million to compensate slave owners for loss of property through emancipation. John Gladstone took his share and bought railway securities (Checkland, 1971, p. 327). In effect, the state borrowed from cautious investors to put money indirectly into the railroads. A similar process took place in France in the rebuilding of Paris by Haussmann in the 1850s. Money raised by the government to compensate those whose property was condemned often found its way out of real estate into railroads and other industrial ventures. One anecdote cannot be suppressed: Madame Haussmann complained that no sooner had she bought a house and settled into it than the government wanted to tear it down to widen the street (Emden, 1938, p. 156). The Bank of France discounted canal and railroad bonds. The British government guaranteed the obligations of the colonial government in India (Thorner, 1950). The separation between government and private finance implicit in the division of Chapter 9 from 10 and 11 is overdrawn.

TAXATION, BORROWING, SELLING ASSETS

If the distinction between private and public finance is overdrawn, so are the lines among taxation, borrowing, and selling assets. Forcible loans approach taxation. Selling a stream of income is borrowing, or selling an asset not yet in hand, whichever way one wants to view it. If the government overassigns a given revenue—a practice more developed in France than in Britain (R. Ashton, 1960, p. 53)—the borrowing or sale of an asset approaches taxation.

FINANCIAL INSTITUTIONS AND THE SOCIOPOLITICAL MATRIX

The conclusion of this chapter—one of the more general conclusions of the entire book—is that while institutions respond to supply and demand or to economic necessity, as the Coase theorem asserts, they do so within a social and political structure that profoundly shapes the outcome. Supply and demand propose; in frequent cases, as in tax farming in France, the social matrix disposes, rejecting an efficient solution resolutely until finally it has to be smashed.

Why no poachers turned gamekeepers in France? Why are the most important reformers, save Sully and Turgot, foreigners? Unhappily the macrosociology that would tell us when and why a society is highly responsive and adaptive, and when rigid and resistant, when and why strong interests will yield a little on short-run narrow gains in the broader or long-run interest, and when not, does not exist.

SUGGESTED SUPPLEMENTARY READING

Bordo and E. White (1991), A tale of two currencies: British and French finance During the
    Napoleonic Wars.
Bosher (1970), *French Finances, 1770–1795.*
Dent (1973), *Crisis in Finance.*
Dickson (1967), *The Financial Revolution in England.*
R. D. Harris (1979), *Necker, Reform Statesman of the Ancien Régime.*
Lodge (1931 [1970]), *Sully, Colbert, and Turgot.*

In French

Chaussinand-Nogaret (1970), *Les Financiers de Languédoc au XVIII siècle.*

10

Private Finance—Individuals and Families

House for sale
He writes in fine Chinese style
The Third generation.

(Eighteenth-century Chinese haiku, quoted in Burke,
Venice and Amsterdam, 1974, p. 110)

SOURCES AND FORMS OF PRIVATE WEALTH

From government we move to private finance. The subject defies simple organization. This chapter deals with the individual, the family household, and the rudimentary business, organized as a proprietorship or partnership. The following chapter turns to the corporate form, needed for larger and more permanent accumulations of capital. Capital arises from savings that require, in the normal case, substantial incomes. Substantial income can be obtained from land, commerce, finance, industry, and the professions. When saved, the resultant capital can be held as land, buildings, inventories, evidences of ownership or debt, and cash. There is also negative wealth in the form of debt, unpaid bills, mortgages on land and buildings, promissory notes, and the like. A crucial aspect of the subject is risk, including the active embracing of risk in investments financed by debt, and more straightforward gambling, in which the chances of gain or loss are both high. There is also risk avoidance through safe investments, avoidance of debt, and insurance. The development of insurance from real to financial forms is an essential aspect of finance that requires a considerable digression.

Wealth has a time dimension in both this and the following chapter, continuity in time is a central issue. Individuals gradually turn away from risk in order to extend the family in time. In the next chapter the corporate form is used to preserve the continuity of a business from one generation to the next.

LAND

Well into the nineteenth century, land was the most important source of income in western Europe and object of investment. This was true of all but a few highly commercialized places with limited land availability, like Amsterdam and Hamburg, and even in Amsterdam there was the occasional exception, such as John Hope, the English banker, who entered upon a process of aristocratization, acquired several estates, and spent his time in the last third of the eighteenth century traveling among them (Buist, 1974, pp. 1, 16). Land had two virtues: in large units with a big house and lavish entertainment it conveyed elite status; in addition, while illiquid, farms could be rented to produce income that was stable and safe compared to that from other investments and could almost always be borrowed against.

Land was occasionally an avenue to more land, as when the duke of Bedford advanced borrowed funds to a syndicate in the seventeenth century to drain the great fens of Norfolk and received 95,000 acres of reclaimed land as his return (Clifford, 1956, p. 50; Stone, 1967, p. 171). Infrequently, ownership of land led into industry, whether in the cutting down of forests for making charcoal and then cast iron in the sixteenth and seventeenth centuries—with disastrous effects on the woodlands (Stone, 1967, pp. 139, 162–69, 180), or in eighteenth- and even nineteenth-century France (Dornic, 1955, p. 171; R. Forster, 1960, ch. 5; Daumard, 1970, p. 368). A number of peers with landed estates exploited coal on their acres or converted mineral rights into coal royalties (Spring, 1951, 1974). The English aristocracy owned and rented out a great deal of urban property, especially in London, much of it originally acquired cheaply or as a gift when Henry VIII stripped the Church of its wealth. But the basis of aristocratic wealth and prestige was the countryside; the way into the gentry or aristocracy was to acquire land. For the most part, merchants, financiers, professional men, and, belatedly, industrialists eagerly undertook the task.

It might be reasoned that there was only a fixed amount of land in Europe and that upwardly mobile wealth holders could obtain it only when someone with the same appetite for landowning was prepared to sell, so that land purchase could not constitute an outlet for savings. Apart from those cases where good agricultural land was enlarged by drainage of marshes and polders, reclamation of waste, and enclosures of commons, land soaked up a considerable volume of savings in two directions. As books dealing with the economic aspects of the aristocracy make clear, a great deal of land was consumed by borrowing against it and spending the proceeds on the good life, to an extent that the debtor occasionally had to yield his acres by selling land to pay down his debts or an avid lender might foreclose (Stone, 1967; R. Forster, 1960). The duke of Cumberland, who claimed to have spent £100,000 of borrowed money on expeditions against Spain and ultimately had to sell an estate, said that he "threw his land into the sea" (Stone, 1967, p. 175). The other outlet represented real capital formation by means of enlarging and extending a country seat. Some part of mercantile and financial investment in the country was productive: Adam Smith noted that "merchants are commonly ambitious of becoming country gentlemen and when they do they are the best of improvers" (1776 [1937], p. 384). Such capital formation increased production for the market. But much money was spent for converting dwellings into stately homes, chateaux, seigneuries, and Hofs, and existing stately homes, and so on, into those more stately. To the extent that calculation of national income includes rent on owner-occupied houses, this added to national income and was productive. It is more properly regarded as conspicuous consumption.

GAMBLING

Aristocratic necessity to borrow on, and sometimes lose, an estate did not come from conspicuous consumption on housing, dress, feasting, military adventure, and formal entertainment alone. Gambling was close to a requirement. An aristocratic attribute to take risks and not to be concerned with mundane safety—values summed up in such slogans as "Never take cover" or "Never count the change" (Pitts, 1963, pp. 241 ff.)—spread ultimately to the middle classes. Much gambling was associated with capital markets; refinements such as puts and calls (options) and trading in futures developed in Amsterdam in the sixteenth century and was gradually diffused to London, Paris, and elsewhere. But aristocratic gambling was usually purer, without the possibility that it might broaden capital markets and make possible hedging against risk. The grandson of Paul Depont considered gambling an investment in his future as he sought to acquire noble status (R. Forster, 1980, p. 53). Gambling moved from a pastime to an obsession in seventeenth-century England; it was as important to play dice and cards as to ride and dance (Stone, 1967, p. 259). In Prussia when the price of grain fell sharply after the imposition of the British Corn Laws in 1818 and mortgages on Prussian estates doubled between 1837 and 1857, the Junkers indulged in one vice in the hope of escaping poverty and boredom: gambling (Stern, 1977*b,* p. 51). It was impossible that it would succeed for them all.

Governments pandered to the gambling instinct (or acquired trait) with lottery loans and *tontines* but on occasion found the activity disturbing. They believed it necessary, for example, to regulate insurance, which was designed to reduce risk, so as to lessen the opportunity to play with risk—for example, to eliminate its use in wagering on the lives of public men by taking out policies on them without an "insurable interest," that is, some possible loss that a policyholder would suffer from the insured's death (Supple, 1970, p. 54).

LAND AS INVESTMENT

Whether useful to establish a merchant's credit (R. Forster, 1980, p. 14) for income, as in the case of the unambitious Sir John Banks who kept adding to his estate with care and deliberation, year after year, until it was worth £170,000 in 1699 (Coleman, 1963, pp. 172–73), or for social ambition and an outlet for relentless drive, as in Sir Horatio Palavicino, whose grasping nature made him hated by his neighbors and tenants (Stone, 1956, ch. 7), land was a good investment. It did not so much make a person rich as help to keep him so. And it was useful for creating a family. Sir Stephen Fox, like most other moneyed men, converted wealth into landed estate, buying it only partly for social position, largely for his descendants. After having had ten children by his first wife, he despaired of having grandchildren and stopped accumulating land, only to resume when he remarried at 77 after his first wife's death and began a new family (C. Clay, 1978, pp. 165–66). Those with a passion for antiquarian demography may be interested in the fact that his grandson by this second line, Charles Fox, the political antagonist of Pitt, had two aunts who died 168 years apart, the first in infancy in 1658, and the second, the much younger sister of his mother, wife of Henry Fox, the paymaster, an aunt who died in 1826 at the age of 86.

The market for land was, on the whole, efficient. In the Mississippi Bubble, appetite for land is indicated by fact that when the regent depreciated the *billet d'état* in May 1720, which proved to be the start of the collapse, François Castanier who had started to *"en terre mes billets"* (convert his notes into land) had used his 30 million beginning October 1719 to buy twenty-three *seigneuries* (large estates) in the dioceses of Aleth and Béziers near Carcassonne in the Languedoc. Purchases undertaken in October and November had largely preceded the rise in price of estates, which took off when others began getting out of Banque Royale notes and Compagnie d'Occident shares (Chaussinand-Nogaret, 1970, p. 147). John Law himself did well briefly, despite no chateau with land; in 1720 before the collapse he owned the Hôtel de Mazarin, office of the Compagnie d'Occident, six houses in the rue Colbert, seven other houses in the place Vendôme, fourteen estates in the provinces, including Roissy, which cost 1 million livres, and so on (Levasseur, 1854 [1970], p. 171). On the other side of the channel when the South Sea Bubble collapsed, John Blunt had six contracts to buy country estates; a colleague, Surman, four (Carswell, 1960, p. 198). Land near London rose to forty-five times its normal annual rent, and prices began to move up and down with South Sea stock quotations to reflect the link between the markets (ibid., p. 159). Visa II and the parliamentary follow-up on the South Sea Bubble, however, meant that land bought with bubble profits did not always stay in new hands.

MERCHANTS

Conventional wisdom has it that fortunes made in commerce tend to go at the next stage into industry. Such seems rarely to be the case. The tendency is rather to move into land or finance or both. This is partly a matter of the risk-return trade-off, with a higher return being exchanged for lower risk, partly for prestige in both land and finance, and to some extent in finance, for higher returns. There are exceptions. In coal and iron in Wales, for example, some of the most substantial entrepreneurs began as merchants in the iron trade, largely from London (John, 1950, ch. 2). In other manufacturing, the role of mercantile equity capital was on the whole minimal.

We have already described the movement from merchant to financier with its many variations. More generally it was a movement from entrepreneurship to *rentier* status. The wealthy in Venice in 1581 got their money from trade; in 1711 from land on *terra firma*. In 1652 the Dutch historian Aitzema quoted the general complaint that the regents were not merchants any longer but derived their income from houses, land, and securities and allowed the sea to be lost (Burke, 1974, pp. 102, 104). In transition, a man such as Sir John Banks under the Stuarts had an income between 1657 and 1669 of £5,680 from rents, £16,300 from trade, and £18,900 from finance (Coleman, 1963, p. 47). Over time trade diminished, finance leveled off, rents rose.

Some small part of the enormous wealth of the Glasgow tobacco lords with a quasi-monopoly of stapling Maryland and Virginia tobacco under the Navigation Acts went into such industry as the Carron iron works or local textiles concerns. By far the greater part went into land and banking. The collapse of the Ayr Bank in 1772, moreover, led to the loss of much of the land because of unlimited liability of shareholders (Devine, 1975).

Many merchants acquired land in the West Indies involuntarily, through failure of planter customers to meet payments on advances for supplies and slaves. John Gladstone, father of William, the prime minister, was one such; he never visited the West Indies (Checkland, 1971, p. 194), John Binney of Bristol another (Pares, 1950 [1968]). Gladstone toyed with the idea of taking over a failed bank in Gloucester in 1825, but the deal fell through (Checkland, 1971, pp. 182–83). The Dolle brothers, originally of the Dauphiné, made money in commerce with the Antilles, by way of the Beaucaire fair, and bought plantations in the West Indies rather than land in France as a sort of vertical integration (Léon, 1963, p. 87). Other voluntary investors in the West Indies were the Jewish traders and financiers of Holland, who were excluded from buying Dutch land (Bloom, 1937, pp. 171, 182). The ordinary, successful Dutch entrepreneur invested in promissory notes, silent partnerships, marine insurance, discounted bills, urban real estate, and governmental and company loans. Cut off from the purchases of offices, honors, and landed estates, he was nonetheless interested in building an endowment safe from the risks of active entrepreneurship (Riley, 1980, p. 62).

Macroeconomic studies of French estates left after death by bourgeois decedents begin systematically only in the nineteenth century. In the eighteenth century one can cite individual cases such as Paul Depont who died in 1746 with an estate valued at 1.3 million livres: 32 percent in land, 25 percent in *rentes,* 20.5 percent in notes and drafts, largely on West Indian debtors, 17 percent for advances to children, and a surprising 4.5 percent in gold and silver coin (R. Forster, 1980, p. 62). His son who died in 1776 left 952,000 livres: 40 percent in land, 41 percent in *rentes,* nothing in notes and drafts, 12 percent in advances, and 6.8 percent in coin (ibid., p. 74).

In the nineteenth century, Daumard's studies of a considerable sample of Paris bourgeois estates show *pierres et terres* (buildings and land) at 49.6 percent in 1820 and 45.5 percent in 1847; financial assets, including *rentes* and promissory notes, 38.3 and 41.6 for the same dates, respectively; Bank of France shares, 3.2 and 2.5 percent; company shares, 2.5 and 1.8 percent; and foreign bonds, 0.7 and 0.7 (1970, pp. 484–85). The proportion of financial assets rose relative to land after 1880, with an internal switch from *rentes* to equity shares, which increased from 21 percent of portfolios in the 1890s to 32 percent in 1910–14, on the one hand, and into foreign bonds on the other (Michalet, 1968, pp. 177, 280). Foreign lending absorbed 2, 4, and 6 percent of national income in 1885, 1900, and 1913, respectively (ibid., p. 210). For some reason, which seems bizarre in retrospect, foreign bonds were regarded more as bonds, and therefore safe, than as foreign and therefore risky.

THE FAMILY

Modern macroeconomic theory provides one theory of consumption called the "life cycle" in which consumption is based on anticipated lifetime earnings rather than current income. Under such a model, a person could end up with zero assets at death by converting wealth into annuities as Adam Smith thought the practice of French *officiers,* and as the duc de Lauzun, childless though married and an aristocrat rather than a parvenu, may furnish an apposite example (R. Forster, 1971, pp. 114–15)—though Forster regards him as an anomaly (ibid., p. 136). The modern version accounts for piling up debt in early years as households accumulate assets such as house and furnishings beyond their capacity to pay out of current earnings, with debt paid off in later life, and net assets either accumulated or not. Lawrence Stone has identified what he believes to be a change in the character of the English family about the beginning of the seventeenth century. Prior to that time, wives were committed to bear children until they died in childbirth, and children so seldom survived the neonatal state that parents could not afford to make an emotional investment in them. With improvement in survival rates, men of substance began to make provision for their wives and children after their death (Stone, 1977). It was not expected that the widow could manage the business, although abundant counterexamples can be found.

A recent study of three Leeds businessmen during the industrial revolution purports to identify a similar property cycle. A man accumulates avidly until a turning point at age 40 when capital is increasingly concentrated outside of his business in preparation for old age (Morris, 1979). Almost the same point was made by Sir Josiah Child in 1688 in his *Brief Observations concerning Trade and the Interest of Money:* "in England, merchants withdraw from trade before old age fearing that he will lose one third of his wealth, if he dies, through the inexperience and ineptness of his wife" (Letwin, 1969, p. 42).

Complete withdrawal may go too far. In France, it is claimed that at least from the beginning of the nineteenth century, all fortunes are divided into two parts: one reserved for investment for a *père de famille*—in urban real estate, purchases of land, or stock exchange bonds. This is said to constitute the reserve, which is not to be disposed of except to establish the next generation in adult life. The other part is set aside for speculation in business, in land, or on the bourse. Adeline Daumard concludes that "the spirit of enterprise thus combined with prudence allows one to get rich without endangering the position of the family" (1980, p. 107).

The rise of family sentiment called for a variety of measures—life insurance for one, safe investments for another. Marine and fire insurance are appropriately discussed with life insurance, despite the fact that the first two cope with risk and the latter extends the family in time.

INSURANCE

Financial decisions are based on risk and return. One way to reduce risk (which lowers return) is to insure. The same end can be achieved more or less without the financial institution. Venice built little ships to divide the risk before it achieved the breakthrough represented by marine insurance (Braudel, 1949 [1972], Vol. 1, p. 306). The three biggest freight handlers in Reval in the winter of 1430 spread their shipments among nine, eight, and seven ships, respectively, given the inability of Hansa merchants to provide financial insurance (Dollinger, 1964 [1970], p. 156). The practice, moreover, was to enter into many short-term and changing partnerships, in both shipowning and trade. This was the normal form of commercial enterprise undertaken both to increase the mass of capital and to reduce risk (ibid., p. 166). Sir Thomas Gresham shipped the proceeds of his loans in Antwerp in behalf of Elizabeth in gold or silver specie, but not more than £1,000 in one bottom or £3,000 with the same messenger if he went by land to Calais and thence to Dover and London (de Roover, 1949, p. 25). During the Anglo-Spanish War of 1740–44, the Dutch provided silver coin to the Royal African Company but only one money chest per ship (Vilar, 1969 [1976], p. 271).

Gradually there grew up the practice of raising capital for larger ships by selling fractional shares. The system was binary, went down as far as sixty-fourths, and was widespread. Heckscher noted that cargoes in Sweden, as well as ships, had many owners in the seventeenth century (1954, p. 113). Moreover, one can find real insurance in literature:

Salarino: ... I know Antonio
             Is sad to think upon his merchandise.
Antonio: Believe me, no. I thank my fortune for it,
             My ventures are not to one bottom trusted,
             Nor to one place; nor is my whole estate
             Upon the fortune of this present year:
             Therefore my merchandise makes me not sad.
             (Shakespeare, *The Merchant of Venice,* Act I, sc. i)

In *Roxana,* a Dutch ship captain never could think of venturing all he had in one bottom, which is why he did not bring his wife on board with him (Defoe, 1724 [1964], p. 275).

The origins of financial insurance are found in Italy in the fifteenth century (Melis, 1975). In the late Middle Ages a primitive form of monetary marine insurance was a loan to a master or merchant proceeding to another port, commonly repayable at the ship's destination and in coin of that realm, with risk of loss being born by the lender (Postan, 1928 [1973], p. 14n). Such loans on ships were called "bottomry" and on cargo "respondentia." They survived into the era of more usual insurance,[1] so that a marine insurance policy on bottomry or respondentia was, in fact, reinsurance (Sutherland, 1933, p. 52).

---

1. Another reference to *Roxana* places a loan on bottomry in context and shows the portfolio of a rich Dutch merchant proposing marriage: "but he produc'd me in Goldsmiths' Bills, and Stock in the *English East India* Company, about sixteen thousand Pounds Sterling; then he gave into my Hands, nine assignments on the Bank of *Lyons* in France, and two upon the Rents of the Town-House in *Paris,* amounting on the whole to 5800 Crowns *per Annum,* or Annual Rent *as 'tis called there,* and lastly the sum of 30000 *Rixdollars* in the Bank of *Amsterdam,* besides some Jewels and Gold in the Box ... for besides all this he shew'd me ... several Adventures he had Abroad, in the

If the Hanseatic League was backward in insurance, the Dutch and the English were not. In Holland, financial insurance was called for by the awkwardness of real insurance—waiting for the slowest ship in a convoy, for example, or dividing cargos among many ships. The Dutch gained a start on the English, and in the Third Anglo-Dutch War British ships were being insured in Amsterdam (Barbour, 1929, p. 34). The English were not far behind. An act as early as 1601, when Venice dominated the field, provided a Court of Assurances that lasted ninety years. Coffee houses began to deal in marine insurance from the middle of the seventeenth century, and by 1680 Lloyd's Coffee House emerged on top. The year 1680 also saw the establishment of the first fire insurance company, the Sun Assurance Company, fourteen years after the great London fire of 1666 (Dickson, 1960). It was quickly followed by the Phoenix in 1681, but that did not survive (Supple, 1970, p. 7).

The next big step in insurance in England came in the South Sea Bubble. Two companies that slipped through the door before it slammed shut in the Bubble Act of June 1720 were the Royal Exchange and London Assurance. In 1721 marine insurance was in three hands—the Royal Exchange, London Assurance, and Lloyd's—though Lloyd's wrote 90 to 95 percent of all marine risks. The Sun, Royal Exchange, and London Assurance wrote primarily fire and life.

Life insurance was often written to protect loans made to others on an annuity basis, that is, to protect the capital of the loan against an early death—rather than to provide for the survivors of the decedent. In the eighteenth century, too, insurance was taken on the lives of public figures as a wager with long odds. This was declared illegal in 1774 (ibid., p. 54). By the middle of the century actuarial tables had been produced and premiums for life insurance based on age came into existence. In marine insurance, premiums were altered for winter and summer, and special risks. Privateers could not get average—an ancient principle going back to the Phoenicians under which any part of the ship or cargo damaged in the interest of the venture as a whole was paid for by assessment on the rest that escaped (Sutherland, 1933, p. 52).

For fifty years there were only three major companies in fire and life insurance, until lawyers found a loophole in the Bubble Act, which let in a series of new. An unincorporated company was formed by establishing a trust to which a large partnership would commit capital and thereby get the advantages of incorporation, including unified ownership of property and action, perpetual succession, transferability of shares, and even limited liability (Supple, 1970, pp. 59–60). A new Phoenix company was formed in 1782, the Equitable Assurance in the same year, the British Fire Office in 1799. This was all preliminary to the big spurt of the early nineteenth century, with eight new companies, including the Globe, the Rock, the London Fire, and the Atlas, formed between 1803 and 1808, and twenty-nine more successfully between 1815 and 1830, plus a great many more that blossomed briefly

---

Business of his Merchandize; as particularly, an eighth share in an *East-India* ship then Abroad: an Account-Courant with a Merchant, at *Cadiz* in *Spain;* about 3000 l. lent upon *Bottomree,* upon Ships gone to the *Indies;* and a large Cargo of Goods in a Merchant's hands, for sale, at *Lisbon* in *Portugal,* so that in his books there was about 27000 l. more, all of which made about 27000 l. Sterling and about 1320 l. a year" (Defoe, 1724 [1964], p. 257) (italics in original).

in the boom of 1823 to 1825 and then wilted (ibid., p. 111). The insurance habit spread widely thereafter as British business, households, and individuals at all incomes above minimum levels sought to protect their assets currently and, in the case of individuals, to protect their families after their deaths.

In France, as indicated earlier, insurance seems to have been about a century behind Britain. Marine insurance developed in the ports on a local basis in the first half of the eighteenth century (Dawson, 1931, cited by Sutherland, 1933, p. 50n; Clark, 1971, ch. 9) with some help from Paris, but it was necessary in the usual case to cover part of a marine risk in London and/or Amsterdam. What is said to have been the first joint stock insurance company in France, in fire and life, was organized by one Etienne Clavière in the boomlet of 1786, along with a number of others. All quickly expired without writing much insurance, having been primarily vehicles for financial speculation (Lüthy, 1961, Vol. 2, pp. 707–15). The growth of insurance in France can be said to have begun only after the Napoleonic Wars, when the old Compagnie des Eaux began to write fire insurance, and James Rothschild, then 24, Jacques Laffitte, and other Paris bankers organized the Compagnie Royale d'Assurance Maritime (Bouvier, 1967, p. 118).

The course of insurance in the rest of northern Europe follows roughly the same pattern as in England. Coverage was available for marine risks in Holland in the seventeenth century (Barbour, 1929, pp. 33–35), and the excitement that helped start the Royal Exchange and London Assurance during the South Sea Bubble communicated itself to both Amsterdam and Hamburg. On 16 July 1720, as South Sea shares began to slip, eighty Jews, Presbyterians, and Anabaptists, denizens of "Change Alley" in London, took off to Amsterdam to mend their fortunes in Dutch insurance, while others left for Hamburg. The Maatschappij van Assurantie was established in Amsterdam in 1720, flourishing for more than two and a half centuries. Twenty other companies were founded in the same year in a manic boom in Middelburg, Rotterdam, and possibly elsewhere in the Netherlands (Spooner, 1983, pp. 24–25). Other insurance companies participating in the boom sprang up in Hamburg and Rouen, and still others were proposed in New York the following year (ibid., pp. 43–45). This last statement does not square with a secondary source that states that the first insurance company in Hamburg was founded in 1765. The point may be that that was the first insurance company to survive. The same writer goes on to assert that at the outbreak of the Napoleonic Wars, Hamburg had thirty insurance companies and the largest insurance market in Europe (Wiskemann, 1929, p. 134). This may well be chauvinism. The usual view—itself possibly chauvinistic or parochial—is that London and Amsterdam competed for ascendancy at the beginning of the eighteenth century and that London pulled ahead before 1755 (Sutherland, 1933, p. 50). The author supports her position by stating that agents of English insurance companies wrote policies in Europe and reinsured them in London, earning 100 percent because of the different rates prevailing in the two markets (ibid., p. 51).

The significant development of large insurance companies in Germany waited for their promotion by the newly founded "great banks" in the middle of the nineteenth century (Riesser, 1911, pp. 71–72).

A detailed study of the Amsterdam market for marine insurance attributes the decline of that market to bankruptcies in the financial crises of 1763 and 1772, plus losses in the Seven Years' War of 1756–63, the American Revolutionary War from 1775 to 1783, and especially the Fourth Anglo-Dutch war from 1780 to 1784 (Spooner, 1983, ch. 7).

The major point of this spotty and parenthetical account of insurance is that financial institutions were needed to cope with risk efficiently and that they developed, at different times in different societies, but largely in spurts, and in parallel with other financial institutions.

TAKING CARE OF OLD AGE AND OF POSTERITY

The theme of investments appropriate for widows and orphans has a history going far back in time—all the way to 2390 B.C. and Mesopotamia, where the Hammurabi code included these lines:

> That the strong might not oppress the weak,
> that justice might be done to the widow and orphan . . .
> I write my precious words on my stele [cylinder] . . .
> To give justice to the oppressed.

Special concern for widows and orphans has been characteristic of all societies, partly to reassure soldiers and others exposed to great risk that if they are killed at an early age, their families will be cared for. If this help is funded, moreover, the monies were available for investment. In the medieval period

if there was any source from which the mercantile community drew its investments, it was the orphans funds, and especially those administered by municipalities. In Northern Europe such funds were employed by municipal authorities in public loans or given out on long term to private merchants. (Postan, 1928 [1973], p. 20)

Preoccupation with the problem is implicit in Charles Wilson's frequent mention of widows and orphans, along with other unsophisticated investors, in his discussion of Anglo-Dutch commerce and finance (1941). Investors in these categories, later characterized as those with trustees who sought "trustee investments," are variously described as "spinsters, retired naval and army officers, magistrates, retired merchants, parsons and orphanages" (ibid., p. 118); "civil servants, magistrates, widows and orphans, and charitable institutions" (ibid., p. 135); "widows, parsons, orphanages, magistrates and civil servants" (ibid., p. 162); "country gentry, wealthy burghers and officials of Amsterdam, widows and wealthy spinsters" (ibid., p. 181); "spinsters, theologians, admirals, civil servants, merchants, professional speculators, and the inevitable widows and orphans" (ibid., p. 202). After 1713 Dutch funds seeking safe investment became so plentiful that they spilled over into Bank of England, South Sea Company, East India Company shares, and British government debt. Estimates of foreign holdings of these securities ranged as high as one-third of the total. Dickson has studied the stock transfer books and found that by approximately 1750 they reached 15 percent. Women's share of total foreign holdings rose from an average of roughly 18 percent in 1723–24 to 29 percent in 1750, as a consequence partly of greater longevity of women and partly of the more rigorous search for stability of income and absence of risk (1967, pp. 322, 325). Some doubt attaches to all such figures, to be sure, because of the widespread practice of holding securities through nominees, which may understate the proportions of securities ultimately owned by foreigners and women. Similar figures seem not to be available for British domestic holdings, although women subscribed 12 percent of the tontine loan of 1693 and 6 percent of the original issue of Bank of England stock in 1694 (ibid., p. 249). By 1750, the three largest subscribers to government debt were the Accountant-General of Chancery, an office created in 1726 to unify the administration of suitors' funds previously under the control of separate Chancery masters, some of whom had speculated with funds in their care in South Sea stock; the poor clergy of the Church of England; and the Commissioners for New Churches (ibid., pp. 292, 295). Dame Sutherland, on the other hand, claimed that propertied classes rarely kept much in securities, holding their wealth largely in land. In 1730, for example, only forty-seven persons owned as much as £10,000 or more in shares of the East India Company, among them three peers, a doctor, a spinster, and a rich widow. The bulk of holders consisted of professional financiers (1952, p. 42).

TRUSTEE SECURITIES

The rise of the railroad and incorporation are discussed in the next chapter. The one led to the other, and together they converted investment from the personal involvement of monied men in a particular enterprise (abutters or prospective users of a canal or railroad, for example, or friends of the shipowner, family of the cotton spinner, neighbors of the iron master) to an impersonal affair, affecting gradually increasing numbers of investors, on the one hand, and of securities on the other. Private companies went public to dislodge the second and third generation below the innovator-owner, permitting them to enter politics or the weekending class. New forms of investment proliferated—the debenture, preference share, and foreign bond—and trustees, pushed by primogeniture to invest increasing amounts of capital, kept looking for outlets (Jeffrys, 1938 [1977], p. 263). Numbers of investors in private companies and public companies other than railroads increased from 50,000 in 1860 to between 230,000 and 500,000 in the first decade of the twentieth century, with the actual number almost certainly near the upper end of the range. Moreover, 80 percent of investors wanted a safe return of 4 to 5 percent. The appetite for outlets led trustees to move into foreign bonds. In the 1850s a country bondholder was a rarity, and a man who lent money to a foreign state was regarded as a lunatic. By the 1870s foreign bonds were bought by the '"provincial investor, the country clergyman, the village probationer, the retired tradesman and the ancient dame" (ibid., p. 393).

WEALTH

In France and Britain, though less so in Italy, Germany, or the United States, men who achieved outstanding wealth came first and foremost from landowning, then from trade and finance, last from industry (Rubenstein, 1977, p. 107, and 1980, p. 22; Daumard, 1970, p. 85). The data come mostly from probate records of estates left in death. These are subject to statistical difficulties: some exclude real estate (Rubenstein, ed., 1980, p. 54). French inheritance taxes did not apply to public funds issued before 1850 in order to compensate investors in government debt ruined by the Revolution (Daumard, 1980, p. 91). Landowners in England, especially the peerage, had the largest fortunes. An 1870 list of two dozen members of the Conseil Général in France with incomes of more than 300,000 francs a year put Rothschild and one of the Pereires at the top, with amounts not specified, followed by Schneider, the steel magnate, with 1½ million francs, the duc de la Rochefoucauld-Doudeauville next with 800,000 francs, and then a long list of aristocrats before coming down to another banker, Edouard André with 500,000 francs, more aristocrats, and some bourgeoisie before the banker, Adolphe Fould, at the 300,000-franc limit (Bergeron, 1978, p. 9). Writing on American fortunes before 1865, Edward Pessen singles out Rothschild in England and Gabriel Julien Ouvrard, the *munitionnaire* and *financier* of the Napoleonic period, as the standard of comparison (1980, p. 168). The wealth of Baron Lionel Rothschild of England was £2.7 million in 1879 (Sheppard, 1971, p. 68). I have seen no figure for any of Ouvrard's several fortunes, although Napoleon once put him in the general class of men who had 30 million francs and were dangerous (Liesse, 1908, p. 19).

Nearer to World War I in France, the electoral rolls of 1911 listing property qualifications with wealth of more than 5,000 francs showed half the names with noble titles. If the level were raised to 10,000 francs, Adeline Daumard guesses that the proportion would be close to two-thirds. Mean fortunes left by heads of large enterprises in Paris in 1911 reached 1.5 million francs, seven times the 1820 level. In contrast, there were only two estates of more than 100 million francs between 1902 and 1913—one in 1905 and one in 1912. These were the years when Adolphe and Gustav de Rothschild died. Each estate was close to 250 million francs (Daumard, 1980, p. 104).

In Italy information on wealth is available for the most part only after World War I. Before the Napoleonic Wars, which destroyed much wealth, especially in such cities as Genoa, Arthur Young thought that the Piedmontese and Milanese were the richest peoples in Europe, but his perspective was distorted by his preoccupation with agriculture and the neat, large farms watered by the Po river (1790 [1969], p. 267). Land and banking fortunes in the interwar period were overwhelmed by industrial wealth amassed by the Agnellis, Pirellis, Presentis, and Falcks among the leaders (Zamagni, 1980, p. 153). The German Junkers were not a wealthy elite (Stern, 1977*b*, p. 51).

There were, of course, numerous industrial fortunes beyond that of Schneider in France. Samuel Fludyer, "probably the richest clothier in England," left £900,000 on his death in 1786. Sir Richard Arkwright who invented the waterframe and exploited it himself was a canny manager and amassed a fortune. Josiah Wedgwood who died in 1795 and left between £500,000 and £600,000 (Rubenstein, ed., 1980, p. 54), and Thomas Brassey, the railroad builder, made it into the millionaire class by the time he died in 1870 (Rubenstein, 1977, p. 107). Each was outstripped by still richer aristocrats and bankers—Fludyer by John Moore, archbishop of Canterbury and an aristocrat, who left £1 million in 1805; Brassey by Lord Overstone, who started with almost £2 million inherited from his father (he and his brother were the two richest commoners in England) and died in 1883, owning £2.1 million in securities and £3.1 million in land (O'Brien, ed. [1971], Vol. 1, pp. 14, 46). Although the fortunes of British landowners cannot be measured directly with those of industrialists and merchants because probated estates exclude land (Rubenstein, 1981, p. 44, table 2.7, and p. 202, table 7.3), it is likely that land as a source of wealth declined with the fall in the world price of wheat after 1880, while fortunes made in business kept rising. James Morrison, a textile wholesaler and warehouseman, died in 1857 leaving an estate of £4 million. His son took over the business and extended its activities into merchant banking. His estate at £10.9 million in 1909 was the largest recorded in Britain to that time. Still later, Sir John Ellerman, who had started out as an accountant, moved into shipping and later into finance, newspapers, brewing, and real estate development, died in 1937 leaving an estate of £36.7 million. This was almost three times that of the next largest of the period, that of a Guinness. Ellerman's son, in turn, died in 1957 with an estate of £57 million, the largest on record in Britain (ibid., p. 45).

Before 1880 industrialists were not only less rich, they were less singled out for elevation to the peerage than bankers or public servants. A letter from Lord Granville to Lord Overstone is revealing. Granville asked Overstone about the propriety of awarding a peerage to Marshall of Leeds, a leading flax spinner, or to Gregg of Manchester in cotton. Overstone countered by suggesting Strutt instead, and, in due course, Strutt was ennobled and Marshall and Gregg were not. In replying to Overstone's nomination, Granville wrote: "I quite approve of the selection being made from the class they represent, but the success of such a step would depend entirely on the character, position and *fortune* [my italics] of the individuals selected from so large a Mass, as the Manufacturers of this country." It should also be observed that Edward Strutt was the son and grandson of manufacturers, not a manufacturer himself (Overstone, 1856 [1971], Vol. 2, pp. 633–35). The sentiment is echoed in *Endymion* by that snob of snobs, Disraeli, who has a character observe that it is possible for society to absorb the nabobs who earned fortunes in India, working with and against the East India Company, but that it was necessary to go slow on industrialists and railroad magnates (Beaconsfield, 1880, Vol. 1, p. 24). For Germany information is scrappy indeed. Ehrenberg recounts the slow progress of the fortune of John Parish, the father, of Hamburg, from 38,000 marks in 1767 (1925, p. 12) to 2 million marks in 1796 (ibid., p. 85). The founder died in 1798, and his namesake, John, took his inheritance of 700,000 marks after heavy losses in 1799 and built up that to 1.5 million marks by 1815 and 3 million by 1829 (ibid., p. 112). Jean de Chapeaurouge of Hamburg had a similar fortune (Böhme, 1968, pp. 70, 74). In Berlin in 1854 there were 6 thaler millionaires (Brockhage, 1910, p. 183). About 1870 Bleichröder was the richest man in Berlin, with an annual income of between 2 million and 2.2 million marks. Only Krupp in the Ruhr had an income of the same order of magnitude (Stern, 1977a, p. 477).

NABOBS

The East India Company's service was one avenue to wealth. Enormous fortunes were piled up by Clive and Hastings. Clive remitted £280,000 to England between

1755 and 1759, £210,000 of which was received upon the enthronement of Meer Jaffier Nabob. In addition, he had an income of £27,000 a year from the same worthy, representing a *jagir* or return on a nominal office. This was the sum owed by the "John Company" to the nabob as rent on some land. When Clive returned to England in 1760, the company was unhappy about paying this amount and stopped it in 1763 (Sutherland, 1952, pp. 80–88). An attempt was made, led by Edmund Burke, to impeach Warren Hastings, governor of Bengal, who was said to have been indifferent to his personal fortune and whose £200,000 was thought by Lord North not to be excessive (ibid., p. 297).

The East India Company was a money tree for many groups: the "writers" or civil servants administering the company's territories in the East, cadets and assistant surgeons in its armies, captains of its ships, and ship's husbands who managed the ships chartered from private owners. All but the shipowners, who usually invested in one or more sixty-fourths of the substantial vessels needed for the long voyage and to carry the men and material necessary for their defense, had nominal salaries but opportunities for personal profit. Ship masters, for example, were paid £60 a voyage but made substantial additional amounts by serving as suppliers to their own vessels, in private trade, and in smuggling. On a voyage of fourteen to eighteen months, a commander should earn £4,000 to £5,000, with the total range running from as low as £2,000 to a high of £12,000 (Sutherland, 1933, pp. 87, 101).

All sorts of property rights accumulated around these opportunities. The role of commander was bought and sold, with prices ranging from £5,000 to £10,000, or possibly, as one claim in a dispute put it, to £20,000 (ibid., pp. 101, 104). Appointment as a writer in India had a monetary value of £3,500, although the company directors used the right of appointment for nepotism rather than profit (Philips, 1940 [1961], p. 15). Once appointed, a man was worthy of credit up to £10,000 to obtain his stock in trade, as he could normally expect to make £30,000 and retire at the age of 45 (Collier, 1963, p. 20). Conflicts of interest abounded, between stockholders and directors who owned shares in ships, despite efforts to prevent it throughout the eighteenth century (Sutherland, 1933, p. 91); between ship captain and owners, writers and company, company and government. The problem of taking profits back to England from India will occupy us in Chapter 14: one aspect is worth noting here—that the company's servants had an incentive to undermine its monopoly and to furnish goods to excluded ships, such as those of Americans, in order to get their illegal funds safely out of India. So sharp were the conflicts and so usual was it for individuals to resolve them in their private interest and against their legal obligation that a German economic historian has singled out the great chartered, monopoly companies as illustrative of the historical emergence of corruption, which he regards as a market transaction with fraud needed to irrigate the system (van Klaveren, 1957, 1958*a*, 1958*b*). Service with (and against) the East India Company of England, and to a lesser extent the other Indies' companies, and other monopolies such as those for the Levant, Africa, and Hudson Bay, produced fortunes of such magnitude that the owners achieved respectability despite the dubious origin of the gains.

CAPITAL NEEDS OF THE INDUSTRIAL REVOLUTION

Investment in industry prior to the spread of the corporation, discussed in the next chapter, was moderate. Initial views of the role of capital in the industrial revolution have been sharply revised by economic historians. Large amounts of capital were needed for chartered companies, like the East India, and for public works. J. H. Plumb has stated that the growth of local authorities was the most important development in the eighteenth century in England and the least stressed. Streets were widened, new approaches built to bridges, such as the London bridge; physical improvements took place in cities throughout England after 1750, plus construction of turnpikes, followed by digging canals (quoted in T. S. Ashton, 1959, p. 97). The needs of industry were minuscule. The opinion of W. Arthur Lewis a number of years ago, echoed by W. W. Rostow, that the industrial revolution (or economic take-off) involved a leap of savings from 5 percent of national income to 15 percent turns out to have been wrong (Lewis, 1955, p. 208; Rostow, 1960, pp. 41ff.). Deane and Cole refuted it initially by estimating that savings rose from 5 or 6 percent of national income in 1750 to perhaps 7 percent by 1800, at which figure they stayed level until the railway boom of the 1830s and 1840s (1967, pp. 261–62). More recent work by C. H. Feinstein has modulated the figures to a degree: the ratio of savings to national income rose from 6½ percent in 1770 to 9 percent by 1790, 8 percent at the end of the war, and 11 percent by the time of the railway boom (1978, Vol. 1, p. 91). Whatever the numbers, one can no longer accept the opinion of T. S. Ashton that held sway for so long:

The importance of the lowering of the rate of interest in the half-century before the industrial revolution has never been properly stressed by historians. If we seek—it would be wrong to do so—for a single reason why the pace of economic development quickened about the middle of the eighteenth century, it is to this we must look. The deep mines, solidly built factories, well-constructed canals, and substantial houses of the industrial revolution were the products of relatively cheap capital. (1948, p. 11)

Capital to start most enterprises came from an individual, his family, friends, neighbors, in very informal ways. For ships, the funds were initially amassed in a given port where the shipowner lived, until the middle of the nineteenth century when the increasing size of ships went beyond the capacity of local markets. Fixed capital in mills was small. Buildings were often rented and frequently converted from other uses, such as abbeys or convents (Fischer, 1962, pp. 209ff.: Lévy-Leboyer, 1964, p. 450). The big need was for working capital; this was often scrounged by buying on credit and selling for cash (Crouzet, ed., 1972; Pollard, 1965). Growth came usually from retained profits. Something depended, of course, on the technique used. In textiles in Britain, plants relying on horse power required an initial capital of only £1,000, water power £3,000 to £5,000, and steam power, a minimum of £10,000 (Chapman, 1971, pp. 61–63).

One can find exceptions. That of the iron and coal mines has been mentioned. The deeper coal mines went, the more capital they needed, not least for keeping the mine free of water by pumping. And one can find the occasional industrial plant, like Bolton & Watt, producing steam engines, that grew very rapidly, in excess of

Table 10.1 Net Real Capital Investment in Prussia, 1816–49 (by sectors in millions of marks at 1913 prices)

Period	Agriculture	Nonagricultural Buildings	Transport	Industry	Total
1816–22	86.5	28.7	7.0	2.8	125
1822–31	70.4	18.7	8.8	5.1	103
1831–40	109.6	52.0	22.5	5.6	189
1840–49	59.9	69.2	73.7*	7.0	209

*Of which 60.9 million railroads.
Source: Tilly (1978).

the profits being generated, went through Bolton's money, that of his wife, and finally turned in desperation to Hope & Company in Holland from which it borrowed £30,000 (Smiles, 1865, pp. 268, 278). They were rare.

Requirements for capital by sectors are illustrated fairly generally in a table for Prussia prepared by Tilly, showing net annual figures (Table 10.1). The numbers bear out Borchardt's contention that Clapham, Henderson, Treue, Dunham, and others who thought that German industry lagged behind British industry because of a dearth of capital were wrong (1961, pp. 401, 420). Some industries, such as textiles, beset by fierce competition from Manchester, did not make substantial profits so as to be able to reinvest. On the other hand, a number of industries with monopoly profits found it impossible to absorb all the savings they generated. The demand for capital picked up with the start of railroad construction in the 1840s, but improvement in transport reduced the need for capital elsewhere in such forms as inventories (ibid., pp. 409, 418).

That industry never absorbed more than 5 percent of the capital available in Germany or more than 10 percent in Britain makes it dubious that the industrial revolution had anything to do with capital markets at all. Adam Smith said that joint stock companies were needed only for a limited number of activities—banking, fire and marine insurance, canals, and waterworks (1776 [1937], p. 713). While Smith was not particularly aware of the industrial revolution that was beginning to take place around him, he did believe that the requirements of factories for fixed capital were small (Pollard, 1964, p. 300n).

THE FAMILY FIRM

Technical demand for capital was thus limited in the early stage of the industrial revolution. So, too, says an important school of thought, was social demand. Few aristocratic persons, with their love of risk as evidenced in gambling, went into industry. Middle-class entrepreneurs in small firms were reluctant to get involved with outside funds for fear that the family's ownership might be diluted and even lost. The argument being maximized in the objective function, to use economic jargon, was not profit but family survival. The nobility sought the same end through entail, *fideikommis,* primogeniture, and other devices that kept land in the family, or tried to. For the middle class the appropriate strategy was not to let a firm become public. Leverage meant a chance for greater profit, but it also implied the risk of greater loss. Fail-safe strategy was to borrow the least possible amount, to abstain from selling equity to outsiders. The mottoes that evolved were "measure," "not too much zeal," " build the family."

Landes, Sawyer, Pitts, and others have tried to explain French economic retardation, or at least alleged French economic retardation, by these bourgeois values operating in the family firm (Landes, 1949). P. Sargent Florence has ascribed British industrial backwardness at the end of the nineteenth century to a somewhat different sort of family firm, with children and grandchildren of the founder, profoundly disinterested in the details, dependent on it for income for the good life, and willing to leave the operation of the firm to "faithful retainers" (1953). Neither view goes unchallenged.

It would take us too far from our main themes to enter into this debate, even though it is well to note it insofar as it relates to the extent that firms in Europe depend on outside finance, and hence to capital markets, and other institutions. By the time of the railroad, there is no choice but to amass capital from many pockets. Industry outgrows the family, if manufacturing and commerce had previously stayed largely within its confines. We thus turn in the next chapter to the subject of the corporation

SUGGESTED SUPPLEMENTARY READING

Rubenstein (ed.) (1980), *Wealth and the Wealthy in the Modern World.*
Spring (ed.) (1977), *European Landed Elites in the Nineteenth Century.*
Stone (1967), *The Crisis of the Aristocracy, 1558–1641* (abridged ed.).

On Insurance

Spooner (1983), *Risks at Sea.*
Supple (1970), *The Royal Exchange Assurance.*
Sutherland (1933), *A London Merchant, 1695–1774.*

In French

Daumard (1970), *Les Bourgeois de Paris au XIXᵉ siècle.*
Michalet (1968), *Les Placements des épargnants français de 1815 à nos jours.*

11

Private Finance—The Corporation

A proposal by several ladies and others to make, print and paint and stain callicoes in England and also fine linens as fine as in Holland to be made of British flax . . . they are resolved as one man to admit no man but will themselves subscribe to a joint-stock to carry on the said trade. (Subscribers must be women dressed in calico.) Subscriptions to be opened April 20, 1720 at the China Shop in St. Martin's near St. Paul's.

("Promotions of the South Sea period, 1719–20," in Scott, *The Constitution and Finance of English, Scottish and Irish Joint-Stock Companies to 1720*, 1911, Vol. 3, p. 450)

PARTNERSHIP AND COMMENDA

The earliest form of business organization above the sole proprietorship was the partnership. It could be a true partnership in which the partners each provided both capital and services, or one or more partners, but not all, could be silent. In the *commenda* (in Italian, in French *commandite,* in German the *Kommanditgesellschaft,* in English the silent partnership), one partner, assuming only two, dominated the other. The partnership could be, in effect, a disguised loan in which labor hired the capital, or a disguised principal/agent relationship with capital hiring the labor (Postan, 1957 [1973], ch. 3). On occasion, partnerships became complex, as in Scottish banks with over 300 "partners," who were actually shareholders using the old nomenclature, or in the Hanseatic practice, shared elsewhere, of merchants forming a large number of short-range and shifting partnerships to diversify interests in various ships and voyages as a form of real insurance in the absence of effective financial institutions.

As the scale of transactions became larger and their nature more complex, there developed in Britain the regulated company, a loose federation of merchants associated for limited purposes. The Staplers or Merchants of the Staple in the fourteenth century maintained quality of product (as Danish cooperatives would do in the late nineteenth century) and provided security to their members by supervising dealings and enforcing contracts in special courts. Merchants of the Staple exported primarily wool, leather, tin, and lead. During the fifteenth and sixteenth centuries there developed further the Merchant Adventurers, exporting finished goods, especially cloth.

Various other ancestors of the joint stock company, and ultimately of the corporation, consisted in: the maone, a large partnership to finance petty conquests of one city-state by another during the Middle Ages; of associations that grew up to provide loans to city-states in return for special privileges, as in the Casa di San Giorgio in Genoa in 1408, the first bank in Europe; various municipal affairs that required charters from monarchs or local lords, paid for them, and obtained bundles of rights that gave a city or borough a quasi-corporate character; the guild, with a wide variety of purposes of a socioreligious nature beyond trade and crafts, essentially a monopoly that excluded nonmembers (J. P. Davis, 1905, Vol. 1).

JOINT STOCK COMPANY

The joint stock company was developed because of the requirements of "distant trade," as Adam Smith called it, that tied up capital in large amounts for extended periods of time (Ehrenberg, 1896 [1928], p. 378). The Hansa, Merchant Adventurers, and initially the Dutch in the fluyt ships dealt along the English Channel and the littoral of the North Sea. With extension of the capacity of ships and longer voyages, more elaborate administrative structures were needed. The Eastland Company began in the fifteenth century with trading rights to Scandinavia, Poland, and the east coast of the Baltic. The Muscovy Company was chartered for the Russian trade in 1553, the same year as the Guinea Adventurers (Richards, 1965, p. 20). As the reach of English shipping extended to the Mediterranean, the Levant Company was created in 1581 with the privilege to trade with Turkey. Finally came the East India Company, an offshoot of the Levant Company, formed in 1599 and chartered by Elizabeth 1 in 1600.

The first agreement of the East India Company was for one voyage only, after which profits were divided. At this stage it was a loose association of merchants, much like the Merchant Adventurers. Gradually the organization grew tighter, and its monopoly position increased. In 1613 £429,000 in capital was raised to cover four voyages; in 1617 it put together £1.7 million for seven voyages. By this time it had 36 ships and 934 stockholders. Only in 1657 did the company become continuous, for the period specified in its charter. Initial charters for joint stock companies in France and England were granted for limited periods of time, though with the possibility and prospect of renewal. Renewals furnished an opportunity for the Crown to extract additional quid pro quos or make new conditions (J. P. Davis, 1905, Vol. 2, ch. 5). The South Sea Company in 1720 sought a perpetual charter, as did the East India Company. Neither got it, though the East India Company succeeded in getting a longer extension to 1733. Charter renewal in 1720 set a limit on its right to borrow by issuing bonds, at £5 million, raised to £6 million in the renewal of 1744 (Sutherland, 1952, pp. 12, 16). The first permanent joint stock company was the Dutch East India Company founded in 1602 (J. P. Davis, 1905, Vol. 2, p. 114).

With the Glorious Revolution of 1688 and the accretion of wealth in London from rising trade, especially with India, came a flurry of joint stock company formation. By 1695 100 new companies had been formed with a capital of £4.5 million in all (Carswell, 1960, p. 10). The formation of the South Sea Company in the new century and the meteoric rise in its stock brought a new burst, with 195 new joint stock companies between September 1719 and August 1720. Trading in the shares of new companies took on a manic character, not uncontaminated with swindles. Daniel Defoe's tract, *The Anatomy of Change-Alley: A System of Stock-*

Jobbing Proving that Scandalous Trade as it is now carried on to be Knavish in its Private Practice and Treason in its Publick (1719), had no effect despite such rhetoric as

> There is not a man but will own 'tis a compleat System of Knavery; that 'tis a Trade founded in Fraud, born of Deceit, and nourished by Trick, Cheat, Wheedle, Forgeries, Falsehoods and all sorts of Delusions, Born in false News, this way good, that way bad; whispering imaginery Terrors, Frights, Hopes, Expectations and then preying on the Weakness of those whose Imaginations they have either elevated or depres'd. (ibid., pp. 3–4)

The stock of an insurance company, either the Royal Exchange or the London Assurance, rose fivefold between February and May 1720. More than 100 bubbles were advertised in May and the first half of June, 23 on June 7, 24 on the ninth, and 15 on the tenth to escape the Bubble Act, signed 9 June to take effect from 20 June (Carswell, 1960, p. 155). As noted earlier, the legislation requiring joint stock companies to obtain a royal charter was enacted not to punish the South Sea Company but to protect it by halting the diversion to newly formed enterprises of cash subscriptions that might otherwise have accrued to its stock (ibid., p. 139). The act was strengthened in 1735 to forbid the sale of stock not owned. It endured to 1824.

Speculation in joint stock companies was assisted by the practice of selling shares against a partial payment, with down payments as low as 5 or 10 percent and full payment delayed until the end of a series of successive calls. Justifications for the practice were (1) that the real investment took place gradually and that capital might better be left in the hands of the investor than idle in those of the company and (2) to provide a margin of protection for creditors of the company by making it possible to make new calls on the shareholders. The effect, however, was to encourage "stags" who bought not because of interest in the project but to benefit from a rise in stock prices, selling out before full payment was made, and sometimes even before the first call.

CANAL MANIA

The first wave of joint stock companies in England under the Bubble Act was for the construction of canals. (Country banks that grew rapidly in the 1750s were partnerships.) Need for effective internal transport led to improvement in the navigation of rivers from 1660 to 1730, with merchants interested in navigation pitted against millers who favored dams, fishermen with weirs, and towns on other rivers fearing diversion of water or loss of traffic. Despite such successes as the Aire & Calder Company that connected Leeds in the interior by canal boat to Hull on the coast (over the opposition of York), river improvement was not sufficient. About 1750 a start was made on canalization. The Duke of Bridgewater canal connecting the coal mines on his estates to Manchester, completed in 1761, spurred the movement. Between 1730 and 1790 when the full mania burst, canals in Britain doubled in length and reached 2,200 miles (Deane, 1965 [1979], p. 79). Demand was largely for transport of coal, which, because of its weight and bulk, could not be moved economically by road. Of 165 canal acts submitted to Parliament between 1758 and

1803, 90 served collieries and 47 iron, copper, lead mines, and their works (Porteous, 1977, p. 17).

The canal mania of 1791–94 was sedate by comparison with the railway mania of half a century later but was still characterized as involving large amounts of capital and wild speculation (Jackman, 1916, p. 394). Between 1791 and 1794 eighty-one canal and other navigation acts were passed. The forty-two new canals built cost £6½ million. Original share denominations were large: £200 was common; shares less than £50 each were rare. In one instance, shares of a canal could not be traded until £15 had been paid in—a device to discourage speculation—but, on the whole, precautions of this sort were not needed (J. R. Ward, 1974, p. 19). To a limited extent, local landowners (but especially the local mercantile community—not London) took the initiative and provided most of the capital (ibid., p. 172; Bagwell, 1974, pp. 17–18). At least 56 percent of the original shareholders buying shares after 1789 retained ownership in 1800. Industrialists, such as Bolton & Watt in steam engines and Wedgwood in china, were deeply interested in promoting the canal system to move their supplies and output more cheaply than with packhorses and, in the case of china, with less breakage.

Contributing to the "canal mania" was the sharp decline in the return on consols after the American War of Independence, from 5.4 percent in 1784 to 3.3 percent in 1792.

COMPANIES PRIOR TO THE RAILROAD

A short-lived flurry of miscellaneous acts of incorporation occurred in the midst of the Napoleonic Wars. In January 1808 alone, forty-two companies projected in the previous year were formed, including seven breweries, five wine companies, four distilleries, several insurance companies, and new enterprises in coal, wool, copper, paper, and clothing (Clapham, 1945, Vol. 2, p. 20). There were no flotations in cotton textiles, a key industry in the industrial revolution, and few in iron. In these industries, companies still relied on local capital, internal finance from plowed-back profits, and bank credit.

A second insurance boom, a century after 1720, began in 1823, following successful promotion of the Alliance Insurance Company. In the first quarter of 1824 alone, 250 private bills were filed with Parliament to establish a wide variety of companies. The boom spread to foreign bonds. In the two years before collapse, 624 company prospectuses were produced, involving a total nominal capital of £372 million. Foreign investment, discussed in the next chapter, added another £52 million. Few of the domestic projects—little more than 100—survived the crash of December 1825 (Smart, 1911 [1964], Vol. 2, pp. 188–89, 295–99).

PROVINCIAL STOCK EXCHANGES

Through the eighteenth century the London capital market had dealt in the securities of only a few firms beyond the "money companies"—Bank of England, South

Sea Company, and East India Company. The bulk of shares in canals and joint stock companies were traded informally in provincial cities. In the second quarter of the nineteenth century, these informal markets became institutionalized with the establishment of the Liverpool Stock Exchange, for example, in 1827, and the Manchester Exchange in 1830. Organized markets developed from auctions of shares of, especially, dock, water, and gas companies (not new issues) to place small blocks of shares, such as those sold by an estate. With the first boom in railway shares in 1836, the provincial stock exchanges expanded rapidly (W. A. Thomas, 1973, p. 28). By 1885 there were twelve provincial stock exchanges and, with extension of incorporation in that year, twenty-one in 1900 and twenty-two in 1914 (Jeffrys, 1938 [1977], p. 371). In 1885 provincial stock exchanges were said to have been very calm, with purchasers acquiring industrial securities not for speculation but to hold (ibid., p. 339).

RAILWAY BOOMS

The first railroad in Britain ran from Stockton to Darlington in 1825. It made little splash. More conspicuous, and with greater impact, was the Liverpool and Manchester line opened in 1830. Five new railway companies were chartered each year from 1827 to 1836, when the number jumped to twenty-nine, followed by seventeen in 1837. Joint stock companies chartered by Parliament then became the rage.

Early railroad shares, like those of canals, were marketed to merchants, gentry, and other men of known substance interested in the success of the venture who could be counted upon to meet calls for payment when they were made (Reed, 1975). Promoters were local and kept tight control. Up until 1845 it was not the London capital market that financed railroads but Lancaster capital (Broadridge, 1969). That only one London banker took a prominent part in the movement was regarded as sufficiently noteworthy by Disraeli to find its way into his novel *Endymion,* in a passage sufficiently pithy in describing the railway boom to be worth extended quotation:

Capital and labor wanted a "new channel." The new channel came and all the persons of authority, alike political and commercial, seemed quite surprised that it had arrived; but when a thing or a man are wanted, they generally appear. One or two lines of railway, which had long been sleepily in formation, about this time were finished. . . . Suddenly there was a general feeling in the country, that its capital should be invested in railways; that the whole surface of the land should be transformed, and covered, as by a network, with these mighty means of communication. When the passions of the English, naturally an enthusiastic people, are excited on a subject of finance, their will, their determination, and resource are irresistible. This was signally proved in the present instance, for they never ceased subscribing their capital until the sum intrusted to this new form of investment reached an amount almost equal to the national debt; and this too in a very few years.

What is remarkable in this vast movement in which so many millions were produced, and so many more promised, was, that the great leaders of the financial world took no part in it. The mighty loan-mongers on whose fiat the fate of kings and empires sometimes depended, seemed like men who witnessing some eccentricity of nature watch it with mixed feelings of curiosity and alarm. Even Lombard Street, which was never more wanted, was inactive, and it was only by an irresistible pressure of circumstances that a banking firm which had an extensive country connection was ultimately forced to take a leading part that was required, and almost unconsciously lay the foundation of the vast fortune which it has realized, and organize the varied connection which it now commands. All seemed to come from the provinces, and from unknown people in the provinces. (1880, pp. 380–81).

In the novel, the banker who took a leading part was named Vigo. In actuality it was Glyn of the bank of that name (Jenks, 1927, p. 130). A number of small provincial banks invested sums of £5,000 to £10,000 in railroads, but Glyn's put £100,000 into the London & Birmingham, possibly, suggests Reed, because of its Quaker promoters (1975, p. 242) although it is hard to see how this would constitute "irresistible pressure of circumstances." Failure of London bankers to turn to railroading should not have surprised Disraeli in 1880. In 1873, in *Lombard Street,* Walter Bagehot summed up the need for new men in new activities: "The rich have income and want to keep it. Any change is risky, 'a bore.' But a new man who has to make his way in the world, knows that changes are his opportunities" (1873 [1978], Vol. 9, pp. 52–53).

In the 1840s a new railroad boom took place, this time a mania. Forty-eight acts were passed by the House of Commons in 1844, 120 in 1845, 272 in 1846, and 190 in 1847, the last involving £40 million of new capital issues. In 1848 the capital sum dropped to £4 million (Evans, 1849 [1969], pp. 37–38). Construction kept on rising after the market turned downward. Panic occurred in 1847 when further capital calls, amounting to £6.15 million issued in the single month of January, found many buyers unable to pay and forced to dump shares. Initial down payments had seldom been higher than 10 percent.

The need to raise more capital to complete construction underway led to further innovations—vendor shares, preference shares, and debentures. Vendor shares were issued to contractors, like Thomas Brassey and their suppliers, in lieu of money payments. They had a subsequent revival after 1886, especially in mining, and are regarded by Jeffrys as "one of the most objectionable devices of modern finance," presumably because they are bought not for investment but for resale when market conditions improve and hang over the market like a pall (1938 [1977], p. 41).

Debentures, especially of railroad companies, were the nearest thing to government bonds in the eyes of the Victorian investor: "the favorite of couples about to marry, the last resort of Trustees . . . the cynosure of the old-fashioned school of investor" (Viscount Goschen, quoted in ibid., p. 349).

Halfway between vendor shares and debentures were preference shares, which developed especially in reaction to the railway mania. Unlike debentures with a fixed rate of interest and common stock with a variable dividend, preference shares share in profits on a preferred basis, ahead of common stock, and generally at a stipulated rate above debenture bonds. The proportion of preference shares in total railway issues was 4 percent in 1845 and 11 percent in 1846; by 1849 it had risen to 66 percent.

Incidentally the use of vendor shares by mining companies is understandable. Mining stocks in the nineteenth century were notoriously speculative. According to Sir William Forbes of the Edinburgh branch of Coutts: "I regard mining as a very deep species of gambling, whereby there has probably been more lost upon the whole than gained" (1803, in Forster and Forster, eds., 1969, p. 161). The same view was held in 1873 when there was a boom in mining shares in Germany. "The exchange is now caught up with mining companies, and mining, as my experience teaches, is the last act of the drama" (Ludwig Bamberger, quoted in Pinner, 1937, p. 208). Again he said that mining (from which along with railroads he made his own fortune) tested all of an individual's ability to distinguish good from bad risks (Zucker, 1975, p. 37). The speculative character of investing in mines came from the large amount of capital required and the long period of time that had to pass before one could be sure that that a discovery would be worthwhile and lead to dividends. An investigation of British investment in overseas mining maintains that frenzied booms and busts in mining shares were an integral part of the Victorian capital market, with yields in Western Australia, for example, ranging from complete loss to a 2,333 percent profit. Paris banks promoted speculation in kaffirs (South African gold-mining shares), borrowing in London to finance their clients. When the London banks stopped discounting this paper in late 1895, the boom collapsed (van Heltern, 1990, esp. pp. 159, 166, 172).

H. G. Lewin's book, *The Railway Mania and Its Aftermath, 1849–52* (1936 [1968]), deals less with financial aspects of railroads than with technical matters, but it does illuminate the character and behavior of George Hudson, the great railway genius of the period, who repeatedly mesmerized himself into committing illegal acts. Hudson was at one time chairman of four separate companies and tended to believe himself above the law. He entered into contracts with companies of which he was himself an owner and officer; raised dividends before making up annual accounts; paid dividends out of capital; altered books; and so on. To be sure, on occasion he would advance money to a railroad from his own funds (ibid., pp. 262, 357–64). Unlike Mirès in France and Strousberg in Germany, he was a railroader rather than purely a financier. Like them, however, he played fast and loose with stockholders' funds.

This may be a suitable place to list other dubious or outright dishonest or illegal practices of corporate finance in this period: paying dividends out of stock sales; issuing new shares before existing shares are fully paid up; using company cash to support its own shares—done especially by banks in the nineteenth and twentieth centuries with disastrous impact on their liquidity, on the one hand, and capital/deposit ratio on the other; issuing shares to insiders with down payments advanced by the company itself. One could also demand a standard of conduct that included full disclosure to existing and potential stockholders (Wirth, 1858 [1890], p. 215).

GENERAL INCORPORATION

The Bubble Act was repealed in 1824 because the British government could no longer adequately supervise a growing number of unincorporated enterprises and because it wanted to remove an unwarranted restriction on joint stock companies. These joint stock companies with parliamentary approval grew from 1824 to 1856 when general incorporation without specific approval became possible, as amounts of capital required for various businesses became larger with the growth of factories and ships, and with the spread of steam power. In addition, even apart from unlimited liability, the disadvantages of large partnerships—lack of continuity and inability to sue and to be sued as a collectivity—loomed larger, particularly as Britain had not developed the form of private partnerships with limited liability and transferable shares. With the coming of the railroads, the pressure on Parliament to approve joint stock companies became intense. In the 1850s and 1860s, moreover, limited liability came to be widely debated. It was unpopular, Bagehot said, not only for banks, where it reduced the security of depositors (and was delayed until after the failure of the City Bank of Glasgow in 1878), but generally with the rich, who found the combined wealth of little stockholders in corporations provided them with greater competition (1862 [1978], Vol. 9, pp. 400, 406). A number of economists were fearful that generalized incorporation would stimulate speculation (Cottrell, 1980, p. 49).

There is something of a debate over the "sudden" coming of the reform of the company law that produced generalized incorporation in 1856. Jeffrys maintained that the proximate cause was found in savers in southeast England who, with surpluses to invest and facing a slowdown in railroads, wanted a reduction of risks before they would undertake investment in manufacturing (1938 [1977]). Contemporary Christian Socialists advocated widening limited liability in order to encourage workmen to invest their savings in industry and thereby to reduce the tension between the owning and the working classes (Cottrell, 1980, pp. 47–48). In the end, the decisive argument was that of freedom of economic activity, plus the fact that a number of companies were incorporating under French or American law to limit shareholder liability (ibid., pp. 51–52). Whatever the proximate cause, however, the basic reason was surely that the amounts of capital required by railroads, mines, shipping companies, banks, and a growing number of industrial enterprises were increasing beyond the capacity of informal markets to provide them.

Modern economics has undertaken a new discussion of limited liability in recent years in the Modigliani-Miller theorem (1958), which holds that limited liability does not alter the totality of risk but merely redistributes it from owners to creditors. The point was not lost on investors in the nineteenth century. One device to share risk between stockholders and creditors, rather than shifting it in big amounts from one to the other, was to issue debentures only up to the unpaid portion of share capital (Jeffrys, 1938 [1977], p. 184). In cotton, as a rule £5 of capital was left unpaid on each share as security for bank loans; in shipping, shares were frequently left one-quarter or one-third unpaid as a reserve to be called upon against accident liability (Jeffrys, 1946 [1954], p. 53).

In any business above the sole proprietorship, moreover, there is likely to be an "agency" problem. The basis for nepotism is that individuals are not likely to cheat their own families, and fixed pricing substituted for the haggling of the marketplace in such institutions as the department store when scale of operations outgrew family size and left open the possibility that an employee would sell too cheaply to someone to whom he was more closely bound than to his employer. The agency problem, in short, is that owner and employee have different interests, and to ensure that the employee carries out the wishes of the employer, the latter must undertake monitoring costs and, if possible, the costs of bonding the employee. A possible argument for incorporation is that monitoring and bonding costs are more readily covered in a corporation where responsibilities of owners and managers (agents) are more sharply defined than in partnerships where they are not—even where the essence of the partnership is one of principal/agent (Jensen and Meckling, 1976). The case is not a strong one, as the East India Company reveals. As was seen in Chapter 10 (pp. 185–86) and will be seen again in Chapter 13 (pp. 230–32), directors, company servants in India, shipowners, and ship captains often placed their own interest above that of the stockholders, and monitoring was highly ineffective.

Adam Smith was very much aware of the agency problem and used it as an argument against joint stock companies:

The directors of such companies, however, being the managers of other people's money than of their own, it cannot well be expected, that they should watch over it with the same anxious vigilance with which the partners in a private co-partnery frequently watch over their own. Like the stewards of a rich man, they are apt to consider attention to small matters as not for their master's honor, and very easily give themselves a dispensation from having it. Negligence and profusion, therefore, must always prevail, more or less, in the management of the affairs of such a company. (1776 [1937], p. 700)

A third advantage of incorporation, this time favoring the stockholder, is the opportunity it affords for diversification of risk. Risk can be diversified, as we have seen, by shifting, multiple, limited-in-time partnerships. Transactions and information costs are lower with incorporation. If a private company is formed, however, with all shares held by a closed group of investors, the gain in diversification is minimal. In any case, the gain from diversification may have to be balanced against the increase in agency cost from separating management and ownership, but this is probably inescapable as the size of productive units grows.

On these scores, there is no need to wonder why limited liability gave rise to debate upon its introduction, even though, at first glance, with the advent of the railroad, the advantages seem overwhelming.

SWEDISH INCORPORATION

As in the case of central banking, pride of place in generalized incorporation went to Sweden. There were joint stock companies in that country before 1848, but their status—except for those chartered by the government—was somewhat doubtful. In 1848 a governmental decree provided recognition of the legal position of the joint stock company. As in other countries, the coming of the railroad with its necessity for a large accumulation of capital posed the initial requirement. The form was quickly extended to the iron and timber trades, expanding under the pressure of wider markets as Britain lowered its duties generally during the 1840s and 1850s, and especially repealed the timber duties (Montgomery, 1939, pp. 88, 91, 101–2).

BRITISH EXPERIENCE WITH INCORPORATION

The Joint Stock Companies Act of 1856 introduced limited liability and the general right of incorporation without a precedent act of Parliament. The right was consolidated in the Company Act of 1862, which also enlarged the scope of the legislation to include insurance companies but not yet banks. A number of empirical studies have been made of the experience under this legislation: of the first 5,000 companies (Shannon, 1932) and of companies formed after 1880 (MacGregor, 1929). In the former case, absorptions, voluntary liquidations, and bankruptcies thinned the ranks, with absorptions (mergers) accounting for the disappearance of half the banks; a third to a half of railroads, land, mining, shipbuilding, and coastal shipping companies; 20 percent of coal, steel, and general engineering; 15 percent in cotton; and only a few companies in gas, water, and local halls. In all, one-sixth of total companies disappeared through absorption. Insolvency was responsible for a higher toll, covering one-quarter of all companies but only one-sixth of those formed prior to 1862. The reason for the brave early start was the financial crisis of 1857, which occurred shortly after the Joint Stock Companies Act and held down the formation of weaklings. Twenty-nine percent of companies formed from 1862 to 1869 failed, especially financial companies that were mowed down in the Overend, Gurney crisis of 1866. Of total companies formed from 1856 to 1866, 39 percent had disappeared after five years, 54 percent after ten years, and only 9 percent existed in their original form in 1932 (Shannon, 1933 [1954], p. 418). The crash of Overend, Gurney (the Corner House) on Black Friday in May 1866 was blamed on the shift of the company from a partnership to a financial corporation under the Act of 1862, and its failure to solve the agency problem. In one view, cheap money and the piecemeal repeal of the joint stock banking laws of 1844 were more responsible for the boom of the 1860s than the Companies Act of 1862, as they led to the establishment of twelve new banks after 1844, which in turn financed a host of new domestic, colonial, and foreign investment companies and banks (Cottrell, 1988, pp. 44–45).

Company capital doubled in amount from 1856 to 1885 and reached £800 million in the later year. Only 20 to 30 percent of this was new. Most represented conversion of private into public companies (Jeffrys, 1938 [1977], p. 92). Public hostility to joint stock companies by this time had changed to acceptance, and industries such as textiles that were new to the corporate form hastened to adopt it. Companies were encouraged to go public by certain extensions of the benefits of incorporation in legislation in 1885, broadening the 1856 and 1862 Acts. Breweries were conspicuous in the process of conversion. Part of the favor enjoyed by the industry came from the spread in France of phylloxera, attacking grapevines and hurting the wine crop, with potential for increasing the demand for beer. The great success of a Guinness issue in October 1886 was "like the firing of a starting pistol." Eighty-six other breweries issued shares publicly until the Baring crisis of 1890 interrupted, and a new wave of somewhat smaller breweries put out shares in the decade of the 1890s until the boom collapsed in 1900. Glyn Mills Bank took a prominent role in the boomlet, as it had in the railroad mania (Cottrell, 1980, pp. 169–70).

By the last third of the century, other industries beside railroads were growing to a size that outstripped informal capital markets, especially steel, cotton, shipping, coal mines, and the new industries of chemicals and electricity. Company promoters came into being, specialized and professional, especially in iron and steel. Most industrial shares were still traded in the provinces. London catered to railroads, iron and steel, the major international companies, government stock, and foreign bonds (ibid., p. 62).

Denomination of the par value of company shares, like that of bank notes, was a matter for careful determination. In the first ten years after 1856, only 16 percent of shares had par values below £5, 52 percent were from £10 to £100, and some thirty companies had shares of £1,000 or above (Jeffrys, 1946 [1954], p. 51). Canal and bank shares were rarely below £25 and railroads £100. Where stock was held mainly locally and by small investors, as in mining and cotton, a usual denomination was £5 or £10. There was a tendency late in the century for denominations to decline. Jeffrys observed that shipping shares were originally denominated at £75 or £100 each in the 1850s, when the owners were largely merchants and shipbrokers in the larger ports. In the 1880s tramp-ship shares came down to £1 to appeal to a wider group of "servant girls and greengrocers" (ibid., p. 53).

The London Stock Exchange, financed by banks and especially by the deposits drawn from abroad, has been criticized, along with the banks themselves, for neglecting industry. It issued stock for old, established companies in old, established industries, primarily to allow the founder's family to get out as private firms went public. After a flurry of investment in the electrical industry in the early 1880s that ended up in bankruptcies, it did little for the new industries, such as bicycles, automobiles, electrical equipment, and chemicals (W. P. Kennedy, 1990, p. 31). New issues were mainly for local governments and public utilities, such as railroads, tramways, telephone and telegraph, electricity generation, and gas and water, both at home and abroad. Venture capital, however, it did not provide, although by loans to brokers it supported the secondary market on the stock exchange for new issues brought out by merchant bankers (Michie, 1990).

THE MACMILLAN GAP

The Macmillan Committee, which wrote a report on finance and industry in 1931, claimed to find a gap then between companies raising less than £100,000 that could use informal local markets in the provinces and those seeking £1½ million or more that had access to the London stock exchange (Committee on Finance and Industry, 1931, para. 404; Frost, 1954). The report stated that no gap had existed before World War I (Committee on Finance and Industry, 1931, para. 377), but this view is not supported by subsequent research, albeit the gap somewhat narrows. Overhead costs of floating an issue in London made that market too expensive for firms capitalized at £100,000 to £500,000, while those at the upper end of the bracket might have difficulty raising funds in the provinces where markets were highly localized (Jeffrys, 1938 [1977], p. 370). The existence or absence of a gap is important on two counts: for the question as to whether British industry was deprived of capital and as a test of the Coase theorem that institutions always spring into being to perform necessary economic tasks. If Coase is right, a gap cannot exist when financial requirements are continuous in size. Other such gaps have been espied, although not necessarily established, in financing foreign trade between the commercial acceptance at one end of the spectrum, usually of three months but occasionally as long as a year, and foreign bonds that usually run ten years or more. In the 1930s government institutions, such as the Export-Import Bank in the United States and the Export Credit Guarantees Department of the Board of Trade in Britain, helped finance the export of durable capital equipment such as machine tools to fill, in part, this "gap" until the much later development of term loans in international lending after World War II.

DID THE LONDON CAPITAL MARKET HANDICAP BRITISH INDUSTRY?

Whether the London capital market was efficient is frequently discussed in terms of whether it starved British industry of capital by diverting an undue share of national savings into foreign loans. Sir Arthur Lewis considered that the predilection of professional investors for foreign bonds as trustee securities over less risky domestic industrial stocks and bonds was irrational and left unexploited opportunities for investment at home (1978, p. 177). The more usual view is that the trouble with British industry lay with the demand, not the supply, of capital, as evidenced by low rates of interest and profit. The return on foreign bonds, for example, was almost two percentage points higher than that on English railroad securities (Lévy-Leboyer, 1977a, p. 113). We return to the subject in the chapters on foreign lending.

FRENCH JOINT STOCK ENTERPRISE

French experience with joint stock companies has been neatly summarized (Freedeman, 1979). From Colbert's Ordinance in 1673, French law was more liberal than British in allowing, in addition to the *société en nom collectif,* an ordinary partnership, the *société en commandite,* a silent partnership after 1830, and a *société en commandite par actions,* a silent partnership with transferable shares. Public registration of *commandites* was required, but permission was not. Companies could also be chartered by the Crown. An attempt was made in 1782 to liberalize the treatment of *sociétés en commandite,* but the Parlement de Paris was jealous of its right to retain jurisdiction over companies like the Compagnie des Indes or the Compagnie d'Occident and rejected the draft code (ibid., p. 5).

Following the collapse of the Mississippi Bubble in 1720, the barn door was locked by the establishment of a bourse to replace the rue Quincampoix and police the market in company shares. The French Revolution, in turn, led to closing of the bourse and suppression of all quasi-public companies such as the Caisse d'Escompte.

In 1804, under the Empire, an attempt was made to simplify industrial organization by permitting only one type of company, the *société anonyme,* a company with bearer shares, which had to be authorized by the government. Public pressure insisted on the restoration of the *société en commandite,* which was done in January 1808. At this time there were fewer than thirty *sociétés anonymes,* including the Enterprise Générale des Messageries, transporting passengers and goods by post-chaise, the Salines "Estarac," manufacturing salt, a large company draining marshes, the chemical and glass company, Saint Gobain, and so on (ibid.).

In the 1820s and 1830s, France went through a period of canal building and a speculative bubble in company formation along with Belgium. The first was financed to a considerable extent by the *hautes banques* (Grosskreutz, 1977); the second, a speculative mania attracting a wide public of petty investors, is illustrated with brilliant realism in Balzac's novel *César Birotteau* (1837 [1972]). In the speculative boom between 1826 and 1838, over 500 companies were registered as *commandites* in two years with a capital of 520 million francs. There were mining shares, railroad shares, and banks, covering both France and Belgium (Lévy-Leboyer, 1964, pp. 632–33). Speculation in the period was also rampant in *biens nationaux.* Lévy-Leboyer asks: "Who is the Frenchman sufficiently irrational to expose his fortune to enterprise when the state offers him a return of 30, 40 or 50 percent in confiscated domains?" (ibid., p. 709). Textile companies of Alsace were financed partly by banks in Paris (as were those in Normandy, largely Rouen) but mainly by banks of Basle, Strasbourg, and Lyons (ibid., pp. 437, 457). The lack of a provincial capital market in France, as compared with Britain, is striking, but then so is French centralization of economic direction in virtually all respects. Capital was available at St. Etienne, a manufacturing town, especially at Lyons, and a capital market was ultimately established at Mulhouse (ibid., pp. 457, 464). The ordinary investor was primarily interested in land and *rentes,* however, and left the finance of manufacturing to Parisian banks and the entrepreneurs themselves.

FRENCH RAILROADS

The first railroads in France were private lines designed to carry coal from mines in St. Etienne in the Upper Loire valley to various points such as Le Creusot and Lyons. These were completed in the late 1820s. In the early 1830s the French legislature entered the picture and passed a law calling for a centrally designed railroad system—in complete contrast to the British network, which grew by itself without overall design. The Corps des Ponts et Chaussées under Louis LeGrand drew up a plan, with Paris as the center of an *étoile,* or star, from which lines radiated to the corners of the country, but the program involved much debate and was not enacted until 1842.

Meanwhile the success of the Liverpool and Manchester line in Britain, opened in 1830, led the Pereire brothers to experiment, first, with a short line for passengers from Paris to St. Germain, and then with one from Paris to Versailles. Completed in 1837, these started a rush to build major lines. A line from Paris to Rouen was organized by a group of French and London bankers, with some finance from British suppliers of construction and rolling stock, such as Brassey who built the right of way and Stephenson who supplied locomotives. Other parts of the *étoile* were let out—to the north to a Rothschild group with which Emile Pereire was then associated, to the southwest (Orléans and ultimately Bordeaux) to a group of French and Swiss bankers, and to Marseilles by way of Dijon and Lyons—the famous Paris-Lyons-Marseilles, or PLM, line—to groups responsible for separate stretches and including Enfantin and Talabot.

French capitalists had abundant funds, but they were timid; British financiers were attracted to French railroads, but British investors were not. This provided a classic opportunity for international intermediation. London merchant bankers, led by Baring Brothers and Company from 1842 to 1845, issued bonds in the City for French railroads that were bought by French investors; the London imprimatur was enough to overcome French hesitation. After the initial learning experience, the French undertook to invest directly at home (Platt, 1984, ch. 2, esp. pp. 24–27).

A mere 600 kilometers had been completed by 1842 when the Le Grand plan was adopted and promulgated (Cameron, 1961, pp. 204–8). Part of the slowness thereafter to mid-century was due to bankers' quarrels, part to the rigidity of the Corps des Ponts et Chaussées, part to the recession of 1847 and the Revolution of 1848. Building reached a virtual halt when the Revolution produced a wave of xenophobia and drove out British engineers and foremen, from railroads and mines alike, killing one British engineer by a stray bullet in a riot (Locke, 1978, p. 145). Earlier, expansion of the mines at Alais in southern France to supply coal for the PLM had waited on a government loan to the railroad, called for when an attempt to raise 14 million francs privately had failed. This finally passed the Chamber of Deputies in 1836 and enabled the mine to continue to expand capacity (ibid., pp. 42–44).

Expansion of the railroad network with financing from the Crédit Mobilier and admission of railroad bonds to direct discounting at the Bank of France have already been discussed. As in Britain, the railroad—which was impossible to start on a small scale like a textile plant (Tilly, 1966, p. 134)—led inexorably to the adoption of generalized limited liability. An element of rivalry with Britain was involved: "The law of 23 May 1863 had as its first motive the necessity of struggling against Britain with equal weapons" (Bouvier, 1973, p. 93). The law provided for general incorporation and limited liability—the *sociétés à responsabilitée limitée* (SARLs)—with an initial limit of 20 million francs. The law lasted only four years before the limit was removed and general permission to form *sociétés anonymes* (SAs) was enacted. Three hundred thirty-eight SARLs were constituted, among the most important of which were the Crédit Lyonnais, formed two weeks after the law had been promulgated, and the Société Générale. The Crédit Lyonnais chose not to go the SA route because its founders did not want to include Paris money, and Paris *financiers,* excluded from participation, might have opposed the granting of an SA to the bank (Freedeman, 1979, p. 138). Bouvier claims that the promoters of the SARL legislation were particularly interested in making it possible to start banks without government permission (1973, p. 93).

The SA, or corporation, has not been wildly popular in France. One hundred fifty-two companies were quoted on the bourse in 1852 and 1,202 a half-century later in 1902. Two thousand three hundred clients had securities on deposit with the Crédit Lyonnais in 1871 and 5,234 in 1880, but most of these doubtless held mainly government *rentes.* The annual average of new issues in SA form was 152 million for the period 1892–96 and 987 million for 1911–13 (Michalet, 1968, p. 179). Major holdings were in railroads and urban transport, rather than such industries as gas and electricity, and were owned by the rich, rather than the modest *petite bourgeoisie.* While rich provincial towns such as Lyons had sophisticated speculation and Lyons was compared in 1889 to a vast rue Quincampoix (Bouvier, 1960, p. 111), the rural capital and mortgage market, which in Britain had moved after the 1880s away from the solicitor and notary into the more professional hands of the banks (Jeffrys, 1938 [1977], p. 332), remained solidly in the hands of the notary in France.

As in Britain, the question was insistently raised as to whether foreign investment starved domestic industry. Lewis was persuaded that it did (1978, p. 176); Cameron observes that capital exports in 1835–38, 1852–56, 1878–81, and 1910–13 coincided with French prosperity as the monies were used to finance exports and that periods of weak foreign investment, such as 1823–33 and 1882–97, coincided with stagnation and depression. He concludes that capital exports were stimulating rather than deleterious to French industry (1961, pp. 504–5). But, as we shall see, some spurts of French lending to Italy, Spain, and Russia occurred in other periods than those listed by Cameron and were largely wasted. Again, the conclusion from low interest rates within France is that the difficulties with French industry lay with the demand for capital, not the supply.

THE VENAL PRESS

For security prices to reflect rational calculations, investors must have access to sufficient information at low cost, and that information must be accurate. Channels of information must be treated like a public good, moreover, and not be up for sale to the highest bidder. Whereas in Britain in 1720, there were hints that some journalists trimmed their views, and even reversed them as Daniel Defoe, twice a bankrupt and often in debtors' prison, did on several occasions, to accommodate some material interest (Novak, 1962, pp. 5, 13, 160 n. 34, 161 n. 50), the press was far more venal for longer on the Continent.

In the boom of 1881 in Paris and Lyons when 125 million issues with a value of 5 billion francs were being promoted, there were 228 financial journals puffing the single market of Paris, according to an estimate, without counting financial bulletins in 95 other political journals. These periodicals were owned by bankers, brokers, important speculators, and more rarely by the large banks. Many were blackmailers, ready to print damaging "news" if they were not bought off (Bouvier, 1960, p. 29). Emile Zola's *L'Argent* has a scene in which Saccard, patterned after Mirès, is offering to open an account for a journalist, Sabatani, and to start a journal of his own to organize publicity for the Banque Universelle, which he had founded and the shares of which he was engaged in distributing (1890, reprinted n.d., pp. 144–46). One journalist is said to have remarked: "Give me 30,000 francs on announcements and I will place all the shares of the worst enterprise you can imagine" (Lévy-Leboyer, 1964, p. 633). The Panama scandal in Paris in 1892 involved a huge amount paid for publicity by the de Lesseps in promoting their securities to finance the venture, with a major portion of the 7 million francs tied to the lottery loan of 1888 used to bribe deputies in the Chamber to vote to give permission for the issue (Simon, 1971).

Bleichröder in Berlin used journalists to disseminate favorable news about issues he was selling and in 1890–91 paid for a trip to Mexico of one journalist, Paul Lindau, while he, Bleichröder, was selling Mexican bonds. Lindau wrote thirty-four articles on Mexico and a book but failed to disclose the source of his support (Stern, 1977a, ch. 11, esp. p. 275).

Stern observes that a critical press developed first in England (and the United States) and then slowly on the Continent, though at the lower end of the spectrum of honesty, company promoters in England were still complaining of the bribes they had to pay in the 1880s to have their projects noticed. One publisher took money not to reveal information in his periodical (Armstrong, 1990, pp. 117, 124). There was still no objective press in France between the wars (Jeanneney, 1975). In the process of improvement, the private short-run good was finally replaced by the public good, valuable in the long run, comparable to the shift from tax farming to centralized governmental tax collection and expenditure. The path was strewn with difficulties, twists, and turns. In particular, there could be competition among public goods, with foreign policy dominating the public good of accurate dissemination of information, and the Russian government, assisted by the Quai d'Orsay, misleading French investors (White, 1933, pp. 280–82).

GERMANY

Joint stock companies were rare in Germany before 1850; Prussian capitalists kept their money in land, mortgages, and government bonds. Incorporation required specific authority from the government in each case and was often refused because of either the prejudice of the Junker bureaucrats, as in the case of banks, or of fear of competition, for example, of sugar refineries. The change came in mid-century and was again initiated by the railroad for which a number of joint stock companies had been created in the 1840s. "The urge to dig new mines, erect new factories, build new railroads, and above all to invest in corporations and to speculate with stocks gripped all classes from peasants to the prince with the noble crown who was the first imperial prince" (Marx in 1851, quoted in Blumberg, 1960, p. 168). Industry thought that credit was inaccessible, and the issue was discussed widely, not only in chambers of commerce but in state parliaments.

In 1851 a *Miteigentümergesetz* (joint ownership law) was passed, and corporations began to be formed, the capital of existing ones increased. It is not known how many were entirely new and how many represented private-held enterprises converted to public form. There are some known instances after 1857 of private companies going public to save the capital of the "creditors," Blumberg says; he probably means the owners since the creditors would lose from a limitation of the owners' liability (ibid., p. 182). From 1850 to 1859, 122 companies were noted in Prussia with a capital of 108 million thalers, of which 81 million was new capital and 21 million increases. Of the 108 million, moreover, 81 million was in mining and iron and steel, 12.5 million in textiles, 6 million in machinery, and 3.4 million in chemicals, including illuminating gas (ibid., 176–77). The comparable figures for Saxony were 89 companies, for a total of 21.4 million thalers, of which 13.2 million consisted of coal mines.

Prussian corporations were formed for the most part in the Rhineland and Ruhr, that is, Rheinische-Westphalia. Mining and the steel industry employed a considerable amount of foreign capital. Forty-two companies in the industry out of a total of forty-nine had extra-Prussian capital in 1860, and fourteen had foreign capital, largely French and Belgian, which was especially strong in the nonferrous metals sector. Amounts involved were not overwhelming: in the Rhineland and Westphalia, extra-Prussian capital accounted to 20 million thalers out of 54 million paid in and 60 million authorized (ibid., p. 184). It was nonetheless lamented. In the Neu-Essener Gewerbeverein *Festschrift* of 1852, Gustav Mevissen bewails French and English participation in German mining, which "enriches foreign capital through the fruit of German labor" (Benaerts, 1933, p. 353). This is the first complaint of industrial *Überfremdung* (excessive foreign control) of which I am aware, although the same complaint can be heard much earlier against the activities of foreign bankers.

Blumberg's patient digging in archives has produced statistics on the occupations of 480 subscribers to the stock of sixty-one of these early companies. The information is surprising because of the prominent role of merchants, when merchants as a class were weak in Germany, and because where merchants were strong, as in Britain and France, they were not prominent among investors in manufacturing or mining, preferring to hold land. The difference may be based on the greater difficulty of achieving high social standing for a bourgeois in Germany through buying land, as compared to the other countries.

Of the total number of investors, 152 or 32 percent were merchants, 71 or 14 percent manufacturers, 62 or 12 percent state officials, 52 or 11 percent bankers, 33 or 7 percent large landowners, and 6 or 1½ percent members of the military (Blumberg, 1960, p. 197). In Silesia the representation of merchants in mining was lower. State officials, somewhat surprising to find on the list, were said to be not upper level but mostly middle and lower–in other words, not Junkers, who were anti-industrial until close to the end of the nineteenth century, but bourgeoisie excluded from noble ranks.

From this start, German business expanded rapidly with bank support plus auto-financing, as detailed in Chapter 7 (pp. 129–30). Some support to small business had been provided by the Royal Seehandlung in the early part of the century. The role of the stock exchanges was limited, however. After contributing to the financing of railroads, they settled back to their old business of state debt and foreign bonds (Brockhage, 1910, esp. ch. 7). The industrial financial paper in a city such as Frankfurt was small (Böhme, 1968, p. 188). It was partly that industry needed very little capital compared with commerce, agriculture, construction, and infrastructure, as already indicated. Partly banks and ploughed-back profits provided industry with its capital needs.

It is well also to bear in mind the German propensity for cartel formation (*Kartellfähigheit*), for concerns and for trusts, that picked up especially in the depression following 1873 (Levy, 1935 [1966], p. 7). Only six agreements have been traced prior to 1870 and fourteen to 1877. Thereafter, 350 cartels were formed to the end of the century, of which 275 survived to World War I (Clapham, 1953, p. 311) and 1,500 to 1925 (Levy, 1935 [1966], p. 15).

Cartels might have been a substitute for large corporations. In actuality they proved to be complements. In addition, German corporations went in strongly for vertical integration, a movement based on fear of being cut off, whether from sources of supply for inputs or from markets for outputs (Niehans, 1977).

German corporate history is thus different from French and British in various respects. Most striking, however, is that the history that took several hundred years in Britain was telescoped into sixty-five in Germany.

SUGGESTED SUPPLEMENTARY READING

Cottrell (1980), *Industrial Finance, 1830–1914.*
Freedeman (1979), *Joint-Stock Enterprise in France, 1807–1867.*
Jeffrys (1938 [1977]), *Trends in Business Organization in Great Britain since 1856.*
Postan (1957 [1973]), *Medieval Trade and Finance,* ch. 3.
Scott (1911), *The Constitution and Finance of English, Scottish and Irish Joint-Stock Companies to 1720.*
van Helten and Cassis (eds.) (1990), *Capitalism in a Mature Economy.*

In German

Blumberg (1960), Die Finanzierung der Neugründungen und Erweiterungen von Industriebetrieben.

12

Foreign Investment—Dutch, British, French, and German Experience to 1914

> She learned, to her horror, that Margaret, now of age, was taking her money out of the old safe investments and putting it into Foreign Things, which always smash. Her own fortune was invested in Home Rails, and most ardently did she beg her niece to imitate her. "Then we should be together, dear." Margaret, out of politeness, invested a few hundreds in Nottingham and Derby Railway, though the Foreign Things did admirably and the Nottingham and Derby declined with the steady dignity of which only Home Rails are capable.
>
> (E. M. Forster, *Howard's End,* 1921 [1948], pp. 13–14)

FOREIGN LENDING

International capital movements in various forms will occupy us for three chapters. The forms are varied: new issues of foreign securities; trade across national boundaries in existing securities, both shares and bonds; foreign direct investment; and subsidies, indemnities, reparations, and payments of substantial purchases such as Louisiana, Alaska, the khedive's shares in the Suez canal, the French rights and the abortive start on the Panama canal. In this chapter, we treat the major foreign-lending countries of Europe in the seventeenth, eighteenth, and nineteenth centuries, that is, from about 1600 to 1914, and specifically Holland, England, France, and Germany. Chapter 13 is devoted to a series of transfer cases by which loans, or subsidies and indemnities that pose the problem in more acute form, are effectively transferred from one country and currency to others. Chapter 14 addresses a series of further questions about foreign capital movements in historical context—the channels in which such lending flows, their occasional shifts, the political nexus, cyclical patterns, rationality of investors, and the like—and brings the account of lending up to the eve of World War I.

DUTCH FOREIGN LENDING

We begin with the Dutch and about 1600, referring the reader interested in earlier Italian, south German, and Flemish (Antwerp) experience back to Chapters 2 and 3. In the seventeenth and eighteenth centuries, Amsterdam dominated international capital markets of Europe with some limited competition from Genoa—quite a bit in one view (Felloni, 1971)—rather more from Geneva. In the nineteenth century London pulled ahead, with strong competition from Paris, less from Frankfurt and Berlin. The Dutch experience can be summed up in a few sentences: in the seventeenth century from 1616 to 1688, its investments were on the Continent and in the Empire, with most of the latter lost in the Second and Third Anglo-Dutch Wars; from 1688, but more especially after the Treaty of Utrecht ending the War of the Spanish Succession, the Dutch invested heavily in Britain. The Fourth Anglo-Dutch War brought halt to that flow and redirected Dutch savings to France and, to a lesser extent, to the United States. Extended occupation of the country in the Napoleonic Wars virtually finished the lending process.

The Seventeenth Century

The earliest Dutch loan on record in our period is the 250,000 florin advance to the elector of Brandenburg in 1616, produced by a single individual from his own resources (Riley, 1980, p. 86). The elector was followed by a series of royal and princely borrowers (Barbour, 1950 [1966], p. 104), and loans were contracted by Denmark, Sweden, Hamburg, Emden, East Friesland, and the Dutch Empire (C. Wilson, 1941, p. 88). On his restoration to the English throne in 1661, Charles II sought a £2 million loan, but owing to the Anglo-Dutch Wars it was not forthcoming. Loans were on the whole organized informally. The heirs of Gabrielle Marcelis in 1681 claimed that he had furnished large sums to the Crown of Denmark from his own funds but also those of his creditors, including merchants, widows, and orphans. The widow of Irgens made a similar claim later on behalf of her late husband (Barbour, 1950 [1966], p. 113). There was also considerable investment in English mortgages: in the last third of the century, four agents indicated that they had advanced sums to English merchants amounting to £390,000, some considerable part of which was secured by mortgages (C. Wilson, 1941, p. 90).

The greater part of Dutch investment in this early period, however, was direct, that is, closely associated with projects of Dutch merchants and engineers. Dutch money was involved, along with English, in the draining of the Great Fen and Hatfield Chase by the Dutch engineer Cornelius Vermuyden. Dutch entrepreneurs, among them the armament maker Louis de Geer, operated widely in Scandinavia in sawmills, mines, shipbuilding, and canal construction. In Russia, Dutchmen started sawmills, paper mills, glassmaking, and postal service. And in France, pottery, cloth, dyeing, distilling, sugar refining, and especially the draining of swamps were some of their interests (Barbour, 1950 [1966], pp. 118–20).

While this investment in productive assets abroad was taking place, the Dutch at home were actively developing an interest in, and capacity for, gambling with paper assets or claims of one kind or another. The tulip mania of 1636—37 was probably the high-water mark in bubbles (Posthumus, 1928 [1969]; Wirth, 1858 [1890], ch. 2; Garber, 1990). The highest price for a single bulb was an Admiral von Enckhuizen, named after a Dutch hero, which sold for the equivalent of £20,000 (Baasch, 1927, p. 234n). The Amsterdam capital market developed sophisticated techniques for trading, including short selling, puts, and calls, that is, options to sell or buy stocks at a stipulated price over a stipulated period of time and future trading cn commodities. Trading in options earned the designation of *Windhandel* (trade in air). Spot commodities could be bought and sold for future semiannual settlement, as well as for cash (ibid., pp. 233–36).

By the end of the century, finance and trade, and finance and entrepreneurship in foreign operations, were beginning to separate. The growing interest in English securities was purely financial. There were also straight financial loans on the Continent. Austria raised 7½ million florins in Amsterdam in six loans, starting in 1695 during the Nine Years' War and continuing to 1704 into the War of the Spanish Succession. Austria simultaneously borrowed some monies from London and Genoa (Riley, 1980, pp. 87–88).

The Eighteenth Century

During the eighteenth century, the Dutch invested heavily in British securities to 1781 when the Fourth Anglo-Dutch War broke out, and then in France when particularly attractive investments in annuities became available under Necker. In these instances, they were investing in securities issued abroad, denominated in foreign currencies. At the same time, the Amsterdam capital market was underwriting securities in florins for Austria, Denmark, Poland, Sweden, Spain, Russia, and the United States. The details of this lending are set out in general—not always with complete clarity—by Riley (1980) and for the Amsterdam merchant-banking house, Hope & Company, by Buist (1974). From the details, several general conclusions emerge:

1. War was the cause of much borrowing by all countries and vastly complicated both borrowing and payment of interest and capital. Austria borrowed annually during the War of the Bavarian Succession (1788–89), although much of this was refunding of loans coming due that had been issued in the 1760s, again in the Turkish War of 1787, and especially during the Napoleonic Wars. When Amsterdam stopped lending in 1793 because of its occupation by French troops, Austria turned to England for loans. When this source was cut off, it withdrew from the hostilities (Riley, 1980, pp. 128–36).

2. Wartime borrowing was complex. The United States bought Louisiana from the impecunious Napoleon in 1803 for $15 million; 3¾ million was offset against U.S. claims on France, leaving $11¼ million due, for which the United States gave the French bonds. Baring Brothers in England, which was at war with France, and Hope in Amsterdam and London bought the American bonds from the French for 52 million francs, with a 6 million franc down payment, and scheduled payments of 2 million francs a month for two years. President Jefferson advanced $2 million or 10 million francs to the U.S. ambassador as a guarantee of that amount of the borrowing and in July 1802 provided a further 2 million francs in drafts on Willing & Francis of Philadelphia. Hope issued a $5 million loan in Amsterdam and Baring a $6½ million loan in England to enable the United States to pay off France. Baring placed $0.5 million of its loan in the United States and took $1 million for its own account. Hope (London) took $1.7 million of the Baring share for its account, and

$0.3 million was transferred to the Amsterdam *tranche*.[1] This was a great success and went quickly to a premium (Buist, 1974, p. 58).

Labouchère of Hope (Amsterdam) proposed that the funds from these loans be made available to Napoleon in Amsterdam to enable him to pay his trade debts to Russia, which would enable Russia to pay down its arrears of interest and amortization owing to Dutch holders of Russian bonds. Hard-pressed for money, Napoleon turned over the 34 million remaining American bonds to Baring and Hope at a discount of 1.675 million francs (ibid., pp. 57–59, 188–92).

A still more complex transaction of Hope & Company involving the Spanish indemnity paid to France by way of Mexico, the United States, London, and Amsterdam will be detailed in the next chapter.

3. While Dutch investors had been deeply speculative in the seventeenth century, the *rentier* of the eighteenth emerged as a creature of strong habits, inclined to rely on the advice of market intermediaries (Riley, 1980, p. 133). The two attitudes may be related and raise a question about the merit of the modern financial assumption of rationality in financial markets solidly founded in adequate information. One observer claimed, "Love of gambling lies deep in Dutch national character. What is remarkable in a country where personal credit is so limited and difficult, and money available only on personal responsibility, one has so much trust in luck and accident. This does not speak well for the wide existence of real economic insight" (Büsch, quoted in Baasch, 1927, p. 240). Ehrenberg's remark on the lack of information available to investors concerning Dutch governmental accounts has been referred to earlier (p. 156).

4. Dealers in foreign securities were continuously engaged in manipulating prices of outstanding issues for purposes of window-dressing, buying bonds in the open market with various funds at their disposal (Riley, 1980, p. 150), begging the debtor to make if not total at least partial payments on interest or amortization, buying back bonds when they fell in price, intervening in the exchange market to influence bond prices (Buist, 1974, p. 170). They worked assiduously on behalf of bondholders, making repeated trips to debtor governments to plead against default, seeking to pay interest in Hamburg, if Amsterdam were cut off by war (ibid., pp. 30, 155). Persistence paid. Talks were adjourned from time to time but never broken off. Discussion of the conversion of various Russian (and Polish) debts to Amsterdam, Genoa, and Antwerp was initially undertaken in 1794 though not completed until November 1797 (ibid., pp. 155–66). After a series of agonizing makeshift payments of one sort and another, Russian bonds, which had fallen as low as 32 in September 1812 at the time of the Napoleonic invasion, worked their way back to 90 in 1819 when early resumption of full payment of interest and principal earned Russia a reputation for credit-worthiness, Buist says, from which it profited down to 1917 (ibid., pp. 251, 274). Hope & Company in Holland, associated with the Orange pro-English party, lost the underwriting of the 1797 conversion loan to de Smeth of the Patriot (pro-French) side but bought heavily of the old bonds in advance and made a profit of 6 million florins or more—whether before or after Russian change of

1. French for "slice" and used to designate segments of loans.

underwriters and, hence, with or without a conflict of interest as opposed to the bondholders is not made clear (ibid., pp. 29, 170).

5. Dutch foreign assets in 1790 were estimated in Holland as worth a billion florins but more realistically as 500 million to 650 million florins, or £30 million to £ 37 million. Of this amount 150 million to 220 million florins represented loans issued by foreign borrowers on the Amsterdam market; the rest were foreign securities bought by Dutch investors abroad (Riley, 1980, p. 16).

The Switch from English to French Securities

About 1780 Dutch investor interest turned from London to Paris. The Fourth Anglo-Dutch War from 1780 to 1784 had something to do with the change; how much is not clear. The Dutch investor of the seventeenth century was uninhibited by considerations of patriotism or economic nationalism. In this period the Dutch were content to trade with the enemy and even invest in privateers that would not hesitate to attack Dutch shipping (Barbour, 1950 [1966], pp. 130–31). Rising national identification through the eighteenth century probably altered this attitude considerably.

More significant were the new opportunities to invest in French *rentes*. The French financial situation in the American War of Independence was critical, and France was having difficulty in raising funds. The state could borrow at 5 percent through intermediaries such as the Hôtel de Ville of Paris, the clergy, or the provincial estates. For direct loans it had to offer more enticing terms, either lottery loans or life annuities. Abbé Terray who had been minister of finance in 1770 and resorted to a partial repudiation—a forcible refunding of 160 million of perpetual debt at 4 percent, which *rente* promptly fell to 60—undertook the so-called Loan of Holland in 1771. This was an annuity calling for a payment of 8 percent a year on one life, or 7 percent on two lives, but could be purchased with the depreciated *rente* of 1770, which brought the return to the investor, and the cost to France, to 12 percent. Even these terms failed to entice the Dutch investor, however, and by 1774 less than one-quarter of the amount offered had been subscribed in Amsterdam (and Geneva). Turgot transferred the remainder to Paris.

The terms of life annuities were based on the assumption that the purchaser would buy the annuity on his own life, and possibly that of his wife in addition, with a median age for the purchaser of 40 years. Before 1754 interest rates had been adjusted to the age of annuitants but, given the difficulties in French finances, not thereafter. When Necker became controller-general in 1777, he borrowed four times on life annuities. The first, the *rente* of November 1778, offered 10 percent on one life and 9 percent for two, two percentage points above the nominal rates of the Loan of Holland. The *rentes* of November 1779, February 1781, and March 1781 offered 10 percent on one life, 9 percent for two, 8.5 percent for three lives, and 8 percent for four, all without distinction of ages. The February 1781 *rente,* like the Loan of Holland, was exempt from the *dîme,* a tax of 10 percent of the yield; the others were not (R. D. Harris, 1979, pp. 125–33).

One great attraction of these *rentes* was the age feature. Well before Necker offered *rentes* on several lives, Geneva bankers had innovated selecting young women of good family—noble or bourgeois—as nominal beneficiaries of the annuity, and then pooling *rentes* on twenty-five, later thirty, young demoiselles, aged 7 to 14, and selling a claim on the group, as in a mutual fund. Various extensions developed—selling shares in the pool on credit, with the annuity paying for installments until the shares were owned free and clear, or, on a single life annuity, the banker guaranteeing the client against the death of the "head" insured in exchange for the *rente* becoming the property of the banker if the client predeceased the "head." It took Geneva bankers ten years to make investors understand the attraction of these schemes; Dutch investors were slower. But the Dutch were quick after 1779 to pounce on Necker's offers of single annuities on multiple heads irrespective of age (Lüthy, 1961, Vo. 2, pp. 471–518).

How overgenerous the terms were can be seen in the fact that in a reform of 1794, life annuities were adjusted to one life only, and then based on a standard of a 52-year-old annuitant. Those aged 40 to 51 had the annual payment reduced by 8 percent, between 30 and 40 by 20 percent, between 20 and 30 by 28 percent, and between 6 and 20 (the age of the *demoiselles genevoises* or *hollandaises*) by 32 percent (R. D. Harris, 1979, p. 130). The barn door was locked, but belatedly.

Dutch interest in French securities picked up immediately with these three *rentes,* to rival the already flourishing Swiss involvement. Dutch holdings of French securities rose from 25 million florins as a capital sum to a flow of income of 12 million florins annually, worth 120 million if capitalized at 10 percent, and worth more or less depending on the rate applicable (Riley, 1980, p. 179). Although Harris makes light of it, it was a bad mistake on Necker's part; it was a mistake on the part of the Dutch as well, because they backed the wrong horse. Dutch investor interest became diverted from Britain, with its industrial revolution, solid finances, and capacity to win wars, to France about to enter on the travail of a revolution and a long, losing war.

Geneva investments in France were estimated at 100 million livres in 1780, yielding 12 million livres annually (Iklé, 1972, p. 14), but there is no figure handy for the volume of response to Necker's open-handedness.

Decline in Dutch trade had begun about or before 1730; that in finance antedated the change in horizon marked by the Fourth Anglo-Dutch War and the *demoiselles genevoises,* going back to the crisis of 1763, when the banks of Arend, Joseph, and Gebrüder de Neufville collapsed, and 1772, when they were followed by Clifford. The void was not filled by Britain until after the Napoleonic Wars.

Horizons and Channels

The historical and analytical point to be made is that investors lack costless worldwide knowledge and, in making choices among investment opportunities, scan limited horizons. These horizons shift from time to time, displaced by some striking innovation, event, or bargain such as the Geneva pooling of "heads" or Necker's annuities on four lives of annuitants of any age. The consequence of limited horizons that change discontinuously is that capital flows take place in deep channels (the same is true of migration). Unlike water flowing evenly over a broad surface, capital moves like water in sluices or conduits, ignoring or bypassing better opportunities on occasion, because of the high cost of obtaining information about them.

ENGLISH FOREIGN LENDING

It has been claimed that England was the only country in the world that never borrowed, and was always lending, and that the first loan made abroad was for £ 500,000 at 8 percent in 1706 for Joseph I, emperor of Germany (the Holy Roman Empire) (Emden, 1938, p. 37). The second part of this claim is credible, although the sum is given elsewhere at £250,000 (Dickson, 1967, p. 333); the first is not. One has only to recall English kings' defaulting to Italian bankers in the fourteenth century, Gresham borrowing in Antwerp for Elizabeth in the sixteenth, or the fledgling Bank of England obtaining a loan from Amsterdam bankers a mere decade before 1706 to regard the statement as hyperbole. The 1706 loan to Joseph, however, was followed by others—for £90,000 in 1710, £250,000 in 1735, and £320,000 more in 1737. These were probably close to subsidies. Dickson has information on the subscribers only of the 1706 loan and the names are mercantile (ibid.). But the loans were for an ally in wartime, as was a loan to the Dutch in the amount of £50,000 in 1749. Subsequent eighteenth-century British governmental loans to Austria during the Napoleonic Wars, amounting to £6.2 million in 1795 and 1797 combined, were in fact regarded by the Austrians as subsidies, despite their form, and Austria stopped payment on them in 1797 (Helleiner, 1965). The capital sum with accumulated interest had built up to £23.5 million by 1821 and was finally settled in cash in 1823 for £2.5 million (Sherwig, 1969, p. 343).

The Baring Indemnity Loans

The second Treaty of Paris after Waterloo imposed an indemnity of 700 million francs on the restored monarchy of France to pay (1) for construction of fortifications in neighboring states (137½ million); (2) 62½ million to the powers contributing troops to the victorious Battle of Waterloo; and (3) 100 million each to Austria, England, Prussia, and Russia, with a fifth 100 million divided among the lesser powers in accordance with their contingents on the field of battle. Holland renounced its share at 28 million, and this was divided between Prussia and Austria. In all, Prussia was to receive 139 million, Britain 125 million, Austria 114 million, Russia 100 million, the rest scattering amounts. Moreover, France was to be occupied for five years, with expenses of occupation borne by the French government, although the possibility was held out of ending the occupation after three years. France was also forced to agree to settle foreign claims as decided by a commission.

To pay these sums, the French government had to overcome major difficulties. The Treasury was bare except for overdue obligations from collectors of taxes. In 1816 the government ran a deficit of 380 million francs, paid for by drawing down cash available from English advances to the Bourbon monarchy, issuing bonds at declining prices, obtaining fresh advances from tax collectors, and so on. The market for government debt declined at home. It looked as though the French government was in no position to pay on the indemnity. The way out of the impasse was a foreign loan.

Messrs. Baring and Hope visited Paris in January 1817 to study the position. By 10 February, negotiating with Messrs. Ouvrard and Laffitte, they had agreed to buy at 55, less a commission of 2.5 francs, enough 5 percent *rentes* to provide the French government with 100 million francs. A second *tranche* was issued in April at a net price of 55.50 francs, and in July another *tranche* at 61.50. By this time French bankers and the French public were becoming interested. Of roughly 300 million francs of the first three 1817 loans, Baring and Hope cut in a group of French bankers—Baguenault, Delessert, Greffulhe, Hottinguer, and Laffitte—for one-third, but these, in turn, sold most of the *rentes* they managed in London (Gille, 1959, p. 35). The *rente* improved to 68 by the end of July. In May 1818, the French government sold almost 15 million of *rentes* (the income stream) to French investors for a capital sum close to 200 million francs. The loan was oversubscribed ten times, with much of the bidding coming from the provinces. Baring Brothers led two more loans in 1818, a 2 million franc, 5 percent *rente* for a capital sum of 25.8 million francs, that is, at 64½, in March 1818, and a 12.3 million *rente,* also at 5 percent and priced at 67, for a capital sum of 165 million francs in September. The 5 percent new issues rose to 87 by 1821 and 89.55 by 1823. The Baring loans had primed the pump (Laffitte, 1840 [1932], p. 102).

The Baring loan did more. It recycled French indemnity payments, and it broadened the horizon of English investors to include foreign lending. Recycling is a concept developed in connection with the large increase in receipts of the Organization of Petroleum Exporting Countries (OPEC) from increases in oil prices in 1973 and 1979. In effect, France borrowed the money abroad to pay the indemnity immediately and effectively paid it much later when it discharged the foreign debt it had contracted. The same process will be used in the Franco-Prussian indemnity payment of 1871 and in the Dawes loan of 1924 and with the same side effect of stimulating new investor interest in foreign bonds.

Following the Baring indemnity, the London market raised loans for Prussia, including the Royal Seehandlung, for Russia, and after the settlement of the 1795 and 1797 debts, for Austria. All three sets of loans were defaulted. The Baring loan to France, on the other hand, was fully paid.

The 1820s

With conversion of domestic British war debt to a lower rate of interest in 1823 and liberation of the American colonies from Spain in the early 1820s, the stage was set for a boom in domestic issues, already discussed, and in foreign loans. Initial British interest in Latin America had been mercantile. When the Portuguese king was driven from the Iberian Peninsula by war in 1810 and went to Brazil, British merchants from Manchester and Birmingham shipped more goods to that market in a few weeks than had been consumed there in twenty years, including, according to legend, ice skates and warming pans (Clapham, 1945, Vol. 2, p. 20). In 1823, 1824, and 1825 heavy investments were made in government bonds of the newly independent countries of Spanish America, especially in Mexico, Peru, Colombia, and Central America. One of the more bizarre loans was issued to a man who called himself Gregor, the caique of Poyais, a new country that he himself founded. Originally, Sir Gregor MacGregor from Scotland, the adventurer had been a general in the Venezuelan army in 1817, left in 1821 to live among the Poyais Indians, and ended by setting up his own country. It (or he) borrowed funds in London in this period on which no interest or capital was ever paid (DNB, 1893, Vol. 13, p. 539; Emden, 1938, p. 40).

Greek independence in 1821 produced loans for that country but, like those for Colombia, at high rates of interest discounted in advance. Guatemala paid no interest on its bonds until 1855, Nicaragua none until 1874, and Greece none until 1879. Colombia defaulted on its 10 percent interest when the first undiscounted payment became due (Emden, 1938, pp. 40–41).

The 1830s

The collapse of the foreign bond market in 1825 and 1826 shifted foreign lending by Britain to commercial advances, largely to the United States, to pay for exports of goods and specie. The boom in the United States was based on rapid expansion of cotton lands to furnish supplies to Europe, but expansion in acreage planted meant a reduction in current output for a time, as resources were diverted from production to clearing land in more western states. The collapse of the boom in 1836 fed back to Europe via Liverpool and Paris.

The 1840s

The 1840s boom occurred largely in railroad investment at home and abroad. British investment in French railroads amounted to £25 million gross, although much of this was bought by French investors who liked to have French securities denominated in pounds sterling (Jenks, 1927, pp. 148–49; Platt, 1984, ch. 2). An English banker, Sir Edward Blount, was resident in Paris negotiating for Thomas Brassey, the railroad builder, the financial terms for Brassey's construction work on French lines. Blount, regarded as the foremost of foreign railway bankers prior to the Pereires and Rothschilds of the 1850s and 1860s, was associated with the Laffitte successor bank that went bankrupt in 1848, headed the Chemin de Fer de l'Ouest after a hiatus between 1848 and 1852 when British capital and labor were unwelcome in France, went on to become, in effect, French and president of the Société Générale when his firm was wound up (Emden, 1938, pp. 129–32). For a man with such an interesting career, his memoirs are surprisingly tepid (1902). The French Revolution of 1848 with its xenophobic attack on English workers occasioned a new displacement of British lending—a shift of the horizon to be scanned—from the Continent to overseas areas (Jenks, 1927, p. 156).

The effect of the shift can be seen in the course of the proportion of a rapidly rising total investment that went to Europe: 1830, 66 percent; 1854, 55 percent; 1870, 25 percent; and 1900, 5 percent (Pollard, 1974, p. 71). A different source gives the proportion of British investment in Europe in 1900 as 10.4 percent (Woodruff, 1966,

p. 152). It has also been held that the Continental system—Napoleon's blockade of Britain that cut it off from the Continent—reoriented British trade from Europe and the United States to the rest of the world, still including the United States (Heckscher, 1922, p. 326). If finance follows trade, the same would presumably apply in that field. But both trade and finance with the Continent were intense in the first half of the nineteenth century, especially exports of cotton textiles, coal and machinery, including locomotives, and finance of railroads. The more definitive break occurred in 1848. British houses floated no loans, however, for German railroads, which were built almost entirely, apart from a small French contribution, with domestic funds (Borchardt, 1991, p. 215, n. 38a).

U.S. borrowing in Britain began in the 1830s at the level of the separate states; most of the Southern members among them later defaulted, if not shortly after 1837, at least during the Civil War, with massive losses for British (and continental) investors. The federal government had borrowed in the Netherlands in the 1790s and in 1803 for the Louisiana purchase. With the outbreak of war with Mexico, it began borrowing in European capital markets more generally. The capital inflow was to rise in the 1850s and spread from London to Continental centers such as Frankfurt where the federal government, the states, and even such cities as Wheeling, Covington, and Sacramento, to say nothing of New York, San Francisco, and New Orleans, were to have their bonds listed over 1854 to 1856 (Böhme, 1968, pp. 160–61). The borrowing shifted from governments to railroads and gradually spread from London by the 1870s to Berlin, Frankfurt, and Vienna. The houses of Morgan, Seligmann, and Drexel fanned out from the United States over Europe to raise money for investment in the United States—an example of pull rather than push.

The 1850s and 1860s

Finance of Indian railroads in Britain with government guarantees has already received attention. One motive for extending these railroads was the Sepoy Mutiny of 1857, which called for more expeditious movement of British troops in the colony and led to the 1858 guarantee. British overseas investment in railroads everywhere in 1854 to 1869 amounted to £150 million, largely in the interest of monopolistic exploitation of the empire, says a historian with a Marxist inclination (Rosenberg, 1934, pp. 151–52).

Then came Civil War in the United States, cotton famine, and attempts to find new supplies. India was one candidate to fill the void. Egypt, which had started the export of long-staple cotton, was another. The overland route to India, moreover, lay across the Suez peninsula and enjoyed a brisk revival when steamships overcame the difficulty that sailing ships could get to Suez from India only three months of the year because of the prevailing winds. With the completion in 1858 of the Alexandria-Cairo railroad, and then the Cairo-Suez line, communication across the isthmus was improved a decade before the opening of the Suez Canal in 1868. In 1856 a Suez-to-Bombay telegraph line was begun to shorten to minutes the two months it took to communicate between London and Calcutta.

The idea of a canal across the isthmus had been explored by Prosper Enfantin,

A Financial Lesson.

"An Eagle stayed his flight, and entreated a Lion to make an alliance with him to their mutual advantage. The Lion replied: 'I have no objection, but you must excuse me for requiring you to find surety for your good faith; for how can I trust any one as a friend who is able to fly away from his bargain whenever he pleases?"—AESOP.

Cartoon by Thomas Nast (19 August 1876), from Morton Keller, *The Art and Politics of Thomas Nast* (New York: Oxford University Press, 1968), p. 187.

the Saint-Simonien, in 1834. One who traveled with him then was Ferdinand de Lesseps (Walch, 1975, p. 36n). De Lesseps started borrowing money to construct the canal in 1858, with little or no initial success. Work was begun nevertheless. Later the Paris market contributed the necessary funds, apart from a major share of the stock acquired by the khedive.

Along with all this activity, the old Egyptian system of finance broke down, and a group of scalawags from all over Europe, but especially from Britain, France, and Germany, descended on Egypt, demanding and getting concessions, forcing loans on Said and on Ismail who succeeded him as khedive in 1863, making unreasonable demands, and especially when they gave up a concession that they had exacted from Egypt but proved worthless, insisting that they be given compensation in a capital sum for yielding it (Marlowe, 1974, pp. 84, 87, 88, 125, 166, 217). Confusion abounded. Egypt earned the sobriquet of "Klondike on the Nile" (Landes, 1958, ch. 3). Rathenau was later to call Berlin in the early 1870s "Chicago on the Spree" (Stern, 1977a, p. 161).

Said and Ismail were profligate viceroys, borrowing in Europe at high interest rates for consumption, for irrigation schemes designed to serve their own estates, for an extravagant fete to celebrate the opening of the Suez Canal, for badly planned public works. The railroads and Suez Canal benefited Europe, for example, not Egypt, and cost Egypt £12 million for shares ultimately sold to the British government under Disraeli for £4 million (Marlowe, 1974, pp. 107–8). In all, the Egyptian government under Ismail (after 1863) borrowed £53 million, received only £32 million, paid £35 million in debt service, but still owed £52 million on capital account and arrears of interest in 1876 when the government finally defaulted (ibid., p. 113). Marlowe (a *nom de plume*) observes that it was easy to castigate the Europeans who made every Ismail initiative contribute to their wealth, but Egyptian mismanagement was itself spectacular. The collapse of the market in cotton after Grant's victories for the North in the summer of 1864—from 30 pence a pound at the end of July to 21 pence in the last week in October (Landes, 1958, p. 214)—contributed to the break in commodity and security prices in Paris in 1864, to crisis in London in 1866, and to the ultimate bankruptcy of the khedive ten years later.

1873 to 1896

The 1850s, 1860s, and early 1870s were a period of railroad building in the United States, brought to a halt by stock market collapse in Vienna in May 1873 and subsequent fall in Berlin and by the bankruptcy of Jay Cooke in New York in September of the same year. From 1873 to 1896 British lending was less exuberant, except for a period from 1885 to 1890 that culminated in the crisis of the Baring Brothers in 1890, when the bankers found themselves loaded with Argentine paper at a time of falling grain prices that prevented Argentina from meeting its obligations. With the low of the cycle in 1896, however, an enormous rise in British lending began, largely to what were later called Regions of Recent Settlement, notably Canada, Australia, New Zealand, and the Union of South Africa, the self-governing dominions, along with the major countries of Latin America, and a number of rich colonies, most notably Malaya with its tin and rubber.

Table 12.1 Foreign Investment of Major Lending Countries, 1825–1913 (in millions of dollars)

Country	1825	1840	1855	1870	1885	1900	1913
Great Britain	500	750	2,300	4,900	7,800	12,100	19,500
France	100	(300)	1,000	2,500	3,300	5,200	8,600
Germany	*	*	*	*	1,900	4,800	6,700
Netherlands	300	200	300	500	1,000	1,100	1,250
United States	n	n	n	n	n	500	2,500

*No estimate available.
n = negligible.
Source: Woodruff (1966, p. 150).

Lévy-Leboyer holds that British lending turned away from Europe after 1875 because of the rise of protectionism in Europe (1977*a*, p. 184), in contrast with the usual date of 1848. The Pollard figures cited earlier show a decline from 55 percent of total investment on the Continent in 1855, to 25 in 1870 and 5 percent in 1900. They justify the Lévy-Leboyer view if one concentrates on the decline in percentage points as percentage of the proportion held at the beginning of the period. The thirty-point drop to 1870 is slightly more than half of the initial proportion; the twenty-point drop to 1900 is 80 percent. More important, however, one can point out that virtually all the new investment was toward noncontinental borrowers, and the overall figures rose enormously (Table 12.1).

These figures have been rendered somewhat suspect as gross rather than net, and not only because of Platt's discovery that London merchant bankers issued securities for foreign borrowers that were bought by the nationals of the same country (1984). International intermediation can take place not only in identical securities, sold and bought by residents of a single country through investment houses abroad, but also by colonial and foreign countries borrowing long and lending short in a foreign financial center. Foreign and colonial bank deposits in London rose from £107 million in 1877 to £1,855 millions in 1914 (Capie and Webber, 1985, Vol. 1, pp. 130, 250, quoted in Michie, 1990, p. 109). While foreign capitalists, including Argentinians and Brazilians, may have bought bonds issued by their local governments in London, such was not the case for the British dominions where the local subjects had confidence in their governments.

FRENCH FOREIGN LENDING

For a long time, naive American students of French foreign lending, including me, thought it had started in 1880 because the dates in Harry D. White's classic thesis, *The French International Accounts, 1880–1913* (1933), begin with that year. Table 12.1, consisting of rough estimates at best, makes clear that the process started earlier. In fact, the spectacular burst between 1855 and 1870 outstripped the British performance in percentage terms, if not in absolute amounts. Cameron's thesis (1961) explores the period of lending in the 1850s and 1860s under the Crédit Mobilier, which has filled many of the pages in this book, and, with the Lévy-Leboyer dissertation (1964), examined early stages of French lending back to the 1830s. Two strands can be disentangled in the early period prior to 1851. First is the gross movement of French capital to Belgium in connection with the first *banques d'affaires* (ibid., ch. 9) plus some lending to Rome, Spain, and Greece in the 1830s when the level of interest rates on French *rentes* declined from 6 to 4¾ percent. Second, a number of French economists claim that Paris played a major role from 1820 to 1840 in international settlements, with Americans and Britons requiring French francs to pay the Continent, and continental merchants outside France needing French francs to pay the Anglo-Saxons (Bouvier, 1973, p. 238, citing Billoret, 1969; Lévy-Leboyer, 1964, pp. 437–44). One important loan of this period was that of the Hottinguer Bank to the United States to enable President Andrew Jackson to operate a corner in cotton for a time but not for long after British import houses stopped buying.

French investment in Belgium was large on a gross basis, and in the early part of the nineteenth century on a net basis as well. To a considerable extent, Belgium was financially a province of France with large two-way movements: French investors bought Belgian securities, and Belgian investors French. Prior to the mid-century boom in France, Parisian and other investors would also invest in Belgian coal mines and industrial enterprises working for the French market. In addition to these mutual relationships, French capital would go abroad through Belgium, in Ruhr mining prior to mid-century, and often in association with tramway investments late in the period. Reciprocally, Belgians placed their capital in Austria, Italy, and Spain to a considerable extent through Paris.

French lending was also offset, in part, by Lyons borrowing from Geneva, and Strasbourg and Mulhouse from Basle (Lévy-Leboyer, 1964, p. 705).

Lending to Czarist Russia

The period of heavy French lending to Austria, Italy, and Spain, starting with the Crédit Mobilier and continuing to the sharp decline in 1864, has been dwelt upon above, especially in Chapters 6 (pp. 110–11) and 8 (pp. 139–42). After 1866 when funds from Paris stopped flowing to Italy and Spain and after the Pereires had been forced out of the Crédit Mobilier in 1868, there was a lull for the Franco-Prussian War and an enormous horizontal shift with the success of the Thiers *rentes,* issued to pay for the indemnity and discussed in Chapter 13 (pp. 235–43). Then followed, as shown in Table 12.1, a reconstitution of French investment that had been liquidated to subscribe to the Thiers *rentes,* plus a modest gain in foreign lending. The boom from 1878 to the crash in 1882 that brought down the Union Générale involved some foreign investment by that bank as an echo of the Crédit Mobilier and Rothschild lending to Austria, Italy, and Spain. But a shift was in process in French investor interest from obligations of Italy, Spain, Portugal, and Austria, to those of Russia, southeast Europe, and South America (Lévy-Leboyer, 1977a, p. 139). By far the most important of these outlets was czarist Russia; it involved a discontinuous shift of horizon that occurred around 1877 and, in effect, a major recycling.

Prior to 1887, Russian debt amounted to 6,250 million rubles, equivalent to 16.6

billion francs or 18.7 billion marks (the ruble being valued at 2.55 francs and 3 marks) (Girault, 1973, p. 139). It was estimated that about one-third of this was owed abroad, and that of the foreign portion, somewhere between six-tenths and two-thirds was owed to Germany. Germany had issued loans for Russia at the time of the Crimean War in 1856 and again in 1877 at the time of the Russian War against Turkey. In the 1880s, however, Russia and Germany had begun to fall out, mostly over trade but increasingly on political lines. Germany had raised tariffs on grain in 1879, and Russia, becoming interested in industrialization, responded by hiking its tariffs on iron. Moreover, Germany was engaged on a course of rapid economic expansion and was interested in pulling back from foreign lending, in some degree, to obtain capital for domestic use. Investors turned from foreign government to domestic industrial issues. Prices of Russian securities in Berlin began to drop.

In the German Foreign Office about this time, Herbert Bismarck, the chancellor's son, proposed forbidding bank advances on Russian securities as an act of economic warfare. A Russian intriguer, resident in Paris, Elie de Cyon, also known as Ilya Fadeyevich Tsion, sought to persuade the Russian government to shift its financial connections from Berlin to the *hautes banques* in Paris (Kennan, 1979, p. 292). In the summer of 1887 Orphans Courts in Germany were instructed not to acquire Russian bonds for the portfolios of their wards, and on 10 November 1887, an order was issued forbidding banks to lend on Russian securities—the famous *Lombardverbot*. Prices of Russian bonds fell further in Germany; some were bought back by Russian investors, a great many by French (ibid., p. 342). As Russian loans matured thereafter, German holders mostly asked to be paid off, and new bonds were sold to French investors, even though German bankers participated in underwriting a number of loans. Most borrowing was for refunding, including a conversion of 1.7 billion francs of railroad bonds taken by Rothschild in Paris in 1889. In the longer run, however, banks like Rothschilds and the *banques d'affaires* were unable to compete in selling Russian bonds to the French public because they lacked the network of branches (Girault, 1973, pp. 149, 178). The big banks such as the Crédit Lyonnais and the Société Générale dominated the field and stuffed Russian bonds into the portfolios of their depositors.

The shift of Russia's creditor from Germany to France was partly political. It was attributable in good measure, however, to the fact that German industrial expansion was vigorous and French was not. The French *rente* was converted from 4½ and 4 percent to 3 percent on a perpetual basis in 1887, and this stimulated French investors to scan a wider field for opportunities to maintain incomes (ibid., pp. 150–51).

The fact that Germany sold Russian bonds and France bought them meant that French capital was, in effect, recycled to Germany, rather than lent to Russia—at least for the period up to 1895, and this explains how France could lend billions of francs to Russia with such a small direct amount of trade with that country. Some part of the explanation for the divergence between financial loans and exports after the French began to lend new money from 1894 may lie in the fact that some fresh loans were used to pay for armaments that were not included in trade returns (Girault, 1977, p. 254).

In addition to Russian bonds denominated in foreign currencies, the czarist government also sold ruble securities in France amounting to 6 billion francs between 1889 and 1914 (Crisp, 1977, p. 269). Added to the 12.4 billion Russian bonds bought in France (Girault, 1977, p. 262), one arrives at 18½ billion francs of Russian bonds bought by the French before the war. Some of this was, of course, repaid before the Russian Revolution. French loss on the remaining bonds plus those sold by southeast Europe and defaulted is estimated at 15 billion or 16 billion gold francs (Lévy-Leboyer, 1977a, p. 139).

GERMAN FOREIGN LENDING

German foreign lending after 1850 has already been touched upon: the substantial loans to Russia, the turning away in 1887, and selling Russian bonds to French investors, or letting Russian bonds run off while the French bought refunding issues. The movement of funds into Italy late in the century, and their subsequent withdrawal, were noted in Chapter 8 (pp. 143–44). What remains is to furnish an account of early German borrowing and lending in the nineteenth century. It is perhaps best characterized by the statement that the separate capital markets, especially Frankfurt, Hamburg, Berlin, and, to a lesser extent, Augsburg, were connected with each other only loosely, and each dealt with the outside world separately. Frankfurt loaned to the rest of Europe and after 1849 traded in U.S. long-term bonds; Hamburg financed trade, especially that with Scandinavia. Berlin borrowed from Frankfurt, and Hamburg from London and Genoa. In addition, it bought foreign bonds to diversify its investments.

An impression of Frankfurt lending can be obtained from tables of partial particulars of loans given by Böhme for about the first half of the century. There is a list of issues by Gebrüder Bethmann from 1794 to 1824, with interest rates but no amounts. Some are foreign—for Austria, Denmark, and Russia, with one stated to be in collaboration with Baring of London, Hope of Amsterdam, Parish of Hamburg, and Geymüller of Vienna; most are for German principalities and cities (Böhme, 1968, pp. 150ff.). A much longer list for M. A. Rothschild gives amounts as well as coupon rate (ibid., pp. 151–53). Amounts are surprisingly small, with only one more than 10 million thalers, and by far the majority under 1 million. These lists, however, omit the major security issues for foreign borrowers, given in another table, which combined new issues with securities listed on the Frankfurt bourse for trading purposes. It is not known, of course, how large German holdings were of securities merely listed. A summary by period and country does show the development of Frankfurt as a capital market for central Europe to one covering all of Europe and the United States (Table 12.2). French and Belgian bonds are mostly for early issues of railroads, presumably merely listed and traded. The thirty-five American issues are those of the federal government, states, and cities, and again are listed and traded.

Prussian state finances were developed under pressure from the Napoleonic indemnity of 1 billion francs levied in 1806 after the defeat at the Battle of Jena and set forth in the Treaty of Tilsit, plus another 120 million francs "contribution"

Table 12.2 Development of Foreign Issues on the Frankfurt Bourse, 1797–1860

Period	Austria	Hungary	Denmark	France/ Belgium	Holland	Italy	Russia	Spain	United States	Other
1797–1800	10	—	2	—	—	—	—	—	—	1
1801–20	4	—	—	—	2	1	1	—	—	1
1821–30	5	—	2	—	—	2	—	4	—	1
1831–40	5	—	—	9	2	—	1	2	—	3
1841–50	7	3	—	3	3	3	4	1	1	1
1851–60	17	3	—	5	1	13	—	2	35	4

Source: Böhme (1968, pp. 156–61).

exacted in November 1809. Prior to that time, Berlin had borrowed abroad as a rule, including (in addition to Frankfurt and Hamburg) Leipzig, Kassel (where the Wittgensteinischer Kontor operated and shared with Rothschilds the management of the wealth of the elector of Hesse-Kassel), Amsterdam, and Genoa (Brockhage, 1910, pp. 34–35). In paying off Napoleon and raising its own army of 250,000, out of a population of 5 million, albeit with the help of British subsidies, Prussia resorted to all sorts of taxes and loans, including forced conversion of supplier credits into long-term loans. After the war, a Prussian state loan was issued in London in 1818 and a Royal Seehandlung loan in 1822. Borrowing continued in Frankfurt and Hamburg. At the same time, however, the Berlin bourse began to quote the prices of foreign government bonds issued in Paris, London, and Frankfurt, although only a few bonds may have found their way into Berlin portfolios.

When the railroad age arrived in 1840, German railroad bonds were sold to foreigners at the same time as Berlin bought Russian, Dutch, Austrian, Italian, and German (extra-Prussia) railroad bonds. There is some dispute as to whether the net was zero or favored Prussian capital exports (ibid., pp. 210–11). What is clear is that until the great banking drive of the 1850s, Germany had a series of very loosely integrated capital markets, some lending net, some borrowing, all interested in diversification through substantial gross movements in both directions. The growth of the great banks after 1853, and especially in 1856, unified the capital market and enabled Germany to hurry to catch up in foreign lending with Britain and France.

SUGGESTED SUPPLEMENTARY READING

Platt (1984), *Foreign Finance in Continental Europe and the USA, 1815–1870.*

On British Lending

Cairncross (1953), *Home and Foreign Investment, 1870–1913.*
Edelstein (1982), *Overseas Investment in the Age of High Imperialism.*
Jenks (1927), *The Migration of English Capital to 1875.*

On Dutch lending

Riley (1980), *International Government Finance and the Amsterdam Capital Market, 1740–1815*.

C. Wilson (1941), *Anglo-Dutch Commerce and Finance in the Eighteenth Century.*

On French lending

Cameron (1961), *France and the Economic Development of Europe (1800–1914).*

White (1933), *The French International Accounts, 1880–1913.*

In French

Girault (1973), *Emprunts russes et investissements français en Russie, 1887–1914.*

Lévy-Leboyer (ed.) (1977b), *La Position internationale de la France.*

In German

Brockhage (1910), *Zur Entwicklung des preussisch-deutschen Kapital-exports.*

13

Transfer Cases

> The next time we defeat the French we'll insist that they let us pay them an indemnity.
>
> (A remark ascribed to Prince Bismarck in Sauvy, *Histoire économique de la France*, 1965, Vol. 1, p. 131)

International capital transfers have two aspects: financial and real. Both are of interest to the financial historian, but perhaps the financial more than the real. They are, of course, interrelated. The financial transfer consists of the means by which a payment is made from the money of one country and received in the money of another, especially in the light of the difficulties of effecting payment entirely in metallic money. These difficulties are primarily two: the lack of availability of sufficient specie and the expense of its movement over distance. The real payment is the development of an export surplus of goods and services on the part of the payer and of an import surplus for the payee. In normal capital flows, discussed in the last chapter, the export surplus typically develops from the excess savings of the lending country, the import surplus from the excess spending (for investment) of the borrower. More interesting pathological transfer cases—the subject of this chapter—arise when there is a financial payment to be made that has a different origin from ordinary savings and investment, typically in subsidies to allies or an indemnity to be paid after defeat in war.

The largest and most interesting such payment prior to 1914 was the 5-billion-franc Franco-Prussian indemnity of 1871–72. As a preliminary to that episode, we furnish potted accounts of several other cases of varying complexity in which significant sums of money (for the time) were transmitted from one country to another through the foreign exchanges. First are two indemnities paid by Sweden to Denmark in the sixteenth and seventeenth centuries. There follow six cases: Palavicino's transfer in 1586 of a subsidy from England to Casimir, son of the elector of the Palatinate, to assist him to raise an army to fight with the French and English against the Spanish; second, the transfer of funds from Spain to Flanders to pay mercenaries fighting for Spain against the Dutch in the Eighty Years' War (1568–1648) of the Counter-Reformation; third, the problem of remitting home the profits of the servants of the East India Company gathered in India in the eighteenth century; fourth, payment of a Spanish indemnity or contribution of 6 million francs a month to Napoleon under an agreement of 20 May 1803, to ensure Spanish neutrality; fifth, payment of £10 million from London to Wellington's army in the Iberian Peninsula; and, finally, the 5-billion-franc indemnity paid by France to Germany at the end of the Franco-Prussian War of 1870–71.

REDEEMING THE FORTRESS OF ALVSBORG

The Treaty of Stettin ending the northern Seven Years' War in 1570 required Sweden to pay 150,000 thalers before the Danes would return the fortress of Alvsborg, which they had captured and continued to occupy. To raise this sum, Sweden subjected all movables in the country to a heavy tax after an inquest said to be more searching than that of Domesday in England (Ward, Prothero, and Leathes, eds. 1906, p. 166). Peasants contributed one-tenth of the value of their property, unburned towns one-twelfth, and burned towns one-eighteenth. Payment of the indemnity was effected in seven Swedish currencies of varying degrees of debasement at their metal equivalents (ibid.).

A generation later, the Alvsborg had to be ransomed again in the Treaty of Knäred (1613). This time payment of 1 million German thalers over six years was called for. Gustavus coined his plate, laid heavy taxes on the countryside, and set aside 30 percent of his revenue for buying copper. To meet the obligation he bought copper, which he sold through merchants in western, northern, and central European markets, primarily Lübeck and Amsterdam. Unfortunately it became necessary to divert a substantial part of the proceeds to other uses and to borrow from Amsterdam to effect the necessary payment on time. The loan was never fully repaid (Heckscher, 1954, pp. 79, 85, 105). This early attempt at recycling an indemnity is worth mention even though it proved unsuccessful.

PALAVICINO AND THE ÉCU SUBSIDY

In his biography of Sir Horatio Palavicino, Lawrence Stone sets out the need to advance 50,000 écus or £15,468 to Frankfurt, to supplement 150,000 écus from the French, to enable Casimir to raise an army of 9,000 knights, 4,000 foot soldiers (*landknechte*), and 10,000 Swiss. French funds were provided partly in bills of exchange from Italian financiers in Geneva, obtained against pledges of Huguenot and Navarrese property as security, and partly in specie shipped to Frankfurt via Hamburg. The smaller English sum was transmitted entirely in bills. Palavicino proceeded from London to Frankfurt by way of Haarlem, Bremen, and Kassel, arriving in Frankfurt before the end of the spring fair of 1586 to raise money there. Before leaving London, he had arranged for the money to be paid to two business agents, Giustiniano and Rizzo, in six equal installments from February to July, and to use the proceeds to buy bills of exchange on Lyons, Rouen, Antwerp, Cologne, and Frankfurt. It was impossible to transfer the whole amount by bills of Frankfurt since too few English businessmen sold goods in that market. Bills on Rouen were readily available, although one had to be careful not to depress the exchange rate too much. The rate on Rouen was 6s 4d per écu compared with 6s 3½d on Lyons. Collecting French money in Rouen, for example, from the Italian financiers on whom the bills were drawn, Palavicino expected to transfer the money further to Lyons with his own bills, paying his French alum monopoly money in Rouen against money in Lyons, which he would then sell in Frankfurt.

When he got to Frankfurt, Palavicino borrowed 30,000 écus on his personal security at the spring fair at the end of March and in early April. The money was obtained largely from Ludvico Perez & Company of Nuremberg, against bills of exchange drawn by Palavicino on his agents in Middleburg, Antwerp, Lyons, and Venice, payable in early June with the funds arriving from London. The rest of the money he borrowed in Frankfurt in May from Antwerp and Cologne bankers, to be repaid in the same way by drafts bought in London on those centers (Stone, 1956, pp. 139–41).

Stone comments that the fact that Antwerp and Cologne were in Spanish hands and that Rouen and Lyons were under the influence of the king of France was not a problem, since politics did not interfere with finance in that day. He also notes that the decline in cloth exports of the Merchant Adventurers to Emden and Hamburg meant that bills on those centers were not abundant (ibid., p. 142). To transfer £15,000 in bills from London to Frankfurt, there need not be an export surplus of the one center on the other, so long as London had an export surplus overall, or capital movements were being directed to London from somewhere. While £15,000 does not seem a large amount, it was so for its day, and skill, plus banking instinct, were needed to find the appropriate routes to make the transfer.

It is of some interest that this transaction was carried out with bills on Rouen and Lyons but not on Paris. A century later, moreover, Daniel Defoe's heroine, Roxana, transferring her fortune from Paris to London, bought bills in Paris on Rotterdam and used them in Rotterdam to buy bills on London (1724 [1964], p. 121). The implication in both cases is that there was not an active market in bills between London and Paris, perhaps because it was suspended by war. At the end of the thirteenth century such a market existed, however, and the Italian bankers, Ricciardi, effected payments back and forth between the two capitals as a matter of normal business (Kaeuper, 1973, pp. 90–91).

ASIENTOS

In the Counter-Reformation, the Catholic Hapsburg Empire, led by Spain, fought against the Protestants, largely Dutch, and in the Spanish Netherlands. The fighting was done with Spanish generals and 5,000 or 6,000 Spanish troops, who were superb fighters. Mercenaries hired in the Spanish Netherlands, Germany, and Italy brought the total army up to 84,000 men in 1572 and 300,000 in 1625 (Parker, 1972, pp. 6, 42). Mercenary soldiers had the disability that they insisted on being paid and if not paid would mutiny. Forty-five mutinies took place in Flanders between 1572 and 1602; the most violent of them brought about the sack of large towns, including Antwerp (ibid., ch. 13, p. 185). It was urgent, therefore, to pay the troops.

The kings of Spain had silver coming to them mainly at this time from Peru (and later Mexico). Much was needed to pay for the goods brought to Seville and Cadiz for transshipment to Spanish America—silver that went partly to the Far East for hoarding and partly to Amsterdam and England, where it was used in considerable quantities to pay for imports of grain, timber, and furs from the Baltic. Some was needed to pay the mercenaries. This was transferred to Flanders by *asientos,* a Spanish word for a right that could be sold or discounted. In 1713, following the War of the Spanish Succession, the South Sea Company in London obtained an *asiento* from Spain to trade slaves to the south Atlantic. The *asientos* used to transfer funds from Spain to the Spanish Netherlands were different.

These *asientos* were of two types: Spanish and Flemish. The Spanish were negotiated by the Council of Finance in Madrid, although most of the actual handling took place at the fair of Medina del Campo near Valladolid. Businessmen exchanged promises to pay local funds at stated times in foreign places, such as Paris, Lyons, Savoy, Frankfurt, or the Genoan fair called Besançon, located for the most part at Piacenza outside Genoa. Flemish *asientos* originated with the Spanish troops in Flanders when the king's governors or captain-generals issued them against local money, often to German bankers such as the Fuggers or Welsers, against subsequent payment in Spain (Lapeyre, 1953, pp. 18–19).

Asientos usually included a license to export silver bought with the Spanish funds. The silver might be shipped for Spanish account from Barcelona to Genoa, converted into gold, and transported via the Spanish Road from Piedmont to Savoy, Franche Comté, and north through Lorraine to Flanders (Parker, 1972, p. 59). Much of the silver went to Flanders by sea—the so-called English Road—from Cadiz to Dover to Flanders, except during outbreaks of war between Spain and England (Attman, 1986, p. 59). Simon Ruiz, the Spanish banker, had a brother in Nantes in France and shipped silver to Flanders through that city and Paris under safe conducts granted by the French with the proviso that one-third of the coin be left in France (Lapeyre, 1953, p. 25). Sometimes silver was used to buy Netherlands currency from the Portuguese, who obtained it with pepper.

The war lasted eighty years, with fighting building up and dying down. In 1572, it cost 1.2 million florins a month while the Spanish were able to provide only 7.2 million in all of 1572 and 1573, so that by July 1576 the troops were owed 17.5 million florins. In September 1575 Philip II declared himself bankrupt, canceled all licenses to export silver, and paid off the *asientos* in *juros,* long-term bonds denominated in reals. By August 1576 the entire army had dissolved in mutiny and desertion (Parker, 1972, pp. 136–37). A more far-reaching bankruptcy occurred in 1596 when the king, attempting to repair his finances, signed *asientos* for a total of 4 million écus, 280,000 a month, but was unable to make good. He revoked licenses for exporting specie on all earlier *asientos* and took over revenues that had been assigned as surety to creditors. The pinch in Flanders was so tight that it was said that the captain-general did not have enough money for lunch. This was the crisis that crippled the Fuggers of Augsburg and caused collapse of Genoan credit (Lapeyre, 1953, ch. 4). In due course the debts were settled with the liberal use of *juros* and the resumption of payments in silver arriving from America. There were later royal Spanish bankruptcies in 1607, 1627, 1647, and 1653, with more *asientos* converted forcibly into *juros.* Spain fought long, hard, and losing battles with the aid of American silver, but it did not retain it as money.

David Hume thought that there was a sort of inevitability about Spain's inability to hold on to its silver:

Can one imagine, that it had ever been possible by any laws, or even any art of industry, to have kept all the money in SPAIN, which the galleons had brought from the INDIES? Or that all the commodities would be sold in FRANCE for a tenth of the price they would yield on the other side of the PYRENEES, without finding their way thither and draining from that immense treasure? What other reasons, indeed, why all nations, at present, gain in their trade with SPAIN and PORTUGAL; but because it is impossible to heap up money, more than any other fluid, beyond its proper level. (1752 [1898], p. 335)

BRINGING A FORTUNE HOME FROM INDIA

The East India Company bought goods, including gold, in India and sold them in Europe. The cost of its goods in India, called in its jargon the "investment," was met by proceeds of European goods sold in India—not a substantial quantity—by silver coin and bullion shipped there, which the company tried to hold down, and by monies borrowed locally. If goods sold well in Europe, the company might find itself borrowing in India and piling up funds in England, above the dividend paid out of its profits. There was thus a transfer problem from normal operations because of unbalanced trade and shortage of specie.

There were two further problems. After 1800 when the Napoleonic Continental system, or blockade, made selling Indian goods to Europe difficult, and it had to carry the war to French colonies in the Indian subcontinent, the company found itself borrowing in India for military operations. These should have been paid by the British government in England, adding to the transfer problem. Payments in Britain were often delayed, however, so that the company piled up net debt in India. This proved to be a particular problem in the nineteenth century. The debt that had been £8.4 million in 1784 rose to £18.2 million in 1802, £27 million in 1806, £32 million in 1808, and ultimately to £40 million in 1828 (Philips, 1940 [1961], ch. 6). The problem was solved in the long run only by ending the monopoly of the East India Company and the British government's taking over the debt, and India as a colony, in 1834.

Transferring to England the private fortunes of the company's servants in India was primarily a problem for the second half of the eighteenth century. Colonel Robert Clive defeated the native forces responsible for the Black Hole of Calcutta at Plassey in 1757 and opened up the question of the Indian succession to rulership as the naweb of Bengal. Native candidates bid against one another with "presents" made to Clive and his circle. Clive himself received 16 lakhs of rupees, each then equal to £11,000, plus his share in a general fund of 12 lakhs of rupees, all from the generous Mir Jafir, who was appointed naweb. Clive also asked for and received a *jagir*, or annuity, of £27,000 a year, which lasted, however, only until Mir Jafir died, which opened up another round of bidding. Other substantial payments after Plassey were £117,000 to Clive's secretary, Mr. Watts, £60,750 to Major Kirkpatrick, and £56,250 to Mr. Walsh, all of whom played key roles. Lesser figures in the inner circle obtained 1 lakh of rupees each. When Mir Casim's young candidate replaced Mir Jafir as naweb and he became his chief adviser, there were no presents on the scale of that given to Clive, but Governor Vansittart was given £58,333, Mr. Howell

£30,937, and five more individuals various amounts down to £15,000 (Holzman, 1926, p. 10).

In addition to presents, the company's servants in India, who were paid nominal salaries, could amass sizable fortunes in perquisites, provided they survived. Surviving took some combination of luck and skill. Of 645 civil servants who went to Bengal, three-quarters of those who came before Plassey died in India and 57 percent overall (P. J. Marshall, 1976, pp. 217–18). Not all who survived reaped big fortunes. Of 178 who got back to Europe, the success of at least 49 was questionable (ibid., p. 254). But others made a great deal of money in various ways: in the "country" (or Asian) trade not monopolized by the East India Company, which concentrated on trade between Asia and Europe; through kickbacks from suppliers to the company; interest earned on monies loaned to the company in India, or to the naweb; through farming the Revenue Department's taxes and banking with the monies while having them in hand. Fortunes of £100,000 were not unusual and, as already noted in Chapter 10 (p. 186), Lord North, as prime minister in England, thought Warren Hastings, as governor of Bengal, modest in limiting his ambition to £200,000. The trick, after surviving, was how to get the money back to England. It could, of course, be invested at high rates of interest in India, but that posed a serious agency problem, whether one would see the capital or the income on it again.

There were two main routes of transfer: buying bills on the East India Company itself or breaking its monopoly by buying bills in India on the Dutch or French companies that furnished them the cash to compete. There were lesser channels as well, such as supplying the company funds in Canton needed for purchases of tea, by selling opium, cotton, and tin to Chinese merchants; sending for sale to London diamonds in which the company did not trade; shipping goods on East India ships in the small amount of cargo space that the company allowed the ships' captains and that they were often willing, at a price, to use for private shipments; advancing monies to ships' captains against certificates payable in London to enable them to provision their ships in India.

For a time the company tried to build its London funds by adding to the investment, that is, shipping more goods and making more profits. This did not prove a success. Moreover, the company and Parliament were unwilling to expand company bills for fear of encouraging still further corruption among its servants in India. In 1773 Parliament fixed an upper limit of £300,000 a year on the amount that could be transferred this way. There were other disadvantages: the publicity that attended use of official channels and the fact that the rate for the rupee slipped through the period of remittances from 2s 3d per rupee to 2s. And while the company paid promptly in the early stages, by 1780 delays in effecting payment were stretching for as long as four years (P. J. Marshall, 1976, p. 222).

The record of how funds were remitted has been put together by Marshall for Clive, for a few other individuals, and for the group as a whole. Clive succeeded in transferring to England £310,000 in all, by means of £41,000 in company bills, £230,000 in Dutch bills, £30,000 in diamonds, £4,000 in certificates on East India ships, £5,000 via Bombay, and £7,000 in a bill drawn upon Laurence Sulivan, a

Table 13.1 Means of Repatriating "Profits" from India, 1757–84

	£
Bills on the East India Company	10,381,000
Company bills via Canton after 1769	1,500,000
Bills via Dutch, French after 1757	4,000,000
Bills on Danes after 1778	750,000
Diamonds after 1765 from Banaras, India	275,000
	16,906,000

Source: P. J. Marshall (1976, p. 255).

leading company director in London (ibid., pp. 235–6). For the group as a whole, Marshall has provided a table (Table 13.1). Miscellaneous other routes contributed perhaps an additional £1 million, making the total amount of private fortunes brought home a tentative £18 million (ibid., p. 255). For about 125 nabobs, this comes to an average of £145,000 each.

THE SPANISH INDEMNITY OF NAPOLEON

In May 1803 renewed war broke out between England and France, which had been at peace since the Treaty of Amiens in 1802. Under its treaty with France, Spain was committed to furnish military assistance. It sought to renegotiate this obligation and ended up, since Napoleon needed money more than men, in an arrangement to provide 6 million francs a month retroactive to May 1803. Of this, 2 million francs was to take the form of supplies and 4 million to be in cash, despite the fact that Spain had no funds, was cut off from its Mexican supplies of silver, and had little or no capacity to borrow in Amsterdam, Hamburg, or Paris (Buist, 1974, p. 284). By September 1804 the shortfall, including old obligations, had reached 116 million francs. Of the 40 million due to the end of October, only 18 million had been received in Paris, and this in the unsalable form of bills drawn on the Spanish Treasury.

Into this impasse entered Gabriel Julien Ouvrard, French *financier* and *munitionnaire,* who had formed a Compagnie des Négociants Réunis (Company of United Merchants). In the course of negotiations with the French and Spanish, he worked out an agreement under which he received Spanish bills from the French Treasury and obtained a monopoly of exports and imports for the Spanish colonies in America for the duration of the war against England, including gold and silver. Armed with these documents, he went to Hope & Company in Amsterdam (ibid., ch. 9). The monopoly of merchandise trade was valueless, given British domination of the Atlantic, but if British permission were granted for the shipment of silver, wanted by Napoleon for his armies and by Britain for India, ways might be found for France to collect its debt. Or if the silver could not be shipped to Europe, it could be sold in the United States against payment in London and Amsterdam arising from the American export surplus with Europe. From London the funds would be remitted to Amsterdam, and from that pivot converted to francs. Spain, as worked out by Ouvrard and Labouchère of Hope, was to pay France by way of Vera Cruz, Havana, New Orleans, Baltimore, New York, London, and Amsterdam.

The system worked remarkably well. By means of American goods, 9½ million guilders (equal to something over 14 million francs) was transferred in 1806 and 10.8 million guilders (16 million francs) at the peak rate in 1807. Hope & Company had agents in Vera Cruz, New Orleans, Baltimore, and New York, the last being David Parish, son of the Hamburg banker, John Parish. Piasters from Vera Cruz were used to make advanced payments on North American goods—largely sugar, coffee, rice, and cotton, although sugar, backed up from India as well, finally became a drug on the European market. Shippers would draw on consignees and deliver the bills to Hope and Baring representatives, who forwarded them to London and Amsterdam for collection. On occasion, Parish would forgo the use of the Mexican silver, draw bills on Baring to be sold to American importers to buy British goods, and use the proceeds to buy American drafts on the Continent. This merely shifted funds from London to the Continent. Funds were sometimes routed through Hamburg where the British deficit with Russia was handled. The transfer from Amsterdam to Paris was regulated by way of Hamburg, Rotterdam, Antwerp, and Frankfurt to reduce the pressure on the Amsterdam-Paris exchange rate. Bankers in these localities drew bills on Hope, which they sold to merchants making payments in Amsterdam, and delivered the counterpart to Hope in Paris (ibid., pp. 318–20).

Piasters were also shipped to Europe as silver, particularly after the death of Pitt (in January 1806) who had opposed this method. They were carried, in fact, on British warships, especially 3,679,835 on the frigate *Diana,* with the French Treasury being paid at the rate of 3.85 francs to the piaster (equivalent to a dollar). The abandonment of American goods in favor of direct silver shipment was partly owing to increasing harassment of the ships of the Baltimore merchant, Robert Oliver, by British men of war (Bruchey, 1956). The need for the subsidy or indemnity stopped in 1808 when Spain went to war against Britain and the duke of Wellington undertook the Peninsular campaign.

BRITISH SUBSIDIES FOR THE PENINSULAR CAMPAIGN

British subsidies to its allies in the Napoleonic Wars amounted to £42.5 million from 1811 to 1816, paid out by John C. Herries, paymaster-general of the British government. Specie was short, and an effort was made at all times to limit its use (Sherwig, 1969, p. 88). From time to time specie was especially scarce, and a movement across the exchange would result in depreciation of the pound and an increase in the agio on gold, as the banking school, notably Thomas Tooke, later contended.

In 1810, with the start of the Peninsular campaign, hard money was needed for Wellington's army and for subsidies to Portugal, and later Spain, which Wellington dispensed from his military chest. Since British commerce was relatively free with Portugal, Spain, and Sicily at the time, Britain should have had little difficulty in raising funds in those localities. In occasional periods of difficulty, depreciation of the exchange rate would stimulate exports to provide bills of exchange, which could be shipped to Wellington for collection (Heckscher, 1922, p. 353). Or if the duke sold bills on London at a discount, they should have been bought up locally by merchants finding it profitable to import from London. Heckscher thought that the difficulty lay not in the basic economic position but in bad organization of payments between England, on the one hand, and Portugal and Spain on the other—an anti-Coase position—and the fact that the British government did not initially take war on the Peninsula sufficiently seriously (ibid., pp. 353–54). The duke of Wellington continuously complained, criticizing the Treasury for sending so little specie—although the guinea was selling in London for 24*s* instead of the par of 21*s*—and claiming that his greatest deficiency was not food but cash. He could get local money by selling local bills but only at a heavy discount—close to 25 percent. The army had not been paid for several months. The duke's specific complaint was that "The want of money in the army is a most serious evil; and we may trace to this want the acts of plunder and indiscipline by which we are disgraced every day" (Sherwig, 1969, pp. 232, 255).

Some gold brought back from India against silver had been minted into guineas there—the last guineas to be coined by Britain and referred to as military guineas. These were sent to Wellington. When they proved insufficient, Herries turned to Rothschild's bank for help. Of the £42.5 million paid out by Herries on the Continent between 1811 and 1815 for troops and subsidies to allies, it is estimated that Rothschild handled at least half. His method was direct. Instead of shipping specie to Spain, or continuing the Wellington practice of discounting bills on London in Spain, he bought drafts on Spain, Portugal, Sicily, and Malta in Paris with gold. Cash went from London to Paris, permitted by Napoleon and Mollien because they thought it would weaken Britain and strengthen France—a mercantilist notion. In Paris it was used to buy bills of exchange on a network of bankers, largely Jewish, in Portugal, Spain, and so on, at prices representing enormous savings as compared with the discounts on bills drawn in these small financial centers on London.

It is not completely clear from various accounts how often Nathan Rothschild acted as Herries's agent and how often as principal. As agent, he would be paid in London, get gold, buy francs, with francs buy bills from Paris bankers on Spanish, Sicilian, and Maltese bankers—an "intricate network of business firms"—who contrived through their connections to get the paper to Wellington "who duly received cash from the bankers" (Corti, 1928, p. 117). On at least one other occasion, in 1811, as principal, he took his own money, plus money entrusted to him by the elector of Hesse-Kassel to buy consols and, in fact, all his credit, bought an entire shipment of gold from the East India Company—£800,000—and bought in Spain at an enormous discount Wellington's bills, which were then paid off at par in London (ibid., p. 118). In his later years, Nathan Rothschild recounted a story of such an operation to Sir Thomas Powell Buxton in 1834, adding, "It was the best business I ever did" (Heckscher, 1922, p. 354). In 1813 Wellington wanted French currency, rather than Spanish or Portuguese, and Rothschild went to Holland with his brothers, collected French coin, which was flooding the Continent, and shipped it along the coast to Wellington's headquarters (Corti, 1928, p. 128). On this occasion it is not specified how he obtained Dutch funds.

THE FRANCO-PRUSSIAN INDEMNITY

Background

Bismarck had financial difficulties in preparing for war against Austria. Appropriations had to be voted by the Prussian Diet, and this was opposed to military aggression. Like Napoleon before him, however, he collected indemnities from defeated countries and others whom he blackmailed, or at least exacted payment from, in return for refraining from aggressive action. In 1864 he collected an indemnity from defeated Denmark (Stern, 1977*a*, p. 53). Preparing for war against Austria, he needed 400,000 thalers to support the Hungarians against their neighbor. He took 100,000 thalers of this from Foreign Office funds and borrowed the remainder from Bleichröder, his personal banker, against the security of a 10,000-thaler-a-day indemnity from Saxony, the price of leaving that state its fiscal independence. When 2½ million of this had been paid, the total was fixed at 10 million, which Saxony borrowed to discharge its debt to Prussia (ibid., pp. 90, 110). He also levied a punitive indemnity of 5 million thalers against Frankfurt-am-Main, which Bismarck detested for its liberalism and independence. After war against Austria had been won, this sum was raised to 25 million, and Frankfurt-am-Main, along with Hanover, Hesse-Kassel and Nassau, was annexed to Prussia (ibid., p. 90).

These monies were still insufficient for war against Austria, so Bismarck arranged—through von der Heydt, the finance minister—for Hansemann and Bleichröder to buy the shares of the Cologne-Minden railroad held by the Prussian government, outside the control of the Prussian Diet. The Prussian army was being mobilized. Stock markets all over Europe were paralyzed in distress. While bankers generally insisted that they wanted peace, the condition under which they flourished, and that they did not lend for warlike purposes, when it came to the crunch Hansemann and Bleichröder acquiesced quietly. They got little credit for it from Bismarck in 1889:

At an earlier time, there was almost no possibility of covering Prussian war loans by national capital, as the example of 1866 made clear, and the Berlin *haute finance* did not feel strong enough as regards capital to muster the courage to risk what they had for the sake of the nation. (ibid., p. 85)

Setting the Indemnity

War between Prussia and France broke out in July 1870, again with depressing effects on financial markets. After a succession of victories, however, the Prussian government had no trouble borrowing through a Hansemann consortium, which offered a loan of 20 million thalers to the public, in both Berlin and London. Bleichröder who, Stern insists on the same page, was no friend of war, and Rothschild of London, took 3 million each, the Diskontogesellschaft under Hansemann 4.3 million (ibid., p. 131). Napoleon III fell in six weeks from the outbreak of war, but the Third Republic of France, under the presidency of Louis Adolphe Thiers, held out until January 1871.

The possibility of exacting an indemnity from France had been discussed as early as August 1870, one month into the hostilities, when the figure of 2 billion francs was mentioned, contrasting sharply with the 700 million francs levied against France in 1815 to cover twenty-three years of Napoleonic aggression. Favre, a French diplomat, is said to have offered Bismarck 5 billion francs if France could keep Alsace and Lorraine. The Prussian State Ministry mentioned a figure of 1 billion thalers or 3 billion francs. Bleichröder thought 4 billion the right amount, 5 billion distinctly too high, and numbers such as the 7 billion or 8 billion mentioned in the press absurd (ibid., p. 149). While this discussion was under way, a 200 million indemnity was levied on the city of Paris. For the indemnity to be paid by France as a whole, Bismarck favored a large amount. He wanted to keep France crippled (Emden, 1938, p. 213). He is also quoted as having said that the more thoroughly France was vanquished, the more stable would be the ensuing peace (Stern, 1977*a*, p. 145).

Parenthetically, it may be suggested that the German basis of comparison for the size of the indemnity was not that levied earlier on France but the reparations paid to France by Prussia after its defeat at Jena in 1806. Between 1806 and 1808, Napoleon squeezed 1 billion francs out of Prussia; its territory was cut in half and its population reduced to 5 million. On top of this, in 1809, he demanded a 120 million franc contribution which was mostly paid by 1812 by means of a 70 million mortgage on royal domain rentals and 50 million in bills of exchange levied on seven Prussian merchants, to be paid off at 4 million a month after November 1808. Payments on the latter amount fell behind (Brockhage, 1910, pp. 38, 41). These were hard times for Prussians, and peasants ate seed. There was this difference between Napoleon and Bismarck in extracting indemnities. Napoleon needed them to keep fighting, pay his armies, provide gratifications to his generals, and, in part, run the French state at home without borrowing or issuing paper money, both of which expedients he detested. His interest was financial, not punitive, and the levies on Italy, Spain, Austria, the Netherlands, and Prussia were often preceded by laying violent hands on coin and beautiful horses to pull the carts to carry it away (Menias, 1969, p. 18). The distinction may be without a difference for the country forced to pay; it has meaning for the exactor. It is, in this sense, that the Franco-Prussian indemnity can be called "an unprecedented ransom" (Landes, 1960, p. 215).

The indemnity was finally fixed in the convention of 26 February 1871 at 5 billion francs, with interest at 5 percent on the unpaid portion (ultimately amounting to 301 million), less the value of French railroads in Alsace and Lorraine, calculated at 325 million, or a net monetary payment of 4,976 million. Five hundred million was to be paid in thirty days from signing of the peace treaty (which took place in May) and 1 billion more in the rest of 1871. Five hundred million more was due by May 1872 and 1 billion each 1 March thereafter, in 1873, 1874, and 1875. The last three payments all bore 5 percent interest; prepayment was allowed in amounts of 100 million francs, with a discount of 5 percent.

Mode of Payment

Payment was accepted by Germany in gold, silver, bank notes of the Bank of England, Prussian State Bank, Royal Bank of the Netherlands, or the Royal Bank of Belgium, in checks on these banks, and in immediately payable bills of exchange of the first rank, presumably on good names, in England, the Netherlands, Prussia, or Belgium. French bills of exchange were explicitly excluded.

There were some ambiguities. South German money was not mentioned in the agreement, and it was not clear initially whether gold and silver could be in bullion or had to be minted. It was later specified that coin was wanted. Since Germany was about to switch from the bimetallic to the gold standard and the price of silver bullion was falling, it was a mistake on the part of the Germans to accept silver coin at a nominal value. The French later bought silver in the open market, presumably in London, and had it minted in Hamburg (Gutmann, 1918, pp. 201–15).

The Paris Indemnity

The Paris indemnity of 200 million francs constituted a dry run for the larger subsequent payment. Bleichröder came to Paris to arrange the details (Stern, 1977*a*, p. 148) that were set out in a convention of 11 February 1871. Fifty million could be provided in French bank notes, 50 million in coin, and the rest in exchange on Berlin and London. The exchange rate was fixed at 1 thaler equal to 3.75 francs; the pound sterling at 25.20 francs. Financing in France consisted of a loan to the city of Paris by the Bank of France in the amount of 210 million francs. The 50 million in coin was not collected immediately, but was replaced by a guarantee fund of bank notes.

When it came to the exchange on London, Bismarck personally—doubtless at the instigation of Bleichröder—specified a list of seven of the Paris banks called upon to guarantee the exchange: Rothschild, Hottinguer, Mallet Frères, A. Fould, Sellières, Pillet-Will, and Marcuard, André. All seven houses were required to endorse each sterling bill, in proportions laid down, with the banks liable for stipulated sums until the exchange had been paid off. Of the 100 million in exchange, 37 million was paid in thaler bills on Berlin, 63 million in sterling. The thaler exchange had a maturity of two months. Sterling exchange was made up of 22.7 million in six-day maturities and 40.3 million in fourteen-day maturities. Provision of the exchange was expeditiously carried out and the whole payment discharged by the end of June 1871 at a cost of about 2 million francs. Purchases of sterling bills drove the exchange rate on London up slightly to 25.3448 francs, presumably because of the short maturities; the thaler-franc rate actually fell from 3.75 to 3.7325 (Gutmann, 1913, pp. 192–98).

Paying the 5 Billion

The convention of Versailles of January 1871 was followed by the peace treaty of Frankfurt in May, and the two documents together specified a schedule of withdrawal of German occupation troops. When the first 500 million had been paid within thirty days from the treaty, the Germans undertook to withdraw from the Somme, the Seine-Inférieure, and the Eure. With the 1 billion further payment by December 1871, the *départements* of Oise, Seine-et-Oise, Seine-et-Marne, and the forts of Paris would be evacuated. On receipt of the additional half billion due May 1872, still further withdrawals would take place, leaving the Germans occupying

Marne, Haute-Marne, Ardennes, Vosges, Meuse, Meurthe-et-Moselle, and Belfort until the last 3 billion had been paid (Thiers, 1904, pp. 181–82). Thiers tried to offer financial guarantees to get the Germans to evacuate French territory faster, since it had been agreed at Versailles in January that financial guarantees could be partially substituted for occupation. In August 1871 the German government stipulated that these guarantees must consist of the signature of the French government guaranteed by the first banking houses of Germany, France, and England, and asked that these guarantees be negotiable on demand. The matter was dropped (ibid., pp. 220, 285).

What is critical, however, was the French drive to get the payment finished and French territory free of occupation as quickly as possible. "Thiers was the soul of the financial operation; he did everything" (Gutmann, 1913, p. 230). In his *Notes et souvenirs* of 1870 to 1873, not memoirs, Thiers asserts that from 1 May 1871, when he started negotiating with the German representative von Arnim, his purpose was to convince the German government that France had the will and the power to pay (1904, p. 285). The contrast is with German reparations to the Allies in the 1920s when Brüning's main purpose was to convince the world, at whatever cost, that Germany was unable to pay the reparations scheduled.

In May 1871 it was agreed that while French exchange was excluded from the indemnity, 125 million in French bank notes were acceptable. These were delivered as follows: 40 million on 1 June, 40 million on 8 June, and the rest on 15 June in denominations of 100, 50 and 20, francs, for further use, beyond the monies in the Paris indemnity, by German troops. Additional payment in gold and silver coin, and German bank notes, which it was agreed would include the south German gulden, along with the thaler and the Hamburg mark banco, and the transfer of the Alsace-Lorraine railroad valued at 325 million francs, completed the 500 million payment due in thirty days.

The First Thiers Rente

Thereafter it was necessary to raise further monies in France to pay the 1 billion due by the end of the year. On 6 June, Pouyer-Quartier, finance minister, announced the sale of a 2,500 million *rente* at 5 percent of which 2 billion was to be for the indemnity, the remainder for general governmental expenses. Subscriptions were to open on 26 June and stay open until the loan was covered but not beyond 30 June. Subscriptions would be accepted as low as 5 francs and above 10 francs in multiples of 10. Issue price was fixed at 82.50. Payments above minimum amounts would be called for in sixteen equal installments beginning July 1871. Thiers recalled later that the government had hoped to raise 1 billion from the public that had already loaned it 800 million, plus another billion from the banks of Paris (1904, p. 193).

The loan was marketed partly directly to the public, in part by banking syndicates. M. M. Warburg in Hamburg first assumed that the loan would be handled by a single French syndicate and wrote to Rothschild as early as 31 May to obtain a piece of the French *rente* to market in Germany. It then appeared that the Berliner

Diskontogesellschaft and Bleichröder were organizing a German syndicate, and Warburg joined that. The Warburg files show that the French government had taken a two-page advertisement in the Hamburg press to advertise the loan, a prelude, say the bank's historians, to "one of the most astonishing financial transactions of modern times" (Rosenbaum and Sherman, 1976 [1979], pp. 70–71).

Before the end of the first day, 2.5 billion had been subscribed in Paris, followed by 1¼ billion coming in the next day from the provinces and later 1,135 million from abroad, including subscriptions from as far away as India, for a total of 4,897 million, or roughly twice the amount called for. The initial payment was calculated to produce 323 million, but advance payments brought the sum to 847 million. Another 467 million was received in August. Europe was astounded (Thiers, 1904, p. 195).

For a 5 percent *rente* issued at 82.5, the cost to the French government was close to 6 percent. Even before the bonds were issued, however, the market bid the issue up to 84.5. In July it rose further to 86.25, and by the end of October to 94.95. Banks and others that bought bonds on speculation made sizable profits.

With these monies—partly foreign exchange, mostly French francs—in hand, the French government set about buying foreign bills to pay down its obligation. Three hundred seventy-five million was paid off in July, 175 million in August, and 510 million in September and October, which with the June payment fulfilled the 1½ billion due by the end of the year. Gutmann has a long footnote setting out the number and the highest and lowest denominations of bills bought in this period. One thousand, nine hundred thirty sterling bills were bought, the lowest at £4, the highest at £1,265,000. Other highest denominations were 2.5 million thalers, 2.5 million Dutch florins, 1.8 million marks banco, and 8 million Belgian francs (1913, p. 226n). The French government established specialized agencies in London, Brussels, Amsterdam, Hamburg, Frankfurt, and Berlin. In December 1872 these agencies held bills of exchange to the value of 417 million francs, of which 142 million had been accumulated in Hamburg (Rosenbaum, 1962, p. 130).

France succeeded brilliantly in raising the French franc equivalent of these payments. The foreign exchange counterpart consisted of two elements: foreign subscriptions to the first Thiers *rente,* on the one hand, and French subscriptions coming from liquidation of foreign securities in French portfolios that were switched into the *rente,* on the other. Despite the initial availability of exchange, a critical passage was encountered in December as the foreign exchanges weakened, presumably as a result of profit taking by foreign subscribers to the *rente.* Gold and silver reserves of the Bank of France fell; the exchange rate on London weakened to the gold export point to such an extent that 80 million francs in gold left for London in a single day (Thiers, 1904, p. 231). The Bank of France sought to substitute bank notes for coin in the internal circulation, issuing denominations of 20, 10, 5, and even 2 and 1 franc notes for the first time. The Bank of France wanted the government to borrow another 1.5 billion francs to pay down its advance at the bank, which had been raised from 1.5 billion to 2.4 billion during the war. Thiers commented that he regarded this idea as "infinite folly," since it would have meant replacing a 1 percent loan with another at 6 percent. Since the government was

'Je t'en avais comblé, je t'en veux accabler' [I have met your demand; let me now crush you].   (*vers connu.*)

Cartoon by Honoré Daumier (1871), from Charivari, 2 August 1871. Reproduced with the permission of the Houghton Library, Harvard University.

comfortably ahead in its schedule of payments to the end of the year, it could halt buying foreign exchange. It did so, and the franc rate recovered.

The next half-billion francs plus 150 million francs of interest on the 3 billion owed in 1873–75 was due on 1 May 1872. The French government proposed to pay this in installments of 80 million francs each first of the month and fifteenth, from 15 January to 15 April 1872, and 90 million on 1 May. As it worked out, it was able to better this schedule. One hundred sixty-one million were paid in January, almost 258 million in February, and 82 million on the principal plus the 150 million of interest on 6 March.

The Second Thiers Rente

Negotiations between the Germans and French were continuous over the possibilities of advancing schedules for payment and withdrawal of occupation troops. Thiers had been wondering as early as October 1871 about the possibilities of getting finished well ahead of 1 March 1875. In May 1872 a proposal for a loan of 3 billion was discussed. There would be three *tranches* of 1 billion each; first a lottery loan, the second a *rente* at 5 percent, and the third, a loan in foreign securities acceptable to the Germans and guaranteed by the French government. Bleichröder reported that Bismarck, possibly on his advice, objected to the lottery loan and the loan in foreign securities, and could understand only a *rente* like that of 1871. Thiers did not dissent (1904, pp. 294–306). Accordingly, the French government began preparations for another major issue.

The second Thiers *rente* for 3 billion to be paid to Germany and an additional 500 million for the discount and expenses was authorized on 15 July to be sold beginning Sunday, 28 July. The terms were for a 5 percent *rente,* issued at 84.50, to be paid in five equal installments on a monthly basis beginning 1 September. In France people stood in line all night for a chance to subscribe. In Paris and the nine other places the loan was offered, the loan was covered thirteen times. The two *rentes,* says Lévy-Leboyer, were covered five times at home and seven times abroad, which presupposes some initial division of the *rentes* into domestic and foreign *tranches* (1977a, p. 12). Subscription to the 1873 *rente* in Berlin and north Germany amounted to 4½ billion, with Berlin alone at 3 billion. Individual subscriptions of as little as 1 million francs were rare; 10 million to 50 million was more usual, and one bank tried to buy 500 million (Gutmann, 1913, p. 238). These sums were not serious, of course, but speculation on the rise in price with the expectation, or hope, of selling the *rente* at a profit before the second call. German bankers had hoped to be cut in on the original issue and earn the underwriters' commission. In the event, after long and harrowing negotiations revealed by the Bleichröder papers, the Rothschild French group cut the Germans, or at least Bleichröder, out of the initial issue, making them evidently more anxious to get on the bandwagon, however belatedly and at higher cost (Landes, 1982). An alternative version is that it was Count Harry von Arnim, the first German ambassador to France after its defeat, who arranged to include Haber, Henckel, and Hansemann in but leave Bleichröder out of what Stern calls the last billion of the indemnity (1977a, pp. 234–35).

The only other competition to the Rothschild syndicate came from J. S. Morgan, the American firm, but well anglicized, in London. This had taken a risk in 1870 in advancing £10 million to the French government after it had moved from Paris to Tours (Sheppard, 1971, p. 80). In 1871 it headed a London syndicate that offered what Jenks called the only serious competition to the Rothschilds (1927, p. 268).

In addition to its underwriting commission, the Rothschild syndicate was guaranteed 25 million francs by the French government for assurance that the subscriptions would produce 700 million of exchange on Germany (Thiers, 1904, p. 323).

The first payment on the *rente,* amounting to 1,100 million, was again larger than required by the terms of the offering. This allowed France to redeem the Marne and Haute-Marne from German occupation six months ahead of schedule.

The large speculative interest in the issue meant that the government's troubles were not over. On the contrary, the Treasury immediately began to worry about how many speculators would sell immediately in August on a when-issued basis, before the 1 September settlement date, and again in September before the payment due on 1 October. It was feared that support might be needed for the franc as well, if profits made by foreigners on resale of the *rente* were returned abroad. The Bank of France raised its discount rate; it and the Treasury prepared to defend the price of the *rente.* The crisis spread to London where the French acquired 200 million francs equivalent in sterling to pay to Germany, at a time when the pound was weak against the thaler. The French readied themselves to advance part of their accumulated gold holdings to the Bank of England and to slow their payments to Germany. The tension was relieved, however, by gold received in London from Australia. An active discount policy helped, and the direct assistance of the French, apart from slowing payment to Germany in sterling bills, was not needed (ibid., pp. 361–63).

With the great success of the second Thiers *rente,* effectively digested, France proceeded to pay off the rest of the indemnity. German exchange had been accumulated prior to marketing the *rente.* Subscriptions in foreign exchange, plus flourishing exports as a result of a good French grain harvest when the rest of Europe had a mediocre crop, provided the rest. The government paid roughly 610 million francs from 29 August to 5 September—200 million in October, 100 million in November, and 200 million in December, which more than anticipated the billion due on 1 May 1873—and then proceeded with 150 million in January 1873, 250 million in February, and 150 million in March, to pay off 250 million in each of six successive months through September 1873, which wound up the 5 billion (Gutmann, 1913, p. 222).

The payment was effected somewhat differently before and after the end of August 1872, according to figures worked up by Gutmann (Table 13.2).

The table fails to indicate a couple of things: first, whether French authorities bought German exchange with sterling, for example, and second, the extent to which the source of foreign exchange was French investors' liquidating their foreign holdings as opposed to foreigners' going long of French francs. On the first score, Morgan notes that of £61 million (1,500 million francs) acquired by the French in sterling, half was converted into German bills and the rest paid to Germany in sterling (Morgan, quoting Léon Say, 1943, p. 183). Even taking these qualifications into account, it seems clear that it was a mistake to believe, as British writers tend to do (Clapham, 1945, Vol. 2, p. 287), that the payment was financed largely through bills drawn on London. On the other hand, the round-about payment through London, and possibly others via Amsterdam and Brussels, make it impossible to accept the view that Germany as a whole—Prussia, Hamburg, and the

Table 13.2 Means of Paying the 5 Billion Franc Indemnity, 1871–73 (by periods in millions of French francs)

Method	1 June 1871–28 August 1872	29 August 1872–5 September 1873	1 June 1871–5 September 1873
French gold coin	109	163	273
French silver coin	63	176	239
French bank notes	125	—	125
German notes and coin	63	42	105
Thaler exchange	312	2,173	2,485
South German gulden exchange	29	209	238
Mark banco exchange (Hamburg)	117	148	265
Dutch gulden exchange	251	79	330
Belgian franc exchange	147	149	296
Sterling exchange	624	13	637
Total	1,840	3,152	4,993

Source: Gutmann (1913, pp. 227–28).

South German Federation—transferred close to three-fifths of the indemnity and Britain, Holland, and Belgium only one-quarter of it (Borchardt, 1976, p. 6).

Effects

An operation of this magnitude was hardly without consequences. Apart from the gold payment itself, availability of foreign exchange that could be converted into gold enabled Germany, however clumsily, to go over to the gold standard. Its total money supply expanded from roughly 2 billion thalers to 3 billion (Taussig, 1927, p. 272). Sixty million were devoted to rebuilding Berlin and touched off a construction boom. The German government took 4.5 billion to repay debts of the states about to be formed into the German Empire, and these monies in the hands of investors casting about for equal or better outlets fed the fires of speculation in railroads and building that spread to Austria and ended only with the stock market collapse of May 1873. In the fashion of Frederick William, father of Frederick the Great, 120 million in gold were sequestered in the Julius Turm (tower) as a war chest, providing a metaphor that came to be used after World War II when a German finance minister, Fritz Schaeffer, hid a budget surplus by prepaying expenditures and delaying receipts.

German inflation was sharp. Price indexes are less than perfect for the period, but the wholesale price level rose from 103 in 1870 to 141 for the average of 1873—much higher in the first months of the year—and prices of industrial materials within the general index went from 121 in 1870 to 167 in 1873 before falling back to 95 in 1879 (Jacobs and Richter, 1935, p. 81).

The accumulation of sterling in rather inexperienced and elated German hands worried Britain. The Germans could have broken the Bank of England if they had wanted to (Clapham, 1945, Vol. 2, p. 287). The Bank of England changed its discount rate twenty-four times in 1873—four times upward from May to 6 June, from 3½ percent to 7 percent, and again in September successively from 3 percent to 9 percent in November. The governor of the Bank of Prussia wrote to the Bank of England, offering a loan of gold "now or at any future time." The governor in London, "politely but curtly" turned down the offer on the ground of impertinence from an upstart (ibid., p. 294).

In France the immediate effect was to leave the country comparatively depressed when all around it were experiencing inflationary expansion. This helped to create the export surplus necessary to transfer the indemnity abroad in real goods and services. But the speculative spirit had been aroused by the enormous profits made in the Thiers *rentes,* especially by banks. From 82.5 in July 1871, the 5 percent *rente* reached 100.5 in 1874 and 120 in 1880 (Lévy-Leboyer, 1977*a,* p. 129) when Gambetta and Léon Say were talking of, and finally managed to pull off, a conversion of 6 billion, with stimulating effects on the 1878–81 boom leading to the collapse of the Union Générale (Bouvier, 1960, pp. 158–61).

The Union Générale boom and bust was one effect. Another was the growing disdain of deposit banks and *banques d'affaires* for industrial loans as contrasted with speculation, mostly in bonds perhaps, but not completely separate from the effort of the Comptoir d'Escompte, which almost went under in its attempt in 1888 to corner the copper of the world.

The longest delayed effect, and perhaps the most devastating, was the precedent created for the aftermath of World War I when France, having forgotten Napoleon's exactions after Jena but recalling having paid the indemnity in 1871–73, a big one, was determined this time, as winner, to collect.

Real Transfer

Money payment of the indemnity was accomplished by recycling. To the extent that French investors sold foreign securities that they wanted, in the long run, to maintain, or that German buyers, exemplifying foreign subscribers as a class, were engaged in short-term speculation only, and expected over time to return to their normal habitat for investment inside German territory, no permanent payment had been made. That came with reversal of the recycling operation, renewed capital exports of French capital to restore portfolio balance, and repatriation of foreign capital after profits in the Thiers *rente* had been taken.

The real transfer is represented by a positive balance in the current account of France above what it would have been if French capital were not to return abroad, and German, Dutch, and Belgian capital were not to be repatriated. The counterfactual calculation of what the balance of payments would have been in the absence of the recycling operation is evidently highly subjective. Two estimates have been provided: one by James W. Angell who believed that long-run equilibrium was reached, with capitalists on both sides of the border where they wanted to be and an accumulated French export surplus of roughly 5 billion francs in about five years after 1873, that is about 1878 or 1879 (1926, app. B, pp. 520–21). A later calculation comes out with a figure of three or four years for transmitting about half the indemnity through merchandise trade, without specifying whether the remainder transferred through the service accounts in the balance of payments occurred simultaneously or extended beyond the initial period (Machlup, 1964*b,* pp. 380–

81). Whichever view one takes, most of the real transfer occurred during the early years of German inflation and French (relative) deflation.

The real transfer took place not only through direct Franco-German trade but in trade with third countries such as Britain. With rising German prices and prices steady in France, Germany became a better place to sell, a poorer place to buy, as compared with France; some British exports were redirected from France to Germany, some British imports from Germany to France. This improved the balance of payments of France and worsened that of Germany, without necessarily affecting that of Britain overall.

Automatic Functioning of Markets

Particularly noteworthy in the light of the subsequent transfer problem with German reparations after World War I was that with no Keynes to tell them that transfer was impossible, the recycling and subsequent real transfer took place without any banker, economist, or government official giving thought to the question of whether transfer was feasible. Later in the 1920s, when economists became concerned about transfer, analytical emphasis was on gold flows, exchange rates, changes in relative price levels, and shifts of purchasing power. In today's world with attention turned to recycling OPEC foreign exchange surpluses, it has become evident how large a role was played in the 1870s by recycling and by the existence of a newly created asset—the Thiers *rentes*—in which people both inside and outside France were willing to trade. Gold and silver turn out to be merely one more form of internationally acceptable asset that could be used to recycle financial movements through the exchanges until the underlying real transfer in goods and services could work itself out automatically.

U.S. PURCHASE OF PANAMA CANAL COMPANY FOR $40 MILLION

In contrast with the $1 billion Franco-Prussian indemnity, which was transferred only 10 percent in gold and silver coin, or 12 percent in gold and silver coin, plus German and French bank notes, the $40 million paid by the United States for taking over the de Lesseps Panama Company, its rights and assets, had to be transferred from the United States to France almost half in specie. The $40 million given to J. P. Morgan & Company on 9 May 1904 was the largest warrant issued by the U.S. Treasury to that time. To transfer to Paris the payment, which represented 10 cents on the dollar for the French company's original investment, J. P. Morgan shipped $18 million in specie to France and bought exchange on Paris for the rest in several European markets (Simon, 1971, pp. 253–54). It is not clear to me whether the difference between 12 and 45 percent is owing to skill or to different circumstances: monetary conditions, the condition of the U.S. balance of payments, or the fact that the payment was too small to produce ancillary changes that would have enabled it to be transferred in real terms, through an export surplus that generated bills of exchange. A French source described New York in 1913 as an entirely secondary financial center, with a money whose stability was in doubt and with only limited markets for money and foreign exchange (Coste, 1932, p. 129). But then J. P. Morgan should have been able to buy bills on Paris with dollars in London.

SUGGESTED SUPPLEMENTARY READING

Buist (1974), *At Spes Non Fracta: Hope & Co., 1700–1815.*
Corti (1928), *The Rise of the House of Rothschild.*
Landes (1982). The spoilers foiled: the exclusion of Prussian finance from the French Liberation Loan of 1871.
Machlup (1964), The transfer problem: variation II.
P. J. Marshall (1976), *East Indian Fortunes.*
Stone (1956), *An Elizabethan: Sir Horatio Palavicino.*

In French

Lapeyre (1953). *Simon Ruiz et les asientos de Philippe II.*
Thiers (1904), *Notes et souvenirs de M. Thiers, 1870–1873.*

In German

Gutmann (1913), *Das französiche Geldwesen im Kriege (1870–1878).*

14

Foreign Lending—Political and Analytical Aspects

> It is better to have loaned and lost than never to have loaned at all.
> (Remark of Leon Frazer, second president of the Bank for International Settlements, oral tradition)

CHANNELS AND THEIR SHIFTS

Chapter 12 has already noted that foreign lending flows in channels deepened by past flows, which channels sometimes change discontinuously. The Thiers *rentes,* described in Chapter 13, produced a shift not between home and foreign investment in general, or within foreign investment from one outlet to another, but directed investment from land and industry to bonds. Since the French budget was balanced after the indemnity had been paid, bonds meant foreign bonds—first Austrian, Italian, and Spanish, plus the shares of banks lending on those securities, then after the Franco-Italian tariff war, as also related, Russian bonds.

Some channels were purely economic, as in the remarkably widespread Belgian investment in railroads and especially tramways, from Italy where Belgian investments in tramways amounted to 121 million lire out of total Belgian investments in Italy of 161 million lire, and total foreign investments in Italy of 493 million lire (Gille, 1968, p. 364), to China where Belgium ran the railways with French participation (Kurgan-Van Hentenryk, 1977, pp. 203–4). Some were purely political, like German investments in Italy sought by Crispi, quickly undone and replaced by French capital when Crispi fell over the Italian defeat at Adowa in the Ethiopian War in 1896. German economic war with Russia culminating in the *Lombardverbot* and selling off of Russian bonds to French investors has been detailed (pp. 221–22). French commitment to Russian borrowing was partly fascination with bonds as such, partly a response to French Foreign Office support of the Alliance against the Triple Entente. The most flagrantly political loan was 1¼ billion francs raised in Paris for Russia in April 1906 immediately following the October Revolution of 1905, which came after Russian defeat by Japan and briefly threatened the collapse of the czarist regime. This was the biggest of all French loans for Russia, the one for which the Russian and French press campaign pulled out all stops (Girault, 1977, p. 251).

Political Rivalry

French, British and German interests elbowed one another in lending to Egypt, and especially in building the Suez Canal. Initially, the British were uninterested, and

Palmerston is said to have described it as something to be palmed off on French capital (Emden, 1938, p. 307). When the bond issue came out, British investors did not subscribe, but French ones most enthusiastically did. One Parisian investor is said to have asked if he could buy Suez shares "on that railroad on an island in Sweden." Told that the Suez company dealt with a canal across an isthmus in Egypt, he said that he still wanted to buy the shares so long as the project was anti-British (ibid., p. 309).

Later when Said, who had borrowed 40 million French francs in 1861 to purchase the 176,602 shares out of 400,000 that had not been moved in the initial offering, was obliged to sell them in 1875 to stave off bankruptcy—if only briefly—Disraeli bought the block out from under the nose of the Crédit Foncier, which already had a large holding and wanted more as security for floating a long-term bond issue (Marlowe, 1974, p. 175). Disraeli made the purchase with a 2½ percent loan from Rothschild granted on the basis of only the government's word, if the usual story is credible (Blake, 1967, p. 556). The securities were worth £24 million by 1900, £40 million by 1914, before being nationalized with derisory compensation by Egypt after the Egyptian-Israeli War of 1956.

Competition picked up after 1870. In a wave of euphoria the Germans started the Deutsche Bank to challenge the preeminence of London in the finance of international trade. While little headway was made on this front, the Deutsche Bank turned early to the Middle East where it encountered the Banque Imperiale Ottomane, founded in 1863 by an Anglo-French group. Rivalry was intense. Of thirty-four important operations from 1881 to 1914—including nineteen loans, seven conversions, and eight issues of Treasury bonds—seven were undertaken by the Deutsche Bank, two by the English Banque Nationale de Turquie, and twenty-five in Paris, of which the Banque Imperiale Ottomane was responsible for nineteen (Thobie, 1977, p. 291). Britain, France, and Germany struggled over the Bagdad-Berlin railroad and Turkish finance generally. Helfferich scored successes in 1908 in getting the railroad underway and in 1911, after an intermediate setback, in getting it financed. The British Foreign Office under Earl Grey was then prepared to let the Germans run the railroad while the British controlled coastal shipping, with the French proposing a wide variety of ambitious and foolish projects beyond the financial capacity of the country (Williamson, 1971, pp. 80–101).

Imperialism

Dutch, Portuguese, French, and British empires existed before 1885 and remnants of a Spanish one, but a new dispensation arrived toward the end of the nineteenth century. Partly, it was French humiliation over loss of the Franco-Prussian War that encouraged them, and especially the military, to turn to West Africa and annex Tunis in 1882 and later Madagascar in 1896 and Morocco in 1912. In good part, the spurt in colonial interest followed from Leopold of Belgium's taking over the Congo in 1876 as a personal business venture with fantastically high profits. The cost of his operations in the Congo over forty years amounted to 40 million francs. The profit amounted to 66 million francs in a single year, 1908, alone (Brunschwig, 1960 [1966], p. 71).

A conference was called in Berlin in 1885 to see what could be done about Leopold and touched off a race for colonies among Germans, French, and British. The British claimed not to be greedy but expressed concern that if large territories in Africa were taken over by continental powers, these territories would be cut off from free trade. There was also the incentive to protect the route to India and to establish coaling stations. Germany was motivated by *Torschlusspanik*—fear that the door would close before it got inside (Stern, 1977*a*, pp. 410, 416).

It is beyond the scope of this book to go any distance into the European imperialism of 1885–1914 or to analyze the extent to which it was undertaken for profit, to escape falling consumption at home, to counter a decline in the domestic rate of interest, or largely for prestige, national honor, "aggressive altruism," discharge of the white man's burden, or the Frenchman's *mission civilisatrice* (Moon, 1927). Our interest is in Lenin's thesis that imperialism was a search for outlets for finance capitalism, with bankers directing governments to expand abroad so as to maintain the rate of profit and that rival efforts in different countries led to war. There is the further point enunciated by J. A. Hobson—that the Rothschilds could have stopped World War I if they had chosen to (1927 [1938], p. 57)—echoed by Eugen Kauffmann, writing in Germany in 1914, that it would be impossible for France to make war without obtaining Rothschild's consent (1914, p. 9).

In the first place, it is hard to make the case that colonies were lucrative for the imperial power—on the average. They were believed to be so. One of the more interesting fixed ideas of Hjalmar Schacht, the German central banker between the wars, was that the most serious loss of Germany in the Treaty of Versailles was that of its African colonies. Schacht wrote and spoke about the subject continuously (for example, 1937). The fixation may have been due to his upbringing in the port of Hamburg where many merchants and bankers were interested in colonies and building colonies of Germans overseas in independent countries such as Brazil (Wiskemann, 1929, p. 187; Rosenbaum and Sherman, 1976 [1979], p. 105; Stern, 1977*a*, p. 397). Göring understood that colonies were a drain on Germany, not a source of income, but in a curious fashion made an exception of the Cameroons (Office of United States Chief of Counsel, 1917 [1946], Vol. 7, pp. 890, 898). Helfferich, the banker, thought the Cameroons valuable as a means of making Germany independent of U.S. supplies of cotton (Williamson, 1971, p. 53). Bismarck was the greater realist whose conversion to colonialism lasted only a short time and thought that "for us Germans, colonies would be exactly like the silks and sables of the Polish nobleman who had no shirt to wear under them" (Stern, 1977*a*, p. 409 and ch. 15 passim). Ludwig Bamberger recognized publicly what Bismarck had told him in private—that the colonial business was a swindle that offered profits to no one but a few entrepreneurs (Zucker, 1975, p. 257).

There were rich colonies; Britain had most of them: the Gold Coast, India, from which the gains in the eighteenth century had been enormous, Malaysia, and the Witwatersrand, which led Britain into the Boer War, somewhat reluctantly, and marked a turning point in British self-confidence, much as the Vietnam War did for the United States. The Dutch had profitable holdings in the East Indies and, of course, Belgium in the Congo. For the most part, however, colonies were a luxury. Investment tended to precede colonization rather than the converse—in Tunis,

Morocco, Egypt (Fieldhouse, ed., 1967, p. 189)—and much more investment took place in independent countries, if the self-governing dominions like Canada be included among them, than in colonies as such. In 1902 French investment in colonial areas consisted of only 2.1 billion francs out of a total foreign investment of 30 billion to 35 billion (Ministère des Finances, 1902, p. 450). Seventy percent of British investment was in politically independent countries—the United States, European countries, Argentina, Uruguay, and so on—17.3 percent in the Dominions, and only 12.7 percent in the dependent empire (Woodruff, 1966, p. 52). If, in modern fashion, one penetrates formal governing arrangements and shifts from imperialism to "neoimperialism," a case could perhaps be made that Argentina was an economic colony of Britain in the 1880s. The same could not be said for the largest bastion of British investment, the United States, or, after the British North America Act of 1867, for Canada either.

BANKERS AND WAR

What bankers say about war themselves does not constitute solid evidence; protestations of love of peace and hatred of war are self-serving. Fritz Stern, Bleichröder's biographer, takes these protestations at close to face value, despite the failure of Hansemann and Bleichröder to resist Bismarck's insistent pressure for help in financing Prussian wars against Austria and France (1977*a*, pp. 73, 306–10, 317–18). Bismarck thought bankers timid, as noted earlier (p. 235). Wolf-Metternich wrote to von Bülow, a successor to Bismarck, "High finance quakes in its boots whenever any kind of political complication crops up" (Robbins, 1939, p. 58). Albert Ballin, Hamburg shipowner, and his friend, M. M. Warburg, the banker, worked frantically in 1914 with the British banker, Sir Ernest Cassel, to stave off war between Germany and Britain (Cecil, 1967, pp. 171, 193). The evidence does not squarely address the issue since Ballin and Warburg were citizens of the all-English city rather than of imperial and imperialist Berlin.

The most penetrating study, somewhat out of date, is Eugene Staley's *War and the Private Investor* (1935), which finds against the Lenin-Luxemburg thesis that finance capital leads to war. The role of steel interests, intent on selling armor plate to a fleet of dreadnoughts to counter the British navy, is far more compelling (Kehr, 1930 [1970]). Beyond economic and financial interests, moreover, there is the purely political, like the kaiser's saber rattling and the 1905 Tangier and 1911 Ajadir incidents. It is these, in Staley's view, that led to war, not financial rivalry. And while no financial or even trade interests produced these politically neuralgic flareups, the incidents themselves had financial consequences. In each instance, the Quai d'Orsay signaled French banks to pull funds out of Germany, or to refuse to list German securities on the bourse, or to withhold lending to Germany (in 1911) to make floating of a Turkish loan in Berlin more difficult (Poidevin, 1977, esp. p. 222; Rosenbaum and Sherman, 1976 [1979], p. 106). Instead of bankers using governments, governments used bankers, who almost inevitably submerged what they articulated as their material interest to what they were told was the national good.

PUSH OR PULL?

The early literature on the "transfer problem" by students of Frank W. Taussig at Harvard in the 1920s concluded that capital movements worsened the terms of trade, that is, the relation of export to import prices, of the capital-exporting country, and improved those of the capital-importing country. Starting from an autonomous capital flow, an initial gold movement from lender to borrower necessary to get change in the balance of payments underway lowered prices in the lending country, raised them in the borrower, and thus worsened the terms of trade for the former and improved them for the latter. Jacob Viner's classic dissertation, *Canada's Balance of International Indebtedness, 1900–1913* (1924), was held to have demonstrated this proposition, more or less. Then came studies by Rostow (1948) and Cairncross (1953) to contend that causation ran the other way—from terms of trade to capital movement. The terms of trade were taken as a proxy for the profitability of investment—export prices at home, import prices abroad. If the terms of trade worsened, it meant that import prices—those of foodstuffs and raw materials so far as Europe was concerned—were rising, and investment outside Europe in such areas as regions of recent settlement was more profitable, investment in manufacturing industry at home less so. If, on the other hand, domestic prices rose more than foreign prices, or fell less, improvement in the terms of trade provided a signal that relative profitability had shifted, and the time had come to switch investment from foreign to domestic projects.

Rostow originally worked with the Juglar cycle of eight or nine years, based on the periodicity of investment in capital equipment. In a subsequent study, his emphasis shifted to the Kondratieff, or fifty-year cycle, with twenty-five years, more or less, of expansion and twenty-five years of contraction (1978). The period 1850 to 1873 was taken as one of expansion, worsening terms of trade, and capital outflow; 1873 to 1896 as a period of contraction, improved terms of trade, and reduced export of capital; followed by another expansion and outflow after 1896 until the upswing was interrupted by war.

Cairncross was content to stay with cyclical flows and shorter cycles. In domestic boom, terms of trade turned favorable and the capital flow declined, in recession, the reverse. At turning points foreign and domestic investment were sometimes, and briefly, positively instead of negatively correlated, as was the normal pattern. At the peak of the upswing at home, capital movements might start abroad before domestic industry had turned down; foreign and domestic investment rose together (for example, from 1871 to 1874 or 1875); and domestic and foreign investment collapsed together in 1890. Apart from these turning points, however, foreign investment had a countercyclical pattern.

Still a third view of the periodicity of European capital movements placed emphasis on migration and construction of housing, postulating that counterposed building cycles in North America and Britain generated waves of migration that gave rise to need for housing. The housing cycle, sometimes called the Kuznets cycle, lies between the Juglar and the Kondratieff, at twenty years in length from trough to peak to trough again (B. Thomas, 1958 [1973]). It generates rhythmical movements not only in migration but also in capital, which flows in parallel. Boom in the United States brought both migrants and capital; when the wave subsided, labor in Europe continued to move off the farm but migrated to cities within a country rather than abroad.

Apart from the first, in which capital moves of its own accord and terms of trade follow, these models are theoretically reasonable and fit particular circumstances but have little broad generality. Trying to apply a model like that of Cairncross, in which British capital moves countercyclically, W. Arthur Lewis finds exceptions and concludes that timing of international investment has been a puzzle, with the "real puzzle" the second half of the 1880s (1978, pp. 178, 180). He might have added that the outflow of British capital after 1905, and especially from 1910 to 1914, is equally baffling in countercyclical terms, because the outflow picked up sharply with expansion of the business cycle at home—a pro-cyclical instead of the countercyclical pattern. British net investment abroad rose from an annual average of £40 million for 1896 to 1900, and £45 million from 1901 to 1905, to £150 million from 1906 to 1910 and £214 million from 1911 to 1913 (Feinstein, 1976, table 15). At the peak in 1914, Britain exported half its national savings. Cairncross notes that if the United States had exported private capital at the same proportions in 1952 that Britain did in 1913, the total U.S. capital outflow would have amounted to $30 billion, or thirty times the actual movement abroad of private U.S. investment (1953, p. 3). The comparison is invalid on two scores: U.S. investment had still some distance to go in recovering from the traumatic experiences of the 1930s. More germane to present interests is that it is not legitimate to take a single peak year as the basis for comparison or extrapolation. As shown below, 1913 capital exports were an outlier, well beyond the range of normal experience.

The difficulty with attempts to generalize the pattern of long-term foreign investment for Europe is that there are two valid models that apply, not simply one consistent one, and that the pattern shifts from one model to the other, from time to time and country to country, in ways not always easy to explain. In one model, savings are a constant flow to be divided annually between foreign and domestic uses according to the strength of relative demands. One can call this a demand model. It fits the Rostovian and Cairncross patterns if one can accept changes in the terms of trade as a valid proxy for profitability of investment at home and abroad. Under it, capital moves countercyclically—abroad when business is dull at home, less so in domestic boom. Counterposed to the demand model is a supply model, under which investment opportunities are abundant both at home and abroad, or more or less equally scarce, and funds will be allocated to both foreign and domestic outlets in increasing amounts as income and savings rise, decreasingly as savings decline with the fall in income. If this pattern fits, foreign and domestic investment are positively correlated with the business cycle, which determines the rise and fall of income and savings.

Whether the demand or the supply model operates in a given country at a given time cannot be foretold with assurance. As a first approximation it is likely after a change in horizon that uncovers new investment opportunities that the supply model will dominate. Investors now scanning a wider horizon will be anxious to exploit recently recognized opportunities abroad. Boom at home will generate investment needs there. As income and savings rise, foreign and domestic investment move up together. This is learning by doing, an expression that will be recognized by students of international trade theory as a valid explanation for historically decreasing costs. The model applies to Britain in 1817 and again in 1823–25, to both France and Britain in 1835 and 1836, to Britain, France, and Germany in the 1850s, 1860s, and early 1870s, and to Britain again in 1910–13. It also applied to the United States, outside the present jurisdiction, during the 1920s when the success of the Dawes loan in June 1924 suddenly widened horizons of American investors and led to an upsurge in domestic and foreign investment from 1924 to 1928. At the time it was said that New York was unskilled at foreign lending as compared with London. The verdict is understandable but amounts to a statement that the country was following a supply instead of a demand model.

The notion that as a country settles down and explores the full range of foreign investment opportunities it will shift from a supply to a demand model of foreign lending fits the British case fairly well—until 1910. The supply model was followed during the first half of the century, and just as one might have expected a transition to the demand model, a shift in horizon produced by the continental revolutions of 1848 called for exploration of a new set of opportunities. The 1885 to 1890 spurt, which Lewis calls the real puzzle, is a reaction to new opportunities in Argentina.

More puzzling to me is how Germany happened to adhere to a demand model after such a short time with the supply pattern from the mid-1850s to 1873. After barely twenty years of conformity to the supply model, Germany in 1873 reduced its foreign lending and even reversed it to bring home funds from abroad to invest in domestic business. In the late 1880s, when boom inside Germany intensified, Germans sold off Russian bonds to France, as noted in Chapter 12 (p. 222), and even unloaded Argentine bonds in London in 1888 and 1889. Various explanations have been given for dumping Argentine bonds: investors became uneasy about Argentina and enamored of gambling in industrial shares at home (Lauck, 1907, pp. 59–60); or they were disturbed by instability in the Argentine exchange rate, at a time when British investors were slow to see its implications (Morgenstern, 1959, p. 523). Shortly after undertaking political investment in Italy, in 1888 (Stern, 1977a, p. 432) and in 1893, the consortium of German banks under Bleichröder's leadership began unloading them (Confalonieri, 1976, Vol. 3, p. 19). Germany bought a considerable amount of foreign securities in such areas as Mexico, as Table 12.1 indicates. But pressure of domestic growth cut down foreign investment in a manner appropriate to an experienced and mature lender when Germany was a relative beginner. The explanation must lie in the intensity of the boom at home, which overcame the normal expectation that a new foreign lender would follow the pro- instead of the anticyclical pattern.

What remains clear, however, is that no single model can be used to explain all European foreign lending behavior.

THE OUTLIER

Also puzzling to me, if not especially to W. Arthur Lewis, is the resumption in Britain of the pro-cyclical model in the years from 1910 to 1913, after adhering to the other countercyclical one from 1870 to 1910, with the exception of a few years at the end of the 1880s. The loans were heavily concentrated in Canada. This flow started slowly after 1896, and picked up gradually as railroads pushed west and new communities borrowed for infrastructure in the London market. The rush of lending at the end, just before the war, rather spoils Viner's analysis (1924), which relies primarily on long-run effects. It appears that the movement was not a rhythmic rise and fall but a surge. In 1913 when it took half of British savings, foreign investment was a bubble, like the earlier lending bubbles in 1825, 1857, 1866, and 1873 (in Germany and Austria, though not in London) and in Paris and Lyons in 1881. The 1913 British bubble would have shortly burst had the outbreak of war not halted its expansion and deflated it prematurely.

DID FOREIGN LENDING STARVE DOMESTIC INDUSTRY?

The question whether British foreign lending was responsible in some degree for the decline of British industry is one that has been debated for practically a century. The debate is too many-sided and far-reaching for easy summary, but a few things can be said. For a considerable time, there was heated argument over whether British industry had in fact declined and, if so, when. The extension of the record into the last quarter of the twentieth century demonstrates that if Britain had not actually declined, as it has not, it at least fell behind in comparison with other industrial countries. Second is the issue whether the City as an institution was geared up to lend more and more abroad because of inertia or was merely responding to the tastes of the moneyed classes, which had lost their appetite for domestic risks (though not necessarily those in mining abroad) and loaned for the most part on standard securities for governments, railroads, and utilities—loans that did little for British export industries (W. P. Kennedy, 1987). Third are the questions of who benefited from lending directed abroad and who paid the penalty, if any. Seeking to test the Lenin-Hobson thesis that financial imperialism was a response to the falling rate of profit at home, a cliometrician and a political historian, studying British capital exports from 1870 to the eve of World War I, the profitability of British business compared with returns on foreign investment, government expenditure on defense in behalf of the empire (and the world?), plus the distribution of costs and benefits of empire at home and abroad, together with the political forces shaping the outcome, conclude that the British middle class paid, and the elite at home, and especially the self-governing part of the empire, which got its defense free, reaped the benefits (L. Davis and Hutterback, 1987). Starvation puts it too strong, but others who approach the issue statistically make the evident point that the export of capital was a force tending to keep the supply price of capital in Britain higher than it otherwise would have been (Matthews, Feinstein, and Odling-Smee, 1982, p. 342).

SMALL, SIGNIFICANT, ANALYTICAL POINTS

Before treating the subject of Anglo-French rivalry in foreign lending and the contest between London and Paris as the world's leading financial center in the nineteenth century, there are a number of questions of analytical interest, and some importance, that cannot be woven readily into a chronological narrative. They are presented discretely in a series.

Foreign Lending Without Money

Like insurance, foreign lending can be conducted without money or monetary institutions. Textbooks in international economics illustrate capital transfers in kind by the example of two tropic islands, where inhabitants of *A* make a loan to *B* without money, in one of three ways: sending prefabricated housing (capital goods); sending food (consumption goods) so that the islanders on *B* can switch from growing provisions to construction; or sending woodsmen to produce lumber and carpenters to fashion it into housing (services). The point is, first, that capital movements are possible under barter and evade all difficulties of transition from financial to real transfer; second, international capital transfers need not be identified with capital goods such as machinery, if the recipient has capacity to transform or reallocate its resources from one sector to another.

European history provides examples of international lending in commodities to add verisimilitude to theoretical discourse. In the 1520s Lübeck made loans to Sweden in kind, that is, in goods, and in the 1550s King Gustav Vasa made loans in both money and goods (Heckscher, 1931 [1953], pp. 213–14). The 1520s loans were repaid, as well as made, in kind and in consumption goods including, in 1532, butter. A payment due in 1527 was postponed, as it happened, because the food gathered for the purpose in Stockholm was suspected of having become tainted (ibid.).

Trade in Existing Securities

Most data on foreign lending relate to new issues of securities. These are the most readily available statistics in systematic form. Platt's point that the compatriots of the foreign borrower may subscribe to the loan issued in a financial center has already been discussed. But they may also buy them later, long after issuance. Failure to take account of trade in existing securities can be misleading. In the interwar period of the twentieth century, an international banker noted that one Dutch loan issued in New York was entirely bought back piecemeal by individual investors the following year when credit conditions had changed (Beyen, 1949, p. 13). An example from the nineteenth century is furnished by a bond issue of 34.4 million marks (3½ percent bonds, issued at 93) borrowed by the city of Hamburg after its devastating fire of 1842. Two Berlin and one Hamburg house underwrote the issue; it was believed that Berlin investors bought most of it. By 1846, however, the bulk of the bonds had been sold back to Hamburg (Brockhage, 1910, pp. 208–9).

The point has probably been made in connection with Dutch purchases of French annuities, Russian sales to France of ruble bonds initially issued in St. Petersburg (Crisp, 1977, p. 267), foreign subscriptions to the Thiers *rente* for speculation, French investor liquidation of holdings of foreign securities, later rebought, German clearing out of Italian securities originally accumulated in 1888 and 1893 for political ends, and German dumping of Argentine bonds in the London market. It nonetheless bears repeating. One is usually reminded, moreover, that in foreign, as in domestic, securities there is a difference between a stag and a bull (in English terminology)—between an investor who buys to sell soon for a capital gain and one who buys to hold. It is, of course, true that securities may be bought with one intention that converts to another. But an investor may rationally choose to hold the securities of his own country issued in a foreign market and denominated in a foreign currency.

The Gibson Paradox (Fisher Effect)

Gibson observed that when commodity prices rose and fell, the rate of interest went up and down. He thought the behavior curious and even paradoxical and gave his name to the phenomenon, discussed by Keynes in *A Treatise on Money* (1930, Vol. 2, ch. 30, sec. 8). In today's analysis the reaction is called the Fisher effect, after Irving Fisher. He observed that inflation and deflation of the price level led to increases and decreases in nominal interest rates as lenders in the first instance, borrowers in the second, sought to protect themselves against getting back less valuable money, that is, money that would have to be spent at a higher price level in the case of lenders, or for borrowers, against having to repay the debt in money worth more (1911 [1966], pp. 56–57). The change in nominal interest rate is a form of indexing the rate of return or the rate of payment for borrowing that in sophisticated financial markets keeps the real interest rate—the nominal rate deflated by the price level—at the appropriate level. Investors who ignored actual or prospective changes in prices were said to have "money illusion"; they confused the nominal rate of interest with the real.

The Fisher effect is discussed for the most part in domestic lending, and it is evident that rather more sophistication is needed to adjust for inflation or deflation in international lending, unless all national price levels happen to move together. In the nineteenth century, moreover, prices fell heavily from 1873 to 1896 and interest rates were low; or, on some showings, prices fell throughout the century from 1815 to 1896, with brief interruptions in the 1850s and in the early 1870s (Saul, 1969 [1972], p. 13). The question then arises as to whether British investors before and after 1896 adjusted interest rates to the course of general prices, and especially whether Russian borrowing from Germany and France was or was not misled up to 1896 by low interest rates that led to excessive borrowing in the absence of realization that repayment was called for in more valuable money.

The answer seems to be that there was no money illusion on the part of capital markets, either in Britain (Harley, 1977) where one would expect sophistication to be high, or in Russian foreign borrowing (Israelsen, 1979). Econometric testing using a variety of price levels and periods produced this conclusion as a robust result. Nineteenth-century investors seem to have been unusually naive in swallowing propaganda put out by venal journalists, interested bankers, and devious foreign offices, and especially in thinking that foreign bonds were more like bonds than they were foreign, and hence were safe. The naiveté was limited to repayment; on the interest rate, the market seems to have known what was happening.

Lending Abroad Interest Earned Abroad

A vulgar error made by journalists, statesmen, and even historians and economic historians is to say, or come close to saying, that such a country as Britain or France relent abroad the interest received on past lending. Lévy-Leboyer narrowly escapes the fallacy when he writes that revenue on French investment just covered new investment (1977a, p. 123), and Bouvier almost falls into the error of saying that French foreign income was reinvested abroad before he backs away and qualifies the statement (1977, p. 447). The general and analytical point, of course, is that no two items in a national balance of payments can be connected unless one has direct knowledge to confirm the relationships, such as of barter of exports against imports, or reinvestment of profits on direct investment. Income on foreign investment not only goes through the balance of payments, where all credits determine all debits, and vice versa, in a general equilibrium framework, but also joins the stream of national income as a whole (Ford, 1958). Investors with foreign bonds clip their coupons, add the receipts to their total income, and make new decisions, first on how much to consume and how much to save, and second on how much of savings to invest at home and abroad. There may be a rough order-of-magnitude relation at certain stages of a country's growth between the flow of earnings on past investment and the amounts newly sent abroad, but when such a relationship exists it is fortuitous. There is no causal connection, either in balance-of-payments theory or in that on foreign investment.

Stock Adjustment Versus Flow Models

For some purposes, analysts make a distinction between stock adjustment models, in which a given store of wealth is divided between home and foreign investment according to changing conditions, and a flow model, in which change occurs largely at the margin, with, as just detailed in the last section, decisions being made as to how much to save out of a given income and how to divide savings of the given year between domestic and foreign investment. At a higher level of generality, the two approaches are related. This year's saving is a new condition to be taken into account in the stock adjustment model; and decisions on how to divide incremental savings must take into account portfolio readjustments made in the recent past. This is not perhaps the place to pursue the point beyond a brief mention, since I have dealt with it elsewhere (Kindleberger, 1981a, pp. 154–60). It is sufficient to say that long-term capital flows more nearly fit the conditions of the flow models, especially for new issues and the demand model, whereas stock adjustment is called for in the realm of short-term movements, by and large, and in long-term models, first, when horizons change, and second, for trade in outstanding securities. Like the choice between supply and demand models in business cycles, however, there is no ultimate truth short of the loftier levels of general equilibrium analysis. There is no escape from changing models when circumstances change.

Beginnings of Direct Investment in Manufacturing

The origins of direct investment and even of the multinational corporation can be traced in finance back to the Italian banks of the fourteenth and fifteenth centuries.

Direct investment is that in which the investor keeps control and makes decisions for foreign enterprise from abroad. A multinational corporation, in the usual sense, is an enterprise that maintains and coordinates business operations in several countries—the minimum being sometimes given as five. The Medici Bank and the Fuggers provide striking examples of these general classes, and the papacy itself is frequently cited as an example of the sort of coordinated operations in a number of countries involved.

Outside of trade and finance, and particularly in manufacturing, there are few examples before about 1850. Enterprise and capital went abroad together in the seventeenth century under the Dutch, as noted in Chapter 12 (p. 209), but it either did not stay, or it cut itself off from its home base. An early-nineteenth-century direct investment by an American merchant named Haviland in china in Limoges in France, undertaken at the end of the 1830s, was of the same sort. The Havilands finally settled down and became French (Kindleberger, 1974*b*, p. 396). Dunning chooses the operations of the North British Rubber Company in Edinburgh of 1856 as the first American direct investment in manufacturing (1958, p. 17), but this ignores the plant established in London in 1852 by Samuel Colt of Springfield, Massachusetts. This, however, failed and was sold to a London purchaser at the end of the Crimean War (Wilkins, 1970, p. 30).

Given the primitive conditions of transport and communication, what is baffling is not why there was so little direct investment in manufacturing before 1850 but how there happened to be so much in finance. Stories of the Rothschilds bringing the news of victory at Waterloo to London by carrier pigeon from France underline the difficulties. News of the Sepoy mutiny in India in 1857 took one and a half months to get to London (Collier, 1963, p. 151). The telegraph had been established within India, though not at that time to Suez. Within India, moreover, it was most unreliable, being easily cut, and breaking down frequently where it crossed rivers (ibid., p. 52).

The telegraph made possible the first efficient direct manufacturing operations in one country controlled from another. Success in money and banking operating in a number of countries, before the telegraph, required having a large number of brothers or cousins, with a single combined interest and thinking more or less alike, to solve the agency problem. In early manufacturing, an extended connection may have been necessary; it was not sufficient. The Siemens & Halske firm, founded in Berlin in 1847, set up branches in London and St. Petersburg in 1851 and 1852, respectively, both under the direction of brothers of Werner Siemens (Kocka, 1969, pp. 59–60). The business started making telegraphic equipment for the military. Another early investment was that of Guppy, an Englishman, in mechanical equipment in Naples in 1860 (de Rosa, 1968). American labor-saving innovations such as the McCormick reaper, cash register, and typewriter were introduced to European consumers and potential partners in joint enterprises at exhibitions, particularly those of 1851 in London and 1865 in Paris.

The rise of direct investment and the multinational corporation picked up after these isolated beginnings with the advent of the steamship and especially the screw-propeller, which increased the speed and frequency and lowered the cost of personal communication—after 1875. Spectacular flowering, of course, awaited the spread of the continental and transatlantic telephone in 1931 and the jet aircraft about 1950.

Strength of National Currencies

A somewhat idiosyncratic theory of direct investment lays special stress on the strength of the currency of the investing country (Aliber, 1970). Countries with strong currencies find investors from all over the world anxious to hold securities denominated in such currencies. The result is that companies domiciled there can raise capital more cheaply than other companies with head offices and equity issued in countries with weaker currencies.

The theory of direct investment more generally states that a company investing abroad must have an advantage over companies in the host country; if such an advantage is missing, the foreign company coming from a distance and having the disadvantage of heavy costs of communication, information, and cultural misunderstanding would be at a sizable disadvantage against local competitors and would not be able to survive. In eclectic views, the advantage can be of any kind; technological lead is considered by some to be the most usual explanation. In Aliber's theory the advantage lies in the strength of the currency, which gives the company an advantage in cost of capital.

By way of slight digression, direct investment is not based on interest rate differences. Such capital movements go through security markets and have no need to be associated with control. In fact, the corporation is at a disadvantage in moving capital alone compared with stock and bond markets (Hymer, 1960 [1976]). Such movements are, for the most part, one-way, after allowance for diversification of risk, whereas much of direct investment represents cross investments, of corporations of country A in B and those of B in A. While there are particular theories to explain cross investments—the exchange of hostages against intense competition in oligopolistic industries (E. M. Graham, 1975)—Aliber contends that his currency theory does it effectively by noting sequential changes under which now one country, now another, has the world's leading currency (1970). At one time the Dutch florin is strong: Royal Dutch Shell, Unilever, Phillips, and so on, invest heavily abroad. Later Holland will lose its role of "top currency," to use Strange's term (1971, p. 5), to another currency, and direct investment will run the other way.

This is not the place to test Aliber's theory of direct investment. The point is raised to see whether it has relevance to portfolio investment, that is, to ask whether there is a currency/return trade-off for lenders and borrowers, separate from the risk/return trade-off.

It has already been noted that investors frequently like to hold securities issued by their government at home in foreign capital markets, even though the return is lower than at home. (The return must be lower abroad than at home or the government or other borrowing entity would have raised the money at home without undertaking a commitment and risk in foreign exchange.) When Italians buy Italian securities in Paris during the *corso forzoso,* for example, they are moved by (1) the rate of interest, which for an existing issue with fixed coupon rate is a function of price, and (2) the strength of the French franc as opposed to the lira, both at the time of purchase and ultimately upon repayment. When the loan is placed abroad at one time and the domestic investor buys it later, yield and currency may not be in conflict because the price of the bond, and hence the yield, may have changed over the interval. It is not clear at this distance whether one frequently got, say, Italian subscriptions to Italian loans issued in Paris in the original underwriting. Similar European subscriptions to European bonds issued in New York occurred after World War II and confirmed the Aliber contention for portfolio investment, if not for direct investment (Kindleberger, 1981*a*, p. 231).

There are other aspects to investment choice than return, risk, strength of currency, and diversification already mentioned, among them size of market for original offerings and breadth of secondary trading, which determines the liquidity available to the investor if he later wishes or is forced to sell. A borrower with need for a large sum of money may be forced to borrow in a limited number of locations because not every market can handle issues above a certain size, as indicated in the discussion of the Macmillan gap (see pp. 200–201). Liquidity is related to rate of return: "A well-margined loan of £1,000,000 against a security which can be realized at an hour's notice can be made at a much lower rate than that which must be charged if facility of realization is not there" (Powell, 1915 [1966], p. 574). Strength of currency is thus only one argument in the complex function determining the gross and net flows of foreign capital. Given the weakness of the statistics and the econometric disabilities of the writer, it is virtually impossible to sort out the various effects either qualitatively or, much more difficult, quantitatively. The financial historian who looks simply at one variable, however, may be led into error.

PARIS VERSUS LONDON AS THE LEADING EUROPEAN AND WORLD FINANCIAL CENTER

Since so little can be proved objectively about effective characteristics, I set out in Table 14.1 a comparison of interest rates in London and Paris, followed by a series of opinions, in which the literature abounds, as to the relative merits of the London and Paris capital markets. The table is for a limited segment of the prewar period and shows that domestic securities were, on the whole, lower yielding in Britain foreign securities lower yielding in France.

Table 14.1 Yields on Various British and French Securities, 1885–1904 (by subperiods in percent per annum averages)

	British		French				
			Domestic		Foreign		
Period	Domestic Rail	Foreign Bonds	Bonds	Shares	Bonds	Suez	Russian Bonds
1885–89	3.29	5.04	3.79	4.27	4.49	3.92	4.93
1890–94	2.97	4.74	3.25	4.00	4.11	3.72	4.13
1895–99	2.61	4.38	3.06	3.56	3.80	2.95	3.84
1900–4	2.98	4.48	3.28	3.91	3.96	3.32	3.92

Source: Lévy-Leboyer (ed.) (1977*b*, p. 113).

In the first place is the view expressed in 1818 by one Chevalier Seguier: "Over the last twenty years Paris has become the principal center for banking operations in Europe, while London is not really a banking city. . . Paris is . . . [where] most English transactions are handled today" (quoted in Braudel, 1979 [1984], pp. 608–9). Braudel is rightly skeptical. Two other French sources put the primacy of France later. Paris was said to have been the international place of compensation from 1820 to 1840—in other words, the pivot for world payments (Bouvier, 1973, p. 238; Lévy-Leboyer, 1964, pp. 437–38). The evidence is elusive. As indicated earlier, Belgium and France had large gross capital movements between them, if much smaller on balance, and France participated with London, in regulating U.S. payments with the Continent. The claim that France also regulated British payments with the Continent, as Amsterdam had done in the eighteenth century up to the Seven Years' War, is more dubious. London no longer needed a relay or financial entrepôt in Europe. It traded directly on merchandise and foreign exchange with Stockholm, St. Petersburg, Hamburg, and Leghorn, if perhaps not with Turin and Geneva.

There is some fairly equivocal support for the Bouvier–Lévy-Leboyer position for the period to 1851. Van Vleck asserts that France was the political nerve center of Europe during the first half of the nineteenth century and then became, from 1851 to 1857, the center from which fluctuations in economic cycles radiated (1943, p. 42). Again, a remark that England became the financial center of the world after the Crimean War had ended in 1856 implies that earlier it was not (Emden, 1938, p. 378). Perhaps there was a center—Paris; perhaps none.

The usual view, however, is that France was not enormously powerful financially before 1848, became so in 1852 with the innovation of the Crédit Mobilier, and ceased to be in 1870 when the Bank of France went off the gold standard at the outbreak of the Franco-Prussian War and stayed off for eight years, although the depreciation was never wide.

Cameron, who traced gross French lending to the period well before 1880, and even before 1850, notes that French foreign capital amounted to approximately 2 billion francs in 1850 and rose 12 billion francs in the next twenty years to absorb between one-third and one-half of net realized savings of the country (1955, p. 461). In a subsequent statement, this estimate is amended or extended to suggest that the portfolio reached 16 billion by 1880. Total loans amounted to 22 billion francs, but repatriations and losses shrank the net figure to 16 billion, somewhat above the usual estimate of 15 billion (ibid., p. 351). Just beyond this period, however, in 1881, falls the fiasco of the Italian stabilization loan of 644 million francs that Paris was unable or unwilling to make "because of lack of buyers" and passed along to London (Lévy-Leboyer, 1977a, p. 129).

In the more usual view, London had then been the financial center of the world (Powell, 1915 [1966], p. 370), or had a monopoly of capital exports up to 1850 (Rosenberg, 1934, p. 38), when France moved in, largely for *gloire*, says the same source of Marxist persuasion, with capital exports in the service of national policies and expansionary commercial interests (ibid.).

The Franco-Prussian War changed all that: it "destroyed whatever chance of rivalry might be left; so that by 1875 London was supreme in cosmopolitan and domestic Money Markets alike" (Powell, 1915 [1966], p. 370). In *Lombard Street,*

Bagehot attributed the change to suspension of the convertibility of the French franc into gold and silver:

But all great communities have at times to pay large sums in cash and of that cash a great store must be kept somewhere. Formerly there were two such stores in Europe, one was the Bank of France and the other was the Bank of England. But since the suspension of specie payments by the Bank of France its use as a reservoir of specie is at an end. . . . Accordingly London has become the sole great settling house of exchange transactions in Europe, instead of being formerly one of two. And this pre-eminence London will probably retain for it is a natural pre-eminence. The number of mercantile bills incalculably surpasses those drawn on any other city. . . . The pre-eminence of Paris arose from a distribution of political power. (Bagehot, 1873 [1978], Vol. 9, pp. 63–64).

The verdict raises questions. No attention is paid to the suspension of convertibility in 1848, and the two near-misses of 1856 and 1864, or, more significantly, to the French having just mounted the biggest financial operation in the world to that time in the first Thiers *rente,* if perhaps Bagehot wrote before becoming aware of the second. This is not to suggest Bagehot was wrong. The criteria are interesting. The Thiers *rente* is presumably dismissed as a political and perhaps a domestic operation. So it was as far as the French household and individual were concerned, investing for patriotic motives instead of the speculative profits sought by foreign investors and banks everywhere. But in enticing the professionals to buy the Thiers *rente,* Paris showed a purely financial skill divorced from both politics and trade.

Several more opinions are worth noting before an attempt to sum up: in his highly statistical study of *International Financial Transactions and Business Cycles,* Oskar Morgenstern states:

Paris emerges in this study as the *strongest* [his italics] financial center in the world before 1914, if the fact that its short-term rate was relatively the lowest is an indication of strength. This conclusion seems to contradict the generally-held opinion that London was the world's money center. (1959, pp. 128, 137)

Reconciliation is sought between these two views by noting that Paris had large stocks of capital and gold while London had the capacity for putting its monetary funds into efficient movement.

A 1932 French study of competition in finance among London, Paris, and New York, with primary emphasis on changes in the early years of the depression of the 1930s, compares London and Paris in 1913 in the following terms: Paris had lower interest rates and was a redoubtable rival to London in long-term lending. The Paris money market was inferior to that of London, however, for a variety of reasons, including an inadequate structure to rival the London three-tiered set of institutions: banks, accepting houses, and bill brokers. Paris was especially handicapped by the practice of bimetallism, which gave the Bank of France the choice of whether it would pay off its notes in gold or silver—whereas in London one could get all the gold one wanted, without hesitation on the part of the authorities or any doubt (Coste, 1932, pp. 20, 77, 83–84).

Lindert emphasizes that London was not alone in serving as a reserve center for lesser financial powers. Before 1914 a number of European countries, especially czarist Russia, held claims on Berlin and Paris as well (Lindert, 1969). In addition, Paris held bills on London, Berlin, and New York (Bloomfield, 1963). Bloomfield goes on to deny that Britain managed the gold standard for the world, rather than for national purposes, at least insofar as can be seen from the inadequate statistical series (ibid., ch. 4, esp. pp. 76–77).

Finally, consider the view of the Italian, Bonelli, writing on the crisis of 1907, who claimed that Paris was the "real" center for regulating world liquidity (1971, p. 42). The action of the Bank of France in the crisis of 1907 in coming to the aid of the Bank of England, though not asked to do so, will be touched upon in the next chapter. Bonelli notes that help to London indirectly helped New York (ibid.). This seems peculiarly a view from a province attached to a secondary and not the primary center. What Bonelli says about Paris in 1907 is all true, to the considerable irritation of the British who insist unduly that they never asked for help (Sayers, 1936, pp. 106–12).

The position can be summarized briefly. London was a world financial center; Paris was a European financial center. London was an efficient financial market, handling an enormous body of transactions on a small monetary base. Paris was a rich money and capital market, efficient in the sense that it could mobilize savings and pour them in a given direction, such as the Thiers *rente* or czarist bonds, but inefficient in its much higher ratio of gold reserves to total financial transactions as compared with London.

SUGGESTED SUPPLEMENTAL READING

Feis (1930), *Europe, the World's Banker.*
Kindleberger (1987), *International Capital Movements.*
Staley (1935), *War and the Private Investor.*
Stern (1977), *Gold and Iron.*

In French

Lévy-Leboyer (ed.) (1977), *La Position internationale de la France.*

15

Financial Crises

J. Bischoffsheim (banker): If I have 10,000 francs and spend 5,000, I have 5,000 francs to invest. If I invest 10,000, I am anticipating next year. If my neighbor makes some foolish investment, he cannot lend to me. If I am forced to sell, I cannot sell at home because all do the same. A crisis arrives.

Question: Can the whole nation act like that? France? England? Bischoffsheim: Most assuredly, yes. A system has been introduced to achieve this result. This consists of small payments at first and other payments greatly delayed. Speculation gets involved. If I have a premium, I sell, and I do not calculate whether I have to furnish the rest. Too often these speculations turn out to be otherwise than was hoped: people remain committed. One succeeds in making the second payment, the third, but the fourth and fifth arrive, and there is trouble.

Ministère des Finances et al., *Enquête,* 1867, Vol. 2, pp. 99–101)

Before we turn to World War I and the financial problems to which it gave rise, it may be well to draw together the threads of discussion of financial crises that have run through the previous chapters. I have produced a book on the subject, beginning, however, only with the South Sea and Mississippi Bubbles (1978*b* [1989]). Present treatment can serve as a summary of scattered observations in previous pages, without an attempt to speculate on the mystery of why financial crises have tended to appear at roughly ten-year intervals for the last 400 years or so.

A number of crucial questions of finance are tied up in the financial crisis. Are monetary and credit markets stable or unstable? Are causes of crises monetary, including mistakes in decisions about minting, banking, debt conversion, unexpected successes such as the Thiers *rente,* and the like, or are they real—war, the end of war, good and bad harvests, waves of investment based on innovations such as the canal, railroad, automobile? Could they be either? Both? Is "overtrading," in the rhetoric of Adam Smith, usually accompanied by "negligence and profusion," always followed by "revulsion and discredit" (1776 [1937], p. 700)? What are the mechanisms for propagating upswing and precipitating collapse? Is it possible by monetary policy, and especially by designation of a lender of last resort—some agency that takes on the public good of providing liquidity when it is especially tight—to mitigate the effects of, or even eliminate, financial crises? Or is it best to leave them alone, to let the fire burn out?

THE MODEL

The macroeconomic system receives some shock—called by Hyman Minsky, who virtually alone of modern economists is interested in financial instability, a "displacement" (1982). This displacement can be monetary or real. What is significant is that it changes expectations in financial markets with respect to the profitability of some range of investments. New profit opportunities are opened up, and people move to take advantage of them. Each individual so moving may be rational, but it can happen, and historically has happened, that the sum total of all the people reacting to the opportunity is excessive. In the course of undertaking new investment, credit is extended. This stimulates business, and credit is extended further. At some point the displacement may lead to business euphoria, to speculation, and to more pervasive credit expansion.

Time and again in these pages it has been stressed that when the macroeconomic system is constrained by a tight supply of money, it creates more, at least for a time. Shortage of gold and silver has led to substitution of copper, pepper, salt—all more primitive commodity monies—or more sophisticated substitutes, such as various forms of paper (and plastic): bank money, bank notes, bills of exchange, especially chains of bills of exchange, bank deposits, open-book credits, credit cards, certificates of deposit, Eurocurrencies, and so on, to bring the process down to the contemporary scene. In this, money broadly defined is endogenous (that is, responsive to events taking place elsewhere in the system) rather than exogenous (that is, determined by events outside the system); or if money is defined so as to be limited to a few means of payment only, its velocity (turnover against national income) increases as money substitutes are increasingly brought into use.

At some stage in the process it becomes clear to a few, and then to more, that the fallacy of composition is at work—that the whole is rather less than the sum of the parts, that credit positions are extended beyond some limit sustainable in the long run, and that maintenance of capital gains depends on getting out of assets rising in price ahead of others. There follows a period of what may be called "distress": "We have no crash at present, only a slight premonitory movement of the ground under our feet," wrote Lord Overstone to his friend, G. W. Norman, on 1 November 1845 (O'Brien, ed., 1845 [1971], Vol. 1, p. 368). From time to time the distress abates. On other occasions it intensifies. More and more speculators seek to get out of whatever was the object of speculation, to reduce their distended liabilities, and switch into money; and more and more it becomes clear that not everyone can do so at once. There is a rush, a panic, and a crash—or perhaps a lender of last resort intervenes to make clear that it will furnish the market all the cash it insists it requires. In this circumstance, perhaps belatedly, panic and distress subside.

DISPLACEMENT

The displacement that gets the most attention in these pages is war, and the end of war. War both cuts off old connections in trade and finance and is likely to require the fashioning of new. The crisis of 1557 resulted from the Spanish and French kings' repudiating debt caused by extensive and prolonged warfare (Ehrenberg, 1896 [1928], pp. 144, 306, 308, 321). That of 1570 was caused by the outbreak of war between Venice and Turkey that demolished the Dolphin Bank in Venice (Spooner, 1972, p. 55). The major financial crisis of 1619 to 1621 was associated with the beginning of the Thirty Years' War, which encouraged minting in Germany and Poland, and particularly monetary adulteration (Kindleberger, 1991a). Or there may be a lag after a war is over. World War I, as we shall see later, produced a boom and bust in 1919–20 as German exclusion from world trade seemed to open up a host of glorious opportunities for French, and especially British, business. Ten years later it was found that the agricultural comeback after the European loss of output during the fighting had been overdone on a world scale. This excessive response took its place among other causes of the 1929 world depression.

Other real causes were good and bad crops, an upsurge in investment in an innovation that built up slowly, as in canals and railways, and discoveries such as the route to India and Columbus's voyages to America—or cheaper transport as provided by the Suez Canal. Substantial displacements of a real sort were the 1793 Reign of Terror in France, independence of the Spanish colonies in America in the early 1820s, and the Revolution of 1848 in France, which diverted investment from old to new outlets.

Between real and monetary displacements were silver discoveries—Potosi in Peru and Guanajucato and Zacatecos in Mexico, and gold in California, Australia, the Witwatersrand, and Alaska. The crisis of 1557 is said to have been the consequence of a switch of economic fuel from gold to silver as the mines of Potosi came into operation (Braudel, 1949 [1972], p. 476). Partly real in terms of a break in British history in India was Plassey with its monetary loot that stimulated speculation in stock of the East India Company and the troubles of the Ayr Bank, which culminated in the financial crisis of 1772.

Monetary displacements can be more narrowly technical. The recession of 1564 was acute but short following Elizabeth I's recoinage (de Roover, 1949, p. 200). Similar shocks to the system from recoinage occurred in 1696, 1763, and 1875 in various countries or from major debt conversion that caused holders of the debt being retired to look for higher-yielding investments. Displacement might consist of an unexpected financial success, such as the Baring indemnity, the Thiers *rente,* or the Dawes loan of 1924.

One cannot forecast or limit the nature of shocks to the system that can start it off in a new direction. These are called dummy variables in econometrics; they lie outside the model.

OBJECTS OF SPECULATION

The model of financial crisis does not require that there be only one object of speculation. In fact, history shows that there are many possible such objects: securities, as in the South Sea and Mississippi Bubbles, canal and railway manias, and both domestic and foreign securities; imported commodities and exports of manufactured goods for distant markets; new banks, insurance companies, building sites, public land, mortgages, housing, foreign exchange, and, to bring the list to the present time, vacation homes, shopping centers, real estate investment trusts (REITs), loans to less developed countries (LDCs), money funds, and so on. In the sixteenth century there were manias in lending to the king, as in the *Grand Parti* in Lyons in

1555; in the seventeenth century the more nearly pure mania in tulips in 1636–37 (p. 209).

A mania confined to one relatively narrow object of speculation is likely to have a good chance of wearing itself out with no monetary consequences. When euphoria and speculation spread from object to object and place to place, the likelihood that the monetary system will feel tremors is substantially increased. Greed or, less pejoratively, appetite for income is highly infectious. Seeing one's neighbors or acquaintances get capital gains, if only on paper, tends to make one less careful. The South Sea Bubble was intimately tied to the Mississippi Bubble, as Carswell shows (1960, ch. 5), and it was earlier noted (p. 181) that as the climax in "Change Alley in London passed, speculators left for Hamburg and Amsterdam." In 1847 profits reaped in railroads led new groups to bid up the price of wheat, given the fortuitous circumstance of the disastrous crop of 1846 combined with the potato crop failure. People, commodities, and national markets interact to reinforce speculation and to make it depart further and further from a rational view of the prospect. When panic starts, moreover, it too is communicated from place to place as one bankruptcy triggers others in firms and banks that have lent to the first.

Milton Friedman has argued on a priori grounds that destabilizing speculation is impossible in the long run, because it involves selling when prices fall and buying when prices rise, and anyone who buys high and sells low will lose money and will not survive economically in a Darwinian sense. Since speculators continue to exist, they must buy low and sell high or indulge in stabilizing speculation (1953a). The demonstration is persuasive neither in theory nor historically. In theory it is possible to have two groups of speculators: a more or less permanent inside group that buys at the bottom and drives prices up, sells at the top, and drives them down; and a larger changing group of outsiders, such as servant girls and greengrocers or, in the idiom of the 1929 stock market crash, waiters and bootblacks, who come into the market late and buy at the top, catch on late to the need to mark down values, and sell at the bottom. They lose money, withdraw to the sidelines, and earn a living again as greengrocers or whatever, saving a pittance or a nest egg so that they, or someone like them, can come back into the market next time. In the Mississippi Bubble, a historian notes, the insiders, masters of capital flight, who directly stimulate the *agiotage,* kept themselves aloof from the fever and realized their gains when they judged the moment to be the most favorable (Chaussinand-Nogaret, 1970, p. 129).

What is interesting is how outsiders and insiders together achieve a periodicity of financial crises roughly ten years apart, from at least 1551 to 1866, when economic theory insists that the outsiders should learn. It is particularly curious that short-term memory is so faulty when long-term memory of financial catastrophes such as the Mississippi Bubble or the German inflation of 1920–23 affects market behavior and governmental policy fifty to a hundred years later. Moreover, one can find abundant reference to old financial crisis: "the crisis of 1857 kept coming back into discussion among Hamburgers and non-Hamburgers when discussing foreign exchange, and even those reading about it would find their hair standing on end" (Böhme, 1968, p. 274).

Historically, the burden of proof runs against a theorist who says that destabilizing speculation is impossible when the record shows displacement, euphoria, distress, panic, and crisis occurring decade after decade, century after century, and noted by such classical observers as Adam Smith in the eighteenth century and Lord Overstone in the nineteenth, quoted with approval by Walter Bagehot (1852 [1978], Vol. 9, p. 273). The Overstone cycle: "quiescence, improvement, confidence, prosperity, excitement, overtrading, CONVULSION [Bagehot's capitals], pressure, stagnation, ending again in quiescence" (ibid.). Bagehot adds: "Common sense teaches that booksellers should not speculate in hops, or bankers in turpentine; that railways should not be promoted by maiden ladies, or canals by beneficed clergymen . . . in the name of common sense, let there be common sense" (ibid., Vol. 9, p. 275). But history demonstrates that common sense in these questions is uncommon, at least at ten-year intervals.

Each individual may be rational, expecting to sell out before the collapse, but the fallacy of composition ensures that not all can be. The two groups of speculators are like early and late signers of chain letters: some win, all in the aggregate lose, if only the paper, ink, postage, and effort, offset perhaps to a degree by the amusement. And the less scrupulous at the margin between the shrewd insider and the mindless outsider finds himself subject to moral testing, failures of which have produced a rich crop of metaphors. Bleichröder said of Bethel Henry Strousberg: "The man is very clever, but his manner of undertaking new ventures in order to mend old holes is dangerous, and if he should encounter a [sudden] obstacle, his whole structure may collapse and under its ruins bury millions of gullible shareholders" (Stern, 1977a, pp. 358–9). The same metaphor is elaborated in Baron James de Rothschild's remark about Emile Pereire: "A man who is in constant monetary straits, stops up one hole while making another and who is compelled to execute a perpetual egg dance among more or less dangerous debit balances, will, in the end, after every fresh success in averting imminent catastrophe, think himself a financial genius" (Emden, 1938, p. 145). Or, as Louis XV said of an able speculator, banker, and financial statesman, Jacques Necker, "He does have a tendency to pull the covers over to his side of the bed" (R. D. Harris, 1979, p. 238).

THE PROPAGATION (AND COLLAPSE) OF EUPHORIA

The spread of financial excitement can take place through one or more of a number of channels: commodity or security markets connected by arbitrage, movements of specie or capital, either short or long term, and psychological contagion (Kindleberger, 1991b). Within a single economy, a boom in one commodity or asset may spread to others, including not only stocks and bonds but commodities and even real estate. Internationally, a particularly prominent role in spreading boom and bust is filled by capital movements that build up and up and are then suddenly cut off. Capital movements linked Medina del Campo in Spain to Genoa and Lyons in one channel, to Antwerp and Lyons in another. The spread of debased money from Italy through Switzerland to the Holy Roman Empire in mosaic Germany and on to Poland and Britain produced the hyperinflation and collapse of the *Kipper- und Wipperzeit*. The British crisis of 1621 had additional contributory factors, such as the overvaluation of sterling against German monies and the undervaluation of silver relative to gold at the mint, which drove it abroad. In various ways, however, inflation and collapse can be seen to spread, unevenly from place to place. Euphoria in Berlin after the Prussian victory over France reverberated to Vienna and then to New York when German and Austrian investors bought American railroad bonds in procyclical fashion. Collapse on 1 May 1873 halted the outflow to the United States abruptly and communicated the crash from Europe in May to New York in September (Kindleberger, 1990*a*).

Complex patterns of crisis have been communicated by abrupt cutbacks in capital flows from France to Spain and Italy in 1866 and again in 1907. The 1866 design is particularly intricate as it combined the end of the Civil War with strongly depressing effects on the price of cotton in Europe and negative impacts on India, Egypt, Greece, and so on, with Prussian mobilization for war against Austria. In the midst of this, but only days after the stock market crisis in Berlin and the *corso forzoso* in Italy (1 May 1866), the Overend, Gurney crash occurred in England on 11 May. British opinion, apart from Hawtrey, who called it "apparently isolated but really a sequel of 1864" (1919 [1927], p. 177), regarded the crisis as local in character. The judgment is difficult to accept, especially as Overend, Gurney had been involved in shipping to Greece, connected with a system of accommodation bills by which Turkey had been financing the Crimean War, and committed to the Spanish merchant firm, Pinto Perez, which went bankrupt on 7 April through the Paris connection (King, 1936, pp. 242, 247–49). Finance companies created in England in imitation of the Crédit Mobilier further contributed to the 1866 collapse and suggested a source of speculative expansion (Cottrell, 1988). Alfred André, a French banker normally resident in Alexandria, spent a week in London after 11 May, reporting that the finance companies had been ruined, that business was paralyzed in Italy, Prussia, Austria, and Russia, and that France was standing up pretty well but only momentarily (Landes, 1958, p. 287). The bankruptcy of the City of Glasgow Bank in 1878 came close to affecting London but was adroitly fended off by the Bank of England (Collins, 1989). The Baring crisis of 1890 that shut down British lending for a time spread liquidation to Australia, South Africa, southern Latin America, and the United States, which had been borrowing heavily from London (Kindleberger, 1985).

Most of the time, however, it is difficult to tell with assurance where a financial crisis originates. R.C.O. Matthews wrote of Britain and the United States in the 1836–39 crisis that it was "futile to draw any hard-and-fast line assigning to either country causal primacy in the cycle as a whole or in individual phases" (1954, p. 69). The statement can be generalized to multicountry complex cases such as 1857, 1866, 1888–93, 1907, and 1929.

DISTRESS

Distress is a term borrowed from corporate finance, where it is used to characterize the period following initial awareness by a company that in the near future it may not be able to meet its obligations (M. J. Gordon, 1971). In extension to the financial system as a whole, it represents increasing awareness of financial markets that prices are high, people are beginning to get out of securities, commodities, or whatever else the particular object of speculation has been, into money, and that one is not far from a rout, a precipitous rush from less liquid assets into cash with such slogans coming to mind as "every man for himself," "*sauve qui peut,*" "*den Letzten beissen die Hunde*" (the dogs bite the one at the rear), or again in German *Torschlusspanik* (a panicky rush to get through the door before it closes). Distress is not so much defined as described—uneasiness, stringency, tension—and particularly with the use of meteorological metaphors—"a thundery atmosphere" (Clapham, 1945, Vol. 2, p. 257), or "one feels again the oppressive atmosphere that precedes a storm" (Rosenbaum and Sherman, 1976 [1979], p. 129).

Distress is not inevitably followed by panic and crash. Overstone's presentiment of disaster in 1845 was premature by two years. Again in April 1853 four years before the crisis of 1857 he wrote to Norman: "I sincerely hope that the Income Tax may disappear in 1860—but the intervening period will give birth to many unexpected events—among them probably a Monetary and Commercial Crisis—is not this inevitable and are not the symptoms of the coming event beginning to show themselves?" (O'Brien, ed., 1853 [1971], Vol. 2, p. 571). One could mark this as a prescient forecast, but in most predictions it is an error to be prematurely right.

How long distress will stretch out before it either fades away or results in market collapse depends, first, on whether there is a lender of last resort (a subject I address below) and, second and importantly, on psychological factors on which it is impossible to generalize. In Vienna in 1873 it was known by the first of the year that the market was overextended and destined to fall, but speculators refrained from dumping securities as they looked forward to the World Exhibition that was to open in that city on 1 May expecting, or at least hoping, irrationally, that in some unexplained way the exhibition would change the underlying situation. The exhibition duly opened on 1 May, and when it was evident that nothing had changed, the stock market collapsed on 5 and 6 May (Wirth, 1890, p. 519). Acute distress in the London discount market that ended with the bankruptcy of Overend, Gurney on 11 May 1866 began in January of that year when a firm of railway contractors named Watson, Overend & Company—no connection with Overend, Gurney except for the coincidence of name—went bankrupt and called attention to difficulties of the much more illustrious homonymic discount house (King, 1936, p. 240).

Euphoria and speculative excess are characterized by a rush out of money, including credit that the system monetized on the way up, into securities, commodities, land, or whatever else, bidding up their prices. After distress of long or short duration, the process is reversed, and the movement starts out of real assets or securities into money. The precipitant varies from case to case, with no generalization possible. The 1857 crisis started in New York with revelation of the embezzlement of most of the capital of $2 million of the Ohio Life & Trust Company of New York by a clerk. The bank had borrowed from other New York banks, and they from Britain (Gibbons, 1859, pp. 244–53; Evans, 1859 [1969], pp. 63–65). Railroad securities fell in price; banks failed in Philadelphia, Baltimore, Liverpool, and Glasgow. Collapse spread to Scandinavia and thence to Hamburg. Just as rising prices encourage borrowing, more purchases, and still higher prices, so falling prices spread bankruptcy. Investors, firms, and banks seek liquidity even at the sacrifice of good assets.

Modern economic theory tends to ignore price changes on the ground that while a change in price produces a gain or loss for one set of economic actors, it simultaneously results in offsetting loss or gain for another. On this score, to worry about prices and price levels is "money illusion," mistaking nominal money values for real values. This fails to take account of dynamic effects of two kinds. From a monetary viewpoint, price increases and decreases stimulate bank expansion and contraction, respectively, and produce macroeconomic change. When price declines lead to bankruptcy, moreover, that bankruptcy spreads through the system in cumulating fashion with results that are not offset elsewhere. In the second place, while one group gains and another loses from price changes, awareness of gain and loss is not likely to be simultaneous or to fall on groups that are identical in behavior. On both accounts, the results of price changes are unlikely to be offsetting. In financial crisis merchants and producers whose prices are falling are painfully conscious of losses and cut their spending well before consumers have become conscious of gains in real income and increase their spending. The effect of falling prices in increasing the value of real balances is also slow to take hold. The real balances and real income effects of falling prices are therefore second-order matters, likely to be overwhelmed by the primary effect of spreading firm bankruptcy and bank failure.

DEALING WITH CRISIS

A few hard-line believers in efficient markets contend that financial crises can cure themselves. When banks, firms, and households need liquidity, the market can provide it if the price is right; that is, if the interest rate goes high enough, some quantity will be available at some price for the most exigent demanders. When the Bank of England raised the discount rate to 10 percent in the crisis of 1847, a fast sloop was sent down the channel after a schooner that had left for America a day or two before with a shipment of gold, with instructions to change course and bring the specie back to England (Andréadès, 1909, p. 334).

Both currency and banking schools in England thought that the market looked too often to the bank for assistance in time of stress, and Lord Overstone, leader of the former, maintained that such support was not necessary: "The resources of the financial system are so great that, even in times of the utmost stringency, large loans are to be had by those offering a sufficient rate of interest" (Morgan, 1943, p. 133). On other occasions, however, Lord Overstone expressed a different conviction: "There is an old Eastern proverb which says you may stop with a bodkin [a dagger or pin to hold up hair] a fountain, which if suffered to flow will sweep away whole cities in its course" (from *Tracts*, p. 23, quoted by O'Brien in 1971, Vol. 1, p. 95). This was an aberrant view; for the most part Overstone held firmly that paper money should fluctuate like metallic, with equal inelasticity, and that there was no cure for panics (ibid., p. 92).

History records frequent examples of interest rates getting up to ½ percent a day, which have been transformed into rates of 185 percent a year, but wrongly since the loans are for a few days only. In the United States in crises, loans have been contracted at 3, 4, and 5 percent a day. Most testimony insists, however, that on these occasions no money is available. Unless the Bank of England is lending, one cannot get money even on consols, the proverbial liquid asset that "you can sell on Sunday" (Bagehot, 1873 [1978], Vol. 9, p. 77; 1866 [1978], Vol. 10, p. 99). The problem is created in part by knowledge that the amount of money available is limited. Sir G. C. Lewis, chancellor of the exchequer, said in a speech on 4 December 1857: "Whenever you impose a limit, there is no question that the existence of that limit . . . in moments of crisis must increase the alarm" (Evans, 1859 [1969], p. 203). For Bagehot, writing on the same crisis, the effect of the limit was shown by "the instantaneous rapidity with which the currency is repaired by its removal" (1858 [1978], Vol. 10, p. 68).

LENDER OF LAST RESORT IN CRISIS

Whether there is a theoretical rationale for letting the market find its way out of a panic or not, the historical fact is that panics that have been met most successfully almost invariably found some source of cash to ease the liquidation of assets before prices fell to ruinous levels. An important question is who has responsibility to provide that cash. There can be stalemate in crisis, generally brief, while large banks, central bank, Treasury, and other bodies debate over which of their number has the responsibility to provide the public good of needed liquidity.

Other techniques have been applied, mostly without success. In 1720 either the Sword Blade Bank or the Bank of England—the record is confused as to which but probably not both—redeemed bank notes, for which convertibility was sought, in sixpences counted out with deliberation (Carswell, 1960, p. 185; Andréadès, 1909, p. 428). The technique was employed again—this time unambiguously—by the Bank of England in 1745 when Bonnie Prince Charlie was advancing into England from Scotland, with the time gained from stalling used to obtain a thousand signatures from merchants agreeing to accept bank notes and forgo insistance on coin (Andréadès, 1909, p. 151). It was also used on a number of occasions in Scotland (Cameron et al., 1967, p. 68). Again, in France in a run on Bons Grasselin, sight obligations payable in money or copper issued by an owner of building sites in Nantes of that name, payment was made only in sous. As a young clerk to M. Grasselin, Ouvrard was impressed when the trick worked and saved his employer from bankruptcy (Liesse, 1908, p. 7).

More usual and somewhat more successful devices are (1) to guarantee the liabilities of the bank or banks in trouble; (2) to close all banks in a bank holiday; (3) to issue Exchequer bills to merchants in trouble on the security of stocks of merchandise, which bills they then discount with the Bank of England or with banks that can rediscount them. The last, in effect, makes the Treasury the lender of last resort rather than the central bank. Guarantee of bank and firm liabilities was used in Hamburg in 1857, without complete success, again in the Baring crisis of 1890, and by the Golddiskontobank in Germany with a *Haftungsgemeinschaft* (community of liabilities) in July 1931.

Thomas Joplin, the Newcastle timber merchant and banking reformer, said apropos of the panic of 1825; "A demand for money in ordinary times, and a demand for it in periods of panic, are diametrically different. The one demand is for money to *put into* circulation; the other for money to be *taken out* of it" (italics in original) (n.d., after 1832, p. 21). It follows that rules for the issuance of money differ between ordinary times, which can be called "trend," and financial crisis, as Joplin saw: "There are times when rules and precedents cannot be broken; others when they cannot be adhered to with safety" (ibid., p. 29). The same thought was expressed with almost identical wording by Bagehot, the rationalizer of the doctrine of lender of last resort:

laying down a hard and fast rule is dangerous . . . no certain or fixed proportion of its liabilities can be laid down as that which the Bank [of England] ought to keep . . . the forces of the enemy being variable, those of the defense cannot always be the same. . . . I admit this conclusion is very inconvenient. . . . The practical difficulties of life cannot often be met by very simple rules. (Bagehot, 1873 [1978], Vol. 9, pp. 207–8)

Bagehot articulated the lender-of-last-resort rule in *Lombard Street* in 1873. A rudimentary version was contained in his first published article, which appeared in 1848:

[It is] the great defect of a metallic circulation that the quantity of it cannot be readily suited to any sudden demand . . . [the power] should only be used in rare and exceptional cases, but when the fact of an extensive *sudden* [italics in original] demand is proved, we see no objection, but decided advantage in introducing this new element (a paper money) into a metallic circulation. (Ibid., 1848 [1978], Vol. 9, p. 267)

Bagehot himself stated that "the orthodox doctrine . . . that there is a period of panic at which restrictions upon the issue of legal tender must be removed" had been laid down by Ricardo (ibid., Vol. 11, p. 149). The ascription is dubious, and if any one at the beginning of the century should be given the credit, it would be Sir Francis Baring who called the Bank of England "a bankers' bank" and used the expression *le dernier resort* (the last resort) in connection with it in 1797, or to Henry Thornton who noted in 1802 that the Bank of England had learned to lend freely in the case of an internal drain (Hayek, 1962, pp. 38–39).

E. V. Morgan contends that the Bank of England was only gradually assuming the role of lender of last resort during the first half of the nineteenth century (1943, p. 240). T. S. Ashton believed the practice went back to the eighteenth, with the bank allowing its discounts of bills to rise in 1734, 1748, 1758–59, 1762, 1764, 1767, 1773, 1778, 1782, 1785, 1793, and 1797 (1959, p. 112). He insists that the practice preceded theory (ibid., p. 111). The practice was not sufficiently developed, however, that the bank did not make frequent mistakes, such as limiting discounts to certain very short-term maturities of bankers' acceptances or restricting discounts to some pro-rata proportion of the monies sought. These limitations typically worsened the crisis, to support the rationalization of Bagehot a century later that one must lend freely, if at a penalty rate. Moreover, it was not firmly established in the eighteenth century what institution in Britain bore responsibility for supporting the market in crisis—the Bank of England through discounting, or the Exchequer through issues of Exchequer bills as in 1793, 1797, and 1810. As late as 1825 the bank wanted the Treasury to be the lender of last resort with Exchequer bills, but the Treasury insisted that it be the bank. With the help of swapping silver against gold coin with France and the discovery of boxes of £1 and £2 notes left over from the period of suspension between 1797 and 1819, the bank just managed to get by without suspending gold payments again.

In France the governor of the Bank of France, Jacques Laffitte, loaned freely in the crisis of 1818, an intuitive lender of last resort. Thereafter, the Bank of France forgot the lesson. In the 1828 crisis in textiles in Alsace, it first limited discounts to 6 million francs and then refused to accept any paper with Mulhouse or Basle signatures. Instead of alleviating distress, these actions spread panic. At the last minute a syndicate of twenty-six Paris banks came to the rescue with a credit of 5 million francs, and Basle furnished 1.3 million more (Lévy-Leboyer, 1964, pp. 470–71). The episode had very much an ad hoc quality. In 1830 after the July Revolution, a receiver-general in the provinces, having loaned 2 million francs to an honest but imprudent bank, thought to refuse a further loan but decided against stinting on the ground that its refusal would have brought down the bank and spread "grave perturbation in the countryside" (Ministère des Finances et al., 1867, Vol. 3, p. 411). The action of the Bank of France in refusing aid to the provincial banks of issue in the crisis of 1847–48—in fact pushing them under in order to take over a monopoly of the note issue—has been recounted in Chapter 6 (pp. 107–8).

Elsewhere on the Continent, for domestic crises, there was less free discounting by central banks than formation of special funds to buttress weak institutions. In Austria, for example, in the crisis of 1873, a fund of 20 million gulden to be loaned on solid securities was assembled, with 3 million from the government, 5 from the Austrian National Bank, 2 from the Creditanstalt—the three largest institutions in the country—and the remainder widely distributed. It proved inadequate, and bank regulations, which fixed the amount of the note issue, were suspended but with a limit for the excess of 200 million gulden. That also failed to do the trick, and after the Bodenkreditanstalt had been saved, the deflation and liquidation were allowed to stretch on in the decade (März, 1968, pp. 178–81; 1982, p. 189). Hamburg's Garantie-Diskontoverein (Guaranty Discount Union) of 10 million marks banco in the 1857 crisis was exhausted in three days, and the crisis was not resolved until help finally came from Austria (Rosenberg, 1934, pp. 128–29). These efforts suffered because they involved fixed amounts, which could be seen in advance to be less than assuredly adequate.

Chapter 5 (pp. 92–94) dealt with suspensions of the Bank Act of 1844 in the crises of 1847, 1857, and 1866, how lifting the limit stopped runs in the first and last cases before the limit had, in fact, been exceeded, and indicated that the excess recorded in 1857 was small. It will be remembered that the question arose whether it would be useful to provide an automatic device for suspension of the bank act, and that was rejected. The lender-of-last-resort role is riddled with this sort of ambiguity, verging on duplicity. One must promise not to rescue banks and merchant houses that get into trouble, in order to force them to take responsibility for their behavior, and then rescue them when, and if, they do get into trouble, for otherwise trouble may spread. Existence of a lender of last resort creates much the same sort of moral hazard that exists in insurance: if the insured knows he is going to be made whole after a loss due to fire or accident, he is likely to be less careful and thereby increase the chances of fire or accident. Moral hazard is not quite so strong in banking, for the lender of last resort has no contract to bail out bad banking. Over time, however, experience builds expectations, which have nearly the force of contract.

A further ambiguity resides in the fact that if it is obliged to lend in crisis, the central bank presumably seeks to follow rules of helping only sound houses with good paper. The dilemma is that if it holds off too long, what had been good paper becomes bad. The lender of last resort and the money market are locked in a sort of prisoner's dilemma, or game-theory relationship, in which each would like to know with certainty what the other was going to do before it chose what it is going to do, and yet each must act without that knowledge.

Lending to sound houses introduces a note of discretion and judgment into last-resort lending, which inevitably gives rise to questions of insider-outsider, favoritism, and prejudice. When the Bank of France refused to lend to the Pereires and forced them out of the Crédit Mobilier in 1868 or when the Paris banking syndicate of Protestant and Jewish *hautes banques* and deposit banks limited their help to the Catholic banker Bontoux in 1882, but came abundantly to the rescue of the Comtoir d'Escompte six years later, there are bound to be questions raised as to whether the establishment took care of its own and rejected the outsiders and pushy upstarts.

THE INTERNATIONAL LENDER OF LAST RESORT

Thus far the lender-of-last-resort discussion has been confined to domestic crises. Since it has been established that speculative booms and crises are propagated from country to country, however, the question arises as to a lender of last resort between nations. Since World War II, the United Nations has established such institutions as the International Bank for Reconstruction and Development (IBRD, or World Bank) and the International Monetary Fund (IMF) to discharge that role, more or less. The historical question presents itself, however, as to what happened before 1913 and, for subsequent chapters, between 1918 and 1945.

Fernand Braudel hypothesizes that the world economy occupies a given geographical space and always has a pole or center represented by one dominant city or city-state, an economic but not necessarily a political capital. Two centers can exist simultaneously for a time, but in due course one supplants another, as Venice was supplanted by Antwerp and the center moved thereafter successively to Genoa, to Amsterdam, to London, and about 1929 to New York (1977, pp. 80–86).

The reigning center at a given time presumably has a responsibility to act as lender of last resort to other countries in financial crisis when trouble threatens to spill over national boundaries. Thus the Dutch came to the rescue of the Bank of England in the second year of its existence, 1695, by rolling over protested bills, albeit charging the healthy discount rate of 10 percent (Barbour, 1950 [1966], p. 125). Outside the periphery-center relationship there may be side rescues, as in the *Silberzug* (train with 10 million marks banco of silver coin sent by Austria to help out Hamburg in the crisis of 1857, after London, Paris, and Berlin had refused to help), or the 1¼ billion bond issue floated in France for the czar in 1906. But who helps the center when it gets into trouble? In words that used to be known to every schoolboy, *quis custodiet custodiam?*

In the discussion of bimetallism in Chapter 4 (pp. 66–67) a series of cases came up in which the two leading financial centers cooperated in stringency. In 1825, when Britain was in trouble, the Bank of France swapped gold for silver. In 1836–39, the Bank of England drew £800,000 in bills on Paris in 1836 and £2 million again in 1839, plus £900,000 more, partly against silver, on the Bank of Hamburg. In late 1846 and early 1847, the Bank of France borrowed 25 million francs (£1 million) from London and sold 50 million worth of *rentes* to the Russian government. In 1860 and 1861, when silver was undervalued in bimetallic France after the gold discoveries of California and Australia, the Bank of France arranged swaps of silver for gold with the Bank of England, the State Bank of Russia, and an Italian source: 50 million francs for the Bank of England, 31 million for Russia, and 9 million for Italy. The bank wanted to be able to pay out gold if its notes were turned in for coin, not silver, for fear that depositors would start a run on silver for export and sale abroad. It borrowed an additional £2 million (50 million francs) from the London market, drawn in gold—half through Rothschilds and the other half divided among five private bankers. The State Bank of Russia had initiated its arrangement because it wanted the silver for coinage. Fending off a potential run successfully was said to have ended a "war of the banks," presumably referring to a lack of cooperation earlier between the Bank of England and the Bank of France (Plessis, 1985*b*, pp. 241–46). In the crisis of 1890 the Bank of England asked the Russian State Bank not to draw on its deposit with the bank for the time being but, on the contrary, to lend it £800,000 in gold; it also drew £3 million in gold on the Bank of France— all this to meet the Baring crisis. In 1907 the Bank of France bought sterling bills with gold shipped to London to help the Bank of England meet a drain from New York, this time to the extent of 80 million francs and without having been asked.

These operations are discussed very little in banking literature, partly perhaps because they were felt to involve a loss of prestige on the part of the borrowing country. Viner calls the 1836 operation of the Bank of England "doubtless reluctant" and adds that the British thought it humiliating (1937, p. 273). Tooke characterized it as a "discreditable expedient," a "circumstance of almost national humiliation" (Clapham, 1945, Vol. 2, p. 220); he was opposed to last-resort lending in all circumstances. In France, Thiers boasted of the generosity of the French toward the British but suggested that the action should not be repeated (Viner, 1937, p. 273). Sensitivity of central banks and governments at this time is also underlined by the Bank of England's prickly negative reaction to the Prussian National Bank's offer to help in 1873 by lending gold.

Such responses to central bank cooperation seem excessive to modern observers who are used to seeing central bank swaps as lender-of-last-resort operations as they have grown up outside the IMF, and in large part in place of IMF help, for countries with broad financial markets. As early as 1867, however, Michel Chevalier, the French economist and public figure, Saint-Simonist adviser to Napoleon III, in a strong minority in the Commission of Inquiry into Money and Credit in Paris in 1867, was prepared to think along these lines. After recommending foreign bills of exchange as a form of central bank reserves along with gold, an un-French idea for the time and on frequent occasion in the twentieth century, he went on to suggest other measures:

One of the most desirable and the simplest is an entente with a great bank of a country and with other countries, such as has been the case on occasion between the Bank of France and the Bank of England. The bank of the country hurt by a crisis would receive aid from the principal banks of the country where affairs go better. Good relations, exchange of assistance between the great banks of different countries would have more happy effects. In states where there are not dominant banks, they could be replaced by groups of banks such as the banks of Scotland. (Ministère des Finances et al., 1867, Vol. 6, 184)

Chevalier was ahead of his time in other respects: "One does not see why the progress of commercial and political relations among the peoples of Europe should not lead to the creation of an international bank, which would have at least one seat in each of the great states" (1850 [1866], p. 653).

ABSENCE OF A LENDER OF LAST RESORT

Once the technique was developed of getting help from a sound bank or banking system in time of crisis, this was almost always done in some fashion or other. There were exceptions: the rescue operations for the South Sea Company in 1720, for the German and Austrian Maklerbanken and Baubanken in 1873, and for the Union Générale in 1882 were all distinctly limited and grudging.

One writer has drawn the conclusion that the collapse of the South Sea Bubble delayed the industrial revolution, which otherwise might have followed closely on the commercial expansion of the seventeenth century. The judgment is speculative. It is clear, however, that absence of a soft landing increases timidity in the commercial world, as evidenced by the strengthening of the Bubble Act in 1734 to forbid bargains where the vendor did not own the stock at the time, that is, short sales. London stopped growing from 1720 to 1750. The reason may have been the absence of a lender of last resort in the earlier year (Carswell, 1960, pp. 270–71).

In Austria in 1873 the government, the Austrian National Bank, Creditanstalt, and the Rothschilds saved the Bodenkreditanstalt only, but "the cumulative forces of deflation were otherwise allowed to wreak havoc unchecked, ushering in thereby a period of extreme entrepreneurial caution and of more than ordinary aversion of banking toward new and untried business ventures" (März, 1968, p. 176). The 1882 collapse of the Union Générale slowed expansion in France, although the crisis was a local one, not reverberating to the Continent as a whole or beyond. How much the readiness of the *hautes banques* to crush their rival contributed to slow French economic growth at the end of the nineteenth century the historian of the episode does not attempt to estimate, as his conclusions are drawn in political rather than macroeconomic terms (Bouvier, 1960, pp. 280–81).

Prior to the first lender-of-last-resort operation that I have noted—the Dutch operation on behalf of the Bank of England in 1695—were financial crises prolonged because of their absence? The same puzzling ten-year periodicity can be found before and after the age of credit banking (A. Marshall, 1924, p. 305; de Roover, 1949, p. 200). Commenting on the periodicity of the sixteenth century, characterized by wars, reprisals, and other disturbances, de Roover says that the depression of 1586–88 was "particularly severe" and that the most severe was that starting in 1620, which lasted four or five years (ibid., p. 201). Other crises singled out for attention include that of 1557 caused by bad harvest in 1556, the Dutch need to export specie to the Baltic to purchase grain (Friis, 1953), and the resumption of war after 1552 that led to expansion of credit, especially in Lyons and Antwerp, with subsequent ruin to those markets when kings defaulted (Ehrenberg, 1896 [1928], p. 307).

It is virtually impossible, however, to compare financial crises before and after about 1700. Earlier crises lacked a lender of last resort, to be sure, but they also lacked a number of important aspects of the elastic credit mechanism that had given rise to subsequent expansions. Apart from bills of exchange, money was metallic and hence inelastic except for debasement, with no bank notes or any bank lending. Need for a lender of last resort grew up with the development of other forms of bank credit than the bill of exchange, which other forms increased the instability—or perhaps one should say probably increased the instability—of the cycle. Real causes interacted with money and credit in both periods, the real causes being war, harvests, and other interruptions to trade. But while the ten-year periodicity makes it appear that similar causes were at work, it is hard to avoid the conclusion that instability of credit played a larger role, real causes a smaller one, after 1700 than before.

DID THE PERIODIC FINANCIAL CRISIS GO AWAY?

Many economic historians contend that financial crises somehow changed in nature late in the nineteenth century and in some views even disappeared altogether. The case is argued from the 1847, 1857, 1866 sequence and the fact that Britain escaped the 1873 crisis in central Europe with help from a highly volatile discount policy. From 1866 on there was no financial crisis in Britain, apart from the isolated collapse of the City of Glasgow Bank in 1878, until 1890 and that was exclusively British, unconnected with the Panama crisis of 1892 in France (Simon, 1971) or the gold run of 1893 in the United States rooted in the parochial Sherman Silver Purchase Act of 1890 (Lauck, 1907). The conclusion ignores the foreign bond bubble of 1913 that probably would have led to a regular financial crisis if outbreak of war had not produced a crisis of very different character (Morgan, 1952, ch. 1). It ignores as well the 1919–20 boom and bust following the end of the war with classic lines of overtrading, revulsion, and discredit, plus, in the opinion of a Danish economist, not undisputed, the absence of a lender of last resort, producing a quasi-permanent depression (Pedersen, 1961 [1975], p. 188; Moggridge, 1982, pp. 173–76).

The same general view is embodied in the statement that France experienced no financial crisis between 1882 and 1924 (Lévy-Leboyer, ed., 1977*b*, p. 30).

The case becomes stronger after World War II when there were no depressions, and very slight recessions when the rate of growth slowed down, from the end of the war until the first OPEC price rise in 1973. This experience produced from Minsky, the economist who emphasizes the instability of credit, the opinion that the vastly increased weight of government in gross national product tended to stabilize the private sector (1982, p. 27). Government in this regard has been called the borrower of last resort, ready to engage in deficit spending and often forced into it by the fall in tax receipts and rise in welfare benefits in recession or depression (McClam, 1982, p. 262). The reasoning is inapplicable to 1880–1914 when the role of government, except in war, was far smaller than today. There is something of a mystery here. British monetary economists would ascribe the absence of crisis after 1866 (ignoring 1890) to the acquisition of central banking experience and skill in manipulating the discount rate. The same could not be said of France where discount rates were left unchanged for decades on end after the 1856–65 interval of active manipulation. Perhaps the French economy was stabilized by stability in England. That the financial crisis model has not been put completely out of its misery, however, is evidenced by the fringe-bank crisis in London in 1973–74 (Reid, 1982), the Third World debt crisis, and the savings-and-loan debacle in the United States.

Whatever the answer, World War I marked a watershed in European financial history. There were later echos to the pre-1866 past in such a financial crisis as 1919–20. On the whole, however, the structure of the financial world had irrevocably altered. Some of the same principles—the doctrine of the lender of last resort with all its qualifications and ambiguities—were still valid. But financial movements were larger, deeper, and different in nature as well as in pervasiveness.

SUGGESTED SUPPLEMENTARY READING

T. S. Ashton (1959), *Economic Fluctuations in England, 1700–1800.*
Bagehot (1873 [1978]), *Lombard Street, Collected Works,* Vol. 9.
Capie and Wood (eds.) (1985), *Financial Crisis and the World Banking System. Journal of Economic Perspectives* (1990), Symposium on bubbles.
Kindleberger (1978 [1989]), *Manias, Panics and Crashes.*
Kindleberger and Laffargue (eds.) (1982), *Financial Crises.*
E. N. White (ed.) (1990), *Crashes and Panics.*

In German

Wirth (1858 [1890]), *Geschichte der Handelskrisen*

For Accounts of Particular (Largely International) Crises

1619–23, Kindleberger (1991*a*).
1719–20, Carswell (1960).
1836–39, Matthews (1954).

1847, Evans (1849 [1969]), Dornbusch and Frenkel (1984).
1857, Evans (1859 [1969]).
1866, Cottrell (1988).
1873, Kindleberger (1984*b* [1985]).
1878, Collins (1989).
1888–93, Kindleberger (1990*a*).

IV

THE INTERWAR PERIOD

The financial history of Europe encounters a marked discontinuity in 1914. The hundred years of relative peace before that watershed saw well-sustained growth and steady development of financial institutions, including the gold standard, joint stock banking, monetary management, and international lending on a world scale. The width and depth of the war from 1914 to 1918—the first to be called a world war—produced monetary disorder on an enormous scale. Efforts to reconstruct the financial system of Europe after the hostilities, moreover, yielded a widely disparate set of results.

Chapter 16 opens with the financial crisis of August 1914 that links the narrative to the analysis of crises in the previous chapter. It then proceeds to the unsophisticated theories of war finance, and lax methods employed, that stored up monetary disorder for almost a decade. The position was complicated by the insistence by France on collecting massive reparations from Germany, after having paid a sizable indemnity to Germany in 1871–72, and by the parallel insistence on the part of the United States that it should collect on the loans to the Allies made during and immediately after the war—the so-called war debts. The war also produced a spectacular increase in the economic and financial power of the United States that rivaled the world position of leadership of western Europe. The story of reparations and war debts is carried to completion in 1932 before returning in three chapters to the 1920s problems of Germany, Britain, and France (with a short section on Italy).

The financial aftermath of war produced sharply different results in Germany, Britain, and France. As Chapter 17 explains, the German mark exploded in hyperinflation. Debate on the exact mechanism continues to the present day and runs parallel to the controversy between the currency and the banking schools in England after the Napoleonic Wars. Monetarists maintain that the inflation came from central bank laxity in printing and issuing money. The balance-of-payments school, on the other hand, holds that the difficulties originated in the reparations imposed on Germany and the country's necessity to import for restocking, which led to exchange depreciation, the rise of the prices of internationally traded goods, and monetary expansion as the last step in the process. A synthesis of the opposing views is offered.

Chapter 18 deals with the restoration of the pound sterling to par in 1925, again echoing the restoration of gold convertibility in Britain a century earlier after the

Napoleonic Wars. Attention is paid to the boom and relapse of 1919–20 and to the efforts of Governor Montagu Norman of the Bank of England to spread the gold exchange standard across Europe and to promote central bank cooperation generally. The pound was restored to par, but at a considerable cost and, as Chapter 20 sets out, failed to hold it. The story of the French franc in Chapter 19 is one of continuous frustration and defeat in collecting reparations and consolidating governmental finances, a brief success in warding off a speculative attack in 1924, and further relapse. The return to power in 1926 of Raymond Poincaré, ousting the left, restored confidence in the currency, which was stabilized, albeit at a severely reduced level. The chapter concludes with an account of the Italian lire, which was deeply devalued like the French franc but nonetheless left overvalued like the pound.

The last two chapters of Part IV deal with the 1929 crash and the slow and uneven recovery after 1933 in a thoroughly disintegrated world. The Wall Street collapse of October 1929 was followed by a sharp decline in security and commodity prices worldwide, making recovery difficult even after the liquidity squeeze that triggered the crash had been alleviated. The price declines made bank positions untenable, especially in countries where mixed banking had permitted banks to own industrial equities. One clearing bank in Britain that started to fail in January 1929 was quietly rescued. Salvage of the two major Italian banks was conducted in secret in the summer of 1930. The first open collapse occurred in the United States with the failure of two second-order banks in November and December 1930, followed by the internationally resounding collapse of the Creditanstalt in Austria in May 1931. Thereafter, deflation spread rapidly—despite attempts at rescue operations and despite the Hoover moratorium of June 1931 effectively ending reparations and war debts. Germany in July, Britain in September, Japan in December, and the United States in March 1933 went off gold. Initial depreciation of the pound sterling in September 1931 failed to raise prices in sterling but depressed them sharply in gold, to the acute discomfort of the gold bloc in Europe and of the United States.

The 1930s form a lugubrious chapter in the monetary history of Europe. The World Economic Conference of June and July 1933 was a failure. Germany turned away from openness to autarky and foreign exchange control, Britain from the gold standard and world trade to the sterling area and empire preference. The one success story, that of Sweden, turns out to have been based only partly on skill, and a great deal on luck, as Britain recovered from the drab 1920s in a building boom that spilled over into booming imports of Swedish timber. When the gold bloc fell apart and the French had to devalue in September 1936, the defeat was sugarcoated with the formation of the Tripartite Monetary Agreement. With some stretch of the imagination, this can be taken as the point of departure for a renewal of international financial cooperation and a reversal of the decade's financial disintegration.

16

War Finance, Reparations, War Debts

Geld spielt keine Rolle [money is no object, or hang the cost].
(Motto of the German General Staff in World War I, quoted in J. Williamson,
Karl Helferrich, 1872–1924, 1971, p. 126)

THE CRISIS OF AUGUST 1914

At the end of July 1914 war looked more and more inescapable. The Bank of England raised its discount rate from 3 to 4 percent on 30 July and with the declaration of war on 31 July to 9 percent that day and 10 percent on 1 August. Panic had taken hold in Vienna on 25 July; by 30 July stock exchanges were closed everywhere except in Paris; there the 31 July settlement was postponed for a month. Paris called credits on London and withdrew £4 million in gold. Three hundred fifty million in sterling bills had been drawn on, and in, London, but payment on them was impossible because of interruption to shipment of goods and difficulties of selling securities or of borrowing. After the Bank of England had advanced £27 million in the last days of July, the chancellor, on 1 August, offered it a bill of indemnity. It was decided that day to extend all bills of exchange accepted before 4 August automatically for one month. Bank holiday—an extra Monday off during the summer, an invention of the banker Lubbock (Emden, 1938, p. 298)—fell on 3 August. The holiday was extended three days to 6 August to avoid the danger of panic. On 13 August the Bank of England said it would discount all approved bills accepted before 4 August, in effect monetizing the material in the bill market (Morgan, 1952, ch. 1; Sayers, 1976, Vol. 1, ch. 5; Clapham [1943] in Sayers, 1976, Vol. 3, app. 3). It was the most pervasive lender-of-last-resort operation to the time.

In the light of subsequent foreign exchange developments, it is ironic to note as an indication of rational expectations and efficient markets that the first reaction in the foreign exchanges was a very weak dollar. The pound went to $6.50 for a time as Europeans dumped U.S. securities and tried to sell cotton. One hundred million sterling of New York City notes largely held in Europe were coming due for which that city tried to acquire European funds against dollars. Foreign exchange was virtually unobtainable in New York. In due course, arrangement was made to ship gold for British account to be held in Ottawa as collateral for a New York loan in U.S. dollars (Morgan, 1952, pp. 21-22). The dollar eventually came back. In due course again the pound and the French franc needed support.

In Berlin there was panic, collapse of security prices, and an internal run on banks that brought deposits down some 20 percent (Holtfrerich, 1980 [1986], p. 61). The suggestion was made that there be a moratorium on all debt. Max Warburg, the Hamburg banker, opposed it firmly with calls to Berlin. Instead, the *Darlehnskassen* (war credit banks) were created to provide liquidity to concerns in difficulty (Rosenbaum and Sherman, 1976 [1979], p. 113). The trouble was short-lived. By the middle of August things began to right themselves. The Reichsbank raised its discount rate from 5 to 6 percent in early August. By December it lowered it again to 5 percent.

HOW TO PAY FOR THE WAR

In November 1939, J. Maynard Keynes wrote three columns in *The Times* of London, which were later made into a pamphlet with the title *How to Pay for the War* (1940). In this he said that in wartime the British gave their people tax receipts, the French gave *rentes,* the Germans gave money. The statement contains considerable exaggeration because Britain financed World War I only half by taxation. It was still a far more valiant effort than either the French at 14 percent or the Germans at 13 percent. While it fits principles of sound finance, moreover, it may have been a mistake in the long run insofar as it encouraged the British in the 1920s to restore the price level to something like prewar orders of magnitude and the pound to par, when Germans and French more readily gave up the task.

Taxation and debt were not the only means of financing war. One could borrow abroad, as well as at home, let foreign assets run down, collect indemnities from foreign countries in Napoleonic and Bismarckian fashion. One could be, and almost inevitably was, forced to consume capital at home, that is, let public structures, industrial and household buildings, and stocks run down through depreciation and consumption, without or with inadequate replacement. The principal means were nonetheless taxation and borrowing. Decision (or nondecision) in this field was fateful for settlement of financial questions after the war was over.

GERMANY'S THEORY OF WAR FINANCE

German war finance was handicapped in 1914 and thereafter by a number of problems, which its finance ministers made too little effort to resolve. First was the assumption that the war would be short and that the enemy could be made to pay, as in 1871 and 1872 (J. Williamson, 1971, p. 126). The French happened to operate on the same assumption—having a defeated enemy pay for one's war—and while it might be true for one country, it could not be true for both. That the French thought their war would be short is illustrated by a 1911 estimate that war against Germany would cost 20 billion francs, as against the ultimate expenditure of 181 billion.

Second, the Germans operated with the same theory that proved disastrous to Necker in the American War of Independence, namely, that it was sound to finance war as a capital asset, by borrowing, provided that interest on debt and annual amortization were included in the regular budget covered by taxation. As explained in Chapter 9 (pp. 168–69), this partial equilibrium view, assuming no repercussions of national budget decisions, fails to fit the general equilibrium problem posed by war expenditure rolling through the entire economy and financial structure. The Germans thought British war finance woefully unsound because that government suspended amortization of national debt during the hostilities (ibid., p. 125).

In the third place, Germany went to war with a federal tax structure ill suited to a major national effort. Since the time of the Zollverein, central bodies in Germany had had customs revenues and some excise taxes, plus, after the formation of the North and South German Bunds, some contributions made by members to the federal bodies. This system was extended to the Reich in 1871. A few additional items of revenue were added at the national level: income from Post, Telephone and Telegraph (PTT) and from the Alsace-Lorraine railroad. In 1913 Prussian revenue alone of 4.2 billion marks exceeded both ordinary and extraordinary revenue of the Reich by some 100 million marks; other states had a further tax income of 2.5 billion (Stolper, Hauser, and Borchardt, 1964, pp. 53–60). Reich debt was 4.9 billion marks, that of Prussia 9.9 billion, of the other states 6.4 billion. The entire field of direct taxation was reserved for states, not the Reich. In 1906 the Reich got a share in inheritance taxes and in 1913 levied a *Wehrbeitrag* (defense contribution) of 1 billion marks, which was repeated in 1914 and 1915. But taxes on incomes and profits, sought by the Socialists, lay beyond the powers of the national government according to the Reich's constitution, even if right-wing interests had wanted to permit them to be levied.

Here is another Coase-theorem-type problem in finance with which European financial history is endowed, or perhaps one should say plagued. If the objective situation of war demands a change in institutions, presumably, if Coase is right, it should be forthcoming. But Karl Helfferich, the Conservative economist who was finance minister for most of the war, made no effort to undertake thorough-going reform of the financial structure. This was left for after the war to his hated rival, Matthias Erzberger, finance minister in the Socialist government, who in 1920 established fiscal sovereignty of the Reich at the expense of the states, which were reduced to little more than provinces (Epstein, 1959, p. 334). Helfferich has been called "a financial Ludendorff" for his failure to change the system that contributed to catastrophic inflation (J. Williamson, 1971, p. 123), and by Erzberger, not entirely fairly according to John Williamson, "the most frivolous of finance ministers" (ibid., p. 298). In any event, he was lulled into inaction by the conviction that borrowing was not inflationary if the ordinary budget was balanced, and by conservative bias that resisted taxing profits and high incomes. At the end of 1915 when he concluded that new taxes were necessary, he imposed them on consumption articles—though not on necessities—for example, tobacco, beer and spirits, first-class rail fares, postal fees. For the most part, he relied on the hope that the French and British would pay for the war. In August 1915 in a speech later mocked, he said: "The instigators of this war have earned this dead weight of billions." At that stage he estimated that wartime accumulation of debt would reach 70 billion marks—it actually climbed to 220 billion by the middle of 1920—and continued: "How this debt is cast off will be the biggest problem since the beginning of the world" (ibid., pp. 129–31). When the time came to solve the problem, he strongly resisted Socialist proposals for taxes on profits, mortgages on real property, or turning over shares of existing industrial enterprises to the state (ibid., p. 360).

The first German war loan was issued in September 1914; the fourth in March 1916. Analysis of the fourth loan indicated that 227,000 large subscribers bought 57 percent of the total; 3 million small subscribers as a group took only 4 percent, suggesting that profits were gaining sharply at the expense of wages and salaries. Government obtained the necessary resources to pursue the war; money played no role in preventing this. It did, however, store up problems for the future. Prices rose from 100 in 1913 to 152 in 1916, 187 in 1917, and 213 in 1919. While the price level rose 113 percent, the fiduciary circulation of currency went up almost six times.

FINANCING THE OUTBREAK OF WAR

The *Wehrbeitrag* of 1913 was only one of many indications that Europe on both sides of hostile borders was preparing financially for trouble. Before the war in Germany the General Staff worried how much finance would be needed to mobilize how many men (Haller, 1976, p. 116). In France in 1911 it was agreed between the government and the Bank of France that when war erupted the Bank would advance 2.9 billion francs to the government immediately. Preparations went further back. In 1890 German authorities prepared texts to allow the Reichsbank to issue 2 billion marks in additional notes above statutory limits in time of war, and to establish *Darlehnskassen,* a new set of intermediaries in the form of lending banks that issued money in the form of *Darlehnskassenscheine.* On 4 August 1914, the Reichsbank acted swiftly in these directions: legislation was enacted suspending the right of redemption of the mark into gold, abolishing the tax on note circulation in excess of 550 million marks, organizing *Darlehnskassen,* and empowering the Reichsbank to include three-month Treasury bills in its reserve against bank notes in circulation, and *Darlehnskassenscheine* in its cash. All this conformed to a theory that the money supply could be expanded at the outbreak of war without untoward effects because of slack in the economy, less readily thereafter. Moreover, the majority of German economists, including Helfferich, did not believe in the quantity theory of money, but subscribed rather to the banking school, especially in its external aspect that price increases are the result of worsening balances of payments and exchange depreciation.

The rich in Britain were willing to pay taxes in the national interest, and the chancellor of the exchequer raised the rate of income tax somewhat at the outbreak of war, and again in 1915, but the Germans and French were not, even though they had passed certain legislation before the war that pointed in this direction. In Germany a *Vermögenszuwachssteuer* (tax on gains in wealth) had been enacted in 1913; it was put into effect only in 1917; and the *impôt cédulaire* (tax on scheduled income) voted after a hard struggle just before the war in France was equally left unused until 1917. German proposals for taxes on gains in income (*Mehreinkommensteuer*) (because income could not be taxed directly) or a war profits tax (*Krieg-*

swinnsteuer) were either defeated or watered down to ineffectiveness. The tax on turnover (*Umsatzsteuer*) was largely evaded. A capital levy other than the *Wehrbeitrag* of pre- and early war days—the *Notopfer* (emergency sacrifice) decided at the end of the war under Erzberger and bitterly attacked by Helfferich—may have stimulated inflation through capital outflows and accelerated depreciation of the exchange rate (Epstein, 1959, p. 342). Neither the Germans, nor the French for that matter, were in a mood for emergency sacrifices in the overall interest.

This then left borrowing. Abundance of liquidity in France and Germany provided by central bank expansion made it easy. In Germany six-month Treasury bonds at 5 percent were issued consistently and refunded from time to time, such as every six months, into war loans. The same system obtained in France, with short-term Treasury notes and bonds of national defense converted from time to time into *emprunts de guerre* (war loans) on a 4 or 5 percent coupon, issued at a varying discount. A synthetic financial history such as this is not the place to worry about the finicky details, but some impression of pile-up of liquidity and debt in the war can be obtained from Tables 16.1 and 16.2 setting out data from the French *Annuaire statistique* on currency in circulation and national debt for four leading countries of western Europe.

The Bradburys and *Darlehnskassenscheine* were forms of money issued outside the central bank. French and Italian debt kept rising after the end of hostilities, the French undertaking reconstruction expenditure for which it was expected that "*Le Boche paiera*" (the Hun will pay). The points need to be borne in mind for later chapters.

FINANCING WAR THROUGH FOREIGN ASSETS AND BORROWING

France, Britain, Italy, and Russia undertook to finance war in part by selling off foreign assets, and especially by borrowing abroad. Much of the borrowing was associated with support of exchange rates, declining under the weight of adverse

Table 16.1 Note Circulation of Selected Central Banks, 1913–21 (annual averages of weekly figures in millions of national currency)

Year	Bank of England (pounds sterling)	Bank of France (francs)	Reichsbank (marks)	Bank of Italy (lire)
1913	28.7	5,665	1,958	1,647
1914	35.6	7,325	2,018	1,828
1915	33.8*	12,280	5,409	2,624
1916	35.4*	15,552	6,871	3,294
1917	40.2*	19,845	9,010	4,660
1918	54.8*	27,531	13,681	7,751
1919	76.4*	34,744	27,887	10,197
1920	114.8*	38,186	52,435	13,525
1921	127.3*	37,352	76,536	14,175

*Does not include currency notes issued by the Treasury (Bradburys), which amounted to £368 million in 1920 and £326 million in 1921.

Source: Ministère de Travail, etc., Statistique Générale de la France (1929, pp. 83*, 333*, 334*, 377*).

Table 16.2 National Debt of Selected Countries, 1913–21 (on specified dates in millions of national currency)

Year	Great Britain (1 March, pounds sterling)	France (1 January, francs)	Germany (31 March, marks)	Italy (30 June, lire)
1913	717	32,974	4,926	15,125
1914	708	33,558	5,158	15,716
1915	1,166	38,861	9,736	18,695
1916	2,397	51,250	30,595	23,851
1917	4,054	79,610	56,659	33,694
1918	5,921	124,338	72,275	60,212
1919	7,481	151,122	92,756	74,496
1920	7,878	240,242	91,710	86,482
1921	7,634	297,368	82,520	92,856

Source: Ibid. (pp. 397*, 398*).

balances of payments. J. P. Morgan & Company in New York, for example, was called upon, beginning in 1915, to support the pound sterling on behalf of the British government at $4.76½, down slightly from the par rate of exchange of $4.866, and to borrow money in the New York bond market for the purpose. The cost of this support to the end of the war amounted to more than $2 billion and was transferred from Morgan to the U.S. government when that country entered the war in April 1917 (Burk, 1988). Further advances for wartime purchases of materiel and imported supplies after the armistice of November 1918 brought the war debt of the British government to the U.S. government to $4.1 billion. The French overall debt was larger—owed more than half to the United States, less than half to Great Britain. Both countries took over some foreign securities owned by their nationals, liquidated a portion of these holdings, and thereby reduced postwar earnings from foreign investment.

German access to external help was more limited. M. M. Warburg placed $3 million of City of Hamburg dollar-denominated Treasury bills in Scandinavia at the outbreak of war (Rosenbaum and Sherman, 1976 [1979], p. 116). The move was imaginative but the amount tiny. The country's assets were for the most part either sequestered, as more and more countries entered the war against Germany, or inaccessible because of the Allied blockade. Germany was able to acquire real resources from occupied territory, such as Belgium, where its cumulative debt at the end of the war, plus marks introduced into the country from Germany, Luxembourg, and Holland, amounted to 6 billion marks (Van der Wee and Tavernier, 1975, p. 39). The Treaty of Brest-Litovsk, signed with the Soviet government in 1917, provided for territorial annexations, though no reparations, but 6 million gold rubles of compensation for German property expropriated in Russia. Germany also sought to control countries like Turkey and Rumania within its trading area by long-term contracts to purchase goods (J. Williamson, 1971, pp. 260–79).

An interesting, if not vital, external relationship of Germany and the Allies was with Sweden. Sweden had goods for sale that the belligerents wanted but had little to offer in exchange. Accordingly, the Swedes found themselves repatriating Swedish securities, representing past borrowings, piling up foreign exchange, making some disclosed and other unrevealed public credits, especially to Germany, and accumulating gold. To resist the net loss of useful goods, the country imposed an embargo on the import of gold. It was not watertight because the Scandinavian Monetary Union of 1885 bound Sweden to accept gold coin from Denmark and Norway. Some gold was shipped by Germany to those countries, minted and reexported to Stockholm, until agreement was reached in 1917 to halt the movement. The gold embargo led to appreciation of the krona, which reached as high as 34 percent against the pound in November 1916, lifting export prices, improving terms of trade, and somewhat dampening inflationary pressures arising from foreign demand for Swedish exports (Heckscher, 1930; *Federal Reserve Bulletin,* January 1920, pp. 35–46).

REPARATIONS

Early in the war the Germans made plans to annex territory and collect reparations from the enemy they expected to defeat. Even Erzberger, who ultimately moderated his views, was an extreme "annexationist" in 1914, wanting to take into the German Empire Belgium and the territory along the channel as far as Boulogne; the iron ore of Briey-Longwy, rich *minette* bodies discovered on the French side of the Lorraine line after the annexation of 1871 had been fixed; parts of Russia; additions to the German Empire in Central Africa; and a huge monetary sum, including 10 billion marks of direct war costs, plus compensation for Russian devastation of East Prussia, gifts to statesmen and generals (on the 1871 precedent), as well as a far-reaching housing program for veterans (Epstein, 1959, pp. 105ff). The Hamburg banker Warburg favored a 50 billion gold mark indemnity to be paid to Germany by the Allies (Schuker, 1976, p. 182n). Helfferich, the finance minister, was regarded as more of an annexationist than the premier, Bethmann, wanting to surround Germany by a system of satellite states, join Austria-Hungary to Germany in economic and political union, and infiltrate Belgium by charging it an indemnity payable in stocks and bonds of Belgian industry (J. Williamson, 1971, pp. 256–58). Annexationist sentiment remained strong even after unrestricted submarine warfare had failed and brought the United States into the war against Germany. The Peace Resolution, introduced by Erzberger in July 1917, called on the Reichstag to instruct the government to sue for peace. Popular opinion was unwilling to accept peace without territorial gains for Germany, however, and the debate over the resolution produced a new government, an interpretation by the new prime minister that robbed the resolution of all force, and an excuse later used by the nationalists that the Social Democratic party had stabbed Germany in the back (Epstein, 1959, pp. 180–83).

VERSAILLES

In the Armistice Convention signed on 11 November 1918, it was agreed that Germany was to pay reparations to the victorious Allies. The amount was left for settlement in the peace treaty. At Versailles in 1919, however, the Big Four—Clemenceau, Orlando, Lloyd George, and Wilson—were unable to agree on a fixed amount. Any sum the Allies would have accepted as not derisory would have frightened the Germans, and the amount was left for later settlement, not out of surrender to the Germans but in a spirit of inter-Allied cooperation (Mantoux, 1952, p. 65). Germany was forced to sign the treaty that ascribed responsibility for starting the war to it. It was agreed in principle that Germany should repair the damage done in the war, consistent with its ability to pay. There were numerous difficult issues, such as whether war damage included pensions to wounded and dependents of those killed and whether to rate Belgian accumulation of German marks at an overvalued exchange rate as equivalent to physical destruction in such areas as northeastern France. There were sharp differences on the Allied side, temporarily resolved by agreement on a five-year provisional settlement from June 1920 until it could be seen how the process was going. The Germans insisted, however, that they had the right to know the extent of the total obligation. A special Reparation Commission was appointed to fix a figure of compensation for war damage, consistent with ability to pay.

This commission reported in January 1921 and suggested that reparations should amount to 226 billion gold marks, plus a 13 percent tax on exports. The Germans found the figure impossible and appealed to President Harding, who backed away from the issue, twisted, turned, and argued. In April 1921 the Reparations Commission fixed an amount of reparations at 132 billion gold marks plus 26 percent in export taxes over forty-two years (Epstein, 1959, p. 381). The German negotiators resisted. In May 1921, the Allies issued an ultimatum to Germany: agree or else. The Germans agreed.

ECONOMIC CONSEQUENCES OF THE PEACE

One of the British financial experts at the Paris negotiations in the spring of 1919 in a not very exalted position was the youthful John Maynard Keynes, who found himself intensely disliking the reparations settlement. He resigned from the British delegation,[1] returned to England, and wrote at great speed and with great brilliance *The Economic Consequences of the Peace* (1919), which changed the course of history. A belated rebuttal, published posthumously, was undertaken by the Frenchman Etienne Mantoux, *The Carthaginian Peace, or the Economic Consequences of Mr Keynes* (1952), taking fierce exception to the emphasis on economic and financial clauses of the Treaty of Versailles, instead of the political and territorial, and challenging Keynes as a prophet.

In *Economic Consequences* Keynes asserted that there were three sources of instability in Europe: its population dependent for its livelihood on a complex and somewhat artificial system of organization; the psychology of capitalist and labor-

---

1. On the same day that Keynes quit the British delegation to Versailles, Lord Cunliffe, no longer governor of the Bank of England, also withdrew, but for the opposite reason. He thought the Germans were being let off too lightly (Sayers, 1976, Vol. 1, p. 109n). Cunliffe was not a lovable man (ibid., p. 66), and Keynes was the only man he ever feared (ibid., p. 103n).

ing classes; and the tenuous character of Europe's claim on overseas food and raw materials. The last point was the extension of an article written before the war in which Keynes claimed that the terms of trade were destined to worsen for Europe because imported food and raw materials were subject to diminishing returns, while exported manufactures would fall in price because of increasing returns or decreasing costs (1912). (The forecast proved wrong, and the analysis was dubious from the start, since falling prices for exports will not worsen welfare if productivity increases as much as, or more than, prices decline.) He noted that Germany was peculiarly dependent on overseas trade, which required ships, foreign investments, and colonies, all taken from it in the Versailles Treaty, criticized Lloyd George and Wilson for not realizing that the most serious problems that claimed their attention were not political or territorial but financial and economic, and that the problems of the future lay not in sovereignties and frontiers but in food, coal, and transport (1919, p. 146). He quoted the statement of the Germans that "those who sign this treaty will sign the death sentence of many millions of German men, women and children," and added, "I know of no adequate answer to those words."

Publication of the book encouraged the Germans to resist paying reparations, in confirmation of the Heisenberg principle that observation affects the thing observed. Moreover, excoriation of Wilson as a "blind and deaf Don Quixote," "an old Presbyterian bamboozled by Clemenceau and Lloyd George," "seldom a statesman of the first rank more incompetent," "his mind slow and unadaptable," helped Republicans in the United States to defeat American ratification of the Versailles Treaty and keep the United States out of the League of Nations. The book abounded in purple passages discussing Clemenceau's boots and gray suede gloves and Wilson's hands "wanting in sensitiveness and fineness." An interesting aspect of these descriptions is that it is now well established that Keynes was in the presence of the Four on only one occasion in a "confused and furious gathering" in which "large numbers of economic advisers" were invited into a drawing room (House and Seymour, eds, 1921, p. 65n, as reported in Mantoux, 1952, p. 45; Duroselle, 1960, p. 115; Salter, 1967, pp. 85–86; Harrod, 1951, p. 236). Keynes, moreover, has been accused of pro-German bias and of hiding his friendship with Carl Melchior, a partner of M. M. Warburg in Hamburg since 1917, who served on the German reparation delegation (Schuker, 1980, p. 126). Having once toyed with reparations to be paid by the Allies to Germany, Melchior and Warburg now proposed that Germany pay 100 billion gold marks without interest in annual installments, the discounted value of the obligation being far below its nominal value, of course, by an amount depending upon the period over which payment would be made and the relevant rate of discount. The proposal was approved on the German side but never submitted to serious negotiation (Rosenbaum and Sherman, 1976 [1979], p. 123).

Keynes's own proposal for German reparations was for $10 billion, as contrasted with the $40 billion at which he calculated the Versailles open-ended arrangement, the nominal amount of $20 billion suggested by Melchior and Warburg, and the $1 billion paid by France in 1871–73. He considered $10 billion the maximum payable but doubted that it could be paid. The proposal included the cancellation of inter-Allied debts, no reparations to be received by Great Britain, German payments to new states of eastern Europe to be guaranteed by the Allies to establish their creditability, and other ex-enemy powers to issue bonds as reparations, also to be guaranteed (1919, pp. 147, 200).

The French Finance Ministry equally wanted German reparations guaranteed. It believed in official recycling, in today's parlance, then called "commercialization of the debt" (Schuker, 1976, p. 19). Germany would issue bonds to be bought by Americans with monies then turned over to reparation claimants. Real reparations would be paid by Germany when and if it paid off the bonds. As it turned out, German reparations were not exactly commercialized, but until the hyperinflation of 1922, and later after the Dawes Plan of 1924, they were paid by Americans, as indicated below.

OCCUPATION OF THE RUHR

Germany had no choice but to accept the ultimatum of May 1921. The will to pay, however, was weak or altogether missing, especially after Keynes's polemic had sunk in. Matthias Erzberger was among the few who acknowledged some German obligation because of the unprovoked invasion of Belgium and voluntary acceptance of the prearmistice contract with its reparation clause (Epstein, 1959, p. 380). The position was unpopular. He was taunted into suing Helfferich for slander after the latter had written three articles entitled "Away with Erzberger," won a nominal settlement of 300 marks but was driven from public life. On 26 August 1921 he was assassinated by right-wing reactionaries—the "symbol of a man who wanted a negotiated peace," popular among the lower classes but the "most hated man among the annexationists and those who wanted no tampering with Germany's social and political structure" (ibid., p. 213). Symmetrically, Helfferich in opposition to the Socialist government in power in the Weimar Republic was described after the war as the "best hated man" in Germany (J. Williamson, 1971, p. 342). The social rift implied by these attitudes contrasts sharply with the unified spirit in which France worked in 1871–73 to get occupation forces withdrawn from French territory.

Seeking to reopen the reparation question, the Germans called for a conference in Cannes in January 1922 to discuss a moratorium. Britain hoped and worked for a revised and reduced schedule and possibly an international loan to stabilize the now-sinking mark (Clarke, 1973, p. 6). In France the moderate Briand government fell and was succeeded by the firm Poincaré team that insisted on adherence to the May 1921 schedule. Impasse widened as the United States Funding Commission, established in February 1922 to negotiate Allied war debt settlements, was specifically forbidden in the authorizing legislation to make reduction in capital amounts (ibid., p. 7). The British were pushing for a monetary conference to be held in Genoa in May to discuss metamorphosing the gold into a gold exchange standard. A blow fell in the east with the signing of the Rapallo Agreement between Germany and the Soviet Union in violation of Versailles and involving mutual cancellation of financial claims, which bode badly for Allied hopes of collecting war debts, or recognition of commercial debts from the successor to the czarist government. In early April the Reparations Commission appointed a committee of bankers to explore the possibility of international loans for Germany. It was scheduled to meet in late May when the question was raised as to whether the committee's terms of reference permitted it to examine Germany's capacity to make reparation payments on the 1921 schedule.

On 2 June the French government decided that the banker's committee could not consider the May 1921 schedule. On 10 June the committee decided that, given the reparation schedule, Germany's credit was not sufficiently high to justify an international loan. On 22 June Walther Rathenau, the German foreign minister who had been cooperating with the Allies in seeking a solution to the reparation question, was assassinated. The three events in combination produced a change in expectations concerning the value of the mark, a subject to be dealt with in the next chapter (pp. 307–8).

In the summer and fall of 1922, German deliveries of reparations in kind, especially coal and telegraph poles, fell into arrears. As the situation deteriorated, French and Belgian troops crossed the border in January 1923 to occupy the Ruhr in an attempt to enforce deliveries. It failed to help. Ruhr miners and workers went on strike. To assist the strikers the German government printed more money. Inflation, which had turned sharply upward in June 1922, reached hyperinflationary levels, and in real terms the money supply shrank as printing presses failed to keep up with prices. In May 1923 the British tried to arbitrate between the French and the Germans, with no success. By August the mark exploded and was replaced in November by an entirely new currency, the Rentenmark. In the spring of 1924 this was replaced by the Reichsmark when the Dawes Plan took effect.

THE DAWES PLAN

By late summer and early fall of 1923 it was clear to the French that occupation of the Ruhr was not working, and they were prepared to contemplate a new approach. This was forthcoming in the appointment of two committees of experts, one under the chairmanship of Charles G. Dawes, a Chicago banker, to reexamine the reparations question, the second, of less consequence, but a sop to French pride, under the leadership of Reginald McKenna, a British banker, to explore the extent to which Germans had exported capital abroad to evade their reparations obligations. The leading American on the reparations committee was Owen D. Young, later president of the General Electric Company and chairman of the Federal Reserve Bank of New York, a largely honorary post, while Dawes who had been ambassador to the Court of St. James in Britain and later was vice-president of the United States, was more of a figurehead. Powerful British experts were Sir Josiah (later Lord) Stamp and Sir Arthur Salter, the latter a civil servant. The committee lined up the British who wanted to moderate reparations against a more intransigent team of French, Belgians, and Italians, with the Americans in the middle trying to arbitrate. Negotiations were tense. Stamp thought that the British position was extreme; another British representative, Lord Bradbury, regarded both Dawes and Young as "unsound" (Schuker, 1976, p. 193). Keynes proposed to the committee that the

United States should guarantee German payment of reparations to the Allies, an idea that Rufus Leffingwell of J. P. Morgan & Company found preposterous (ibid., p. 176), although his partner, Dwight Morrow, a Francophile, wanted to take the burden off Germany by lending the French the money to buy German coal, coke, and dyes with dollars (ibid., p. 290). In March 1924 after the French had been helped through a currency crisis with a Morgan loan (discussed below in Chapter 19, pp. 341, 343), they stiffened their opposition to withdrawing from the Ruhr, to the anger of the British. A continuous French refrain was that they wanted German reparations to be based on pledges of productive assets, such as railway and industrial bonds.

After long and difficult negotiation, the Dawes Plan was agreed and made public in April 1924. It provided for a reparation schedule starting at 1 billion gold marks for the first year, rising to 2.5 billion in the fifth, with some room for changes if gold prices moved up or down by 10 percent. The total amount to be paid in the long run was left open. A Reparations Agency was established in Berlin to oversee German government finances, the raising of the amounts due in marks and their transfer into foreign exchange, with power to intervene if difficulties arose. The Reichsbank was reorganized to support a new German currency, the Reichsmark, which replaced the Rentenmark, with a mandatory limit of 40 percent cover against demand liabilities, three-quarters in gold, one-quarter in foreign exchange. (The British had wanted a higher ratio of foreign exchange but were overruled by the Americans.) Finally, provision was made for an initial recycling operation, for a loan of 800 million Reichsmarks, to be sold in a number of markets. The British insisted that international bankers would not be able to sell the loan unless French and Belgians withdrew from the Ruhr and this was finally accomplished. The Morgan representative, in turn, insisted that French investors had to subscribe some part of the Dawes loan to instill confidence in American investors; the French thought it unjust to make them lend Germany money to pay reparations (ibid., p. 153). In France and in Belgium the prime ministers had to call in private bankers and apply heavy pressure to get them to handle their shares of the Dawes loan. Even the British public objected to lending to Germany (Clarke, 1967, pp. 67–68).

The Dawes loan was not to recycle the entirety of German reparation, as the French sought, but merely to prime the pump. In this it succeeded beyond expectations. The New York *tranche* of about half the total, or $110 million, was a phenomenal success, being oversubscribed eleven times. It marked a discontinuity in American foreign lending, being followed by a wave of foreign loans, at first to Germany and German industrial firms and thereafter more widely in Europe, Latin America, and Australia (Feis, 1950, p. 42). The flow of foreign loans from New York to German borrowers provided foreign exchange needed for Germany to pay reparations to France and Britain—for a time. This was not exactly commercialization of reparations in the French model in which German government bonds would be sold to American investors to raise funds that Germany would pay France. It approached it closely, however. As the German government raised the Reichsmark equivalent of reparation payments in the domestic capital market, and through a budget surplus, it increased interest rates. This diverted firms, states, and municipalities from the domestic to foreign capital markets, and especially New

York, and provided both an offset to deflationary fiscal efforts of the central government and the foreign exchange necessary to pay reparations.

The recycling aspect of German borrowing was not recognized at the time. Discussion of the transfer problem, rife in academic circles, focused on real transfer—how the Germans would develop an export surplus so as to pay reparations to the Allies in goods and services. On the Franco-Prussian indemnity model, this would occur only when Germany paid off its foreign loans—something that would not happen. In the famous Keynes-Ohlin transfer debate, Keynes argued that elasticities of demand for German exports and imports were too low to enable transfer to be achieved readily (1929 [1947]); Ohlin, a Swedish economist, countered that Keynes's analysis omitted reference to shifts in purchasing power—downward in Germany as the country raised the Reichsmark equivalent of the payment and upward in receiving countries as they spent the proceeds—a point about spending changes that later came to be regarded as Keynesian analysis (1929 [1947]). Ohlin failed to note, however, that to the extent that the governmental surplus in Germany, or the private surplus borrowed by government, was offset by corporate, state, and municipal investment financed by foreign loans, no decline in purchasing power in the paying country took place. To the extent, moreover, that reparations were used in the receiving country not to undertake new reconstruction—that had been virtually completed by 1924—but to retire debt, the increase in spending posited by Ohlin would not take place either, at least not in the first round. Whether additional spending occurred later would turn on what followed in the capital market when the debt was retired.

The Dawes loan was significant in one other respect in that it marked a renewal of American interest in European matters, at least in financial circles, after the withdrawal implicit in Senate rejection of the Versailles Treaty.

THE YOUNG PLAN

Before the onset of the 1929 depression, and even before it had been noticed that the rise in the New York stock market in mid-1928 was diverting American investor interest from foreign bonds to domestic stocks, S. Parker Gilbert, the reparation agent-general in Berlin, in his regular report of June 1928, proposed reconsideration of reparation arrangements with a view especially to winding up the Berlin agency and restoring fiscal autonomy to the German government. There were also questions of fixing a total amount for German reparations and beginning the process of withdrawing occupation forces from the Rhineland. In September it was agreed to appoint a new committee of experts to meet in February 1929, with Owen D. Young as chairman. Negotiations in Paris among the experts were again stormy, with demands by Schacht for the restoration of German colonies and dismantling of the Polish corridor, on one side, and French threats to withdraw short-term balances from Germany, on the other. In August 1929 when the draft agreed in June went to the political level at a meeting in the Hague, tension between Philip Snowden, British chancellor of the exchequer, and Henri Chéron, French finance minister, resulted in a sharp exchange that prompted threats to withdraw swollen

French balances from London. In all this acrimony, the Young Plan was finally put into effect in April 1930, six months after the New York stock exchange had suffered a grievous collapse.

The Young Plan differed from the Dawes Plan in a number of respects. The reparation bill, starting at 1,650 million gold marks and rising to a steady figure of 2,500 million in the fifth year, was fixed to last for fifty-nine years, for a total of 121 billion gold marks with a present discounted value of 37 billion. Annual payments were divided in two, one part unconditional, the remainder postponable in event of transfer difficulty. A $300 million Young loan was projected, with two-thirds of the proceeds divided among Germany's creditors, one-third paid to Germany. A new institution was created to help transfer the first year's Reichsmark payment, the Bank for International Settlements (BIS), located at the European railroad junction of Basle, Switzerland. The transfer was purely notional: the German payment would be invested by the Bank in Germany; receiving countries obtained deposits on the books of the BIS, which they were expected to regard as an asset but not to spend or cash. Germany continued to pay interest on the BIS investment in fully convertible foreign exchange, both through the moratorium on reparations and the standstill period after July 1931 when other foreign payments were blocked. It was the major earning asset of the BIS, which served as a monthly meetingplace for European central bankers, a source of information, and a place for exchange of views that German central bankers valued and protected from possible aggression by political forces. When war broke out in 1939, the French government insisted on withdrawing its deposit under the Young Plan.

In June 1930, when the time came to float the Young loan, international capital markets were no longer in the triumphant mood that greeted the Dawes loan six years earlier. The New York *tranche* was barely covered; when the loan was issued, it went to a discount.

Fourteen months after the signing of the Young Plan to settle German reparations for fifty-nine years, on 19 June 1931, the Hoover moratorium, postponing reparations and war debts for a year, effectively killed the former forever. A conference held at Lausanne in the summer of 1932 buried the remains. At that conference, Germany agreed to deliver to the BIS for the benefit of reparation recipients $3 billion Reichsmark gold bonds, with a nominal value of $715 million, which the Bank was forbidden to sell for three years, and then only at a price above 90. The bonds bore 5 percent interest and a 1 percent sinking fund. Any bonds that remained in the hands of the BIS after fifteen years were to be canceled. No bonds were ever sold. The present discounted value of the bonds in 1932 at the depth of the depression was almost certainly zero.

REPARATIONS PAID

Estimates of the reparations paid by Germany have been provided by the Reparations Commission and by Germany. Divided by periods, the numbers are summarized in Table 16.3. Differences between the two estimates under the Dawes and Young plans are due to the inclusion of interest, along with principal, in German

Table 16.3 German Reparation Payments, 1918–32 (by period and estimator in billions of Reichsmarks)

Period	Estimated by Reparation Commission	Estimated by German Government
11 November 1918 to August 1924	9.6	42.0
Dawes Plan	7.6	8.0
Young Plan	2.8	3.1
Other	0.8	14.6
Total	20.8	67.7

Source: Mantoux (1952, p. 152).

estimates. For the other periods, German estimates include such items as work done by German prisoners of war, industrial disarmament within Germany, and, for the early period, the value of the German fleet scuttled at Scapa Flow. Military equipment yielded by the defeated to the victorious armed forces is usually regarded as war booty rather than reparations. Since the German navy sank its fleet, moreover, even if the cost could conceivably be regarded as paid by Germany, it could hardly be thought of as received by the Allies.

A detailed breakdown of the two estimates to the end of 1924 is available in Holtfrerich (1980 [1986], p. 147).

ECONOMICS AND POLITICS OF REPARATIONS

In June 1928 as the stock market started its climb, the United States stopped lending at long term to the world. For a time Germany borrowed short to finish industrial, municipal, and state projects and to continue to pay reparations. For the most part it was subjected to strenuous deflation. Domestic income and imports fell faster than exports in the years from 1928 to the middle of 1931. Unemployment rose to 15 percent of the work force and reached 1.9 million, whereas when the insurance fund had been established in 1927 the highest imaginable figure had been 800,000. Heroic deflation produced an export surplus and transferred reparation payments. Some economic observers, notably Viner and Machlup, have on occasion said that the experience proves how malleable balances of payments are, although Machlup later backed off considerably from his original position (Machlup, 1950 [1964], p. 81n, and 1980, pp. 128–31; Viner, 1952, p. 182).

Deflation produced by the cutoff in American lending was enhanced by the brutal policies, beginning in March 1930, of Heinrich Brüning, German prime minister, who was determined to show the Allies that it was impossible for Germany to pay, even if he had to destroy the economy and the political system to do so. In the early 1920s, Germany had been resolved not to pay on the basis of Keynes's demonstration. A decade later it sought to mount its own demonstration of impossibility. While French intransigence in the matter of receiving reparations and American intransigence in war debts compounded the problem, Mantoux's question remains open: could the Germans have paid reparations in the amount of the May 1921 ultimatum if they had loyally tried to? The answer is probably no.

WAR DEBTS

Commercial loans, reparations, and war debts created an impossible situation in international finance in the 1920s. France benefited from reparations, wanted to get rid of war debts, and had minimal interest in commercial lending. Germany had no interest in war debts, detested reparations, and welcomed commercial borrowing. Britain was prepared to cancel out reparations and war debts but not commercial lending. The United States had no interest in reparations, wanted to collect war debts, but at the same time wanted to sustain commercial lending. In the intricate, game theoretic circumstances, it seems inevitable that reparations and war debts would be wiped out and likely that they would pull down commercial debts in the destruction.

The British were consistent advocates of cancellation of war debts. For centuries in war they had advanced subsidies to their allies, and when they departed from the practice in 1795 and 1797 and helped Austria through loans, they lived to regret it. Keynes called for cancellation in *Economic Consequences of the Peace* and in other journalistic writing, published in *Essays in Persuasion* (1931). In the latter volume he offered a table of the network of debts as of 1919; which showed that the United States was owed £1,900 million (roughly $8.5 billion at $4.50 to the pound); Britain was ahead by £900 million nominally but far less if one realistically wrote off the Russian obligation on which the chances of collection were virtually nil; France was behind by £700 million, counting all obligations equally but falling £160 million further back if Russian debts are ignored (Table 16.4).

In August 1922 the British reacted to this position with the Balfour Note addressed to the United States and their Allies, stating that receipts from German on reparations account and war debts collected must be equal to payments made on war debt account to the United States. If the country was to pay the United States about £35 million a year and collected reparations, later fixed under the Dawes Plan at £24 million a year, it would require France, Italy, and others to pay £11 million a year.

The United States took the firm position that war debts and reparations were entirely unconnected. The debts had been contracted without thought of what the

Table 16.4 Inter-Allied War Debts, Estimated as of 1919 (in millions of pounds sterling)

Loans to	From United States	From United Kingdom	From France	Total
United Kingdom	842	—	—	842
France	550	508	—	1,058
Italy	325	467	35	827
Russia	38	568	160	766
Belgium	80	98	90	268
Serbia, etc.	20	20	20	60
Other Allies	35	79	50	164
Total	1,900	1,740	355	3,995

Source: Keynes (1919 [1931], p. 31).

borrowers might or might not collect from others. For a borrower to insist that it would pay only if it could collect from a weak debtor would be unilaterally to foist a weak asset on the United States when it originally had a strong one. Automatic offsetting is tolerable only when all debtors have the same (good) credit standing, and the intermediary, passing through what it is owed to its creditor, stands behind the debt.

Keynes found the U.S. view, and even the Balfour stand, absurd. If Italy paid its full debts and Germany £100 million a year, under the Balfour Note the United Kingdom would get nothing, France would receive £32 million, and the United States £58 million, which he felt to be unjust. Moreover, if the Dawes Plan failed, the Balfour Note would require France to pay Britain even if it received nothing from Germany (1925 [1931], p. 63).

The U.S. position was not quixotic or arbitrary but had roots in public opinion, not unconnected with the impact made by *The Economic Consequences of the Peace,* which pictured Europe as greedy and cynical and the United States as easily gulled. This was the source of the congressional instruction to the United States War Debts Commission in February 1922 not to reduce the capital sums of these debts—although changes in interest rates are, of course, the equivalent insofar as they reduce the present discounted value of a debt.

Under the authority conferred by Congress, the commission reached its first debt settlement on 1 May 1923 with Finland and the last with Yugoslavia on 3 May 1926. France was only four days ahead of Yugoslavia on 29 April (Moulton and Pasvolsvy, 1932, p. 82). A typical settlement was that with Britain, the second reached, in June 1923. The debtor undertook to pay the full face amount plus interest from 19 April to December 1922 in sixty-two equal annual installments with interest at 3 percent for the first ten years and 3½ percent for the following fifty-two, all this in U.S. gold coin or the equivalent. Sixty-two years was substituted for the original congressional authorization, which had been limited to twenty-five years. Concessionary interest rates brought down present discounted value (PDV) of settlements more for less developed countries such as Italy and Yugoslavia. For Great Britain the original advances amounted to $4.1 billion and the PDV at settlement $3.8 billion; for France the two sums were $3.0 billion and $2.2 billion, respectively, and for Italy $1.6 billion and $0.5 billion (ibid., p. 163). The reader who thinks the last sum minuscule should recall that it was half the nominal amount paid by France to Germany in the "unprecedented ransom" of 1871. The inflation of U.S. prices, to be sure, had made the real value considerably less.

THE MORATORIUM OF JUNE 1931

U.S. insistence that there was no connection between reparations and war debts repeated through the 1920s did not survive the moratorium of 19 June 1931, except in the shakiest of forms. Finland kept paying its war debts on the nail for the public relations value; the sum was small. Hoover pressured the French to pay after the year's moratorium had run out, and Herriot fell from power in the French Chamber on 14 December 1932 when he proposed meeting the installment due the next day. The British paid on 15 December 1932, and again, but this time in depreciated silver, on 15 June 1933. It was the end of the line.

SUGGESTED SUPPLEMENTARY READING

Epstein (1959), *Matthias Erzberger and the Dilemma of German Democracy.*
Hardach (1977), *The First World War.*
Keynes (1919), *The Economic Consequences of the Peace.*
Mantoux (1952), *The Carthaginian Peace.*
Moulton and Pasvolsky (1932), *War Debts and World Prosperity.*
Schacht (1931), *The End of Reparations.*
Schrecker (1978), *The Hired Money.*
Schuker (1988), *American "Reparations" to Germany.*
J. Williamson (1971), *Karl Helfferich, 1872–1924.*

In French

Artaud (1978), *La Question des dettes interalliées et la reconstruction de l'Europe (1917–1929).*

In German

Haller (1976), Die Rolle der Staatsfinanzen für die Inflationsprozess.

17

German Postwar Inflation

> It is a close matter whether it is worse to be lost in the woods (without a theory) than in one's theory, pursuing its internal consistence to the point where contact with reality is lost.
>
> (J. H. Williams, An economist's confessions, 1952)

German hyperinflation after World War I has been a favorite topic in the financial history of Europe. After a substantial literature had grown up about it contemporaneously, another burst of interest occurred in the early 1930s, producing books by Frank D. Graham (1930) and Costantino Bresciani-Turroni (1931 [1937]). With deflation in the 1930s, concern for inflation languished until World War II when it, and other European inflations, were studied by the League of Nations as part of postwar planning, the principal author being Ragnar Nurkse (League of Nations, 1946). Rediscovery of money and the rise of monetarism awakened new interest in the case in the second postwar period, producing an important article by Philip Cagan (1956) and a later book-length study by two Danish economists, Karsten Laursen and Jørgen Pedersen (1964). With the breakdown of Bretton Woods, a turn to flexible exchange rates, and the jolt of worldwide inflation after 1973, new attention turned to the case, and German inflation is now studied by monetarists concerned with international economics, such as Jacob Frenkel (1977), by general historians like Gerald Feldman (1977) and Charles Maier (1975), and for the first time by a German economic historian—the other major studies having been by foreign economists—Carl-Ludwig Holtfrerich (1980 [1986]). In the vast outpouring of interpretations and disputes, one must tread warily.

THE SCHOOLS

The two main bodies of analysis explaining German hyperinflation are the balance of payments and the monetary. The former is congruent with the banking school in the bullion controversy in England in the early decades of the nineteenth century and with the Hats in Sweden half a century earlier (see pp. 132–33). They maintained that the troubles began with the balance of payments and the exchange rate and, especially in the German case, with reparations and the necessity of a depleted country to restock its warehouses with imported raw materials at the end of the war. The balance of payments turned adverse, and the exchange rate fell to an undervalued level, driving up foreign trade prices. The price rises spread to prices in general, and this forced the monetary authorities to expand the money supply to avoid unemployment. The exchange rate led the process; money supply brought up the rear. German authorities, notably Karl Helfferich, belonged to this persuasion immediately after the war, blaming inflation on reparations and hence on the Allies. Less committed emotionally but following the same analytical path were many outside observers, such as John H. Williams (Malamud, 1980), James W. Angell (1926), and Laursen and Pedersen (1964). As a committed conservative and rabid opponent of the Socialists, Helfferich also blamed inflation on the workers who were using it as a means of proletarianization; first came depreciation from reparation and French violence; then, with the rise in imported prices, an unconscionable demand for higher wages, which spread to higher prices generally and increased demand for currency; and finally calls upon the Reichsbank to make more currency available (J. Williamson, 1971, pp. 382–83). Laursen and Pedersen (1964, passim) follow this sequence also in laying stress on the role of wages in following prices and forming the connection between exchange depreciation and monetary expansion.

The monetarists, on the other hand, have affinity with the currency school in nineteenth-century England, led initially by Ricardo and later by Lord Overstone (see pp. 64–65, 91–92), who blamed the agio on gold (depreciation of sterling), on the Bank of England's loose ways in issuance of money. The eighteenth-century Swedish analogue is the Caps. The initial fault was that of the Reichsbank in overissuing money or, in some versions, of the government, which ran a large budget deficit that had to be monetized by borrowing from the Reichsbank. Irresponsible policies of the government, central bank, or both raised prices internally, which turned the balance of payments adverse and led to depreciation of the exchange rate. In some versions, purchasing power parity—the relationship between domestic prices and those in other countries—was maintained rigidly, so that the rise in domestic price was communicated directly to the exchange rate, without the need for a change in the balance of payments or with undervaluation or overvaluation being considered possible. An early postwar adherent to this school was Gustav Cassel, a Swedish economist, who formulated the modern but rigid version of purchasing power parity (1924, p. 184). A major monetarist explanation at the end of the 1920s was the work of Bresciani-Turroni (1931 [1937]). Most recently, the point of view has been examined with more refined techniques—those of econometrics, not uniformly accepted by others—by Cagan (1956) and Frenkel (1977).

THE FACTS

The facts of European wartime finance were put forward rather broadly in Chapter 16. In more detail, German money supply rose during and after World War I, as shown in Table 17.1.

The floating debt for broadly the same dates is shown in Table 17.2 and, finally, a price level and several measures of exchange rates in Table 17.3. The trade-weighted index of exchange rates on a nominal basis is lower than the dollar index because of the depreciation of Germany's European trading partners against the dollar, as shown in Figure 17.1. The deflated trade-weighted index is a measure of

Table 17.1 Money Supply in Germany, 1914–23 (on selected dates in millions of marks)

Date	Currency in Circulation	Reichsbank Deposits	Joint Stock Bank Deposits	Savings Bank Deposits	Postal Check Assets
June 1914	6,323	858	8,392	20,302	258
December 1918	33,106	13,280	29,981	29,981	295
December 1919	50,173	17,072	54,601	36,981	2,763
December 1920	91,629	21,327	84,526	44,563	7,108
December 1921	122,963	32,906	n.a.	49,932	11,019
June 1922	180,716	37,174	n.a.	n.a.	21,476
December 1922	1,295,228	550,526	n.a.	163,020	175,552
June 1923	17,393,000	8,953,000	n.a.	n.a.	n.a.

n.a. = not available.
Source: Holtfrerich (1980 [1986], table 11, pp. 52–54).

Table 17.2 Floating Debt of the German Reich, 1914–23 (on selected dates)

Date	Floating Debt (in millions of marks)	Held Outside the Reichsbank (in percent)
July 1914	0.3	0.0
December 1918	55.2	50.7
December 1919	86.4	52.2
December 1920	152.8	62.3
December 1921	247.1	46.5
June 1922	295.3	37.0
December 1922	1,495.2	20.0
June 1923	22,019.8	16.7
November 1923	191,580,465,422.1	0.9

Source: Ibid. (table 20, pp. 67–68).

Table 17.3 German Price Level and Exchange Rates, 1914–23 (on selected periods and dates) (1913 = 1)

Date	Wholesale Prices	Dollar Exchange Rates	Trade-Weighted Exchange Rates, 14 European Countries and United States	
			Nominal	Deflated by Relative Prices
June 1914	0.99	0.998	n.a.	n.a.
1914 average	1.05	1.017	n.a.	n.a.
1915 average	1.42	1.16	n.a.	n.a.
1916 average	1.52	1.32	n.a.	n.a.
1917 average	1.79	1.57	n.a.	n.a.
1918 average	2.17	1.43	n.a.	n.a.
1919 average	4.15	4.70	n.a.	n.a.
1920 average	14.96	15.01	7.01	1.91
June 1921	13.66	16.51	6.62	1.67
December 1921	34.87	43.72	16.7	1.75
June 1922	70.30	75.62	25.5	1.40
December 1922	1,475	1,807.8	539.4	1.62
June 1923	19,985	26,202	6,831.0	1.77

n.a. = not available.
Source: Ibid. (tables 1 and 2, pp. 17, 23–24).

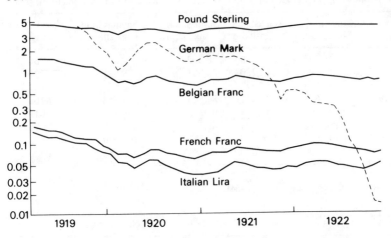

Figure 17.1 Monthly average exchange rates of European currencies in U.S. dollars, 1919–22 (on logarithmic scale). Source: Board of Governors of the Federal Reserve System (1943, Sec. 663–n81. Taken from Figure 2 in Holtfrerich (1980 [1986], p. 20).

the purchasing power of the mark, with 1 the equivalent of the 1913 level. An attempt to calculate purchasing power parities during the war by comparing the first two columns runs up against the difficulty that both price level and exchange rate were artificially controlled. Various items in the cost-of-living index such as grain were subsidized, and the dollar exchange rate was controlled by the Reichsbank until September 1919.

One more caveat is called for in discussing purchasing power parities, a subject that will arise in subsequent chapters treating the pound sterling and the French franc: that structural changes in a country's international economic relationships make it unlikely that the equilibrium relationship between domestic and foreign prices translated through the exchange rate will be the same after the war as before (Metzler, 1947 [1978]). Since Germany had lost a great deal of manpower and some exporting territories, such as Upper Silesia and Alsace-Lorraine, along with income from foreign investments, and had to pay reparations, an exchange rate equivalent to 1913 in purchasing power terms would almost certainly be overvalued in 1919. Exactly how much the 1913 rate would have to be devalued to produce equilibrium in the changed circumstances of the immediate postwar period, however, is virtually impossible to establish with any precision.

A SINGLE MODEL?

Table 17.3 has been divided into annual averages for the war years and half-yearly periods thereafter against the possibility that a monocausal explanation focusing exclusively on either the balance of payments or the money supply will fail to penetrate to the heart of the matter. Philip Cagan, for example, a monetarist, believes that the demand for money is stable in real terms at all times and that the public will try to hold balances that maintain their purchasing power, based on its expectations about inflation. These expectations, in his judgment, are formed on the basis of past inflation. If such a stable demand for real money could be proved, hyperinflation could not be blamed on a fickle public's suddenly dumping money as it spent for goods and foreign exchange, so that hyperinflation would have to be caused by persistent government deficits and printing of money (Cagan, 1956).

There is considerable debate about the formal character of Cagan's econometric proxy for inflationary expectations needed to establish his money demand function. One critic maintained that under rational expectations they should be formed not by past price behavior but by current additions to the money supply. When the data were tested in this way, no stable demand for money could be found (R. L. Jacobs, 1975). In reply, Cagan with Kincaid argued that the public's expectations about future price changes were based on the behavior of prices as they responded to pressures from whatever source: money creation, deficits in the budget, exports or exchange depreciation (Cagan and Kincaid, 1977). By admitting the last two factors into consideration, Cagan gave away some of the monetarist case and moved a distance from pure monetarism to the balance-of-payments position. Sargent and Wallace (1973) tried to restore the monetarism explanation with rational expectations, but this involved discarding the other monetarist assumption about a stable demand function for real money. Rationality required the public to believe that the government, in trying to acquire real resources, will keep on printing money. As prices rise and the government prints more money, the public spends it faster and faster. In this form of the analysis, inflation leads to money creation, not vice versa.

THE COURSE AND CONTROL OF INFLATION AFTER WORLD WAR I

In his book written for the League of Nations during World War II (League of Nations, 1946), Nurkse showed for Germany, but for a wider range of Europe as well, including Poland, Hungary, Austria, and so on, that both balance-of-payments and monetarist positions could be right but in series rather than at the same time. In his generalized discussion, countries of Eastern Europe devastated by war and trying to build new countries had to undertake large expenditures at home. In Poland, for example, a new infrastructure was needed, especially for the railroad system to be fashioned as a unified structure out of the odds and ends of Russian, Austrian, and German remnants. Taxes were limited by the need to build new bureaucracies and practices; foreign borrowing was initially unavailable. The only recourse was the inflation tax, that is, to print money.

In the initial stages, inflation was monetarist. Government deficits and central bank purchases of government securities against currency and deposits were the autonomous factors moving the system and leading to depreciation of the currency. Depreciation, moreover, gave rise to the expectation at home and abroad, not wholly rational perhaps, that decline would be temporary and would be followed by appreciation to the original level. Foreigners bought Polish zlotys, Hungarian pengos, Austrian schillings, and German marks as a speculative investment, in some cases with eleemosynary overtones, to the extent that the country in question was one from which they or their forebears had originated. There was some pure speculation: the French, for example, do not emigrate, but a great many francs were acquired in 1919–20 by foreigners hoping for appreciation. The comment is offered by a historian that they did not want to sell and take their losses and hung on until there was actual panic (Schuker, 1976, p. 67). In Nurkse's analysis (League of Nations, 1946), they held on, perhaps in increasing distress, until expectation of eventual appreciation was conclusively dispelled by some event or events. They then finally reversed positions when realization dawned that the prospect of appreciation was an illusion. Foreigners, and perhaps domestic holders as well, rushed to sell, and the rate plummeted.

In this generalized historical account, in the first stage when the exchange rate is depreciating but domestic assets are being acquired by foreigners, internal inflation proceeds faster than the depreciation, the exchange rate is overvalued, despite its depreciation, there is an import surplus financed by capital inflow, and the monetarist explanation is valid. When expectations are drastically reversed, and foreigners and domestic holders sell domestic currency for foreign exchange, the exchange rate falls faster than domestic prices rise, an export surplus develops as a result of undervaluation of the exchange rate—which export surplus allows some capital to escape the country—and the balance-of-payments explanation comes into its own.

As depreciation and internal inflation accelerate in hyperinflation, after a time central bank printing presses find it impossible to keep up. The real money supply declines. Sooner or later, the domestic population stops using local money as a unit of account and starts pricing in foreign exchange. The old monetary system explodes. People spend nominal balances as fast as possible, unwilling to hold assets shrinking in value.

In the absence of foreign speculation—a capital inflow—the international overvaluation postulated by Nurkse could not take place. An acute observer of foreign exchange history, in fact, has recently claimed that, in the general model, undervaluation occurs in the early stages of inflation with flexible exchange rates and is followed by overvaluation—the exact contrary of the Nurkse model (Bernholz, 1982). Under flexible exchange rates, an initial autonomous capital outflow will drive down the country's currency until either the outflow is cut off by the rising price of foreign exchange or an export surplus develops, which allows it to be transferred abroad. Rising foreign trade prices are communicated to the price level as a whole, and the export surplus, if continued, will raise the money supply. In the later stages of inflation under flexible exchange rates, domestic inflation takes over and accelerates. Prices rise, the currency is overvalued at the old rate, and the trade balance worsens. Bernholz finds striking evidence for this sequence in a series of inflationary episodes, including the Hats and Caps in Sweden and Russian depreciation in the nineteenth century. In neither of these episodes were speculative capital inflows produced as a response to the initial depreciation or reversed themselves in the second stage. In the German case, he seeks to support the model with a table drawn from Bresciani-Turroni, produced here as Table 17.4. The comparison based on 1918 raises questions as to the extent the pegged exchange rate and the subsidized price level were in equilibrium in that year. In the lower part of Table 17.4, a similar problem arises from the choice of a single day, 31 July 1923, as a

Table 17.4 Bank Notes in Circulation, Dollar Exchange Rate and Internal Prices in Germany, 1918–23

	Bank Note Circulation	Internal Prices	Exchange Rate
	(1918 = 1)		
October 1918	1.0	1.0	1.0
October 1919	1.625	2.105	4.07
February 1920	2.039	5.063	15.032
October 1920	2.897	5.412	10.342
May 1921	3.061	5.268	9.44
October 1921	3.734	9.3	22.76
July 1922	7.61	38.699	74.784
October 1922	18.112	206.266	482.357
June 1923	651.119	7040.896	16677.58
	(31 July 1923 = 1)		
31 July 1923	1.0	1.0	1.0
14 August 1923	2.67*	3.913	2.454*
15 September 1923	73.02	206.832†	82.06
23 October 1923	12026.0	85000.0	50763.0
30 October 1923	57339.0‡	109938.0	66031.0‡
30 November 1923	131778.0	853664.6	381679.4

*15 August 1923.
†18 September 1923.
‡31 October 1923.
Source: Bernholz (1982, p. 29, derived from Bresciani-Turroni, 1931 [1937]).

base. There is no basis for judging that this day was representative of the days and weeks immediately before and after it and so serves well as a basis for judging the relative behavior of internal prices and the exchange rate on the dollar during the hyperinflation of 1923. Choice of a different day is likely to have produced a substantially different result.

From 1918 through June 1923, in the upper part of the table, it appears that the Bernholz model with external inflation leading internal, applies to about February 1920. Thereafter to June 1922, internal prices rise faster than the exchange rate, leaving the exchange rate overvalued on the basis of February 1920, if not on that of October 1918. From July 1922, on the other hand, the exchange rate got out ahead of internal prices, and a fortiori of the bank note issue.

Putting the entire account together, one starts with depreciation and undervaluation, which awakened expectations that the exchange rate would rise again. This led to a capital inflow, an import surplus, and overvaluation. The exchange rate recovered, as shown in Figure 17.1, and then stayed relatively steady until the spring of 1921 when the Allies delivered the ultimatum to Germany forcing it to accept the 121 billion gold mark reparation bill. A drastic decline took place to October 1921, after which the rate was relatively steady until June 1922. The Bernholz table, reproduced as Table 17.4, goes straight from October 1921 to the following July and fails to record the break in June. This was the triple shock of the French government, the bankers' committee and the assassination of Rathenau, noted in the previous chapter (see p. 293). The assassination, especially, "shocked persons in Allied countries into thinking more clearly," and the rate on the dollar went from

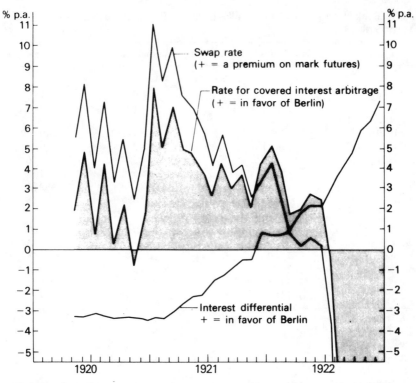

Figure 17.2 Possibilities of covered interest arbitrage between London and Berlin, 1920–22 (on the basis of contemporary private discount rates). Sources: Swap rates calculated on basis of mark forward rates in London: monthly rates for May to December 1920 from J. M. Keynes, The forward market in foreign exchanges, *Manchester Guardian* Commercial Supplement, *Reconstruction in Europe*, 20 April 1922, pp. 11–15; weekly data from January 1921 in Paul Einzig, *The Theory of Forward Exchange* (London: Macmillan, 1937), pp. 449 *ff*. Private discount rate Berlin: *Statistisches Jahrbuch für das Deutsche Reich*, Vol. 43 (Berlin: Statistisches Reichsamt, 1923), p. 269; private discount rate London (three-month bank bills): *Statistical Abstracts for the United Kingdom, 1913-29* (London: HMSO, 1931), p. 205. Taken from Figure 8 in Holtfrerich (1980 [1986], p. 291).

332 to 355 on the day it occurred (Felix, 1971, pp. 173, 175). Overall the exchange rate went from 275 marks to the dollar in May to 370 on 30 June, 400 on 1 July, to 2,000 by August, and 7,000 by November (J. Williamson, 1971, p. 372). The blows of June reversed any lingering expectation that the rate might recover and marked a definite shift from the monetarist to the balance-of-payments explanation of inflation and from an overvalued exchange rate to an undervalued one. Reichsbank deposits and other measures of money supply leaped upward, as Tables 17.1 and 17.2 indicate. Internal and external inflation leapfrogged one another, but the dollar rate went up a multiple of twenty-four times between June and December 1922, whereas the money supply rose sixteen times as measured by currency in circulation, Reichsbank deposits fifteen times, the floating debt five times, and so on.

One further bit of evidence testifies to the importance of June 1922 as the time when expectations about the future of the mark were drastically altered: the behavior of forward exchange rates as shown in Figure 17.2. The data are not nearly as good as analysts would like—with forward rates dug out of records of banks somewhat on the sidelines so that they may not constitute a good sample, and interest rate differentials between London and Berlin complicated by chaos in the latter market and the difficulty of establishing a representative short-term instrument available to all participants in the market. While the data must be regarded with suspicion, they show an unambiguous change in June 1922, when the forward rate on Berlin went from premium to discount, and covered interest arbitrage shifted from inward to outward, despite a rapid rise in the interest differential in favor of Berlin.

Franco-Belgian occupation of the Ruhr is sometimes taken as the turning point in German inflation. It surely was for hyperinflation when stability in the system vanished as government, firms, and households all tried to run deficits simultaneously (in terms of elementary macroeconomics, the $C + I + G$ curve cut the 45 degree line from below and the system exploded). Government provided funds to striking miners by printing it. Tax collections in the Ruhr melted. The system got completely out of control, and the currency was virtually abandoned in favor of transacting in foreign exchange, a practice that had begun as early as October 1922 (Holtfrerich, 1980 [1986], p. 75). People sought foreign currency by all manner of devices. Sailors off foreign ships were mobbed for foreign currency they might sell (Rosenbaum and Sherman (1976 [1979], p. 127). And from a novel:

Jules made his first money selling U.S. telephone books in Germany during the inflation so that all the Schwartzes, all the Finkelsteins, all the Grumbachers, all the Schmidts, all the Epsteins, all the Müllers wrote to their namesakes and begged them to send them a couple of dollars. They buying the telephone books at $2 and selling them for $5 did good business. (Stead, 1938, p. 345)

The account is fiction, but financially informed fiction. At the end, the forces driving up internal inflation faster than exchange depreciation were those who bought goods in Germany and shipped them abroad to acquire foreign funds directly, completely bypassing the foreign exchanges. The choice between internal and external inflation to see which led and which followed ultimately became uninteresting. But the difference between the Nurkse and Bernholz models turns on the expectations (first inelastic, then elastic, first, that is, thinking the currency would come back after falling and then thinking it would not) of foreigners.

FOREIGN HOLDERS OF MARKS

A critical issue between the monetarists and the balance-of-payments theorists is whether there is a difference in the demand for German money between foreign speculators and domestic holders, which latter group, to be sure, may choose to speculate for or against their own currency. Cagan's analysis assumes a single demand for German money, lumping foreign and domestic holders together. Holtfrerich emphasizes the different uses to which the two groups put German money and the alternatives against which they weighed the decision whether to hold it.

Domestic holders needed German money to carry out daily transactions of earning and spending, as well as for any speculative demand; foreign demand for German marks is only to a small extent for transactions in German goods, services, and other assets; the main alternative to German marks was the money of some country other than Germany, plus real or financial assets outside Germany. The McKenna Committee noted that during the five-year period from 1918 to 1923, more than a million individual accounts had been established in Germany for foreigners. These, for the most part, had "not been immediately utilized and had undergone a process of shrinkage through the depreciation of mark values that amounted to veritable evaporation" (*Report of the Second Committee of Experts, 1924* [1925], p. 504). The committee concluded that Germany had benefited from the sale of mark credits by an amount of 7 million to 8 million gold marks, plus selling abroad 600 million to 700 million more gold marks equivalent of German currency, or a total from the two sources of 7.6 billion to 8.7 billion gold marks (ibid., p. 505).

Holtfrerich has pursued the matter into the archives of the committee and the personal working papers of Leonard P. Ayres, an American bank economist serving as an expert on the committee, to observe that foreign deposits of the largest eight banks in Germany constituted 20 percent of all deposits in December 1918, 35 to 36 percent in the three Decembers succeeding that date, but declined from 36 to 11 percent between 1922 and the end of 1923, underlining the difference in behavior of foreign and domestic holders of mark balances (1980 [1986], p. 287).

This view of the role of foreign attitudes toward the mark does not go undisputed. In a comment on a paper by Holtfrerich in 1979, Jean Debeir, in particular, challenged the idea that one can usefully distinguish between foreign and domestic holders of a national money. Foreigners, for example, include foreign branches of German banks, which respond to the view of their head offices; domestic marks in Germany similarly include those belonging to the branches in the country of foreign banks. Some mark deposits of foreigners may be covered by foreign exchange held by German banks (1982, pp. 133–34). Foreign and domestic holders of marks read the same news on wire services and, insofar as they are sophisticated, money dealers are likely to form the same sets of expectations. In such circumstances, it is futile to separate domestic from foreign holders; in fact, the tendency to regard speculation as foreign is present in all countries and part of xenophobic myth.

This may, however, be another case (such as that noted in Chapter 15, p. 267) in which participants in a speculative market should be divided into groups: sophisticated speculators, on the one hand, where Debeir is undoubtedly right that differences between Germans and foreigners are not great; and the outside, unsophisticated mass, where few Germans put money abroad in the early postwar period, and a very large number of foreigners bought marks after the original decline because they thought, or hoped, the rate would recover. Americans had the lion's share of mark holdings. Their losses were estimated by Ayres at $770 million or 3.2 billion gold marks (Holtfrerich, 1980 [1986], p. 287). Of the million mark accounts, if that estimate is correct as to order of magnitude, only a small proportion can have belonged to banks, bankers, dealers, and sophisticated speculators. To insist that the demand for mark currency as deposits is the same for the large outside group as for Germans is understandable in a school that is unwilling to divide speculators into groups and insists, on a priori grounds, that speculation is always stabilizing. A loss of $770 million—again assuming that the number is approximately correct as an order of magnitude—is proof of destabilizing speculation, buying high and selling low, or even not selling at all as values decline to zero, but certainly, after June 1922, not buying any more. According to legend, the game rooms of Milwaukee and Chicago in the late 1920s were papered with German currency and bonds.

During the second half of the 1920s, following the success of the American *tranche* of the Dawes loan, American investors and banks loaned $3 billion to Germany. The movement began in bonds, but when the Wall Street stock market boom started in the spring of 1928, German borrowers turned to bank loans. Like speculation in German currency and deposits from 1919 to 1922, all ended in partial or complete default (McNeill, 1986). Thus Americans "paid reparations" to Germany (Schuker, 1988).

OTHER COUNTRIES

In our formulation, Hungary lies outside the range of Western Europe, but one can observe the same phenomenon of a two-stage inflation in that country—one stage in which expectations about the exchange rate at home, but especially abroad, were inelastic, that is, as the rate depreciated, people thought that it would return to its old level, followed by a stage in which expectations were reversed and turned elastic, with the market concluding that decline in the rate was a signal that there would be further decline (League of Nations [Nurske], 1946, pp. 65–68). In the first stage, the monetarist view of inflation was correct; the exchange rate was overvalued, creating an import surplus finance by a capital inflow. After reversal in expectations, sales of pengos by foreigners and domestic holders plunged the exchange rate down, raising internal prices, extending the governmental deficit, and enlarging the money supply at galloping rates that ended four years after the start in hyperinflation. For this second part of the process, the balance-of-payments explanation was valid.

Of particular interest is that the stage of hyperinflation that took four years to attain after World War I was reached in thirteen months after World War II. Once bitten, twice shy: the market had learned from the first experience and was much more sophisticated (Nogaro, 1948). It is one of the disabilities of social science that experiments cannot be repeated because the necessary material has been altered by the first effort.

The Austrian problem after World War I was particularly critical since the old Austro-Hungarian Empire had much of its hinterland lopped off and formed into new states—Hungary, Czechoslovakia, Poland, Yugoslavia, Rumania, Bulgaria, and so on—leaving Austria a hydrocephalic state—a head without a body. It had limited reparations to pay and the far more difficult task of transforming the country from one that served as the capital of an empire to a small state that had to live by itself presented grave difficulties. The solution—only temporarily successful and collapsing in the 1929 depression—was an internal stabilization effort under international auspices, organized by the Economic and Financial Department of the League of Nations, and two international stabilization loans. Among the international servants of the effort was Per Jacobsson of Sweden, later economist of the Bank for International Settlements and, still later, managing director of the International Monetary Fund (IMF). The League of Nations staff in Austria can be thought of as a forerunner of IMF stabilization advice to countries with balance-of-payments and stabilization problems after World War II. The economist staff of the Economic and Financial Department of the League of Nations in the interwar period, organized under Sir Arthur Salter and then Alexander Loveday of Britain, was small as compared with modern international institutions, but unsurpassed for quality, including John Condliffe, Gottfried Haberler, Folke Hilgerdt, Martin Hill, James Meade, Ragnar Nurkse, Bertil Ohlin, and Jan Tinbergen—all, but Meade, from small countries such as Australia, Austria, Latvia, the Netherlands, New Zealand, and Sweden, three of those that survived beyond 1968 winning the Nobel prize in economics established only in that year, the three hundredth anniversary of the foundation of the Riksbank.

A distinction of interest is drawn by Edouard März, the late Austrian economic historian, between the stabilization effort in which the proceeds of the League of Nations loan were doled out piecemeal by the league commissioner for purely financial purposes, while Marshall Plan assistance, almost thirty-five years later, put the emphasis on real investment (1982, p. 190).

SOCIAL ASPECTS OF GERMAN INFLATION

Even on the monetarist interpretation of German inflation that surely applies to considerable parts of the period, especially from early 1920 to the spring of 1921, and again in the spring of 1922, the question may be asked as to whether the authorities had a wide range of policy choice—the government as to whether to balance the budget, the Reichsbank as to how much of government debt to monetize. Do monetary and fiscal authorities make decisions on policy on the basis of free selection from a wide variety of alternatives, so that inflation is the result of mistakes in policy, or are they hemmed in, pressured, and constrained by forceful political interests in society? Did Helfferich, as finance minister during the war, have the option of a much higher level of taxes, which would have left less inflammable material about after the war? Did Havenstein, the postwar president of the Reichsbank from 1921 to 1923, have carte blanche?

Keynes has written cogently on this subject. In *A Revision of the Treaty* published in early 1922, he wondered whether any German government could balance the budget:

Once this issue is faced . . . the struggle will be bitter and violent for it will present itself to each of the contending interests as an affair of life and death. The most powerful influences and motives of self-interest and self-preservation will be engaged. Conflicting conceptions of the end and nature of society will be ranged in the conflict. A government which makes a serious attempt to cover its liabilities will inevitably fall from power. (1922, p. 55, quoted by Malamud, 1980)

In the *Tract on Monetary Reform* of 1924, Keynes pointed out that inflation was a struggle between the active and working elements in the community and the *rentier* or bondholding class, in which, after a war, the former resist handing over to the latter more than a certain proportion of national output. To restore the currency to par is to make fixed charges on the national debt unsupportable. The alternatives then are repudiation—a violation of the implicit contract entered into during the war—a capital levy, or currency depreciation. Capital levy, he suggests, is resisted, and has never been tried on a large scale (1924, p. 72). Certainly it was proposed frequently in Germany after World War I, as in Britain after the Napoleonic Wars. Socialist draft legislation provided for an *Erfassung der Sachwerte* (seizure of real assets). One form of capital levy called for a mortgage on all real property, another for turning over to the state a portion of the shares of existing enterprise. The Reichstag would not accept any such capital levy as a solution to the state's difficulties even as late as 1923 (J. Williamson, 1971, pp. 358–60, 380).

Keynes is impressed that it is impossible to impose a capital levy that he thinks more expedient and just but relatively easy to expropriate the bondholder by currency depreciation—in this context both internal and external. Medium fortunes lost half their real value in Britain, seven-eighths in France, eleven-twelfths in Italy, and virtually the whole in Germany and the succession states of Austria and Hungary. "Small savers suffer quietly, as experience shows, these enormous depreciations . . . when they would throw out a government which had taken from them a fraction of the amount by more deliberate and juster methods" (1924, pp. 16, 71–72). This is an assertion that "wealth illusion" exists.

Lacking in Keynes's analysis, which regards currency depreciation as equivalent to a capital levy, is the distinction between wealth in real form and equity ownership, on the one hand, and fixed claims of bondholders, on the other. That distinction was not lost on the Socialists, as the concept of a capital levy as an *Erfassung der Sachwerte* makes clear. Currency depreciation wipes out the *rentier* but leaves owners of real property and equities intact, or even better off because of the elimination of their liabilities. In a classic book, Alexander Gerschenkron (1943) has shown how the landowning Junker class survived war, peace, deflation, inflation, and all sorts of tribulations (until the territorial settlement after World War II). In the iron and steel industry, inflation suited the interests of the Thyssens and Stinnes, despite the rise in wages, as they paid off their debts and invested heavily in new plant (Feldman, 1977).

The research of Holtfrerich, however, shows that the distribution of income and wealth was narrowed in Germany as a result of the inflation rather than widened, as many opinions, both Marxist and non-Marxist, had held. The ratio of skilled wages to those of common labor narrowed from 145 percent in 1913 to 106 percent in 1923; wages of high governmental officials fell more than 60 percent in real terms, whereas junior officials lost only 30 percent (1980 [1986], p. 235). The view that the middle class lost out to the proletariat and the rich owner of enterprise is supported if one thinks of skilled labor and the bureaucracy as the middle class, but middle-size business and middle-size farmers gained on balance. The *rentier* class suffered: incomes from interest and rent fell from roughly 15 percent of national income in 1913 to less than 3 percent in 1925 (ibid., p. 268).

But these are outcomes: what was critical was that the postwar position made it necessary for sectors in society to struggle over income distribution, including within that general question, the issue of whether deflation and unemployment would saddle a major share of the load on the working class, as contrasted with the *rentier*. Keynes observed in 1922 that the choice between inflation or deflation comes down to an agonizing outcome of a struggle among interest groups, although he put it the other way around:

If the present exchange depreciation persists and the internal price level becomes adjusted to it, the resulting distribution of wealth between classes will amount to a social catastrophe. If, on the other hand, there is a recovery in the exchange, the cessation of the artificial stimulus to industry . . . based on the depreciating mark may lead to a financial catastrophe. (1922, p. 105)

STRUCTURAL INFLATION

This view approaches today's social theory of inflation, which is sometimes called structural (Hirsch and Goldthorpe, eds., 1978). One hundred percent of the population wants 110 percent of national income. Various sectors have monopoly power—ability to tax or print money for government, ability to raise prices for farmers and for business enterprise, ability to raise wages for labor. In today's version, *rentiers* can raise their interest return, but only on new saving contracts. In the circumstance, social harmony is achieved briefly by allowing a balance-of-payments deficit of 10 percent of national income by issuing 110 percent of national income in money terms until this is frustrated by running out of reserves and depreciation of the exchange rate. Or one can start from equilibrium, in which each interest is content with its share of national income, and impose a new burden. Inflation takes place as each group tries to resist any portion of the burden falling on it. The resistance of separate groups may include resistance to taxation, in which case the government, in order to maintain its share of real output, runs deficits and prints money.

Fundamental to the analysis is that inflation can be stopped if one sector of society—say, the *rentier*—is weak and the burden is not too large. It can then be dumped on the weak sister. Deflation may also win out if unemployment and wage reductions can be imposed upon labor. The issue can be postponed if foreigners fail to recognize what is going on and contribute real resources in the form of capital inflow. When that contribution stops, however, and foreign investors plus domestic owners of liquid wealth change their expectations and try to escape, the monetary system must be discarded in favor of a new one.

What this analysis concludes is that the German hyperinflation of 1921–23 was much more than a financial phenomenon and had deep roots in the sociopolitical condition of the German peoples, unwilling to bear the burdens of war, reparations, or supporting their compatriots in the Ruhr by explicit sharing decisions, but rather printing money and letting the chaotic inflation tax decide the outcome (Olson, 1987).

'The Fruits of Labor.'

Cartoon by George Grosz (1923), from Imre Hofbauer (ed.), *George Grosz* (London: Nicholson & Watson, 1948), p. 58.

THE RENTENMARK

As early as October 1922 it was apparent that the mark no longer served the functions of money as store of value and unit of account. The country started to spend marks as fast as they were received, on occasion daily and even twice daily, and to fix prices in marks on the basis of the exchange rate on the dollar. With the occupation of the Ruhr in January 1923, the position worsened, and steps began to be taken to substitute a new German money for the mark. The first proposal from Helfferich was for a Roggenmark (rye mark, or mark based on a fixed quantity of grain). There is a long history of proposals for currencies based on commodity reserves that comes down to the present day, but this did not appeal to the German government of 1923 on the ground that the rye crop is highly variable, and consequently so is the price, so that the grain would not serve well as currency reserve. In October 1923 the Socialist financial theorist, Rudolf Hilferding, who was finance minister in a Stresemann cabinet, proposed a Gold Note Bank, to be equipped with 180 million gold marks and empowered to issue twice that amount in bank notes. This amount was clearly too small in relation to a currency that had been 6 billion in 1914. Hans Luther, who succeeded Hilferding as finance minister, then combined the Helfferich and Hilferding plans into one and produced the Rentenbank and the Rentenmark. The operation was managed by Hjalmar Schacht of the Reichsbank.

The intention was to produce a transitional currency to replace the thoroughly discredited mark. In the absence of sufficient gold and the presence of highly variable harvests of rye, it was decided to substitute the productive land of Germany as backing for the new currency, in the form of a mortgage on that land to the amount of 3.2 billion gold marks. The value of the farm and industrial property was determined on the basis of the 1913 *Wehrbeitrag,* a modest capital levy. The holder of the mortgage was a new central bank, the Deutsche Rentenbank, independent of the government. The Reichsbank stopped issuing currency, and the Rentenbank took over the outstanding enormous issue at the rate of 1 billion marks for 1 Rentenmark. Of the 2.4 billion Rentenmarks put out, half went to the government and half to the public. In due course, this circulation was raised to the total value of the mortgage, that is, 3.2 billion (Born, 1977, pp. 420–21).

Success has many fathers; failure is an orphan. The several political parties in Germany pushed the claims for authorship of the Rentenmarks, each for a separate candidate: the Socialists behind Hilferding, the German National People's Party behind Helfferich. The German Democratic party backed the claims of Schacht and the German People's party those of Luther. Luther in his memoirs gives a provenance that sounds more plausible. He claims that the idea came from a civil servant, later a state secretary in the Ministry of Justice, one Franz Schegelberger (Pentzlin, 1980, pp. 30–31).

The Rentenbank invites comparison with the English National Land Bank, which existed briefly before the formation of the Bank of England (Richards, 1965, pp. 116ff.), with John Law's Banque Royale and its land in Louisiana, and with the *assignats* (see pp. 98–100, 101). None made a great success, but in the emergency produced by hyperinflation, some action had to be taken. Helfferich felt that the difference between the *assignats* and the Rentenmark was that the former were assignable to specific plots of land, whereas the latter were not (J. Williamson, 1971, p. 388). The point is without interest. The major difference from the French experience was that after the explosion of the mark, the German government began to balance its budget in the new medium, without the disastrous lag in hyperinflation between expenditure and receipt of taxes and the Rentenbank restricted the issue of currency as the French had not (Franco, 1990, esp. p. 183). Very shortly there was an inflow of capital again, helped by the success of the Dawes loan. The struggle over distribution of income and wealth had been temporarily resolved, or pushed aside. Stinnes, the steel company, after flourishing through inflation, failed in 1925 under stabilization and had to be reorganized. Hyperinflation proved an exhausting climax, but it furnished the basis for a new start.

The mortgage on agricultural and industrial land that constituted the only asset of the Deutsche Rentenbank was not very different from a capital levy, which the Reichstag had continuously rejected. In the exhaustion of wiping out the old currency and issuing a new, the similarity was hardly noticed. Even Helfferich, who had bitterly opposed a capital levy, claimed credit for the Rentenmark. The mortgage of 3.2 billion gold marks, however, was a small proportion of German wealth estimated at some 150 billion gold marks, down from 310 billion in 1913 (Holtfrerich, 1980 [1986], p. 27, esp. fn. 6/30). In 1948, in the monetary reform after World War II, the level of the mortgage on real property, including structures as well as land, was to be 50 percent, and on financial assets 90 percent. But on this occasion the wealth destroyed by war had been a far greater fraction than half.

THE GOLDDISKONTOBANK

One curiosity produced by the dying days of hyperinflation was a new bank, a subsidiary of the Reichsbank, needed to finance foreign trade in stable currency since the mark could no longer serve in that capacity. Its capital was denominated in foreign exchange, that is, as 10 million British pounds of which only 1.25 million was paid in. The bank played a minor role in international trade until 1931, when it blossomed briefly as a sort of Reconstruction Finance Corporation to assist banks in the deflation of that year. In the same year it changed its capitalization from pounds sterling to 200 million Reichsmarks, this before 21 September when the pound went off gold (Born, 1977, p. 465).

COLLECTIVE MEMORY

How much reparations laid down in the Versailles treaty, French occupation of the Ruhr, the hyperinflation that wiped out the upper middle class of *rentiers* and officials, and unemployment from 1928 to 1932 each contributed to the collapse of the Weimar Republic and the rise of the Nazi party to power in Germany in 1933 is a question on which it is easy to have opinions but hard to have assurance. To a considerable extent, the phenomena were interrelated. What is clear, however, is that the impact of inflation on the German psyche went deep. In 1931 the left wing of the German political spectrum was firmly opposed to changing the exchange rate, even if only to devalue in consonance with the pound sterling and avoid the deflationary pressure of Reichsmark appreciation. In debate with Wladimir Woytinsky, Hilferding regarded the former's position that depreciation would help with exports and unemployment as "nonsense" (Woytinsky, 1961, p. 467). The Socialists hammered away at the slogan "no tampering with the currency," as labor remembered the race between wages and inflation, and trade union officials recalled how union funds had evaporated overnight (Sturmthal, 1943, pp. 87–88).

The memory was still strong after World War II, more than half a century after the event. The German trade-off between inflation and unemployment was very different from that of the British, who had suffered in the 1920s from unemployment and deflation, as we explore in the chapter that follows. Like the Mississippi Bubble of John Law, which put the French off banks for more than a hundred years, these experiences shaped policy choices for periods of time measured in half-centuries, whereas the ordinary financial crisis takes a population a mere decade to forget and enter happily into another. A question to be addressed in Chapter 22, moreover, is whether the successful coping with the aftermath of the much more severe World War II was the result of policy lessons learned in the 1919–23 inflation or of a different objective situation of the interest groups involved.

SUGGESTED SUPPLEMENTARY READING

Bresciani-Turroni (1931 [1937], *The Economics of Inflation.*
Cagan (1956), The monetary dynamics of hyperinflation.
Holtfrerich (1980 [1986], *The German Inflation, 1914–1923.*
Laursen and Pedersen (1964), *The German Inflation, 1918–23.*
McNeill (1986), *American Money and the Weimar Republic.*

18

The Restoration of the Pound to Par

If the economic and, in particular, the monetary problems we are facing today have a startling resemblance to those which were the subject of contention for two generations a century ago, the experience of the Napoleonic and post-Napoleonic days has an interest for us in two respects. The two periods illuminate one another, and we can pass from the depreciated exchanges of 1797–1819 to those of 1914–1925 . . . with the feeling that our comprehension of the past and present is increased by comparing one with the other.

(Gregory, introduction to Tooke and Newmarch, *A History of Prices,* 1838 [1928], Vol. 1, p. 8)

GETTING BRITISH FINANCE UNDER CONTROL

At the end of the war, the British money market, like the French and the German, was awash with liquidity. Half the war had been financed by deficits, and these had been monetized to a considerable extent. The national debt had risen from £650 million to £7,800 million. Almost one-third of the debt matured in five years or less and one-fifth within three months. The struggle to control the national budget and contain the debt was to last three years (Moggridge, 1972, p. 24). In that period, governmental expenditure fell by 60 percent and taxation rose 27 percent, together turning a deficit amounting to £1,690 million, or 65 percent of total expenditure in the fiscal year 1918–19 into a small surplus by 1920–21. Debt under five years fell from one-third of the total to one-fifth. Bank deposits fell by 2 percent and currency in circulation by 14 percent. In March 1919 the Bank of England ceased providing official support for the pound. In December 1919 the Treasury switched from a system of issuing Treasury bills "on tap," that is, borrowing at short term by continuously feeding three-month bills into the market in a steady stream, to a weekly tender or auction in which a stated amount of bills is sold on a specific day to the highest bidder.

THE 1919–20 BOOM

Mopping up excess liquidity took time; meanwhile there was enough to finance a sizable boom. From the armistice in November 1918 to the end of April 1919, business in Britain paused for breath and then took off in an expansion that lasted until the summer of 1920 and fell back in early 1921. The period has been characterized as "frenzied finance" (Youngson, 1960, p. 44). The "displacement," to use the jargon of Chapter 15, was the realization that German competition had been knocked out—for a time—in coal, steel, shipbuilding, shipping, and cotton textiles on the Continent. Restocking the economy drove the prices of raw materials and semifinished goods sky high, a movement that spread to the market for capital assets. Prices for houses rose sharply, as rentals became unavailable because of rent controls.

A wave of mergers took place in steel and cotton textiles. In 1918 the United Steel Company was formed from a number of smaller enterprises and expanded still further in 1920 to create United Steel Corporation Group. The Amalgamated Cotton Mills Trust was put together in 1919, Crosses & Heaton and Joshua Hoyle & Sons in 1920. Excitement ran parallel to that immediately after other wars—1763 in Holland and London, 1816 in Britain, 1871 in Berlin and Vienna. In March 1920 at close to the peak, cotton mills were bought and transformed into new companies at £4 a spindle, when the current cost of installation was £3 and prewar capitalization had run at £1.

Thirty new companies in shipping were floated in a single month with £4 million in capital. Experienced shipowners sold; ignorant bought, financing acquisitions with bank loans. In 1921 after the bubble had burst, ships that had been bought for £24 10s a ton were down to £5 10s (Youngson, 1960, p. 45). Kleinworts, a banking house that helped finance the boom, and especially to promote integration backward from shipbuilding into steel and coal, found itself involved for the next thirty years, with no successes to show for it (Diaper, 1990).

Capital costs in steel had been £4 to £4 10s a ton of capacity in 1890 and had worked up to £6 10s to £7 by 1910. After the war there was a leap to £10 and £12 a ton. Most takeovers and mergers were financed by banks, which, when the loans were slow to be paid off, ended up owning debentures or even shares. They were forced to take an interest in industry that their experience had not equipped them to do, except in the brief flurry of finance companies that ended in 1866. Bank advances rose 81 percent from January 1919 to April 1920, or by £385 million, and there was another £50 million increase in commercial bills discounted. Students of the period note that the credit policy of the banks was in no way conservative and that it was spurred by a competitive spirit (W. A. Thomas, 1978, pp. 60–61; Tolliday, 1987, p. 177). Of the borrowing companies, United Steel, in particular, took on heavy liabilities in interest and preference dividends, with the consequence that the whole decade of the 1920s was dominated by a struggle for cash to pay debt charges (Andrews and Brunner, 1951, p. 80).

Speculative excitement from the spring of 1919 to the summer of 1920 led to overcapitalization in a number of British industries. This, combined with the return of the pound sterling to par, were the causes of the slump from the end of 1920 and early 1921 to 1923, and of doldrums that extended all the way to 1931. The reader is warned against overstating the position. Difficulties were largely concentrated in traditional industries—coal, cotton, ships, and steel—and located in parts of the country, largely the north and Scotland and Wales, that came to be known as "depressed areas." On the other hand, new industries sprang up in the south, near London, in automobiles, electrical equipment, other durable consumers' goods, and chemicals, with a considerable gain in productivity, and some growth in national income, as labor slowly transferred from old industries and locations to new (Kahn, 1946; Sayers, 1950).

Having risen 40 percent from January 1919 to a peak in 1920, wholesale prices then fell sharply by 50 percent to January 1922, with the cost of living declining by half as well, and wages almost as much—38 percent between January 1921 and December 1922. Helping to compress wages were sliding-scale agreements under existing union contracts that were symmetrical and—for the last time—worked in both directions. Jørgen Pedersen and I have asserted that if a lender of last resort had acted to halt the downward plunge of prices, ensuing difficulties would have been reduced (Pedersen, 1961 [1975], p. 188; Kindleberger, 1978*b* [1989], p. 214). This view is not shared by Moggridge, who maintains rather that the difficulties of the postwar period in Britain were structural, not a product of financial crisis or inadequate liquidity during the crash, and that what was needed was a program of reconstruction assistance of the character of the Marshall Plan after World War II (1982, p. 176).

Milton Friedman and Anna Schwartz claim that the 1920–21 depression origi-nated in the United States, as proved by the gain in gold in that country during the period (1963, p. 360). The same claim is later made for 1929 (ibid., ch. 10; Schwartz, 1981, pp. 21–24). The test is satisfactory in neither instance. Prices rose sharply in a bubble worldwide in the rush to rebuild stocks. Which countries gained or lost gold was determined less by changes in income and current accounts in bal-ances of payments than by capital flows, only loosely connected with the question of identifying the initial source of the crisis—an exercise of no particular interest or value. Prices rose worldwide because of limited output and an upswing of demand; they fell when it was clear that liquidity had been strained and that production had responded quickly, even in excessive measure. The British depression was exacer-bated by the bubble in security prices based on rosy prospects for exports that were quickly dashed by a strike of coal miners in the second quarter of 1921, the forward surge of Scandinavian shipbuilding to fill the gap left by German decline, and the rise of cotton-textile production and consequent exports in Japan and India.

The foregoing is the conventional view shared by Keynesians and monetarists—that the 1919 depression was demand led. Three other points are worth making, however. First, the eight-hour day came into being in Europe at the end of the war, not only in the victors—France and Britain, as in the United States—but also in Germany. Connected with this general movement was a number of Communist-led strikes. Second, J. A. Dowie has shown that while weekly wages rates rose in Britain less slowly than the cost of living, hourly wages rose faster, conveying an impression of wage push (1975). Dowie also is impressed by the spurt to prices given by the depreciation of March 1919 when the peg in the dollar-sterling rate was let go. This gave a fillip to the rise of wholesale prices in Great Britain, compared with the United States, widening the spread from 107 in April 1919 to 123 in December of the same year (ibid., p. 447).

The third element of less than straightforward demand-pull based on restocking, booming export markets and easy credit is a series of dark hints that the Soviet Union was trying to undermine capitalism through inflation by one means or another. Keynes quoted Lenin to the effect that inflation was the surest way of defeating the capitalist system, although it is impossible to find a statement to that effect in Lenin's writings (Fetter, 1977). The period was one of great nervousness over bolshevism in the face of demobilization and industrial unrest, and there is journalistic evidence that Communist sympathizers were hopeful that their cause would gain through inflation. It is most unlikely that the Soviet Union or its agents could have contributed to inflation in Western Europe, despite rumors of their counterfeiting Western currencies. A competent economic historian, H. R. C. Wright, engaged in looking into the question, found some smoke but no fire.

THE CUNLIFFE REPORT

As early as January 1918, well before the end of the war was clearly in view, the British government appointed a Committee on Currency and Foreign Exchanges after the War, under the leadership of Lord Cunliffe, then governor of the Bank of England, to chart a path for the restoration of the pound to gold convertibility at the old par rate of £3 17s 10½d per ounce of gold, 0.917 fine. There was no question whether this should be done, or consideration of alternatives such as a floating currency or a return to the gold standard at a higher price for gold and lower price for sterling (Pigou, 1948, p. 68). The questions addressed were: when—at the end of the war or later—and how? In 1931 after the depreciation of the pound sterling in September, Tom Johnston, a Clydedale member of Parliament and editor of the Independent Labour party journal *Forward,* expressed surprise, saying, "They never told us we could do that" (Moggridge, 1969, p. 9). This view somewhat exaggerates the position, as Sayers points out, because there were what some called "devaluation-mongers" as early as November 1921 (1976, Vol. 1, p. 135).

The Cunliffe Committee's report appeared in August 1918 and set out a description of the classic gold standard mechanism of adjustment, with inflows and outflows of gold automatically correcting the balance of payments and maintaining the appropriate supply of money through their effects on prices and trade balances. The committee urged far-reaching withdrawal of government from domination of money and capital markets, a budget surplus that would allow the redemption of debt, and the restoration of an active discount policy at the Bank of England to manage its gold reserve when parity had been restored.

It was recognized that the postwar version of the old standard would have to differ in some particulars from earlier practice because of the rise in prices and the relative shortage of gold as compared with 1913. To economize gold, it was proposed to return to the gold bullion standard, with coin used to settle international imbalances but not freely available internally. This suggestion had originated with David Ricardo after the Napoleonic Wars and been resurrected by Gideon Maria Boissevain, a Frenchman, who won the prize offered by Sir H. M. Meysey Thompson for the best essay on "The money question" at the Paris Monetary Congress of 1889 (Boissevain, 1891 [1977]). As a further measure to economize on gold, it was proposed to encourage lesser money markets to hold their reserves in foreign exchange instead of gold. Ralph G. Hawtrey, a Treasury civil servant, wrote an article urging adoption of what came to be known as the gold exchange standard (1922). The Bank of England tried to persuade the world to adopt this at the Genoa Conference of the spring of 1922. An earlier conference on international financial questions had been held in Brussels in 1920.

BRUSSELS CONFERENCE, 1920

In the summer of 1920, the Council of the League of Nations issued a call for an international financial conference to be held at Brussels. Originally scheduled for 23 July of that year, it was finally held from 24 September to 8 October. Thirty-four countries were represented, not only members of the league but also a number of ex-enemy countries and newer states. The United States sent an observer. Papers were presented by a number of financial experts—by Professor Gustav Cassel on exchange stabilization and the purchasing power parity theory of the foreign exchanges; by M. Delacroix, a former Belgian prime minister and minister of finance, who proposed the establishment of an international bank of issue, which would exchange interest-bearing gold bonds for genuine securities of European states, furnished to it with satisfactory guarantees, thus intermediating between investors to whom the countries acquiring gold bonds sold them and the borrowing states; and, finally, by A. C. Pigou, Cambridge economics professor, on the difficulties of floating international loans in the disturbed circumstances of the period. Four committees were constituted in fields of public finance, currency and exchange, international trade, and international credits. The final outcome was a recommendation to the League of Nations Council, based on a scheme of M. Ter Meulen of Hope & Company in Holland, for governments in Europe to borrow on the basis of guarantees provided by certain assets, which would be segregated as surety for the lender.

The recommendation of the Brussels Conference to the League of Nations resulted in no action of any kind. The same outcome would be repeated in the World Economic Conference of 1933 when numerous creative ideas were put forward, especially by the smaller countries, for nations of the world to establish innovative sorts of banks to finance trade and investment. Then, as earlier, no such proposals came from the countries—the United States and France in 1933—with resources sufficient to carry them to fruition.

It was recognized early at the Brussels Conference that no settlement of the issues at stake was likely when the amount and method of paying German reparations had not been determined and when questions of reparations and inter-Allied debts were excluded from consideration (*Federal Reserve Bulletin*, 1920, p. 1277). In addition, the American observer accurately conveyed the sentiment of the United States, which was unhelpful. On 28 September, early in the deliberations, he reminded the delegates of the negative attitude of the former secretary of the treasury, Carter Glass, confirmed by his successor, Mr. Houston, that aid in the form of credit or otherwise from the United States was not to be forthcoming.

I do not go beyond my authority for a statement of our governmental position with regard to the possibility of Government loans and refer you to those authorized statements. Beyond that there will always be the friendly and charitable spirit of the American people; that has been enormous, it continues, and my personal faith is that it will continue, and yet, after all, the result of charity can be but small. Further, there is the possibility of relations in the ordinary business way. America is a business nation. America is always ready for business, and America will be ready to do business even more than she is now doing with Europe whenever conditions are such that business can be done, but at present it is my personal view that Americans will find it difficult to convince themselves in large numbers and to great amounts that Europe under present conditions is a good business risk. I ask you, gentlemen, to bear in mind that Americans as a whole have never accustomed themselves to sending their money into foreign countries. . . . We . . . have always found opportunities for investment at home and have never grown into the habit of sending our money abroad. (Ibid., p. 1292)

It would be hard to find a more discouraging statement, a more accurate one, or one that contrasts so completely with the attitude of the United States after World War II.

GENOA CONFERENCE, 1922

It was not the League of Nations but France and Britain that sponsored the Genoa Conference in the spring of 1922 in order to obtain the participation of the United States. The meeting was designed partly with an eye to international economic recovery from the recession of 1921 and partly to plan for resumption of the gold standard. Again, thirty-four countries attended, mostly European, with Germany and Russia (which had not been present at Brussels) for the first time on the basis of equality—but, in the event, not the United States, which continued to be fearful of involvement in European political affairs. A British draft presented to the conference had been amended and cleared in advance by experts from Belgium, France, Italy, and Japan and provided for the gold bullion standard, with foreign exchange held along with gold in central bank reserves. It was proposed that major countries would hold their reserves entirely in gold, while other countries would be encouraged to hold foreign exchange claims on gold centers. The Belgians greeted this agreement with enthusiasm, contemplating that after their currency had been restored to convertibility, Brussels could hope to become a gold center (Van der Wee and Tavernier, 1975, p. 87). Gold centers were expected to cooperate with one another so as to coordinate the demand for gold and prevent undue fluctuations in its purchasing power. Some countries, it was recognized, would be unable to reestablish old gold parities, although all were encouraged to fix some parity. The Bank of England was asked to convene a meeting of central bankers to work out an international convention to translate the principles into practical rules. It was especially hoped that the United States would participate in this effort (Clarke, 1973, pp. 5–14).

THE GOLD EXCHANGE STANDARD

At the time of Genoa, the gold exchange standard was regarded as a new concept. Research by Peter Lindert shows, however, that it was already widely established by 1913. Foreign exchange reserves were calculated on various bases, the most comprehensive of which produced a world total of $1.6 billion in 1913, as compared with world gold reserves for the same year of $4.9 billion (Lindert, 1969, pp. 23–25). Lindert regarded the increasing tendency for the world to hold sterling as an indication of Britain's rising deficit in international payments rather than as the outcome of a normal and healthy process of international financial intermediation in which countries chose to use the same money as a store of value that they employed as a medium of exchange, and borrowed at long term when necessary to replenish foreign exchange reserves—that is, borrowing long and lending short when the City of London lent long and borrowed short. (In the case of the dominions, the process was one of continuously borrowing short to finance imports and then, from time to time, refunding the accumulated short-term obligations into long-term loans.) Whether the case of 1913 is regarded as international financial intermediation or a rising deficit in the British balance of payments, there can be no doubt that there is a sharp difference between a situation in which countries hold a foreign currency automatically and as a natural outgrowth of their spending patterns, on the one hand, and one where the country on which claims are held applies persuasion or pressure to get them to do so, as Britain was doing in the 1920s and the United States, in turn, would do in the 1960s.

The Genoa Conference, like Brussels, failed to achieve a lasting result, and for broadly the same reasons set out in the last two chapters in connection with reparations, war debts, and the collapse of the mark after June 1922—the difficulty of finding a middle ground on which various countries objectives could be reconciled and compromised. About this time, Benjamin Strong, governor of the Federal Reserve Bank of New York, began to wonder whether central bankers of different languages, customs, and beliefs, and with different problems—each of whom had to give first priority to his home mission—could ever cooperate. As an alternative he wondered whether it might not be a superior strategy to think in terms of key currencies to be stabilized one at a time (Clarke, 1967, pp. 40–41). Nor did failure of the Genoa Conference to produce a follow-up convention drawn by central bankers stop further steps to restore the pound to par.

By way of parenthesis, the "key currency" concept was developed fully after World War II by John H. Williams, Harvard University economist and vice-president of the Federal Reserve Bank of New York, in opposition to the Bretton Woods legislation authorizing the United States to participate in the World Bank and the International Monetary Fund. Like the Genoa Conference, Bretton Woods was an attempt to repair the entire international monetary system at one fell swoop. Williams favored the one-at-a-time approach, which he termed "key currency" (1947 [1978]). He had used the expression "key countries" as a member of the Preparatory Commission of Experts before another global effort, the World Economic Conference of 1933 (*Documents diplomatiques français,* 1966, Vol. 2, p. 386). Clarke's use of the term "key currencies" in his 1967 book about 1922 may have represented current vocabulary at the time of writing. Although the discussion based more closely on Strong's papers in 1922 does not use the expression, the meaning is the same, especially, "Countries should be treated individually, or, at most, in groups whose problems were similar" (Clarke, 1973, p. 15). One could perhaps argue, however, against "groups whose problems are similar" being treated together, in favor of groups of countries with strong financial interconnections.

If the reader will indulge further extension of the parenthesis, note that there was no criticism of the gold exchange standard in the 1920s similar to those of Jacques Rueff or Robert Triffin after World War II. They characterized it as (1) a swindle in which financial centers buy up goods, services, and assets from the outside world and pay for them with claims on themselves, which they have no intention of requiting (Rueff and Hirsch, 1965); or (2) as an "absurdity" since it involves countries in piling up deficits to provide additions to reserves of the system, with a consequent shortfall of liquidity when these countries correct their balances of payments (Triffin, 1958). I accept neither of these criticisms, which ignore international financial intermediation of the sort that occurs widely and is approved within countries, and believe that the difficulty with the gold exchange standard lies rather in its instability because of Gresham's law (Kindleberger, 1981*a*, pp. 63–64, 287–89). But this is not the place to make the case.

THE CHAMBERLAIN-BRADBURY COMMITTEE

A Labour government took power for the first time in British history in the fall of 1923 on an issue of tariffs. The Conservatives, bemused by the attraction of empire preference, were contemplating departure from the traditional British position of free trade and raising tariffs in order to have something to lower in favor of the commonwealth. The country chose to stay with free trade and voted the Conservatives out, Labour in. The exchange rate, which had risen to $4.63 at the end of 1922 and $4.70 in January 1923 with the French and Belgian occupation of the Ruhr, because of a flight of French capital from Paris to London, now fell to $4.30 as it was felt that the Labour government would take unsound financial measures to combat rising unemployment. In February 1924, however, the Labour government announced its adherence to the principles of the Cunliffe Report, and the downward movement in the exchange rate was halted. At this stage the Bank of England pressed the government to appoint a committee of experts under the chairmanship of Austen Chamberlain, followed in the chair, when Chamberlain became foreign minister, by Lord Bradbury, to make recommendations on two questions: (1) how to consolidate the Treasury notes (Bradburys) with the Bank of England fiduciary issue when the time came to do so and (2) what to do when the Gold and Silver Act expired at the end of 1925. The committee took testimony from many witnesses, among them Keynes and McKenna, who alone opposed a return to par.

Keynes argued against the deflation needed to return the pound to par on the ground, expressed in the *Tract on Monetary Reform* (1924), that it would transfer wealth from the taxpayer and worker to the *rentier*. While he would have preferred a managed currency, he recognized that this possibility was unlikely to be accepted and argued, for the most part, for postponement or, if that were unacceptable, for devaluation, that is, a return to gold convertibility at a price for gold tied to existing exchange rates and commodity prices. His testimony was not entirely consistent. At one point he opposed revaluation to par on the ground that it would be inflationary. Adoption of the gold standard would turn management of the British price level over to American authorities. If the United Kingdom lost gold to New York, inflation would result there and be communicated back to Britain. The argument evoked a proposal, which had been seriously put forward in 1923, deliberately to ship $100 million in gold to the United States to cause inflation there and relieve pressure on the British balance of payments. The idea was rejected by Montagu Norman in November 1923 as impractical. The Federal Reserve system could too readily sterilize the gold, that is, take it into the monetary base but sell off an equal amount of government securities to leave the total base, and the prospect of inflation, unchanged.

Some testimony before the Chamberlain-Bradbury Committee was based less on impartial expert analysis than on perceived or real interests. Much had its roots in considerations other than economic. Industry, for example, was said to have wanted the old gold standard restored because it was fearful of managed money and wanted a resumption of capital outflows and the stimulus they gave to exports (Perrot, 1955, pp. 49–50). In a later view, however, it has been made clear that industry was not consulted, as the City dominated the press and public opinion (Boyce, 1988). The purported industrial analysis ignored, first, that the Bank of England had established informal restrictions over new capital issues for foreign borrowers in November 1924 and, second, that the high exchange rate implicit in the old gold price called for capital inflows rather than permitting outflows. The City viewed restoration to par as an answer to the challenge of New York as a world financial center (Costigliola, 1977), a theme that is echoed in Churchill's defense of the action in April and May 1925. But, for the most part, what was involved was wounded *amour propre,* self-esteem, the need "to face the dollar in the eye" (*The Times,* 6 May 1925, quoted in Perrot, 1955, p. 35), an expression taken up by all the journalists. A French economist-demographer called the return to gold "a question of prestige, a question of dogma . . . almost a question of religion" (Sauvy, 1965, Vol. 1, p. 121). The leading British economic historian of the action claims that the views involved were essentially moral and based on deep faith in the gold standard (Moggridge, 1969, p. 68). One finds here an echo of Lopez's remark about the bezant, the Ottoman coin of the first millennium after Christ: it was "more than a lump of gold. It was a symbol and a faith" (1951, p. 214).

In the *Tract on Monetary Reform,* Keynes had tried to answer the argument based on "sacredness of contract" in relation both to currency depreciation and capital levies, claiming that it overlooked the essential difference between the right of the individual to repudiate a contract, which must be circumscribed, and the right or duty of the state to control vested interests when they threatened the general welfare. The state, he said, must revise what is intolerable. The continuation of an individual society depends on moderation in the pursuit of interests. Absolutists of contract, he went on, had denounced death duties, income tax, and state intervention in questions of land tenure, game laws, Church establishment, feudal rights, and slavery. They were the real parents of revolution (1924, pp. 75–76). The discussion went to the core of the question of vested interests in financial questions that are ostensibly technical, that is, to the differences among private, collective, and public goods. It evoked little response.

As in 1819, destabilizing speculation after the fall of the Labour government in October 1924 over a question unrelated to finance had pushed the exchange rate up to the point where the difference between the market and parity was "trifling." Most purchasing power parity calculations showed that sterling was 10 to 12 percent overvalued, but it was generally felt that this gap would be readily narrowed by a rise in prices in the United States. In his speech to the House of Commons presenting the Gold Standard Bill of 1925, Winston Churchill, as chancellor of the exchequer, stated that there was only a five-point difference between the United States and the United Kingdom in what he called "index figures" and claimed that a discrepancy of this width had existed before the war on one occasion in 1907, without producing strain on the exchange rate (1925 [1974], Vol. 4, p. 3602). Recent calculations have confirmed the wider measurement: wholesale prices produced an overvaluation of only 3 percent, because of the law of one price, which keeps the prices of internationally traded goods continuously in line with the exchange rate; on the basis of broader indexes, however, the overvaluation ran 10 to 12 percent (Officer, 1976, p. 21). Here again, however, as in the German and French cases, a question arises as to whether adequate attention was paid to the changes in the British financial position during the war, including the rise of rival industries in established British export markets and a worsening of £1.6 billion in the balance of international indebtedness, because of claims on weak debtors that could not be offset against liabilities to strong and exigent creditors.

DOWN TO THE WIRE

Strong pressure for stabilization at par came from the United States and additional pressure by example from a number of countries inside and outside the empire. Sweden went back on gold in March 1924, "tired of waiting." The Dawes loan of June 1924 promised a new German currency. Hungary obtained a stabilization loan in the summer of 1924, and the Union of South Africa announced its intention of going on the gold standard on 1 July 1925. The Australian currency was put on gold and went to a premium. Holland and Switzerland were planning resumption (Clarke, 1967, p. 80). The pressure built up. The reconstruction period after the war was drawing to a close in 1925. It was time to act.

Montagu Norman, continuously reelected governor of the Bank of England in opposition to a tradition that had earlier kept the position a rotating one, testified before the Chamberlain-Bradbury Committee in the summer of 1924, and again in January 1925, as he had testified before the Cunliffe Committee and would again before the Macmillan Committee. In all cases, he strongly defended an early return to par, called by Moggridge "the Norman conquest of $4.86." In discussion with Strong in New York he was more circumspect. In 1923 Strong had felt obliged to raise the discount rate of the Federal Reserve Bank of New York, action that threatened to draw funds from London (Clarke, 1967, p. 31). In December 1924 he raised the rate again, asking Norman whether the Bank of England wanted to lead or follow. Norman said "follow," with a 1 percent increase at the Bank of England on top of a ½ percent rise in New York so that it would appear that the Bank of England's hand had been forced (ibid., p. 88). The governor of the Federal Reserve Bank urged restoration of the pound to par; he distrusted the "devaluationist," who had been given encouragement by the text of the Genoa resolution, saying, "I fear him and his patent remedies" (Clarke, 1973, p. 15).

Strong was ready to help in the task of revaluation, first, by maintaining interest rates low in New York and transferring international borrowing there from London, second, by inflating domestically, although in this he failed to persuade his colleagues on the Federal Reserve Board in Washington; and, third, by a stabilization credit. This last was arranged to the extent of $200 million from the Federal Reserve Bank of New York and $300 million privately placed with J. P. Morgan & Company, the latter being cut to $100 million by the British Treasury because it objected to the fee charged (Clarke, 1967, pp. 72, 75, 82). As it worked out, the New York credits were not drawn upon. Governor Norman was prepared to do so, but his colleagues thought they should return to gold on their own resources without help, which might weaken self-reliance and discipline (ibid., p. 77).

In the change of government in the fall of 1924, Winston Churchill became chancellor in place of Philip Snowden. In January 1925 he widely circulated a minute (short memorandum) to civil servants, including Norman at the Bank of England and Lord Bradbury, Otto Niemeyer, and Ralph Hawtrey at the Treasury, as devil's advocate and in the spirit of the Keynes-McKenna position, asking for their considered judgment on the wisdom of the return of the pound to gold, when to do it, and whether it would not be possible to obtain better terms from the United States. There is a debate among historians as to whether this request for opinions was a genuine attempt to collect views or merely to build the record by covering all possibilities. Moggridge maintains that the exercise was window dressing (1972, pp. 66–67). In his biography of Churchill, Martin Gilbert holds that the broadside was inspired by genuine doubts (1977, ch. 5).

Niemeyer was asked again to comment on an article by Keynes in *The Nation and Athenaeum* for 21 February 1925, entitled, "The return towards gold," and, in particular, on the issue as to whether France with its financial embarrassments but a low exchange rate was not better off than Britain with its unemployment. Niemeyer was the wrong person to ask if Churchill wanted any other answer than strong, confident advocacy of a quick return to gold, but Niemeyer suited Churchill in a way that Montagu Norman did not (Sayers, 1976, Vol. 1, p. 134).

On 17 March Churchill gave a dinner party at which the guests included Bradbury, Grigg, Keynes, McKenna, and Niemeyer and stirred up a further debate on the issue. Bradbury and Niemeyer argued strongly for a return to gold at par and Keynes and McKenna for postponement. Grigg, who was not as fully committed as the first two and gives the fullest account, concluded that Niemeyer and Bradbury had by far the best of the debate and that the arguments of Keynes and McKenna paled beside theirs (1948, p. 182). If this account is credible, it would be neither the first nor the last time that the winner of a debate had the worse of the arguments.

Three days later, the prime minister, the chancellor of the exchequer, and the secretary of state for foreign affairs, meeting with Montagu Norman, Lord Bradbury, and Sir Otto Niemeyer, agreed to the return to gold. The matter went to the entire cabinet as part of the budgetary review and was announced in the budget speech of 25 April 1925. As with tax changes, it took effect from the moment of announcement, although the legislation was debated in Parliament on 4 May and the king signed the legislation on 14 May.

Insight into the relationship between Churchill and his advisers is afforded by a passage in his speech before the House of Commons on 4 May:

I do not pose as a currency expert. It would be absurd if I did; no one would believe me. I present myself here not as a currency expert but as a Member of Parliament with some experience in dealing with experts and weighing their arguments, as the Minister who has behind him what, I believe, is, and what I dare say the right honorable Gentleman believes is, on the whole, the finest expert opinion in financial matters, in Treasury matters in the whole world. . . . When the men who have managed the currency so well, according to the opponents of the present Bill, tell me that they can manage the currency no longer on this basis, and tell me that it would have been impossible to have managed it so far as they have unless they had always had the return to the gold standard as a goal to steer towards . . . surely this opinion should carry great weight. (Churchill, 1925 [1974], Vol. 4, p. 3597)

Churchill also acknowledged Keynes's opposition in "searching and brilliant" articles in *The Nation* but quoted a sentence from his article of 2 May: "If we are to return to gold and in the face of general opinion that is inevitable, the Chancellor and the Treasury and the Bank have tried to do so along the most prudent and far-sighted lines which are open to them."

THE ROLE OF THE CITY

While Churchill insisted that he was not a currency expert, his perhaps subconscious prime reason for supporting the return to par emerges in two speeches given in the spring of 1925. In the budget speech of 28 April, which announced the decision only incidentally, he gave as a leading reason:

. . . the revival of international trade and inter-Imperial trade. Such a revival and such a foundation is important to all countries, and for no country is it more important than to this island whose population is larger than its agriculture or its industry can sustain, which is the centre of a wide Empire, and which in spite of all its burdens, has still retained if not the primary, at any event the central position in the financial systems of the world. (Churchill, 1925 [1974], Vol. 4, p. 3562)

In his speech of 4 May he goes on:

We are not only the financial center of the world; we are also the center of a wide Empire. (ibid., p. 3598)

And later

If the English pound is not to be the standard which everyone knows and can trust, and which everyone in every country understands and can rely on, the business not only of the British Empire, but of Europe as well, might have to be transacted in dollars instead of pounds sterling. I think that would be a great misfortune. (ibid., p. 3599)

Churchill does not quite use the expression "dollar standard" as a replacement for sterling and gold. The words can be found, however, in the *Tract on Monetary Reform* (Keynes, 1924, p. 215). Britain was conscious of the approach of the end of an era and was striving to stave it off.

COMPARISON WITH 1819

Apart from Acworth, who makes only the most glancing reference to 1925 in writing the introduction to his book on the resumption of specie payments in 1819 (1925, p. v), and the epigraph from Gregory at the head of this chapter, for a time I had found no references to the earlier experience in the major analyses. Accordingly I asked Donald Moggridge whether anyone in British governmental discussion had been alive to the analogy and got from him the friendly private reply, "Only Hawtrey," with the further remark that no one paid attention to his comparison. Moreover, Hawtrey thought that resumption in 1819 had been a great success and cited Peel, quoting Locke against Lowndes in 1695, to the effect that adoption of the market price of silver (in 1819 gold) would have been a fraud on the public creditor, Hawtrey adding that "it would have been a mean-spirited course to go back on the century-old standard on account of so trifling a premium on gold" (1919 [1927], p. 351).

There were other economists with a historical view, however, and a number of journalists, in a discussion Perrot calls "very scholarly," which I had overlooked (1955, p. 35). In his 2 May 1925 article for *The Nation,* Keynes noted that the bullion standard provided in the legislation was the same as that recommended in 1819 by Ricardo. *The Economist,* of the same day, observed that the seven years taken to restore parity in 1925 were longer both than had been envisaged by the Cunliffe Commission, and than were required after the Napoleonic Wars. It added that monetary troubles were less generalized in the world a century earlier and that British finances were less entangled with those of other countries than currently. Perrot characterized as "less scholarly" a remark in *The Times* of 29 April, commenting on the announcement of resumption, that the procedure had been modeled in its principal points on that which had been so successful in 1819. A few days later, in the issue of 2 May, the financial editor of *The Times* attacked members of the Labour party who opposed the return to par for fear of its repercussions on British industry and the working class, by saying, "Like the 500 [Birmingham] merchants who signed a petition a hundred years ago against the return of gold, you worry about the immediate present in neglecting the long-run future" (Perrot, 1955, p. 36).

PRICES AND WAGES

Appreciation of the pound from \$3.40 at its lowest to \$4.866 at par was thought to leave it no more than 10 percent overvalued, although, as has already been pointed out, this calculation assumes that the same relationship of prices as in 1913 would restore equilibrium in 1925, a questionable hypothesis in the light of the substantial structural changes brought on by the war. The short-run position was satisfactory. In the spring of 1925, the Bank of England had £153 million in gold and had set aside $92 million in the fall and winter of 1924 and $166 million in 1925 to meet the war debt payments due 15 June and 15 December of that year (Clarke, 1967, p. 90). But the price level was still out of line. If prices and wages would not go up in the United States, they would have to go down in Britain. Moreover, the British focused too exclusively on developments in relation to the United States and ignored foreign exchange and financial outcomes in France.

Prices and wages did not rise in the United States, and it became necessary to force them down in Britain. After deep cuts in 1921, the process was painful. An attempt to lower wages in coal led to a second coal strike following that of the spring of 1921. The coal strike of 1925 widened into a general strike of all unions in 1926. The government broke the strike but at a heavy cost in deepening social fissures in the country. The working class was resentful—of politicians, of the City, and of foreign countries.

In October 1925 the Bank of England lowered its rediscount rate to 4½ percent and felt strong enough the next month to relax the unofficial restrictions on foreign loans in the London market. By December, however, the exchanges looked weak, and bank rate was raised back to 5 percent. The action evoked a strong protest from Churchill, the chancellor of the exchequer, on the ground that it would increase the growing unemployment. Thereafter, the rediscount rate was changed only once in three years, down again to 4½ percent in April 1927. Sayers asserts that it was not that bank rate would not reduce prices and wages but that it was not allowed to do so. He concedes that increasing the rediscount rate would not have had much effect on capital movements vis-à-vis the Continent (Sayers, 1976, Vol. 1, pp. 215–17). The contrast is with 1873 when the rate was changed twenty-four times within a year: twice a month in 1873 as opposed to once in thirty-six months from 1926 to 1928.

CENTRAL BANK COOPERATION

Governor Norman and, from 1926, Emile Moreau, the governor of the Bank of France, had been rivals for spheres of influence among central banks on the Continent. Norman was a friend of Hjalmar Schacht, who was no friend of France. Schuker puts it more polemically when he says that Norman, who had spent two happy years in Germany, loved the Germans and passionately despised the French (1976, pp. 114, 291). Moreau regarded Norman's direct dealings with the national banks of Poland, Italy, Rumania, and others, and even those indirect contacts through the Financial Delegation of the League of Nations with Austria and Hungary, as unfriendly to the Bank of France. Later, in 1928, he wanted to divide Europe into spheres of financial influence (Moreau, 1954 [1991], pp. 443). Before that date, but after undervaluation of the French franc (discussed in the next chapter) was firmly established, the bank's sterling balances had built up from £5 million in November 1926, £20 million at the end of February 1927, £60 million in April, and £160 million at the end of May. Moreau was in a position to get his way by threatening to convert the sterling balances owned by the Bank of France into gold (L. V. Chandler, 1958 [1978], p. 371; Clarke, 1967, p. 111). A confrontation took place between Norman and Moreau in May 1927. The French asked the British to raise interest rates to slow withdrawal of French private funds from London and their exchange for francs; the British asked the French to fix a legal parity for the franc in the hope that that would slow the movement of French capital to Paris from London. The French were unwilling to stabilize because they had not settled on a final rate. Norman maintained that he could not raise interest rates, given the state of British unemployment. The public and the government would erupt in a storm, especially Churchill at the Exchequer (Moreau, 1954 [1991], pp. 290ff.).

Into this impasse, the Federal Reserve Bank of New York entered with a two-stage compromise. In the first instance, it provided the French with some gold against sterling from its London gold holdings, as the French tried to work their sterling balances a little lower. As part of this operation, the Bank of France altered its buying prices for dollars and sterling to discriminate against sterling in favor of dollars, so that if it had to furnish francs to the market, it would acquire dollars rather than sterling. Second, at a meeting held in July 1927 at the Long Island home of Ogden Mills, the American secretary of the treasury (with Norman, Schacht, and Strong present for the Bank of England, the Reichsbank, and the Federal Reserve Bank of New York, respectively, and Charles Rist representing Moreau of the Bank of France), it was agreed that instead of raising interest rates in Europe, the Federal Reserve would lower them in New York. The New York bank also agreed to make gold available to Europe in New York at the price of gold in London, in order to hold down the drain on the Bank of England's reserve, and to buy more of the Bank of France's sterling with dollars (Moreau, 1954 [1991], p. 331). In carrying out the main feature of the agreement, the bank bought $200 million in government securities in open-market operations from July to September and in August lowered its discount rate by ½ percent to 3½ percent.

A number of observers have regarded this action as fateful, blaming it for the subsequent rise in the stock market, the crash of October 1929 that followed, and the Great Depression of the 1930s. The judgment is excessive and is matched by extreme opinion on the other side by Friedman and Schwartz that the stock market crash played no role in the depression (1963, pp. 291ff.). A number of points may be made about the episode:

1. The New York central bank did not choose international over domestic objectives in lowering interest rates in the summer of 1927. This was not a "dilemma situation" where domestic policy calls for one course of action, international cooperation for another. The year 1927 was one of recession in the United States; world commodity prices were slipping from their 1925 levels; expansionary pressure was desirable in the short run on both domestic and international scores.

2. The managed gold standard calls for adopting an average level of interest rates that suits the world as a whole, and then for separate countries to decide whether to fix small differences for domestic rates from that average—higher for countries with weak currencies, lower for such countries as the United

States with abundant reserves. July 1927 was the precedent for the meeting of finance ministers—they could have been central banks—at Chequers on 22 January 1967 trying to agree on an international level of interest rates (Kindleberger, 1981*a*, p. 116), the occasions in the 1970s when the United States argued for lower interest rates in Europe to assist expansion at home, or the position later when European countries asked the United States for lower interest rates ("Europeans assail US high rates," *New York Times,* 4 March 1981). The Long Island meeting can be regarded as a forerunner of proposals today for a Federal Reserve Open-Market Committee with European members, or an Atlantic Open-Market Committee to set interest rates for the world financial system as a whole (Kindleberger, 1981*a,* e.g., p. 29).

3. It would be difficult to call the central bank cooperation forthcoming from the July 1927 Long Island meeting a brilliant success. It bought time, but little was done with that time to improve the position. Franco-British wrangles continued. Benjamin Strong died in October 1928. Herbert Hoover, who was much less sympathetic to European problems and called Benjamin Strong a "mental annex to Europe," was elected president of the United States in November 1928. Central bank cooperation, never deeply rooted, wilted even before the hot sun of 1929, and the torrid blasts of 1931.

A. J. Youngson has defended the return of the pound to par. "What wrecked the gold standard was the self-regarding unwisdom of French and American monetary policies" (1960, pp. 233–34). Perhaps. Perhaps, however, in monetary policy, as in driving an automobile, one must conduct oneself defensively, taking into account the possible, or even the likely, unwisdom of others. In the British case, Churchill explicitly raised the question as to whether the return to parity had been made after extracting a high enough price from the Americans. No thought was given to the question of what the French would do and whether their action would dovetail into the pattern planned for the pound.

SUGGESTED SUPPLEMENTARY READING

Boyce (1988), Creating the myth of consensus: Public opinion and Britain's return to the gold standard, 1925.
Clarke (1967), *Central-Bank Cooperation, 1924–31.*
Clarke (1973), *The Reconstruction of the International Monetary System.*
H. Clay (1957 [1979]), *Lord Norman.*
Howson (1975), *Domestic Monetary Management in Britain, 1919–38.*
Keynes (1931), *Essays in Persuasion.*
League of Nations (Nurkse) (1944), *International Currency Experience.*
Moggridge (1972), *British Monetary Policy, 1924–1931.*
Sayers (1976), *The Bank of England, 1891–1944,* Vol. 1, chs. 7–9.

In French

Perrot (1955), *La Monnaie et l'opinion publique en France et en Angleterre, 1924–36.*

19

Stabilization of the Franc

Each time the franc loses value, the Minister of Finance is convinced that the fact arises from everything but economic causes. He attributes it to the presence of foreigners in the corridors of the Bourse, to unwholesome and malign forces of speculation. The attitude is rather close to that of the witch doctor who attributes the illness of cattle to the "evil eye," and the storm to an insufficient quantity of sacrifices made before some idol.
(Keynes, preface to the French translation of *A Tract on Monetary Reform,* 1924)

Like Britain and Germany, France ended the war with a swollen money supply, a large debt, only moderate taxes, but, in contrast with Germany, the hope and expectation that the Germans would pay for war damage and reconstruction. Such taxes as existed were for the most part indirect. A war profits tax and an exceptional war tax had been voted in 1916. These were followed by an increase in inheritance taxes in 1917. The income tax agreed before the war also took effect in 1917 over the protest of banking and financial groups but was not collected efficiently. Accumulated tax liabilities were sufficiently high in the 1920 recession, moreover, for the Ministry of Finance to be afraid that it would drive companies and households into bankruptcy if it pushed collection hard; this led solvent taxpayers to avoid or evade the income tax on the ground that they did not want to become suckers. The income tax was in fact called *l'impôt des poires* (the suckers' tax) (Schuker, 1976, pp. 65, 70). The French had a long tradition of escaping taxes, with businesses keeping several sets of books, and the tax administration, despairing of ascertaining accurately what a given income might be, shifting over to taxation based on "visible signs of wealth," that is, numbers of houses, automobiles, servants, race horses, and the like, as a surrogate for income. During the war, taxes failed even to cover the ordinary budget, amounting to 52.3 billion francs in 1918—26.1 billion of civil expenses plus 26.2 billion of debt service—although the criterion, as earlier noted (see pp. 284–86), is a dubious one. Total expenditure during the war amounted to 225 billion francs and borrowing to 187 billion.

After the war, reconstruction was undertaken immediately without waiting for the receipt of reparations: "*le Boche paiera*" (The Hun will pay). Reconstruction expenditures were included in the extraordinary budget where they were balanced by reparation receipts still to be collected (Jeanneney, 1977, p. 61). The government deficit in 1919 amounted to 42 billion and was eliminated only over a number of years. It declined little at first, amounting still to 25 billion in 1922, but thereafter fell to 9 billion in 1924 and 5 billion in 1925, before reaching balance in 1926. Reconstruction expenditure declined both absolutely and as a percentage of national income, falling on the latter basis from 15 percent of income in 1921 to 3 percent of a larger and rising income in 1925. The French rejected reparations in the form of work of labor battalions from Germany: they wanted money. In 1919 the country adopted the eight-hour day; wage rates rose with the cost of living and wage costs still more.

Not only was the debt large and growing, even if at a declining rate. Much was short term. An attempt was made to limit direct monetization of government debt through a ceiling on Bank of France advances to the government imposed in December 1920 in the François-Marsal Convention between the Bank of France and the minister of finance, after whom it was named. Under the convention, the ceiling started at 27 billion, which was to last until December 1921, when it was to be reduced to 25 billion, and by 2 billion a year thereafter. The government did its best and got advances down to 24.6 billion in May 1922 and then to 21,089 million at the year end before they got out of hand again. A second ceiling applied to currency in circulation, which had mounted from 27.5 billion francs average in 1918 to 37.3 billion in 1921. This was fixed at 41 billion francs.

One source of pressure on the note circulation was the requirement of occupied German territories—the Saar, Palatinate, and Rhineland in particular—since the Ruhr was flooded with marks printed by the Reichsbank, and even the neighboring unoccupied areas (Debeir, 1978, pp. 37ff.). The collapse of the mark created a vacuum into which francs were drawn. With the institution of the first stage of currency reform, the Rentenmark in the fall of 1924, exchanges of Rentenmarks against francs created a new supply of ammunition in the hands of German banks. How large the circulation of francs in German areas was is unknown. There had been a suggestion that a special money be issued for the Rhineland's 10 million inhabitants, with an obvious need for a circulation of a dozen billion francs equivalent or more (ibid., p. 38).

The year 1924 saw increases at the Bank of France in advances to the government, discounts to the market, and currency in circulation. Already by the summer of 1924 both ceilings had been secretly violated. It was easy to violate that on advances to the Treasury. The Treasury merely borrowed from banks, which rediscounted the notes at the Bank of France, which recorded them as obligations of the banks, not of the Treasury. The ceiling on note circulation was more complex. Data on the circulation consisted of notes issued by the Paris head office of the Bank of France plus notes issued by its branches, which counted them as of a different day of the week. The figures were cooked by shipping notes from head office to branches, or branches to head office, just in time to keep them out of the tabulation.

The system was impossible to sustain, and the new government of the Cartel des Gauches under Edouard Herriot as prime minister and Etienne Clémentel, finance minister, considered many possible avenues. One, advised strongly by Pierre de Moüy, director of the Mouvement Général des Fonds (General Movement of Funds), was to ask Parliament for authority to raise the ceilings. Another was to consolidate the two ceilings, permitting the Bank of France to raise its note ceiling any time *bons du Trésor* (Treasury bonds) declined (because investors wanted to be paid in cash). Other less serious palliatives were to encourage the use of checks instead of notes—somewhat akin to the Bank of France's conservation of its gold and silver reserves through issuing bank notes at the time of the Thiers *rente* (see p.

239), to reduce the cash balances of all public accounts, to issue new monies for Madagascar and the Saar, or to sell a big stock of copper in the arsenal at Bourges worth 500 million francs (Jeanneney, 1976, pt 3, ch. 2, pp. 217, 226). In the end, the Herriot government temporized fatally until at the beginning of October an under-governor at the Bank of France discovered what his superiors had been doing and demanded that Clémentel be informed. In December, Robineau, the governor, felt obliged to inform the regents of the Bank of France, most of whom, under the leadership of François de Wendel, were opposed to the left government in power and had been reluctant to pledge the gold of the Bank of France as a guarantee of a new Morgan loan. While the position was finally regularized by raising the ceilings in April 1925, inflation had proceeded much further, and the Cartel des Gauches had lost its momentum. The historian of François de Wendel's service as a regent at the Bank of France wrote a second popular book in 1977, when Mitterrand first ran for president of France, to draw the lesson for a new left-wing government that temporizing in the early stages of a new government determined on a new course could be disastrous (Jeanneney, 1977).

Floating debt had been minuscule in France in relation to *rentes* in 1913 but approached half the combined total by January 1919 and was still 45 percent from 1923 to 1926. Inability to fund the floating debt, as much as anything, lay at the root of France's problem. That inability, due to the unwillingness of the French investor to give up liquidity, is reflected in monthly averages of the lows of the 5 percent *rente* of 1920: 84.75 in 1922; 82.75 percent in 1923; 68.75 percent in 1924, and 58.75 percent in 1925. French investors refused to buy more *rentes* and get "locked in" to illiquidity, that is, unable to sell *rentes* for cash except at a price that would sink. The result was that, each two weeks as another batch of six-months' bills became due, the capitalist had the option of rolling them over into new six-months' bills or demanding cash, which required the Ministry of Finance to sell bills to the Bank of France and enlarge the circulation. It also posed the possibility, even the likelihood, that the capitalist would use the currency to buy foreign exchange, driving down the rate.

THE EXCHANGE RATE

The French franc had been pegged in New York at 5.4 to the dollar, somewhat below the 1913 gold standard parity of 5.18, or 25.22 to the pound. As in the case of the pound, this was done with the help of a Morgan loan later taken over by the American government and incorporated in the war debt. The peg was removed in March 1919, and the franc fell roughly in half, from 5.5 to 11. In the boom of 1920 it moved still lower to 16 to the dollar but recovered in 1921 after the collapse of raw material prices eased the weight of the French import bill. The profile for the year was 17 to 10 and back to 12. A considerable volume of foreign bull speculation had taken place from 1919 to 1920, based on the inelastic expectation that when reconstruction, reparations, and war debts were settled, the franc would return to its old par (Schuker, 1976, p. 67). In 1921 and 1922, however, there was no progress toward the solutions of war debts or reparations, and the franc weakened in the latter year to 22. The year 1923 saw, first, a recovery during the first enthusiasm for occupation of the Ruhr, but when it became clear that this did not provide a solution to anything, relapsed again from 15 to 19.

Liquidity in the money market made speculation against the franc easy. Cash was owned or easily obtained by Frenchmen and readily borrowed by foreigners. News suggesting that France was having difficulty in solving its financial problems—German intransigence, banker unwillingness to provide loans to Germany for recycling German reparations, American insistence on collecting war debts, disclosure that the government had violated the ceiling on borrowing from the Bank of France, the fall of a cabinet, or the resignation of a minister—led to renewed weakness of the currency. Albert Aftalion produced a "psychological theory of foreign exchange," based on speculation, which related the course of the currency to news breaks and even rumors (1927). The school was a distant cousin of the banking school of a hundred years earlier in Britain that blamed the agio on gold (depreciation of sterling), not on the money supply but on the subsidies given by Britain to its allies and the state of the harvest. The theory confused symptoms with causes. The French were unable to raise taxes to pay for reconstruction because the public believed that Germany would pay. The French government was unable to make the Germans pay, whether by negotiation, such as inducing them to borrow in the United States and substitute an obligation to the United States for one to France, or by force, such as the occupation of the Ruhr. It was unable to borrow at home at long term to finance the deficit and to clean up the accumulation because the public did not trust it.

There were further problems. The Versailles Treaty had guaranteed Alsace-Lorraine industry free access to the German market for five years, after which Germany would be able to negotiate access on the basis of equality, and the end of this five-year period was approaching in 1924. The iron and steel industry was acutely conscious of prospective competition with German industry, wanted an undervalued currency to help meet it, and did not hesitate to talk the franc down publicly (Debeir, 1978, pp. 32–34). While the franc was actually declining in January 1924, moreover, the industry shifted to invoicing its export sales in Swiss francs or sterling and defended the practice by invoking the necessity to sell in a stable money. There was also some question as to whether iron and steel firms repatriated the proceeds of their export sales or held them abroad (ibid., p. 36).

The fact that first the Poincaré government and then that of Herriot had violated the ceilings of advances to the Treasury and on the Bank of France's note circulation made the speculative position more tangled. As the news—impossible to hide completely—began to leak out at the end of 1924 and through early 1925, speculation against the franc increased. Schuker agrees with Pierre de Moüy that it would have been possible to face the public down on the ceilings, pointing out that the limits had symbolic merit only and did not represent critical economic values (1976, pp. 32, 87). Perhaps this would have been possible immediately after the Herriot government took power in June 1925. But, by the fall, the right wing was harping on the need for confidence. The election loss of Poincaré and the Bloc National was bad enough for confidence. An increase in "inflation," as higher numbers on advances and the note circulation were called, would have hurt it more. The

French public was not ready to cast away symbols. That was all it had. The French had no policy to solve the reparation tangle through occupation or to overcome their difficulties in budgetary balance and debt management. When violation of the ceilings was revealed at the Bank of France in early 1924, the Poincaré government sought to tidy up with a tax program, introduced on 17 January, raising all imposts 20 percent, the so-called *double decime* or double tithing. The Chamber of Deputies dawdled and did not pass the program until 18 February, and then the Senate obstructed it. The government then tried to raise a 3 billion franc long-term loan. This failed. Between inability to raise taxes and inability to borrow either from the market, which refused to give up liquidity, or from the Bank of France because of the François-Marsal Convention, it had no room to maneuver. This left 30 billion in long-term debt coming due, plus 50 billion of short maturities (six months or less), equal to 10 billion to be financed each month. Accordingly, when a speculative attack on the franc took place, it was easily escalated into panic. Panic began on 4 March 1924.

THE 1924 PANIC

French public opinion was persuaded that the speculative attack on the franc originated in Germany as a government plot. French diplomatic channels in Nuremberg, the Rhineland, Holland, and Switzerland all mentioned governmental involvement. The Reichsbank was said to have orchestrated meetings of banks in Berlin and Frankfurt to set out the order of the day. Poincaré showed a document, which cannot now be located, to Edouard de Rothschild, the banker, and François de Wendel, the steel magnate of Lorraine—both regents of the Bank of France—purporting to be instructions given by Chancellor Stresemann to bankers at the Hotel Adlon in Berlin on 4 March (Jeanneney, 1978, pp. 9–11). Schuker considers it unlikely that the German or the British government was involved (1976, pp. 96–97). He can find no documents to that effect and thinks monetary chaos in Germany in late 1923 and early 1924 kept the German government too preoccupied with its own affairs to stir up trouble elsewhere. Jeanneney finds this reasoning weak. A secret attack would leave no trace in the archives. He noted that the archives contain no statement to the effect that the German government did not participate in planning the attack. Jeanneney's evidence for the suggestion that the British government might be involved is a report from a French diplomatic representative in Rome that the British credits (to French borrowers?), normally renewable for three months, had suddenly been called in November 1923 (1978, p. 12). This, in turn, is far from conclusive.

That there was German and Austrian speculation is not denied anywhere, not even in Germany and Austria: the only question is whether it bore the imprint of government design. A number of operators had made substantial profits speculating against German, Austrian, and Hungarian currencies, now all stabilized, and thought to apply their proved techniques anew. A syndicate was organized about January 1924 at the Amsterdam branch of the Mendelssohn Bank, directed by one Mannheimer (Philippe, 1931, pp. 25–26). Closely linked was a banking group in

Vienna, of which the leading figure was a man named Bosel who ran the Union Bank. The group presumably assembled francs from all over occupied Germany and borrowed widely of the floating supply, including from Paris through British and American banks, notably, among the latter, the Guaranty Trust and the Equitable Trust Company, both connected with J. P. Morgan & Company, and for the Bosel group, from the Banque de l'Union Parisienne. To get francs, these Parisian banks discounted at the Bank of France, where discounts rose from 2 billion to 4 billion francs between the end of September and the beginning of January, with the discount rate unchanged at 5 percent. When the bank finally raised the rate on 10 January—a slim ½ percentage point—the modesty of the gesture convinced European bankers that the Bank of France had no serious intention of defending the currency. One Dutch banker called it a joke *(plaisanterie)* (Debeir, 1978, p. 35).

The French government initially responded to the speculative attack by a series of measures directed against symptoms rather than causes. It prohibited the export of meat and vegetables, which, stimulated by the depreciating franc, greatly aroused the ire of the French public; expelled some foreigners taking advantage of franc undervaluation—the French public later attacked tourists in the streets, so frustrated and angry had it become; required telegrams of a financial character to have any cipher accompanied by a clear text; closed commodity exchanges, where forward prices for primary products reflected the market's negative view of the franc. In its entirety it was a program that Maurice Bokanowski, an adviser to the prime minister, Raymond Poincaré, found lacking in all coherence (Schuker, 1976, pp. 82–83).

At the end of January, Finance Minister Lasteyrie forbade French banks, including the French subsidiaries of foreign institutions, to grant extensions or new loans in francs to foreigners (Jeanneney, 1978, p. 21). This slowly began to pinch foreign speculators, although it had no effect on Frenchmen with abundant funds. The technique of the foreign speculator then became selling francs in quantity to the extent that they could amass them from the world's floating supply—on the smaller and thinner exchanges on the Continent and in New York after continental markets had closed, to push down quotations and provoke the French public into dumping its enormous supply of francs when it saw the lower prices the following morning.

COUNTERATTACK

Plans to counterattack had been put forward, in one instance as early as November 1923. One proposal for a government monopoly of all foreign exchange transactions is reminiscent of the Royal Exchanger recommended by the mercantilists in sixteenth- and seventeenth-century England. This was advanced by a journalist, one M. Phiouze, and rejected out of hand by J. Seydoux, the head of the commercial department in the French Foreign Office and financial expert in Poincaré's personal cabinet (Debeir, 1978, p. 43). For a time, Seydoux thought that the crisis would be short and that it was necessary to tolerate it for the sake of full employment and brisk export demand. Gradually it became clear that counterattack was necessary. Bokanowski, who planned it, met with Poincaré, the prime minister, and

Millerand, the president, on 1 and 2 March and on the fifth day after panic had broken out, with the finance minister, Lasteyrie, and a team from Lazard Frères, including Raymond Philippe, Michel Lazard, plus the banker Robert Wolff.

Without the possibility of swapping spot sales against forward purchases in interest arbitrage, as banned by Lasteyrie at the end of January, the forward rate had gone to 140 to the pound on 8 March. At the same time, it was impossible to borrow francs to sell spot, with speculators looking for them not only in the smaller markets of Europe, such as Madrid and Athens, but in Constantinople, Cairo, Rio de Janeiro, and Buenos Aires. The rate of interest on such francs went to 40 percent.

The cabinet met on Sunday, 9 March, and at the end of the meeting a communiqué was issued stating that the Bank of France and the banks of the country would intervene in the struggle in which certain foreign syndicates had enlisted against French money (Jeanneney, 1978, p. 23). Meanwhile, the French government had borrowed $100 million from J. P. Morgan & Company at 4½ percent for three months.

CONDITIONALITY

The French had originally appealed to Thomas Lamont of J. P. Morgan, asking for a loan of $50 million to support the exchange; Lamont thought the sum too small to achieve the desired result and offered $100 million but wanted gold as security for the loan and an agreement by the French government to push for immediate and complete passage of its tax measure in the Senate (Schuker, 1976, p. 108). He also demanded a slowing of expenditure on the devastated areas of northeastern France and avoidance of new expenditures. These conditions led ultimately to the downfall of Poincaré's center-right government in the regular elections of May 1924, despite the success of the squeeze against the speculators, and raise, for the period, the question of conditionality of assistance, which is so prominent an issue of International Monetary Fund loans to developing countries, and will feature prominently in my account of rescue operations of the 1930s

Misunderstandings arise easily in these loans, and participants even misunderstand their own motives. The banker will claim to be judging the conditions necessary for the loan to achieve its purpose and for the bank to be repaid. Lending other people's money, in the bank's view, calls for circumspection. The borrower for whom the conditions are laid down frequently feels that his temporary weakness is being taken advantage of, and, in particular, what purport to be economic or technical market conditions are, in fact, deeply political in nature, stated perhaps by bankers but coming essentially from the foreign government and designed to carry out ulterior motives of ideology or foreign policy. In these circumstances gratitude for help seldom comes unmixed with other emotions.

THE SQUEEZE

Support for the franc came from the Morgan fund on 12 March. For the first two days the defenders, Morgan and Lazard Frères, had their hands full trying to hold

'PHEW! THAT'S A NASTY LEAK. THANK GOODNESS IT'S NOT AT OUR END OF THE BOAT.'

Cartoon by David Low (1932), from his *Autobiography* (New York: Simon & Schuster, 1957), p. 243. By permission of *The Evening Standard*/Solo.

the franc at 123 to the pound, the quotation on 8 March, and close to 25 to the dollar. They then worked it up to 116 to the pound. By 19 March steady buying of francs with dollars, and with pounds bought for dollars, brought the rate to 84.45, with the speculators running for cover, by 24 March to 78.10, just about 15 to the dollar, and at the end of April to 61. At this price, counterattackers stopped buying francs and turned to sell them against foreign exchange to speculators trying to cover short positions. They very quickly recovered the whole $100 million to pay off the Morgan loan and more.

The franc bounced around during the May elections, falling from a high of 68 to the pound to 74, and in June to 80–85 when the Left Cartel had won. This time bankers like Philippe and political leaders like Caillaux agreed not to use the Morgan fund but to support the franc to the extent of an extra $22 million accumulated by Lazard Frères and held outside the Bank of France. This was effective. Political turmoil, however, left no opportunity to take advantage of the success of the squeeze to gain open water for plain sailing.

GERMAN AND AUSTRIAN LOSSES

Selling francs at anything up to 140 to the pound and having to buy them back in the range of 78 to 61 proved expensive for German and Austrian banks. Estimates of losses are highly uncertain, but the Mendelssohn Bank is said to have lost 10 million florins and Mannheimer 6 million more for his personal account. The shares of the Barmer Bankverein used by the syndicate fell from 1,000 marks to 240. The Deutsche Länderbank of Berlin failed. A Reparation Agency estimate suggested that Germany lost altogether some 400 million gold marks (Debeir, 1978, p. 47).

Damage was even more extensive in Austria where the Allgemeine Industriebank, the Austro-Polnische, and the Austro-Orientbank all failed, along with the private Union Bank of Bosel. On 16 March the *Wiener Morgenzeitung* said that the speculators had been caught like "ants in the honey" (Jeanneney, 1978, p. 24). A leading scholar of Austrian banking noted that between March and June 1924, the Austrian National Bank lost about one-third of its foreign exchange and built up its discounts threefold as a result of "ill-fated speculation against the franc in which almost the entire Austrian banking community participated." The episode was the "opening shot of a series of bank failures culminating in the breakdown of the Creditanstalt in the spring of 1931." The League of Nations commissioner who had refused to make releases from the stabilization loan for investment in Austrian industry was willing, in his lender-of-last-resort role, to hand them out to Austrian banking via the Austrian National Bank (März, 1982, pp. 190–91).

The 1924 squeeze was a short-lived triumph. Little advantage was taken of it. It serves, nonetheless, as an example of destabilizing speculation and a paradigm of what can be done by authorities, acting as a lender of last resort, if they succeed in reversing the expectations of speculators. The operation was repeated later by Italy in 1964, by the United Kingdom in 1976, and briefly, by the United States on 31 October 1978 (Dornbusch, 1982, p. 220). To keep speculators' expectations reversed in the longer run, however, the authorities must adopt effective means of monetary and fiscal stabilization. This may be more than the average set of politicians can accomplish in a given sociopolitical state.

MORE CONDITIONALITY

The Herriot government, which succeeded Poincaré, was equally constrained by the inconsistent demands of the French public for lower taxes, increased spending, unlimited liquidity, and a stable money. It was clearly less competent in financial matters. The budget improved, as called for under the conditions of the Morgan loan, but no progress was made in funding short-term debt or settling war debts. French agreement to the Dawes Plan and the Dawes loan was dragged from them grudgingly and with bad grace. With the rise of the pound toward par, moreover, French capital found it profitable to speculate in favor of the pound, which incidentally meant going short of the franc.

The Morgan loan had been renewed once for three months in the midst of the battle. It came due for a second time on 12 September 1924. The question of whether to renew, and on what terms, again raised agonizing issues of conditionality on which it is normal to expect differences of view among the participants. Should the loan be extended to six months, be converted into a long-term loan, and, in either case, under what conditions? An American scholar notes that the private Morgan correspondence shows great sympathy for the French plight as the partners reiterated the conditions that they believed were required for successful stabilization and the limits of what the bank could do, bearing in mind the safety of the funds entrusted to it by depositors and stockholders (Schuker, 1976, p. 141). A diverging French view notes the profitability of the loan to the American bank because of the reduction in interest rates in New York at the beginning of 1924 (Debeir, 1978, p. 46) and observes that the Morgan Bank on 8 November 1924 pictured the American market as unable to supply $100 million if the budget were not balanced, but on 26 November found itself able to supply $350 million, after (1) a secret letter from the prime minister promising to balance the budget, but (2) above all, a "much more stimulating offer from a rival bank, Dillon Read" (Debeir, 1982, p. 135).

In any case, the Department of State interposed a new obstacle, its informal objection, expressed to bankers who asked for its opinion—and all did—to loans to countries that had not reached a settlement of their obligations under war debts to the United States (Jeanneney, 1977, p. 126).

THE CRISIS OF 1926

The Herriot government stumbled along. Having reached 18 to the dollar at the peak after the squeeze, the franc fell during 1925 to 21 in July, 25 in November, 27 in December. There were ten ministers of finance between September 1924 and July 1926 in almost as many governments. A new government would be formed, generally of the Left Cartel headed by Herriot, and present a budget to the Chamber of Deputies, which the chamber would refuse to pass. When the government failed to get advances from the Bank of France, it would fall, and the process would be repeated with a minimally changed cast. A budget was passed in a Briand government in the spring of 1926 under Raoul Péret, minister of finance, but at this late stage it did no good. The franc kept slipping. At the end of April 1926 the French government ate humble pie and settled its war debt with the United States in order to qualify for a new private loan from Morgan. It also settled with Britain. The franc fell further, from 29 to the dollar in May to 31 in June.

On 1 June Péret appointed a Committee of Experts to prepare a new program for the stabilization of the franc. One staff member, Jacques Rueff, served as a member of a similar committee appointed thirty-two years later by President de Gaulle. Before the committee's report was finished, Péret was gone, and a new minister, Caillaux dismissed the governor of the Bank of France, Robineau, whom he had tried unsuccessfully to get rid of on two previous occasions (Jeanneney, 1976, p. 265, n. 53). He contemplated seeking powers that would enable him to dismiss the whole Board of Regents of the Bank of France, persuaded as he was that the bank's policies were based on political and ideological grounds rather than economic and financial ones (ibid., p. 263).

In Robineau's place, he appointed the canny, cards-close-to-the-chest Emile Moreau. On 17 July the Briand cabinet fell, and one of Herriot's succeeded. That lasted four days. The franc sank like a stone from 173 to the pound in mid-June to 180 in early July to 240.25 to the pound and 49 to the dollar (almost 2 cents per franc) at the low on 21 July. The leftist Herriot government was then followed by a right-center government under Poincaré, who served as his own finance minister. The atmosphere changed.

The Committee of Experts' report, published 3 July, had recommended a conventional program of higher taxes, lower spending, and an early attempt to refund the floating debt. Poincaré reversed the committee's recommendations on taxes, lowering those on income and raising levies on consumption. The purpose was to appeal to the capitalist class in France, to persuade it to repatriate its money. A loan was negotiated with Dillon, Read, not J. P. Morgan & Company, but like the British credit from the Federal Reserve Bank of New York and J. P. Morgan the year before, there was no need to draw on it. Instead Poincaré drew on French capital piled up abroad.

The cumulative import surplus of France in 1919 and 1920 had amounted to 23 billion francs. This had been financed partly by foreign borrowing and partly by a speculative capital inflow. By 1921–23, the annual balance-of-payments deficit was down to 2 to 2½ billion. With the capital outflows of 1924, 1925, and 1926, however, the undervalued franc permitted or resulted in the transfer of French capital abroad in amounts of roughly 1½ billion francs a year. How much capital had been accumulated abroad was impossible to estimate. At some stage, however, when it was judged that the bottom had been reached, this capital was prepared to take its profits and return to France.

As the strong man of French politics, Poincaré produced the necessary change in expectations, convincing French owners of foreign balances that the future course of the franc had changed from down to up. By 26 July the rate recovered from 240 at the low to 199, the next day to 196, the dollar over the two days from 49 to 40.5 (francs per dollar).

STABILIZING THE FRANC

As the franc rose in the foreign exchange market, questions presented themselves as to whether, when, and how to stabilize the franc. On 7 August the chamber passed a law permitting the Bank of France to intervene in the market to hold down the value of the franc. To Moreau, governor of the Bank of France, such an operation meant giving up all hope of restoring the currency to par at 25 to the pound and roughly 5 to the dollar (Moreau, 1954 [1991], pp. 67–68). Poincaré gave up hope less quickly, along with the anti-American, anti-German, and strong nationalist, François de Wendel, iron and steel tycoon and leader of the right among the regents of the Bank of France, who continued to cling to the hope of a return to the prewar age of gold (Jeanneney, 1976, p. 317). But Moreau was unwilling to buy sterling—supply francs to the market to hold it down—if sterling was likely to continue to fall in price, that is, the franc might move higher. He wanted an agreement with the government indemnifying the Bank of France for any losses experienced in exchange operations. This was not concluded until September and, in the meantime, the franc was subjected to what now is called "clean floating." Moreau's attitude would strike modern central bankers as stiff-necked and old-fashioned; today central bankers intervene in the exchange market now on one side, now on another, without any attention to nominal profit and loss. In slowing a one-way movement such as was in store for the franc, as the Deutsche Bundesbank or the Bank of Japan undertook after 1974 to slow the decline of the dollar, central banks may incur large losses buying foreign currencies, which then fall in price, or would have losses if they were to value the foreign exchange at market instead of cost, losses large enough to wipe out the entire capital of the central bank if it were operated on the rules of a private profit-making institution. But central bankers are providers of a public good and are today expected to ignore the rules applicable to the private market. This outcome has a bearing on the question as to whether it is possible to have destabilizing speculation. If the private market makes profits and officials end up with losses that they ignore, destabilizing speculation is possible on the Friedman criterion without dividing the speculators into two groups.

As in Britain, there were again purchasing power parity calculations—by Quesnay for the Bank of France in August 1926, giving a range of 131 to 196 to the pound with a preferred narrow band of 160 to 170 (Moreau, 1954 [1991], p. 90); and by Jacques Rueff, privately for Poincaré, in November 1926 when the franc was already up to 130, giving a range of 115 to 145 and a preferred rate of 120 (Rueff, 1959 [1991], p. 5).

In October the rate was between 160 and 170 and started to recover further. Moreau wanted a higher rate for the franc so as not to wipe out too much of the income and wealth of *rentiers* through rising prices; on the other hand, pressure began to come from businessmen, especially in the exporting automobile industry, not to let the rate get too high. In its report of 3 July, the Committee of Experts had warned against a high rate, which would produce a deflation like that being experienced in Britain. Norman visited Moreau twice at the end of July, but there was no talk of the appropriate rate. Other Britishers had divided views; McKenna believed that the franc should be raised to a higher level, Sir Arthur Salter that it should not be allowed to rise too far (Moreau, 1954 [1991], pp. 51ff., 54ff., 146, 155). In November when Léon Jouhaux, head of the Confédération Générale de Travail, the national trade union federation, protested about rising unemployment in export industries, the franc was stabilized de facto at close to the rate recommended by Rueff: 124 francs to the pound and 25.51 to the dollar, or 3.92 cents per franc.

At this rate, however, the franc was seriously undervalued. Purchasing power parity calculations had failed to take into account structural changes and, especially, the existence of a large amount of French capital abroad, which in the normal course of a stabilization would return to its regular "habitat" (to use a modern expression in monetary analysis) when the dust had settled. To transfer this capital inward in real terms, that is, in the form of an import surplus, the exchange rate should have been allowed to go considerably higher at some cost to export- and import-competing industry. At the rate chosen, the private capital inflow had to be contained by the Bank of France through piling up dollars and especially overvalued sterling as a countervailing official capital outflow, foreign exchange that the Bank of France hid by tucking it into "miscellaneous assets" on its balance sheet.[1] The rate was even lower than that which would have produced zero balance on current account in the balance of payments. The current account was in surplus from 1927 to 1930. With the franc seriously undervalued and the pound overvalued, the sterling balances of the Bank of France piled up and an unstable position developed, compounded by rising British and American short-term loans to Germany.

By May of 1927, the Bank of France had £70 million and began to convert it from sterling into gold, to the discomfiture of the Bank of England. But the British Treasury had £600 million of war debts in the form of French Treasury bills and threatened to dump them on the market. Moreau then backed down and in June 1927 agreed to hold £70 million to £80 milion in London balances, representing an estimate of bull speculation in the franc from outside the country, which might be expected to be reversed when the currency was finally stabilized (Clarke, 1967, pp. 118–119, 167). In August 1927 after the Long Island accord, however, Moreau rather subtly undertook swap operations, selling spot sterling to the French money market against purchases of forward, at rates attractive to the market. This maneu-

---

1. The Bank of France was not alone in concealing a portion of its international reserves. When the pound was restored to par in 1925, the Bank of England squirreled away a holding of dollars, hidden under "other securities" in the Issue Department. This amounted only to £5 million by the end of 1925, but rose to £21 million by the end of 1926, to £42 million by the end of 1927 and to £45 million in June 1928 before it became necessary to draw on it in defense of the pound (Sayers, 1976, Vol. 1, pp. 218, 223, 227). In the tension of the summer of 1929, with the Federal Reserve Bank of New York raising its discount rate, the Bank of England sold dollars to stave off the necessity to raise its rediscount rate while waiting for the outcome of the Hague Conference.

ver accomplished two objectives. It mopped up excess liquidity in the Paris market, and it made it appear that the sterling held for French accounts in London was owned by private individuals and firms when it was actually due to be delivered to the Bank of France when the contracts were concluded. The swap operations started at a level equivalent to $100 million in September and rose to the equivalent of $600 million by the following June. At that time, the Bank of France started to let the contracts run out instead of renewing them and received spot sterling under its earlier commitment. It then asked the Bank of England for gold for sterling accruing to it from the market, as if it had been produced by current transactions and not by a capital transaction. The Bank of France *Annual Report* for 1929 went so far as to say that it had not taken the initiative in acquiring gold against sterling (ibid., pp. 121, 148, 166). These forward operations were undertaken only in limited amounts, however; spot sterling held by the bank at the time of the New York stock market crash in October 1929 amounted to £97 million (ibid., p. 167).

De facto stabilization was legalized by a stabilization law of 25 June 1928. This was enacted to cut off speculation in favor of the franc by those who thought the rate undervalued and possibly, on that account, to be revalued. It was preceded by a tense discussion through June, both within the Bank of France and between the governor of the bank and the premier, M. Poincaré. Within the bank, two of the most powerful regents, de Rothschild and de Wendel, powerful in both wealth and politics, were opposed to stabilization at 125 to the pound and wanted the franc raised in value. They stayed away from the final meetings of the regents on 21 and 23 June (Moreau, 1954 [1991], pp. 518–19), and de Wendel voted against the measure in the Chamber of Deputies. For a time, Poincaré, too, held out for upward revaluation and even threatened to resign if the bank, with the support of most of his cabinet, pushed ahead. In his turn, Moreau said he would resign if there were no stabilization law (ibid., pp. 506–21). The legislation was submitted without a resignation and passed; Moreau wrote in his dairy on 23 June:

We are experiencing a historic day . . . restoring a healthy currency to France, and remedying, as far as possible, the damages caused by the war and postwar periods. . . . (Ibid, p. 519)

The essential tasks after the stabilization will be to defend the results against the improvidence and demagogy of the politicians, to reorganize the Paris market so that it will become one of the premier markets of the world, and to coordinate and extend the activities of our banks abroad. (Ibid, p. 525)

There is some question whether the Bank of France was required, under the new legislation, to hold its reserves exclusively in gold, or could legally continue to maintain its stock of foreign exchange. The bank sought to give the impression that it was required by law to hold only gold, but Clarke denies that its authority was limited in this fashion. Its total exchange holding, both spot and forward, at the end of 1928 in sterling and dollars amounted to £1.2 billion, equal to half its total assets. By this time, however, there was a decisive shift on the part of both French and Germans to settle international balances in gold and to abandon the gold exchange standard (Clarke, 1967, p. 141).

LESSONS OF THE FRENCH EXPERIENCE

Two major points emerge from French stabilization in 1926 and 1982, the first related to the possibility of destabilizing speculation, the second having to do with the drawbacks of the gold exchange standard.

In *International Currency Experience,* written for the League of Nations, Ragnar Nurkse regarded the attack on the French franc over 1924–26 as a classic example of destabilizing speculation (League of Nations, 1944, p. 118). Milton Friedman took strenuous objection to this characterization, arguing partly on the a priori grounds noted in Chapter 15 and partly against a definition of destabilizing speculation running in terms of selling when the price falls and buying when the price goes up (1953*a,* p. 176). If a currency is far above its equilibrium level, he believed it is not destabilizing to sell when the price falls. To drive the price in the direction of the equilibrium level can, in fact, be regarded as stabilizing. In the case of the franc, however, speculation drove the currency from 5.5 cents in 1924 to 2 cents at the low in July 1926 from which, when it had come back to 3.92 cents, it was still undervalued. Speculation may have initially driven the franc toward the equilibrium rate, but the rate quickly went well past it. Most (but not all) students—for example Aliber (1962)—are content that even with its demonstration of French financial incompetence in the 1920s, the history of the franc reveals destabilizing speculation.

In the second place, the episode is frequently used to illustrate the grave weaknesses of the gold exchange standard. But the difficulties of the 1920s went deeper than a gold exchange standard and into inappropriate exchange rates, both for the pound and the franc, to say nothing of the mare's nest of reparations, war debts, and commercial debts. The instability of the gold exchange standard is part of the instability of money in general, resting on Gresham's law. To minimize transactions costs in transactions of very different sizes, it is necessary to have more than one money. With two or more monies, not freely convertible into one another without limit, in the way that two $5 bills can be exchanged for one $10, and vice versa, there may be tipping points as expectations about the possibilities of getting back and forth, at a stable price, from one to the other, change. Do not blame the gold exchange standard; blame money.

ITALY IN THE 1920s

Like France in the first half and Britain in the second, Italy had an economically troubled decade in the 1920s. It started with the 1919–20 boom in which the four major banks—the Banca Commerciale Italiana, Credito Italiano, Banca di Roma, and the Banca Italiana di Sconto—lent heavily at medium and long term to industry, bought Italian equities, and got badly hurt when security prices fell in 1921. Worst hit was the Banca di Sconto. A rescue attempt was undertaken in November 1921, with 600 million lire put together by a consortium consisting mainly of the Bank of Italy, with help from the other two much smaller banks of issue, the Bank of Naples and the Bank of Sicily, and 10 million each from the other three commercial banks, sometimes called "mixed banks" or "banks of ordinary credit" (Sraffa, 1922, p. 187). When this sum proved insufficient, the Bank of Italy sought to raise more, but the mixed banks refused to go along, whether because of their own lack of liquidity or because of financial rivalry is nowhere stated in the secondary literature. That there was rivalry was clear. The Perrone brothers of the Ansaldo shipbuilding and steel combine who were closely linked to the Banca Italiana di Sconto, and lost heavily when it collapsed, had tried to get control of the Banca Commerciale Italiana (Clough, 1964, p. 205), forcing its principal stockholders as a defensive measure to form a special corporation, Consorzio Mobiliare Finanziario (Comofin), to which the Banca Commerciale Italiana turned over its prime investments in Lombard and Venetian companies to keep them out of range of a takeover (Toniolo, 1980, p. 201). The Ansaldo company was rescued, if not the Perrone brothers or the Banca Italiana di Sconto, and so was the Banca di Roma, also involved with the Ansaldo firm, which had a difficult passage in 1923. The Banca di Roma was salvaged, to use the word that is current in Italian, at the instance of Mussolini, as widely conjectured, as a payoff to the Vatican for its neutrality in the 1922 March on Rome, because the Banca di Roma was the "keystone of the national Catholic banking and credit network" (Maier, 1975, p. 427).

The Bank of Italy's rescue operations of 1921 left it with 1,300 million lire of dubious assets taken over from the Banca Italiana di Sconto and other operations. Earlier, at the start of the war in December 1914, the Italian government had formed a Consorzio per le Sovvenzioni su Valori Industriale (Consortium for the Support of Industrial Securities) to buoy the weak capital market at the time of liquidity squeeze. In March 1922 it enlarged this to add a Sezione Speciale Autonoma (Special Independent Section) to take over the assets acquired by the Bank of Italy in trying to save the Banca Italiana di Sconto. Between 1922 and 1926, these institutions sold off 4,400 million lire of securities to enable them to reduce their debt to the Bank of Italy. Then came another bout of inflation.

QUOTA NOVANTA (90 TO THE POUND FOR THE LIRE)

The short-run success of the British in getting the pound to par in 1925 and the turnaround in the franc in July 1926 were not lost on Mussolini. The lira had been 19 cents in 1913 but emerged after the war at 10.2 cents. Inflation in 1920, after controls and stabilization support were removed, dropped it to 4.73 cents, or about 100 to the pound sterling. In 1924, along with the franc, it sank lower to 3.36 cents, close to 150 to the pound. American pressure to raise the level of the lira and to stabilize it was intense, as part of the campaign of Benjamin Strong and the House of Morgan to promote economic recovery in Europe (Migone, 1980, pp. 179–99). G. Volpi, the finance minister, tried thereafter to bring it back to his goal of 120, establishing for the purpose an Istituto Nazionale per i Cambi con Estero (National Institute of Foreign Exchange) to take over monopoly trading in foreign exchange as called for in the mercantilist proposals for a Royal Exchanger in England (Toniolo, 1980, pp. 184–86). By this time it was necessary to settle war debts with the

United States, if one hoped to get a stabilization loan from J. P. Morgan. This was done in November 1925, and in January 1926, Italy also settled its war-debt account with Britain. J. P. Morgan & Company then led a syndicate that issued a stabilization loan of $100 million at 94.5. The prospects for an improvement in the lira looked bright until the final attack on the French franc. In May 1926 the Italians gave up defending the lira under weight of a heavy supply, and the exchange rate dropped 16 percent between April and August (ibid., pp. 102–8). In August the Bank of Italy took over the two smaller banks of issue, the Bank of Naples and the Bank of Sicily, to tidy up for the defense of the lira. On 18 August, Mussolini gave a speech from a balcony in Pesaro, as the opening gun in the *battaglia di lira.*

The low quotation for the lira, coinciding with the low of the franc at 240 to the pound, was 153 to the pound. On 27 August after the Pesaro speech it was still 149.13 (ibid., p. 110). Deflation was about to start. The Morgan loan proceeds were transferred from the Bank of Italy to the Treasury in September. The discount rate was raised to 5 percent. By mid-September the lira had improved to 130, by 1 October to 128, and by the end of the month to 110. On 6 November all public debt of less than seven years was subject to forced conversion into a long-term *Littorio* bond. Short-term debt of the government fell from 27 billion to 6 billion lire.

Revaluation on this scale, and the deflation necessary to achieve it, was opposed by everyone—industrialists, bankers, J. P. Morgan, the City of London—but Mussolini was dug in (Maier, 1975, p. 574). The rate question arose specifically when Norman and Strong were negotiating with Stringher in December 1927 over a stabilization loan. The first two thought the contemplated level too high but, observing that it had already been reached at 90 to the pound and 5.263 cents against the dollar and receiving assurances from Stringher that it could be held, let the rate stand as an Italian responsibility (Meyer, 1970, p. 52). The commercial banks, moreover, had been wobbly at the beginning of the year. At the request of the minister of Finance, Volpi, and of the governor of the Bank of Italy, Stringher, the four largest among them formed a Società Finanziamento Titoli (Company for Financing Securities), borrowed 500 million lire from the Bank of Italy, and used it trying to bid up a few stocks they had bought at high prices in 1919 and 1920. They lost 200 million lire more and pleaded to the Bank of Italy that they could not pay interest on their loan (Toniolo, 1980, p. 205). Not only did Italian industry have trouble borrowing in these circumstances, owing to the weakness of the capital market, but deflation of prices in general also reduced profits and the possibilities of industry financing itself with internally generated funds.

The deflation produced one bank collapse of interest for international lender-of-last-resort operations. The Banca Italo-Britannica, the fourth or fifth largest bank in Italy, was owned, and presumably controlled, by the British Italian Banking Corporation, which had three of the London big five (at that time) joint stock banks among its eighty stockholders. It experienced irregularities from 1926 on, having bad luck with speculations and being hurt by the deflation caused by the *quota novanta.* When the Wall Street boom in early 1929 tightened interest rates, the Banca Italo-Brittanica suffered deposit withdrawals. Although they had no special legal responsibility beyond that of any other stockholder, the three big banks in London, plus the Bank of England, put together £2 million to save it but found by

April that its losses were bigger than first realized and went to Italy to get a local contribution to the salvage operation from the Italian government and the Bank of Italy. Pressured heavily by Niemeyer, the Italians finally dug up £1 million, although the Bank of Italy was very unhappy at the abysmal character of the paper it received in return. The Banca Italo-Britannica's assets were finally sold at a net loss of £3 million, of which the Bank of England's share was £250,000. This was rationalized as the cost of saving London from threatened shame (Sayers, 1976, Vol. 1, pp. 259–62). A great deal more shame was approaching down the pike.

The *quota novanta* of Mussolini imposed strenuous deflation on Italy well before the turndown of business in Germany in mid-1928, when long-term lending from the United States was cut off, and still further in advance of the stock market crash of 1929, which ushered in the Great Depression of the twentieth century.

SUGGESTED SUPPLEMENTARY READING

Dulles (1929), *The French Franc, 1914–1928.*
League of Nations (Nurkse) (1944), *International Currency Experience.*
McGuire (1926), *Italy's International Economic Position.*
Moreau (1954 [1991]), *The Golden Franc: Memoirs of a Governor of the Bank of France.*
Schuker (1976), *The End of French Predominance in Europe.*
Stringher and Volpi (1927), *The Financial Reconstruction of Italy.*

In French

Debeir (1978), La Crise du franc de 1924.
Jeanneney (1978). De la Speculation financière comme arme diplomitique.
Philippe (1931). *Le Drame financier de 1923–1928.*

In Italian

Toniolo (1980), *L'economia dell'Italia fascista.*

20

The 1929 Depression

It is never safe to dogmatize about human behavior. And as human behavior is the subject-matter of all economic theory, we are bound to recognize that there is no conclusion in the field of economics that may not be stultified by conduct sufficiently irrational and perverse. But that is not a good reason for abstaining from action and letting things drift in crisis, or for deliberately taking what according to all rational standards is the wrong course.

(Hawtrey, *The Art of Central Banking,* 1932, p. 239)

EUROPE AND THE UNITED STATES

The 1929 depression requires us to shift focus somewhat to the United States, although not nearly as much as many American economists would think necessary. *The Great Depression Revisited* (Brunner, ed., 1981), the second book with that title (see Van der Wee, ed., 1972), assumed that the depression was caused by, and occurred almost entirely in, the United States. The international aspects, and any suggestion that it had much to do with Europe, are waved away. In addition, the analysis concentrates exclusively on the question as to whether the depression was caused by changes in the money supply or by nonmonetary factors, and specifically one, a change in spending, that is, on the debate between the monetarists and the Keynesians. It is my contention that both models are too restrictive, insofar as they ignore "overtrading" and the instability of credit, as discussed in Chapter 15 (pp. 264–65) and evidenced in history over several centuries, and especially as they ignore the complex international interaction spreading extreme tightness in liquidity and driving down world commodity prices. The depression was communicated from country to country partly by rapidly shifting capital movements, partly by falling prices of internationally traded goods, which had nothing to do, in the short run, with monetarist or Keynesian analysis but fit easily into the Hawtrey mold of *Currency and Credit* (1919 [1927]), putting emphasis on the necessity for dealers to dump stocks of commodities when credit becomes tight. Moreover, the need to choose between the origin of financial crisis in one market or another, in the United States as Friedman and Schwartz insisted (esp. Schwartz, 1981, pp. 21–24) or Europe as Herbert Hoover preferred to believe (1952, Vol. 3, pp. 61–62), was rejected in earlier chapters and is irrelevant in 1929. There is enough blame to go around.

Two recent books do emphasize the international character of the depression as Snowden in England, Brüning in Germany, Hoover in the United States, and Laval in France undertook deflationary policies in support of the gold standard (Temin, 1989; Eichengreen, 1992). This is a distinct improvement over the former standard "it-was-all-the-fault-of-U.S.-monetary policy" model, but it is still insufficiently subtle in my judgment. It should also be recorded as a gain that Milton Friedman, after reading Moreau's *Memoirs* in English, would now extend responsibility for initiating the depression from the United States alone for its failure to follow gold standard rules, to the failure of both the United States and France (1991, p. xii).

THE SETTING

The international financial position at the end of the 1920s was highly unstable. Overvaluation of the pound and undervaluation of the French franc had piled up sterling in the nervous hands of French authorities. Reparations were being paid through the vulnerable mechanism of continued American loans to Germany and, in turn, were needed to pay debt service on government loans by the United States as the American government insisted. European recovery in the production of grain and sugar especially, but also semifinished and finished manufactures in the face of expansion of production outside Europe undertaken during the war, had led prices, particularly agricultural prices, to turn soft as early as 1925. In this position depression was ushered in by the rapid rise in the New York stock market in the second quarter of 1928 which cut off long-term lending by the United States to Europe, particularly Germany, and to the world periphery represented primarily by Argentina, Australia, Chile, and Latin America generally. Three-million-share days had been recorded in the New York stock market twice in 1925 and three times in 1926. On 1 March 1928, the market turned over 4 million shares. Brokers' loans, used to finance clients' purchases on margin—for example, 10 percent down and 90 percent borrowed—rose from $3.6 billion on 30 June 1927 to $4.9 billion on 30 June 1928, and $6.4 billion at the end of the year. Funds sucked into the security markets, directly into securities or by way of brokers' loans, tightened interest rates and cut off foreign lending. The rise in New York stock prices attracted investors from Europe and the rise in interest rates some short-term lending. Deficiencies of the data make the swing in capital flows impossible to estimate precisely for the periods before and after 30 June 1928, as contrasted with entire calendar years, which are less relevant and interesting. For long-term investment, however, based on figures worked out by Heywood Fleisig (1969, 1972), there was something like a swing of $2 billion between the outflow in the eighteen months before 30 June 1928 and the following fifteen months to 30 September 1929 on the eve of the crash when capital flowed inward. New issues in New York dropped sharply, especially for Germany, Asia, and Oceania but remained positive. Trade in existing securities changed from an outflow to an inflow (Kindleberger, 1973 [1986], pp. 58–59).

The peak of U.S. real output was reached in the second quarter of 1929, and production eased off in the third. Whether the stock market absorbs funds gives rise to debate. On the one hand, it is argued that for every buyer who puts money into the stock market, a seller takes it out, so that the stock market cannot reduce the money supply. The counterargument is that an additional dollar diverted from expenditure on goods and services to the stock market, either to buy shares or to lend on call, is subtracted from expenditure on real output, whereas the seller of the security in a stock market boom is likely to hold the money received from his sale idle awaiting a new opportunity to go back into the market. While the overall money supply is unchanged, within the total there is a shift from what Keynes in the *Treatise on Money* (1930) called the "transactions circulation" to the "financial circulation." If one is reluctant to disaggregate the money supply, the same effect on output is reached through a decline in income velocity, that is, the rate at which total money turns over against national income.

THE 1929 CRASH

The stock market rose in 1929, despite efforts of the Federal Reserve Board to talk it down and despite the board's action in increasing the discount rate in August 1929. Depression had set in in Germany in 1927 when Schacht's campaign against German borrowing in New York began to take hold (McNeill, 1986, ch. 5). There followed a switch to short-term loans (James, 1986, p. 136). With the start of the Wall Street boom in U.S. stocks, long-term lending from New York fell still further. Depression had been endemic in Germany in 1926 and 1927, but the higher interest rates necessary to attract short-term funds pushed production still lower. Unemployment rose from 355,000 in the summer of 1928 to 1.9 million in 1929. The Frankfurt Insurance Company failed in August 1929. Suddenly tighter money in Britain in September, ascribed by a French historian to the action of the Bank of France in pulling gold out of London because of French irritation with Snowden at the Hague meeting on the Young Plan noted earlier (pp. 295–96) (Néré, 1968, pp. 77–78) produced a bankruptcy of the Hatry Investment Trust, a high-flying enterprise that bought up companies with monies borrowed from banks, got into trouble when prices fell, tried to use fraudulent collateral, and was caught out. The Bank of England raised its discount rate from 5½ percent to 6½ percent on 26 September 1929—a response to Wall Street, says Sayers, and not to Hatry or The Hague (1976, Vol. 1, p. 229). Pressure spread to Scandinavia where all discount rates were hiked up into line. As early as August, Montagu Norman had expressed worry that Britain might be forced off gold, a sign of "distress." When the stock market crash came on Black Thursday, 24 October, and Black Tuesday, 29 October, he felt a certain relief (H. Clay, 1957 [1979], pp. 252–54).

The decline in the New York stock market from an average level of 316 in September, on the base of 1926 as 100, to 147 in December, and particularly the heroic declines of 24 and 29 October, have been ascribed by one exponent of "rational expectations"—a theory holding that markets always reflect faithfully what is likely to happen, based on the information available to them—to realization by the market that forces resisting the drive to raise American tariffs had been defeated. That knowledge is thought to have sunk in as a consequence of a particular vote on 23 October on a tariff on carbides, reported on the inside pages of the daily press (Wanniski, 1977, pp. 133–36). The analysis is hard to swallow. Although some monetarists are prepared to admit the Hawley-Smoot tariff as one of the few nonmonetary forces contributing to the Great Depression (Meltzer, 1981; Schwartz, 1981), the usual view in economic analysis is that tariffs raise prices, divert spending from imports to domestic goods, and, in the first instance at least, are expansionary rather than a force for contraction. In a dynamic world, it can happen that retaliation is so severe as to hurt exports more than the tariffs reduce imports. For the market for securities to produce such a reading more than six months in advance of the event and mark down prices of manufacturing companies by very large percentages strains credulity. Nor is it likely that deflation from that cause would spread to primary products immediately or to imported raw materials and foodstuffs, most of which are not subject to tariffs. The suggestion that foreign retaliation for United States action in raising tariffs under the Hawley-Smoot tariff was particularly concentrated against American farm exports and helps account for their 66 percent decline from 1929 to 1932 (Meltzer, 1976, p. 460; R. J. Gordon and Wilcox, 1981, p. 82) has virtually no historical basis. The evidence—the monetarists cite none—makes it clear that retaliation was directed to American manufactures and to such services as motion picture rentals (J.M. Jones, 1934).

A less involuted explanation of the crash is that the stock market got severely extended on the basis of call loans, including a considerable but immeasurable quantity from Europe. Brokers' loans are divided in the statistics into three categories: New York banks, out-of-town banks, and all other. "All other" represents both nonbanks in the United States, including in 1929 many manufacturing and productive businesses that had put their idle cash into the market to earn high interest rates on a liquid asset that could be called on no notice—any day—and foreign lenders. It appears that with the credit strain in London, foreign loans were called—loans by "all others" dropped $120 million in the two weeks ended 23 October—and call money rates went up sharply. At this stage, business lenders began to worry and started to pull out their loans, fearful of the possibility that in a sharp sell-off with falling prices, the stock market might be closed, as it had been in the crash of 1873, and their liquid loan would turn into a frozen asset. Seeing the nervousness of the call money market, New York banks—which had been slowing their contributions to call loans to get ready to take over in case "out-of-town banks" and "all other," which felt no responsibility for the steadiness of the market, withdrew—cut down on other lending to prepare for trouble in stocks. In so doing, they extended the decline in stock prices to commodities.

In the business practice of the 1920s, many exports to the United States were sold through commission agents on arrival. Goods would be shipped to, say, New York, with title retained by the foreign exporter, and sold on organized exchanges in the United States. If buyers were cut off from normal sources of credit, they would be less able to make regular purchases, and sellers, unwilling to store the goods or to divert them to other markets, would have to mark prices down. This is the only way to make sense of the decline in wholesale prices to the end of the year, closely timed with the stock market crash and worldwide, by no means limited to the United States. No explanation relying on the U.S. money supply or the failure of the U.S. money supply to rise in the eighteen months prior to October 1929, or on changes in spending on housing (Barber, 1978; Gordon and Wilcox, 1981), or on automobiles (Rostow, 1978, pp. 335–36) can account for these declines in wholesale prices between August 1929 and September 1930: 22 percent in Japan; 16 percent in Canada; 15 percent in the United Kingdom: 14 percent in Italy, and 12 percent in both the United States and Germany (Schwartz, 1981, table 5, p. 24). For particular internationally traded goods, monthly average prices declined by this range in the three months between September 1929 and December (Table 20.1).

Imported commodities sold on consignment experienced greater price declines than export products produced in the United States and financed in the interior. Corn may have suffered more than wheat and cotton because it depended especially on export markets in Germany and Cuba, as did its product, lard, and these countries were already hard hit from the cutoff in capital imports in the case of Germany and from the earlier decline in the price of sugar for Cuba. Cuban sugar, moreover, was largely owned in the United States and financed in advance of import, which may account for its lesser decline among imported commodities. *The Economist* of 8 February 1930 produced a depressing review of business conditions under the title "The fall of prices" (1930, p. 286). Contemporary observers regarded price changes as important, even though some monetary theorists today—notably the monetarists—dismiss them as irrelevant.

Another product that depended on easy credit for its sales was automobiles. U.S. production fell from 622,000 in March to 416,000 in September as interest rates tightened, and then to 319,000 in October, 169,000 in November, and 92,500 in December, a total decline over the nine months of 83 percent, as banks rationed credit to customers to safeguard the market in brokers' loans. The figures are confused by a massive seasonal fluctuation due to model changes, which occurred annually in these years, but the low point was usually November, not December. Even if we assume that half of the decline was the result of seasonal variation, no monetary or Keynesian theory can explain a collapse of 40 percent, or 25 percent between March and September, as well as can a theory based on instability of credit and its freezing in crisis.

U.S. imports also fell with surprising speed, from $396 million in September 1929 to $307 million in December, a decline compounded of a sharp price decline of 15 percent or so, but also a deep cut in volume. Here again the money supply

Table 20.1 Changes in United States Prices of Selected Commodities, September–December 1929 (in percentages)

Imported Commodities		Exported Commodities	
Cocoa	−15.4	Corn	−14.1
Coffee	−13.1	Cotton	−5.6
Copper	−9.3	Wheat	−3.6
Hides	−18.4		
Lead	−8.8		
Rubber	−25.7		
Silk	−10.0		
Sugar	−6.9		
Tin	−10.1		
Zinc	−16.7		

Source: Calculated from Kindleberger (1973 [1986], p. 143).

and the investment function, that is, the monetarist and the Keynesian explanations, fail to explain why.

RESPONSE TO THE CRASH IN THE UNITED STATES

There were two reactions in the United States to the stock market crash. The first was taken by George Harrison, Benjamin Strong's successor as president of the Federal Reserve Bank of New York, who violated instructions from the Federal Reserve Board in Washington and proceeded to buy $160 million of U.S. government securities in the week after 30 October, well above the regular limit of $25 million a week, and followed that with $210 million more in the rest of November. This was a lender-of-last-resort operation to ease liquidity in the crunch. The Federal Reserve discount rate was quickly lowered to 5 percent on 1 November and 4½ percent on 15 November. In Washington, President Hoover reduced taxes and asked firms not to lower wages, Keynesian policies briefly maintained. He pushed ahead with the signing of the Hawley-Smoot tariff in June 1930, a measure now interpreted by monetarists as deflationary because of retaliation but normally regarded as expansionary.

None of this did much good in raising prices, which proved to be the intractable core of the matter. The usual monetarist, and even Keynesian, view is that unless there is money illusion, prices do not count: losses for one group in deflation are offset by gains for another. That proposition ignores dynamic aspects, both asymmetry between groups and lags. Declines in prices spread bankruptcy, first of firms, then of banks. Real income gains do not lead to the creation of new firms and banks. And losses from price declines are immediate and recognizable, whereas benefits of rising real income through falling prices take time to spread through the system and are adjusted to slowly. By the spring of 1930 the money supply had not started its decline in any serious way, interest rates were well down, but security and commodity prices kept sagging, making the weight of debt ever more heavy. The process is best described as "structural deflation," more or less symmetrical, but with opposite sign to structural inflation of the cost-push variety in which rising prices cannot be ascribed, in the first instance, to either monetary expansion or to upward shifts in spending.

THE POSITION IN EUROPE

At least four countries in Europe were experiencing depression before the stock market crash in New York: Germany, Britain, Italy, and Austria. In Germany, deflationary pressure was caused by the halting of long-term lending and its replacement by short-term loans that could readily be cut off or withdrawn. British unemployment in depressed areas came from weakening exports, a heavy load of debt left over from 1920, and high interest rates required to prevent foreign capital from leaving. Italy suffered from the self-inflicted wound of the *quota novanta,* and Austria from a weakened banking structure stretching back to the amputation of its hinterland in the Treaty of St. Germain, on the one hand, and the losses suffered by banks in the 1924 squeeze on the French franc on the other.

The New York stock market crash was communicated to security markets in Europe, along with the associated decline in internationally traded commodities. The 32 percent fall in New York stock prices between the September average and the December, after a rebound from the November low, was exceeded in Canada with a decline of 33 percent, matched in Belgium with 30 percent, and echoed in declines in other markets running 16 percent in Britain, 15 percent in the Netherlands, 14 percent in Germany, 11 percent in France, 10 percent in Switzerland, 8 percent in Sweden. The fall in Germany came on top of an earlier decline between June 1928 and September 1929 of 15 percent. Reduced share prices weakened the position of European banks, which owned industrial stocks as well as made loans on them.

Unemployment in Germany led to political crisis early in 1930. The 1.9 million unemployed of 1929 overstrained the resources of the Reichsanstalt für Arbeitslosenversicherung (German Unemployment Insurance Fund), which had to borrow from the government to meet its commitments. Socialists and unions proposed raising the contributions of bureaucrats who were protected from unemployment by contract, and clashed with the German Peoples' party representing government workers. From the end of March onward, no government was able to govern with a majority (Born, 1967, pp. 39–42). Heinrich Brüning, who had taken office as prime minister in the March crisis, undertook a strong deflationary program, governing by decree under an emergency provision of the Weimar Constitution. When the Reichstag in June tried to abrogate his powers, he called for new elections in September, two years before they were constitutionally required.

The September elections produced large, unwelcome gains for the Nazi party, and foreign deposits in German banks, which at 8.9 billion Reichsmarks constituted 40 percent of major liabilities, started to leave. Deposits in commercial banks declined 330 million Reichsmarks in August, 225 million in September, 720 million in October. German credit had been weakened by the near failure of the Young loans in June 1930, but the Brüning government managed to borrow $125 million in October from a syndicate headed by Lee, Higginson & Company, a Boston banking firm. Share prices of German banks began to sag, and a number of them, notably the Danat (Darmstädter & Nationalbank), the Commerz & Privatbank, and the Deutsche & Diskontogesellschaft, formed from mergers in the 1920s, supported their shares by purchases in the market with cash, lowering ratios of reserves to deposits and of capital to deposits. The Berliner Handelsgesellschaft used M. M. Warburg to borrow further from New York and supported its stock with outside rather than internal funds (Born, 1967, pp. 60–61). Spending cash reserves to buy back its own stock was also undertaken by the Creditanstalt in Vienna, the only significant Austrian bank remaining after a series of forced mergers starting in 1924. The Bodenkreditanstalt had taken over the bankrupt Union Bank and the Verkehrbank in 1927 and itself was absorbed into the Creditanstalt in 1929, with 90 million schillings of capital but 140 million of accumulated losses. The Creditanstalt, it was said, was demoralized at that time by easy access to foreign short-term credits.

Brüning's political reaction to the Nazi gains in September was to seek foreign policy success in three directions: a heightened campaign against reparations; an armament program that included construction of a pocket battleship, the so-called *Panzerkreuzer* (armored cruiser); and a Zollunion (customs union) with Austria, announced in March 1931. The internal reaction was tepid, but that in the rest of Europe was strongly negative. It was communicated to Germany and to Austria by withdrawals of foreign funds.

THE SALVAGING OF ITALIAN BANKS

The announcement on 11 May 1931 that the Creditanstalt had impaired its capital is generally taken as the start of the great deflationary spiral from 1931 to 1933. It was the first difficulty to be made public. Already in Italy, however, in secret, the Bank of Italy and the government had been bailing out a series of banks from the summer of 1930, including the second leading "mixed bank," the Credito Italiano (Toniolo, ed., 1978, pp. 284–85). The Banca Populare di Vovara was reorganized in a convention of 12 September 1930 by absorbing 75 million of bad securities into the Istituto di Liquidazione of the Bank of Italy. Other operations followed: the Banca delle Venezie was liquidated, the Banca Agricola Provinciale di Rovigo was infused with new liquidity, and the Banca Toscana of Florence was reorganized.

A decree law of December 1930, not published, gave the Bank of Italy power to issue further bank notes in operations connected with the Istituto di Liquidazione. Four days later the Istituto itself was reorganized, and the following day, the last of the year, there began discussions for a major rescue operation for the Credito Italiano. These were concluded in February 1931 with the division of the bank into a bank of ordinary credit, on the one hand, and a Societá Finanziaria Italiana (SFI), which took over the Credito's industrial participations on the other. The cost of these latter had been 1.01 billion lire, their market value 550 million, leaving a loss of 460 million lire, divided 120 million for the Credito Italiano as a capital write-off and the rest for the Istituto di Liquidazione, which proved to be almost entirely a pure subsidy. The new mixed bank, the Banca Nazionale di Credito, was permitted to continue to hold shares of electrical, telephone, and mortgage companies, on the dubious assumption that these did better than other industrial shares (Toniolo, 1980, pp. 215–16).

At the outset of these troubles, A. Mosconi, the Italian finance minister, made optimistic by a small increment in reserves of gold and foreign exchange, relaxed controls over the foreign exchanges in March 1930. The step proved unwise as Mosconi had failed to anticipate a move to pay off foreign debts.

THE CREDITANSTALT

Italian difficulties produced little or no ripple effect because they were unknown. The same cannot be said of those of the Creditanstalt, which announced on 11 May 1931 that it had lost more than half its capital—the criterion under Austrian law by which a bank was declared failed. Its losses amounted to 140 million schillings, its capital to 125 million, and its published surplus to 40 million. On 12 May the Austrian government announced a program to rescue the bank with 160 million schillings—100 million from the federal government, 30 million from the National Bank, and 30 million from the Rothschild group with which the bank had always been identified, largely from Amsterdam. The action failed to allay concern, and a run started, both foreign and domestic. The Austrian National Bank's notes in circulation rose from 305 million in the week ended 7 May to 1,038 million on 15 May and to 1,141 million on 31 May (Pressburger, 1969, pp. 83–87).

Austria was unable to save the Creditanstalt and the schilling alone and turned for help to the Bank of England, the League of Nations, and when these institutions begged off, the year-old Bank of International Settlements. On May 29 the BIS arranged a credit of 100 million schillings ($14 million) from ten of the strongest central banks and its own funds. The Austrian government had asked for 150 million schillings. Negotiations to put together the 100 million had taken from 14 May to 29 May, a delay probably caused by French objection to Austrian participation in the Zollunion with Germany, a matter in suspense then as the French government had raised at the International Court of Justice at the Hague the question of whether Austrian participation in such an arrangement with Germany was legal under the provision of the Treaty of St. Germain, which forbade the political union of Austria with Germany. The 100 million credit was exhausted in five days, and the Austrian National Bank sought another. This was also arranged, subject to the condition that Austria obtain a private 150 million schilling loan from abroad. At this stage, the French insisted that to qualify for a loan, the Austrian government must renounce the Zollunion with Germany. The Austrian government refused and fell. Still under pressure, the Austrian National Bank raised its discount rate to 6 percent on 8 June and 7½ percent on 16 June. This was the day that Governor Norman of the Bank of England, thoroughly incensed at the Bank of France for mixing politics and finance, went ahead on his own with a 100 million schilling loan on a seven-day renewable basis (Clarke, 1967, p. 188). This gallant gesture was without much effect on France or Austria and itself became frozen. It was finally paid off in August when the League of Nations arranged for a 250 million schilling loan from seven governments.

A historian of the episode concludes that the Creditanstalt was so riddled with bad foreign loans, many of them taken over from the bankrupt Bodenkreditanstalt when that failed in 1929, that it was a mistake to try to save it. Under the Bagehot rule, the lender of last resort is called upon for help with illiquidity but not with insolvency (A. Schubert, 1981, p. 178). There is a rule, however, that Bagehot did not consider in the circumstances of British banking in 1870: some banks are too big to be allowed to fail. Their failure is likely to spread, through bank runs, as happened in the case of the Creditanstalt—not to the other Austrian banks, as it happened, but through runs by foreign depositors on banks in other countries. The Creditanstalt had more than half of the bank deposits in Austria, and its failure threw unwelcome light on the financial fragility of all of Central Europe.

THE RUN ON GERMANY

The run on Austria triggered others on Hungary, Czechoslovakia, Rumania, Poland, and Germany. The question was raised in the German press as to whether

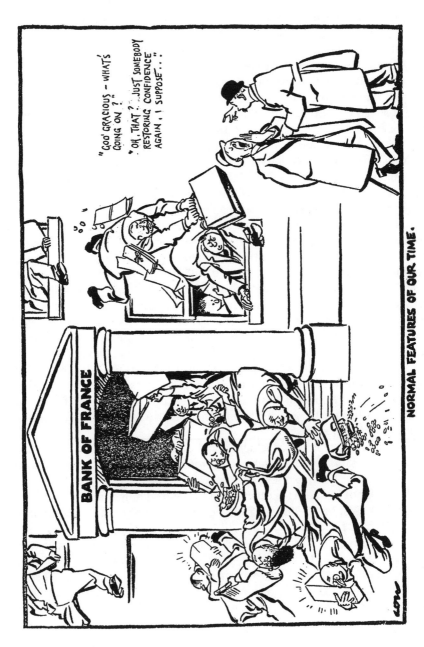

NORMAL FEATURES OF OUR TIME.

Cartoon by David Low (29 May 1935), from *The Evening Standard*. By permission of *The Evening Standard*/Solo.

Americans knew the difference between Austria and Germany (Bennett, 1962, p. 117). In May 288 million Reichsmarks of foreign credits were called. The Danatbank lost 97 million, the Dresdener Bank 79 million, the Deutsche Bank 50 million, and the Commerz & Privatbank 36 million (Born, 1967, p. 67). Large losses were posted at the end of May for Karstadt, the department store, and for Nord Stern, a prominent insurance company. In the first six days of June the Reichsbank lost gold and foreign exchange of 164 million Reichsmarks more.

Brüning, the prime minister, took strong deflationary steps under this authority to govern by decree, invoked again in March 1931, but thought it necessary for domestic political reasons to assert that Germany had reached the limit of its ability to pay reparations. The deflationary measures led to an attempt by the Socialist and Communist parties to recall (in an *Aufruf*) the powers to govern by decree. The announcement on reparations, intended solely for home consumption, stimulated a renewed run on the Reichsbank's foreign exchange reserves. At this critical time, President Hoover, on 19 June, made the suggestion that all countries should agree to a one-year moratorium on both reparations and war debts. Thomas Lamont's papers show that the idea came from a memorandum by Rufus Leffingwell of J. P. Morgan & Company, which Lamont read over the telephone to Hoover on 5 June (Ferguson, 1981, p. 581).

The French had not been notified of the projected moratorium in advance of the announcement, despite independent recommendations from Thomas Lamont by telephone from New York and one by Dwight Morrow in the White House that this should be done. Taken by surprise, they were unwilling to agree without discussion. This took three weeks, even with the fortuitous presence in Europe at the time of both Secretary of State Henry Stimson and Secretary of the Treasury Andrew Mellon. The French raised the valid legal question as to whether it was legitimate to declare a moratorium on unconditional reparation payments of the Dawes and Young plans, as well as on the conditional payments, rather akin to discussing who really owns a house and who should call the fire department when the building is going up in smoke. While the discussion went on, the Reichsbank was drained of gold and foreign exchange down to its 40 percent legal limit.

The run on Germany was exacerbated by the troubles of the Danatbank, which were, in turn, critically affected by those of a firm named Nordwolle. Nordwolle was a speculative enterprise that made the mistake of going long on wool at the beginning of 1931 with funds largely borrowed from the Danat. When wool continued to fall further—from 86 cents (U.S.) a pound in December 1930 to 80 cents in March 1931 and 75 cents in June—Nordwolle sought to hide its losses by transferring the wool at cost to a Dutch subsidiary, Ultramarine. Two days after the Hoover moratorium was announced, the losses of Ultramarine, Nordwolle, and the Danatbank were revealed. The run on the Reichsbank's reserve, slowed by the moratorium, picked up. With the limit reached, the Reichsbank cast about for a loan.

Already in February 1931, Hans Luther, now president of the Reichsbank, had proposed a big loan to fund U.S. bank claims on Germany to the extent of $350 million to $475 million. There was no noticeable response. Pierre Quesnay, a Bank of France official on leave to work at the Bank for International Settlements (BIS), put forward the idea at the time that the British should float a long-term loan in

France—in francs, that is, bearing all the exchange risk. This did not appeal to the British, possibly because such a loan might prove dysfunctional in calling attention to the weakness of sterling and encouraging withdrawals of short-term credits, possibly because they felt they would be led into making political concessions to the French (Clarke, 1967, pp. 178, 180). In his turn, Norman offered the proposal that a bank of international cooperation be formed, to be managed by the BIS, to issue bonds in the United States and France with the funds to be re-lent to governments and private entities. The French were profoundly uninterested: if French money were to be loaned out, it would be by French management. The United States was equally unenthusiastic. Echoing the French, J. P. Morgan & Company felt that bankers would be unwilling to yield their judgment to an international institution, and Jay Crane, vice-president of the Federal Reserve Bank of New York in charge of foreign exchange, thought that such an institution would attract only second-class customers (ibid., pp. 179–80).

On 24 June President Luther of the Reichsbank managed to put together a loan of $100 million: $25 million each from the United Kingdom, the United States, France, and the BIS. Luther had wanted much more, $500 million or $1 billion, but the French would not go along without political conditions such as that reparations would be resumed in a year, and the British, thoroughly disliking the idea of lending money to Germany to pay France, were unwilling to accept political conditions (ibid., pp. 194–96). This may have been an excuse rather than a reason, since British lending capacity was shrinking. When it proved that $100 million was all he could get, and then only to 16 July, Luther tried to keep the amount and terms quiet, lest the market should learn how limited his ammunition was. In this he was unsuccessful (Born, 1967, p. 82).

Equally unsuccessful were attempts to keep hidden the troubles of the Danatbank. Its head, Jacob Goldschmidt, was an outsider in banking circles, having come in from the stock exchange. There was little love lost between him and the others, and especially Oskar Wasserman of the Deutsche Bank & Diskontogesellschaft. Wasserman was unwilling to cooperate with other banks in establishing a new bank institute with 50 million Reichsmarks, half to be used to pay off foreign claimants and half to add to domestic bank capital. If a bank were threatened, he said, the Reich should take over its liabilities, but the bank should be liquidated. When a Swiss newspaper mentioned on 6 July that a large German bank was in trouble, moreover, Wasserman named the Danatbank so as not to have it thought it was his own institution. Born calls this "putting the outsider to the sword" (ibid., pp. 88, 96).

On 11 July the Landesbank of Rhine Province failed, freezing credits of a number of communes, and the municipal deposits of Cologne and Dusseldorf. At a cabinet meeting that night, with representatives of finance and industry present, Wasserman of the Deutsche Bank wanted a three-day moratorium, Reinhart of the Commerz & Privatbank a moratorium on foreign payments. On 13 July the Danatbank failed. This led to a run so severe that many banks limited their payments to 100 Reichsmarks to a depositor, or 20 percent of the amounts requested. That evening a two-day bank holiday was called for the fourteenth and fifteenth. On the morning of July 14 the Dresdener bank said that it was illiquid. A standstill was imposed on foreign credits since many foreign creditors called for the full amount of their balances for the moment of the banks' opening.

The problems of the Dresdener Bank were met by a *Haftungsgemeinschaft* (communal guarantee of liabilities) organized on 18 July under the aegis of the Golddiskontobank but without guarantees from either the Reich or the Reichsbank. Only the Danatbank was left out "From today's standpoint it is incomprehensible that the Reichsbank would let it fail" (Irmler, 1976, p. 287). Deposits of the forty-three other participating banks of all kinds and sizes, national and provincial, were guaranteed first up to 15,000 Reichsmarks, then to 50,000, finally to 100,000. In practice, as with the suspension of the Bank Act of 1844 in England in 1847 and 1866, it was not needed because it was available. By 3 August only 38.3 million Reichsmarks of liabilities looked as though they might need help; by 6 August the amount had shrunk to 3.6 million Reichsmarks. A few days later the whole arrangement was terminated (Born, 1967, pp. 115–16).

The government also arranged for an Akzept & Garantiebank (Acceptance and Guarantee Bank) to provide a third signature for paper to make it eligible for discounts at the Reichsbank—exactly like *comptoirs d'escompte* in France in 1848. By the end of 1931, the Akzept & Garantiebank had lent its name to credits of 1.6 billion Reichsmarks, of which 1,360 million Reichsmarks was still outstanding at the end of 1932. Thereafter, with recovery under the Nazi regime, the amount was quickly reduced and the institution dismantled in 1936.

HEROIC ACTION TO BREAK THROUGH CONSTRAINTS

A deep philosophical issue lies in the question of whether individual actors—their personalities and the decisions they take, more or less on their own—are critical to historical outcomes or whether they are usually constrained by circumstances and conditions over which they have little control. The depression starting in 1929 provides a series of necessarily inconclusive tests bearing on the problem. In numerous cases, political actors were hemmed in by laws, such as the ceiling on advances to the government by the Bank of France, and the inability of the government to fund the floating debt, or the gold reserve rules of the Federal Reserve system in the United States. Those who believe in bold action to overcome restraint argue that a heroic actor should announce boldly to the public that he knew that what he was going to do was illegal, but that force majeure required breaking the law (Schuker, 1976, pp. 138–139; Friedman and Schwartz, 1963, p. 322). President Roosevelt is sometimes cited as one who acted heroically, and not always with complete comprehension of where he was going (as in his messages to the World Economic Conference of 1933).

In the German depression, the question is whether Brüning was fenced in by international circumstances and domestic politics, as Borchardt believes (1979 [1991], ch. 9), or had some room to maneuver if he had had the intelligence to find a way and the skill and courage to pursue it (Holtfrerich, 1982b, 1990a, 1990b). The debate has continued in Germany without a resolution. In a number of views, the gold standard takes the blame as constraint because it was regarded as out of the question for such politicians as Snowden in Britain, Hoover in the United States, Brüning in Germany, and later Laval in France to defy the unwritten rules of the gold standard game.

A classic example of the clash between orthodox adherence to the rules and heroic action to break them is given in an account of a meeting in the Reichsbank on 15 and 16 September 1931 to discuss a proposal of Wilhelm Lautenbach, a high-ranking civil servant who has been called a German pre-Keynesian Keynes, to have the government borrow from the Reichsbank funds to spend on public works (Borchardt and Schötz, eds., 1931 [1991]). The edited transcript of the meeting had lain virtually unnoticed in the archives of the Friederich List Gesellschaft, a conservative nonprofit policy organization, under the auspices of which, and those of the Reichsbank, the meeting had been called. The conferees, called to the meeting at short notice, included government and central bank officials and distinguished academic economists such as Gerhard Colm, Walter Eucken, Hans Neisser, and Wilhelm Röpke. The timing was dramatic—two months after the Standstill Agreement introducing exchange control into Germany and less than a week before the pound sterling abandoned gold. The interest lies not only in the high level of economic policy debate, with frequent anguished interruptions by Hans Luther, president of the Reichsbank, but also in the fact that two years later, Adolf Hitler—and to a certain extent, even before him, Fritz von Papen—stumbled into similar public works policies that produced a boom in Germany and cured the devastating unemployment.

Cartoon, *facing page*: "On the left, above, the Italian Finance Minister is indulging in decidedly dangerous tricks. Messrs. Pierpont Morgan and Owen Young cling together in perfect harmony and describe vast figures on the ice; Mr. Morgan, however, by way of precaution, holds firmly crossed the hands of his partner. The German Finance Minister, Dietrich, seems to have made a slip [he had recently announced that Germany could pay no more reparations]. The spectacle causes great anxiety to M. Moret, Governor of the Bank of France, but moves him to circumspection.

Much greater freedom of movement is shown by Mr. McGarrah, the President of the Basle B.I.S., as becomes one with his connections. Dr. Melchior (Germany) convulsively grasps him by the hat. The Belgian, M. Francqui, spins round without end about his own ideas and explanations, to which he can't get anybody to pay attention. Mr. MacDonald doesn't know where to turn next; in trying to make a beautiful figure of the £ he has put his leg out of joint.

Dr. Luther, director of the Reichsbank, is up to the neck in cold water; on his head Dr. Brüning balances like a great question mark. MM. Laval and Flandin describe elegant figures together: but look out! there's danger near. Mr. Neville Chamberlain is completely dislocated. The sprightly Lord Snowden has got Mr. Montagu Norman, Governor of the Bank of England, by the beard and twists him round. Mr. Hoover is not taking part in the sport, and tries to brush out all the figures on the ice. So as not to catch cold, he's wrapped his feet in the rags of "Prosperity." His Secretary of the Treasury, Mr. Mellon, who's in a bit of a fix himself, is trying to explain the situation to him." (Westwood, 1932, p. 52).

FIGURE SKATING ON THE FROZEN CREDITS.

Cartoon by Alois Derso and Emeric Kelen (?1931), from H. P. Westwood, *Modern Caricaturists* (London: Lovat Dickson, 1932), p. 48.

THE RUN ON STERLING

The end of the line for the Reichsmark and the beginning of the end for the pound sterling occurred on 13 July. Publication of the Macmillan Committee Report on that day is sometimes given credit for starting the run, but this is exaggeration as the press took little notice of its figures of foreign claims on London, which were, in any event, grossly underestimated at £279 million at the end of 1927, and £302 million in 1931. David Williams estimates the June 1931 total as £640 million (1963, p. 527n). The members of the Macmillan committee disagreed over whether they should devalue, as Ernest Bevin recommended, or impose tariffs on British imports, as the other members, including Keynes and McKenna, thought desirable.

More significant for its impact on the pound was the May report, issued 31 July, and calling for a cut in the dole (unemployment benefit). The recommendations of the committee headed by Sir George May were uncompromisingly deflationist, wanting the prospective budget deficit of £120 million, including provision for a sinking fund on the expenditure side, eliminated. The report called for foreign loans, an effort already underway, with $125 million borrowed at the end of July from both the Federal Reserve system and from Paris, the latter divided between the Bank of France and the commercial banks. The Bank of England lost $200 million in foreign exchange and gold in supporting sterling during the month of July. Widespread unemployment had made it give up the use of an increase in discount rates. In addition, monetary authorities in Paris and New York warned that to raise the discount rate above the 4½ percent set at the end of July might have a perverse effect in increasing the rate of withdrawals (Sayers, 1976, Vol. 2, p. 405). The rate was thus left unchanged for the seven weeks of crisis. Governor Norman became nervously ill on 29 July and did not recover until after Britain had gone off gold two months later.

The bank's losses kept up during August, and new borrowing was undertaken from New York and Paris—this time $200 million each. The bankers were reluctant to grant the credit until the recommendations of the May Committee had been carried out. The Labour government sought to cut the dole, but the party split, bringing down the government on 24 August. It was replaced by a National Government led by Ramsay MacDonald of the Labour party and with Philip Snowden, also Labour, again as chancellor of the exchequer. Ernest Bevin and the trade unions withdrew into opposition, attacking the conditions attached to the loan, which was granted on 28 August, as a "bankers' ramp" (in American "racket") (Johnston, 1934). On 10 September the new government introduced its budget with economies of £70 million and new taxation of £80 million, more than enough to balance the budget if national income were maintained at the same level.

One incident that contributed to the run against sterling was the so-called Invergorden mutiny, a demonstration of personnel at a naval base over the pay cuts that took place on 16 September and was magnified by the domestic and foreign press into something more nearly resembling the Sepoy mutiny of 1857 (Divine, 1970). Europe, in particular, was moved by the notion that the Royal Navy, that great British institution, was tottering.

The role of smaller central banks calls for mention. Each separately was unimportant, had no impact, and hence no responsibility for the system. If all acted in the same way, however, their combined efforts could be substantial enough to make a considerable difference. In their book on the National Bank of Belgium, Van der Wee and Tavernier devote a revealing chapter to the question of sterling as seen by a small central bank. Along with the French franc, the Belgian franc had been stabilized at an undervalued level, and by the beginning of 1930, after paying off its stabilization loans to the United States, the National Bank had £25 million in sterling, representing some 62 percent of its foreign exchange. During the year it became nervous about this sum. Yield was unimportant as compared with liquidity and security, and the bank began, slowly and deliberately, to convert sterling into gold and dollars (Van der Wee and Tavernier, 1975, pp. 238–39). In mid-July 1931 it made what it regarded as a helpful gesture to the Bank of England, saying that it would hold the gold bought with sterling under earmark at the bank in London and ship it to Belgium only as circumstances permitted (ibid., p. 237). The relief for the British and cost to Belgium were both close to zero. The Belgian National Bank then proceeded to convert sterling into gold to the point where the Bank of England would have been willing to complain (Baudhuin, 1946, Vol. 2, pp. 249–50).

After the pound had gone off gold while the National Bank still held £12.6 million, it lost the delicacy of feeling that had inhibited it during the summer. On 22 September it converted $106.6 million held in dollars into gold at the Federal Reserve Bank of New York at one swoop. It also formed a consortium of bankers with 1 billion Belgian francs ($50 million) ready to intervene in the foreign exchange market in the event of a panic, but panic did not occur, and it quickly negotiated with the government to take over any loss it might suffer on its sterling holding, to which request the Treasury rather rashly acceded (Van der Wee and Tavernier, 1975, pp. 240–41). From 22 September on, the National Bank of Belgium was committed to the pure gold standard.

The Bank of France is sometimes charged with having pushed the British off gold. The accusation cannot be evaluated thoroughly but is probably untrue. Private Paris banks had reduced their sterling from £40 million to £10 million on 21 September. The earlier amount may have been held partly against forward sales, and hence fell when, if it did, the Bank of France failed to renew its swaps and took delivery of sterling for conversion into gold. The Bank of France's spot holdings of sterling fell from £80 million to £65 million on 21 September (Clarke, 1967, p. 225; £62 million in another account—Mouré, 1991, p. 70). Clément Moret, who by this time had succeeded Moreau at the Bank of France, defended holding the sterling, stating to the regents on 22 September that the bank had been constrained by its international responsibilities as a central bank (ibid., p. 71). As a banker, however he wanted his losses made good. He appealed first to the Bank of England, which turned him down, suggesting that he seek compensation from the French Treasury as the sterling had been accumulated for the most part between 1926 and 1928 when the bank was stabilizing the franc as a matter of public policy. An arrangement with the Treasury was finally reached, although it passed Parliament with difficulty. The Treasury gave the bank a bond maturing on 31 December 1945, some fourteen years after the trouble, so that the bank would not have to show the loss on its books (ibid., p. 72). In the world of floating exchange rates after 1973, central banks keep foreign exchange reserves on the books at cost, without a qualm. The two central banks patched up the dispute, and the British awarded Moret a decoration in October (Leith-Ross, 1968, p. 139n). The decision to go off gold on 21 September 1931 came when British reserves of gold and foreign exchange, having declined £200 million, stood only £5 million above the sum of Bank of England forward contracts to deliver foreign exchange, the loans of July and August, and central bank credits (Clarke, 1967, p. 216).

STERLING DEPRECIATION

Sterling depreciation was particularly violent to the surprise of such knowledgeable folk as the finance minister of Belgium who shared the general opinion that the pound would be quickly established on the gold standard at a parity not far away (which is why he was prepared to underwrite the National Bank's loss on sterling) (Van der Wee and Tavernier, 1975, p. 241). British authorities made no attempt to manage the rate, however, and many people in the market apparently thought that the pound would undergo an adjustment in relation to its prewar parity comparable to those of the French franc and the lira. The rate fell from $4.86 to $3.75 before rebounding to $3.90, and then went off again to $3.25 at the low in December, and averaged $3.47 for that month. Twenty-five countries, largely in the empire, in Scandinavia and Eastern Europe, and intimate trading partners such as Argentina, Egypt, and Portugal, followed the pound down. Such a country as Canada split the difference between the pound and the U.S. dollar. For countries that chose to cling to old parities, however, there was an appreciation of roughly 40 percent against the sterling bloc, which proved to be strongly deflationary. Sir James Grigg, British Treasury official, noted that Britain went off "not in a genteel way, but with a catastrophic fall of 30 percent or more which destroyed whatever basis of coherence the world had at that time" (1948, p. 184).

Like the National Bank of Belgium, the rest of the gold bloc converted dollars in one fell swoop for the little countries and, more slowly but no less inexorably, for the Bank of France. The Bank of France sold $50 million on 22 September, $25 million in 1 October, the same amount 8 October, $20 million on 15 October. From mid-September to the end of October, the Federal Reserve system lost $755 million in gold, and an internal memorandum of the board in December 1931 referred to the precipitous action of the central banks of Belgium, Switzerland, and the Netherlands as "panic" (correspondence of the Federal Reserve Bank of New York, 18 December 1931). More than $350 million was taken by the Bank of France to mid-December.

The Federal Reserve Bank of New York responded to this loss of reserves by raising its discount rate on 9 October and again on 16 October, 1 percentage point each time, bringing it from 1½ to 3½ percent. With hindsight this is universally regarded as a serious mistake in monetary policy, which deepened the depression in the United States and in the entire world outside the sterling bloc. One adviser objected (Despres, 1973, p. xii). The monetary authorities could plead that they had no choice because their free gold was limited: the rules of the system required Federal Reserve liabilities to be backed by gold for a minimum of 40 percent and the rest eligible paper, that is, bankers' acceptances. With the depression, the volume of bankers' acceptances had shrunk and the shortfall had to be made up in gold, thus reducing the amount of "free gold" above the 40 percent requirement. After the passage of the Glass-Steagall Act in February 1932, government securities could be substituted for eligible paper. But this is another case where institutional inhibitions would have been swept aside if there had existed coherent leadership and cohesive followership. The Glass-Steagall bill could have been passed six months earlier, or consonant with the Schuker view of the François-Marsal Convention in France, the Federal Reserve system with the approval of the administration and the leaders in Congress, could have said that the force majeure required it to violate the regulation, as Harrison had violated his instructions in 1929.

Deflation communicated to the United States by the British precipitous deflation was not confined to dollar conversions into gold by panicking central banks. There was simultaneously a direct price effect. When an exchange rate changes, prices of internationally traded goods have to adjust in some fashion. In a world of inflation, depreciation tends to raise prices of international goods in the depreciating country and leave them broadly unchanged in the appreciating one. In a world of deflation, on the other hand, depreciation leaves export, import, and import-competing prices unchanged and lowers them in the appreciating currency. A comparison of prices for specific commodities in dollars between September 1931 and March 1932 shows some aberrations but, on the whole, demonstrates the latter proposition (Table 20.2). The three commodities that least conform to the theoretical expectation are coffee, cotton, and wheat. Coffee had already fallen 64 percent in price between September 1929 and September 1931 and was subject to a Brazilian valorization scheme. Cotton, in turn, had declined 42 percent between March 1931 and September of the same year. Wheat was about to decline 32 percent from March to December 1932. For all three the timing is off, but neither the direction of the movement nor its extent. Of the rest, cocoa, tin and wool were sterling-bloc commodities, which rose in varying degrees in sterling prices and hence did not decline by the full extent of the appreciation of the dollar. Most of the others— copper, corn, hides, lead, rubber, silk, and zinc—fell by roughly that appreciation and, to the extent there was production in the United States, spread deflation in that country.

Depreciation of the pound afforded an opportunity for the Germans to dismantle

Table 20.2 Changes in Average Dollar Prices of Specified Internationally Traded Commodities between September 1931 and March 1932 (in percentages)

Cocoa	—	Hides	−29	Tin	−11
Coffee	+12.5	Lead	−29	Wheat	—
Copper	−31	Rubber	−34	Wool	−10
Corn	−23	Silk	−33	Zinc	−25
Cotton	+10	Sugar	−19		

Source: Calculated from Kindleberger (1973 [1986], p. 139).

their exchange control apparatus, then in embryo, and to avoid deflationary pressure from appreciation of the mark. The opinion has been expressed that the British and French applied pressure against such a course and also that the Germans chose to hold the mark high so as to keep down the local currency cost of its foreign debts (Hodson, 1938, p. 90). The fact seems rather to have been that collective memory of 1923 prevented those in authority from undertaking exchange depreciation, since it would have been interpreted by the public as inflationary. Monetary heretics were prepared to contemplate devaluing along with sterling: Rudolf Dahlberg, Wilhelm Grotkopp, Albert Hahn, Edgar Salin, W. Woytinsky (Grotkopp, 1954, ch. 5, esp. pp. 198ff.) The great majority of all political persuasions was opposed, not only financial experts such as Luther and Schacht and conservative politicians like Brüning, but Rudolf Hilferding, the Socialist financial expert. Fritz Naphtali, a leading Socialist expert, thought it necessary to let the crisis run its course (Sturmthal, 1943, pp. 86–87). Albert Hahn later asked: "If the 5 percent upward revaluation of the Deutschmark in 1956 produced such opposition in export and import-competing industry, what must the deflationary pressure of the 40 percent revaluation of 1931 have felt like?" (1963, p. 80). The debate continues. It has been argued on econometric evidence that a 20 percent depreciation of the Reichsmark would have raised national income 18 percent (Schiemann, 1980).

THE EXCHANGE EQUALIZATION ACCOUNT (EEA)

Debate within the Macmillan Committee as to whether the pound should be devalued or import duties raised produced a typical outcome. Just as after the German cabinet debate of July 1931 as to whether to have a domestic bank holiday or a moratorium on foreign credits, they did both. The pound declined rapidly as importers rushed to stock up before the Import Duties Act of 1932 would be passed and take effect. Then from the low of $3.25 in mid-December, after what is called more than a half-century later "overshooting," it turned around. Partly the market was relieved that French sterling waiting to be sold no longer hung over it. The Bank of England made clear that it had accumulated the exchange needed to pay off the credits of the summer of 1931. Paul Einzig, a widely known and respected journalist on financial matters, thought the time propitious for stabilizing the pound in terms of gold—at $3.50 for sterling—with a view to regaining London's place as a leading financial center (1933, p. 56). (He was later to change his view and bitterly attack advocates of stabilization.) As the pound rose from $3.50 to $3.80, however, there were anguished cries from industry engaged in exports or competing with imports. The latter had gained first from the Import Duties Act that imposed a tariff on most imports (but exempted those coming from the Empire) and then, in prospect, from the establishment of an Import Advisory Committee with the task of recommending further increases in particular duties, which it proceeded to do. Appreciation of the pound had no such buffer to protect exporters. Hence in April 1932, the government established an Exchange Equalization Account (EEA) to manage the exchange rate, especially to keep it down, and to protect the domestic monetary position (Howson, 1980, p. 55).

The EEA was launched by endowing it with the right to create sterling in the form of Treasury bills, on tap, in the amount of £150 million. As capital inflows from abroad tended to bid up the pound, the EEA could issue sterling bills to the market, which would either be held by foreigners directly or by the banks in which foreigners kept deposits. The bills were used to buy foreign exchange, which was then converted into gold. If foreign funds were withdrawn, the EEA would use the gold to buy foreign exchange, which was then furnished to the market against Treasury bills, thus undoing the original operation. Meanwhile, the foreign capital had been sterilized and prevented from having an impact on monetary conditions generally.

One aspect of EEA operations was the secrecy, which was felt desirable as a means of counteracting speculation. Under the gold standard when the market could see each week the state of the central bank's reserves and tell when limits were being approached, and especially when the reserves were running out, central banks felt handicapped. Additional reserves in a secret account were therefore regarded as an advantage in managing a currency. Various analysts worked out complex calculations based on the Treasury statement of total bills, subtracting tender bills and allowing for tap bills issued to other government departments, such as pension funds and the like, to attempt an estimate of tap bills used by the EEA. There was always some uncertainty in these calculations, however. The value attached to secrecy at that time contrasts sharply with today's insistence by believers in rational expectations that the authorities should communicate firmly and clearly to the market what monetary policies are, so that the market can adapt to them and help bring about their realization.

Equipped with sterling created on demand, the EEA was in an excellent position to cope with a capital inflow, that is, to supply sterling to demanders, but would have been helpless before an outflow since sterling cannot be used to buy sterling. For an outflow it would have had to have been created with a supply of gold and foreign exchange. The United States Stabilization Fund, created in 1934 out of the gold profit from revaluation of the U.S. gold stock from $20.67 an ounce to $35.00, could have handled an outflow but was helpless before an inflow, which was what, in the event, it had to contend with. To get dollars to provide to foreigners, it had to sell gold to the Federal Reserve system and enlarge the monetary base, an outcome it was designed (ineffectively) to prevent. A Dutch stabilization fund, created in 1936, was equipped with half gold and half guilders though, of course, its capacity to handle a one-way movement was limited to half its capital.

The EEA prevented the pound from rising very high until the dollar went off gold. Thereafter, faced with a heavy outflow of capital from the gold bloc, it decided that the way to divert that flow from Britain to the United States was to allow the pound to be bid up to the point where it looked expensive as compared with the dollar.

THE JAPANESE YEN AND THE DOLLAR

Depreciation of the pound in the fall of 1931 was followed by a run on the Japanese yen, which had been stabilized in terms of gold as recently as July 1929. On 14

December 1931 it prohibited the export of gold; on 17 December it abandoned the standard. Speculators then turned to the United States, which was sinking rapidly into deeper and deeper depression. The events of those months do not belong in an account of European finance, beyond mentioning that as President Hoover was succeeded by Roosevelt on 4 March 1933, the banks in the United States were closed in a "holiday" to halt a panic and run. For a time, gold exports were prohibited except under license. On 12 April 1933 President Roosevelt accepted the Thomas amendment (by an inflationary senator) to a farm bill, which allowed him, among other things, to change the price of gold. The government shortly stopped issuing licenses to export gold. The dollar then fell from $3.24 to the pound in the first half of April to $3.86 and on 31 May to $4.00. The big question in the world then became not, What is the exchange rate of the pound? but What is that of the dollar? But the corner of the depression had been turned.

SUGGESTED SUPPLEMENTARY READING

Eichengreen (1992), *Golden Fetters.*
James (1986), *The German Slump.*
Kindleberger (1973 [1986]), *The World in Depression, 1929–1939.*
Temin (1989), *Lessons from the Great Depression.*

In German

Borchardt and Schötz (eds.) (1991), *Wirtschaftspolitik in der Krise.*
Born (1967), *Die deutsche Bankenkrise, 1931.*
Grotkopp (1954), *Die grosse Krise.*

21

The 1930s

On their return [from the Second Preparatory Commission meeting for the World Economic Conference] Day and Williams spoke rather hopefully. In Washington on January 31 they outlined the elements of a general settlement they believed to be obtainable. The United States was to reduce its claims against foreign debtors; Great Britain was to promise to keep the value of the pound stable; France was to give assurance that it would eliminate quotas for imports; and Germany was to end its control over payments to foreigners. . . . I did not believe that was a negotiable bargain.
(Feis, *1933: Characters in Crisis,* 1966, p. 76)

THE WORLD ECONOMIC CONFERENCE, 1933

The idea of a World Economic Conference went back to 1930 when Chancellor Brüning proposed to the American ambassador, Sackett, that the interrelated questions of disarmament, reparations, war debts, debt retirement, tariffs, and currency stabilization should be dealt with in one package, on a political basis rather than by economic experts. The Laval-Hoover discussions of October 1931 and a MacDonald-Hoover discussion of May 1932 carried the matter forward to a degree, although the United States undertook to block any discussion of war debts, which led France and Britain to exclude reparations. In May 1932 the League of Nations adopted a proposal of the International Labor Organization calling for the conference, and this was put into effect by the Lausanne Conference on reparations in a resolution of July of the same year. A Preparatory Commission met in October 1932 and again in January and February 1933. By this time, Herbert Hoover had been defeated for the presidency by Franklin Roosevelt, who was anxious to postpone the discussion until his domestic program had gotten underway.

In the Preparatory Commission, in the International Labor Office, and at meetings held in Washington between experts and heads of state and American officials, all sorts of specific proposals were put forward: for an international program of public works; for an international credit institution to finance deficits in national balances of payments; for stabilization of currencies. Most came from smaller countries—Turkey, Poland, Belgium. The British, however, proposed an international fund of $1,500 million to $2,000 million for making loans to central banks in exchange for reductions in trade controls. The United States expressed great skepticism on international financing, saying that Congress would oppose financing other countries' programs. U.S. initiative was confined to a tariff truce until the end of the conference, but most countries, including the United States, wanted to hold out exceptions, so that the agreement failed to amount to much.

During the spring of 1933 the dollar went off gold, with the result that the stabilization problem became less one of sterling than of the dollar. The step was taken while Prime Minister Ramsay MacDonald was crossing the Atlantic to discuss the World Economic Conference with President Roosevelt. James Warburg of the White House staff proposed a plan for stabilization of the dollar at a depreciation of 15 to 25 percent, after which the pound, dollar, and French franc would be fixed in relation to one another and managed by a three-country stabilization fund. The British thought 15 percent depreciation of the dollar excessive, the French that the three-country fund ran the risk of losses in exchange dealings for the French Treasury, which would not be acceptable to the Chamber of Deputies. President Roosevelt himself was relieved when the agreement fell though, since depreciation of the dollar had been lifting the prices of American commodities and securities.

As the June date of the conference approached, various countries became more and more skeptical. The British thought they had better move to an empire rather than a world solution. The French noted that their earlier proposals for public works had received no support from other countries and that such domestic public works as they had tried had failed to raise prices. An adviser to President Roosevelt, Raymond Moley, thought that recovery was a domestic, not an international, question. Schacht from Germany wanted to put colonies on the agenda. But President Roosevelt, especially, became euphoric over the rise in prices that came from depreciation of the dollar. Exchange rate stabilization was taken off the agenda of the world conference but made the subject of a special negotiation by central banks parallel to the general conference.

The conference opened in London on 12 June with a round of formal speeches, that of U.S. Secretary of State Cordell Hull delayed by redrafting in Washington to deemphasize international solutions to the economic problems of the United States, and with a contest between the United States and France over the election of the chairman of the financial committee. Meanwhile, central bankers were drafting an agreement for stabilization of the dollar for the duration of the conference—at $4.00 to the pound and 4.8 cents to the franc, with a 3 percent margin either way and agreement of the three major central banks to support their currencies by selling gold up to a limit of 4 million or 5 million ounces, equivalent at $20.67 an ounce to $80 million to $100 million. The rate chosen, $4.00, had been recorded by the market on 31 May, but by 15 June the dollar had fallen to $4.15. When word of the agreement was leaked to the press, almost certainly by the French (Mouré, 1991, p. 106, esp. n. 107), the dollar recovered to $4.02 and U.S. stock and commodity markets, which had been rising with depreciation, declined. This led President Roosevelt to reject the agreement. He sent Moley to London to work out a compromise. By the time Moley arrived, a watered-down version of intention to stabilize in the long run had been agreed by experts on various delegations, with no mention of rates. This was cabled to Roosevelt, who was vacationing in New Brunswick, Canada. By this time, the dollar was $4.33, and stock and commodity prices had risen again. Roosevelt rejected the compromise in two messages, on 1 July and 3 July, both strongly worded, calling exchange stabilization a specious fallacy, artificial, a fetish of central bankers, and various other unkind things. It broke up the conference. British Empire countries met in a formal conference and formed the sterling area. The gold bloc of France, Belgium, the Netherlands, Switzerland, and, nominally, Italy solidified (Mouré, 1991, ch. 3). Any hope of Germany's emerging from the standstill agreement and from the increasing exchange control was lost.

The United States kept on experimenting with exchange depreciation, including deliberately raising the U.S. price of gold in order to force the dollar down—in line with theories derived by George Warren, an agricultural economist, from the Greenback period in the United States from 1861 to 1879—until in early 1934 President Roosevelt became bored with it and fixed the price of gold at $35.00 an ounce, up from $20.67, which had obtained with interruptions for 100 years. In the early period after April 1933, while the dollar was declining from $3.24 to $5.00 to the pound, the experiment was a success. Instead of lowering prices in appreciating countries, it raised them in the depreciating United States. But there was little that could be done to raise prices on an international level. After the World Economic Conference had broken up, Moley talked in London to Walter Lippmann and J. M. Keynes about a proposal for a new international currency unit—to be named the dinard, the value of which would be stabilized in terms of commodities. None of them, however, knew how this would be done (Feis, 1966, p. 211).

STERLING BLOC

A Conservative minority in Britain had been arguing in favor of pulling back from world status to economic leadership within the empire as early as the turn of the century. In the 1920s L. S. Amery was leader of the empire group, with its slogan developed by Bruce of Australia, "Men, money and markets." "Men" implied a scheme for assisted migration to the Empire. "Money" represented, primarily, preference for empire borrowers in the London capital market but could also be extended to include sterling bloc arrangements. "Markets," of course, referred to empire tariff preferences as was ultimately agreed at the Ottawa Conference of the summer of 1932 (Drummond, 1975, p. 92).

There had been pressure for discussion of exchange rates at the Ottawa Conference largely from Canada and Australia. The issue had arisen first in 1920–22 before the pound had been revalued. In 1923 the Imperial Economic Conference suggested stabilization of intra-imperial exchange rates. London made no response to these initiatives. In 1932 the British authorities again wanted no commitment for their country. If dominion governments wanted to stabilize their respective rates, they were free to do so (ibid., pp. 211–13). At the World Economic Conference, Commonwealth leaders met thirteen times—but on commodity regulation, not finance. The sterling area evolved naturally in the way the Treasury authorities had envisaged in 1932, with each dominion making up its own mind about the exchange rate. Canada threaded its way between the pound sterling and the U.S. dollar; the Union of South Africa, the world's largest gold producer, clung to the

U.S. dollar in 1931 but devalued to the level of sterling in December 1932 because of a flight of capital. The sterling bloc extended beyond the British Empire, encompassing Scandinavia, Egypt, a number of other countries of the Middle East, such as Persia (Iran) and Iraq, and Argentina.

In the fall of 1933 the United States asked the British whether they would be interested in stabilizing the pound-dollar rate. Governor Norman at first thought that, while there was no possibility of de jure stabilization, a working de facto arrangement was possible. It quickly became clear, however, that the British were not ready to contemplate a fixed level for the pound. The gold bloc was under siege, and capital was escaping thence to Britain and the United States, making it useful to maintain a floating rate and the Exchange Equalization Account. Capital controls limited the amount of lending abroad. They had been installed under the aegis of the Bank of England in August 1931 when foreign investments were forbidden. During the conversion of war loan from July to September 1932, all new security issues were banned. In May 1933 restrictions on foreign lending were extended to purchases of existing securities in foreign markets. In July of the following year, the regulations were relaxed in favor of empire and sterling-area countries and for specific foreign loans, which would be highly beneficial to British industry. Finally, in April 1936, an advisory committee was established from the City to supervise foreign lending (Morton, 1943 [1979], p. 250).

War loan conversion in 1932 was an outstanding success. The Bank of England's discount rate had been raised to 6 percent just before the pound went off gold in September 1931, maintained at that level until February 1932, and then reduced in a series of steps to 2 percent by June. Overhanging the market, however, was the 5 percent war loan callable from 1929 to 1947, in the amount of £2,087 million or 27 percent of the total national debt and 38 percent of British securities quoted on the London stock exchange. It was proposed to redeem this with a 3½ percent issue, not callable for twenty years with a £1 premium offered to holders of war loan who agreed to the exchange before 31 July. Those asking for cash redemption were required to announce that intention by 31 August, and the entire exchange was to take place on 1 December 1932. The success was enormous. Of the outstanding issue, £1,921 million, or 92 percent was converted, and only £192 million paid off in cash. Without the 5 percent bonds hanging over the market, interest rates came down sharply. The £1 premium for announcement before 31 July was intended to prevent the security from becoming a 5 percent five-month bill (Nevin, 1955, p. 92; Howson, 1988, pp. 239–43).

Conversion to the 3½ percent interest level, plus improvement in British terms of trade as imported raw material and food prices fell from 1931 more than the prices of manufactured exports, led to a housing boom. Cheap food gave Britons extra income to spend. The substantial backlog of unsatisfied demand in housing accumulated since the war meant that the income would be used on construction. Cheap money enabled it to be readily financed.

In these circumstances, the British economy was comfortable during the 1930s, as it had not been in the 1920s, and the authorities were in no hurry to give up their freedom of action through international agreement. Great Britain had turned away from its world role to withdraw within the commonwealth.

SWEDISH MONETARY POLICY

Sweden tried to hold on to the gold parity of the krona when Britain went off gold in September 1931 but managed to do so only for a week. Thereafter, it depreciated the krona to the level of the pound sterling. A group of economists met in October 1931, and as a result of their deliberations Professor Gunnar Myrdal brought out a book (1931) in Swedish with the equivalent title in English of *Methods of Meeting the Monetary Crisis*. The book emphasized the possibility that normal means of manipulating the discount rate and controlling long-term interest rates might be perverse and that there was need for a positive "international margin" to be gained by exchange depreciation and discrimination against imports. The Riksbank and the Treasury announced a policy of stabilizing the level of internal prices. There was a brief setback to public confidence with the suicide of Ivar Kreuger, the Swedish match swindler, in May 1932, but a new government took power in September with Ernst Wigforss as finance minister, interested in public works to stimulate employment. Depreciation of the currency, public investment financed out of loans, and the Riksbank's easy-money policy each played a part in producing a vigorous recovery that lasted through the 1930s (B. Thomas, 1936, ch. 5).

For a time considerable mystique attached to the Swedish experience. Irving Fisher hailed the experiment as proof that any country could stabilize its internal price level (1934). In his preface to Brinley Thomas's account of the Swedish experience, Hugh Dalton stated that "external factors, such as the rise in certain export prices, have helped a little. But primarily the recovery is due to internal action" (B. Thomas, 1936, p. x). Swedish theory, Thomas's study, and a paper by a Danish economist, Carl Iversen (1936), have underlined the importance of a positive position in the balance of payments, in this instance produced by the building boom in Britain with its insistent demand for Swedish lumber. But it is hard to fault the view that while policy was not sufficient to produce recovery and Sweden had the advantage of being a small state the exchange rate of which did not have external effects, its policies were well designed and broadly agreed. Smallness helps in this as well, since reconciliation of interests is more readily carried through in a small state than in a large one.

GERMAN FOREIGN EXCHANGE CONTROL

The German Standstill Agreement of July 1931 expired in January 1932. It was inevitably renewed. German unwillingness to depreciate the Reichsmark with the pound sterling, and the subsequent 40 percent overvaluation, led to the necessity to build a system of controls—on imports, on foreign use of credits in German banks, on German sale of Reichsmarks to foreigners. The entire network threatened to curtail trade until trade was restored by various clearing agreements.

The theory of clearing agreements is simple. A German importer pays Reichsmarks into an account at the Reichsbank. Whether the foreign exporter is paid immediately in local currency or must wait depends on policy in the exporting country. A Danish expert distinguishes broadly two procedures. First, the foreign central bank can take over the blocked Reichsmarks and pay out local currency immediately to the exporter, thus expanding the money supply. This has the disability of increasing national income in the exporting country and having it spill over into imports in general, not solely from Germany. Andersen (1946) calls this the payments principle. Or, second, the central bank can make the exporter wait until some importer in the country is able to buy goods from Germany and buys the blocked Reichsmarks with local currency, which the central bank then pays out to the original exporter. This constitutes the so-called waiting principle.

Exchange control, as developed in Germany, was divided in other ways. Some transactions took place at the appreciated official rate of exchange and others at exchange rates that diverged by various amounts. In addition to pure clearing arrangements for trade, moreover, there were so-called payments agreements in which a German trading partner, such as Switzerland, would insist on reserving a portion of the proceeds of German exports to Switzerland to pay down German obligations to Swiss creditors. The essence of the system was discrimination and market separation. The Germans, for example, were anxious to prevent Reichsmarks in a Yugoslav clearing account from being transferred to purchase exports to another country, which might be bought anyhow with convertible exchange; or goods in which Germany had a monopoly position, such as instruments and optical equipment, being bought with cheap Reichsmarks instead of free foreign exchange. Incremental exports such as toys, musical instruments, pharmaceuticals, and the like might be sold with special marks withdrawn from Standstill Accounts (Sperrmarks) or so-called Aski-marks (from the initials of Auslands-Sonder-Konto für Inlandskredit, or Special Foreign Accounts for Internal Credit); and special rates would be established to encourage, say, travel, with Reisemarks (travel marks), which could be used for trains and hotel and restaurant bills but not for such purchases as cameras, for which the full rate had to be paid. There were strong incentives for German customers to use cheap marks for purchases, which Germany tried to restrict to expensive marks for sale in convertible foreign exchange, such as dollars.

The system of exchange control developed slowly and in empirical fashion. Once in place, it could be used for a variety of purposes, much like a system of tariffs and subsidies on exports and imports: to improve the balance of payments, to raise revenue, to extract monopoly rents from exports and monopsony (buyer monopoly) bargains in imports. Governmental revenue is enhanced by taxing both exports and imports, for example, or selling exchange to importers at a much higher rate than that at which it is purchased from exporters. To improve the balance of payments, a country restricts imports and pushes exports, whether by tariffs or appropriately chosen exchange rates, or if the object of the exercise is to import without exporting—to improve the balance of payments in a particular way—borrowing from abroad, one can import freely at subsidized rates but make exporting difficult by limiting the export of goods wanted abroad to high rates. To maximize monopoly advantage and improvement in the terms of trade, one charges high exchange rates for goods in inelastic demand abroad and offers very low ones for importing goods in inelastic supply.

Germany was widely accused of having exploited southeastern Europe by importing freely while restricting exports to "aspirin and harmonicas," available only at high exchange rates. Started as a means to protect the balance of payments as an instrument of monetary policy, exchange control became "a device for regulating the direction, composition, volume and the terms of international trade" (Child, 1958 [1978], p. 208). A sharp and acrimonious debate broke out in *The Banker* for May and June 1941 between F. C. Benham, who had asserted that Germany had paid high prices for imports from the Balkan countries while charging competitive prices (1939 and 1940), and Paul Einzig, who contended that Germany had exploited those countries mercilessly. The data, such as they are, support Benham as far as the terms of trade were concerned (Neal, 1979; Kindleberger, 1956, pp. 114–22). The most recent investigation concludes, though the verdict is contested in the same publication, that Benham was right and Einzig wrong (Milward, 1981; Wendt, 1981).

BILATERALISM

Preferences in the sterling area and clearing forced world trade more and more into a bilaterally balanced mode. The overall ratio of trade to national income declined as countries undertook campaigns to persuade their citizens to "Buy British" or "Buy French," adopted discriminatory rules for governmental purchases favoring local suppliers, as well as piled up tariffs, preferences, quotas, and clearing and payments agreements. The ratio of imports to national income declined 10 percent in the United Kingdom, 30 percent in Germany, and 40 percent in Italy (League of Nations [Meade], 1938, pp. 107–8). Within the shrunken volume of trade, moreover, the proportion balanced multilaterally declined, and that balanced bilaterally gained. In 1928 bilateral balancing of export and import values between pairs of countries covered 70 percent of world merchandise traded, with 25 percent multilaterally balanced, and the 5 percent remaining covered by trade in services or capital movements (League of Nations [Hilgerdt], 1941). A later study emphasized the shrinkage in multilateral, and rise in bilateral, settlement without giving precise figures. Trade through clearing agreements amounted to 12 percent of the world total and 50 percent of that of Germany plus a long list of countries in southeastern Europe (League of Nations [Hilgerdt], 1942, p. 70). In 1928 the European pattern of trade had produced a large German surplus in manufactures inside Europe, needed to balance its import surplus in primary products with the rest of the world, especially Latin America and the United States, while Britain had a deficit within Europe, offset by a substantial surplus with the rest of the world, arising, especially, from interest and dividends on investments in the empire and Latin America. The development of exchange control altered this system of settling trade payments, forcing Germany much more nearly to balance its payments within and without Europe, and cutting down on the extent to which Britain offset its deficit within Europe by a surplus outside. The League of Nations study by Hilgerdt did not provide 1938 figures for comparison with 1928, but a later study on a somewhat different basis puts the reduction in multilateral balancing at 20 percent, that is, from 21.2 percent of world trade in 1928 to 16.9 percent in 1938 (Thorbecke, 1960, p. 82).

Exchange controls worked imperfectly. The incentive to defeat the system, whether by exporting capital when it was forbidden or by using cheap currency in place of dear for exports, or overvalued exchange rates instead of undervalued in buying imports, produced continuous pressure to violate the rules, to arbitrage between markets that authorities sought to keep separate. One indication of this is the continuous increase in the penalties for violating exchange controls until, in both Germany and Italy, they included the death penalty, reminiscent of the medieval punishments imposed by governments for adulteration of monies, or mislabeling sealed sacks of coins (p. 23 above). Black markets for Reichsmark bank notes existed in various cities outside Germany, for example, and an oral tradition has it that the three main illegal methods to take capital out of Germany—bribing a Reichsbank official to deliver foreign exchange, by smuggling out bank notes through bribing a foreign diplomat for the use of his pouch, or obtaining and smuggling the bank notes oneself—were all kept in line through arbitrage, to such an extent that any event that affected the black market rate in one method was immediately communicated to the other two. It was also said that the demand for Reichsmark currency in, say, Amsterdam was provided by British secret-service operatives who wanted to smuggle it back into Germany to meet their expenditures.

THE GERMAN DISEQUILIBRIUM SYSTEM

German rearmament called for special financing techniques, somewhat along the lines of the Lautenbach proposal that, despite some academic support, had been rejected in September 1931 by Reichsbank and government officials (Borchardt and Schötz, eds., 1991). Total expenditure on rearmament has been variously estimated at a high of 90 billion Reichsmarks, announced by Hitler when he was trying to frighten the Allies, to Schacht's estimate of 34 billion Reichsmarks at the end of 1938, which frightened him. In the early period from 1934 to 1936, before tax receipts rose sharply, about half was financed by a special form of paper called *Mefo-Wechsel* (Mefo-exchange), "Mefo" being an acronym for Metallische Forschungsgesellschaft (Metal Research Company), a straw firm, the stockholders of which were Siemens, in electrical equipment, and Gutehoffnungshütte, Krupp, and Rheinmetall in iron and steel. *Mefo-Wechsel* was a three-month paper, generally extended to five months in all, drawn by small firms with limited capital supplying material to the Wehrmacht, "accepted" by Mefo, and then discounted at the Reichsbank, or sold to the capital market. At the height in 1936, this paper outstanding amounted to 12 billion Reichsmarks, but it was reduced to 6 billion at the end of March 1938. When the private demand for it dried up, another form of short-term paper was issued from April 1938, *Lieferschatzanweisungen* (supplier Treasury bills). These amounted to 4 billion by the outbreak of the war (Hansmeyer and Caesar, 1976, pp. 391–92, 392n).

The heavy financing of the rearmament effort by the Reichsbank was regarded by its president, Hjalmar Schacht, and many of his board, as inflationary and very dangerous. While the balance of payments was held in check by exchange controls, and many prices were set by government authorities, the Reichsbank felt under pressure. One of Schacht's biographers ascribes his resistance to the financial methods being followed as political in nature, and cited a letter of 1 September 1938, from Schacht to the finance minister, warning against the economic war that would be unleashed by an attack on Czechoslovakia (Pentzlin, 1980, p. 183). In January 1939 the directorate of the Reichsbank wrote to the Reichschancellor saying that *limitless* spending (italics in original) was producing inflation—this was at a time when the theory of suppressed inflation, or the disequilibrium system, had not been elaborated—and setting out four requests akin to demands: (1) that all deficit spending be eliminated; (2) that the finance minister be given control over all spending—to take it away from the Göring Four-Year Plan organization and from the army; (3) that price and wage controls be imposed; and (4) that all claims on the money and capital market be left to decisions of the Reichsbank (Hansmeyer and Caesar, 1976, pp. 383–84). Hitler's reaction was to dismiss Schacht, Ehrhardt, Vocke, and Blessing among the Reichsbank officials and to continue the disequilibrium system with financial pressure high but under more or less effective controls. (After World War II, the German central bank acquired independence from government. Immediately after the first war, however, the Reichsbank had been unable to resist governmental demands, especially under Hitler (Holtfrerich, 1988, esp. pp. 116, 124, 138).

The role of the commercial banks in this was a passive one, since leadership in the flow of credit to armament, after the early period of reflation along Baade-Tarnow-Woytinsky and Lautenbach lines had come to an end, lay in *Mefo-Wechsel* and the Reichsbank. The German government, which at the peak in 1931 had owned 91 percent of the stock of the Dresdener Bank, 70 percent of the Commerz, 67 percent of the Norddeutschebank, and 35 percent of the Deutsche Bank, was able to sell them off to the private market. The heavy liabilities of the banks to foreign creditors were eroded by liquidation at derisory exchange rates through the controls. The banks had an unheroic but profitable run throughout the rest of the decade.

In contrast with the German banks, the Creditanstalt in Austria, which had owned 65 percent of the national capital of Austrian enterprises, ended up entirely owned by the Austrian government, with no opportunity to sell it off.

ITALY

Italy was a member of the gold bloc in name only as it was forced to buttress its overvalued rate for the lira with foreign exchange control and bilateral clearing. This had begun slowly after the *quota novanta* of 1926, was relaxed in March 1930, but strengthened and reorganized in May 1933 on the eve of the World Economic Conference and again in January 1935 after gold losses in 1934. This last provided the occasion for establishing a governmental monopoly over exchange trading in an Istituto Nazionale per i Cambi con Estero (Toniolo, 1980, pp. 184–86).

But if Italy was like Germany in operating an overvalued currency with exchange control, it diverged from its 1936 Axis partner in the realm of banking. The troubles of the Credito Italiano at the turn of the year had been followed by similar difficulties of the Banca Commerciale Italiana in the summer of 1931 when the bank was forced to borrow from the Bank of Italy against the collateral of its branches in New York and London (ibid., p. 229). At that time, the Bank of Italy required it to segregate its industrial assets in the Società Finanziaria Industriale Italiana (Sofindit), which had been created in the spring of 1930, merge it with another subsidiary, Consorzio Mobiliare Finanziario (Comofin), formed in the early 1920s to protect its prize industrial assets from takeover by the Perrone brothers, and to quit altogether the field of industrial finance. This left a problem as to how industry would be financed in the absence of healthy profits, a vigorous capital market, or banks prepared to lend equity capital. The answer came in the form of a new governmental creation, the Istituto Mobiliare Italiano (IMI), established in January 1933, which, however, was not very active as compared with the Istituto per la Ricostruzione Industrial (IRI) created in the same month.

The IRI was perhaps patterned after the Reconstruction Finance Corporation, established by President Hoover in the United States in December 1931, but had a somewhat different proximate origin. Its immediate task was to take over from the Bank of Italy its claims on the Istituto di Liquidazione, with frozen assets dating back to the outbreak of World War I, and especially others acquired in the 1921 recession. It went further and acquired the Società Finanziaria Italiana (SFI), which had been hived off from the Credito Italiano, and Sofindit of the Banca Commerciale Italiana, ending up with a capital of 10,369 million lire, or 22.5 percent of the nominal capital of all Italian firms, and an interest in the three major banks and in firms controlling 48.5 percent of the capital of the country (ibid., pp. 248–49).

The initial intention had been to use IRI as a holding company, which would gradually unload its securities as private markets returned to health. But recovery was slow, IMI's activity was limited, and the problems of organizing the financial side of Italian industry would not wait. IRI had to provide more capital to the leading banks. In March 1934 a series of conventions were drawn up empowering IRI to take steps to organize the industrial assets in its portfolio. Thereafter, it began to regroup them by industry—telephones, shipping, metallurgy, shipbuilding, machinery, munitions. In 1936 the hope of selling the securities back to the private market was abandoned. New legislation forbade banks of ordinary credit to take on industrial participations, just as the Glass-Steagall Act of 1933 in the United States had excluded commercial banks from underwriting securities or other investment banking. The 1936 Italian law barred commercial banks from taking part in the management of private corporations—a reversal of the patterns established in the 1860s and 1890s when first the French and second the German banks had established mixed banking in Italy. The importance of government in managing industry through IRI, however, owed far less to corporatist economic theory, to the extent that it existed, than to the circumstances of a weak capital market, several overextended forays into industrial finance by mixed banks, and the need to provide a second- or third-best solution to the problems of providing industrial capital.

THE GOLD BLOC

Although Italy was nominally a member of the gold bloc, its pattern of economic recovery was sharply different. The gold bloc had roughly the same membership as the Latin Monetary Union—France, Belgium, the Netherlands, Switzerland, and Italy in name only—but it was a defensive arrangement rather than an optimum currency area. Failure of the World Economic Conference, development of German foreign exchange control, withdrawal of Britain into the commonwealth preferential area, and depreciation of first the yen and then the dollar left the gold bloc countries to find their way as best they could. A meeting was held in Paris on 8 July 1933, but the bloc was more a facade than a reality (Van der Wee and Tavernier, 1975, p. 258).

France pioneered in quota restrictions as early as 1930 to protect its peasant farmers. Tariffs had failed to raise wheat prices, as the only response to them seemed to be lower prices in Australia and Argentina with heavy supplies overhanging the market and inadequate storage facilities. France therefore switched from price to quantitative restraint. Quotas spread from foodstuffs to other articles, and as trade agreements began to exchange quota reductions, unwanted quotas were imposed to have bargaining counters to give away.

Quotas were not foreign exchange control, however, and the French response to overvaluation of the franc after the depreciation of sterling and the dollar was primarily deflation. Prices declined from 462 in 1931 to 347 in 1935 (July 1914 = 100) and national income in money terms from 331 billion francs in 1930 to 221 billion in 1935. Between September 1921 and September 1936 there were sixteen changes of government or changes of finance ministers within a government. Successive governments would try to balance the budget by cutting payments to pensioners and veterans and wages of government employees, meet bitter resistance, and fall. Pensioners' real income increased 46 percent and that of government employees 19 percent, but any attempt to reduce them evoked fierce opposition based either on money illusion or a well-organized collective that disregarded the national interest (Sauvy, 1967, Vol. 2, p. 137).

Like France, Belgium had enjoyed prosperity after devaluation in 1926, not only through 1929 but well into 1930 before deflationary pressure struck. Falling prices set various banks, industrial firms, and agricultural cooperatives sliding toward bankruptcy from which the government and the National Bank of Belgium tried to rescue them by one means or another. From early in the spring of 1934 Léon Dupriez began to argue that the position of the Belgian franc was untenable and that it would be wise to attach Belgium to the sterling zone at an exchange rate of 140 to the pound (Van der Wee and Tavernier, 1975, p. 170). All political parties, including the Socialists, were at first opposed, and in November 1934 a government was formed committed to the retention of the old parity. More banks weakened, and a new Flemish Kredietbank was formed by the merger of the Algemeene Bankvereeniging and the Bank voor Handel en Nijverhied. One by one various political and financial leaders—Paul van Zeeland; Vice-Governor of the National Bank Emile Francqui; Prime Minister Theunis—came to the conclusion that devaluation was inevitable. The governor of the National Bank, Louis Franc, held out until the second week of March 1935, when capital flight led to a loss of reserves amounting to close to 1 billion Belgian francs. A delegation visited Paris where the French authorities tried to dissuade the Belgians from adopting exchange control, claiming that it would be the first step to devaluation, and offering to lend it 1 billion Belgian francs instead. The delegation declined this. Prime Minister Theunis resigned; van Zeeland was appointed in his place and began preparing for devaluation.

There were three possible routes: first, to attach the Belgian franc to the pound at a rate based on purchasing power parity calculations produced at Louvain by Dupriez and Robert Triffin. This called for a devaluation of 28 percent. A second alternative was to devalue by about 25 percent and float. A third was to devalue in terms of gold. Except for two regents, the National Bank favored staying with gold on the ground that the other two courses were too uncertain. Devaluation in terms of gold was adopted in April 1935 with remarkable effect—rising prices, employment, foreign trade, and international reserves.

The defection of the Belgians from the gold bloc led to speculative pressure on France after the fall of the Flandin government on 31 May. The British EEA supplied sterling to the market against francs, with which it bought gold. There was some fear, however, that the parallel rush from francs into dollars might overwhelm the facilities for shipping gold to New York, so that the United States agreed to supply $150 million in cash against gold earmarked in Paris. It was not a loan so much as a convenience but helped the French resist pressure on the currency. The Bank of France's trader was able to put in an appearance at the bourse with sang-froid, offering dollars freely and selling only $34 million (Clarke, 1977, p. 10). A mini-squeeze, it gained a few months to the end of the year.

THE TRIPARTITE MONETARY AGREEMENT

Continued deflation in France under frequently changing governments led in the spring of 1936 to a series of sit-down strikes participated in by Socialists and Communists alike in a Popular Front. These strikes brought down the Sarrault government on 4 June and led to the Popular Front government of Léon Blum from 5 June. On the next day the governor of the Bank of France, J. Tannery, was dismissed and E. Labeyrie appointed on a temporary basis. On the following day, the Matignon Accord was signed between labor and industry, providing for increases in wages, three-week vacations, and a forty-hour week. Wages rose 12 percent, on the average, immediately and wholesale prices from 375 (on the 1913 base) to 420 between May and September.

The program of the Popular Front was empty of precise detail. It called for repression of trusts, control of speculation, suppression of fraud, and, especially, repudiation of inflation. It said nothing about devaluation. The Socialists were not doctrinaire in opposition to devaluation, but the Communists were. Blum received private advice favoring devaluation from Pierre Quesnay. Paul Reynaud, Charles Rist, and Louis Germain-Martin were advocating it publicly. Vincent Auriol, the finance minister, insisted that France should devalue only in the context of a general stabilization (Mouré, 1991, pp. 246–47). There was no program for handling the deficit in the French balance of payments or the capital outflow provoked by the sitdown strikes.

Clarke reports that the U.S. Treasury official, Harry D. White, discussed gold bloc devaluation with the British in the spring of 1935, expressing concern that when they did devalue they would devalue too much (Leith-Ross, quoted by Clarke, 1977, p. 15). In these views, White was ahead of the U.S. secretary of the treasury, Henry Morgenthau, a man whose understanding of international finance was weak, and of the British who were still resisting any suggestion that the pound sterling should be stabilized. While the British did not acknowledge that the pound had been allowed to decline too far in 1931, they felt strongly that the United States had devalued excessively in 1934 and was gaining gold in the years since. Bit by bit, however, the prospect of excessive devaluation of the French franc made Americans and British both see some merit in discussing the question of French prospective devaluation with each other and with France.

An American view of the negotiations leading to the Tripartite Monetary Agreement is set out in a paper by Stephen Clarke (1977). A day-to-day account French account from the Matignon Agreement of June to the climax of 26 September 1936 by Mouré (1991, ch. 6, esp. pp. 227ff.) includes the attempts by both the Americans and the French to persuade the British to stabilize the pound as part of the cover for the devaluation of the franc. In the light of these differences, the content of the agreement was limited. Each country agreed to stand ready to consult the others on foreign exchange operations and to hold one another's currency for twenty-four hours before converting it into gold. This was just a short step beyond Belgium's help to Britain in 1931 in not shipping gold acquired with sterling, but holding it under earmark in London, and light-years away from the swaps through which central banks held each other's currencies for periods of three months (albeit subject to an exchange guarantee) after March 1961. A French economist-historian asserts that the agreement engaged the central banks to nothing and, coming two years too late, had no result (Sauvy, 1967, Vol. 2, p. 225). Agreement to consult, however, and help provided to the French government in diverting attention from the failure of the Popular Front, marked a turning point in international monetary cooperation after the depths to which it had sunk in the first half of the decade.

Holland and Switzerland clung to their 1913 parities all through the 1920s and 1930s. They were consulted during the course of the negotiations and adhered to the Tripartite Monetary Agreement after devaluing their currencies.

THE GOLD SCARE

The Tripartite Monetary Agreement stopped a speculative movement out of the French franc into gold but gave rise to an opposite movement out of gold into national currencies, especially the dollar. The increased price raised the value of existing gold reserves by 69 percent. It also stimulated gold mining, despite restraining action on the part of the Union of South Africa, which imposed taxes to siphon off part of the extra profit, hitting especially hard at rich ores in an effort to extend the life of its mines. Upcountry Indian bazaars, which had for years been a sinkhole for hoarded gold, turned from a "sink" to a "spigot" and, with China, dishoarded $1½ billion (Graham and Whittlesey, 1939 [1978], p. 16). A certain amount of jewelry was melted down. As war clouds gathered in Europe, capital first drifted and then poured toward the United States, transferred in gold. The U.S. gold stock rose by almost $10 billion from January 1934 to June 1939. The mass movement produced a sense in the market in the spring of 1937 that the price of gold would be reduced. When this was contemplated, there was a rush of private hoards out of gold into money, especially dollars, a movement in which some of the smaller central banks, notably the Swiss National Bank, joined.

The gold scare was another manifestation of Gresham's law. When doubt attaches to the long-run stability of the price between two monies, the market will dump the overvalued in exchange for the undervalued one. There was great pressure on the authorities to take some action, and statements, such as that by President Roosevelt on 9 April 1937 that no action was contemplated, failed to calm the market. The period from the Tripartite Monetary Agreement to September 1937, when the New York stock market broke to usher in the 1937–38 recession, was characterized by gold sterilization on the part of Federal Reserve authorities, which underlined how uncomfortable the United States was made by the gold inflow, and by a wide-ranging literature in economic and business circles, pro and con a change in the gold price. In the event, the monetary authorities failed to change the price and rode the storm out, stabilizing the price at the level chosen in February 1934. Whether this was due to firm resolution, which overcame the uncertainties of the market, or fear of difficulties in managing the gold "loss" from lowering the price on existing reserves is not evident from the historical record, although the unimportance of the paper loss, and easy means for handling it, were apparent to later observers (League of Nations [Nurkse], 1944, p. 133)

In a reference that eludes me, Harry G. Johnson, after World War II, suggested that there was something inevitable about this episode. When a country such as the United States wants to raise the price of gold (depreciate the dollar), it must do so in a credible manner. It is therefore important to depreciate by more than the equilibrium amount so as to convince the market that it will not have to depreciate again. The result is that it gets the price of gold too high and the price of the dollar too low, thus setting up expectations of a reversal partway. Mundell went somewhat further and suggested that an exchange crisis from overvaluation is resolved only when the country in question achieves undervaluation but that this results in overvaluation of another currency. In this manner, a currency (national) crisis tends to escalate into a structural crisis, which leads on into a systems crisis, calling for a fundamental reorganization of the international monetary system (Mundell, 1969). The difficulty with these generalizations is that they rest on one historical example only. In the case of the French franc, great care was taken in September 1936 not to depreciate by too wide a margin, with the result that—in the absence of more fundamental macroeconomic reforms—it became necessary to devalue again a year later.

And yet there is something to the view that successive depreciations of the pound sterling, the yen, the dollar, and the gold bloc were each excessive and communicated overvaluation and deflation to the rest of the system in a system of overshooting, not by the private market alone, but by the monetary authorities who condoned the rates when they did not actually choose them. Rolfe and Burtle (1973) state that there was no competitive exchange depreciation in the 1930s but rather a general depreciation against gold that had the effect of raising prices in money terms. That was the outcome. The process, however, was one excessive depreciation after another in which each country would emerge from its own deflationary problems at the expense of the system as a whole, with the whole more than the sum of the parts.

THE VAN ZEELAND REPORT

The prospect of a change in the price of gold was not the only thing altered by the recession of 1937 and armament boom of 1936–39. In April 1937 the British and French governments asked Paul van Zeeland, no longer prime minister of Belgium, to prepare a report on the possibilities for restoring world trade. The report was made public in January 1938. It called for reciprocal tariff reductions, along the lines of the Reciprocal Trade Agreements Act of 1934 in the United States; substitution of tariffs for quotas; gradual dismantling of clearing agreements; removal of controls over capital exports in creditor countries and over financing of foreign trade in debtor countries. It was suggested that the Bank for International Settlements should finance trade through a multilateral clearing arrangement, or a common fund, while exchange controls were being dismantled. Long-run hope for control of "hot money"—capital flows motivated by a search for safety or for exchange rate profits rather than responding to differences in rates of interest—was sought in the reestablishment of the gold standard on which a beginning should be made by extending the Tripartite Monetary Agreement to guarantee exchange rates for six months rather than the existing twenty-four hours. The reenthroning of gold was the final step in the series of recommendations, not the first.

Very quickly, however, European efforts turned from reconstruction of the economy after its disintegration in the years from 1929 to 1936 to preventing further breakdown in war. Like the recommendations of so many conferences, committees, and individuals, the van Zeeland report ended up in a pigeon-hole.

SUGGESTED SUPPLEMENTARY READING

Arndt (1944), *The Economic Lessons of the Nineteen-Thirties.*
Cairncross and Eichengreen (1983), *Sterling in Decline.*
Clarke (1977), *Exchange-Rate Stabilization in the Mid-1930s.*
Howson and Winch (1977), *The Economic Advisory Council, 1930–39.*
Journal of European Economic History (1984), Banks and Industry in the Interwar Period.
Mouré (1991), *Managing the Franc Poincaré.*

In French

Sauvy (1967), *Histoire économique de la France entre les deux guerres (1931–1939)*, Vol. 2.

In German

Deutsche Bundesbank (ed.) (1976), *Währung und Wirtschaft in Deutschland, 1876–1975*, esp. papers by Irmler, and Hansmeyer and Caesar.

In Italian

Toniolo (1980), *L'economia dell' Italia fascista.*

V

AFTER WORLD WAR II

The concluding chapters bring the history into the postwar period. For the most part, they are concerned with wartime and immediately postwar finance and are designed to provide a contrast with the experience after World War I. Chapter 22 on German finance introduces a topic hitherto neglected: the financing of armies in the field with distinctive bank notes, special exchange rates, and convertibility problems. It focuses attention on the German mobilization of the resources of Europe, as a whole, through various devices. The major theme of the chapter, however, is the contrast between the German inflation after World War I and the effective and equitable monetary reform of 1948.

The contrast with war debts after World War I is provided in Chapter 23 by a discussion of lend-lease, the Anglo-American Financial Agreement of 1946, and the Marshall Plan of 1947 to 1952. Only passing attention is paid to the United Nations program of relief and rehabilitation through the United Nations Relief and Rehabilitation Administration (UNRRA); reconstruction through the International Bank for Reconstruction and Development (IBRD); and achieving payments stability through the International Monetary Fund (IMF)—all widely discussed in economic literature elsewhere. The contrast between the worldwide approach embodied in this program and the key currency and key region philosophies inherent in the British loan and the Marshall Plan is, however, a major theme.

Chapter 24 introduces the unfinished story of European financial integration and touches on new institutions, such as the Eurocurrency and Eurobond markets, which are actually worldwide, as well as those more narrowly European. In extension of a theme of the entire book, I conclude that European monetary integration waits on political unification, rather than constituting an avenue to it.

The final chapter attempts to put the emerging European financial system into a world setting. If the Venetian ducat and Florentine florin were followed by the Spanish peso, the Amsterdam gulden, French livre tournois, British pound, and American dollar, what is next? Does the dollar have staying power as the world's financial center moves—where? London? Frankfurt? Paris? Brussels? Tokyo? Will the world currency and the world financial center go separate ways, as the Eurodollar took its stand in London? Will the écu be European money only or international? Tokyo and the yen? Although no answers will be furnished to these questions, they are nonetheless worth raising and speculating about, if economic historians are perhaps reluctant to speculate on the currencies themselves.

22

German Finance in and After World War II

It is necessary to make clear the kind and extent of the financial charges which Germany had imposed on France as a result of the occupation. . . .

1. France was to place at the disposition of the German military command in France as a deposit for each day of occupation the sum of 20 million Reichsmarks, calculated as 400 million francs, payable in advance every ten days. . . .

2. And that was not all. Entirely in addition to these payments, every ten days France had to settle and pay directly the expenses of lodging and quartering the troops stationed on French territory. . . . The total of such expenses varied during the occupation; in 1942 they came to about 500 million francs per month; in 1944 they were 1,000 million francs per month.

3. Entirely outside these military expenses the French Treasury had to meet another charge which resulted from the operations of the Franco-German clearing. Under a special agreement reached in November 1940 the French Treasury advanced to the French exchange office in francs such sums as were necessary. In 1942 the monthly charge was on the average about 4,000 million francs; in 1944 it reached 7,000 million francs. At the end of the occupation in July 1944, the grand total of these advances was 165,000 million francs.

4. To complete the picture it should be recalled that under decision of the German military command, taken in the days just after the occupation of Paris, the value of the Reichsmark had been set at 20 francs. It bore no relation to the true value of the two currencies at that time, the mark being worth barely over 10 or 12 francs.

(Statement of Pierre Cathala, Minister of Finance and National Economy of France, 1942–44, in *France during the German Occupation, 1940–1944*, 1957, Vol. 1, pp. 79–81)

GERMAN STRATEGY

Even more than in World War I plans, German strategy rested on Blitzkrieg—an overwhelming superiority in armament based on stocks rather than production, a war of movement as opposed to stalemate in trenches. There was financial preparation. A law of 15 June 1939 suspended the gold-cover rules for the Reichsbank. On 4 September, immediately after outbreak of war, wage, income, and excise taxes were raised, in sharp contrast to the two-year delay after 1914. Another dissimilarity was the continuous funding of short- into long-term debt by secret negotiation with banks, savings banks, insurance companies, and so on, rather than periodic public refundings with bonds sold to the public with fanfare. This was a Nazi technique called "noiseless finance" (Hansmeyer and Caesar, 1976, p. 403). Liquidation of the Rentenbank was interrupted so as to make available *Rentenbankscheine* to supplement the coinage. *Reichskreditkassen* (national credit offices) were established to issue *Reichskreditkassenscheine* (special bank notes) to be used in occupied territories, not within Germany.

German financial performance in World War II was superior to that in World War I but far from optimal. Forty-eight percent of government expenditure was raised by taxation, as opposed to 13 percent in 1914–18. An additional 12 percent was extracted from the occupied territories—primarily France, Belgium, and Holland—for little was obtained from Eastern Europe. *Reichskreditkassenscheine* were actually sold by German troops in southeastern Europe to those in France because their purchasing power was higher there (Milward, 1977, pp. 137, 148). Nonetheless, the Reich budget deficit rose from 5.1 billion Reichsmarks in 1938–39 to 240.3 billion at the end of the war, Reich debt from 31 billion Reichsmarks to 380 billion (at the end of the fiscal year 1944–45), the short-term portion of the debt to 241 billion Reichsmarks, or 64 percent of the total, and the money supply from 4.3 billion Reichsmarks to 56.4 billion. At the outbreak of war, a *Preisstopp* (price freeze) fixed all prices at the 1 October 1936 level, which was maintained with only minor upward adjustments until the postwar monetary reform of 21 June 1948, that is, for almost twelve years. With totalitarian government and a submissive population, Germany operated the most far-reaching suppressed inflation in a disequilibrium system that Europe has ever experienced.

OCCUPATION FINANCE

Invading German troops were closely followed by *Reichskreditkassen,* which issued notes used by the German authorities and by troops until more formal arrangements could be made for "occupation costs," on the one hand, and clearing arrangements, on the other. Initially the monies were intended primarily to allow troops to live off the land and to buy up civilian inventories, which were all that were thought useful in Blitzkrieg. After 1942, when England and the Soviet Union proved not to be readily overwhelmed, German authorities settled down to extract production and labor from occupied territories by various means. The epigraph at the head of the chapter summarizes the techniques used at the government-to-government level in France. Similar procedures were followed in Belgium, to which was added the independent, uncoordinated operations of various German agencies and services, especially the Luftwaffe, in black market purchases in Belgium that were tolerated, and even encouraged, by the German officials because they offered a more effective way to get goods (Gillingham, 1977, ch. 5). Belgium was initially charged occupation costs of 1 billion Belgian francs a month, raised in 1941 to 1.5 billion, plus a German deficit in the clearing that reached 1 billion Belgian francs a month in the second half of 1941 and rose further to 2.5 billion by March 1942.

How much Germany gained from occupied territories during the war can be estimated—like the German payment of reparations after World War I (see p. 297)—only within wide margins of error. Estimates are strongly affected by subjective considerations. The U.S. Strategic Bombing Survey calculated the foreign contribution from the beginning of 1940 to the end of 1943 at 104 billion Reichsmarks. In an independent estimate, Burton Klein put the figure at 85 billion Reichsmarks (Milward, 1971, p. 272). French figures for their own country come to 862.5 billion francs—roughly 43 billion Reichsmarks at the official rate of 20 francs to the Reichsmark—of which 641 billion represented occupation costs and 221 billion was largely the clearing deficit of Germany (ibid., table 59, p. 271). These figures fail to include war booty—that is, material taken over by the German armed forces from the defeated military, or the value of work performed by forced labor from occupied territories inside Germany in excess of subsistence. The Belgian official statement to the Nuremberg Tribunal judging Nazi war crimes put total losses at 175 billion Belgian francs. A Belgian Finance Ministry estimate produced a figure of 145 billion Belgian francs. Gillingham calculated occupation costs and the unrecoverable Belgian surplus in clearing at 133 billion Belgian francs, and a Belgian economist, Fernand Baudhuin, put the figure at 35 billion of 1939 Belgian francs, or roughly 70 billion of current francs (Gillingham, 1977, p. 182). The title of a book by a Belgian radical, Fernand Demany, written first in Flemish (1945) and then in French (no date), was *On a volé 64 milliards: l'histoire de la Banque d'Emission* (They have stolen 64 billions: The history of the Bank of Emission). The Banque d'Emission was created to replace the Banque Nationale de Belgique, which fled into exile with the Belgian government. It provided Belgian franc counterparts for payments of occupation costs and out of the Belgo-German clearing (ibid., pp. 68ff.).

The Gillingham estimate, he notes, should be reduced to the extent that German agencies bought goods and services at black market prices, but increased because of undervaluation of the Belgian franc, not the initial undervaluation arising from setting the exchange rate at 12.5 Belgian francs to 1 Reichsmark, as opposed to the prewar value of, perhaps, 7 or 8 Belgian francs (ibid., p. 189), but that from whatever percentage of undervaluation remained after Belgian prices had risen because of choice of this rate.

While German troops in occupied areas were provided with *Reichskreditkassenscheine* at overvalued rates to enable them to live well in the local economy until prices rose to offset the exchange rate, a different money—*Wehrmachtsbehilfsgeld* (army emergency money)—was issued to German troops in friendly or satellite countries such as Bulgaria, Hungary, or Rumania. This was denominated in marks and could be spent locally at regular exchange rates equal to those in the clearing but was given a higher value when used in army canteens or remitted back to accounts in Germany. It was intended to discourage spending in the local economies of friendly countries, whereas spending by German troops in occupied enemy countries was encouraged (Southard, 1946 [1978], p. 116).

ALLIED MILITARY EXCHANGE RATES

Allied policies also made a distinction in military exchange rates between liberated and enemy areas. All Allied and liberated areas wanted the local currency overvalued against the dollar, and the dollar undervalued, in order to maximize dollar earnings of the Allied country from expenditures by American logistical units and troops. The French, for example, wanted a rate in North Africa of 49 francs to the dollar, which prevailed before the fall of France, whereas the market was close to 75. At 50 francs to the dollar, the amount of money available to soldiers for recreational spending would have been cut 33 percent, to the detriment of troop morale—a problem encountered many times above in this history when armies were either not paid at all for long periods or paid in monies that they regarded as less than the best. Discussion of the appropriate exchange rate for the lira ranged from 33⅓ to the dollar to 200, before settling on 100 to the dollar, at which it was overvalued; that for the German Reichsmark, when Germany was finally occupied, ranged from 5 to 40 cents (ibid., pp. 117–18). In the end, the Allied armies resisted the pressure of friendly nations to overvalue their currencies, not always with complete success, and settled on 10 cents per Reichsmark or occupation mark, a considerable distance from the official 40 cent rate and from the 25 cent rate widely judged to be the prewar equilibrium level. Ten cents did more or less justice to the inflationary position reached in Germany during the war, with low fixed prices of rationed goods, and black market prices much higher.

There were many more problems of army finance than the exchange rate, although that was critical. When liberated countries obtained control over their former territories, governments were expected to furnish local currency to British and American armies on a generous basis, with settlement for the amounts made available being reserved for the general financial negotiation at the end of the war. In the case of the United States, settlement was made under lend-lease, with Allied government advances to the U.S. forces for expenditure in France, Belgium, and ultimately the Netherlands, included as reverse lend-lease, to be cleared against any U.S. positive claim for material and supplies furnished to European governments. Local monies provided to British forces were similarly noted and reserved for overall postwar settlement. Before local governments had control of the central bank or Treasury, however, invading armies would issue either special Allied Military Government money, printed up prior to invasion or, in the case of the United States in Italy, special yellow-seal dollars, distinct from ordinary U.S. currency, which bears a blue seal. For a time yellow-seal dollars sold in Italy at discounts of 45 to 55 percent from blue-seal dollars because it was not known whether the United States would redeem them—as it might not have done if the territory had been retaken by German troops (ibid., p. 153n).

Another problem was whether to redeem foreign currencies acquired by Allied military personnel. To the extent that such soldiers, sailors, and airmen obtained part of their pay in local currency, failed to spend all of it, and wanted to convert the remainder back into dollars, there was no problem. To the extent, however, that local currencies were acquired by black market operations—selling off army rations or stolen supplies, cigarettes from home, or even relieving Axis military paymasters of their payrolls—and that the proceeds were turned in for redemption in dollars or pounds, often with the claim that the large amounts of cash represented winnings at dice or poker, the military by redeeming such funds in dollars was, in effect, financing luxury imports or capital exports for the inflated Continent. Southard recounts the exploits of American airmen shuttling between Cairo and the Italian theatre, who would buy gold sovereigns in Egypt for $18 or $20, sell them in Italy for the equivalent (at the overvalued exchange rate) of $55 or $60, convert the proceeds into dollars or sterling, and repeat the process. One person was caught at a Naples airport with almost a quarter of a million dollars worth of sterling, British Military pounds, and dollars (ibid., p. 125).

The remedy for this hemorrhaging was either to redeem no foreign currency at all or to issue each member of the armed forces with a paybook in which was recorded how much pay he had drawn against local currency and limiting conversion back into dollars to that amount—regardless of winnings at poker or dice. As it was, American armed forces acquired what was euphemistically called "a surplus of foreign currencies in the troop-pay account" (actually a shortage of dollars), about which little has been written but which in one version is said to have amounted to $530 million (Rundell, 1964, cited by Milward, 1971, p. 349). Rumors of economists in government at the time put the U.S. loss in the European theatre of war at $450 million, to which was added another $300 million paid out in Japan, with £100 million or so lost by the British government. Milward states that it can only be assumed that this was a method of providing extra pay for soldiers serving abroad, a more sophisticated form of loot (ibid.). A legal argument was made that American forces could not follow British practice in withholding some pay due (Southard, 1946 [1978], p. 169). It is, however, a theorem of philosophy that the simpler reason is more likely to be accurate than the sophisticated, and the likelihood is that the loss was the result of stupidity in high army circles, a failure to see that the key to the situation was how much, if any, local currency the army was prepared to redeem in dollars or pounds.

Confusion over the issue in the U.S. press and public was enormous, as it was long thought that the action of the U.S. Treasury under Secretary Morgenthau and Assistant Secretary Harry D. White in making the plates for printing occupation marks available to the Soviet Union was responsible for the U.S. losses. This misinterpretation had the consequence that German monetary reform was held up after the war to ensure that the Soviet Union did not get access to plates of the new Deutschemark currency, when how many occupation marks were in existence, or by whom they had been produced, had nothing to do with how many marks U.S. military paymasters redeemed in dollars.

Parenthetically it may be noted that the British Parliament made good the loss in their troop pay account by voting an appropriation to bring it back into balance, whereas in the United States the military worked their way out of the deficit bit by bit over a number of years by paying out marks for purchases of goods and services made in Germany for the occupation forces and voted in dollars, crediting the corresponding dollars to the troop pay account. If the deficit had not existed, dollars voted for support of the occupation administration would have been earned by the German economy. Since Germany was receiving aid from the United States for most of this time, it made no difference to the United States as a whole, or to Germany, but the U.S. Army budget gained at the expense of the foreign aid budget and with a distinct loss for financial integrity. The episode is reminiscent of the U.S. Treasury, under Secretary Morgenthau, saying that it would make a profit on the million pounds bought from the Soviet Union on 26 September 1936 at $4.91, and then when the pound sank further to $4.78, crediting the account with the gold-handling charges during the ensuing years of gold scare until the loss had been made up. That the Russian access to the occupation-currency plates had nothing to do with the case is attested to by the fact that loss was recorded also in Japan, although the Russian armies did not take part in that occupation or have access to occupation yen. The contrast of British and American experience is with the German practice of issuing *Reichskreditkassenscheine* to troops that could be spent only outside the country and were inconvertible into Reichsmarks.

POSTWAR MONETARY REFORM

Despite the attempts of the combatants to raise more of government expenditure at home with taxation, Europe ended the war swimming in currency. In liberated and conquered areas there had been no hesitation in using inflation to acquire resources for the pursuit of war, on the one hand, and the recreation of armed forces on the other.

Almost as soon as a country was liberated by Allied armies and the government in exile or a new government free of German influence had taken over, decisions had to be made as to whether to do anything about the monetary system. There was no thought this time of returning to prewar parities with postwar monetary supplies. The issue was debated within the French Resistance, with Pierre Mendès-France, the Socialist reformer, recommending a massive blocking and currency conversion, whereas neoliberals, such as René Courtin and Emmanuel Monick, objected to a permanent amputation of money in circulation on the ground that it would be "unpopular, unfair, arbitrary and ineffective." They preferred a massive loan to soak up purchasing power (Kuisel, 1981, pp. 182–83). Later in the government as minister of the economy, Pierre Mendès-France proposed a drastic program of monetary reform with a new issue of bank notes and a heroic reduction in bank deposits (Bouvier, 1988, p. 93). The discussion was conducted in secret with Governor Monnick of the Bank of France. The bank fought against the program on the ground of impracticality and was supported in the cabinet by René Pleven at the Treasury. President de Gaulle ultimately decided against Mendès-France, who resigned in April 1945. François Bloch-Lainé, a high Treasury official, concluded well after the event that Mendés-France had been right and Monick and Pleven wrong, stating that the bank was like the general staff, fighting the last war (Bloch-Lainé and Bouvier, 1986, ch. 2, esp. p. 81). He does, however, blame Mendès-France for writing a polemical memorandum on the subject. In his memoirs, Mendès-France puts the onus on the Bank of France (1985, vol. 2, pp. 149–51).

Failure to adjust the money supply to the existing price level meant by default adjusting the price level to the money supply. There was a big wage increase in 1945 and galloping inflation from that year to 1951 at 34 percent a year (Bloch-Lainé and Bouvier, 1986, pp. 41, 68, 73). Stabilization was finally achieved, more or less, with Marshall Plan funds. The inflation in France, as in Italy, resulted in a redistribution of wealth between debtors and creditors and between owners of claims denominated in money and owners of real property and equities.

New monies were printed and exchanged for old in order to invalidate large black market hoards, which were not converted for fear of questioning about the owners' activities during the German occupation. A one-for-one conversion initiated in French Corsica in 1941 and carried out in Metropolitan France in June 1945 reduced the currency in circulation from 549 billion francs on 31 May 1945 to 444 billion on 2 August. Continued substantial deficits in government accounts and the need to finance them by borrowing at the Bank of France permitted the circulation to expand again to 580 billion francs by the end of December 1945. The French franc, which had been 5 to the dollar in 1913 and 19 in 1928, went to 48 and 75 during the war, to 119 after the war, and finally in the devaluation of 1958 to 500 plus. At this stage, it was decided to change it nominally by 100 to 1 back to 5 to the dollar. The practice was one that prevailed on a more extravagant scale in Latin America, where the Brazilians, for example, devalued the reis time and time again until they divided by 1,000 and called the new currency the milreis, and then after continuous depreciation of the milreis, divided by 1,000 again and called it the cruzeiro. Illustrating the difficulty of changing the unit of account in a country, French adults continued to reckon in "old francs" long after 1958, whereas children and tourists shifted over to the new, finding it easier to think in terms of 100 new francs than 10,000 old.

Italy had planned to undertake a currency exchange, but plates for the new money were stolen and the effort had to be abandoned (Clough, 1964, p. 292n). It also planned a capital levy, but this was converted into a percentage added regularly to the tax on private and corporate wealth, which was, in any event, consistently underpaid. The Italian lira declined from 5 to the dollar in 1913 to 19 at the time of the *quota novanta* in 1926, 100 in the invasion of Sicily and 225 in January 1946 (when the purchasing power parity was far lower) (ibid., p. 293). When allowed to be traded freely, the lira dropped to 600 to the dollar in September 1946 and for a time reached 900 in 1947 before settling back to 600.

In France and Italy, then, monetary reform was nominal or very limited, and the social effects of inflation on various holders of wealth and recipients of income were generally allowed to work themselves out.

BELGIAN MONETARY REFORM

More thoroughgoing, but still far from radical, was the monetary reform undertaken in Belgium. The government-in-exile returned to Brussels in September 1944 with its plans already formulated. It was hoped to cut the money supply, which stood roughly 250 percent above prewar levels—bank notes were up 350 percent and current accounts in banks only 125 percent—to the price level rather than let prices rise. The exchange rate had been agreed in London: 176.6 to the pound and 43.70 to the dollar, as compared with roughly 145 and 30 before the war. A new currency had been printed in England. In early October all notes over 100 Belgian francs were frozen, while a census of cash was carried out in five days and a start made in distributing the new currency (Dupriez, 1947, p. 17). Two thousand Belgian francs per family member were exchanged immediately. More was exchanged slowly, but amounts above certain limits, which varied depending upon whether they were in notes, post office accounts, or bank accounts, were blocked permanently to the extent of 60 percent and 40 percent provisionally, to be released at the discretion of the minister of finance. Some 10 billion to 13 billion of the 300 billion Belgian francs was not turned in at all. Blocked funds could be used to pay new special taxes, which included those on wartime profits, running as high as 100 percent for collaborators with Germany, plus the value of the goods sold, a tax on exceptional wartime profits of noncollaborators running up to 80 percent, and a capital levy of 5 percent, with exemptions of 40,000 francs for each man and wife and 10,000 to 15,000 for each additional child (ibid., pp. 32–33). The special taxes could be paid by corporations issuing capital stock to the Belgian government, which undertook not to sell it without offering it first to the issuing company.

The immediate exchange reduced the note circulation from 300 billion Belgian francs in September 1944 to 57.4 billion in October, from which it rose to 75 billion at the end of December. Further substantial expansion took place to the end of March 1945—27 percent—with 14 percent more through June, 11 percent to September, and 13 percent to December. This rapid growth was the consequence, partly of expenditures of British and American troops using Belgium as a base and partly of the restocking of the Belgian economy. Since Belgium had been overcome quickly by German forces in May 1940, it had not exhausted its reserves in fighting. When the tide of battle swung the other way, moreover, German troops pulled eastward through the country quickly, and Belgium was able to serve as host to British and American armies. Payment for supplies, billets, and service went on reverse lend-lease, which vastly exceeded lend-lease to the Belgian government and was settled in foreign exchange. The country therefore emerged from the war with abundant reserves of foreign exchange and gold.

Belgian gold had, in fact, been captured and taken by the Germans when the Belgians were trying to move it to safety and when it was in France under French protection. Belgium sued the French government in American courts to recover the loss, charging that the French had neglected to take adequate precautions, and was awarded the full amount out of French stocks under earmark in the United States. As it turned out, all German gold acquisitions from the Allies during the war were recovered, so that neither France nor Belgium lost in the long run. In the short run, however, the French were obliged to make up the Belgian loss.

There were all sorts of administrative problems in the currency reform and special taxes, some dealing with foreign assets (both those recorded in a special census that the Germans had taken and those not disclosed for patriotic or other reasons), questions of bonds not registered in order to avoid ordinary taxation, whether the capital levy applied to single-premium, life insurance contracts, or the like.

Other monetary conversions were undertaken by Denmark in July 1945, in the Netherlands from July to October 1945, in Norway in September 1945, Czechoslovakia in October, Finland and Austria in December 1945. The Danish conversion had the principal purpose of eliminating German holdings of kroner. In most cases, reform consisted of part conversion and part blocking, with various conditions under which the blocked portion could be used. Capital levies were involved in few instances. An American expert who made a study of currency reforms in the spring of 1946 stated that opinion was general that a major mistake was made in delaying a capital levy, which meant continued blocking and uncertainty as to what the relationship between real wealth and the monetary superstructure would eventually be (Metzler, 1946 [1979], p. 368).

GERMAN MONETARY REFORM

Allied policy in Germany after that country's defeat combined various objectives—denazification, demilitarization, and democratization. In the economic and financial field, one strand of policy emanating largely from the U.S. Treasury Department emphasized that the occupation forces should take no steps to improve the German condition, beyond those necessary to prevent such disease and unrest as might endanger the occupation forces. This expected and rather welcomed the prospect of the rapid deterioration of the Reichsmark and uncontrollable inflation in Germany (Wandel, 1979, p. 321). The Office of Military Government of the United States (OMGUS) and the Department of State were interested relatively early in two major financial developments: in planning for a new central bank to replace the Reichsbank and in monetary reform. Manuel Gottlieb of the Finance Division of OMGUS suggested a local currency conversion as early as September 1945—the war had ended in May but the Potsdam Agreement among the occupying powers had been reached only in mid-August—and Joseph Dodge, the head of the division, was discussing extinguishing all debt in Germany with Adolf Weber, the German economist, in November 1945, the month in which he drew up a plan for a decentralized central banking system, based on the *Länder,* to replace the Reichsbank (ibid., pp. 322–23). In early 1946 on the recommendation of the U.S. occupation staff in Berlin, the Department of State appointed a commission consisting of Gerhard Colm, Joseph Dodge, and Raymond Goldsmith to prepare a plan for monetary reform in Germany.

Dodge was a banker from Detroit, Colm an economist of German origin who had emigrated to the United States and served as a high civil servant in government, Goldsmith a statistician who had similarly grown up in Germany and experienced the inflation of 1921–33 at firsthand before emigrating to the United States. With a staff of seventeen, the commission began its work in March 1946, had a first draft completed in April, and a final report, with seventeen appendixes, finished on 20 May 1946 (Colm, Dodge, and Goldsmith, 1946 [1955]). In drawing up the report, the commission consulted thirty German plans prepared by various experts and quasi-experts, on which the German participants, without political power, had been unable to agree. The Colm-Dodge-Goldsmith plan called basically for a 10:1 conversion of the currency and all debts in the financial system, plus a capital levy called *Lastenausgleich* (equalization of burdens or war losses)—far more drastic than the 5 percent capital levy of the Belgian authorities or similar imposts that could readily be converted from a tax on capital to a modest one on income.

FOUR-POWER AGREEMENT

The Potsdam Agreement of August 1945 committed the occupying powers—the United Kingdom, United States, France, and the Soviet Union—to treat Germany as a single economic unit. This agreement broke down slowly for a variety of reasons not germane to monetary reform, but its residue was the basic reason for the delay from May 1946 to June 1948 in effecting monetary reform.

One stumbling block was the printing of a new currency. For a large, modern country, printing a new currency is likely to take six or eight weeks or more because of the great quantity of notes of small denomination that must be produced, the need to manufacture suitable paper in adequate quantity, and so on. Specialized presses are required, and these are few in number throughout the world. The only suitable presses in Germany were those of the Reichsdruckerei (Imperial Printing Office) in Leipzig in the Soviet zone of occupation; the Western occupying powers were wary of confiding the task of printing the German currency to that zone, especially in the light of the earlier and continuing misunderstanding of the American public over the consequences of transmitting the plates to print occupation marks to the Soviet Union. For months the Allied Control Council in Berlin wrangled over where to print the new currency, whether in Leipzig or abroad—that is, in London or New York. At the end, as the rift between the Western occupation powers and the Soviet Union widened, the decision was taken by the Western powers to print it in England. Military secrecy was preserved so as not to induce the German public to get rid of its Reichsmarks precipitously, and the process went forward under the code name Operation Birddog (Möller, 1976, p. 444). The graphic design was American, with figures and border design similar to those of the dollar bill, and cogwheels, marble columns, pensive titans, and bare-breasted women taken over from designs used in producing American stock certificates (Wandel, 1979, p. 328).

While the argument was ostensibly about the detail of where to print new currency under adequate supervision to ensure that the Soviet Union did not produce an extra supply for its own use, the basic issue went far deeper. The Western powers and the Soviet Union were embarked on diametrically opposed courses in banking: the West had opened preexisting banks; the Soviet Union built a system of entirely new banks, which it tried to extend into the West as a means of controlling the economy (Möller, 1976, pp. 438–39). Moreover, for the Soviet Union to agree to a plan for German monetary reform applicable to all four zones would have robbed it of the freedom to apply an inflation tax in the Soviet zone of occupation. Arthur Marget, director of the U.S. Financial Division in the Allied Council for Austria in Vienna, had obtained a stunning victory in an early vote in the Allied Council that all new issues of money in Austria were to be made by the Austrian government after authorization by the Allied Council. This measure deprived the Soviet Union of the right to issue new money in the Soviet zone of occupation in Austria and made it wary of financial agreement in the much more important case of Germany. So long as the Western powers remained committed to treating Germany as a single economic unit, the Soviet Union had a veto over monetary reform. The note-printing issue was a convenient facade behind which to hide.

It is profoundly significant that the final split of Germany between the Federal

Republic in the West and the People's Republic in the East came about over the issue of introducing the new currency into the three western sectors of Berlin. This led the Soviet Union to blockade Berlin from the western zone and the West to respond with the airlift. Money is a critically sensitive aspect of sovereignty, and the inability to work out a four-power solution in this field signified and symbolized deeper division.

BLACK MARKET AND PRIVATE COMPENSATION

Cigarettes were first used as money—a medium of exchange and unit of account— by German soldiers in occupied areas in 1942 (Hansmeyer and Caesar, 1976, p. 422). They were further widely used by Allied military personnel in German prisoner-of-war camps, with economist prisoners recording the inflationary bubbles that occurred when a collection of delayed Red Cross packages laden with cigarettes arrived in a bunch (Radford, 1945). In the extreme disequilibrium system of Germany from 1945 to the spring of 1948, cigarettes were one form of money and soluble coffee and silk stockings other, but less satisfactory, substitutes—stockings because they were too high in value for small transactions and not uniform in size, coffee because of the difficulty of measuring it for odd amounts. Cigarettes came in cartons of ten packages, packages of twenty cigarettes, and individual cigarettes, which were occasionally divided. They were, moreover, a disappearing money since some fraction such as one-fourth or one-fifth was consumed on each turnover, a disappearing money such as a number of monetary cranks had recommended for introduction during the 1930 depression to speed velocity of circulation. The source of new supplies was occupation forces who sold cigarettes to the German economy against all sorts of more or less valuable services and goods.

In addition to the cigarette market, there was a real black market against Reichsmarks, both German issued and those put out by the occupation forces. This had only 10 percent of transactions but 80 percent of monetary turnover; prices in it were 100 times the level of the *Preisstopp* (Hansmeyer and Caesar, 1976, p. 423). Effective money in official transactions was not the Reichsmark but the ration card. Currency was redundant; virtually everyone had enormous quantities of it. The official price level meant that many firms recorded losses on all sales as, for example, when it cost 31 Reichsmarks to mine a ton of coal and the official price was 15 Reichsmarks. Losses were financed by continuous bank loans, which companies had no prospect of paying off but which it was expected would be regularized ultimately by monetary reform.

Between the official white market where ration cards dominated and the black lay a gray market of "private compensation" or barter. Coal miners were partly paid in so-called *Deputat-Kohle* (coal allowance), a reversion to the truck system, or wages in kind, which was highly valuable to miners since they could barter coal for food and other goods and services. Mines even paid pensions in coal. Miners were given extra rations because of the importance of coal to the economic recovery of Europe as a whole and their inability to sustain the heavy work at the average German ration of 1,550 calories a day. An attempt was made to provide these extra rations solely in a hot meal served at the mine, but workers insisted on being able to bring extra calories home to be shared with their families. Coal mines would exchange coal for cement, timber, and other supplies in private compensation. An inefficient but flourishing barter economy thus grew up alongside the stunted money economy. And employees had no interest in safeguarding company property, which was worthless if sold for money or exported through official channels, for which the company could receive only money. Trainloads of coal would be slowed down going through cities and towns to allow the local citizenry to climb into the wagons and shovel coal over the side to be salvaged later, or the locomotive engineer would brake sharply as he rounded a curve near a town to spill coal out of wagons through centrifugal force.

One measure of the inefficiency of an economy in which money does not function is the exchange between countryside and city. The winter of 1946–47 was a harsh one for Europe with floods, freezing, and, for Germany, the lowest priority of all the countries of Western Europe, scarce food supplies. Normal breadgrains in international trade were in desperately short supply, the local potato crop ruinous, and the German housewife was handed corn (maize) in her rations, which she did not know how to use in baking or porridge. Farmers were reluctant to sell potatoes and meat for money, which was worthless, but would barter them for the possessions of city folk. Instead of potatoes being shipped to the cities in railroad freight cars to be distributed in bulk through jobbers to grocery stores, city dwellers would trek individually to the countryside at the weekend, carrying books, lamps, appliances, and the like to barter for potatoes brought back to the city in passenger trains in kilo lots in rucksacks.

Some factory and artisan production, moreover, went into hiding in cellars and storage sheds rather than into trade or the shop window. The *Wirtschaftswunder* (economic miracle) consequent on monetary reform was partly a movement of goods already produced in secret into the open (Abelshauser, 1975), although the incentive that working for valuable money gave to the German economy furnishes a striking example of supply-side economics.

THE REFORM

In theory, monetary reform was simple, consisting of two major steps: conversion of currency and debts at a ratio of 10 Reichsmarks for one new Deutschemark and a fund for the equalization of war losses, built with a capital levy, the *Lastenausgleich,* which would correct at least part of the inequity as between owners of debt and owners of real assets and shares of corporations. In practice, there were many problems to be settled. When the decision was taken to introduce monetary reform into the Western zones alone, a group of German experts from the bizonal area, which had been working in the background since the fall of 1947, was assembled and segregated in an army barracks in Rothwesten, beginning in April 1948, to work out the details over the course of thirty meetings in forty-nine days (Möller, 1976, pp. 445–46). The Allied liaison officer was a 25-year-old American economist, Edward Tenenbaum, who applied pressure on the German group to work out the numerous laws, announcements, proclamations, and instructions, which came to twenty-two detailed documents, and who negotiated between the German group and the Allied Control Council, or the Western members. Milton and Rose Friedman in *Free to Choose* (1980, p. 56) assert that the currency reform was the work of Ludwig Erhard, who believed in a modified economy, the so-called *Sozialmarktwirtschaft,* and therefore reflected the beneficent outcome of the market forces when government is held far from them. Mrs J. Kipp Tenenbaum, widow of the liaison officer, takes vigorous exception to this view (1980). Ludwig Erhard was the author of one of thirty plans for monetary reform and was not a member of the Rothwesten group. He was not present when the reform was announced by Jack Bennett (who, by this time, had replaced Joseph Dodge as director of the U.S. Finance Division) with Tenenbaum at his side. The notion that Erhard insisted on immediate freedom of markets from price control against the will of the Allies is characterized by a German financial consultant to OMGUS as "legend" (Sauermann, 1979, p. 316). A bit on the other side of the debate. Möller observes that there was a dispute as to whether price controls should be relaxed step by step or once and for all. Those who were for step-by-step relaxation were concerned with hunger and unrest. Erhard, representing the Freiburg-im-Breisgau school of Walter Eucken, won but not with the sweeping victory he later claimed. Food, agricultural prices, and most raw materials were still controlled on 24 June 1948 when the *Preisstopp* of 1939 was lifted. While textiles and clothing had price control removed, they were still rationed for a time (Möller, 1976, p. 458).

The issue goes deeper than the question of price control. Monetary reform is not something that can be left to the market to work out. Enormous numbers of problems must be solved in time-consuming legal, administrative, and analytical work. It is absurd to regard German monetary reform as an argument against government; only government can provide the public good of stable money, although it is evident that it does not always do so.

This account of the major role of Tenenbaum and the limited one of Erhard is confirmed in the memoirs of Otmar Emminger, who was president of the Bundesbank in the 1970s. He also makes the point that only an occupation regime could undertake so drastic a monetary reform. Other countries were left with a large money overhang that acted in each case as a leg shackle *(Klotz am Bein)* (1986, p. 23).

Conversion of all money and debts at 10:1 made an exception for the first 60 Reichsmarks of currency per capita, but all debts meant all debts. The text is set forth in Department of State documents (1950, pp. 492–511). The debts of the Reich—mortgages, bank loans, insurance policies—were written down, 10:1. The German experts held out for a time for conversion only of government debt, with private debt excluded from the measure and converted from Reichsmarks to Deutschemarks one for one (Pfeiderer, 1979, p. 361). The point was probably of minimal practical importance since, with money in great surplus, private debtors had, for the most part, paid off their creditors.

Banks, insurance companies, and similar financial institutions shrank to one-tenth their size on both sides of the balance sheet, although items such as buildings and fixtures on the asset side, and capital on the liability, were affected rather by the

Lastenausgleich. The military government had decreed at the beginning of the occupation that all debts must be contracted in Reichsmarks; now it was laid down that they must be in Deutschemarks. There were problems in the treatment of pensions and interest obligations, for overdue taxes and wages that should have been paid before 21 June and for taxes that had been prepaid, not to mention special treatment for released prisoners of war, Danish refugees, *Volksdeutsche* expelled from territory taken over by the Soviet Union and Poland, and the refugees from the Soviet zone of occupation and United Nations nationals. A particular problem was that the liabilities of the banking system were written down less than their assets, leaving banks with capital impaired (Möller, 1976, p. 456). Of crucial importance was the problem of dealing with Berlin where the trizonal authorities insisted on introducing the Deutschemark into their sectors of the city, which were open to the Soviet sector. Even after the whole list of documents had been finished on 18 June, it proved necessary to promulgate eleven supplementary ordinances to the currency law dealing with the Deutschemark and forty-two to the conversion law to the end of the year.

The *Lastenausgleich* was designed as a mortgage on all real property and equity holdings, equal to 50 percent of their value. Fifty percent is far different from the 90 percent by which debts were reduced. In defense of the round number, it can be said that the value of real assets and equities was highly uncertain both at the time of the *Lastenausgleich* and as they might develop in the future and that a 90 percent mortgage might threaten some assets then, or in the short-term future, with negative values. Fifty percent was also well above the timid levels of 5 or 10 percent, which characterized capital levies in other monetary reforms. A fund was set up to hold the mortgages and to receive interest on them plus repayment of principal. The fund used these monies to pay people who suffered major losses during the war— wounded veterans, widows, orphans, air-raid casualties, owners of damaged property, and those whose savings had been all but wiped out in the currency and debt conversion. Payment priority was based on need, not legal precedence.

At the last minute, the American authorities insisted on separating monetary reform and *Lastenausgleich,* leaving the latter to be enacted by the German authorities before 31 December 1948 as a task "of the greatest urgency." This was not because of "hesitation to impose currency reform" on the part of Americans and Germans as some have alleged (Maier, 1981, p. 343n). It was on the entirely personal initiative of the U.S. Secretary of the Army, Kenneth Royall, in nominal charge of the occupation forces, based on his ideological objection to capital levy as contrary to the American, or capitalistic, way of life. The Department of State and the Allied Control Council had wanted to have the *Lastenausgleich* enacted during the occupation, on the ground that a new German government would be frail when it took office and that a measure so far-reaching in ostensible effect on property might be difficult for it to enact without weakening its hold on authority. German experts at Rothwesten regarded *Lastenausgleich* as an integral part of the scheme. Owing to the intransigence of the secretary of the army, however, the compromise was reached that the Germans would do it, although the Allied Control Council put a time limit on the action and stated that it was an urgent necessity. In the event, not nearly so much time as the end of the year was needed. After intense debate, the *Lastenausgleich* was agreed without damage to the political fabric and put into effect on 2 September 1948.

SOCIAL BASES OF INFLATION AND MONETARY REFORM

I regard the German monetary reform of 1948 as one of the great feats of social engineering of all time. Contrast runs with the inflation of 1923; comparisons with the switch from the mark to the Rentenmark and from the Rentenmark to the Reichsmark in 1923 and 1924 are basically uninteresting (Pfleiderer, 1979). What accounts for the difference between the two postwar episodes: the quality of monetary policies or something more deep-seated?

In 1921–23 inflation had its roots less in the technicalities of money creation and exchange depreciation caused by reparations and restocking than in the fundamental inability of various groups in Germany to agree on how to share the burdens of war and reparations. As Chapter 17 (pp. 312–14) tried to demonstrate, Junkers, iron and steel magnates, and propertied classes, on the one hand, and laboring men and women on the other, were deeply divided on this basic issue. There was fundamental disagreement on the right, both with the republic and with the Socialists. The lack of social cohesion is illustrated particularly by such a politician as Helfferich and the assassinations, partly instigated by him, of Erzberger and Rathenau. A leader like Wilhelm Cuno, who accepted the republic, although a shipowner, had lines of communication open to Americans and British, and tried to effect compromises on the major issues, was shunted aside (Rupieper, 1979, passim, but esp. p. 259).

In contrast, World War II saw the destruction of all interest groups in Germany. The Junkers lost their base in agricultural land east of the Oder-Neisse line. German finance and industry had been compromised by allowing themselves to be co-opted by the Nazis, whose foreign and military policies had proved a failure. There was no effective collective interest left to defend its position (Olson, 1965, 1987). In these circumstances a national policy that achieved more or less equity among classes and functional groups was produced by experts fairly readily. The difference was not in understanding what needed to be done. In the *Kipper- und Wipperzeit* after the hyperinflation from coinage debasement had been halted, there was no sense of how to achieve equity among varying groups. But that issue, as noted above (pp. 29–30), was overwhelmed by the horrors of the Thirty Years' War. In Britain after the Napoleonic Wars, the same issues of equity had arisen and were understood, but the clash of various interests made it impossible to reach a solution. In Germany it was otherwise: the vacuum of powerful interests and the assertion of responsibility by the occupying powers—in spite of Secretary Royall and the French who held out until the last minute (Möller, 1976, pp. 446)—made it possible for reasonable policies to be adopted.

If one looks hard, one can find disagreements and opposition to the overall plan on the German side. The dispute over the release of price control has already been mentioned. Domes and Wolffsohn claim that there was considerable disapproval of currency reform in Germany, with trade unions, in particular, protesting and organizing mass demonstrations for which 9 million people turned out. They note that in June 1948, Germans complained most frequently that reform should have taken social factors into account and were critical of the destruction of savings and the asymmetry of treatment between businessmen and capitalists, on the one hand, and the common people, on the other. In July 1948 a public opinion poll recorded that 79 percent of West Germans thought that the reform had given special advantages to certain strata—62 percent picking out businessmen, 38 percent manufacturers, and 20 percent "capitalists" (Domes and Wolffsohn, 1979, p. 351). In private conversation, Knut Borchardt has told me that there were political struggles as to who among various claimants—widows of veterans, wounded, owners of destroyed property, those whose Treasury bonds had been decimated (in the sense of being cut to 10 percent), on the one hand, and labor unions, pensioners, and other needy groups on the other—would be compensated in what order from the *Lastenausgleichfond.* I have not seen any other dissatisfaction with the reform, but Möller, like Emminger, states that so thorough-going a reform in a country with such sharp conflict and inability to compromise would not have been possible without the military regime and without a population that had nothing to lose and doubted its prospects for economic and political reconstruction (1976, p. 437).

I conclude that the difference between 1923 and 1948 was not so much in the expertise of the economic and financial planners, though one must admire the skill of the Colm-Dodge-Goldsmith team and of the Rothwesten group, its German predecessors, and the Allied Military Government under Bennett and Tenenbaum, as in the different social situation—1923 heavy with powerful interests that survived the war and fought to reduce their share of the burden, and 1945–48 with political and economic groupings disorganized and helpless to protect themselves, creating a political vacuum in which policy in the general interest was possible.

GERMAN BANKING DECENTRALIZATION

Western occupying powers revived banks in their respective zones, while the Soviet Union ripped out the old network and established an entirely new banking system. Both actions were in contravention of the Potsdam provision for treating the four zones of occupation as a single economic unit.

In addition, various branches of the Reichsbank in the West were initially formed into separate *Land* banks. This system with a separate central bank for each *Land* and therefore four each in the British and American zones of occupation, survived the Bizonal Agreement between the Americans and the British of December 1946. In due course, however, as France joined the bizonal arrangements and monetary reform approached, a single entity was formed, the Bank Deutscher Länder (Bank of German States), patterned somewhat after the Federal Reserve system and organized in March 1948. Hamburg and Düsseldorf in the British zone and Frankfurt-am-Main in the American were more or less equal money and capital markets at the time, until in due course Frankfurt pulled ahead. Banks like the Deutsche and the Dresdener, from having spread their managements around, eventually came to concentrate them in Frankfurt. With deliberate speed, the Bank Deutscher Länder was converted in 1957 into the Deutsche Bundesbank with centralized direction, again located in Frankfurt.

The centripetal character of banking is illustrated in this gradual organization of German banking into a hierarchical structure despite the efforts of occupation authorities, largely at American instigation, to decentralize the system and to root it widely in the states.

Considerable interest attaches to why the apex of the structure ended up in Frankfurt, the administrative capital of the American zone, instead of Düsseldorf in the British. Düsseldorf started out as the major security market in Germany, and banking has typically been drawn to securities, as in downtown New York or the City of London. With the rise of the multinational corporation, however, there is a tendency for banks to be pulled more closely to head offices of such companies. This accounts for the movement of most major banks in New York City to the midtown area in the 1960s and 1970s and probably explains the Darwinian choice of Frankfurt over Hamburg, the trading city, and Düsseldorf with its emphasis on securities. It goes without saying that the ancient administrative and financial capital of Berlin had to be superseded, and the new capital of the Federal Republic at Bonn was a most unlikely substitute, having been, prior to its choice as capital, a provincial town. Cologne, close to Bonn, was a potential rival of Frankfurt. The fact that the headquarters of American military forces were located in Frankfurt, however, attracted there the German offices of American multinational corporations, and led by a somewhat meandering path to the emergence of Frankfurt as the new financial capital of West Germany. With the reunification of East and West Germany in 1990, a new question arose whether (a) government and (b) banks would be drawn to Berlin, from Bonn and Frankfurt respectively.

REPARATIONS IN CAPITAL ASSETS

At Yalta in February 1945, Stalin proposed that Germany be charged $20 billion in reparations—one-half to be paid to the Soviet Union, the other to be divided among the Western Allies. Winston Churchill resisted the proposal vigorously. Seeking a compromise, President Roosevelt was prepared to accept it, but only as a basis for initial discussion by a Reparations Commission to be appointed by the Soviet Union, the United Kingdom, and the United States.

After the end of the war on 8 May 1945, the Reparations Commission met in Moscow in July. By this time, however, the reparations issue had been caught up in a tangle of war booty, restitution, and the principle of treatment of Germany as a single economic unit. War booty in international law is generally restricted to property of defeated armed forces; in the wake of its armies, however, the Soviet government extended the concept to cover civilian property, which it seized and loaded on flat cars for shipment to the Soviet Union—not only military equipment produced, for which title had not yet passed from civilian producer to the German armed forces, but machine tools, equipment such as trucks, and even light and plumbing fixtures ripped out of ceilings or off walls and floors. Until war booty acquired by the Soviet Union could be circumscribed, discussion of reparations was impossible.

Restitution involved large questions of equity, especially as between restitution and reparations. In Anglo-Saxon, and generally Western, law, recognizable stolen property belongs to the rightful owner and has to be returned to him. Moreover, the Allied governments during the hostilities had announced that they would regard German purchases of existing assets, particularly art treasures but also gold, as made under duress, and therefore equivalent to robbery. Since the individual seller might be a collaborationist, the Allies did not presume to determine who the rightful owner was but undertook only to return recognizable property to the jurisdiction from which it had been taken, leaving the determination of ownership to authorities there.

There were exceptions to the principle of restitution. The German economy needed some railroad cars to enable its economy to function. To let Allied countries seize German railroad cars within their boundaries as reparations and claim restitution of their railroad cars in Germany, when efficient railroad practice provided for easy exchange on a rental basis, would have damaged the occupation. A special regime was decreed for gold. It was assumed that not all gold taken by the Germans, and possibly paid by them for purchases from neutrals, would be recovered, and it seemed arbitrary to restore recognized gold in toto and leave those whose gold was not recovered with only a general claim. Accordingly, the Allies worked out an arrangement comparable to general average in marine insurance, the so-called gold pot, into which all recovered gold would be put and against which all claimants of gold stolen by the Germans would have a proportionate claim. It is ironic that Reichsbank records were so complete that all gold looted by Germany could be identified as to its disposition and recovered, so that claims against the gold pot were paid in full.

A special dispensation was later worked out to deal with gold recovered from concentration camps: the principle that property of the dead should revert to the state was set aside because of the higher principle that a criminal cannot expect to benefit from his crime. This gold, taken from victims in the camps, was turned over to the Intergovernmental Committee on Refugees to rehabilitate and settle nonrepatriable victims of German aggression (Department of State, 1950, pp. 429–30).

The Soviet Union had a powerful case in equity that restitution, as a principle, favored those countries that failed to put up effective resistance to German attack, the property of which was therefore available for capture or purchase, intact, and penalized the Soviet Union, which had resisted the Wehrmacht with scorched earth and was therefore entitled only to reparations. Identifiable property was restored 100 percent; a claim for reparations would entitle a country only to a small percentage of the loss suffered.

Given stalemate in the Reparations Commission, questions of war booty, restitution, and reparations were turned over to the meeting of the heads of state at Potsdam, from 17 July to 2 August 1945. There it was decided, reluctantly by the British and American governments, that a zonal reparations agreement was inescapable. The Western Powers insisted on, and the Soviet Union conceded, the principle of treating Germany as a single economic unit, despite its division into four zones of occupation, and also on the so-called first-charge principle that the first charge on the proceeds of exports out of any zone of Germany would be the cost of imports into any zone of Germany. The point was to prevent the Soviet Union from taking food and raw materials out of current production in the Eastern zone of occupation without payment, while the United States and Britain had to feed and stock the Western part of the country. Reparations would then come out of capital equipment not needed by a peaceable German economy. Quadripartite experts would calculate the level of industry that would give the Germans a standard of living no higher than the average of the bordering countries—an appalling assignment for economists—and capital equipment in excess of this amount was then to be made available for removal as reparations. Since the Soviet zone was relatively agricultural and less industrialized than the Ruhr, especially, it was agreed that in addition to the removals from its own zone under the Level-of-Industry Agreement, it would be entitled to 25 percent of the equipment removed from the Western zones, although for three-fifths of this it undertook to make reciprocal deliveries of foodstuffs and raw materials. The Soviet Union undertook to take care of Poland's entitlement to reparations out of its share. Remaining Western removals were to be divided among Allied countries, other than the Soviet Union and Poland, at an Inter-Allied Reparations Agency established in Brussels.

In addition, German foreign assets in Allied countries were confiscated by them under a so-called Safe-Haven Program, designed to root out German commercial interests abroad, some of which were held to have engaged in espionage. German assets in Austria were divided between the Soviet Union and the West, again on a zonal basis. The Western Powers were entitled to any claim they were able to collect on German property in neutral countries; agreements with Sweden and Switzerland dealt with claims for the restitution of gold for the gold pot and with distributing the proceeds of German assets liquidated in these countries. The settlement with Switzerland on German assets provided that the proceeds should go half to the Swiss government to meet its claims against Germany and half to the Allies to be used for the rehabilitation of countries devastated or depleted by war (ibid., p. 408n). In all cases, German owners of property abroad received in its place a claim against the German government or against the Fund for the Equalization of War Losses.

The program of capital equipment removals did not last long. Having found that second-hand capital equipment that had stood in the open for months was not very useful, the Soviet Union switched to reparations from current production from its zone of occupation, withheld reciprocal deliveries, but continued to press for capital removals from the West. In May 1946 Lucius Clay, commander of the U.S. Occupation Forces, halted reparation deliveries to the Russians because agreement on the level of industry "became meaningless" as a result of its "exploitation of Eastern Germany" (1950, p. 320).

The U.S. effort to prevent its paying German reparations failed for the second time. After World War I, American private investors lent German firms, states, and local governments, plus the central government in the American *tranches* of the Dawes and Young loans, the money that was used to pay reparations to France,

Britain, Belgium, and others. After World War II, the same process was repeated in real rather than financial terms. The U.S. military provided foodstuffs to the American zone of occupation and most of the British zone after the Bizonal Agreement of December 1946, under an appropriation for Government and Relief in Occupied Areas (GARIOA). Across the country in the East, the Soviet Union took food and raw materials out as reparations.

SUGGESTED SUPPLEMENTARY READING

Department of State (1950), *Germany, 1947–1949.*
Dupriez (1947), *Monetary Reconstruction in Belgium.*
Gillingham (1977), *Belgian Business in the Nazi New Order.*
Milward (1971), *The New Order and the French Economy.*
Milward (1977), *War, Economy and Society, 1939–1945.*
Richter (ed.) (1979), Currency and economic reform.
Southard (1946) [1978]), *The Finances of European Liberation.*

In German

Deutsche Bundesbank (ed.) (1976), *Währung und Wirtschaft in Deutschland, 1876–1975.*
Emminger (1986), *D-mark, Dollar, Währungskrisen.*

23

Lend-Lease, the British Loan, the Marshall Plan

> The task of statesmanship is to build a new international order on the basis of freedom for individual countries to regulate their external economies effectively. The old international order was based on *laisser-faire* and has broken down for good. Nothing but failure, futility and frustration can come from the attempt to set it up again.
>
> (Henderson, *The Inter-War Years and Other Papers,* 1943 [1955], p. 293)

> If an international system is to be restored it must be an American-dominated system, based on *Pax Americana.*
>
> (Condliffe, *The Reconstruction of World Trade,* 1940, p. 394)

LEND-LEASE

Reparations, which had been such a difficult problem after World War I, were virtually eliminated after World War II by the program of capital equipment removals, which went a certain distance before it got caught up in the cold war and was quietly swept under the rug. War debts had been forestalled earlier by the Lend-Lease Agreements of March 1941.

The principle of lend-lease was simple enough: the United States would provide its allies with goods and services, mostly military equipment, and agreed to settle accounts after the war on some generous basis. In return, recipients of aid under Article 7 of the Lend-Lease Agreements agreed to participate with the United States in constructing a multilateral world trading system after the war, different from the bilateralism that prevailed during the 1930s. A set of broad principles along these lines had already been accepted by President Roosevelt and Prime Minister Winston Churchill in the Atlantic Charter, signed on a battleship in Placentia Bay in Newfoundland in August 1941.

The Atlantic Charter and Article 7 evoke memories of 1802, when, after the Treaty of Amiens, the British sought to conclude a treaty on commercial questions with the French, only to have the first consul, later the emperor, Napoleon I, say, "Not so fast. I will not sacrifice French industry. I remember the distress of 1786" (the year of the Anglo-French Eden commercial agreement) (Thiers, 1894, Vol. 2, pp. 105–6). It also evokes memories of British efforts later, when the Napoleonic Wars had been resumed, to obtain agreement from recipients of British subsidies— Austria, Prussia, Russia, and Spain—to change their commercial, military, and diplomatic policies and for Portugal and Spain to end the slave trade. The initiative failed: Prussia made a few concessions, and Portugal agreed to end the slave trade north of the equator in return for another subsidy of £300,000 (Sherwig, 1969, pp. 311, 313). Brougham asked Parliament: "After a war of unexampled suffering, how come the glorious peace it purchases comes without restoring our foreign markets and France, Prussia and Russia keep out our products?" In 1835 a member of Parliament, Cogden, echoed the complaint: "We should have insisted on free trade as an indemnity for winning the war" (Acworth, 1925, pp. 121–22).

While simple in principle, the Lend-Lease Agreement with Britain had a number of sticky aspects. In the first place, the U.S. Treasury Department thought that the American public would be upset by generous provision of aid without some sort of means test or gesture appropriate to a pauper, and, led by Secretary Henry Morgenthau and Assistant Secretary Harry D. White, insisted that Britain should sell one of its prime investments in the United States. Lever Brothers was spared because of its partial Dutch ownership. Brown, Williamson, in tobacco, escaped by borrowing a substantial sum from the Reconstruction Finance Corporation in Washington to be paid off out of future profits, and sold the dollars to the British government. Finally, both sets of authorities fixed on the American Viscose Company, a subsidiary of the British company Courtaulds, engaged in the manufacture of rayon, and despite the mother company's vigorous protests and after considerable delay, it was finally put on the block in March 1941 after the Lend-Lease Act had been passed. The experience was illuminating to economists who are wont to theorize about the value of capital assets. Generally regarded as worth £32 million, it was sold in the New York market in a new issue, sponsored by Morgan Stanley and Dillon Read, for a net of $54.4 million, or £13.6 million. Commissions on the promotion were high and gave rise to grumbling in Britain about an American "bankers' ramp." Courtaulds demanded compensation from the British government of £44.1 million, including $50 million for goodwill. It was offered £16.7 million. Arbitration between these extremes produced an award of £27.15 million plus interest. The historian of Courtaulds comments wryly that it cost the British taxpayer £13.6 million to satisfy Secretary Morgenthau (Coleman, 1969*a*, Vol. 2, ch. 15, quotation from p. 487).

A series of problems turned on British needs. One aspect was that British aid requirements under lend-lease differed depending upon whether Britain continued to service its customary export markets, which were still available. It wanted to do so to maintain market position and be ready with a running start in export competition after the war. On the other hand, the resources that might go to this effort might better be devoted to military ends, leaving those export markets unserved by their customary British suppliers perhaps inclined to switch to American sources. The problem is conceptually soluble if one knows the length of the war; the substitutability in production of export goods for military supplies, and vice versa; costs of diversion, first, to war materiel and then back again; inertia in export markets, which makes a buyer, once having shifted, reluctant to shift back again; plus some appropriate shadow rate of interest. In practice, the issue was one of constant haggling, inching, and irritation on both sides.

Apart from military questions, the prospective balance-of-payments problem was the British government's main obsession during the war (Dobson, 1986, p. 59), and the Economic Section under the war cabinet started to plan for this "fundamental problem" as early as February 1941 (Cairncross and Watts, 1989, ch. 7).

Another problem was shipping space, which in many respects was a tighter bottleneck than finance. Should it be used for extra food to build stocks in Britain in order to make sure that no sudden burst of German success in submarine warfare would critically depress the British standard of living, or was it well to take some risk in this regard for the sake of delivering to British beachheads and docksides higher stocks of tanks, guns, landing craft, and fuel? Since the risks were being taken by the British, it is easy to understand that they might have had a somewhat different outlook on the trade-off between food and guns as candidates for ship tonnage than the American government.

Basic misunderstanding about lend-lease, however, came over its ending. Roosevelt died in the spring of 1945, to be succeeded as president by Harry S. Truman, a former senator, who appointed another senator, James F. Byrnes, as secretary of state. The story in the Department of State, at the time, was that Truman and Byrnes decided to cancel lend-lease on their way to the Potsdam Conference in July 1945, to make good on a Roosevelt commitment to the Senate, and vehemently refused to reconsider when the economic side of the department pointed out the mess that would be involved. In his *Memoirs* President Truman gives a rather different story, saying that Acting Secretary of State Joseph Grew and Leo Crowley, the foreign economic administrator, presented him with a memorandum on 8 May, VE day, and that he signed it without giving it too much thought—a mistake, as he confessed. Crowley then proceeded to unload Russian ships still in American ports to remove lend-lease material from them. Stalin thought that the action was anti-Soviet. The British complained bitterly but had to comply (Truman, 1955, Vol. 1, p. 227).

In an authoritative economic history of the war, a rather muddled passage on the lend-lease settlement with Britain leaves the inference that the United States was rather less than generous, and far less generous to Britain than was Canada, which canceled all British obligations to Canada under its Mutual Aid Agreement (Milward, 1977, pp. 351–52). That may be so, or at least it is a British view. An American expression of opinion puts it that the generosity of the settlement "surpassed expectations" (Gardner, 1980, p. 208). Reverse lend-lease brought the $30 billion of American aid to the United Kingdom down by about $4 billion. Some $6 billion of surplus property in Britain, and lend-lease goods not yet transferred, were sold at 9 or 10 cents on the dollar for $532 million. A full charge was made for prime peacetime goods in the pipeline that Britain chose not to cancel, for $118 million. This and the $532 million, or a total of $650 million, was financed by a 2 percent fifty-year credit. The remaining $20 billion was canceled. The 2 percent fifty-year credit bore the same terms as the British loan of 1946, to be discussed below, and was less onerous than the 2⅜ percent twenty-eight-year credits charged to other countries in lend-lease settlements. The British credit contained further, what the others did not, provision for waiver of interest in the event of balance-of-payment difficulties (as did the British loan and as other settlements did not). The contrast is with 1923 when the war debt settlement with the British was at nearly commercial terms and other debtors were given concessions.

The British bargained hard in the lend-lease settlement, wanting to bring into the bargain retroactively the $6 billion the country had spent on armaments in the United States before the lend-lease legislation had been enacted. "This was of course politically impossible for the United States government" (ibid., p. 175). A subsequent observer saw no reason why the United States should provide tanks on lend-lease for British crews, rather than Britain providing crews on reverse lend-lease for U.S. tanks, evoking the thought of early silent partnerships (see p. 190), which sometimes involved management hiring capital and sometimes capital hiring management (Milward, 1977, p. 351). Since the obligation by Britain to the United States under wartime transfers had been written off, the point is academic.

A side issue of some analytical interest was that Canada was anxious not to accept lend-lease from its giant neighbor and yet needed balance-of-payments help in meeting its enormous program of aid to Britain. The solution was reached in a meeting between Mackenzie King, Canadian prime minister, and President Roosevelt, in Hyde Park, New York, in December 1941, that components and materials from the United States needed by Canada for incorporation in war production for British account would be paid for by United States lend-lease to Britain but shipped from the United States to Canadian plants (Department of State *Bulletin,* 1941, pp. 494–95). This could be regarded as real intermediation by Canada between the United States and Britain, or as Canada recycling a debt to the United States to a British debtor.

The end of war in Europe left more to be settled than lend-lease. Military relief had been provided by the United States to friendly countries in the zone of combat, and after VE day in May 1945, occupied countries had received minimal aid under an appropriation for Government and Relief in Occupied Areas (GARIOA), administered by the military. After the war, the U.S. military took the position that they were not in the business of furnishing aid to Allies, despite their clear role in the occupation, and suddenly sent out bills to friendly governments that had received military relief. This transferred the question to diplomatic channels to be settled with lend-lease or, in the case of such countries as Austria, Italy, and Germany with which the Allies had been at war, in peace treaties. Settlements with Austria and Italy (which had been regarded as the enemy, had switched sides or been liberated, and had received some military relief before being transferred to UNRRA) were inevitably complex.

THE OVERALL POSTWAR PLAN

Postwar economic planning was conducted initially by national governments and on an international basis between the American embassy in London and British governmental departments (Penrose, 1953). Two of the major international institutions, the World Bank and the International Monetary Fund (IMF), emerged from a broad international conference held in Bretton Woods in July 1944, which considered a joint Anglo-American draft based on earlier American (the White Plan) and British (the Keynes Plan) proposals. The intellectual history of these ideas, as noted in Chapter 21 (pp. 375–77), went back to the 1930s.

The overall notion adopted by the United Nations, largely at American urging, was to proceed from relief (food, clothing, and emergency shelter), to rehabilitation (particularly reconstituting stocks of primary products), to reconstruction. When this stage had been reached, the world economy posed a number of tasks: to elaborate a code for trade, to provide for the financing of trade imbalances, and to restore the movement of capital from developed countries to the poorer countries of the world to assist their development.

Relief and rehabilitation were the tasks of the United Nations Relief and Rehabilitation Administration (UNRRA); reconstruction was the assignment of the World Bank, formally known as the International Bank for Reconstruction and Development (IBRD), which thereafter was to turn to long-term loans to developing countries. The code for world trade was the product of meetings at Geneva, London, and, ultimately, Havana in 1948, which produced the draft charter of the International Trade Organization; this proved stillborn and was replaced by a less formal General Agreement on Tariffs and Trade (GATT). Current account imbalances in payments between countries—it was assumed that capital movements would be controlled if they proved disturbing—were to be financed by the IMF, which also had the task of setting and managing the structure of world exchange rates.

UNITED NATIONS RELIEF AND REHABILITATION ADMINISTRATION (UNRRA)

UNRRA's start as an operating agency was achieved by equipping it with surplus stocks of military and civilian supplies already in existence. The first contribution or *tranche* consisted of goods with a value of $2.6 billion, of which the United States furnished 72 percent, Britain 12 percent, Canada 6 percent, the Soviet Union 2 percent, and the remainder scattered. When the time came in August 1945 to vote in London a second *tranche* for UNRRA, another $2.6 billion, certain difficulties arose. Canada withdrew, saying that it would rather provide aid to Britain, which as a benefactor of UNRRA could not be a beneficiary. The United States added the Canadian 6 percent to its own share. The Soviet Union, which was likewise a benefactor and not a beneficiary, although on account of its devastation not a prominent aid giver, stated that it was not prepared to support a second *tranche* for UNRRA unless Belorussia and the Ukraine, regarded as separate countries for United Nations purposes, received UNRRA assistance. Finally Britain, as a condition of its favorable vote, insisted that Austria and Italy be shifted from military aid, where it paid half, to UNRRA where its contribution would be 12 percent. With only one vote in seventeen on the UNRRA Council, the United States was forced to accede to these conditions to keep UNRRA operational. The experience helped to shape new rules under the Marshall Plan two to three years later, under which the United States made one agreement with Europe as a whole and a separate agreement with each country receiving American aid.

While IBRD and IMF articles of agreement had been signed in 1944, the institutions could not begin operation until these documents had been ratified by a sufficient number of countries, and this took time. In the meantime, reconstruction could not wait. As one expedient, the United States enlarged the capital of the Export-Import Bank from $0.7 billion to $3.5 billion, of which $1 billion of the increase was known to be set aside as a loan for the Soviet Union. The Export-Import Bank had been created in 1934 primarily as an aid for exports during the depression, particularly to provide intermediate-term financing for heavy and long-lived equipment, which did not fit ordinary three-month financing, and in the absence of an effective international long-term capital market. The $2.8 billion increase in capital was quickly used up in loans to Europe, especially in connection with lend-lease settlements. The earmarked $1 billion for the Soviet Union was released to general purposes as the cold war took over. Leo Crowley, director of the Export-Import Bank, claimed that the Soviet loan application had been lost.

When the United States refused to participate in a third *tranche* of UNRRA, on the ground that it contributed the bulk of the aid but had only a minuscule voice in its use under circumstances where no widely agreed principles of allocation could be invoked, that country voted a special $350 million in post-UNRRA relief. Although Poland and Yugoslavia lie outside the geographical scope of this work, politics appeared to enter into post-UNRRA relief when U.S. Department of Agriculture experts decided that these countries no longer needed relief and rehabilitation, when to most observers the reason for halting assistance to them was not so much a change in economic conditions as the rapidly intensifying cold war.

The IBRD and IMF finally opened for business in the spring of 1946. This was a time when a number of European countries were running out of dollars needed to pay for vital supplies of foodstuffs and raw materials. Emergency loans from the Bank and drawings on IMF quotas were made by France, the Netherlands, and Britain, even though there were no reconstruction plans for the bank to approve or short-term balance-of-payments deficits needing temporary IMF financing. As throughout financial history, in emergency rules must be bent.

BRITISH LOAN

In testimony before Congress on the Bretton Woods legislation, John H. Williams, who divided his time between the Harvard University Department of Economics and the Federal Reserve Bank of New York where he was vice-president in charge of research, opposed the fund on the ground that it sought to restore the payments position of the world as a whole, whereas in his opinion it was desirable to proceed to revive key currencies, one at a time (1947 [1978]). The analytical basis of his view rested on the proposition that currencies were arranged in hierarchical structures, not on the basis of equality all at the same level, and that it was necessary to repair those at the apex of the structure before tackling others lower down that depended on the key currencies. The idea went back in Williams's thought to the Preparatory Commission for the World Economic Conference of 1933 and to Benjamin Strong's views in the 1920s, as recounted by Clarke (1973, p. 15), also called a "country-by-country approach," based on the view that different countries had accomplished varying amounts of progress on the way to stabilization (Chandler, 1958 [1978], p. 278), although keyness and different rates of progress are not identical.

There could be no doubt that after the dollar, the pound sterling was of critical importance in terms of keyness. It was the pivot of the sterling area and, in the not-too-distant past, had been the unit of account and medium of exchange for a large portion of world trade and the world's largest money and capital market. But while Williams viewed a large loan for the pound as an alternative to the IMF, Keynes—who had negotiated the Bretton Woods Agreement for the British and helped, from his seat in the House of Lords, to steer the legislation through Parliament—wanted both. In September 1945, with Lord Halifax, the British ambassador to the United States, he undertook to negotiate a loan with Secretary of the Treasury Fred Vinson, who had replaced Morgenthau when Truman became president, and with William L. Clayton, the under secretary of state for economic affairs. After laborious negotiation, a loan of $3,750 million was agreed in December 1945, ratified by Congress at the conclusion of an intense debate, and signed into law on 15 July 1946. The agreement provided that the British would render the pound convertible within a year, negotiate with holders of sterling balances to get them to write down claims on Britain, and end discrimination against American exports by the end of 1956. Passage of legislation in the Congress was assisted by the deepening of the cold war and the impression in Washington that a vote for the Anglo-American Financial Agreement, as the loan instrument was called, was a vote against the Soviet Union.

The British adopted currency convertibility, as required by the agreement, on 16 July 1947 but were able to sustain it for only seven weeks. A number of things account for the failure: the disastrous winter of 1946–47, described in chapter 24 (see p. 404); the size of the loan; British failure to achieve a solution of sterling balances; and technical mistakes in handling British foreign exchange control. Most of all, the timing was unrealistic. A British memorandum of June 1947 blamed the financial position on world dollar shortage that increased the drain on British official dollar holdings, estimated at the time of the loan to have reached $100 million a month in 1947 and over $300 million a month in April and May of 1947. Europe, Asia, and Latin America were all holding on tightly to such dollars as they possessed or could earn and were not using them to buy British goods. Moreover, Britain had to lay out dollars for such purposes as helping India to buy grain. The memorandum stated that no manipulation could solve the problem for Britain; what was needed was world recovery to bring the supply structure back into balance again (Department of State, *FRUS, 1947,* 1972, pp. 17–24).

The sum of $3¾ billion may or may not have been too small in December 1945. It clearly became so in July 1946 when the United States lifted price controls, and American wholesale prices rose from 111 in May 1946 to 141 in December (1935–39 = 100). Gardner's book on sterling-dollar negotiations contains a facsimile of a page of notes used by Clayton in discussion with Vinson to determine the amount of the loan, which is fascinating in the picture it presents of bargaining on the American side (1980, p. 200). There are a number of estimates of British balance-of-payments figures, past and prospective, a typed list of forecast deficits for five successive years that appear to have summed to $6 million, but three of the figures and the total are written over in ink to make them add up to $5 billion, and the original typescript is not completely legible. On the left is a notation "Keynes 5," and underneath it "4.3," which seems to have been Clayton's proposal. On the bottom, under some geometric doodles, is "3 billions" which was presumably Vinson's opening bid, and then "4,500" and several "4s" here and there, along with a "3.8," that appears to have been the compromise reached, rounded down to $3,750 million. Keynes and Clayton may have been right on the amount of the loan necessary in economic terms; Vinson was surely correct politically, as a crippling amendment in the Senate was defeated only 45–40, so that a switch of three votes would have beaten the administration proposal.

Sterling balances had been built up rapidly by heavy British spending in India and the Middle East during the war. For the British to pay in sterling for Indian troops outside their country was understandable, but for Britain to pay in sterling for local expenditure in India, which had little foreign exchange content, added enormously to Indian claims. The Indian government insisted that the sterling be used as far as possible to buy out British investments in India. Despite an effort along these lines, Indian holdings rose from £259 million in the middle of 1942 to £1,321 million at the end of 1945 (Milward, 1977, p. 349). Egypt and the Sudan, comprising the rear British area of much of the fighting in North Africa between Montgomery and Rommel, together accumulated a claim of more than £500 million; smaller but significant amounts were piled up by Iraq, Portugal, Argentina, and so on. In total, sterling balances in the hands of former colonies and less developed countries amounted to more than £3 billion. Independent dominions had similar claims on Britain, but these they wrote off in sizable amounts as aid to the mother country. Article 10 of the Anglo-American Financial Agreement recorded the intention of Britain to negotiate agreements with major holders of sterling to write off some, block others, rendering some released at once, others more slowly (for text, see Gardner, 1980, pp. 387–92).

As it transpired, the British government failed to take effective action on sterling debt. It was widely thought at the time that the country was reluctant to lose face in asking forgiveness for its debts from countries it had once governed as head of the British Empire or had held in tutelage. Two somewhat different views have been put forward. A knowledgeable journalist states that the British rejected the "American proposal"—although as part of an agreement it was more than that—for fear of a world slump and the wish to have purchasing power available to sustain British employment, if only in the hands of India, Egypt, and others (Fry, introduction to Bolton, 1970, p. 15). If so, the thought proved less than astute. "Unrequited exports," as the expression went, that is, exports that produced neither foreign exchange nor any imports though they reduced outstanding debt, proved to be a serious drain on British real resources for years after the war.

The other view blames the Bank of England for reversing the procedure implicit in the agreement that called, first, for blocking of sterling and, second, for convertibility, and undertaking convertibility first with only a hope, never realized, of blocking the sterling balances (Pressnell in Thirlwall, ed., 1976, p. 95). Keynes's death in 1946 removed the man who negotiated the agreement and might have been a strong protagonist for the original program. A left-wing position objected to the proposed convertibility, favored retention of trade controls, and was disposed not to block the sterling of the poor countries of the sterling area on grounds of equity (Balogh in ibid., p. 96).

At the technical level, there is little direct evidence. Contemporary newspaper discussion and an oral tradition held that Bank of England exchange control for capital movements had large gaps through which such countries as Belgium and Argentina were able to get large amounts of dollars against sterling well before convertibility was introduced in July 1947. Argentine balances were drawn down, in part, by Britain's selling its holdings of Argentine railroads to the government of that country. One particular loophole was said to have been trade in "kaffirs" (South African gold-mining shares), and especially security arbitrage between the kaffir markets of London and Johannesburg. If movement of capital from Britain to the Union of South Africa was forbidden, without censorship of mail to prevent mailing of securities between two countries it would be vital to cut off arbitrage in the kaffir market. Without arbitrage, the purchase of kaffirs in London and their sale in Johannesburg would raise prices in the former and lower them in the latter, until the loss from exporting capital would be sufficient to attract an offsetting import of capital by those who bought cheap in South Africa and sold dear in Britain so that no net capital movement would take place. If arbitrage was allowed to keep prices of securities in line with the exchange rate, buying in South Africa, selling in London, and remitting the proceeds of the latter sale back to South Africa through a permitted arbitrage account, the last stage in the process would constitute the capital outflow. Since South Africa was not a part of the sterling area and its currency could be sold for dollars, evasion of British foreign exchange control via Johannesburg was possible so long as security arbitrage was authorized.

THE TRUMAN DOCTRINE

Well before Britain was committed by terms of the loan agreement to adopt sterling convertibility, it could see that the position was dangerous. The memorandum of June 1947 given to the American government has been mentioned. Still earlier, the British government cast about for ways to save dollars and thought it necessary to retrench on its military and diplomatic commitments. On Friday, 21 February 1947, the British first secretary in Washington informed the Department of State that his country was no longer in a position to furnish Greece with the military assistance that country needed to resist Communist aggression, while economic aid to be provided by the United Nations to the amount of £20 million was clearly inadequate to enable Greece to achieve internal stability. The British government, he said, would be unable to furnish Greece assistance after 31 March 1947. If Greece and Turkey, which was also threatened, were to be able to hold out against internal and external Communist attacks, it was necessary for the United States to pick up the burden of assistance Britain was forced to lay down. This was the start of the "fifteen weeks" from 21 February to 5 June 1947, in which the United States moved strongly to assume responsibility for countering the deterioration of European capacity and will to resist Soviet overt and covert aggression (J. M. Jones, 1955).

The Council of Foreign Ministers (CFM) of France, the Soviet Union, the United Kingdom, and the United States met in Moscow from 10 March to 24 April. It failed to achieve agreement on any issue. In a speech before a joint session of Congress on 12 March, President Truman asserted what came to be known as the Truman doctrine—the determination of the United States to render all necessary aid to Greece and Turkey. The Senate passed the administration's bill on 22 April and the House of Representatives on 15 May; the president signed it into law on 22 May. Under Secretary Clayton was in Europe from 8 April to 19 May, negotiating the draft of the international trade organization and helping the United Nations Economic Commission for Europe get under way. Late spring was the low period of a disastrous year for European agricultural output, as the last of the old crop was rapidly being consumed, and the new crop looked unpromising. Mr. Clayton was deeply impressed by what he deemed to be the breakdown of economic connections between the city and the countryside. Secretary of State George C. Marshall returned from the frustration of the CFM meeting in Moscow, arriving in Washington on 28 April, consulted with Clayton and with Under Secretary Dean Acheson, determined that a new start should be made in promoting economic recovery in Europe, and directed the Policy Planning Staff of the department, under George Kennan's chairmanship, to work out a plan.

THE MARSHALL PLAN

The result was the speech of 5 June 1947 at the Harvard commencement, indicating to Europe that if it were to produce a coordinated and cooperative plan for economic recovery that required financial assistance, the United States would consider favorably attempting to provide the assistance. In due course, Foreign Minister Ernest Bevin of Britain met in Paris with his counterparts, Georges Bidault of France and V. M. Molotov of the Soviet Union. The Soviet representative stated categorically that European response to the American initiative should be to form a list of separate national demands for assistance and present them to the United States, rather than to prepare a plan for cooperating in achieving recovery. When this was rejected by Bevin and Bidault, Molotov withdrew from the exercise and withdrew the participation of the countries of Eastern Europe, especially Poland and Czechoslovakia, which had initially responded positively. The exit of the Soviet Union was viewed with considerable relief by both Western Europeans and the United States due to the difficulty of working cooperatively with that country.

The withdrawal of the Eastern bloc meant that the program of recovery could not be drawn up by the newly organized Economic Commission for Europe in which the Eastern countries were active members. Accordingly, a new group—the Committee for European Economic Cooperation (CEEC)—was formed and spent the summer preparing a program and a schedule of needed financial assistance for submission to the United States. The original draft produced a program of assistance for four years amounting to $30 billion—somewhat along the lines that had been advocated by Molotov. When Clayton and Lewis Douglas, the American ambassador to Britain, suggested that this was more than could reasonably be considered, the amount was cut to $16 billion. In the fall and early spring the U.S. government produced a legislative submission to Congress, outlining a program of aid for seventeen European countries, including Greece and Turkey, with balance-of-payments estimates covering four and a quarter years from 1 April 1948, including forecasts in real terms of exports and imports of these seventeen countries in twenty-six specified commodities. The amount of aid deemed desirable for the first fifteen months, the last quarter of the 1947–48 fiscal year, and the entire year to 30 June 1949, was $5.2 billion. While the legislation was going through the time-consuming congressional processes, a special program of "interim aid" was quickly passed in the amount of $597 million.

The Marshall Plan served as a compromise between the overall recovery program implicit in the Bretton Woods institutions—the World Bank and the IMF—and the key-currency approach of the British loan. Europe was a key region. Later, special help came for the rest of the world in the Point-Four program of aid for economic development set out in President Truman's Inaugural Address of January 1948. There was a suggestion of a key country or key currency within the key region: when Clayton and Douglas visited the British government at the end of June 1947, Mr. Bevin urged that the United States establish a financial partnership with the United Kingdom and that the two countries together provide a European recovery plan (Department of State, *FRUS, 1947,* 1972, pp. 269–70). Mr. Clayton's reaction was that the needs of Britain should be fitted into those of Europe as a whole.

One special consideration of the British problem, however, was that the United States took over the major share of external finance of the bizonal administration of Germany. This had been formed in December 1946 by merging the British and American zones of occupation, with the total cost split 50–50. Already that agreement had eased the burden on Britain because the British zone of occupation in the Ruhr had a far larger import bill than the more southerly and less populated American zone. The new arrangement provided that Britain would finance the limited volume of imports that were obtainable in sterling but that the United States, from 1 November 1947, would pay the rest (Department of State, 1950, p. 453).

MARSHALL PLAN ISSUES

Planning Versus Markets

Some confusion prevailed in the early stages of developing the European Recovery Program, as the Marshall Plan was officially known, as to how far European economic institutions were expected to develop along planning lines and how much the program of cooperation consisted of a restoration of the free working of markets and ordinary macroeconomic stability. France had established the first of a number of four-year plans in 1946 in the so-called Monnet Plan. Messrs. Clayton and Douglas, who provided guidance for the CEEC in drawing up the program, laid heavy emphasis on the decontrols, nondiscrimination, and the restoration of efficient operations of free markets helped by macroeconomic stability and buttressed by commodity aid, rather than planning in the "indicative" French sense of pointing out where the economy was likely to go, or in the Soviet "imperative" sense of detailing what should be produced and in what amount. In one field, there was a semblance of planning in which governments and private companies worked closely together—in the petroleum industry and particularly, on the scale and siting of new oil pipelines and refineries—although even here the Italian nationally owned petroleum company, Ente Nazionale Idrocarburi (ENI), went its own way. In other industries—despite a considerable amount of industry (and, in France, banking) that had been nationalized immediately after the war for one reason or another, despite socialist governments in a number of countries, and despite the open espousal of planning in France—emphasis was on reducing obstacles to international trade and making markets for goods and services work. At this early stage, virtually no attention was paid by the CEEC or U.S. missions to the functioning of markets for labor or capital.

Amount of Aid

Initial calculations of the amount of aid necessary for European reconstruction were based on estimates of balance-of-payments deficits anticipated in the several years after 1947 and the available means of financing them. Somewhat later it was pointed out by Fritz Machlup that the reasoning was, to a degree, circular. If aid or expendable reserves were not available, there could be no deficit; aid determined the deficit—the amount by which European spending exceeded what Europe produced—rather than the other way around (1950 [1964]). This reasoning hardly applied to 1946 and 1947, however, when a measure of the deficit implicit in a program of economic recovery was revealed by the extent to which European countries were willing to run down their reserves, or borrow on market terms, to get the resources they felt they needed.

Aid required by the state of the balance of payments raised a question that became salient later in connection with the development of younger countries: the difference between the savings gap and the foreign exchange gap as potential or actual bottlenecks in recovery or growth. When a country has a capacity to reallocate resources among industries, and the prospective deficit in the balance of payments can be reduced by saving more, thus spending less directly on imports and releasing domestic resources that can be transferred into additional exports, any balance-of-payments deficit is the result of a savings gap and can be eliminated by reducing spending and increasing saving. The lower real income is in relation to some historic level, making it difficult to compress expenditure on domestic product and imports, however, the more the gap is in foreign exchange, and not merely in savings.

The issue was raised in both Europe and the United States, especially by economists who felt that "dollar shortage" was, in the words of Sir Roy Harrod, "one of the most absurd phrases ever coined," and "one of the most brazen pieces of collective effrontery that has ever been uttered" (1947, pp. 42–43). British observers, believing in the existence of a dollar shortage, blamed it on a tendency of the United States to fall into depression. American detractors of the idea of a dollar shortage, such as Gottfried Haberler, Friederich Lutz, and Henry Hazlitt, found the difficulty in excess consumption and investment in Europe. They thought that it could be eliminated by "balancing the budget and depreciating the exchange rate to the purchasing-power parity," as isolationist Senator Joseph Ball of Minnesota recommended during the course of the debate on the European Recovery Program in

Congress, or, more generally, "stop the inflation and adjust the exchange rate" (Haberler, 1948, p. 444). The greater generality of "stop the inflation" lies, of course, in the fact that today there would be less emphasis on fiscal policy (balance the budget) and more on monetary policy (fix the money supply). The debate resembles that between the banking and currency schools in Britain at the end of the Napoleonic Wars (see pp. 64–65). Believers in dollar shortage followed the banking school in insisting that the balance-of-payments deficit had structural origins, while the opposition took the view that the balance of payments was fairly malleable and could be corrected by some appropriate combination of restrictive internal macroeconomic policy and finding the right exchange rate.

Allocation of Aid

The balance-of-payments deficit of a country depends, at least to some degree, on internal policies. To the extent that these are adjustable by authorities, the deficit forecast for a given country is not immutably fixed by economic variables, unless these are rigidly constrained by political and social factors. In this circumstance, allocation of a given amount of aid by the United States could be divided among a number of countries in Europe in a virtually unlimited number of ways. The problem, once the United States had hinted to the CEEC as to how much would be a good amount to ask for, was how it should be divided.

There is no unique criterion. One basis might be to bring each country back to its historical level of living by an equal percentage. Or one could allocate more to the slowest-recovering countries until all end up, after diminishing returns have worked their will, recovering at the same equal rate. Or one could choose an equitable standard and give more aid to the poorest countries, less to the richest, and try to bring them all to the same level of living. In the absence of any single agreed criterion, the economic historian is tempted to say that the allocation was the outcome of a political process, based on power and prestige, but this explains very little. In actuality, the allocation seems to have been based on some shifting amalgam of the historic, the desirable, and the feasible. The historic relates to past levels of living; the desirable to the need for countries that had lagged behind to get more assistance; and the feasible to the capacity to use assistance effectively in reconstruction. The initial allocation was probably dominated by the historic, and Britain got the lion's share of aid. There were a number of anomalies. Such a country as Turkey was insufficiently ambitious, it was said in the corridors, and was told to take back its initial calculations and raise them by some substantial power. It was also said that Sweden was embarrassed in finding itself—a neutral in the war and doing well—being regarded as entitled to American aid.

With the initial allocation somehow agreed, an acute dilemma arose for the following year. If foreign aid were designed to finance balance-of-payments deficits, the worse a country performed, the more aid it would be entitled to receive. Such a model has strongly perverse effects on incentives; effective policy would be penalized by taking away assistance, incompetence rewarded by giving it more. After debating the issue at length and muddling through in the second year, the Organization for European Economic Cooperation (OEEC), which operated the Marshall

Plan in Europe, chose to take the amount of aid made available by the United States in the third and fourth years and divide in the same proportions as in the second, thus ensuring that a country would benefit from an effective performance and suffer from a poor one.

Financing Overall Deficits or Deficits with the United States

A central aspect of European economic cooperation was to halt the process by which various countries in Europe discriminated against intra-European trade in order to earn dollars to use in payment for goods from the United States, especially goods in inelastic world supply such as bread-grains, coal, petroleum, farm machinery, and the like. Each country tried to sell in dollars in Europe and, to the extent that it could get dollars, push those exports but not pay for imports from Europe in dollars and, if required to, to buy as little as possible. Where balances in bilateral trade had to be cleared in dollars, the incentives were the same despite clearing. At one stage in the planning process in Washington, in forecasting European trade prospects, country committee experts added up lists of intra-European exports and imports and found that projected European exports to Europe exceeded projected European imports from Europe by more than a billion dollars—a statistical impossibility. It was also reported that in a Franco-Danish trade negotiation, the French export team reached a bargain with the Danish import group by which France sold Denmark a sizable number of vacuum cleaners, while the Danish export team achieved the same success in vacuum cleaners with the French import contingent— a result similar to a game of American football with the two-platoon system, both sides with strong offensive teams and weak defense, and consequent high scoring. The waste of real resources involved in discriminating against European countries was clearly illustrated in the case of bizonal imports from overseas into the Ruhr by way of Hamburg, a much more circuitous route than via Rotterdam but one that could be paid for in local currency, whereas the Dutch authorities demanded dollars for the transit from Rotterdam to the German border.

The problem can be illuminated with a simple example. Assume two recipients of aid, Britain and France, with a combined deficit with the United States of 300 units of some currency and an imbalance of 100 units between them.

Balance of Payments Surplus ($+$) or Deficit ($-$)

	With the United States	Within "Europe"	Total
Britain	-200	$+100$	-100
France	-100	-100	-200
Total	-300	$-0-$	-300

In early attempts to deal with this problem, the United States sought to make some aid available as "offshore purchases," in the example buying 100 units of a good in Britain with dollars and delivering it to France. It could then finance the British overall deficit of 100 and the French deficit with the United States of 100, for a total of 300 when the offshore purchase is added in. This technique was found to be awkward because of its ad hoc character and the difficulty of identifying goods of the kind and amount that would produce the sought-after result. It was particularly helpful in the Rotterdam-Ruhr transit question just mentioned and in Italy, which had useful fruit and vegetables for sale in Europe that other countries, such as Germany, wanted but were unwilling to spend scarce dollars for.

There followed the Intra-European Payments Scheme (IEPS), in which the United States sought to finance either the deficit with the United States or the overall imbalance, conditional upon the appropriate financing of intra-European trade. The cost is the same, as the example shows—300 units either way. Suppose the United States finances the deficit with the United States. It makes 100 available to France unconditionally and 200 available to Britain on the condition that it provide 100 to France without payment. This solution is upsetting to the French since they cannot be sure that the British, having all the dollars they need and lacking incentive, will in fact make the scarce goods needed by France available. The French would prefer a system under which the United States financed total deficits, with 100 unconditionally for Britain, and 200 units for France, conditional upon the French using 100 units of their U.S. aid to buy goods in Britain. The British with a deficit of 200 with the United States, only half certainly financed, find this disagreeable: what if the French should take the money and cut down on imports within Europe, spending these units on some old or newly discovered wants elsewhere?

The unsatisfactory character of the IEPS led, in June 1950, to the establishment of the European Payments Union (EPU), a device to make the proceeds of exports anywhere in Europe the equivalent of dollars so that there would be equal incentive to export inside as well as outside the Continent.

European trade after the war had taken place largely under bilateral trading arrangements. Attempt had been made to multilateralize these clearings. Two types of what were called "compensations" were recognized: first category and second category. Taking three countries as an example, let us suppose that the Netherlands has an export surplus of 10 with France, France a surplus of 15 with Belgium, and Belgium a surplus of 5 with the Netherlands. On this showing, a first-category compensation is possible of 5, reducing the unpaid bilateral surplus of the Netherlands with France to 5, that of France with Belgium to 10, and wiping out the Belgian gross surplus with the Netherlands altogether. Total bilateral balances after this operation have been reduced from 30 to 15. Second-category compensation would take place if France succeeded in persuading the Netherlands and Belgium to transfer 5 of the French claim on Belgium to the Netherlands against the Dutch surplus with France. This would reduce bilateral imbalances from 15 to 5. The Netherlands would agree to the canceling only if it believed that Belgium was as reliable a debtor and Belgium only if it believed that the Netherlands was no more exigent a creditor than France. The technical staff of the Bank for International Settlements in Basle worked through a fairly limited number of first-category compensations and proposed and gained acceptance for a much wider number, but not all of the second-category possibilities.

Like offshore purchases, the system of multilateralizing bilateral imbalances was contrived and artificial, as opposed to dealing automatically, and without self-con-

"Try to think of something that doesn't require dollars."

Cartoon by Starke (undated), from Martin Rosenberg and William Cole (eds), *The Best Cartoons from Punch* (New York: Simon & Schuster, 1982). Reproduced by permission of Punch.

sciousness, in international money. The EPU sought to achieve this more advanced state with the help of a one-time credit from the United States.

This ingenious scheme called for members of the EPU to trade with each other in multilateral clearing with the EPU as a group, not clearing with separate countries, and to have a single settlement for each country at the end of a month, partly in dollars and partly in credit according to a prearranged formula. Each country was given a negotiated quota, divided into five equal *tranches.* How much of a country's credit or debit balance with EPU would be settled in dollars or credit depended upon which *tranche* it was operating in, on a cumulative basis, and whether as creditor or debtor. The schedule was as shown in Table 23.1. The largest quota was that for Britain (which also included the sterling area), $1,060 million; next, at $520 million, was France. As inspection of the table will reveal, it could happen that the EPU be asked to pay out to creditors more dollars than it was receiving in dollars from debtors, if most of the participants were operating in the second or third *tranches.* More than five hundred million dollars of capital from the United States enabled the EPU to tide over such situations. On a couple of occasions in the history of the EPU, its capital was almost entirely paid out in this process, but the movement of a number of countries—debtors into the fifth *tranche,* or creditors back to the first—brought dollars flowing back to the fund and kept it afloat.

The EPU went into operation in June 1950. This was also the month of the outbreak of war in Korea that brought about a sudden sharp rise in commodity prices, especially Asian primary products such as tin, rubber, wool, silk, tea, and so on, from which it was feared that Europe and the United States might be cut off. It coincided with the relaxation of German credit restrictions, two years after monetary reform, that gave rise to heavy borrowing by German industry for rebuilding stocks of raw materials. Imports shot up. The country exhausted its quota in short order and was given an additional allotment, provided that the banking system reapplied credit restraint. Since the restocking was a once-and-for-all operation, this proved a success, and Germany quickly moved back up the debtor column and down the creditor to become a persistent creditor. Buying heavily of raw materials in the early stages of the Korean boom proved a wise investment, too. British markets seem to have thought that raw material prices were coming down quickly and

Table 23.1 European Payments Union Schedule of Settlement

Tranche of National Quota	Debtors Percentage Paid in		Creditors Percentage Received in	
	Dollars	Credit Received	Dollars	Credit Granted
1	10	90	0	100
2	30	70	50	50
3	40	60	50	50
4	50	50	50	50
5	70	30	50	50
Average	40	60	40	60
Beyond quota	100	0	100	0

held off even regular replacements. This improved the balance of payments in the short run. By the first quarter of 1951, however, they had reduced inventories to dangerously low levels and had to build them back up at peak prices.

Success of the EPU led many observers and some authors of the scheme to claim too much. The fact that the $500 million plus worked out to be the right amount was a compound of skill and serendipity in debatable proportions. Beyond that, the EPU had two fortuitous factors working for it. In principle, it was a mistake to balance trade inside Europe rather than the trade of each country with the world as a whole, reestablishing the prewar pattern in which some countries earned surpluses inside Europe that were needed to pay for deficits with overseas countries. In practice, the facts that the United States was financing deficits in dollars for persistent debtors and that Britain brought the sterling area into the scheme with it meant that the EPU was practically a world arrangement. Proposals for other regional clearing unions in Asia or Latin America were seen to lack these essential elements. In the second place, the EPU rested on the hypothesis that each country balanced its trade in the union over some considerable period of time and that, in the long run, there would be no persistent debtors that had exhausted their quotas and had to pay 100 percent of deficits in dollars and no persistent creditors entitled to receive 100 percent dollars. As it happened, there were a number of persistent debtors—initially especially Austria, Greece, and Turkey—but their above-quota deficits were taken over by the United States as direct aid under the European Recovery Program (ERP), thereby enabling the persistent creditors to be paid off. A fund that is not fed continuous infusions on this basis would quickly break down unless it happened to have no persistent imbalances.

Depreciation of the pound sterling, the Deutschemark, and a number of other currencies against the dollar in September 1949, after recovery had progressed some distance from the depths of the winter of 1947, helped move European currencies toward convertibility. The final step was taken at the end of the 1950s when President de Gaulle of France depreciated the franc in 1958, moved to the "new franc," and Britain seized the occasion to restore the pound to convertibility. The EPU had outlived its usefulness. It was dismantled in 1960 in favor of a loose European Monetary Arrangement (EMA), calling primarily for consultation on currency matters among the European members of the OEEC. Outstanding credit and debit balances were consolidated into long-term loans. The capital of the EPU, originally provided by the United States, was set aside to make loans for special needs of underdeveloped members of the OEEC. The OEEC itself was broadened beyond its original European framework into an Organization for Economic Cooperation and Development (OECD) with the addition, as regular members, of Canada and the United States initially, and later Japan and Australia. The new organization serves as an agency for organizing world responsibilities of developed countries and, in particular, to deal with such questions as aid to economic development in Third World countries, guidelines for multinational corporations, and coordination of macroeconomic policy. In due course, less and less attention was paid to OECD Working Parties Number 2 and 3 on macroeconomic policy as the question of stability was elevated to the economic summit among three to seven heads of state: the United States, Britain, France, Germany, Italy, Canada, and Japan.

The detailed negotiations in establishing EPU and guiding it through a series of crises have been set out by two participants in a book with the subtitle *Financial Diplomacy in the 1950s.* (Kaplan and Schleiminger, 1989). Striking about the history is the give-and-take among the various countries in seeking to reach solutions to practical problems. The contrast is with the World Economic Conference of 1933 where there was little real negotiation, although its failure may be blamed on the imperious intervention of President Roosevelt with a nonsensical message, if perhaps his political unwillingness to be committed made some sense; and with the Bretton Woods Agreement of 1944, which history regards as a bargain largely between Harry Dexter White of the United States and John Maynard Keynes of the United Kingdom, but an impartial Belgian observer asserts was dictated by White (van Dormael, 1978).

Counterpart Funds

Government-to-government loans in the post–World War II period have been made decreasingly in money that the recipient could spend as it wished. Except for the British loan made in money, and beginning with lend-lease, such loans have been transferred in kind, with lender and borrower setting up joint procurement machinery in the United States—leaving aside offshore purchases—and none of the donor's money actually reaching the aid-recipient's hands. The thinking behind this requirement was based on the primitive financial notion that sound banking required the lender to ensure that proper use was made of the proceeds of his loan. The idea embodied the fallacy of misplaced concreteness. What the banker needs to know is that the borrower is using all his resources efficiently, both those borrowed and those already under his control. It was on this basis that such a banker as J. P. Morgan was said to lend not on specific commitments in fine print and their particular merits but on character.

Under the Marshall Plan, if not lend-lease, goods received as aid were not used by the receiving government for the most part but were introduced into normal commercial channels by being sold. From these sales, the aided government received considerable sums of its own money, raising the question of how to handle them.

A significant error in congressional understanding, comparable to that over the printing of occupation currency, was that these funds somehow should belong to the United States. If this were to have been the case, the transactions would not consist of aid at all but would represent an export sale for local currency. In the course of legislating the ERP, the U.S. administration fought hard against this idea but ended up by compromising to the extent of agreeing that 5 percent of counterpart funds should belong to the United States, to be spent by it in the recipient country in ways approved by the local government. Some considerable amounts were spent on embassy buildings and official residences, and especially on the entertainment of visiting congressmen. Since no normal economic use could be made of the monies, they had an implicit high rate of depreciation and were lavishly thrown around, contributing measurably to the demoralization of both the U.S. foreign service and Congress, and wasting some of the aid-receiving country's resources.

For the rest, the United States recognized that the funds belonged to the receiving state but wanted to make sure that they were used in ways that contributed to macroeconomic stability. An optimal use, for example, would be to retire government debt to the central bank, shrinking the money base. The import surplus provided by aid in this circumstance would have the same effect as one under the gold standard, paid for by gold exports that reduced the money supply. At the other extreme, if the government regarded the funds as an ordinary budget receipt and spent them, they would add to money income through the Keynesian multiplier, and part of the increase would spill over again into imports. In this case, improvement in the balance of payments would be temporary. In an intermediate position, counterpart funds could be regarded as additional savings available from abroad and used for capital formation in productive projects designed to improve the balance of payments in the long run, if not the short. The strings retained by the U.S. (Treasury) representative over the use of these funds were designed to influence European national policies in anti-inflationary directions.

With such a country as Greece, the system worked well. The Greek finance minister, let us say, under pressure from his cabinet colleagues to increase outlays for this project and that, could point to counterpart funds and claim that, unless his country followed restrictive policies, the United States would not release the monies for sought-after purposes. At the other extreme, the British government chose not to make any requests to the U.S. Treasury attaché in London for spending the counterpart funds, allowing them to pile up unused, and, if necessary, prepared to expand the money supply at the Bank of England to carry out existing policies. They resented the hold on policy sought through counterpart funds as patronizing.

There were some critical moments. In France, for example, the government would be unable to borrow from the Bank of France because of statutory restrictions, unable to raise taxes in the Chamber of Deputies for political reasons, and, on occasion, would be dependent upon counterpart funds to meet regular expenses. For the United States to refuse to release counterpart funds would be to bring down the government, an exercise in conditionality equivalent to that of the bankers in the British rescue loan of 1931, or to some IMF stabilization loans today. It will readily be understood that there were differences of opinion within the U.S. government over the wisdom of refusing to release counterpart funds for ordinary expenses as a matter of high principle at whatever political cost within France or in Franco-American relations, and the more expedient and benevolent line of bending with the breeze.

For the most part, in such a country as France, counterpart funds were released to the government to help finance investment under the Monnet and successive plans. From 1945 to 1954, counterpart funds contributed close to one-half of the deficit of the French Treasury (Baum, 1958, p. 58 and table 10, p. 56). The Commissariat au Plan used these monies as released, together with the accumulation of savings funneled into the Caisse des Dépôts et Consignations from savings banks all over France, as a means of enforcing the plan on the part of those companies that did not have capital funds through internally generated profits or ready access to the capital market.

Structural Versus Keynesian Unemployment

Keynes's *General Theory,* written in 1936, had been intellectually absorbed in some degree in the late 1930s, with the brilliant illustration of German recovery through armament expenditure, but was refined and extended during the war in a mathematical and geometric model. Some of its lessons were misleading, as in the widely held belief among American economists that the end of the war and the sharp decline in government expenditure would bring about a depression with widespread unemployment (Hagen, 1949). The Harriman Report—produced in the United States to investigate the feasibility of the Marshall Plan in terms of the availability of resources in the United States and the possibilities of achieving recovery in Europe—used a sophisticated analysis of consumption, investment, and multipliers for the first time on an international scale. Moreover, the young American economists who staffed ERP offices in Europe in the first days of the Marshall Plan were well versed in Keynesian analysis. Those in the American group in Rome in 1948 found themselves in a sharp difference of opinion with Deputy Prime Minister, former Governor of the Bank of Italy, later President of the Republic, and leading Italian economist Luigi Einaudi.

Italy had suffered strenuous inflation during the war, an inflation that continued into 1946 and 1947 as business borrowed from commercial banks, and government financed its deficit at the Bank of Italy. At the end of May 1947, Prime Minister Alcide De Gasperi reorganized his government, including as deputy prime minister and budget minister, the then governor of the Bank of Italy, Professor Einaudi. Einaudi and his successor at the bank, Donato Menichella, put together a program of monetary deflation, which took effect in August. Despite almost 2 million unemployed, inflation was proceeding at the rate of 5 to 7 percent a month. A broad program of stabilization was undertaken, including higher discount rates, high reserve requirements for banks, restrictions on Treasury borrowing from the central bank, dismantling of exchange control, and its replacement with depreciation of the lira. When ERP officials arrived in 1948, they expressed concern that more aggressive government spending was required to achieve full utilization of Italian industrial capacity, including fuller employment. This attitude was echoed by the United Nations Secretariat of the Economic Commission for Europe.

The Italians insisted that their problem was not one of deficient demand but of structural imbalance. Unemployment, which reached 2.19 million in March 1947, was largely the consequence of shortages of raw materials and fuel, on the one hand, and of fixed capital, on the other, relative to the enlarged labor supply. Wage rates higher than the marginal product of workers could not be lowered on political grounds, and given the fixed character of capital equipment, it was impossible to change factor proportions in the short run, in any event. To expand spending in these circumstances would speed up inflation without correcting unemployment. The Marshall Plan was needed to raise the capital stock to the appropriate proportion to the labor supply, all the while maintaining restrictive monetary and fiscal policies. It was a foretaste of the supply-side disagreement with Keynesian policies that broke out especially in the United States in the 1980s, though without inclusion of the hocus-pocus about incentives and tax cuts.

As with many other conventional accounts, this summary of the Marshall Plan experience has been questioned by revisionists. One conservative monetarist view echoes those economists who objected at the start—Harrod, Haberler, Hazlitt, and Lutz (see p. 424), to name a few—on the ground that the market could have righted itself if governments had adopted appropriate fiscal and monetary policies: balanced budgets, tight money, and devalued or perhaps floating exchange rates (Cleveland, 1984). An eminent British economic historian blames European governments for unduly encouraging domestic investment without regard to balance-of-payments consequences and maintains that the terrors of the bad winter, spring, and summer of 1947 in Europe were grossly overstated (Milward, 1984, ch. 1). A general historian of Europe believes that contemporary observers overstated the likelihood of irreversible (in the short run) Communist takeovers in France and Italy (Maier, 1981). Perhaps so, but I have strong doubts. It seems to me that U.S. memories of the mess that was made after World War I—especially war debts and reparations—produced policies of positive help for stricken allies, and enemies too, that proved their worth. The years from 1950 to 1973 in Europe, and over much of the rest of the world as well, produced a sort of supergrowth that has been called a "golden age" that would have been unlikely if Europe had been left to recover by itself (Kindleberger, 1987, esp. ch. 14).

DEVALUATION OF THE POUND

The IMF stood on the sidelines during the Marshall Plan, as far as Europe was concerned, sending observers to meetings of the OEEC dealing with such issues as the EPU, but in the wings rather than at the center of the stage. For the most part, it handed out credits and advice to less developed countries. Exchange parities were fixed, and especially the pound at \$4.02. Convertibility of the pound, required within a year of July 1946 by the terms of the British loan, lasted a brief seven weeks. Under the Marshall Plan, countries were pushed by U.S. Economic Cooperation missions to relax their discrimination against American exports.

In 1949 industrial production in the United States dipped a bit and, with it, income-elastic imports of the United States from Britain. The British government reimposed restrictions on dollar imports into the sterling area in August 1949. In September of the same year it shifted to a new exchange rate, \$2.80, informing the IMF rather than requesting permission. Similar adjustments against the dollar were made by other countries, mostly smaller in amount, and notably by Germany. It would not be until 1958, however, that the pound was made fully convertible. By that time, the movement for European integration that has been a persistent theme of the Marshall Plan was getting under way.

SUGGESTED SUPPLEMENTARY READING

Diebold (1952), *Trade and Payments in Western Europe.*
Ellis (1950), *The Economics of Freedom.*

Gardner (1980), *Sterling-Dollar Diplomacy in Current Perspective.*
J. M. Jones (1955), *The Fifteen Weeks (February 21–June 5, 1947).*
Kindleberger (1987), *Marshall Plan Days.*
Maier and Bischof (eds.) (1991), *The Marshall Plan and Germany.*
Milward (1984), *The Reconstruction of Western Europe, 1945–51.*

24

European Financial Integration

Anyone who wishes to escape from the pessimistic conclusion that nobody is going to be in command, and that therefore the historic world is returning into chaos, will have to fall back to the point we started from, and ask himself seriously: Is it certain as people say that Europe is in decadence; that it is resigning its command; abdicating? May not this apparent decadence be a beneficial crisis which will enable Europe to be really, literally Europe? The evident decadence of the *nations* of Europe, was this not *a priori* necessary if there was to be one day possible a United States of Europe, the plurality of Europe substituted by its formal unity.

(Ortega y Gasset, *The Revolt of the Masses,* 1930 [1932], p. 152).

ECONOMIC INTEGRATION

While the notion of European integration is an old one, it received a fillip from the Marshall Plan. The congressional preamble to the Economic Cooperation Act of 1948 called on Europe to follow the American example and form a Continent-wide economic market. In a speech of 31 October 1949, Paul Hoffman, U.S. administrator of the Marshall Plan, echoed the same thought, urging Europe to "integrate." Nor was the idea exclusively an American one. Its French origins went back to Saint-Simonism and were echoed after World War II by Jean Monnet and his technocratic followers.

As economists and others thought about it, there proved to be many degrees and levels of economic integration. There was first "functional integration," illustrated by special regimes for special functions such as mails, or transport, or rivers that flow through a number of countries. Here the high point was the European Coal and Steel Community (ECSC), originated by Jean Monnet and put forward in 1950 by French Finance Minister Robert Schumann as a device for ensuring peaceful cooperation in heavy industry between Germany and France. The more usual form of economic integration advocated for Europe, however, was a customs union.

The Rome Treaty of 1957 forming the European Economic Community (EEC) among Belgium, France, Germany, Italy, Luxembourg, and the Netherlands called for a customs union among the signatories, for freedom of movement of factors of production—labor and capital—and for several new institutions designed to offset adverse effects of the new arrangements on parts of any country, notably a European Social Fund, a European Investment Bank, and a fund for assisting the economic development of former colonies of European powers. These three institutions were designed to modify a market outcome, especially as it might favor parts of France, Germany, and Italy near the epicenter of the community and react against southwest France, southeast Germany, and southern Italy; the overseas fund was a price exacted by France and Italy, with former colonies, from Germany, which had none.

Rejecting an invitation to join the EEC in 1957, the British formed a European Free-Trade Area (EFTA), made up of the peripheral states of Western Europe: Norway, Denmark, Sweden, Austria, Switzerland, and Portugal, along with Britain. The British reason for refusing to join the Common Market was, partly, its special relation to the United States and, partly, its membership of the British Commonwealth. In due course these extra-European ties were seen to have limited value, and Britain applied to join the Common Market, failing to be accepted in 1963 when President de Gaulle said "no," but ultimately gaining admittance on 1 January 1973 along with Denmark and Ireland. Norway originally proposed joining but backed out when a referendum showed that political sentiment was on balance opposed. The adherence of Britain, Denmark, and Ireland to the EEC broke up EFTA in which Britain had been the leading spirit.

Definitions of economic integration start with free trade (Tinbergen, 1954; Machlup, 1977); Balassa went further and specified the absence of all government discrimination affecting the movement of goods and factors (1961). This requires harmonization of a variety of policies in countries engaged in the process of integration, including taxation, qualitative regulation such as standards, pure food and drug laws, and the like. A still more far-reaching definition is factor price equalization, especially the equalization of wages and salaries for labor, and of interest rates for capital (Myrdal, 1956). This is an ideal standard rather than an operational goal. Expanding trade by means of removal of tariffs in customs unions and/or promotion of free movement of factors of production can move toward factor price equalization, as protection and restrictions may move away from it. Given discrimination by geography and by peoples, however, customs unions and free movement of factors are not likely to achieve complete factor price equalization even when governments are nondiscriminatory. Geography separates countries by distance, which are equivalent to tariffs in preventing equalization of goods prices, needed under rigorous conditions for trade to succeed in bringing about factor price equalization. And where governments do not discriminate, people may, preferring, say, to live where they were born, know the language, and feel comfortable, rather than to migrate for a gain in real income.

One qualification must be admitted to the definition of economic integration as factor price equalization. Integration means oneness, and equalization of factor prices must be brought about by direct joining of relevant markets, rather than by external factors and markets. The point is central to the recent history of financial integration in Europe. Things equal to the same thing are equal to each other, but they are not necessarily integrated. If wage differences between France and Germany are narrowed by a floating supply of Yugoslav, Spanish, and Turkish labor, this will move France and Germany toward factor price equalization but can hardly be said to constitute integration. The same is true of corporate enterprise, where greater equality of corporate profits within the EEC may be achieved by American multinational corporations, alert to opportunities in various European national markets, and ready to move from one to another, or at least to direct expansion to the most profitable countries. And, especially, external factor markets have been important in the field of capital where the Eurodollar—or more generally the Euro-currency market—external to each country in Europe, tended to equalize interest rates among members of the EEC without much in the way of capital movements directly from one capital market in Europe to another and without creation of a dominant capital market for all of Western Europe.

EUROPEAN CAPITAL MARKETS

During the 1950s and 1960s, European borrowers turned to New York to obtain funds, borrowing long, and selling the dollars to their central banks, which often added them to reserves. Under the liquidity definition of equilibrium in the balance of payments used by the U.S. government, this produced a "deficit," and the U.S. government was unhappy about it. While European borrowers issued loans in the New York market, a sizable proportion of them was bought there by European investors, the buyer accepting a lower yield than was available in all markets but Belgium, the Netherlands, and Switzerland—presumably in exchange for a more liquid asset, that is, one with a broader secondary market and therefore better likelihood of being converted into cash, if necessary, without a sharp price decline. Belgium, the Netherlands, and Switzerland maintained interest rates below those of other European countries, and below New York, by limiting access of foreign borrowers to their capital markets, although for Belgium and the Netherlands this contravened Article 67 of the Treaty of Rome. The purpose was partly to maintain interest rates low for governmental borrowing and, in the case of Switzerland, which limited foreign borrowers to 60 million Swiss francs or less than $15 million, to achieve diversification for Swiss investors through many small foreign loans rather than a few large ones.

Speaking before the American Bankers' Association meeting in Rome in 1962, the U.S. secretary of the treasury, Douglas Dillon, claimed that European capital markets were riddled with monopoly that diverted local borrowers to New York. With competition, he suggested, Europeans would borrow in Europe and the deficit in the U.S. balance of payments would be relieved. The same view was expressed in a study of European capital markets by the Joint Economic Committee of the U.S. Congress (1964, esp. p. 130). A somewhat different view held that Europe and the United States had sharply different preferences for liquidity and that Europe tended to borrow long and lend short in New York to acquire the liquidity sought after in Europe and available in the United States (Kindleberger, 1965 [1966]). This was international financial intermediation of the sort normal in domestic markets, so that lending long and borrowing short (within moderation) should not be regarded as leading to deficit for leading financial centers. This view of the matter was not widely accepted (Hague, 1966, pp. 550–64; Lamfalussy, 1968, pp. 171–77). The two views are not unrelated, however, since more competitive and closely joined capital markets in Europe would provide greater liquidity to satisfy European needs.

The American attempt to blame the balance-of-payments deficit on deficiencies in European capital markets led to new European research. A study of capital markets by the EEC in 1966 was addressed largely to impediments to the effective functioning of national markets and their availability to foreign borrowers. The Segré Report (as it was called, after the chairman of the group of experts and the principal author, Claudio Segré) found that national markets in Europe discriminated in favor of domestic borrowers, especially national governments, as against foreign, especially in regulations governing the investment of funds of savings banks and insurance companies, assistance for housing, and the like. Few European securities were listed on stock exchanges outside the countries where the issuing company was domiciled. The report concluded that little progress had been made in establishing a European capital market, which, it held, was desirable in the interest of both borrowers and lenders. Detailed studies of national capital markets were made on a wider basis by the OECD Committee for Invisible Transactions (invisible, that is, in the balance-of-payments sense). These studies again emphasized the narrowness of European national capital markets and their domination by national governments and recommended strengthening the links between national capital markets, especially secondary ones (*Capital Markets Study: General Report,* 1967, p. 15).

THE EURODOLLAR MARKET

About 1957 or 1958, European banks, notably in London and Switzerland, began to deal in dollars. The origin of this trading is variously ascribed to (1) the move of Sir George Bolton, Bank of England foreign exchange trader and executive director from 1948 to 1957 to the moribund Bank of London and South America (BOLSA), and his insight that opportunities for trading in sterling were limited so that he switched the bank into dollar borrowing and lending (Fry, 1970, pp. 32–37); (2) realization that Regulation Q in the Federal Reserve system in the United States, setting ceilings on interest rates payable on time deposits, did not apply to deposits in New York belonging to foreign banks or to foreign branches of New York banks, with the result that a depositor of dollars could earn a slightly higher return by transferring funds from New York to Europe without exchange risk so long as he kept them in dollars (Gilbert and McClam, 1970, pp. 361ff.); and (3) the convenience of trading in dollars during daytime hours in the European time zones, plus the safety for such depositors as the Russian state bank in holding its dollars in non-American banks where the chances of their being affected by political incident were reduced.

An early academic controversy turned on whether the Eurocurrency or, less formally, the Eurodollar market, created money. Shift of a dollar deposit to a European bank (or European branch of an American bank) could be regarded as an increase in reserves in the Eurodollar market, which could be loaned and reloaned to borrowers who put the money back into the system or paid it to people who did so, thus expanding the money supply in multiple fashion, comparable to an increase in primary reserves of a national banking system, as, say, Milton Friedman held (1969 [1970]). Or the process might be cut off by the original borrower's spending the dollars in the United States so that they would not be redeposited in the Eurocurrency market. In this case, the possibilities of multiple expansion were limited, in the manner of savings banks or savings and loan associations in the United States, where the recipient of the funds borrowed generally does not return them to the savings and loan system (Klopstock, 1968, pp. 3–9). The issue turns on whether the Eurodollars borrowed are returned to the Eurocurrency market. The answer is that in the early stages of the market, dollars were borrowed by those who wanted dollars to spend as dollars; later, as the market broadened and thickened, some dollars were borrowed for stockpiling against future need and reinvested in the market, and others were sought by Europeans who were not unwilling to go short of dollars, wanted local monies for spending in Europe, and sold the dollars to a central bank against local funds. When the central bank redeposited the dollars in the Eurodollar market, a basis was laid for relending and multiple expansion. In the early stages of the development of the institution, Klopstock was right and the multiple-expansion ratio was limited; as the practice developed of redepositing the funds in European banks, the Friedman position gained validity.

The Eurodollar market is a misnomer in a sense additional to the fact that it is not limited to dollars. It is no longer restricted to Europe. A Eurocurrency is any currency borrowed and lent outside the country that uses that currency, and the Eurodollar market today exists in Canada, the Bahamas, Singapore, Japan, Hong Kong, and the Middle East, as well as in London, Zurich, Brussels, Luxembourg, Hamburg, and so on. The market, in fact, travels around the world daily, shifting to the Antilles and Canada when business hours close in Europe, then to Singapore, Tokyo, Hong Kong, next to Bahrain, before opening the next day in Europe. It is, of course, a wholesale market, with individual transactions in millions of dollars, or at the minimum hundreds of thousands, highly competitive, working on slender margins, with a very large gross of interbank transactions and a much smaller net claims on, and liabilities to, nonbanks.

To the extent that European countries have become closely associated with the Eurocurrency market, then, they are integrated into a wider unit than Western Europe. The tension as to whether Europe is an integrated unit by itself, or a set of separate countries each integrated in varying degrees into the world—which for financial purposes means the dollar system, on the one hand, and the Bretton Woods system on the other—has been continuous. In 1963 Italy turned for assistance through swap arrangements to the United States in Washington, rather than to the EEC in Brussels (de Cecco, 1969). The swap network that developed in Basle after March 1961 as a lender of last resort was worldwide rather than European (Coombs, 1976, ch. 5). (Under swap arrangements, two central banks exchange claims on each other for a limited period of time, such as six months, enabling the one in trouble to spend the currency of the other to meet a drain.) In the early postwar period European financial arrangements, such as the European Payments Union (EPU) or the European Monetary Arrangement (EMA), had no provision for lender-of-last-resort assistance. In this circumstance, Europe might have been integrated for trade finance, but its separate countries had to be connected to world financial institutions for broader financial needs. A point to be noticed as it bears on monetary planning is that both the Eurodollar market and the Basle swap network grew up more or less spontaneously, in evolutionary Darwinian fashion, rather than emerging from the drawing boards of economist planners.

THE EUROBOND MARKET

Parallel to the Eurocurrency market for money and mainly time deposits, there developed a Eurobond market in which borrowers issued bonds in a given currency or unit outside the country of that money. The market was partly stimulated by the onerous registration requirements of the Securities and Exchange Commission in Washington, partly by the Interest Equalization Tax (IET) imposed in the United States in 1963 on bond interest to stop European countries' borrowing in the United States. From 1963 to 1973 Eurodollar bonds were issued exclusively in Europe. In 1973, when the United States repealed the IET and all restrictions on capital movements out of the United States, a given dollar bond could be issued simultaneously in New York and other European capitals.

Eurobonds were offered mostly in dollars, to some extent in Deutschemarks, on occasion in French francs, and also in European units of account (EUAs) (Genillard, 1970, p. 331). "Unit of account" was the name given to the units used to calculate balances in the EPU in 1950 and was initially equal to $1. In 1961 it was reorganized as a composite of seventeen currencies to hedge the borrower against changes in the currency of the lender and the lender against changes in the currency of the borrower. Pushed particularly by the Kreditbank of Brussels and used for loans syndicated by Belgian or Luxembourg banks (Kirschen, 1969, pp. 59–60), it was intended to form an imaginary unit of account for European transactions. "However, the complexity of the formula, and the fact that it has not always met with an enthusiastic response from the monetary authorities, has not permitted it so far to emerge as the ideal forerunner of a common European currency" (Genillard, 1970, p. 331). For the five years from 1974 to 1978 "composite and dual currencies" (which include EUA) were responsible for only 2.3 percent of total Eurobond issues ($1.1 billion), as contrasted with 58 percent in U.S. dollars, 25.5 percent in Deutschemarks, 5 percent in Canadian dollars, 4 percent in guilders, and the rest scattered (Wood, Gundy & Company, 1979).

With the adoption of the European Monetary System in 1979, the unit of account was replaced by the European currency unit (ecu), and efforts were made to issue debt in ecu and even to encourage the establishment and use of ecu deposits. Bond issues for the European Community and the European Investment Bank were increasingly denominated in ecus rather than dollars, but progress has been slow. In the first six months of 1991, for example, international bonds in Europe were issued 31 percent in dollars, 13 percent each in ecus and Deutschemarks, 10 percent in sterling, 10 percent in all other EMS currencies, 11 percent in yen, and 10 percent in all other (*The Economist,* July 13, 1991, p. 83). Composite currencies that are not used in ordinary commercial and financial transactions may serve as a unit of account in debt instruments or in measuring central bank reserves. They are awkward, however, since they involve fairly complex foreign exchange transactions in buying and selling debt instruments.

EUROPEAN MONETARY UNIFICATION

Two forces contributed to the drive to European monetary unification: (1) continuation of the integration movement in its various aspects—commercial, economic, financial, possibly political; and (2) growing weakness of the dollar as a world currency. On the first score, history reveals that unification, or integration, proceeds by stages, with customs union typically the first step, followed by "economic union," in which a number of ancillary policies are harmonized, followed at the peak by monetary union. There is even a question as to whether monetary union can precede or necessarily follows political unification, so difficult it is otherwise to produce the coordination of sensitive instruments, close to the core of sovereignty, such as monetary and fiscal policy. In Germany and Italy in the nineteenth century, as we have seen (see pp. 121, 138), monetary unification followed the achievement of political unity, in each case driven by a dominant state, Prussia and Piedmont, respectively. This is not the interpretation, however, of a German economic historian who regards the various steps to monetary unification short of the establishment of the mark and the Reichsbank as a case of monetary unification preceding and leading to the political foundation of the German Reich (Holtfrerich, 1988).

The second reason, the weakness of the dollar, is discussed in the next chapter.

OPTIMUM CURRENCY AREAS

Early in postwar financial history, economic discussion began over what constituted an appropriate area to have an independent currency and, in particular, what the criteria were for an "optimum currency area." Mundell, who first advanced the topic, thought in terms of factor movements. If one portion of a wide area had unemployment and factors were immobile so that the unemployment could not be cured by migration, it might be useful for the depressed area to devalue its currency as a substitute, increasing exports, diverting expenditure from imports to import substitutes produced at home, and increasing employment through the foreign trade multiplier. On his criterion, the touchstone was factor mobility (Mundell, 1961). McKinnon countered this notion with the suggestion that it would not help a limited area to devalue if, in fact, it traded heavily with the outside world and was unable to prevent its citizenry from recognizing that the rise in export and import prices needed to divert spending from foreign to domestic goods, right the balance of payments, and expand employment represented a decline in the level of living of a size sufficient to induce labor to try to raise wages and capital to raise the rate of interest. If these efforts were successful, devaluation would help neither the balance of payments nor employment. Hence his criterion for an optimum currency area was one that traded intensely within itself and had limited commercial contacts with the outside world (McKinnon, 1963). On the Mundell criterion, Canada was too large to be an optimum currency area since migration between the two coasts—the Maritime provinces and British Columbia—and the interior was limited. On the McKinnon basis, on the other hand, Canada was too small to be an optimum currency area, since so much of its trade was with the United States and other foreign countries.

Europe fits uneasily into this analysis, devised by one-time Canadians especially for application to North America. Indigenous factors of production are relatively immobile, as already noted, but a considerable degree of mobility has been achieved through outside factors. Germany, for example, handled the unemployment that began in 1974 when OPEC raised the price of oil by allowing its foreign labor force to run down. Moreover, while European internal trade has increased more rapidly than external trade since the Treaty of Rome, the volume of extra-European imports is still sizable and in certain categories (such as petroleum, grain, coffee, rubber, wool, and the like) is critical to the European standard of living, and hence impossible to overlook.

There is still another criterion of an optimum currency area. There must be a set of institutions to operate it (Kenen, 1969). This implies a mechanism for arriving at political choices and making political as well as technical decisions. In recognition of the need to strengthen decision making in this area, the EEC Commission in February 1969 recommended to the heads of state (the EEC Council) that a group should be established to work under the chairmanship of Pierre Werner, prime minister of Luxembourg, to examine various aspects of the "realization by stages of economic and monetary union" in the EEC.

ECONOMIC AND MONETARY UNION (EMU)

The Werner group produced a preliminary report, consulted a Committee of Experts staffed largely by European central banks, and ultimately emerged with a *Report to the Council and the Commission on the Realization by Stages of Economic and Monetary Union in the Community* (EEC, 1970). The plan called for three stages, of which only the first was set forth in any detail. During the first stage, the report called for "concertation" of short-term policies, especially in matters of budgets, fiscal policy, financial markets—generally eliminating remaining restrictions—and domestic monetary and credit policy. In addition, a beginning was to be made in the development of a common external policy, with consultation in advance in dealings with the IMF, the swap network, and in dollars. In particular, the first stage provided for narrowing exchange rate variations within Europe to a range more constricted than that authorized by the IMF.

The first stage was scheduled to start on 1 January 1971 and to run for three years. In the second stage, it was agreed to harmonize medium-term policies, in addition to the short-term policies already harmonized in the first, and to establish a European Monetary Cooperation Fund (EMCF, but usually referred to by the acronym of its initials in French, FECOM) under the control of the governors of the participating central banks. FECOM would take a portion of the reserves of each central bank and use the whole as a fund for intervening in support of weak exchanges and to repress unwanted exchange rate fluctuations. In the third and final stage, FECOM was expected to become the instrument for managing the aggregated foreign reserves of the community as a whole—perhaps, it was hinted, evolving into a supra-European central bank. In any event, the third stage was expected to witness the establishment of a single community currency, to be realized by 1980, ten years from the initiation of the process.

In discussions about the path of financial integration, experts initially divided into so-called economists, who believed that coordination of economic policy had to precede monetary unification; monetarists, who sought irreversible monetary commitments that were expected to force policy coordination; and institutionalists, who thought it necessary, first and foremost, to construct the political and administrative machinery for European-wide decision making (Oort, 1979, p. 193).

As it happened, the target of 1980 for the establishment of a single European currency was overly ambitious. Years of gradual convergence of rates of inflation and smaller and smaller devaluations from successive parities for the separate currencies elapsed before the original six countries of the EMS even approached that goal. European economists kept proposing a series of new plans. One was called the All-Saints Day Manifesto of 1973, calling for a new "parallel currency" (parallel, that is, to the national Deutschemark, French franc, pound sterling, lira, etc.), to be called the "Europa" and to be issued by a Euroagency that would ultimately evolve into a Europe-wide central bank. Another Study Group on Optimum Currency Areas, the so-called "Optica Group," produced a report offering detailed provisions for the transition to a new European currency, with limits on exchange rate changes, rules for intervention, and the like (EEC, 1977; Basevi, 1979). Friederich Hayek, Roland Vaubel, and Pascal Salin took a more radical stand, urging that the parity system be abandoned altogether, that central banks in Europe should borrow, if at all, only in private markets, withdrawing from the IMF and giving up FECOM and the swap arrangement, that European central banks should abstain from foreign exchange intervention to limit fluctuation in rates, and cease acting as lenders of last resort in foreign exchange crises (Hayek, 1972; Vaubel, 1979, p. 183; Salin, 1980). In some versions of these ultramonetarist recommendations, countries are called upon to abandon sovereignty over money and the designation of legal tender, allowing "currency choice," that is, freedom of individuals in all countries to conduct business—buying, selling, contracting, and holding any money at all—and to encourage countries, banks, firms, and individuals to offer their own private monies for use by the market (Bronfenbrenner, 1980). These views are based on a belief that government has private purposes of its own, in addition to providing the public good of monetary stability; that Gresham's law is a danger only because monies are fixed in price and will not be harmful if exchange rates are flexible, with no official intervention (Vaubel, 1977); that speculation is generally stabilizing; that there is no need for a lender of last resort; and that any possible economies of scale in economizing on information and transactions costs from maintenance of a single money are outweighed by the tendency of the issuer to indulge in irresponsible inflation.

A number of these ultramonetarists wanted to give up entirely on the idea of a central bank. So popular did such discussion become that one economist, who had previously worked for the Bank of England, wrote a generalized defense of central banking. It was needed, he asserted, to provide surveillance over the payments mechanism (Goodhart, 1989). A bank's depositors may be able to judge the value of the bank's investments, but they have no way of evaluating the bank's loans, which are not traded on markets with public quotations. It might be possible to convert banks into mutual funds, the liabilities of which, used as money, would fluctuate in price. With banks, given the difficulty of judging asset values, it would place too heavy a burden on depositors to ask them to determine whether a bank that offers a higher interest rate on deposits than the competition is more efficient than others or so weak that it needs an infusion of new deposits to stay alive (ibid., p. 30).

More broadly, competitive monies or mutual fund liabilities that fluctuate freely against one another within a country or a currency area pose a question as to whether there is any money at all. In most definitions, money is the one asset whose price does not change, except as the reciprocal of a weighted average of all other prices.

EUROPEAN MONETARY SYSTEM (EMS)

While debate over parallel currencies and currency choice was under way, Roy Jenkins, the former British president of the European Commission, in a Jean Monnet lecture in October 1977, launched a new drive for European monetary integration by calling for a European Monetary System (EMS). The trial balloon was followed by a new plan of the German chancellor, Helmut Schmidt, for a "zone of monetary stability" in Europe, which was discussed, first, in the EEC Council in April 1978, later at a summit meeting between Schmidt and the French president, Giscard d'Estaing, and finally adopted by the EEC in Brussels in December 1978, to start on 1 January 1979. That start was delayed for two and a half months by one of a series of Franco-German disputes over agriculture.

The EMS differs from the EMU in a number of particulars. It introduced the ecu as a parallel currency, provided two measures to aid in narrowing fluctuations of national exchange rates, constituted a European Monetary Fund, and provided a system of credit facilities for mutual payments support.

Established as a unit of account for the EMS, the ecu was made up of fixed amounts of the several currencies: 0.828 Deutschemarks, 1.15 French francs, and so on. As the exchange rates among the several currencies varied against one another, in narrower and narrower margins, the percentage each currency contributed to the ecu was adjusted.

Starting out as a unit of account and parallel currency, the ecu is intended to become a single currency, substituting for the national monies of the European Community at some time between 1997 and the year 2000, according to the decision of the EC Maastricht Summit Meeting of December 1991. First, the Common Market had to reach the stage of completion at which customs officials were no longer needed at border crossings since harmonization would have been achieved in all or most of the regulations and taxes that differed among member countries. The EC White Paper of 1985 on the Completion of the Common Market set forth the agreement that this would be accomplished by the end of 1992, to make for a new start on 1 January 1993. Capital markets, it was similarly agreed, would be free of controls by July 1990. When the ecu became the only European currency, some time before 2000, all assets and liabilities would be denominated in ecus, which would be legal tender throughout the community. The process of the ecu replacing the other currencies raises once again whether money is what the state declares is money (the legal tender or Georg Knapp view), or money is what people use for spending and record keeping, so that the transition to the ecu would occur piecemeal in a Darwinian fashion.

There remain a series of questions to be resolved on the road to European monetary and financial integration: the regulation of banks; the status of latecomers joining the Common Market—Greece, Spain, and Portugal, plus any countries of the former Socialist bloc that might apply for and be granted membership; whether there should be a central bank, and if so, its character and location; whether membership in EMS and substitution of the ecu for the national currency are irreversible commitments, needed for credibility, or whether it would be possible to opt out of particular aspects of the agreement, as the British insisted at Maastricht and which was allowed them but not others; whether at some stage the commission will concern itself deeply in the fiscal policies of member countries to prevent pressures on the others through excessively expansionary or contractive budgets. In the view of a number of economists, effective integration requires a fiscal mechanism by which transfers are made automatically from region to region, with rich persons and rich areas paying more in taxes and receiving less in benefits than poor persons and areas.

BANKING REGULATION

Harmonization of national banking regulation is most readily achieved by deregulation. From the late 1940s to the 1970s, there was not much change. Deregulation began with the Treaty of Rome in 1957 and picked up pace in 1973 with a European Commission directive imposing freedom of establishment across state lines for financial institutions, a directive first proposed in 1965. In 1977 the first banking directive laid down the principle of home country control of financial institutions, including within control responsibility for the international obligations of an insolvent bank. Interest in the question arose from the collapse of the Herstatt bank in Germany in 1974, with substantial paper abroad in the process of collection. Numerous exceptions had to be made to the principle of home country responsibility, especially in deposit insurance, explicitly excepted in the Second Banking Directive of 1989, since deposit insurance requires bank supervision and the home country cannot audit branches and subsidiaries abroad of its home banks (Dermine, 1990). This exception would appear to have been a response to the Italian refusal to accept responsibility as lender of last resort for the 1982 failure of the Luxembourg branch of the Banco Ambrosiano. Antitrust policy is evidently another exception to home country control, but this, while only loosely applied, falls under the original provisions of the Treaty of Rome. An indication of the complexity of harmonization of financial regulations is that the Second Non-Life Directive (insurance) issued in June 1989 was fifteen years in the negotiation! (Fitchew, 1990, exclamation point in the original).

Deregulation in Europe and in OECD countries generally in the 1970s and 1980s was followed by financial innovation, consolidation at home, extension abroad, and some change in standards. The Second Banking Directive adopted the universal bank as a basic model (Steinherr, 1990, p. 59), as specialized financial firms were taken over by banks (except in Italy, where the 1936 prohibition on banks' underwriting securities remained in force). In London, the "Big Bang" of 1 October 1986 started with the breaking down of the wall between stock jobbers and brokers, with the abandonment of fixed commissions, inducing leading banks everywhere to establish subsidiaries in London, often to undertake activities such as security trading, forbidden in their own country (e.g., Italy and the United States). As it turned out, the Big Bang proved a disappointment. The collapse of the New York stock market on 19 October 1987 produced sharp declines in share prices in Europe as well as in New York. Together with a similar plunge of stock prices in October 1989 and protracted loss of investor interest in equities, a number of banks and investment houses that had scrambled to London in preparation for unregulated trading pulled back in part or in whole.

Some skepticism has been voiced over innovations in finance, on the ground that the innovators tend to underprice them in order to gain acceptance, and hence lose money (Cross Report, 1986). The point is general. New banks that enter an existing market tend both to pay too much for their money and accept undue risks in an effort to break into the markets of established banks with long-standing ties to their customers, as demonstrated by the experience of the "fringe banks" in London that had to be rescued by the Bank of England in 1974 (Reid, 1982). Following the collapse of the Franklin National and the Herstatt banks at about the same time, the Cooke Report recommended new and higher standards of capital adequacy and solvency. This was followed in July 1988 by an agreement reached at the Bank for International Settlements among the leading countries, including Canada and the United States, along with those in Europe, on minimal capital standards, well above existing levels in some countries.

THE EUROPEAN CENTRAL BANK

At Maastricht in December 1991, the twelve-member EC agreed on a three-phase process of monetary union. The first had already been taken on 1 July 1990 when monetary policies were coordinated and capital restrictions abandoned. The second is to begin 1 January 1994, with still narrower ranges of movement of exchange rates and activation of FECOM, which will ultimately be transformed into the central bank.

The third stage is more complex. In 1996 community governments will determine what member countries have met strict "convergence criteria, measured by deviations of interest rates, price levels, budget deficits and exchange rates from the Community standard." If a majority of the existing members have met the standard, they can decide by a two-third majority to establish the single currency and the central bank as early as 1 January 1997. All but the United Kingdom will take part at least by the end of 1999. The United Kingdom reserves the right to make its decision at a later date whether to take part.

While the decision has been taken by all but the United Kingdom, presumably it can be changed if overwhelming forces rendered it necessary. There are still economists who believe that a central bank is not needed and that the market can regulate itself if left to itself. The argument put forward by Goodhart (1989) and the verdict of history, which has consistently created central banks since 1668, runs to the contrary. One strongly held view is that national central banks should coordinate to the limited extent of ensuring that they jointly create the requisite amount of money for the world in the aggregate (McKinnon, 1989). For the most part, however, mainstream economics holds that European monetary integration implies, in the long run, a European central bank. The questions are whether it should be (1) a loose confederation of national central banks or a single unified institution whose writ runs into each separate country; (2) a dominant central bank that absorbs the central banks of the other members of the community, as the National Bank of Prussia took over the other note-issuing institutions of the states forming the Reich and was renamed the Reichsbank; (3) whether the European central bank, federal or unified, should be independent of government or of the European Commission and the European Parliament or subject to political control; and (4) where the European Central Bank, if there were one, would be located.

The decision at Maastricht postpones the resolution of these questions to at least 1 January 1994, when the second phase of monetary unification occurs, a sizable portion of central bank reserves are pooled and denominated in ecu, and work on the design of ultimate central banks becomes serious. One pattern is that of the Federal Reserve system of the United States as it was envisaged in the original act in 1913—twelve regional banks cooperating under the leadership of a board in Washington. This model appeals especially to the Germans who call their country a federation (*Bund*) and their central bank a Federal Bank (*Bundesbank*). In the United States, however, reality departed from the original design. Because of the financial exigencies of World War I, the New York bank, operating in the major capital market of the United States, became the focus of major changes in monetary policy, with the eleven other regional banks—some like Chicago and San Francisco with significant capital markets—tagging along.

One Bundesbank official questions whether there is a need or an inevitability for financial markets to be organized asymmetrically, with a dominant center and the other satellite markets dependent on it (Rieke, 1989, p. 346). Means of communication may have developed by the late 1990s to the point where face-to-face communication in a single financial center is no longer the likely evolutionary outcome, but financial history suggests otherwise (Kindleberger, 1974 [1978]). As in the United States, the Bank Deutsche Länder evolved from an institution linking three banks into the Bundesbank, a unified institution, firmly anchored in Frankfurt. A federation of European central banks would be likely to coalesce into a single bank (with regional branches) at a single center. Friedman regards a system of linked national central banks as an "utter mirage" (1992, p. 255). Goodhart observes that the centripetal tendency in banking has been kept at bay only in Canada and Scotland (1989, p. 35), but, I would add, not for long.

The site of the eventual European central bank is partly a locational, partly a financial, and partly a political question. In location, face-to-face communication requires easy transport, which in today's world means accessibility to a major airport. It is ironic that the Bank for International Settlements was located in Switzerland, at Basle, near the *Drei-Ecke* (three-corner) touching of the borders of France, Germany, and Switzerland, because in 1930 Basle was a major rail center. Central bank travel by air began in 1931, when Hans Luther, president of the Reichsbank, flew from Berlin to Paris and London to beg for loans to save the mark. Even thirty years ago, one heard remarks such as: "if it is not within forty-five minutes of a jet airport, it doesn't exist."

In finance, the major centers among which a choice of a European center would be made are London, Paris, Frankfort, Brussels, Milan, and, if Switzerland were to join the community, Zurich and possibly Geneva. London, with the skills and despite a limited pool of domestic savings, has gradually emerged as the leading center for Eurocurrency dealings. The capital markets of Frankfurt and Milan are underdeveloped, in the German case because universal banks and thick capital markets are substitutes, not complements. A Deutsche Bank economist also notes that West Germany was slow in deregulating and even imposed a withholding tax on interest and dividends in 1988, to repeal it a year later following a capital outflow. The German transfer tax was scheduled to be abolished on 1 January 1992, but this may be too late (Walter, 1990). The same observer notes that Paris has been making strenuous efforts to remove restrictions in order to attract financial business and that Frankfurt has a major advantage over London and Paris in that its employees speak foreign languages. In addition, it is likely to have charisma as the seat of the EMS, but if London came fully into the EMS, it would probably end up as the pivotal financial center (ibid., esp. pp. 150, 154–55).

An economist is not entitled to a guess about the politics. The location of the European central bank may well be traded for other prestigious advantages, or it may, in a deadlock among major contenders, be awarded to an outside candidate, such as Amsterdam or Brussels.

Would a European central bank be subject to close governmental supervision and direction? Here the issue seems to be joined between the Germans, who pride themselves on the independence of the Bundesbank, and most of the other members. The case for independence in Germany came from two disastrous inflations in and after World Wars I and II and the widely held view that politicians are prone to favor the inflation tax over a tax that has to be legislated. The argument against is that all national policy is essentially political, and that just as war is too important to be left to the generals, so monetary policy should not be handed over to unaccountable bankers. While legislative requirements differ substantially, practice more nearly converges. Those central banks nominally under the direct supervision of governments rarely are directed how to behave, and those ostensibly independent are not unmindful of political pressures (Toniolo, ed., 1988, with papers on a number of European central banks; and *New York Times,* 1991, pp. D1, D5).

The issue, as so much in this question, turns on prestige and matters of sovereignty. Despite the view that monetary unification in Germany paved the way for political unification (Holtfrerich, 1989), I judge that the delicate balance of power in monetary policy between elected officials and appointed central banks cannot be settled until some time after political unification results in agreement on what powers are ceded from existing nations to the new Europe.

EASTERN EUROPE

The tearing down of the Berlin wall and the political and economic collapse of the Socialist bloc in Eastern Europe lie outside the scope of this work. They have relevance for it, however, to the extent that they have an impact on the political and economic unification of Western Europe. The key may lie in Germany, where *Ostpolitik*—German policy regarding its national unification and the necessity, as some see it, to stabilize countries to the east, and aid the former Soviet Union to ensure the withdrawal of its troops from Germany—may divert the attention of the German authorities away from the completion of the economic and monetary union on schedule—the Common Market by 1 January 1993 and the monetary union by 1 January 2000.

Poland, Hungary, and Czechoslovakia want to join the Common Market, as Spain, Portugal, and Greece have done, with concessions regarding the speed with which they take up member obligations but without greatly diluting the unity of the West and North. The European Free Trade Area of Norway, Sweden, Finland, Austria, and Switzerland is negotiating to join the customs union, creating another list of issues requiring resolution. Width is likely to subtract from depth. The outcome can be perceived only dimly. Historical evolution, it seems to me, however, is likely to move in the direction of delay in meeting the rigorous schedules laid down but not to foreclose the relentless movement to unification.

SUGGESTED SUPPLEMENTARY READING

deCecco and Giovanni (eds.) (1989), *A European Central Bank.*

Fair and de Boisseu (eds.) (1990), *Financial Institutions in Europe Under New Competitive Conditions.*

Revista di Politica Economia (1991), Building the New Europe—I—Single Market and Monetary Unification in the EEC Countries.

Toniolo (ed.) (1988), *Central Banks Independence in Historical Perspective.*

25

Europe in the World Financial System

> The unity we need now must be a unity based on explicit treaty and voluntary agreements. But the idea is the same. Ultimately the world will see one *code de commerce*, and one money as the symbol of it.
>
> We are, as yet, very distant from so perfect an age. . . . I fear the attempt to found a universal money is not possible now; I think it would fail because of its size. But I believe we could get as far as two moneys, two leading commercial currencies, which nations could one by one join as they chose, and which, in after time, might be combined; and although this may fall short of theoretical perfection, to the English mind it may seem the more probable for that very reason.
>
> (Bagehot, *A Universal Money, Collected Works,* 1868 [1978], Vol. 11, pp. 65–66).

INTERNATIONAL MONEY

Earlier chapters have traced the shift of international money from the bezant of the Middle Ages to the Venetian ducat and Florentine florin in the Renaissance and then to the Spanish peso, Dutch gulden, British pound sterling, and American dollar, with various challenges from the French livre (later franc) and the German thaler (later mark). In the typical case, a given market became an entrepôt trading in goods; the country grew rich and strong; finance elsewhere used the national currency as an international one. At some stage the leading trading country slowed down in foreign commerce and picked up in finance, typically lending abroad to earn interest and profits to help pay for its imports. There may or may not have been a state purpose behind these transitions. It has been widely held that at the heyday of sterling, the British government clung to laissez-faire and did not intervene in furthering the interests of the City beyond providing the Royal Navy to patrol the seas. The same was not true of England in the seventeenth and eighteenth centuries when vigorous policies such as the Navigation Acts were put in place to overcome its commercial rival, Amsterdam.

World trade and finance typically have a center or core. Fernand Braudel and Immanuel Wallerstein write of a center and the periphery and of the need from time to time to "recenter" world trade and finance (Braudel, 1979 [1984], ch. 1; Wallerstein, 1980, chs. 3, 6). The financial world order evolves in hierarchical form, with a leading, primary, or, in political science verbiage, hegemonic state at the top or center. Transitions from one nation's primacy to that of another were often the result of war. Even when war was not directly involved in recentering, on occasion it hastened the decline of one economy and the rise of another, as World Wars I and II did for British with its pound sterling and the United States with the dollar.

The transition from sterling to the dollar was extended in depression, as Britain was unable and the United States unwilling to take on the roles that fall to the lot of the leading economic power, especially the maintenance of open markets for goods and serving as a lender of last resort in finance. The question posed by the weakness of the dollar since about 1968 and the gradual development of the European ecu, if it should reach completion, is, What next? A place must be found in the equation, too, for the Japanese yen.

THE STERLING STANDARD

Sterling had the advantage as international money in the nineteenth century in that it appeared to be something quite different and objective from a national money taking over an international role—the gold standard with more or less agreed rules. The dollar standard in turn was disguised as the Bretton Woods agreement among the nations of the world. Studies of the gold standard in recent years have questioned how it really worked (deCecco, 1984; Bordo and Schwartz, eds., 1984; Goodhart, 1989, chs. 14, 15). It remains remarkable, however, that Bank of England official reserves were very small and yet supported a large volume of claims on sterling. Confidence was the key, and confidence depended less on the visible reserves behind short-term claims on London than on Britain's position as the workshop of the world and the British Navy as guardian of the world's peace. In the period from 1873 to 1914, Britain overloaned abroad twice—once in the five or so years leading up to the Baring crisis of 1890 and again from 1910 to 1913 in the manic boom of foreign bond issues that was interrupted by the outbreak of war.

The City held the monetary reserves of much of the rest of the world, as liabilities, including especially those of the commonwealth and the colonies with currency boards. Some viewed the latter arrangement as Britain borrowing from its disadvantaged colonies, but that is not the only possible interpretation. The colonies borrowed long term as well. Britain loaned long and borrowed short, in classical financial intermediation as a—or should one say "the"—world financial center. A financial center lends long and borrows short, as the City did for the rest of the United Kingdom and the world, without difficulty so long as confidence is maintained and the lending is not recklessly overdone. The system is hierarchical, not symmetrical, pluralistic, or federal.

THE DECLINE OF THE DOLLAR

There is no need to recite the emergence of the dollar and the Bretton Woods system at the end of World War II, as the world, led by the United States, sought to correct the errors of the 1920s and 1930s. More relevant to the question of a new world financial order is to record the decline of the dollar, which followed from a loss of confidence and from a critical mistake in monetary policy.

The United States paid little attention to its balance of payments in the 1950s. The current account was positive, and if the surplus was exceeded by foreign aid

and loans by an amount running $2 billion to $4 billion a year, the amounts served
to provide liquidity to the rest of the world as the dollars piled up in New York. The
system worked well. Major European currencies became convertible into dollars in
1958 when the extended transitional period of the Bretton Woods institutions
finally ended. At that point, however, economists redefined balance-of-payments
deficits to cover not only losses of gold but also increases in U.S. short-term liabilities to foreigners. No account was taken of U.S. short-term claims on the rest of
the world, much less long-term claims. It was implicitly assumed that foreign claims
on the dollar were likely to be encashed momentarily, while U.S. short-term assets
were illiquid. On the "liquidity" definition, the United States had been in balance-
of-payments deficit as early as 1951 or 1952, at a time when it felt on top of the
world.

At the end of the 1950s, the world impression was that the dollar was strong, and
as late as 1971 a political scientist, Susan Strange of the London School Economics,
still regarded the dollar as the "top currency" (1971). Confidence was beginning to
ebb, however. In the late 1950s, Robert Triffin worried about what would happen
to world liquidity when the United States corrected its "liquidity deficit," and new
gold production went into hoarding. He argued for replacing both gold and dollars
in international reserves with a synthetic unit of account, worries that finally
resulted in the creation by the IMF of the Special Drawing Right (SDR) (Triffin,
1958). Others countered that the liquidity definition of equilibrium in the U.S. balance of payments was strongly misleading. Banking centers were not, in this view,
in deficit when they lent long and borrowed short, providing liquidity to the rest of
the world. The United States, in effect, was acting as a bank, and banks were not in
disequilibrium when their deposits rose each year along with loans (Despres, Kindleberger, and Salant, 1965 [1981]). This view made a solid point but was too optimistic; along with increases in loans and deposits, banks need a parallel rise of
reserves. Given the loss of confidence, however, new gold was sold to hoarders, and
central banks took additions to reserves in and even converted dollars into gold—
a case of Gresham's law at work. Various central banks withdrew from the gold pool
set up in London in 1960 to hold down the price of gold. The French government
undertook to convert dollars into gold as a means of disciplining the United States,
until it found itself in need of dollars to support the franc, and, hesitant to sell gold
for dollars, undertook official borrowing of dollars in the Euro-bond market (Kindleberger, 1972 [1985]). In 1968 the United States broke up the gold pool and
adopted a two-tier system for gold, permitting the private price to rise above the
official $35.00 an ounce price at which central banks ostensibly traded—although
strong pressure was exerted against foreign central banks changing dollars for gold,
and a number of financial instruments with exchange guarantees were made available by the U.S. Treasury to official dollar holders to forestall gold purchases. As in
the summer of 1931, the smaller countries of Europe, led by Belgium, the Netherlands, and Switzerland, went ahead in converting dollars to gold, leading to the
Connolly shock of August 1971 under which the secretary of the treasury imposed
a 10 percent import surtax in an effort to devalue the currency, a move finally
agreed to at the Smithsonian Conference in Washington, D.C., in December. The
United States raised the gold price first to $38.00 and then to $42.50 as a concession

to the French and widened the permissible range of fluctuation against the dollar, under IMF auspices, from 1½ to 2¼ percent. None of these measures succeeded in buttressing confidence in the dollar, and in February 1973 that currency was set free to float. European dependence on the dollar in these circumstances was seen as a source of weakness, and the movement to a European currency—an economic and monetary union—began to gather urgency.

THE BLUNDER OF 1970–71

Contributing to the breakdown of the Bretton Woods system in August 1971 was an enormous outflow of dollars to the Eurocurrency market in 1970 and the first months of 1971, the consequence of an important mistake in monetary policy. The reelection campaign of President Nixon was scheduled for 1972, and his administration was understandably anxious to have the American economy prosperous by then. As a contribution to this goal, the Federal Reserve system in 1970 started to lower interest rates, at a time, however, when the Bundesbank was seeking to restrict inflation in West Germany by raising interest rates there. If the two money markets had been completely separate, separate policies could have been carried out, but they were joined through the Eurodollar market. Dollars flowed from New York to London with its higher rates, and German borrowers, pinched by still higher rates, refinanced outstanding loans through the Eurodollar market in London. The dollars borrowed there were sold for Deutschemarks to the Bundesbank, which redeposited them in the Eurodollar market. The more that German borrowers took up in London, the more dollars flowed there from New York. The liquidity-definition balance-of-payments deficit of the United States rose from a $2–4 billion a year average in the 1960s to $20 billion in 1970 and $30 billion in 1971. The gap between U.S. and German interest rates was not closed until March 1971 (Emminger, 1986, pp. 174–75). By this time, world banks, awash with funds, started looking for new lending outlets. This initiated the boom in syndicated bank loans to sovereign states, especially in Latin America, well before the November 1973 price rise of the Organization of Petroleum Exporting Countries that led to so-called recycling of Arab profits from oil deposited in Eurodollars and re-lent to oil-consuming countries. The boom in lending went largely unnoticed in the 1970s as trusting bankers maintained that sovereign states do not repudiate their loans. The awakening occurred only in August 1982 when Mexico failed to meet its interest payments.

AFTER THE FALL

Floating of the dollar from the spring of 1973 surprised economists in a number of respects. In the first place, those whose knowledge went back to the 1930s expected that flexible exchange rates would inhibit capital flows because of exchange risk. This proved not to be the case. Quantity turned out to be more important than price. If one needed a substantial amount of capital—for example, $250 million was a substantial amount of money in 1973 (though not today)—it was necessary to borrow dollars (Kindleberger, 1975 [1981]).

Second, economists thought that the floating dollar would lose the role of international unit of account, standard of deferred payment, store of value, and means of payment. While the dollar's functions as international money in these capacities were nibbled away at the edges, it was not displaced in them for lack of a satisfactory alternative. The SDR of the IMF planners was designed as an addition to central bank reserves, not for spending; central banks that drew on the fund did so in national currencies that were spendable. Some economists hoped that the SDR would replace gold and dollars entirely in central bank reserves and in time would be held in private bank accounts, spent and received as international money, as is now planned for the ecu in Europe at the end of the century. That never happened. The original purpose of the unit—to add to world liquid reserves—was seen to be remedied by borrowing national currencies, especially the dollar. The initial creations and allocations of SDRs in 1968 were not repeated.

That leaves other national currencies. The Deutschemark and the Japanese yen have been studied as international currencies, with the conclusion that, until recently, neither country envies the role and both have discouraged the international use of their currencies. A study of the Deutschemark, in fact, contains an appendix of West German measures to restrict capital inflows, with strong measures beginning in the early 1970s, and only very gradual relaxation in the 1980s (Tavlas, 1991, pp. 36–37). An unofficial study of the yen as an international currency notes that Japan has experienced massive outflows of capital but imposes limits on the use of the yen by foreigners (Tavlas and Ozeki, 1991). In neither case has there been normal international banking, that is, financial intermediation in the form of lending long and borrowing short by allowing the proceeds to remain on deposit in local currency until used. As Table 25.1 shows, while the dollar has lost some of its dominance over national currencies used in bank lending, external bond issues, and Eurocurrency deposits, it is still used more than all other leading currencies together, and four times, more or less, the rate of use of the leading competitor in each instance.

A leading Japanese civil servant who later became the president of the Bank of Tokyo predicted in 1986 that Tokyo would become an international market using mainly the currency of its home country and would undoubtedly take over part of the role played by the U.S. dollar. He added, however:

If history were to repeat itself, America's rapid accumulation of external liabilities today would be pushing it toward a lesser role as a key-currency nation, and Japan—together with the Federal Republic of Germany, no doubt—would be moving to the fore. The cycles of history, however, are more complex than this. Japan has neither the potential nor the inclination to take over the role of a key-currency nation. The same, I presume, is true of Germany. (Kashiwagi, 1986, pp. 7, 10)

One clue to the lack of challenge of the dollar's position is found in the fact that both Japan and Germany have helped fill the deficit in the U.S. balance of pay-

Table 25.1 Relative Currency Shares of External Assets, 1980s (percent)

Asset Type and Currency	1981–84(Avg)	1985	1986	1987	1988	1989
Shares of external bank loans						
Deutschemark	1.7	2.1	3.0	2.4	2.2	3.2
U.S. dollar	83.3	62.5	67.0	65.1	69.9	77.0
Pound sterling	3.1	3.4	6.4	14.7	14.1	6.4
Yen	5.9	18.5	16.1	10.8	5.6	5.3
Swiss franc	1.2	3.0	2.1	0.7	0.3	0.4
ecu	1.3	7.1	2.2	2.4	2.8	4.6
Other	3.5	3.4	3.2	3.9	5.1	3.1
Denominations of external bond issues						
Deutschemark	6.3	8.5	8.0	8.0	10.1	6.4
U.S. dollar	63.2	54.0	53.9	38.8	41.2	51.9
Pound sterling	3.4	4.0	4.6	7.8	9.4	6.8
Yen	5.7	9.1	10.4	13.7	8.4	8.3
Swiss franc	14.7	11.3	10.7	12.9	11.1	7.5
ecu	1.7	5.2	3.4	4.0	4.9	5.2
Other	6.7	7.9	9.0	14.8	14.9	13.9
Denominations of Eurocurrency deposits						
Deutschemark	11.4	11.4	12.8	14.2	13.3	13.9
U.S. dollar	74.0	67.9	63.5	58.2	60.1	59.7
Pound sterling	1.4	2.0	2.1	2.8	3.4	3.1
Yen	1.8	3.4	4.5	5.8	5.5	5.5
Swiss franc	5.8	6.4	7.2	7.7	5.4	4.9
ecu	0.5	2.6	2.6	2.8	3.0	3.2
Other	5.2	6.2	7.2	8.4	9.2	9.7

Source: Tavlas (1991, p. 32). Various minor qualifications are ignored.

ments by buying U.S. Treasury securities, but they have been content to do so in dollars, and accept the foreign exchange risk, rather than insist on lending only in their own currencies.

THE ECU

If the ecu becomes the single European currency on schedule—perhaps realists might insist, the Deutschemark disguised as the currency of all Europe, as the Prussian thaler became the German mark of 1871—what then? Will the ecu outstrip the yen in international dealings and displace the dollar as international money? Much depends on whether the Europe of 2000 is bent on a prestigious role, as the French have been, or more like Germany after its two defeats, content to be a follower of the leadership of others. German ambitions may focus on *Ostpolitik* more than a policy of building the new United States of Europe, more deeply concerned with the national identity than with the *gloire* that consistently motivates the French.

In other publications I have discussed the future of world finance, whether the ultimate decline of the dollar, slow or fast, will be replaced by new national currency taking over, as sterling took over from the gulden, and the dollar from sterling; if so, which one, and whether Japan or Europe will provide the international public goods of open markets, steady capital flows, international money, and a lender of last resort; whether the habits of cooperation among leading nations—the Group of 3, or 5, or 7, or 10—will continue to manage world finance cooperatively in a regime, as the political scientists use the term, left over from the days of U.S. leadership; whether the world will break up into dollar, yen, and ecu blocs; or whether, as in 1918 to 1939, the world will stumble along economically until another, perhaps unsuspected country, emerges as the economic and financial leader (Kindleberger, 1991c). There are those who feel confident that the United States will remain the world's political, economic, and perhaps financial leader (Nye, 1990; Nau, 1989); others see at least relative decline as inevitable (P. Kennedy, 1987). In my judgment, the latter have the better of the argument, although little in economics is inevitable.

When it comes to a new international money to replace the dollar, if it be replaced within the near-term future, I find it impossible to fasten on a firm prediction—whether a universal currency such as Bagehot predicted a century and a quarter ago, continued cooperation under the habits built up under Bretton Woods, and then perhaps a revival of Europe that brings it back to the world eminence it enjoyed in the three centuries before the twentieth. The safest prediction is that there will be another transitional period, like that between the world wars, after which a new continental or national leadership will emerge. Chaos theory and evolution hold that mutations are unpredictable. There may well be chaos. One can hope that there will be no major wars among contestants for dominance; that game is not worth the candle. There will be crises, and surprises.

Glossary

acceptance. A bill of exchange, or draft, becomes an acceptance when the payer, on whom the bill is drawn, "accepts" it by affixing his signature, in effect recognizing the obligation.

accommodation bills. Bills drawn by an individual without an underlying trade transaction. The payer accepts, allowing the payee to discount the bill, as an accommodation. It is, in effect, merely a promissory note.

agency costs. Expense undertaken by employer to ensure that employees (agents) take care of employer's and not their own interests.

agio. A premium above the normal long-run price, especially in gold and foreign exchange.

annuity. A contract under which an investor receives a stipulated sum each year for life in exchange for a capital payment.

arbitrage. Simultaneous purchase and sale, normally in different places, or currencies, sometimes for delivery at different times, with no price risk.

asiento. Spanish word for right to undertake specified trade.

Aski-marks. Marks usable only for limited purposes, from *A*usland-*S*onder-*K*onto für *I*nlandskredit (Special Foreign Accounts for Internal Credit).

assignats. Literally assigned objects; French money issued during the Revolution, in which bank notes were "assigned" (at first) to particular parcels of land taken over from the Crown, the nobility, or the Church by the Revolutionary government.

average. *See* general average.

balance-of-payments school. Proponents of view that inflation is caused by need to make payments abroad, such as subsidies or reparations leading to depreciation of the currency, and thereby rising foreign trade prices, which spread to internal prices.

bank money. Transferable deposits in banks, originally based on deposits of coin, that usually traded at a premium over ordinary money (coin) because they were redeemable in coin of uniform and high-quality weight and fineness.

bank rate. In Britain the discount rate of the Bank of England, used historically as the central instrument of monetary policy.

banking school. Strand of thought in first half of nineteenth-century Britain, believing that it was not inflationary and deflationary to allow the money supply to rise and fall with the rise and fall of production and trade.

banque d'affaires. Literally, a business bank, French term for a type of bank that made long-term loans to, and often held ownership in, industry, as contrasted with commercial or joint stock banks that made only short-term advances, at least in theory.

biens nationaux. Literally national goods or assets, land and buildings seized in the French Revolution from the king, the nobility, and the Church, and used as backing for the issuance of the *assignats* (q.v.), and later as an object of speculation.

bill of exchange. Evidence of indebtedness, drawn by the seller on the buyer in a commercial transaction, sometimes accepted by the buyer, and sold or discounted by the seller of the goods to collect his money in advance of the time of payment by the buyer.

billion. Billion in this book follows American usage and means one thousand million.

billon. Metal for making coin with a minimum of silver and a strong adulteration of copper.

bimetallism. A standard under which money is related to two precious or semiprecious metals, usually gold and silver, or occasionally silver and copper.

BIS. Bank for International Settlements. An international bank established under the Young Plan of 1930 to assist in transferring German reparations to the Allies. It has developed into a club of central bankers, and a source of expert help in European monetary matters and carefully produced statistics on the Eurodollar market and financial questions generally.

blackening. Adulteration of silver money with copper.

bottomry. A loan made on the security of a ship that is forgiven if the ship is lost—a form of insurance.

bourse. An organized market or exchange, housed in a building or regular meeting place, for trading securities, and, in some countries, foreign exchange (q.v.)

"call up." Under bimetallism (q.v.), when coins of one metal are overvalued and those of the other undervalued, adjustment is possible either by lowering the metal content of overvalued coins, which is "crying down," or raising the denomination of undervalued coins, which is "calling up."

cambi. Italian for bill of exchange or foreign exchange (q.v.)

CEEC—Committee for European Economic Cooperation. Formed in the summer of 1947 that drew up the program of European Economic Recovery presented to the United States for funding under the Marshall Plan.

chains of discounts. A method of credit expansion in which *A* draws bills on *B, B* on *C, C* on *D,* etc., and all discount such bills with banks. These are accommodation or finance bills (q.v.), that is, promissory notes rather than bills arising from commercial transactions. The Dutch expression for the practice is *Wisselruiterij,* the German *Wechselreiterei.*

Chamber of Justice. A special court in sixteenth-, seventeenth- and eighteenth-century France after the end of a war or the death of a monarch, to examine individuals who might have profited unduly in the recent past and to levy fines on them.

City, the City of London. An incorporated borough of Greater London, which contains the financial district in commerce, banking, insurance, etc.

clearing. The process of cancelling offsetting evidences of indebtedness, such as checks, notes, trade payments, etc., so as to economize on payments in money.

commandite. A silent partnership in which, as a rule, one or more partners provides the entrepreneurship, and another, the silent partner, the capital. The word is French. The Italian word is *commenda.*

conditionality. The attachment of conditions to making a loan, sometimes on how the loan is to be spent, sometimes on other action to be taken by the borrower, such as balancing the national budget, depreciating the exchange rate, etc. The lender is often thought by the borrower to be unduly harsh or political in the conditions attached.

consols. An abbreviation for "consolidated" British debt, which is borrowed in perpetuity.

conversion. The process of calling in debt at one rate of interest when permitted by the terms of the loan, and replacing it with lower-interest obligations, when permitted by the conditions of the capital market.

convertible debentures. Bonds that can be converted into equity shares under conditions specified when the bonds are issued.

counterpart funds. Monies obtained by post–World War II governments receiving foreign aid from selling the goods received in their national markets. Terms of aid may specify how the aid-receiving country can use such funds, or subject them to the aiding institution or country's approval.

court banker. A banker who lends especially to kings, princes, aristocracy, etc.

"cry down." *See* call up.

currency school. A group of financial and economic thinkers in Britain who started out in 1810 with the view that the depreciation of sterling (or the premium on gold) was the result of overissuance of Bank of England notes. In due course, the currency school stood for the position embodied in the Bank Act of 1844 that the bank note circulation should be limited to a small fixed amount, plus whatever gold might be held in the Bank of England.

debenture. A long-term, fixed-amount debt in the form of a bond.

deposit bank. This term is used both for the early public banks of the sixteenth century in Italy and Spain and the seventeenth century in Holland, Germany, and Sweden, which issued bank notes against deposits of coin on the basis of assayed values; and for the large private banks in the second half of the nineteenth century in France and Germany, which acquired depositors through deposits of bank notes, but also through loans.

[to] discount. Selling a claim on a third party to a bank or discount house, which deducts the interest in advance.

diversification. An attempt to reduce risk by spreading wealth among a variety of assets.

douceur. Literally, a sweetener. An extra payment to obtain special consideration or to avoid charges of usury.

draft. An order by a seller, directing the buyer to pay under certain (agreed) conditions. *See* bill of exchange.

dry exchange. A bill of exchange (q.v.) drawn as if it were based on international trade but actually permitting payment in the local country. Designed to evade charges of usurious dealings. In reality, a promissory note at interest.

ECE—Economic Commission for Europe. The first regional commission of the United Nations established at Geneva in 1947.

ecu—European Currency Unit. A composite currency formed under the European Monetary System established 1 January 1979, with the acronym having the same spelling as the old French gold coin, the écu, equal to 3 livres.

EEA—Exchange Equalization Account. A fund established in Britain in 1932 to prevent the pound sterling from appreciating, to sterilize hot-money movements into and out of Britain so that they would not affect the domestic money base, and to enable the authorities to intervene in the foreign exchange market without disclosing their operations as, for example, would have been the case if the Bank of England undertook the intervention.

EEC—The European Economic Community or European Common Market. Established in 1957 under the Treaty of Rome. Originally consisting of France, Western Germany, Italy, Belgium, the Netherlands, and Luxembourg, it was enlarged in 1973 to include the United Kingdom, Denmark, and Ireland.

EMCF—European Monetary Cooperation Fund. An entity established under the European Monetary Union in 1970 among the Six to manage a part of the central bank reserves of the members. Usually referred to by the acronym of its initials in French, FECOM (q.v.).

EMS—European Monetary System. The system designed to replace the EMU beginning 1 January 1979, with a parallel currency, issued by the European Monetary Fund alongside national currencies.

EMU—Economic and Monetary Union. The proposed highest stage of economic integration of the EEC under the Werner Plan of 1970.

ENI—Ente Nazionale Idrocarburi. The Italian state monopoly in oil.

EPC—European Parallel Currency. *See* ecu and EMS.

EPU—European Payments Union. A clearing fund established in June 1950, under the European Recovery Program, to prevent discrimination in favor of the dollar and against European currencies.

EUA—European Unit of Account. A basket of various European currencies, the mix of which has been altered from time to time, originally used for the issuance of bonds.

Eurodollar. Originally dollar deposits in banks in Europe, including the branches there of American banks. More recently, dollars anywhere in the world outside the United States and, more generally, a term used for Eurocurrencies, which are deposits in a given country denominated in any currency but that legally used there.

Exchequer bills. *See* Treasury bills.

fair. A gathering of merchants twice or four times a year in the Middle Ages, originally primarily to buy and sell goods but, in a number of cases, broadened to trade in bills of exchange (q.v.), coin, and bullion and to borrow and lend internationally.

[to] **farm** (as in particular taxes). To pay the entity owed a given tax a fixed sum in exchange for being allowed to keep all the taxes one can collect.

FECOM—Fonds Européen pour Coopération Monétaire. *See* EMCF.

finance bills. *See* accommodation bills.

financial intermediation. The act of simultaneously borrowing and lending, undertaken by a person, financial institution such as a bank, or even a country, which lends through foreign bonds and holds foreign deposits, and sometimes even selling foreign bonds abroad to the nationals of the borrowing country.

financier. In eighteenth-century France, this word, literally translatable as a financier, meant something much more. A *financier* was one who had bought an *office,* that is a post created by the king and endowed with a commission, that was typically involved either in paying the king's expenditures or receiving his revenues. The *financiers* held these monies for considerable periods of time and invested them for their personal benefit while they were in possession.

Fisher effect. The tendency of the rate of interest to fall with falling commodity prices, and to rise when prices are rising, so as, in effect, to index interest payments. Named after the economist Irving Fisher.

forced circulation. Repudiation of a government or central bank obligation to redeem paper notes in coin, so that the notes are obliged to remain in circulation. In Italian, *corso forzoso.*

foreign exchange. Initially a bill of exchange (q.v.) providing payment in foreign money. In due course, the expression came to mean all types of foreign means of payment except specie (q.v.).

forward market. Market in which futures (q.v.) are traded.

Fronde. The *Fronde* (literally "slingshot') was an uprising in the middle of the seventeenth century in France by lesser nobility against the more exalted, especially *financiers* (q.v.) and *officiers* (q.v.).

futures. A contract to buy or sell a financial asset (or a commodity) in the future at a price fixed in the contract. Traded in forward or futures markets (q.v.).

general average. An ancient practice of levying a charge against ship and cargo to pay damage to any cargo hurt in the interest of the voyage as a whole, such as a deck cargo jettisoned to lighten the vessel. The contrast is with "particular average," accidents to a cargo or ship unrelated to the safety of the voyage, where the loss must be borne by the particular cargo or its insurer.

Gibson paradox. Another name for the Fisher effect (q.v.).

GmbH—Gesellschaft mit beschränkende Haftung. A German company with limited liability.

gratifications. Bonuses given for outstanding performance, especially by Napoleon to his generals.

Gresham's law. A generalization, erroneously named after Sir Thomas Gresham, Queen Elizabeth's exchanger at Antwerp, that bad money, that is, especially coin that is clipped, rubbed, sweated, or overvalued at the mint, drives good money (that is, undervalued) out of circulation. The mechanism is that those receiving overvalued money spend it as rapidly as possible, whereas undervalued money is hoarded, melted down, or exported to foreign countries where its value is higher.

Haftungsgemeinschaft. Literally, a community of liabilities. An undertaking by a group to guarantee the liabilities of a bank or firm in difficulty.

hyperinflation. Inflation of prices that picks up speed and becomes explosive.

IBRD—International Bank for Reconstruction and Development. The World Bank established at Bretton Woods in 1944, located in Washington, D.C., that makes loans to assist developing countries.

IMF—International Monetary Fund. An institution established at Bretton Woods in 1944, along with the IBRD (q.v.), also located in Washington, D.C., that assists countries in payment difficulties by furnishing credits.

IMI—Istituto Mobiliare Italiano. Literally, Italian Security Institute. Established by the Italian government in January 1933, to assist business by furnishing credit.

intermediation. The act of standing between borrowers and lenders, by borrowing from the latter and lending to the former, for the purpose of bridging time preference (the lenders want to lend short, and the borrowers to borrow long), or risk (the lenders do not trust the credit of the borrower, preferring that of the intermediary). Applied typically to banks, but in early European financial history to individuals, including notaries, lawyers, financiers, and rich men.

investment bank. A bank engaged in making long-term loans to industry and/or in underwriting security issues for such firms in the capital market.

IRI—Istituto per la Recostruzione Industriale. Literally, Institute for Industrial Reconstruction. A fund of government credit, established in January 1933, in Italy to take over frozen loans previously assumed by the government or in the hands of the banks. Patterned initially after the Reconstruction Finance Corporation (RFC) in the United States. Whereas the RFC was liquidated, it has remained active and is actively engaged in managing Italian industry.

joint-stock company. British term for a corporation with limited liability.

juros. Perpetual bonds denominated in pesos, issued by the Spanish monarchy in the sixteenth and seventeenth centuries when they could not meet their obligations in silver under *asientos.*

Keynesianism. The view that there may be times when national markets will, of themselves, fall on depressed circumstances, and that an active policy of government spending, sometimes stretched to include bank expansion, can usefully increase income and employment and stimulate industry, agriculture, and trade.

Kipper- und Wipperzeit. A period in Germany and Poland at the beginning of the Thirty Years' War, 1618–48, when mints competitively produced very debased coinage.

Lastenausgleich. Literally, equalization of burdens. A device in West Germany as part of the Monetary Reform of 1948 for imposing a 50 percent mortgage on real property and equities, to bring their owners into a more equitable relationship with owners of debt (such as Reich bonds), whose claims were written off by 90 percent.

legal tender. Money designated by the government as acceptable in payment of all debts, public and private.

lender of last resort. The institution, usually government or central bank, that stands ready in financial crisis to lend to banks, or occasionally business firms, that are in long-run sound condition but are in immediate need of liquidity to meet their obligations.

lottery loan. A loan in which some bonds, chosen by lot, are paid off more handsomely than others, either at higher rates of return or sooner.

Ltd.—Limited. A firm with limited liability in the United Kingdom.

Macmillan gap. A discontinuity, discovered in the Report of the Macmillan Committee of 1931, between small amounts of capital that business is able to raise in local markets and substantial amounts that are efficiently dealt with by issuance of securities in the London capital market. In-between-sized firms were believed to have great difficulty in obtaining capital.

mercantilism. A broad and somewhat vague nationalistic school of thought that believed in a positive balance of payments as an objective of policy—hence, subsidization of exports and protection against imports, accumulation of gold and silver, and, more positively, elimination of internal barriers to trade.

merchant bank. Private banks that typically developed from mercantile operations, often retained dealing in commodities along with money, and usually restricted themselves to a small, specialized clientele.

mixed bank. The Italian expression for what the Germans called a "universal bank," that is, a bank that not only made short-term loans but also bought bonds and shares from industrial companies and often voted the shares of clients that they held in safekeeping.

monetarism. The school of thought that believes that the amount of money in a country or system is a main determinant of economic activity, and especially of the price level.

money illusion. The mistaken belief when prices are changing that money amounts, such as money incomes, represent real incomes.

munitionnaire. A supplier of munitions (or other equipment and food) to the armed services under contract.

nabob. An English civil servant with the East India Company who acquired wealth in the service and then returned to England.

numéraire. A somewhat ambiguous word meaning "cash" or "ready money" to economic historians, and the "unit of account" (q.v.) in which prices and values are reckoned to economists.

OECD—Organization of Economic Cooperation and Development. The successor to the OEEC (q.v.), enlarged to include the United States, Canada, Japan, and Australia, and evolving as the major economic organization for developed countries and their problems, including those vis-à-vis developing countries.

OEEC—Organization for European Economic Cooperation. The organization formed by seventeen European states receiving aid under the European Recovery Program of 1948 to supervise cooperative recovery efforts, including those to eliminate discrimination in trade.

officier. French word for a holder or purchaser of an office. *See financier.*

OPEC—Organization of Petroleum Exporting Countries. An organization of the major oil-exporting countries, originally formed to resist falling world prices of oil and, ultimately, in 1973 and 1979, pushing through major price increases.

optimum currency area. The concept that there is some optimum size of an area that should have a single currency and that some areas are too big to have but one money, others too small. Economists differ as to what constitutes the optimum.

parallel money. A money issued by a group of countries together, along with their separate national monies, with the intention of encouraging competition among the various monies for public confidence and use.

particular average. *See* general average.

Physiocrats. A school of thought in France and Italy in the eighteenth century that believed that the strength of any economy lay in agriculture and that the agricultural sector ought to be encouraged, especially by eliminating restrictions on exports. Its motto was *"laisser faire, laisser passer,"* (leave them alone and let their goods pass).

PLM. The French railroad from Paris to Lyons and Marseilles.

protest. If a bill of exchange (q.v.) is not paid by the payee, its holder "protests" it and seeks payment from the drawer or from any intermediate party that has endorsed it.

PTT. Post, telephone, and telegraph.

public bank. The public deposit banks of the seventeenth century that accepted deposits of all sorts of coin of varying weights and fineness and issued uniform "bank money" against them.

public good. A good provided to a whole society, the consumption of which by any member does not significantly diminish the amount available for others. Illustrations include national defense, lighthouses, effective macroeconomic policy, sound money.

quantity theory of money. The belief that changes in the quantity of money will be reflected primarily in changes in prices, since the volume of output and employment fluctuates only within narrow limits around some "natural rate," and the velocity of money is fixed in the longer run.

rational expectations. Starting as an assumption used in econometrics to replace that which held that the forces at work yesterday will be at work today and tomorrow, by one which said that the market would respond to policy measures in ways that can be deduced from simple economic models, "rational expectations," as concept, has evolved into the view that market prices accurately reflect all the knowledge available to intelligent participants in the market.

real-bills doctrine. This is the view, held by the banking school (q.v.) and opposed by monetarists (*see* monetarism), that it is safe to allow the money supply to grow with the underlying volume of trade, that is, to lend on real bills (but not accommodation bills (q.v.) or finance bills) representing the movement of goods from seller to buyer.

recourse. When a bill or draft is protested because the payee is unable to make good on his commitment, the holder of the bills takes recourse to a previous holder or to the drawer. Some bills are discounted without recourse.

régie. An institution in which an agent works for a principal in managing property, collecting taxes, making payments, with all income above a stipulated salary going to the principal instead of a "tenant" or farmer, paying a fixed fee, taking the risk, and accepting the loss or profit from any shortfall or gain above that fee.

rente. An annual fixed payment, in perpetuity, sometimes for a lifetime, and sometimes subject to call and conversion (q.v.). The term is usually applied to the income, but sometimes to the capitalized sum at which the income is bought and sold.

rente viagère. A lifetime *rente* or annuity.

respondentia. Loan made on the cargo of a ship and forgiven if the cargo is lost at sea. Corresponds to bottomry (q.v.).

risk. Chance of loss owing to accident, failure of a debtor, change of an exchange rate, etc.

SA—Société anonyme. Literally, anonymous society. French for "incorporated."

SARL—société anonyme à responsibilité limitée. Joint stock company (q.v.) with limited liability.

scrivener. British equivalent of the French *notaire,* or notary. An official who recorded deeds, loans, mortgages, etc., and often evolved into a banker.

SDR—Special Drawing Rights. Form of international reserve issued by the IMF (q.v.) from time to time upon the votes of its directors to member countries and usable by them in settling international balances.

seignorage. The difference between the value of coin, or other form of money, and its cost of production, including (in the case of coin) both metal and minting expense. When the mint privilege was limited to the lord or *seigneur,* seignorage was a "right of the *seigneur.*" Modern banks are said to earn seignorage to the extent that interest on deposits and the costs of services rendered to depositors fall short of interest on loans by more than the normal rate of profit.

specie. Gold or silver money.

speculation. The purchase, or sale, of an asset, usually with borrowed money, for the purpose of making a profit from a change in its price, as contrasted with its purchase for income or use.

Sperrmarks. Literally, blocked marks. A bank balance in Germany after the Standstill Agreement of July 1931 (q.v.), that could be used only for limited designated purposes.

spot. A purchase or sale for immediate delivery, as opposed to one for term, forward, or future settlement.

Standstill Agreement. An agreement in July 1931 between Germany and countries with loans to, and deposits in, that country which recognized that Germany was unable immediately to repay such loans and deposits.

staple. A designated commodity in the Middle Ages, with staplers being merchants authorized to trade in that commodity, and stapling consisting of bringing such commodity to a central place for sale and distribution.

state theory of money. The view held by Georg F. Knapp, a German economist of the turn of the twentieth century, that money consisted only in what the state declared to be legal tender.

sterilize. The act of monetary authorities of preventing gains or losses of international reserves from affecting the money base of a country, by offsetting measures of monetary policy, such as selling central-bank security holdings in the open market when gold reserves rise, to prevent a rise in commercial-bank reserves.

structural inflation/deflation. The view that inflation is caused by rising prices ahead of increases in money, which follow and are endogenous, as opposed to the quantity theory of money (q.v.) that regards changes in money as exogenous. On the inflation side, the reasons may be increases in wages, short crops, depreciation of the exchange rate, or a slowdown in productivity. Structural deflation may arise from bumper harvests, and especially from currency appreciation that reduces prices and leads to bank failure and reductions of the money supply by that means.

swaps. A forward contract matched by a spot transaction (q.v.), or vice versa. This is a form of exchange arbitrage (q.v.), in which a purchase of foreign exchange (q.v.) for spot delivery, for example, is offset by a future sale at a fixed price, so that all exchange risk is eliminated.

symmetallism. A proposal that money be made of an amalgam of two metals, such as gold and silver, so as to moderate or eliminate the instability in bimetallism (q.v.) that arises from Gresham's law (q.v.).

tally. Evidence of debt used in early modern times, consisting of notched hazel sticks, split, with one piece given to the lender and the other retained by the borrower.

tap bills. British Treasury bills (q.v.) continuously available to government funds, and hence on tap, as contrasted with weekly public auctions of bills, for which buyers tender bids.

tax farming. The purchase of the right to collect a given tax for a stipulated sum, with the purchaser entitled to keep any amount collected above what is contracted to be paid.

tender bills. Treasury bills (q.v.) sold at weekly auctions or "tenders."

tontine. A form of annuity loan named after an Italian, Lorenzo Tonti, clerk to Cardinal Mazarin in France in the seventeenth century, under which the interest on a loan would be divided among surviving members of the lending group, until the death of the last, who before that time was receiving all the interest.

traité. Literally, treaty. A contract between the king of France and some *traitant,* specifying certain duties and the payment therefor.

tranche. Literally, slice. The segment of a loan issued at a particular time, place, in a particular currency, etc. Also the fraction of a line of credit, similarly divided.

transactions costs. The cost of carrying out particular transactions.

transfer problem. The process of transferring capital payments from one country to another in real terms, that is, in a net export surplus of goods and services, after starting with a financial transfer.

Treasury bills. Short-term Treasury borrowing by means of discounted bills, that is, the lender paying the capital sum less the rate of discount. The system was invented by Walter Bagehot in the late nineteenth century to replace Exchequer bills, where daily interest was added to an initial capital sum to the date of maturity.

unit of account. Function of money to serve as a yardstick for measuring prices, values, and wealth.

universal bank. *See* mixed bank.

universal money. Attempt in the nineteenth century to standardize the coins of various countries so as to make one set of coins acceptable in many countries.

usance. Customary delay between the drawing of a sight bill (bill of exchange, q.v., payable at sight) and the due date, depending upon the normal time for transporting the bill, which varied for pairs of cities depending upon the distance and means of transport between them.

usury. Charging of interest, later of excessive interest, forbidden by the Koran and by the European Church for varying lengths of time.

vendor shares. Shares of stock used to pay suppliers of inputs to companies in the process of formation, instead of cash.

Visa. The name given to two special Chambers of Justice in France in 1715 and 1720, the former after the death of Louis XIV, the latter after the collapse of the Banque Royale of John Law.

Währung. German for currency.

Wechsel. German for bill of exchange (q.v.) (Dutch *Wissel*).

Conversion Tables—
Equivalences and Exchange Rates
for Specified Coins and
Currencies at Specified Dates

The equivalences and exchange rates provided in these tables are intended to afford only an approximation of rates for conversion of various money sums mentioned in the text from time to time and should be used with the greatest caution. All currencies were debased throughout the present millennium against precious metal, as indicated by the fact that a pound sterling (and the French livre—almost exactly the same as a franc—and the Italian lira) was originally a troy pound of silver, worth today something on the order of $120. Moreover, there were frequent adjustments of separate state and principality currencies in terms of one or another precious metal, or both, and hence against one another. A proper study of monies and exchange rates before modern times calls for skills found in few economists and economic historians, and the information gathered here may be, in significant part, misunderstood by me. For separate discussions of individual currencies in the early part of our period, see Feaveryear (1963), Spooner (1972), and McCusker (1978).

Table 1 Dutch and Spanish Money, Sixteenth Century

Dutch Money (Sixteenth Century)	Spanish Money (Sixteenth Century)
1 Flemish pound = 20 schellings	1 peso = 450 maravedi
1 schelling = 12 grooten	1 ducat = 375 maravedi
1 Flemish pound = 5 Carolus gulden	1 piece of 8 (reals) (strong peso or piastre) = 272 maravedi
1 Carolus gulden = 20 stivers	1 real = 44 maravedi
1 Dutch ducat = 42 or 43 stivers	
1 Rhenish florin = 1 gold gulden	

Sources: Ehrenberg (1896 [1928], p. 12) for Dutch money, and Vilar (1969 [1976], pp. 78, 81, 130, 137, 138) for Spanish money.

Table 2 European Currencies, About 1760

English money	*Florentine money*
1 pound = 20 shillings	1 scudo = 7 lire
1 shilling = 12 pence	1 florin = 5 + lire

Table 2 European Currencies, About 1760 (cont.)

French money	*Imperial money* (Holy Roman Empire)
1 livre = 20 sous	1 reichsthaler = 2 gulden
1 sou = 12 deniers	1 gulden = 60 kreutzer
1 écu = 3 livres	1 groschen = 3 kreutzer
1 louis d'or = 23 livres	1 Imperial ducat = 4 gulden, 20 kreutzer

These currencies had the following equivalents in French livres:
1 English pound = 23 livres or 1 louis d'or
1 Florentine scudo = 5.68 livres
1 Imperial reichsthaler = 3 livres or 1 écu
1 Imperial ducat = 6.50 livres

Sources: de Roover (1966, p. 188), for Florentine money, and R. and E. Forster (eds.) (1969, p. 410).

Table 3 Approximate Equivalents of Silver Coins in English Pounds Sterling, About 1776

Amsterdam	*Hamburg*
ducatoon of 63 stuivers = £0.29	reichsthaler = £0.25
riksdaalder of 50 stuivers = £0.23	thaler = £0.13
leeuwendaalder of 42 stuivers = £0.19	mark = £0.07
gulden (florin) of 20 stuivers = £0.09	
Copenhagen	*France*
rigsdaler = £0.22	écu blanc of 6 livres = £0.26
krone (4-mark pieces) = £0.14	½ écu (crown of exchange) = £0.13
England	*Spain*
crown = £0.25	peso de plata antigua (piece of 8, 1728–72) = £0.23
shilling = £0.05	peseta de vellon of 4 reales = £0.05

Source: McCusker (1978, table 1.1, p. 10).

Table 4 Approximate Equivalents of Basic Gold Coins in English Pounds Sterling, About 1766

Amsterdam	*Hamburg*
ryder = £1.28	ducat = £0.47
ducat = £0.48	
Copenhagen	*France*
ducat of 4 marks = £0.48	louis d'or—pre-1726 = £0.84
current ducat of 12 marks = £0.37	—post-1726 = £1.02
England	*Spain*
guinea = £1.05	pistole (doblon)—post-1722 = £0.83

Source: Ibid. (table 1.2, pp. 11–12).

Table 5 Exchange Rates 1880 in Terms of French Francs

1	Belgian franc, Swiss franc, Italian lira and Spanish peso =	1	Ff
	Egyptian piaster	0.31	Ff
	British pound sterling	25.22	Ff
	Dutch florin	2.60	Ff
	Austro-Hungarian florin	2.50	Ff
	German mark	1.11	Ff
	U.S. dollar	5.18	Ff

Source: Banco di Roma (1980, p. 22).

Table 6 Average Exchange Rates, December 1926 and Years 1936, 1950, and 1991, for Specified Countries (in U.S. cents per unit)

Country	Unit	December 1926	1936	1950	1991
Austria	schilling	14.08	18.79	n.q.	8.56
Belgium	Belgian franc	2.78	3.38	1.99	3.27
France	old franc	3.95 (old)	6.11 (old)	0.29 (old)	17.7 (new = 100 old)
Germany	RM, DM	23.80	RM40.30	DM23.84*	60.2
Italy	lira	4.44	7.29	n.q.	.00081
Netherlands	guilder	39.99	64.48	26.23	53.42
Spain	peseta	15.24	12.31	n.q.	.009
Sweden	krona	26.72	25.63	19.33	16.5
Switzerland	Swiss franc	19.32	30.19	23.14	69.6
United Kingdom	pound sterling	485.12	497.09	280.07	176.7

*Based on quotations beginning 26 June 1950.

n.q. = not quoted.

Source: Federal Reserve Bulletin: various issues.

Bibliography

Where two dates are given, the first is generally that of the original publication, either the first edition of an English work, that of the original work in the case of translations, or sometimes the only edition where a classic work has been reprinted.

Abel, W. (1966), *Agrarkrisen und Agrarkonjunktur: Eine Geschichte der Land- und Ernährungs-wirtschaft Europas seit den hohen Mittelalter* (Hamburg-Berlin: Parey).

Abelshauser, W. (1975), *Wirtschaft in Westdeutschland, 1945–49: Rehabilitation und Wachstum-bedingungen in der amerikanischen und britischen Zone* (Stuttgart: Deutsche Verlag).

Acworth, A. W. (1925), *Financial Reconstruction in England, 1815–1822* (London: P. S. King).

Aftalion, Albert (1927), *Monnaie, prix et change* (Paris: Sirey).

Agmon, Tamir, and Kindleberger, Charles P. (eds.) (1977), *Multinationals from Small Countries* (Cambridge, Mass.: MIT).

Albion, Robert Greenhalgh (1939), *The Rise of New York Port (1815–1860)* (New York: Scribner's).

Aliber, Robert Z. (1962), Speculation in the foreign exchanges: the European experience 1919–1926, *Yale Economic Essays,* vol. 2, pp. 171–245.

Aliber, Robert Z. (1970), A theory of direct foreign investment, in Charles P. Kindleberger (ed.), *The International Corporation,* pp. 17–34.

American Economic Association (AEA) (1947), *Readings in the Theory of International Trade* (Philadelphia, Pa: Blakiston); for the Keynes—Ohlin transfer controversy, see chs. 6 and 7.

Andersen, P. Nyboe (1946), *Bilateral Exchange Clearing Policy* (Copenhagen: Einar Munksgaard).

Anderson, B. L., and Cottrell, P. L. (eds.) (1974), *Money and Banking in England: The Development of the Banking System, 1694–1914* (Newton Abbot: David & Charles).

Andréadès, A. (1909), *History of the Bank of England* (London: P. S. King).

Andrews, P. W. S., and Brunner, Elizabeth (1951), *Capital Development in Steel* (Oxford: Blackwell).

Angell, James W. (1926), *The Theory of International Prices: History, Criticism and Restatement* (Cambridge, Mass.: Harvard University Press).

Armstrong, John (1990), The rise and fall of the company promoter and the financing of British industry, in J. J. van Helten and Y. Cassis (eds.), *Capitalism in a Mature Economy,* pp. 115–38.

Arndt, H. W. (1944), *The Economic Lessons of the Nineteen-Thirties* (London: Oxford University Press).

Artaud, Denise (1978), *La Question des dettes interalliées et la reconstruction de l'Europe (1917–1929)* (Paris: Librairie Honoré Champion), Vols. 1 and 2.

Ashton, Robert (1960), *The Crown and the Money Market, 1603–1640* (Oxford: Clarendon Press).

Ashton, T. S. (1948), *The Industrial Revolution, 1760–1830* (London: Oxford University Press).

Ashton, T. S. (1953a), The bill of exchange and private banks in Lancashire, 1790–1830, in T. S. Ashton and R. S. Sayers (eds.), *Papers in English Monetary History,* pp. 37–49.

Ashton, T. S. (1953b) The crisis of 1825: letters from a young lady, in T. S. Ashton and R. S. Sayers (eds.), *Papers in English Monetary History,* pp. 96–108.

Ashton, T. S. (1959), *Economic Fluctuations in England, 1700–1800* (Oxford: Clarendon Press).

Ashton, T. S., and Sayers, R. S. (eds.) (1953), *Papers in English Monetary History* (Oxford: Clarendon Press).

Attman, Artur (1986), *American Bullion in the European World Trade, 1600–1800* (Gotenborg: Kungl. Vetenskap- och Vitternets-Samhället).

Baasch, Ernst (1927), *Holländische Wirtschaftsgeschichte* (Jena: Gustav Fischer).

Bagehot, Walter (1978), *The Collected Works of Walter Bagehot*, ed. N. St. John-Stevas (London: *The Economist*), vols. 9–11. Original dates are cited in the text.

Bagwell, Philip S. (1974), *The Transport Revolution from 1770* (London: Batsford).

Baker, Norman (1971), *Government and Contractors: The British Treasury and War Supplies, 1775–1783* (London: Athlone Press).

Balassa, Bela (1961), *The Theory of Economic Integration* (Homewood, Ill.: Irwin).

Balderston, T. (1977), A comment on "German business cycles in the 1920s," *Economic History Review,* 2d ser., vol. 30, pp. 159–61.

Baldy, Edmond (1922), *Les Banques d'affaires en France depuis 1900* (Paris: Librairie Générale de Droit et Jurisprudence).

Balzac, Honoré de (1837 [1972]), *César Birotteau* (Paris: Le Livre de Poche).

Banco di Roma (1980), Italia 1880: le banche a Roma, *In Villaggio, Rivista Mensile di Informazione del Banco di Roma,* vol. 11, pp. 18–28.

Barber, Clarence L. (1978), On the origins of the great depression, *Southern Economic Journal,* vol. 44, pp. 432–56.

Barbier, Jacques A., and Klein, Herbert S. (1981), Revolutionary wars and public finances: the Madrid Treasury, 1784–1807, *Journal of Economic History,* vol. 41, pp. 315–40.

Barbour, Violet (1929), Marine risks and insurance in the seventeenth century, *Journal of Economic and Business History,* vol. 1, pp. 561–96.

Barbour, Violet (1950 [1966]), *Capitalism and Amsterdam in the 17th Century* (Ann Arbor, Mich.: University of Michigan Press; 1966 paperback ed.).

Basevi, Giorgio (1979), Summary of the Optica 1976 proposals for exchange-rate management, in Samuel I. Katz (ed.), *US—European Monetary Relations,* pp. 184–91.

Baudhuin, Fernand (1946), *Histoire économique de la Belgique, 1914–1938,* 2 vols. (Brussels: Etablissement Emile Bruyes).

Baum, Warren C. (1958), *The French Economy and the State* (Princeton, N.J.: Princeton University Press).

Bautier, Robert-Henri (1971), *The Economic Development of Medieval Europe* (New York: Harcourt Brace Jovanovich).

Beach, W. Edwards (1935), *British International Gold Movements, 1881–1913* (Cambridge, Mass.: Harvard University Press).

Beaconsfield, Earl of (Benjamin Disraeli) (1880), *Endymion,* 3 vols. (New York: Appleton).

Benaerts, Pierre (1933), *Les Origines de la grande industrie allemande* (Paris: Turot).

[Benham, F. C.] (1939), *Southeastern Europe—A Political and Economic Survey,* Special Memorandum No. 48, London and Cambridge Economic Service in collaboration with the Royal Institute for International Affairs (London: Oxford University Press).

Benham, F. C. (1940), The terms of trade, *Economica,* n.s. vol. 7, pp. 360–76.

Bennett, Edward W. (1962), *German and the Diplomacy of the Financial Crisis, 1931* (Cambridge, Mass.: Harvard University Press).

Bergeron, Louis (1978), *Les Capitalistes en France (1780–1914)* (Paris: Gallimard).

Bergier, Jean-François (1979), From the fifteenth century in Italy to the sixteenth century in Germany: a new banking concept? in Center for Medieval and Renaissance Studies, *The Dawn of Modern Banking,* pp. 105–30.

Bernholz, Peter (1982), *Flexible Exchange Rate in Historical Perspective,* Princeton Studies in International Finance, no. 49 (Princeton, N.J.: Princeton University Press).

Beyen, J. W. (1949), *Money in a Maelstrom* (New York: Macmillan).

Bigo, Robert (1947), *Les Banques françaises au cours du XIXe siècle* (Paris: Sirey).

Billoret, J.-L. (1969), Système bancaire et dynamique dans un pays à monnaie stable: France, 1816–1914, thesis, University of Nancy.

Binney, J. E. D. (1958), *British Public Finance and Administration, 1774–92* (Oxford: Clarendon Press).

Bisschop, W. R. (1896 [1968]), *The Rise of the London Money Market, 1640–1826* (reprinted London: Frank Cass).

Bisson, Thomas N. (1979), *Conservation of Coinage, Monetary Exploitation and Restraint in France, Catalonia and Aragon, c. 1000–1125 A.D.* (Oxford: Clarendon Press).

Blake, Robert (1967), *Disraeli* (Garden City, N.Y.: Anchor Books).

Bloch-Lainé, François, and Bouvier, Jean (1986), *La France restaurée (1944–54): Dialogue sur les choix d'une modernization* (Paris: Fayard).

Bloom, Herbert I. (1937), *The Economic Activities of the Jews of Amsterdam in the 17th and 18th Centuries* (Williamsport, Pa.: Bayard Press).

Bloomfield, Arthur I. (1959), *Monetary Policy under the International Gold Standard, 1880–1914* (New York: Federal Reserve Bank of New York).

Bloomfield, Arthur I. (1963), *Short-Term Capital Movements under the Pre-1914 Gold Standard,* Princeton Studies in International Finance, no. 31 (Princeton, N.J.: Princeton University Press).

Blount, Sir Edward (1902), *Memoirs of Sir Edward Blount* (London: Longmans Green).

Blumberg, Horst (1960), Die Finanzierung der Neugründungen und Erweiterungen von Industriebetrieben in Form der Aktiengesellschaften während der fünfziger Jahrhunderts in Deutschland, am Beispiel der preussischen Verhältnisse erläutert, in Hans Motteck (ed.), *Studien zur Geschichte der industriellen Revolution in Deutschland* (Berlin: Akademie Verlag), pp. 165–208.

Board of Governors of the Federal Reserve System (1943), *Banking and Monetary Statistics* (Washington, D.C.: National Capital Press).

Bogucka, M. (1980), The role of Baltic trade in European development from the XVIth to the XVIIIth centuries, *Journal of European Economic History,* vol. 9, pp. 5–20.

Böhme, Helmut (1968), *Frankfurt und Hamburg, Des Deutsches Reiches Silber und Goldloch und die Allerenglishste Stadt des Kontinents* (Frankfurt: Europäische Verlagsanstalt).

Boissevain, Gideon Maria (1891 [1977]), *The Money Question. An Essay which Obtained the Prize Offered by Sir H. M. Meysey Thompson, Bart, at the Paris Monetary Congress of 1889* (reprinted Westport, Conn.: Greenwood).

Bolton, Sir George (1970), *A Banker's World: The Revival of the City, 1957–70. Speeches and Writings of Sir George Bolton,* ed. Richard Fry (London: Hutchinson).

Bonelli, Franco (1971), *La crisi del 1907: una tappa dello sviluppo industriale in Italia* (Turin: Einaudi).

Borchardt, Knut (1961 [1991]), On the question of a capital shortage in the first half of the 19th century in Germany, in Borchardt, *Perspectives on Modern German Economic History and Policy,* ch. 1.

Borchardt, Knut (1976), Währung and Wirtschaft, in Deutsche Bundesbank (ed.), *Währung und Wirtschaft in Deutschland,* pp. 1–53.

Borchardt, Knut (1979 [1991]), Constraints and room for maneuver in the great depression of the early thirties: toward a revision of the received historical picture, in Borchardt, *Perspectives on Modern German Economic History and Policy,* pp. 143–60.

Borchardt, Knut (1980), Zur Frage der währungspolitischen Optionen Deutschlands in der Weltwirtschaftskrise, in Knut Borchardt and Frank Holzheu (eds.), *Theorie und Politik der internationalen Wirtschaftsbeziehungen,* pp. 165–81.

Borchardt, Knut (1991), *Perspectives on Modern German Economic History and Policy* (Cambridge: Cambridge University Press).

Borchardt, Knut, and Holzeu, Franz (eds.) (1980), *Theorie und Politik der internationalen Wirtschaftsbeziehungen* (Stuttgart: Gustav Fischer).

Borchardt, Knut, and Schötz, Hans Otto (eds.) (1931 [1991]), *Wirtschaftspolitik in der Krise* (Baden-Baden: Nomos).

Bordo, Michael, and Schwartz, Anna J. (eds.) (1984), *A Perspective on the Classical Gold Standard, 1821–1931* (Chicago: University of Chicago Press).

Bordo, Michael, and White, Eugene N. (1991), A tale of two currencies: British and French finance during the Napoleonic wars, *Journal of Economic History,* vol. 51, no. 2 (June), pp. 303–16.

Born, Karl Erich (ed.) (1966), *Moderne deutsche Wirtschaftsgeschichte* (Cologne/Berlin: Kiepenheuer & Witsch).

Born, Karl Erich (1967), *Die deutsche Bankenkrise, 1931, Finanzen und Politik* (Munich: Piper).

Born, Karl Erich (1977), *Geld und Banken im 19. und 20. Jahrhundert* (Stuttgart: Kröner) translated by B. R. Berghahn as *International Banking in the Nineteenth and Twentieth Centuries* (Leamington Spa: Berg).

Bosher, J. F. (1970), *French Finances, 1770–1795: From Business to Bureaucracy* (Cambridge: Cambridge University Press).

Bouvier, Jean (1955 [1970]), The banking mechanism in France in the late 19th century, in Rondo Cameron (ed.), *Essays in French Economic History,* pp. 341–69.

Bouvier, Jean (1960), *Le Krach de l'Union Générale, 1878–1885* (Paris: Presses Universitaires de France).

Bouvier, Jean (1961), *Le Crédit Lyonnais de 1863 à 1882, les années de formation d'une banque de dépots,* vols. 1 and 2 (Paris: SEVPEN).

Bouvier, Jean (1967), *Les Rothschilds* (Paris: Fayard).

Bouvier, Jean (1973), *Un Siècle de banque française* (Paris: Hachette).

Bouvier, Jean (1977), A propos des approches micro- et macro-économiques des exportations des capitaux avant 1914 in M. Lévy-Leboyer (ed.), *La Position internationale de la France,* pp. 443–52.

Bouvier, Jean (1988), The Banque de France and the state from 1850 to the present day,' in Gianni Toniolo (ed.), *Central Bank Independence in Historical Perspective,* pp. 73–104.

Bovill, E. W. (1958), *The Golden Trade of the Moors* (New York: Oxford University Press).

Boyce, R. (1988), Creating the myth of consensus: public opinion and Britain's return to the gold standard, 1925, in P. L. Cottrell and D. E. Moggridge (eds.), *Money and Power,* pp. 173–97.

Boyer-Xambeau, Marie Thérèse, Deleplace, Ghislain, and Gillard, Lucien (1986), *Monnaie privée et pouvoir des princes: L'économie des relations monétaires à la Renaissance* (n.p.: Presse de la Fondation Nationale des Sciences Politiques).

Brailsford, H. N. (1961), *The Levellers and the English Revolution,* ed. Christopher Hill (Stanford, Calif.: Stanford University Press).

Bratchel, N. E. (1980), Regulation and group consciousness in the later history of London Italian merchant colonies, *Journal of European Economic History,* vol. 9, pp. 585–610.

Braudel, Fernand (1949 [1972]), *The Mediterranean and the Mediterranean World in the Age of Philip II,* vols. 1 and 2 (New York: Harper & Row).

Braudel, Fernand (1977), *Afterthoughts on Material Life and Capitalism* (Baltimore, Md.: Johns Hopkins University Press).

Braudel, Fernand (1979 [1984]), *The Perspective of the World,* vol. 3 of *Civilization and Capitalism, 15th–18th Century* (London: Collins).

Bresciani-Turroni, C. (1931 [1937]), *The Economics of Inflation: A Study of Currency Depreciation in Post-War Germany, 1914–1923* (London: Allen & Unwin).

Brezis, Elise, and Crouzet, François M. (1990), The role of the *assignats* during the French Revolution: Evil or rescuer? Brandeis University, Department of Economics, Working Paper no. 267/90.

British Parliamentary Papers (1847 [1969]), *Causes of Commercial Distress, Monetary Policy, Commercial Distress:* Vol. 3, *Report of the Select Committee, House of Lords;* Vol. 4: *Report from the Select Committee on the Operation of the Bank Acts and the Causes of the Recent Commercial Distress with Proceedings, Minutes of Evidence, Appendix and Index, 1857–59* (Shannon: Irish University Press).

Broadridge, S. A. (1969), The sources of railway share capital, in M. C. Reed (ed.), *Railways in the Victorian Economy,* pp. 184–211.

Brockhage, Bernhard (1910), *Zur Entwicklung des preussisch-deutschen Kapital-exports* (Leipzig: Duncker & Humblot).

Bronfenbrenner, Martin (1980), The currency-choice defense, *Challenge,* vol. 23 (January–February), pp. 31–36.

Brown, William Adams, Jr. (1940), *The International Gold Standard Reinterpreted, 1914–1934,* 2 vols (New York: National Bureau of Economic Research).

Bruchey, Stuart W. (1956), *Merchant of Baltimore, 1783–1819,* Johns Hopkins University Studies in Historical and Political Science (Baltimore, Md.: Johns Hopkins University Press).

Brunner, Karl (ed.) (1981), *The Great Depression Revisited* (The Hague: Martinus Nijhoff).

Brunschwig, Henri (1960 [1966]), *French Colonialism, 1871–1914: Myths and Realities* (New York: Praeger).

Buist, Marten G. (1974), *At Spes Non Fracta: Hope & Co., 1700–1815, Merchant Bankers and Diplomats at Work* (The Hague: Martinus Nijhoff).

Burk, Kathleen (1988), A merchant bank at war: the House of Morgan, in P. L. Cottrell and D. E. Moggridge (eds.), *Money and Power,* pp. 155–72.

Burke, Peter (1974), *Venice and Amsterdam: A Study of Seventeenth Century Elites* (London: Temple Smith).

Cagan, Philip (1956), The monetary dynamics of hyperinflation, in Milton Friedman (ed.), *Studies in the Quantity Theory of Money,* pp. 25–117.

Cagan, Philip, and Kincaid, George (1977), Jacobs' estimates of the hyperinflation model: comment, *Economic Inquiry,* vol. 14, pp. 111–18.

Cairncross, Alec (1953), *Home and Foreign Investment, 1870–1913* (Cambridge: Cambridge University Press).

Cairncross, Alec, and Eichengreen, Barry (1983), *Sterling in Decline: The Devaluations of 1931, 1949 and 1967* (Oxford: Blackwell).

Cairncross, Alec, and Watts, Nita (1989), *The Economic Section, 1939–1961: A Study in Economic Advising* (London: Routledge).

Cameron, Rondo (1955), L'Exportation des capitaux français, 1850–1880, *Revue d'histoire économique et sociale,* vol. 33, pp. 346–53.

Cameron, Rondo (1956), Founding the bank of Darmstadt, *Explorations in Entrepreneurial History,* vol. 13, pp. 113–30.

Cameron, Rondo (1961), *France and the Economic Development of Europe (1800–1914)* (Princeton, N.J.: Princeton University Press).

Cameron, Rondo (ed.) (1970), *Essays in French Economic History* (Homewood, Ill.: Irwin).

Cameron, Rondo (ed.) (1972), *Banking and Economic Development: Some Lessons of History* (New York: Oxford University Press).

Cameron, Rondo, with the collaboration of Crisp, Olga, Patrick, Hugh T., and Tilly, Richard (1967), *Banking in the Early Stages of Industrialization: A Study in Comparative Economic History* (New York: Oxford University Press).

Cantillon, Richard (1755 [1958]), *Essai sur la nature du commerce en général* (Paris: INED).

Cantor, Norman F. (1971), *Perspectives on the European Past: Conversations with Historians* (New York: Macmillan),

Capie, Forrest, and Webber, Alan (1982), *A Monetary History of the United Kingdom, 1870–1982,* vol. 1: *Data Sources and Methods* (London: Allen & Unwin).

Capie, Forrest, and Wood, Geoffrey E. (eds.) (1986), *Financial Crises and the World Banking System* (London: Macmillan).

Carnegie Endowment for International Peace (1930), *Economic and Social History of the World War: Sweden, Norway and Iceland in the World War* (New York: CEIP).

Carswell, John (1960), *The South Sea Bubble* (London: Cresset Press).

Carus-Wilson, E. M. (ed.) (1954), *Essays in Economic History,* 4 vols (London: Arnold).

Cassel, Gustav (1924), *Money and Foreign Exchange after 1914* (New York: Macmillan).

Cassis, Youssef (1984), *Les Banquiers de la City à Londres a l'époque Edouardienne, (1890–1914)* (Geneva: Droz).

Cassis, Youssef (1985), Bankers in English society in the late nineteenth century, *Economic History Review,* 2d ser. vol. 39. no. 4 (May), pp. 210–29.

Cassis, Youssef (ed.) (1992), *Finance and Financiers in European History, 1880–1960* (Cambridge: Cambridge University Press; Paris: Editions de la Maison des Sciences de L'Homme).

Cecil, Lamar (1967), *Albert Ballin: Business and Politics in Imperial Germany, 1888–1918* (Princeton, N.J.: Princeton University Press).

Center for Medieval and Renaissance Studies, University of California in Los Angeles (1979), *The Dawn of Modern Banking* (New Haven, Conn.: Yale University Press).

Chandler, George (1964 [1968]), *Four Centuries of Banking (Martin's Bank)* (London: Batsford).

Chandler, Lester V. (1958 [1978]), *Benjamin Strong, Central Banker* (reprinted New York: Arno Press).

Chapman, S. D. (1971), Fixed capital formation in the British cotton manufacturing industry, in J. P. P. Higgins and S. Pollard (eds.), *Aspects of Capital Investment in Great Britain,* pp. 57–107.

Chaussinand-Nogaret, Guy (1970), *Les Financiers de Languédoc au XVIIIe siècle* (Paris: SEVPEN).

Checkland, S. G. (1948), The Birmingham economists, 1815–1850, *Economic History Review,* 2d ser., vol. 1, pp. 1–19.

Checkland, S. G. (1971), *The Gladstones: A Family Biography, 1764–1851* (Cambridge: Cambridge University Press).

Checkland, S. G. (1975), *Scottish Banking: A History, 1695–1973* (Glasgow: Collins).

Cheong, W. E. (1974), The crisis of the great East India houses, 1830–34, *Revue internationale de l'histoire de la banque,* vol. 9, pp. 106–33.

Chesterton, G. K. (1904 [1950]), *The Napoleon of Notting Hill* (New York: Devin-Adair).

Chevalier, Michel (1834 [1838]), *Lettres sur l'Amérique du Nord,* 3d ed., 2 vols. (Brussels: Société Belge de Librairie).

Chevalier, Michel (1850 [1866]), *Cours d'économie politique,* Vol. 3: *La Monnaie,* 2d ed. (Paris: Capelle).

Chevalier, Michel (1859), *On the Probable Fall in the Value of Gold, the Commercial and Social Consequences which May Ensue and the Measures which It Invokes,* 3d ed. (Manchester: Alexander Ireland).

Child, Frank C. (1958 [1978]), *The Theory and Practice of Exchange Control in Germany: A Study of Monopolistic Exploitation in International Markets* (reprinted New York: Arno Press).

Churchill, Winston S. (1974), *Winston S. Churchill, His Complete Speeches, 1897–1963*, Vol. 4: *1922–28*, ed. R. R. James (London: Chelsea House). Original dates of speeches are cited in the text.

Clapham, Sir John (1945), *The Bank of England: A History*, 2 vols. (Cambridge: Cambridge University Press).

Clapham, Sir John (1953), *The Economic Development of France and Germany, 1815–1914*, 4th ed. (Cambridge: Cambridge University Press).

Clark, John G. (1971), *La Rochelle and the Atlantic Economy during the Eighteenth Century* (Baltimore, Md.: Johns Hopkins University Press).

Clarke, Stephen V. O. (1967), *Central-Bank Cooperation, 1924–31* (New York: Federal Reserve Bank of New York).

Clarke, Stephen V. O. (1973), *The Reconstruction of the International Monetary System: The Attempts of 1922 and 1933*, Princeton Studies in International Finance, no. 33 (Princeton, N.J.: Princeton University Press).

Clarke, Stephen V. O. (1977), *Exchange-Rate Stabilization in the Mid-1930s: Negotiating the Tripartite Agreement*, Princeton Studies in International Finance, no. 41 (Princeton, N.J.: Princeton University Press).

Clay, Christopher (1978), *Public Finance and Private Wealth: The Career of Sir Stephen Fox, 1627–1716* (Oxford: Clarendon Press).

Clay, Sir Henry (1957 [1979]), *Lord Norman* (reprinted New York: Arno Press).

Clay, Lucius D. (1950), *Decision in Germany* (Garden City, N.Y.: Doubleday).

Cleveland, Harold van Buren (1984), "If there had been no Marshall Plan . . . ," in Stanley Hoffmann and Charles Maier (eds.), *The Marshall Plan: A Retrospective* (Boulder, Colo.: Westview Press), pp. 59–64.

Clifford, Henry C. (1956), *The Draining of the Fens*, 2d ed. (Cambridge: Cambridge University Press).

Clough, Shepherd B. (1964), *The Economic History of Modern Italy* (New York: Columbia University Press).

Coase, Ronald H. (1937), The nature of the firm, *Economica*, n.s., vol. 4, pp. 386–405.

Coase, Ronald H. (1960), The problem of social cost, *Journal of Law and Economics*, vol. 3, pp. 1–44.

Cohen, Benjamin J. (1981), The European monetary system: an outsider's view, *Princeton Essays in International Finance*, no. 142 (Princeton, N.J.: Princeton University Press).

Cohen, Jon S. (1966 [1977]), *Finance and Industrialization in Italy, 1894–1914* (reprinted New York: Arno Press).

Cohen, Jon S. (1967), Financing industrialization in Italy, 1894–1914: the partial transformation of a late comer, *Journal of Economic History*, vol. 27, pp. 363–82.

Coleman, D. G. (1963), *Sir John Banks, Baronet and Businessman: A Study of Business, Politics and Society in Later Stuart England* (Oxford: Clarendon Press).

Coleman, D. G. (1969a), *Courtaulds: An Economic and Social History*, 3 vols. (Oxford: Clarendon Press).

Coleman, D. G. (ed.) (1969b), *Revisions in Mercantilism* (London: Methuen).

Collier, Richard (1963), *The Sound of Fury: An Account of the Indian Mutiny* (London: Collins).

Collins, Michael (1988), *Money and Banking in the United Kingdom: A History* (London: Croom Helm).

Collins, Michael (1989), The banking crisis of 1878, *Economic History Review*, 2d ser., vol. 42, no. 4 (November), pp. 504–27.

Colm, Gerhard, Dodge, Joseph M., and Goldsmith, Raymond W. (1946 [1955]), A plan for the liquidation of war finance and the financial rehabilitation of Germany, *Zeitschrift für die gesamte Staatswissenschaft*, vol. 3, pp. 204–43 (German text pp. 244–84).

Committee for Invisible Transactions, Organization for Economic Co-operation and Development (1967), Capital Markets Study, *General Report* (Paris: OECD).

Committee on Finance and Industry (1931), *Report* (Macmillan Report), Cmd. 3897 (London: HMSO).

Committee on the Working of the Monetary System (1959), *Report* (Radcliffe Report), Cmnd. 827 (London: HMSO).

Condliffe, J. B. (1940), *The Reconstruction of World Trade: A Survey of International Economic Relations* (New York: Norton).

Confalonieri, Antonio (1976), *Banca e industria in Italia*, Vol. 1: *Le premesse: dall' abolizione del corse forzoso all caduta dei Credito Mobiliare;* Vol. 2: *Il sistema bancario tra due crisi;* Vol. 3: *L'esperienza della Banca Commerciale Italiana* (Milan: Banca Commerciale Italiana).

Coombs, Charles A. (1976), *The Arena of International Finance* (New York: Wiley—Interscience).

Cope, S. R. (1978), The Stock Exchange revisited: a new look at the market in securities in London in the eighteenth century, *Economica*, vol. 45, pp. 1–22.

Corti, Count Egon Caesar (1928), *The Rise of the House of Rothschild* (New York: Blue Ribbon Books).

Coste, Pierre (1932), *La Lutte pour la suprématie: les grandes marchés financiers: Paris, Londres, New York* (Paris: Payot).

Costigliola, Frank C. (1977), Anglo-American financial history in the 1920s, *Journal of Economic History*, vol. 37, pp. 911–34.

Cottrell, P. L. (1972), The international financial society: the investment bank in England, 1856–1880, paper given at the Economic History Association's annual meeting in Canterbury, England (April).

Cottrell, P. L. (1980), *Industrial Finance, 1830–1914: The Finance and Organization of English Manufacturing Industry* (London: Methuen).

Cottrell, P. L. (1988), Credit, morale and sunspots: the financial boom of the 1860s and trade-cycle theory, in Cottrell and D. E. Moggridge (eds.), *Money and Power*, pp. 41–71.

Cottrell, P. L., and Moggridge, D. E. (eds.) (1988), *Money and Power: Essays in Honour of L. S. Pressnell* (London: Macmillan).

Crick, W. F., and Wadsworth, J. E. (1936), *A Hundred Years of Joint-Stock Banking (Midland Bank)* (London: Hodder & Stoughton).

Crisp, Olga (1977), Russian public funds in France, 1888–1914, in Maurice Lévy-Leboyer (ed.), *La Position internationale de la France*, pp. 263–74.

[Cross Report] Bank for International Settlements (1986), *Recent Innovations in International Banking*, prepared by a Study Group Established by the Central Banks of the Group of Ten Countries (Basle: Bank for International Settlements).

Crouzet, François (ed.) (1972), *Capital Formation in the Industrial Revolution* (London: Methuen).

Crouzet, François, Chaloner, W. H., and Stern, W. M. (eds.) (1969), *Essays in European Economic History, 1780–1914* (New York: St. Martin's Press).

[Cunliffe Report], British Parliamentary Reports on International Finance (1978), *The Cunliffe Committee (1918) and the Macmillan Committee (1931) Reports* (reprinted New York: Arno Press).

Dahmén, Erik (1970), *Entrepreneurial Activity and the Development of Swedish Industry*, translated by Axel Leijonhufud (Homewood, Ill.: Irwin).

Daumard, Adeline (1970), *Le Bourgeois de Paris au XIXe siècle* (Paris: Flammarion).

Daumard, Adeline (1980), Wealth and affluence in France since the beginning of the nineteenth century, in W. D. Rubenstein (ed.), *Wealth and the Wealthy in the Modern World*, pp. 91–121.

Dauphin-Meunier, A. (1936), *La Banque de France* (Paris: Gallimard).

Davis, John P. (1905), *Corporations: A Study of the Origins and Development of Great Business Combinations and Their Relations to the State* (New York: Putnam's).

Davis, Lance E., and Huttenback, Robert A. (1986), *Mammon and the Pursuit of Empire: The Political Economy of British Imperialism, 1880–1913* (Cambridge: Cambridge University Press).

Davis, Ralph (1973), *The Rise of the Atlantic Economies* (Ithaca, N.Y.: Cornell University Press).

[Dawes Plan], Rufus C. Dawes (1925), *The Dawes Plan in the Making* (Indianapolis, Ind./New York: Bobbs-Merrill). *Report of the First Committee of Experts (Dawes Plan)*, pp. 299–489; *Report of the Second Committee of Experts, 1924 (McKenna Committee)*, pp. 490–509.

Dawson, W. R. (1931), *Marine Underwriting at Rouen, 1727–42* (London: Lloyd's).

Day, John (1978 [1987]), The great bullion famine of the fifteenth century, in Day, *The Medieval Market Economy* (Oxford: Blackwell), pp. 1–54).

Day, John (1986), The history of money in the writings of Marc Bloch, in Mario Gomes Marques and M. Crusafont I. Sabater (eds.), *Problems of Medieval Coinage in the Iberian Area* (Aviles: Sociedad Numismatica Avrilesina, Instituto de Sintra).

Deane, Phyllis (1965 [1979]), *The First Industrial Revolution* (Cambridge: Cambridge University Press).

Deane, Phyllis, and Cole, W. A. (1967), *British Economic Growth, 1688–1959* (Cambridge: Cambridge University Press).

Debeir, Jean Claude (1978), La Crise du franc de 1924: un exemple de spéculation "international," *Relations internationales*, no. 13, pp. 29–49.

Debeir, Jean Claude (1982), Comment on Carl L. Holtfrerich, "Domestic and foreign expectations and the demand for money during the German inflation, 1920–1923," in Charles P. Kindleberger and Jean-Pierre Laffargue (eds.), *Financial Crises,* pp. 132–36.

DeCecco, Marcello (1969), The Italian payments crisis of 1963–64, in Robert A. Mundell and A. K. Swoboda (eds.), *Monetary Problems of the International Economy,* pp. 383–89.

DeCecco, Marcello (1975), *Money and Empire: The International Gold Standard, 1890–1914* (Oxford: Blackwell).

DeCecco, Marcello (1984), *The International Gold Standard: Money and Empire,* 2d ed. (London: Frances Pinter).

DeCecco, Marcello, and Giovanni, Alberto (eds.) (1989), *A European Central Bank: Perspectives on Monetary Unification After Ten Years of the EMS* (Cambridge: Cambridge University Press).

De Mattia, Renato (ed.) (1977), *Storia del capitale della Banca d'Italia e degli istituti predecessori,* vol. 3 in 2 prs. (Rome: Bank of Italy).

Defoe, Daniel (1719), *The Anatomy of Change-Alley: A System of Stock-Jobbing Proving that Scandalous Trade as it Is Now Carried On to be knavish in its Private Practice and Treason in its Publick* (London: E. Smith).

Defoe, Daniel (1724 [1964]), *Roxana, the Fortunate Mistress* (London: Oxford University Press).

deJong-Keesing, Elizabeth Emmy (1939), *De economische crisis van 1763 te Amsterdam* (Amsterdam: N. V. Intern).

Dent, Julian (1973), *Crisis in Finance: Crown, Financiers and Society in Seventeenth Century France* (New York: St. Martin's Press).

Department of State (1941), *Bulletin,* vol. 4.

Department of State (1950), *Germany, 1947–1949: The Story in Documents* (Washington, D.C.: United States Government Printing Office).

Department of State (1972), *Foreign Relations of the United States (FRUS), 1947,* 5 vol. (Washington, D. C.: United States Government Printing Office).

Dermine, Jean (1990), Home country control and mutual recognition, in Donald D. Fair and Christian de Boissieu (eds.), *Financial Institutions in Europe,* pp. 287–303.

Despres, Emile (1973), *International Economic Reform: Collected Papers of Emile Despres,* ed. Gerald M. Meier (New York: Oxford University Press).

Despres, Emile, Kindleberger, C. P., and Salant, W. S. (1965 [1981]), The dollar and world liquidity: a minority view, *The Economist,* reprinted in C. P. Kindleberger, *International Money,* pp. 42–52.

Deutsche Bundesbank (ed.) (1976), *Währung und Wirtschaft in Deutschland, 1876–1975* (Frankfurt: Knapp).

Devine, T. (1975), *The Tobacco Lords* (Edinburgh: Donald).

Diaper, Stephanie (1990), The Sperling combine and the shipbuilding industry: merchant banking and industrial finance in the 1920s, in J. J. van Helten and Y. Cassis (eds.), *Capitalism in a Mature Economy,* pp. 71–94.

Dickens, Charles (1848 [1864]), *Dealings with the Firm of Dombey and Son, Wholesale, Retail and for Exportation* (London: Oxford University Press).

Dickens, Charles (1857 [1894]), *Little Dorrit,* 2 vols. (Boston: Houghton Mifflin).

Dickson, P. G. M. (1960), *The Sun Insurance Office* (London: Oxford University Press).

Dickson, P. G. M. (1967), *The Financial Revolution in England: A Study in the Development of Public Credit, 1688–1756* (New York: St Martin's Press).

Dictionary of National Biography (DNB) (1893) (London: Oxford University Press).

Dictionnaire de biographie française (1954), vol. 6 (Paris: Latouze & Ane).

Diebold, William, Jr. (1952), *Trade and Payments in Western Europe* (New York: Harper).

Dillen, J. G. van (ed.) (1934), *History of the Principal Public Banks* (The Hague: Martinus Nijhoff).

Disraeli, Benjamin, *see* Beaconsfield, Earl of.

Divine, David (1970), *Indictment of Incompetence: Mutiny at Invergordon* (London: Macdonald).

Dobson, Alan P. (1986), The Export White Paper, 10 September, 1941, *Economic History Review,* 2d ser., vol. 39, no. 1 (February), pp. 59–76.

Documents diplomatiques français, 1932–1939 (1966), 1st ser. (1932–35), Vol. 2 (15 November 1932–17 March 1933) (Paris: Imprimérie Nationale).

Dollinger, Philippe (1964 [1970]), *The German Hansa* (Stanford, Calif.: Stanford University Press).

Domes, Jürgen, and Wolffsohn, Michael (1979), Setting the course for the Federal Republic of Germany: major policy decisions in the bizonal economic council and party images, 1947–49, *Zeitschrift für die gesamte Staatswissenschaft,* vol. 135 (September), pp. 332–51.

Dornbusch, Rudiger (1982), Comment on Paul Coulbois, "Central banks and foreign-exchange crises today," in Charles P. Kindleberger and Jean-Pierre Laffargue (eds.), *Financial Crises*, pp. 216–21.

Dornbusch, Rudiger, and Frenkel, Jacob A. (1984), The gold standard and the Bank of England in the crisis of 1847, in Michael Bordo and Anna J. Schwartz (eds.), *A Retrospective on the Classical Gold Standard*, pp. 233–64.

Dornic, François (1955), *L'Industrie textile dans Le Maine et ses débouchés internationaux, 1650–1815* (Le Mans: Editions Pierre-Belon).

Doubleday, Thomas (1847), *A Financial, Monetary and Statistical History of England from the Revolution of 1688 to the Present Time* (London: Effingham, Wilson).

Dowie, J. A. (1975), 1919–20 is in need of attention, *Economic History Review*, 2d ser., vol. 28, pp. 429–50.

Drummond, Ian M. (1975), *Imperial Economic Policy, 1917–1939: Studies in Expansion and Protection* (Toronto: University of Toronto Press).

Duffy, Ian P. H. (1982), The discount policy of the Bank of England during the suspension of cash payments, 1797–1821, *Economic History Review*, 2d ser., vol. 35, pp. 67–82.

Dulles, Eleanor L. (1929), *The French Franc, 1914–1928: The Facts and Their Interpretation* (New York: Macmillan).

Dunning, John H. (1958), *American Investment in British Manufacturing Industry* (London: Ruskin House).

Dupriez, Leon H. (1947), *Monetary Reconstruction in Belgium* (New York: King's Crown Press).

Durand, Yves (1971), *Les Fermiers généraux au XVIIIᵉ siècle* (Paris: Presses Universitaires de France).

Duroselle, J. -B. (1960), *De Wilson à Roosevelt* (Paris: Colin).

Eagly, Robert F. (1971), *The Swedish Bullionist Controversy: P. N. Christiernin's Lecture on the High Price of Foreign Exchange in Sweden (1761)* (Philadelphia, Pa.: American Philosophical Society).

The Economist (London), various issues.

Edelstein, Michael (1982), *Overseas Investment in the Age of High Imperialism: The United Kingdom, 1850–1914* (New York: Columbia University Press).

Ehrenberg, Richard (1896 [1928]), *Capital and Finance in the Age of the Renaissance: A Study of the Fuggers* (New York: Harcourt Brace).

Ehrenberg, Richard (1925), *Das Haus Parish in Hamburg* (Jena: Gustav Fischer).

Eichengreen, Barry J. (1992), *Golden Fetters: The Gold Standard and the Great Depression* (New York: Oxford University Press).

Einaudi, Luigi (1936 [1953]), The theory of imaginary money from Charlemagne to the French Revolution, in F. C. Lane and J. C. Riersma (eds.), *Enterprise and Secular Change*, pp. 229–61.

Einzig, Paul (1933), *The Comedy of the Pound* (London: Kegan Paul).

Ellena, V. (1880), La statistica di alcune industrie italiane, *Annali di Statistica* 2d ser., vol. 13.

Ellis, Howard S. (1934), *German Monetary Theory, 1905–1933* (Cambridge, Mass.: Harvard University Press).

Ellis, Howard S. (1950), *The Economics of Freedom* (New York: Harper).

Emden, Paul H. (1938), *Money Powers of Europe in the Nineteenth and Twentieth Centuries* (New York: Appleton—Century).

Emminger, Otmar (1986), *D-mark, Dollar, Währungskrisen: Erinnerungen eines ehemaligen Bundesbankpräsident* (Stuttgart: Deutsches Verlaganstalt).

Epstein, Klaus (1959), *Matthias Erzberger and the Dilemma of German Democracy* (Princeton, N.J.: Princeton University Press).

Ernst, H. (1905), *Eine schweizerische Bundesbank* (Winterthur: Geschwieter Ziegler).

European Economic Community (EEC), Commission (1966), *The Development of a European Capital Market* (Segré Report) (Brussels: EEC).

European Economic Community (EEC), Council and Commission (1970), *Report to the Council and the Commission on the Realization by Stages of Economic and Monetary Union in the Community* (Werner Report) supplement to *Bulletin II-1970* of the EEC (Luxembourg).

European Economic Community, Commission, Study Group on Optimum Currency Areas (Optica Group) (1977), *Inflation and Exchange Rates: Evidence and Policy Guidelines for the European Community* (Brussels: EEC).

Evans, D. Morier (1849 [1969]), *The Commercial Crisis, 1847–48,* 2d ed. (reprinted New York: A. M. Kelley).

Evans, D. Morier (1859 [1969]), *The History of the Commercial Crisis 1857–58 and the Stock Exchange Panic of 1859* (reprinted New York: A. M. Kelley).

Fair, Donald E., and deBoissieu, Christian (eds.) (1990), *Financial Institutions in Europe Under New Conditions* (Dordrecht: Kluwer).
Faure, Edgar (1977), *La Banqueroute de Law, 17 juillet 1720* (Paris: Gallimard).
Feaveryear, Sir Albert (1931 [1963]), *The Pound Sterling: A History of British Money,* 2d ed., revised by E. Victor Morgan (Oxford: Clarendon Press).
Federal Trust for Education and Research (1972 [1973]), *Report on European Monetary Integration* (prepared by Giovanni Magnifico and John Williamson), reprinted as an appendix to Giovanni Magnifico, *European Monetary Unification,* pp. 199–222.
Feinstein, C. H. (1976), *Statistical Tables of National Income Expenditure and Output of the United Kingdom, 1855–1965* (Cambridge: Cambridge University Press).
Feinstein, C. H. (1978), Capital formation in Great Britain, in P. Mathias and M. M. Postan (eds.), *The Cambridge Economic History of Europe,* vol. 7, pt. 1, pp. 28–96.
Feis, Herbert (1930), *Europe, the World's Banker* (New Haven, Conn.: Yale University Press).
Feis, Herbert (1950), *The Diplomacy of the Dollar, 1919–39* (New York: Norton).
Feis, Herbert (1966), *1933: Characters in Crisis* (Boston, Mass.: Little, Brown).
Feldman, Gerald D. (1977), *Iron and Steel in the German Inflation, 1916–25* (Princeton, N.J.: Princeton University Press).
Felix, David (1971), *Walther Rathenau and the Weimar Republic: The Politics of Reparations* (Baltimore, Md.: Johns Hopkins University Press).
Felloni, G. (1971), *Gli investimenti finanziari genovesi in Europa tra il seicento e la restaurazione* (Milan: Giuffre).
[Felloni, G., ed.] Atti della Società Ligure de Storia Patria (1991), *Banchi pubblici, banchi privati e monti de pietà nell 'Europa preindustriale,* 2 vols. (Genoa: Società Ligure di Storia Patria).
Ferguson, Thomas (1981), Critical realignment: the fall of the House of Morgan and the origins of the New Deal, Ph.D. dissertation, Princeton University.
Fetter, Frank Whitson (1965), *Development of British Monetary Orthodoxy, 1797–1875* (Cambridge, Mass.: Harvard University Press).
Fetter, Frank Whitson (1977), Lenin, Keynes and inflation, *Economica,* vol. 44, pp. 77–80.
Fetter, Frank Whitson (1980), *The Economist in Parliament, 1780–1868* (Durham, N.C.: Duke University Press).
Fieldhouse, D. K. (ed.) (1967), *The Theory of Capitalist Imperialism* (London: Longman).
Fischer, Wolfram (1962), *Der Staat und die Anfänge der Industrialisierung in Baden, 1800–1850* (Berlin: Duncker & Humblot).
Fisher, Irving (1911 [1966]), *The Purchasing Power of Money: Its Determination and Relation to Credit, Interest and Crises,* rev. ed. (reprinted New York: A. M. Kelley).
Fisher, Irving (1934), *Stable Money: A History of the Movement* (New York: Adelphi).
Fitchew, Geoffrey E. (1990), The European regulatory and supervisory framework, in Donald E. Fair and Christian de Boissieu (eds.), *Financial Institutions in Europe,* pp. 27–38.
Fleisig, Heywood W. (1969), Long-term capital flows and the Great Depression: the role of the United States, Ph.D. dissertation, Yale University.
Fleisig, Heywood W. (1972), The United States and the non-European periphery during the early years of the Great Depression, in Herman Van der Wee (ed.), *The Great Depression Revisited,* pp. 145–81.
Florence, P. Sargent (1953), *The Logic of British Industry: A Realistic Analysis of Economic Structure and Government* (London: Routledge & Kegan Paul).
Flux, A. W. (1910), *The Swedish Banking System* (Washington, D. C.: United States Government Printing Office for the National Monetary Commission).
[Forbes, Sir William] (1803 [1969]), A Scottish banking house (memoirs of Sir William Forbes), in Robert and Elberg Forster (eds.), *European Society in the Eighteenth Century,* pp. 154–65.
Ford, A. G. (1958), The transfer of British foreign lending, 1870–1913, *Economic History Review,* 2d ser., vol. 11, pp. 302–8.
Forster, E. M. (1921 [1948]), *Howard's End* (New York: Knopf).
Forster, Robert (1960), *The Nobility of Toulouse in the Eighteenth Century: A Social and Economic Study* (Baltimore, Md.: Johns Hopkins University Press).
Forster, Robert (1971), *The House of Saulx-Tavanes: Versailles and Burgundy, 1700–1830* (Baltimore, Md.: Johns Hopkins University Press).
Forster, Robert (1980), *Merchants, Landlords, Magistrates: The Depont Family in Eighteenth Century France* (Baltimore, Md.: Johns Hopkins University Press).
Forster, Robert, and Forster, Elberg (eds.) (1969), *European Society in the Eighteenth Century* (New York: Walker).

Fox, Edward Whiting (1971), *History in Geographic Perspective: The Other France* (New York: Norton).

Foxwell, H. S. (1909), preface to A. Andréadès, *History of the Bank of England*, 2 vols. in 1 (London: P. S. King).

France during the German Occupation, 1940–1944: A Collection of 292 Statements on the Government of Maréchal Pétain and Pierre Laval (1957), 3 vols. (Stanford, Calif.: Stanford University Press for the Hoover Institution on War, Peace and Revolution).

Franco, Gustav H. B. (1990), Fiscal reform and stabilization: four hyperinflation cases, *Economic Journal*, vol. 100, no. 399, pp. 176–87.

Freedeman, Charles (1979), *Joint-Stock Enterprise in France, 1807–1867* (Chapel Hill, N.C.: University of North Carolina Press).

Fremdling, R., and Tilly, R, (1976), German banks, German growth, and econometric history, *Journal of Economic History*, vol. 36, pp. 416–24.

Frenkel, J. A. (1977), The forward exchange rate, expectations and the demand for money: the German hyperinflation, *American Economic Review*, vol. 67, pp. 653–70.

Frenkel, J. A., and Johnson, H. G. (eds.) (1976), *The Monetary Approach to the Balance of Payments* (Toronto: Toronto University Press).

Fridlizius, Gunnar (1957), *Swedish Corn Exports in the Free Trade Era: Patterns in the Oats Trade, 1850–1880* (Lund: Gleerup).

Friedman, Milton (1953a), The case for flexible exchange rates, in Milton Friedman, *Essays in Positive Economics*, pp. 157–203.

Friedman, Milton (1953b), *Essays in Positive Economics* (Chicago, Ill.: University of Chicago Press).

Friedman, Milton (ed.) (1956), *Studies in the Quantity Theory of Money* (Chicago, Ill.: University of Chicago Press).

Friedman, Milton (1969 [1970]), The Eurodollar market: some first principles, in Herbert V. Prochnow (ed.), *The Eurodollar Market*, pp. 272–93.

Friedman, Milton (1991), foreword to Emile Moreau, *The Golden Franc*, pp. x–xiv.

Friedman, Milton (1992), *Money Mischief: Episodes in Monetary History* (New York: Harcourt Brace Jovanovich).

Friedman, Milton, and Friedman, Rose (1980), *Free to Choose* (New York: Harcourt Brace Jovanovich).

Friedman, Milton, and Schwartz, Anna Jacobson (1963), *A Monetary History of the United States, 1867–1960* (Princeton, N.J.: Princeton University Press).

Friis, Astrid (1953), An inquiry into the relations between economic and financial factors in the sixteenth and seventeenth centuries. I: The two crises in the Netherlands in 1557, *Scandinavian Economic History Review*, vol. 1, pp. 191–241.

Frost, Raymond (1954), The Macmillan gap, 1931–53, *Oxford Economic Papers*, vol. 6, pp. 181–201.

FRUS (Foreign Relations of the United States), *see* Department of State.

Fry, Richard (1970), introduction to Sir George Bolton, *A Banker's World*

Galbraith, John Kenneth (1975), *Money: Whence It Came, Where It Went* (Boston, Mass.: Houghton Mifflin).

Gapinski, James, and Rockwood, Charles (eds.) (1979), *Essays in Post-Keynesian Inflation* (Cambridge, Mass.: Ballinger).

Garber, Peter M. (1990), Who put the mania in the tulipmania? in Eugene N. White (ed.), *Crashes and Panics*, pp. 3–32.

Gardner, Richard N. (1980), *Sterling—Dollar Diplomacy in current Perspective: The Origins and Prospects of Our International Economic Order* (New York: Columbia University Press).

Gascon R. (1971), *Grand commerce et vie urbaine au XVIe siècle: Lyon et ses marchands*, 2 vols. (Paris: S.E.V.P.E.N.).

Gasslander, Olle (1962), *History of the Stockholms Enskilda Bank to 1914* (Stockholm: privately printed).

Gayer, Arthur D., Rostow, W. W., and Schwartz, Anna Jacobson (1953), *The Growth and Fluctuation of the British Economy 1790–1850: An Historical, Statistical and Theoretical Study of Britain's Economic Development*, 2 vols. (Oxford: Clarendon Press).

Genillard, Robert L. (1970), The Eurobond market, in Herbert V. Prochnow (ed.), *The Eurodollar Market*, pp. 316–47.

Gerschenkron, Alexander (1943), *Bread and Democracy in Germany* (Berkeley, Calif.: University of California Press).

Gerschenkron, Alexander (1962), *Economic Backwardness in Historical Perspective* (Cambridge, Mass.: Harvard University Press).

Gibbons, James S. (1859), *The Banks of New-York, Their Dealers, the Clearing House and the Panic of 1857* (New York: Appleton).

Gilbert, Felix (1980), *The Pope, His Banker and Venice* (Cambridge, Mass.: Harvard University Press).

Gilbert, Martin (1977), *Winston S. Churchill,* Vol. 5: *1922–1939: The Prophet of Truth* (Boston, Mass.: Houghton Mifflin).

Gilbert, Milton, and McClam, Warren (1970), Regulations and policies relating to the Eurocurrency market, in Herbert V. Prochnow (ed.), *The Eurodollar Market,* pp. 348–411.

Gille, Bertrand (1959), *La Banque et le crédit en France de 1815 à 1848* (Paris: Presses Universitaires de France).

Gille, Bertrand (Vol. 1, 1965; Vol. 2, 1967), *Histoire de la Maison Rothschild,* Vol. 1: *Des origines à 1848;* Vol. 2: *1848–1870* (Geneva: Droz).

Gille, Bertrand (1968), *Les Investissements français en Italie (1815–1914)* (Turin: ILTE).

Gille, Bertrand (1970), *La Banque en France au XIXe siècle: recherches historiques* (Geneva: Droz).

Gillespie, Charles Coulston (1980), *Science and Polity in France at the End of the Old Regime* (Princeton, N.J.: Princeton University Press).

Gillingham, John (1977), *Belgian Business in the Nazi New Order* (Ghent: Jan Dhondt Foundation).

Girault, René (1973), *Emprunts russes et investissements français en Russie, 1887–1914* (Paris: Colin).

Girault, René (1977), Investissements et placements français en Russie, 1880–1914, in Maurice Lévy-Leboyer (ed.), *La Position internationale de la France,* pp. 251–62.

Goldsmith, Raymond (1969), *Financial Structure and Development* (New Haven, Conn.: Yale University Press).

Good, David M. (1977), National bias in the Austrian capital market before World War I, *Explorations in Economic History,* vol. 14, pp. 141–66.

Goodhart, Charles (1972 [1986]), *The Business of Banking, 1891–1914,* 2d ed. (Aldershot: Gower).

Goodhart, Charles (1989), *The Evolution of Central Banks* (Cambridge: Cambridge University Press).

Gordon, M. J. (1971), Towards a theory of financial distress, *Journal of Finance,* vol. 26, pp. 347–56.

Gordon, Robert J., and Wilcox, James A. (1981), Monetarist interpretations of the Great Depression: an evaluation and critique, in Karl Brunner (ed.), *The Great Depression Revisited,* pp. 49–107.

Gould, J. D. (1970), *The Great Debasement: Currency and the Economy in Mid-Tudor England* (Oxford: Clarendon Press).

Graham, Edward Montgomery (1975), Oligopolistic imitation, theories of foreign direct investment and European direct investment in the United States, Ph.D. dissertation, Graduate School of Business Administration, Harvard University.

Graham, Frank D. (1930), *Exchange, Prices and Production in Hyper-Inflation: Germany 1920–1923* (Princeton, N.J.: Princeton University Press).

Graham, Frank D., and Whittlesey, Charles R. (1939 [1978]), *Golden Avalanche* (reprinted New York: Arno Press).

Great Britain, Parliamentary Debates (1810 [1978]), *Report from the Select Committee on the High Price of Gold Bullion (1810), Ordered by the House of Commons to Be Printed, 8 June 1810* (reprinted New York: Arno Press).

Gregory, T. E. (1928), introduction to Thomas Tooke and William Newmarch, *A History of Prices.*

Gregory, T. E. (1936), *The Westminster Bank Through a Century,* 2 vols. (London: Westminster Bank).

Grigg, P. J. (1948), *Prejudice and Judgement* (London: Cape).

Groseclose, Elgin (1934 [1976]), *Money and Man: A Survey of Monetary Experience,* 4th ed. (Norman, Okla.: University of Oklahoma Press).

Grosskreutz, Helmut (1977), *Privatkapital und Kanalbau in Frankreich, 1814–1848: Eine Fallstudie zur Rolle der Banken in der französischen Industrialisierung* (Berlin: Duncker & Humblot).

Grotkopp, Wilhelm (1954), *Die grosse Krise: Lehren aus der Überwindung der Wirtschaftskrise, 1929–32* (Düsseldorf: Econ-Verlag).

Gutmann, Franz (1913), *Das Französiche Geldwesen im Kriege* (1870–1878) (Strasbourg: Karl J. Trübner).

Haberler, Gottfried (1948), Dollar shortage, in S. E. Harris (ed.), *Foreign Economic Policy for the United States*, pp. 426–45.

Hagen, Everett E. (1949), The reconversion period: reflections of a forecaster, *Review of Economics and Statistics*, vol. 31, pp. 178–81.

Hague, D. C. (1966), Summary of the debate, in Roy Harrod and D. C. Hague (eds.), *International Trade Theory in a Developing World*, pp. 393–564.

Hahn, L. Albert (1963), *Fünfzig Jahre zwischen Inflation und Deflation* (Tübingen: J.C.B. Mohr [Paul Siebeck]).

Haller, Heinz (1976), Die Rolle der Staatsfinanzen für die Inflationsprozess, in Deutsche Bundesbank (ed.), *Währung und Wirtschaft in Deutschland*, pp. 115–55.

Hamilton, Earl J. (1934 [1965]), *American Treasure and the Price Revolution in Spain, 1501–1650* (reprinted New York: Octagon Books).

Hamilton, Earl J. (1945), The foundation of the Bank of Spain, *Journal of Political Economy*, vol. 53, pp. 97–114.

Hamilton, Earl J. (1968), John Law, *International Encyclopedia of the Social Sciences*, vol. 9 (New York: Free Press), pp. 78–81.

Hamilton, Earl J. (1969), The political economy of France at the time of John Law, *History of Political Economy*, vol. 1, pp. 123–49.

Hansmeyer, Karl Heinrich, and Caesar, Rolf (1976), Kriegswirtschaft und Inflation (1936–1948), in Deutsche Bundesbank (ed.), *Währung und Wirtschaft in Deutschland*, pp. 367–429.

Hardach, Gerd (1977), *The First World War* (Berkeley, Calif.: University of California Press).

Hargreaves, Eric Lyde (1930 [1966]), *The National Debt* (reprinted London: Arnold).

Harley, C. Knick (1977), The interest rate and prices in Britain, 1873-1913: a study of the Gibson paradox, *Explorations in Economic History*, vol. 14, pp. 69–89.

Harris, Robert D. (1979), *Necker, Reform Statesman of the Ancien Régime* (Berkeley, Calif.: University of California Press).

Harris, S. E. (1930), *The Assignats* (Cambridge, Mass.: Harvard University Press).

Harris, S. E. (ed.) (1948), *Foreign Economic Policy for the United States* (Cambridge, Mass.: Harvard University Press).

Harrison, Joseph (1978), *An Economic History of Modern Spain* (New York: Holmes & Meier).

Harrod, Roy (1947), *Are These Hardships Necessary?* 2d ed. (London: Hart-Davis).

Harrod, Roy (1951), *The Life of John Maynard Keynes* (London: Macmillan).

Harrod, Roy, and Hague, D. C. (eds.) (1966), *International Trade Theory in a Developing World* (London: Macmillan).

Harsin, Paul (1928), *Les Doctrines monétaires et financières en France du XVIe au XVIIIe siècle* (Paris: Alcan).

Harsin, Paul (1933), *Crédit public et banque d'état en France du XVIe au XVIIIe siècle* (Paris: Droz).

Hawtrey, Ralph G. (1919 [1927]), *Currency and Credit* (London: Longmans, Green).

Hawtrey, Ralph G. (1922), The Genoa Resolution in currency, *Economic Journal*, vol. 32, pp. 290–304.

Hawtrey, Ralph G. (1932), *The Art of Central Banking* (London: Longmans, Green).

Hawtrey, Ralph G. (1938), *A Century of Bank Rate* (London: Longmans, Green).

Hayek, F. A. (1962), Introduction to Henry Thornton, *An Enquiry into the Nature and Effect of the Paper Credit of Great Britain*, pp. 13–59.

Hayek. F. A. (1972), *Choice in Currency: A Way to Stop Inflation*, Institute of Economic Affairs Occasional Papers, no. 48 (London: IEA).

Heckscher, Eli F. (1922). *The Continental System: An Economic Interpretation* (Oxford: Clarendon Press).

Heckscher, Eli F. (1930), Sweden's monetary history, 1914–1925, in its relation to foreign trade and shipping, in Carnegie Endowment for International Peace, *Economic and Social History of the World War: Sweden, Norway and Iceland in the World War*, pp. 127–278.

Heckscher, Eli F. (1931 [1953]), Natural and money economy, as illustrated from Swedish history in the sixteenth century, in F. C. Lane and J. C. Riersma (eds.) *Enterprise and Secular Change*, pp. 206–28.

Heckscher, Eli F. (1934), The Bank of Sweden in connection with the Bank of Amsterdam, in J. G. van Dillen (ed.), *History of the Principal Public Banks*, pp. 161–90.

Heckscher, Eli F. (1935 [1983]), *Mercantilism*, Swedish original, 1931; English translation by Mandel Shapiro, 2d rev. ed., E. F. Söderlund (ed.) (1955) (New York: Garland).

Heckscher, Eli F. (1950), Comment on Charles Wilson's "Treasure and trade balances," *Economic History Review,* vol. 3, pp. 219–28.

Heckscher, Eli F. (1954), *An Economic History of Sweden* (Cambridge, Mass.: Harvard University Press).

Hegelund, H. (ed.) (1961), *Money, Growth and Methodology: Papers in Honor of Johan Åkerman* (Lund: G.W.K. Gleerup).

Helfferich, Karl (ed.) (1900), *Ausgewählte Reden und Aufsatze uber Geld- und Bankwesen.* (Schriften des Vereins zum Schutz der deutsche Goldwährung, Band 1) (Berlin: Guttenberg).

Helfferich, Karl (1921–23 [1956]), *Georg von Siemens, Ein Lebensbild aus Deutschlands grosser Zeit,* revised and shortened edition of the 3-volume 1921–23 work (Krefeld: Richard Serpe).

Helleiner, K. F. (1965), *The Imperial Loans: A Study in Financial and Diplomatic History* (Oxford: Clarendon Press).

Henderson, H. D. (1943 [1955]), *The Inter-War Years and Other Papers* (Oxford: Clarendon Press).

Hidy, Muriel E. (1939 [1978]), *George Peabody, Merchant and Financier, 1829–1854* (Ph.D. dissertation, Radcliffe College; published New York: Arno Press).

Higgins, J.P.P., and Pollard, S. (eds.) (1971), *Aspects of Capital Investment in Great Britain, 1750–1850* (London: Methuen).

Higgs, Henry (ed.) (1925–26 [1963]). *Palgrave's Dictionary of Political Economy,* 3 vols. (reprinted New York: A. M. Kelley).

Hilgerdt, Folke, *see* League of Nations.

Hirsch, Fred, and Goldthorpe, John (eds.) (1978), *The Political Economy of Inflation* (Cambridge, Mass.: Harvard University Press).

Hirschfeld, Gerhard, and Kettennacker, Lothar (eds.) (1981), *Der "Führerstaat": Mythos und Realität* (Stuttgart: Klett for the German Historical Institute, London).

Hobson, John A. (1927 [1938]), *Imperialism: A Study* (London: Oxford University Press).

Hodson, H. V. (1938), *Slump and Recovery, 1929–37* (London: Oxford University Press).

Hoffmann, Stanley, et al. (1963), *In Search of France* (Cambridge, Mass.: Harvard University Press).

Holtfrerich, Carl-Ludwig (1980 [1986]), *The German Inflation, 1914–1923: Causes and Effects in International Perspective* (translated from the German by Theo Balderston) (New York: Walter deGruyter).

Holtfrerich, Carl-Ludwig (1982*a*), Domestic and foreign expectations and the demand for money during the German inflation, 1920–1923, in Charles P. Kindleberger and Jean-Pierre Laffargue (eds.), *Financial Crises,* pp. 117–32.

Holtfrerich, Carl-Ludwig (1982*b*), Alternative zu Brünings Wirtschaftspolitik in der Weltwirtschaftskrise, *Historische Zeitschrift,* vol. 236, pp. 605–31.

Holtfrerich, Carl-Ludwig (1988), Germany, 19th century to present, in Gianni Toniolo (ed.), *Central Banks' Independence in Historical Perspective,* 105–39.

Hotlfrerich, Carl-Ludwig (1989), The monetary unification process in nineteenth-century Germany: Relevance and lessons for today, in de Cecco and Giovanni (eds.), *A European Central Bank,* pp. 216–41.

Holtfrerich, Carl-Ludwig (1900*a*), Economic policy options and the end of the Weimar Republic, in Kershaw (ed.), *Weimar: Why Did German Democracy Fail?* (London: Weidenfeld and Nicholson), pp. 58–91.

Holtfrerich, Carl-Ludwig (1990*b*), Was the policy of deflation in Germany unavoidable, in Jürgen Baron von Kruedener (ed.), *Economic Policy and Political Collapse: The Weimar Republic, 1924–1933* (London: Berg), pp. 63–80.

Holzman, James M. (1926), *The Nabobs in England: A Study of the Returned Anglo-Indian, 1760–1785* (Ph.D. dissertation, Columbia University; New York: privately printed).

Hoover, Herbert (1952), *The Memoirs of Herbert Hoover,* Vol. 3: *The Great Depression, 1929–1941* (New York: Macmillan).

Hoselitz, Bert F. (1956), Entrepreneurship and capital formation in France and Britain since 1700, in Bert F. Hoselitz, *Capital Formation and Economic Growth* (Princeton, N.J.: Princeton University Press for the National Bureau of Economic Research), pp. 306–22.

House, E. M., and Charles Seymour (eds.) (1921), *What Really Happened at Paris* (New York: Scribner's).

Hovde, B. J. (1943 [1972]), *The Scandinavian Countries, 1720–1865: The Rise of the Middle Classes* (reprinted Port Washington, Wis.: Kennikat Press).

Howson, Susan K. (1975), *Domestic Monetary Management in Britain, 1919–38* (Cambridge: Cambridge University Press).

Howson, Susan K. (1980), The management of sterling, 1932–39, *Journal of Economic History, vol. 40, pp. 53–60.*

Howson, Susan (1988), Cheap money and debt management, 1932–51, in P. L. Cottrell and D. E. Moggridge (eds.), *Money and Power,* pp. 227–89.

Howson, Susan K., and Donald Winch (1977), *The Economic Advisory Council, 1930–39: A Study in Economic Advice During Depression and Recovery* (Cambridge: Cambridge University Press).

Hughes, J.R.T. (1960), *Fluctuations in Trade, Industry and Finance: A Study in British Economic Development, 1850–1860* (Oxford: Clarendon).

Hume, David (1752 [1898]), *Essays, Moral, Political and Literary,* 2 vols. (London: Longmans Green).

Hundert Jahre im Dieste der deutschen Wirtschaft: eine Rückblick zur Erinnerung an die Grundung der Mitteldeutschen Creditbank am 29 Februar 1856 (1956) (Frankfurt: privately printed).

Hyde Park Agreement (1942), Department of State *Bulletin,* vol. 4, pp. 494–95.

Hymer, Stephen H. (1960 [1976]), *The International Operations of National Firms* (Cambridge, Mass.: MIT).

Iklé, Max (1972), *Switzerland: An International Banking and Finance Center* (Stroudsberg, Pa.: Dowden, Hutchinson & Ross).

Irmler, Heinrich (1976), Bankenkrise und Vollbeschäftigungspolitik (1931–1936), in Deutsche Bundesbank (ed.), *Währung und Wirtschaft in Deutschland,* pp. 283–329.

Israelsen, L. Dwight (1979), The determinants of Russian state income, 1800–1914: An econometric analysis, Ph.D. dissertation, Massachusetts Institute of Technology.

Iversen, Carl (1936), The importance of the international margin, in *Explorations in International Economics: Notes and Essays in Honor of F. W. Taussig* (New York: McGraw-Hill), pp. 68–83.

Jackman, William T. (1916), *The Development of Transportation in Modern England* (Cambridge: Cambridge University Press).

Jacobs, A., and Richter, H. (1935), Die Grosshandelspreise in Deutschland von 1792 bis 1934, *Sonderhefte des Institut für Konjunkturforschung,* no. 37 (Berlin), pp. 7–111.

Jacobs, Rodney L. (1975), A difficulty with monetarist models of hyperinflation, *Economic Enquiry,* vol. 13, pp. 337–60.

James, Harold (1986), *The German Slump: Politics and Economics, 1924–1936* (Oxford: Clarendon).

Jeanneney, Jean-Noël (1975), Sur la vénalité du journalisme entre les deux guerres, *Revue français de science politique,* vol. 25, pp. 717–38.

Jeanneney, Jean-Noël (1976), *François de Wendel en république: l'argent et le pouvoir, 1914–1940* (Paris: Seuil).

Jenneney, Jean-Noël (1977), *Leçon d'histoire pour une gauche au pouvoir: la faillite du Cartel (1924–26)* (Paris: Seuil).

Jeanneney, Jean-Noël (1978), De la spéculation financière comme arme diplomatique: à propos de la première bataille du franc (novembre 1923–mars 1924), *Relations internationales,* no. 13, pp. 5–27.

Jeffrys, J. B. (1938 [1977]), *Trends in Business Organization in Great Britain since 1856* (Ph.D. dissertation, London School of Economics; published New York: Arno Press).

Jeffrys, J. B. (1946 [1954]), The denomination and character of shares, 1855–1885, in E. M. Carus-Wilson (ed.), *Essays in Economic History,* vol. 1, pp. 344–57.

Jenks, Leland H. (1927), *The Migration of English Capital to 1875* (New York: Knopf).

Jensen, Michael C., and Meckling, W. H. (1976), Theory of the firm, agency costs and ownership structure, *Journal of Financial Economics, vol. 3, pp. 305–60.*

John, A. H. (1950), *The Industrial Development of South Wales, 1750–1850: An Essay* (Cardiff: University of Wales Press).

Johnston, Thomas (1934), *The Financiers and the Nation* (London: Methuen).

Jöhr, Adolf (1915), *Die schweizerischen Notenbanken, 1826–1913* (Zurich: Institut Orell Füssli).

Joint Economic Committee, United States Congress (1964), *A Description and Analysis of Certain European Capital Markets, Economic Practices and Policies,* paper no. 3 (Washington, D.C.: United States Government Printing Office).

Joint Economic Committee, United States Congress (1979), *The European Monetary System: Problems and Prospects (A Study Prepared for the Use of the Subcommittee on International Economics of the Joint Economic Committee and the Subcommittee on International Trade, Investment and Monetary Policy of the Committee on Banking, Finance and Urban Affairs,*

U.S. House of Representatives, Written by Ben W. Crain and Lloyd C. Atkinson (Washington, D.C.: United States Government Printing Office).

Jones, D. W. (1972), Merchants, financiers and interlopers: the London mercantile community and the Nine Years' War, 1688–1697, paper delivered to Economic History Society in Canterbury (April); mimeo.

Jones, Joseph M. (1934), *Tariff Retaliation: Repercussions of the Hawley-Smoot Bill* (Philadelphia, Pa.: University of Pennsylvania Press).

Jones, Joseph M. (1955), *The Fifteen Weeks (February 21–June 5, 1947)* (New York: Viking).

Joplin, Thomas (1832), *An Account and History of the Currency Question, together with an Account of the Origin and Growth of Joint Stock Banking in England* (London: James Ridgeway).

Joplin, Thomas (n.d., after 1832), *Case for Parliamentary Inquiry into the Circumstances of the Panic, in a Letter to Thomas Gisborne, MP* (London: James Ridgeway).

Joslin, D. M. (1954 [1962]), London private bankers, 1720–1785, in E. M. Carus-Wilson (ed.), *Essays in Economic History*, vol. 2, pp. 340–59.

Josseau, J. B. (1860 [1884]), *Traité du Crédit foncier* (Paris: Marchal, Billiard).

Journal of Economic Perspectives (1990) Symposium on Bubbles, vol. 4, no. 2 (Spring), pp. 13–101.

Journal of European Economic History (1984), Banks and Industry in the Interwar Period, vol. 13, no. 2 (Fall), Special Issue.

Judge, A. V. (1926), Philip Burlamachi: a financier of the Thirty Years War, *Economica*, vol. 6, pp. 285–300.

Juglar, Clément (1860 [1967]), *Des Crises commerciales et leur retour périodique en France, en Angleterre et aux Etats Unis* (reprinted New York: A. M. Kelley).

Kaeuper, Richard W. (1973), *Bankers to the Crown: The Ricciardi of Lucca and Edward I* (Princeton, N.J.: Princeton University Press).

Kahn, Alfred E. (1946), *Great Britain in the World Economy* (New York: Columbia University Press).

Kaplan, Jacob J., and Schleiminger, Günter (1989), *The European Payments Union: Financial Diplomacy in the 1950s* (Oxford: Clarendon).

Kashiwagi, Yusuke (1986), The emergence of global finance, 1986 Per Jacobsson Lecture (Washington, D.C.: Per Jacobsson Foundation).

Katz, Samuel I. (ed.) (1979), *US-European Monetary Relations* (Washington, D.C.: American Enterprise Institute).

Kaufmann, Eugen (1914), *La Banque en France* (Paris: Giard & Brière).

Kehr, Eckhard (1930 [1970]), Imperialismus und deutscher Schlachtflottenbau, excerpts from *Schlachtflottenbau und Parteipolitik, Berlin, 1930*, in H. U. Wehler (ed.), *Imperialismus*, pp. 289–308.

Kellenbenz, Hermann (1958), *Sephardim an der unteren Elbe: ihre wirtschaftliche und politische Bedeutung von Ende des 16. bis zum Beginn des 18. Jahrhunderts* (Wiesbaden: Steiner).

Kenen, Peter B. (1969), The theory of optimum currency areas: an eclectic view, in Robert A. Mundell and A. K. Swoboda (eds.), *Monetary Problems of the International Economy*, pp. 41–60.

Kennan, George F. (1979), *The Decline of Bismarck's European Order: Franco-Prussian Relations, 1875–1890* (Princeton, N.J.: Princeton University Press).

Kennedy, Paul (1987), *The Rise and Fall of the Great Powers: Economic Change and Military Conflict from 1500 to 2000* (New York: Random House).

Kennedy, William P. (1987), *Industrial Structure, Capital Markets and the Origins of British Economic Decline* (Cambridge: Cambridge University Press).

Kennedy, William P. (1990), Capital Markets and industrial structure in the Victorian economy, in J. J. van Helten and Y. Cassis (eds.), *Capitalism in a Mature Economy*, pp. 23–51.

Keynes, John Maynard (1912), Return of estimated value of foreign trade of the United Kingdom at prices of 1900, *Economic Journal*, vol. 22, pp. 630–31.

Keynes, John Maynard (1919), *The Economic Consequences of the Peace* (London: Macmillan).

Keynes, John Maynard (1922), *A Revision of the Treaty* (New York: Harcourt Brace).

Keynes, John Maynard (1924), *A Tract on Monetary Reform* (New York: Harcourt Brace).

Keynes, John Maynard (1929 [1947]), The German transfer problem, in American Economic Association, *Readings in the Theory of International Trade*, pp. 161–69.

Keynes, John Maynard (1930), *A Treatise on Money*, 2 vols. (New York: Harcourt Brace).

Keynes, John Maynard (1931), *Essays in Persuasion* (London: Macmillan). Original dates of essays in this collection are cited in the text.

Keynes, John Maynard (1936), *The General Theory of Employment, Interest and Money* (New York: Harcourt Brace).

Keynes, John Maynard (1940), *How to Pay for the War: A Radical Plan for the Chancellor of the Exchequer* (New York: Harcourt Brace).

Kindleberger, Charles P. (1956), *The Terms of Trade: A European Case Study* (New York: Technology Press/Wiley).

Kindleberger, Charles P. (1965 [1966]), Balance-of-payments deficits and the international market for liquidity, in Kindleberger, *Europe and the Dollar*, pp. 1–26.

Kindleberger, Charles P. (1966), *Europe and the Dollar* (Cambridge, Mass.: MIT).

Kindleberger, Charles P. (ed.) (1970), *The International Corporation: A Symposium* (Cambridge, Mass.: MIT).

Kindleberger, Charles P. (1971 [1981]), The pros and cons of an international capital market, in Kindleberger, *International Money*, pp. 225–42

Kindleberger, Charles P. (1972 [1985]), The international monetary politics of a near-great power: two French episodes, 1926–1936 and 1960–1970, in Kindleberger, *Keynesianism vs. Monetarism*, pp. 119–28.

Kindleberger, Charles P. (1973 [1986]), *The World in Depression, 1929–1939*, rev. ed. (Berkeley: University of California Press).

Kindleberger, Charles P. (1974a [1978]), The formation of financial centers, in Kindleberger, *Economic Response*, pp. 66–134.

Kindleberger, Charles P. (1974b [1984]), Origins of U.S. direct investment in France, in Kindleberger, *Multinational Excursions*.

Kindleberger, Charles P. (1975 [1981]), Quantity and price, especially in financial markets, in Kindleberger, *International Money*, pp. 256–68.

Kindleberger, Charles P. (1978a), *Economic Response: Comparative Studies in Trade, Finance and Growth* (Cambridge, Mass.: Harvard University Press).

Kindleberger, Charles P. (1978b [1989]), *Manias, Panics and Crashes: A History of Financial Crises*, rev. ed. (New York: Basic Books).

Kindleberger, Charles P. (1979 [1985]), The international causes and consequences of the Great Crash, in Kindleberger, *Keynesianism vs Monetarism*, pp. 274–86.

Kindleberger, Charles P. (1980 [1985]), Keynesianism vs. monetarism in 18th and 19th century France, in Kindleberger, *Keynesianism vs Monetarism*.

Kindleberger, Charles P. (1981a), *International Money: A Collection of Essays* (London: Allen & Unwin).

Kindleberger, Charles P. (1981b), Review of Karl Brunner (ed.), *The Great Depression Revisited*, *Journal of Economic Literature*, vol. 19, pp. 1585–86.

Kindleberger, Charles P. (1982), Sweden in 1850 as an "impoverished sophisticate": comment, in Kindleberger, *Keynesianism vs. Monetarism*, pp. 240–43.

Kindleberger, Charles P. (1984a), *Multinational Excursions* (Cambridge, Mass.: MIT Press).

Kindleberger, Charles P. (1984b [1985]), International propagation of financial crises: the experience of 1888–93, in Kindleberger, *Keynesianism vs. Monetarism*, pp. 226–39.

Kindleberger, Charles P. (1985), *Keynesianism vs. Monetarism and Other Essays in Financial History* (London: Allen & Unwin).

Kindleberger, Charles P. (1987), *Marshall Plan Days* (Boston: Allen & Unwin).

Kindleberger, Charles P. (1987b), *International Capital Movements* (Cambridge: Cambridge University Press).

Kindleberger, Charles P. (1988), *The International Economic Order: Essays on Financial Crisis and International Public Goods* (Cambridge, Mass.: MIT Press).

Kindleberger, Charles P. (1989 [1990]), Spenders and hoarders: the world distribution of Spanish silver, 1550–1750, in Kindleberger, *Historical Economics*, pp. 35–85.

Kindleberger, Charles P. (1990a [1990b]), The panic of 1873, in Kindleberger, *Historical Economics*, pp. 310–25.

Kindleberger, Charles P. (1991a), The crisis of 1619 to 1623, *Journal of Economic History*, vol. 51, no. 1 (March), pp. 149–75.

Kindleberger, Charles P. (1991b), International (and interregional) aspects of financial crises, in Martin Feldstein (ed.), *The Risk of Financial Crises* (Chicago: University of Chicago Press).

Kindleberger, Charles P. (1991c), Dangerous times: would the leader of the world economy stand up, *The International Economy*, vol. 5, no. 6 (November–December), pp. 58–62.

Kindleberger, Charles P., and Ditella, G. (eds.) (1982), *Economics in the Long View: Essays in Honour of W. W. Rostow* (London: Macmillan).

Kindleberger, Charles P., and Laffargue, Jean-Pierre (eds.) (1982), *Financial Crises: Theory, History and Policy* (Cambridge: Cambridge University Press).

King, W.T.C. (1936), *History of the London Discount Market* (London: Routledge).

Kirschen, Etienne-Sadi (1969), *Financial Integration in Western Europe* (New York: Columbia University Press).

Klaveren, Jacob van (1957), Die historische Erscheinung der Korruption in ihren Zussamenhang mit den Staats- und Gesellschaftsstructuren betrachtet, *Vierteljahrschrift für Sozial- und Wirtschaftsgeschichte,* vol. 44, pp. 289–324.

Klaveren, Jacob van (1958*a),* Die historische Erscheinung der Korruption: II, Die Korruption in der Kapitalgesellschaften, besonders in grossen Handelskompanien, *Vierteljahrschrift jür Sozial- und Wirtschaftsgeschichte,* vol. 45, pp. 438–68.

Klaveren, Jacob van (1958*b),* Die historische Erscheinung der Korruption: III, Die internationalen Aspeckte der Korruption, *Vierteljahrschrift für Sozial- und Wirtschaftsgeschichte,* vol. 45, pp. 469–504.

Klaveren, Jacob van (1969), *General Economic History, 100–1760: From the Roman Empire to the Industrial Revolution* (Munich: Gerhard Kieckens).

Klein, P. W. (1984), "Little London," British merchants in Rotterdam during the 17th and 18th centuries, in D. C. Coleman and Peter Mathias (eds.), *Enterprise and History: Essays in Honour of Charles Wilson* (Cambridge: Cambridge University Press), pp. 116–34.

Klopstock, Fred H. (1968), The Euro-dollar market: some unresolved issues, *Princeton Essays in International Finance,* no. 68 (Princeton, N.J.: Princeton University Press).

Kocka, Jürgen (1969), *Unternehmungsverwaltung und Angestelltenschaft am Beispiel Siemens, 1847–1914: Zum Verhältnis von Kapitalismus und Bürokratie in der deutschen Industrialisierung* (Stuttgart: Ernst Klett Verlag).

Komlos, John (1978), The *Kreditbanken* and German growth: a postscript, *Journal of Economic History,* vol. 38, pp. 476–79.

Komlos, John (1979), Financing innovation and the demand for money in Austria-Hungary, 1867–1913, paper presented to the workshop in economic history, University of Chicago (16 November).

Krantz, Frederick, and Hohenberg, P. M. (eds.) (1975), *Failed Transitions to Modern Industrial Society: Renaissance Italy and Seventeenth-Century Holland* (Montreal: Interuniversity Center for European Studies).

Krüger, Alfred (1925), *Das Kölner Bankiergewerbe vom Ende des 18. Jahrhunderts bis 1876* (Essen: G. D. Baedeker Verlag).

Kuisel, Richard F. (1981), *Capitalism and the State in Modern France: Renovation and Economic Management in the Twentieth Century* (Cambridge: Cambridge University Press).

Kurgan-Van Hentenryk, G. (1977), Un aspect de l'exportation des capitaux en Chine, les entrepreneurs franco-belges, 1896–1914, in Maurice Lévy-Leboyer (ed.), *La Position internationale de la France,* pp. 203–13.

Labasse, Jean (1955), *Les Capitaux et la région: étude géographique. Essai sur le commerce et la circulation dans la région lyonnaise* (Paris: Colin).

Laffitte, Jacques (1840 [1932]), *Mémoires de Laffitte (1767–1844)* (Paris: Firmin-Dutot).

Lamfalussy, Alexandre (1968), *Les Marchés financiers en Europe* (Paris: Presses Universitaires de France).

Landes, David S. (1949), French entrepreneurship and industrial growth in the nineteenth century, *Journal of Economic History,* vol. 9, pp. 45–61.

Landes, David S. (1958), *Bankers and Pashas* (Cambridge, Mass.: Harvard University Press).

Landes, David S. (1960), The Bleichröder Bank: an interim report, *Yearbook V* (London: Leo Baeck Institute), pp. 201–20.

Landes, David S. (1982), The spoilers foiled: the exclusion of Prussian finance from the French Liberation Loan of 1871, in Charles P. Kindleberger and G. Ditella (eds.), *Economics in the Long View,* vol. 2. pp. 67–110.

Lane, F. C., and Riersma, J. C. (eds.) (1953), *Enterprise and Secular Change: Readings in Economic History* (Homewood, Ill.: Irwin).

Lapeyre, Henri (1953), *Simon Ruiz: les asientos de Philippe II* (Paris: Colin).

Lauck, W. Jett (1907), *The Causes of the Panic of 1893* (Boston, Mass.: Houghton Mifflin).

Laursen, Karsten, and Pedersen, Jørgen (1964), *The German Inflation, 1918–23* (Amsterdam: North-Holland).

Law, John (1705), *Money and Trade Considered: With a Proposal for Supplying the Nation With Money* (Edinburgh).

League of Nations (James E. Meade) (1938), *World Economic Survey, 1938/39* (Geneva: League of Nations).

League of Nations (Folke Hilgerdt) (1941), *Europe's Trade: A Study of the Trade of European Countries with Each Other and with the Rest of the World* (Geneva: League of Nations).

League of Nations (Folke Hilgerdt) (1942), *The Network of World Trade: A Companion Volume to "Europe's Trade"* (Geneva: League of Nations).

League of Nations (Ragnar Nurkse) (1944), *International Currency Experience: Lessons of the Interwar Period* (Princeton, N.J.: League of Nations).

League of Nations (Ragnar Nurkse) (1946), *The Course and Control of Inflation after World War I* (Princeton, N.J.: League of Nations).

Lefebre, Georges (1939 [1967]), *The Coming of the French Revolution* (Princeton, N.J.: Princeton University Press).

LeGoff, Jacques (1979), The usurer and purgatory, in Center for Medieval and Renaissance Studies, *The Dawn of Modern Banking*, pp. 25–52.

Leighton-Boyce, J.A.S.L. (1958), *Smiths, the Bankers, 1658–1958* (London: National Provincial Bank).

Leith-Ross, Sir Frederick (1968), *Money Talks: Fifty Years of International Finance* (London: Hutchinson).

Léon, Pierre (1963), *Marchands et spéculateurs dauphinois dans le monde antillais du XVIIIe siècle: les Dolle et les Raby* (Paris: Belles Lettres).

Letwin, William (1969), *Sir Josiah Child, Merchant Economist* (Boston, Mass.: Baker Library, Harvard Graduate School of Business Administration).

Levasseur, E. (1854 [1970]), *Recherches historiques sur le système de Law* (reprinted New York: Burt Franklin).

Levy, Hermann (1935 [1966]), *Industrial Germany: A Study of Its Monopoly Organizations and their Control by the State* (Cambridge: Cambridge University Press).

Lévy-Leboyer, Maurice (1964), *Les Banques européennes et l'industrialisation internationale dans la première moitié du XIXe siècle* (Paris: Presses Universitaires de France).

Lévy-Leboyer, Maurice (1968), Le rôle historique de la monnaie de banque, *Annales, Economies, Sociétés, Civilisations,* vol. 28, pp. 1–8.

Lévy-Leboyer, Maurice (1977a), La balance de paiements et l'exportation des capitaux français,' in Maurice Lévy-Leboyer (ed.), *La Position internationale de la France*, pp. 75–142.

Lévy-Leboyer, Maurice (ed.) (1977b), *La Position internationale de la France: aspects économiques et financiers, XIXe–XXe siècles* (Paris: Ecole des Hautes Etudes en Sciences Sociales).

Lewin, Henry Grote (1937 [1968]), *The Railway Mania and its Aftermath, 1949–52* (reprinted New York: A. M. Kelley).

Lewis, W. Arthur (1955), *The Theory of Economic Growth* (Homewood, Ill.: Irwin).

Lewis, W. Arthur (1978), *Growth and Fluctuations, 1870–1913* (London: Allen & Unwin).

Li, Ming-hsun (1963), *The Great Recoinage of 1696–1699* (London: Weidenfeld & Nicolson).

Liesse, André (1908), *Portraits des financiers: Ouvrard, Mollien, Gaudien, Baron Louis, Corvetto, Laffitte, de Villèle* (Paris: Alcan).

Liesse, André (1909), *Evolution of Credit and Banks in France* (Washington, D.C.: United States Government Printing Office for the National Monetary [Aldrich] Commission).

Lindert, Peter H. (1969), *Key Currencies and Gold, 1900–1913,* Princeton Studies in International Finance, no. 24 (Princeton, N.J.: Princeton University Press).

Lo Romer, David G. (1987), *Merchants and Reform in Leghorn, 1814–1868,* (Berkeley, Cal.: University of California Press).

Locke, Robert R. (1978), *Les Fonderies et forges d'Alais à l'époque des premiers chemins de fer, 1829–1874* (Paris: Rivière).

Lodge, Eleanor C. (1931 [1970]), *Sully, Colbert, and Turgot: A Chapter in French Economic History* (reprinted Port Washington, Wis.: Kennikat Press).

Loon, Henrik Willem van (1930), *R. v. R.: The Life and Times of Rembrandt van Rijn* (New York: Liverright).

Lopez, Robert Sabatino (1951), The dollar of the Middle Ages, *Journal of Economic History,* vol. 21, pp. 209–34.

Lopez, Robert Sabatino (1956), Back to gold, 1252, *Economic History Review,* 2d ser., vol. 2, pp. 219–40.

Lopez, Robert Sabatino (1979), The dawn of medieval banking, in Center for Medieval and Renaissance Studies, *The Dawn of Modern Banking*, pp. 1–24.

Lüthy, Herbert (Vol. 1, 1959; Vol. 2, 1961), *La Banque protestante en France de la révocation de l'édit de Nantes à la révolution,* Vol. 1: *Dispersion et regroupement (1685–1730);* Vol. 2: *De la banque aux finances (1730–1794)* (Paris: SEVPEN).

Luzzatto, Gino (1934), Les banques publiques de Venise, siècles XVI–XVIII, in J. G. van Dillen (ed.), *History of the Principal Public Banks,* pp. 39–78.

Luzzatto, Gino (1957 [1969]), The Italian economy in the first decade after unification, in F. Crouzet, W. H. Chaloner and W. M. Stern (eds.), *Essays in European Economic History,* pp. 203–25.

Luzzatto, Gino (1963), *L'economia italiana dal 1861 al 1914,* Vol. 1: *1861–1894* (Milan: Banca Commerciale Italiana).

Macaulay, Thomas Babington (1849–51) (1906), *The History of England from the Accession of James the Second,* 5 vols. (London: Dent).

McClam, Warren D. (1982), Financial fragility and instability: monetary authorities as borrowers and lenders of last resort, in Charles P. Kindleberger and Jean-Pierre Laffargue (eds.), *Financial Crises,* pp. 256–91.

McCloskey, Donald N. (1976), Does the past have useful economics? *Journal of Economic Literature,* vol. 14, pp. 434–61.

McCloskey, Donald N., and Zecher, J. Richard (1976), How the gold standard worked, 1880–1913, in J. A. Frenkel and H. G. Johnson (eds.), *The Monetary Approach to the Balance of Payments,* pp. 357–85.

McCusker, J. J. (1978), *Money and Exchange in Europe and America, 1600–1775, a Handbook* (Chapel Hill, N.C.: University of North Carolina Press).

MacGregor, David H. (1929), Joint stock companies and the risk factors, *Economic Journal,* vol. 39, pp. 491–505.

McGuire, Constantine E. (1926), *Italy's International Economic Position* (New York: Macmillan).

Machlup, Fritz (1950 [1964]), Three concepts of so-called dollar shortage, in Fritz Machlup, *International Payments, Debts and Gold,* pp. 110–35.

Machlup, Fritz (1964*a), International Payments, Debts and Gold* (New York: Scribner's).

Machlup, Fritz (1964*b),* The transfer problem: theme and four variations, in Fritz Machlup, *International Payments, Debts and Gold,* pp. 374–95.

Machlup, Fritz (1977), *A History of Thought on Economic Integration* (London: Macmillan).

Machlup, Fritz (1980), My early work in international monetary problems, in Banca Nazionale del Lavoro, *Quarterly Review,* no. 133, pp. 113–46.

McKay, John P. (1976), *Tramways and Trolleys: The Rise of Urban Mass Transport in Europe* (Princeton, N.J.: Princeton University Press).

McKinnon, Ronald I. (1963), Optimum currency areas, *American Economic Review,* vol. 53, pp. 717–25.

McKinnon, Ronald I. (1973), *Money and Capital in Economic Development* (Washington, D.C.: Brookings Institution).

Macmillan Committee, *see* Committee on Finance and Industry.

McNeill, William C. (1986), *American Money and the Weimar Republic: Economics and Politics on the Eve of the Great Depression* (New York: Columbia University Press).

Maier, Charles S. (1975), *Recasting Bourgeois Europe: Stabilization in France, Germany and Italy in the Decade after World War I* (Princeton, N.J.: Princeton University Press).

Maier, Charles S. (1981), The two postwar eras and the conditions for stability in twentieth-century Europe, *American Historical Review,* vol. 86, pp. 327–52.

Maier, Charles and Günter Bischof (eds.) (1991), *The Marshall Plan and Germany* (New York: Berg).

Malamud, Bernard (1980), John H. Williams on the German inflation: the international amplification of monetary disturbances, paper delivered at 8th Brooklyn College Conference on Society in Change (10–12 March), mimeo.

Mantoux, Etienne (1952), *The Carthaginian Peace, or the Economic Consequences of Mr. Keynes* (New York: Scribner's).

Marion, Marcel (1926), *Ce qu'il faut connaître des crises financières de nôtre histoire* (Paris: Boivin).

Marjolin, Robert (1941), *Prix, monnaie et production, essai sur les mouvements de longue durée* (Paris: Presses Universitaires de France/Alcan).

Marjolin, Robert (1981), *Europe in Search of Its Identity* (New York: Council of Foreign Relations).

Marlowe, John [pseudonym] (1974), *Spoiling the Egyptians* (London: Deutsch).

Marshall, Alfred (1924), *Money, Credit and Commerce* (London: Macmillan).

Marshall, P. J. (1976), *East Indian Fortunes: The British in Bengal in the Eighteenth Century* (Oxford: Clarendon Press).

Martin, D. A. (1977), The impact of mid-nineteenth century gold depreciation upon western monetary standards, *Journal of European Economic History,* vol. 6, pp. 641–58.

März, Eduard (1968), *Österreichische Industrie-und Bankpolitik in der Zeit Franz Josephs I, am Beispiel der k. k. priv. Österreichischen Creditanstalt für Handel und Gewerbe* (Vienna: Europa Verlag).

März, Eduard (1982), Comment on D. C. Moggridge, "Policy in the crises of 1920 and 1929," in Charles P. Kindleberger and Jean-Pierre Laffargue (eds.), *Financial Crises,* pp. 187–94.

Mathias, Peter (1979), *The Transformation of England: Essays in the Economic and Social History of England in the Eighteenth Century* (New York: Columbia University Press).

Mathias, Peter, and Postan, M. M. (eds.) (1978), *The Cambridge Economic History of Europe,* Vol. 7: *The Industrial Economies: Capital, Labour and Enterprise* (Cambridge: Cambridge University Press).

Matthews, P. W., and Tuke, Anthony W. (1926), *History of Barclay's Bank, Ltd.* (London: Blades, East & Blades).

Matthews, R.C.O. (1954), *A Study in Trade-Cycle History: Economic Fluctuations in Great Britain, 1832–1842* (Cambridge: Cambridge University Press).

Matthews, R.C.O., Feinstein, C. H., and Odling-Smee, J. C. (1982), *British Economic Growth, 1856–1973* (Oxford: Clarendon).

Maynard, Geoffry (1962), *Economic Development and the Price Level* (London: Macmillan).

Meade, James E., *see* League of Nations.

Melis, F. (1975), *Origini et sviluppi della assicurazioni in Italia* (Rome: Istituto Nazionale delle Assicurazioni).

Meltzer, Allan H. (1976), Monetary and other explanations of the start of the Great Depression, *Journal of Monetary Economics,* vol. 2, pp. 455–72.

Meltzer, Allan H. (1981), Comments on "Monetarist interpretations of the Great Depression," in Karl Brunner (ed.), *The Great Depression Revisited,* pp. 148–64.

Mendès-France, Pierre (1985), *Oeuvres,* vol. 2 (Paris: Gallimard).

Menias, G.P. (1969), *Napoléon et l'argent* (Paris: Les Editions de l'Epargne).

Metzler, Lloyd A. (1946 [1979]), Recent experience with monetary and financial reform, app. O to the Colm-Dodge Goldsmith Plan of 10 June 1946, in *Zeitschrift für die gesamte Staatswissenschaft,* vol. 135, pp. 365–71.

Metzler, Lloyd A. (1947 [1978]), Exchange rates and the International Monetary Fund, in Lloyd A. Metzler, Robert Triffin, and Gottfried Haberler, *International Monetary Policies,* pp. 1–45.

Metzler, Lloyd A., Triffin, Robert, and Haberler, Gottfried (1978), *International Monetary Policies* (reprinted New York: Arno Press).

Meuvret, Jean (1947 [1970]), Monetary circulation of the sixteenth and seventeenth centuries in Rondo Cameron (ed.), *Essays in French Economic History,* pp. 140–49.

Meyer, Richard H. (1970), *Banker's Diplomacy: Monetary Stabilization in the Twenties* (New York: Columbia University Press).

Michalet, Charles-Albert (1968), *Les Placements des épargnants français de 1815 à nos jours* (Paris: Presses Universitaires de France).

Michie, Ranald G. (1990), The stock exchange and the British economy, 1870–1939, in J. J. van Helten and Y. Cassis (eds.), *Capitalism in a Mature Economy,* pp. 95–114.

Migone, Gian Giacomo (1980), *Gli Stati Uniti e il fascismo: alle origini dell'egemonia americana in Italia* (Milan: Feltrinelli).

Milward, Alan S. (1971), *The New Order and the French Economy* (Oxford: Clarendon Press).

Milward, Alan S. (1977), *War, Economy and Society, 1939–1945* (Berkeley, Calif.: University of California Press).

Milward, Alan S. (1981), The Reichsmark bloc and the international economy, in Gerhard Hirschfeld and Lothar Kettennacker (eds.), *Der "Führerstaat,"* pp. 377–411.

Milward, Alan S. (1984), *The Reconstruction of Western Europe, 1945–51* (London: Methuen).

Milza, Pierre (1977), Les Relations financières franco-italiennes au début du XXe siècle, in Maurice Lévy-Leboyer (ed.), *La Position internationale de la France,* pp. 243–50.

Ministère des Finances (1902), *Bulletin de statistique et de legislation comparée.*

Ministère des Finances et Ministère de l'Agriculture, du Commerce et des Travaux Publics (1867), *Enquête sur les principes et les faits généraux qui régissent la circulation monétaire et fiduciaire,* 6 vols. (Paris: Imprimérie Impériale).

Minsky, Hyman P. (1982), The financial instability hypothesis: capitalist processes and the behaviour of the economy, in Charles P. Kindleberger and Jean-Pierre Laffargue (eds.), *Financial Crises*, pp. 13–47.

Mintz, Ilse (1951), *Deterioration in the Quality of Foreign Bonds Issued in the United States, 1920–1930* (New York: National Bureau of Economic Research).

Mitchell, Wesley C. (1944 [1953]), The role of money in economic history, in F. C. Lane and J. C. Riersma (eds.), *Enterprise and Secular Change*, pp. 199–205.

Modigliani, F., and Miller, M. H. (1958), The cost of capital, corporation finance and the theory of investment, *American Economic Review*, vol. 48, pp. 162–97.

Moggridge, D. E. (1969), *The Return to Gold, 1925: The Formulation of the Policy and Its Critics* (Cambridge: Cambridge University Press).

Moggridge, D. E. (1972), *British Monetary Policy, 1924–1931: The Norman Conquest of $4.68* (Cambridge: Cambridge University Press).

Moggridge, D. E. (1982), Policy in the crises of 1920 and 1929, in Charles P. Kindleberger and Jean-Pierre Laffargue (eds.), *Financial Crises*, pp. 171–87.

Mokyr, Joel (1977), *Industrialization in the Low Countries, 1795–1850* (New Haven, Conn.: Yale University Press).

Möller, Hans (1976), Die westdeutsche Währungsreform von 1948, in Deutsche Bundesbank (ed.), *Währung und Wirtschaft in Deutschland*, pp. 433–83.

Mollien, François Nicholas (1845), *Mémoires d'un ministre du Trésor Public, 1780–1815*, vols. 1–4 (Paris: Fournier).

Montgomery, Arthur G. (1939), *The Rise of Modern Industry in Sweden* (London: P. S. King).

Moon, Parker T. (1927), *Imperialism and World Politics* (New York: Macmillan).

Moreau, Emile (1954 [1991]), *The Golden Franc: Memoirs of a Governor of the Bank of France: The Stabilization of the Franc (1926–1928)*, translated by Stephen D. Stoller and Trevor C. Roberts (Boulder, Colo.: Westview).

Morgan, E. Victor (1943), *The Theory and Practice of Central Banking, 1797–1913* (Cambridge: Cambridge University Press).

Morgan, E. Victor (1952), *Studies in British Financial Policy, 1914–1925* (London: Macmillan).

Morgenstern, Oskar (1959), *International Financial Transactions and Business Cycles* (Princeton, N.J.: Princeton University Press).

Morris, R. J. (1979), The middle class and the property cycle during the Industrial Revolution, in T. C. Smout (ed.), *The Search for Wealth and Stability*, pp. 91–113.

Morrison, Rodney K. (1967), Financial intermediaries and economic development: the Belgian case, *Scandinavian Economic History Review*, vol. 15, pp. 56–70.

Morton, Walter A. (1943 [1979]), *British Finance, 1930–1940* (reprinted New York: Arno Press).

Moss, David J. (1981), The Bank of England and the country banks: Birmingham, 1927–33, *Economic History Review*, vol. 34, pp. 540–53.

Motteck, Hans (ed.) (1960), *Studien zur Geschichte der industriellen Revolution in Deutschland* (Berlin: Akademie Verlag).

Moulton, Harold G., and Pasvolsky, Leo (1932), *War Debts and World Prosperity* (Washington, D.C.: Brookings Institution).

Mouré, Kenneth (1991), *Managing the Franc Poincaré: Economic Understanding and Political Constraint in French Monetary Policy, 1928–1935* (Cambridge: Cambridge University Press).

Mun, Thomas (1664 [1965]), *England's Treasure by Forraign Trade, or the Balance of Trade is the Rule of Our Treasure* (reprinted New York: A. M. Kelley).

Mundell, Robert A. (1961), A theory of optimum currency areas, *American Economic Review*, vol. 51, pp. 637–65.

Mundell, Robert A. (1969), The crisis problem, in Robert A. Mundell and A. K. Swoboda (eds.), *Monetary Problems of the International Economy*, pp. 343–49.

Mundell, Robert A. (1989), The global adjustment system, in *Rivista di Politica Economica*, Year 79, 3d ser., no. 12 (December), pp. 351–464.

Mundell, Robert A., and Swoboda, A. K. (eds.) (1969), *Monetary Problems of the International Economy* (Chicago: University of Chicago Press).

Murphy, Antonin E. (1983), Richard Cantillon—an Irish banker in Paris, in Murphy (ed.), *Economists and the Irish Economy* (Dublin: Irish Academic Press), pp. 45–74.

Myrdal, Gunnar (1956), *An International Economy: Problems and Prospects* (New York: Harpers).

Nau, Henry R. (1990), *The Myth of America's Decline: Leading the World Economy into the 1990s* (New York: Oxford University Press).

Neal, Larry (1979), The economics and finance of bilateral clearing agreements: Germany, 1934–38, *Economic History Review*, n.s., vol. 32, pp. 391–404.

[Necker, Jacques] (1781), *State of the Finances of France Laid before the King by Mr Necker, Director-General of the Finances, in the Month of January, 1781* (London: G. Kearsley et al.).

Nef, John U. (1945), *Industry and Government in France and England, 1540–1640* (Philadelphia, Pa.: American Philosophical Society).

Nelson, Benjamin (1949), *The Idea of Usury: From Tribal Brotherhood to Universal Otherhood* (Princeton, N.J.: Princeton University Press).

Néré, J. (1968), *La Crise de 1929* (Paris: Colin).

Neuberger, Hugh, and Stokes, Houston H. (1974), German banks and German growth: an empirical view, *Journal of Economic History*, vol. 34, pp. 710–31.

Neuberger, Hugh, and Stokes, Houston H. (1976), German banks and German growth: a reply to Fremdling and Tilly, *Journal of Economic History*, vol. 36, pp. 425–27.

Neuberger, Hugh, and Stokes, Houston H. (1978), German banks and German growth: reply to Komlos, *Journal of Economic History*, vol. 38, pp. 480–83.

Nevin, Edward (1955), *The Mechanism of Cheap Money: A Study of British Monetary Policy, 1931–1939* (Cardiff: University of Wales Press).

The New York Times, various issues.

Niehans, Jürg (1977), Benefits of multi-national firms for a small parent economy: the case of Switzerland, in Tamir Agmon and Charles P. Kindleberger (eds.), *Multinationals from Small Countries*, pp. 1–39.

Nishimura, Shizuya (1971), *The Decline of Inland Bills of Exchange in the London Money Market, 1855–1913* (Cambridge: Cambridge University Press).

Nogaro, Bertrand (1948), Hungary's recent monetary crisis and its theoretical meaning, *American Economic Review, vol. 38, pp. 526–42.*

North, Douglass C., and Thomas, Robert Paul (1973), *The Rise of the Western World: A New Economic History* (Cambridge: Cambridge University Press).

North, Michael (1990), *Geldumlauf und Wirtschaftskonjunktur im südlichen Ostseeraum an der Wende zur Neuzeit (1440–1570)* (Sigmaringen: Jan Thorbecke Verlag).

Novak, Maximilian E. (1962), *Economics and the Fiction of Daniel Defoe* (Berkeley, Calif.: University of California Press).

Nurkse, Ragnar, *see* League of Nations.

Nye, Joseph S., Jr. (1990), *Bound to Lead: The Changing Nature of American Power* (New York: Basic Books).

O'Brien, D. P. (ed.) (1971), *The Correspondence of Lord Overstone*, vol. 1–3 (Cambridge: Cambridge University Press). Original dates are cited in the text.

O'Brien, Patrick K., and Keyder, Caglar (1978), *Economic Growth in Britain and France, 1780–1914: Two Paths to the 20th Century* (London: Allen & Unwin).

Office of the United States Chief of Counsel for the Prosecution of Axis Criminality (1914 [1946]), *Nazi Conspiracy and Aggression* (Washington, D.C.: United States Government Printing Office), vols. 1–8.

Officer, Lawrence H. (1976), The purchasing-power-parity theory of exchange rates: a review article, *IMF Staff Papers*, vol. 23, pp. 1–60.

Ohlin, Bertil (1929 [1947]), The reparation problem: a discussion, in American Economic Association, *Readings in the Theory of International Trade*, pp. 170–78.

Olson, Mancur, Jr. (1965), *The Logic of Collective Action* (Cambridge, Mass.: Harvard University Press).

Olson, Mancur, Jr. (1979), The political economy of comparative growth rates, in James Gapinski and Charles Rockwood (eds.), *Essays in Post-Keynesian Inflation*, pp. 137–59.

Olson, Mancur (1987), Some observations about the Weimar Republic and possible parallels to the developed democracies today, in Peter Koslowski (ed.), *Individual Liberty and Democratic Decision-Making* (Tübingen: J.C.B. Mohr [Paul Siebeck]).

Organization for Economic Cooperation and Development (OECD), Committee for Invisible Transactions (1967), *Capital Markets Study*, 7 vols. (Paris: OECD).

Origo, Iris (1957), *The Merchant of Prato: Francesco di Marco Datini* (New York: Knopf).

Ortega y Gasset (1930 [1932]), *The Revolt of the Masses* (New York: W. W. Norton).

Outhwaite, R. B. (1969), *Inflation in Tudor and Early Stuart England* (London: Macmillan).

Overstone, Lord, *see* O'Brien, D. P. (ed.).

Pares, Richard (1950 [1968]), *A West-India Fortune* (reprinted New York: Archon Books).

Pareto, Vilfredo (1895 [1965]), *Le Marché financier italien, 1891–1899* (annual articles, reprinted Geneva: Droz).

Parker, Geoffrey (1972), *The Army of Flanders and the Spanish Road, 1567–1659: The Logistics of Victory and Defeat in the Low Countries' Wars* (Cambridge: Cambridge University Press).

Pedersen, Jørgen (1961 [1975]), Some notes on the economic policy of the United States during the period 1919–1932, in Jørgen Pedersen, *Essays in Monetary Theory and Related Subjects,* pp. 188–210.

Pedersen, Jørgen (1975), *Essays in Monetary Theory and Related Subjects* (Copenhagen: Samfundsvidenskabeligt Forlag).

Pedersen, Jørgen, and Laursen, K. (1964), *German Inflation, 1918–1923* (Amsterdam: North-Holland).

Penrose, E. F. (1953), *Economic Planning for Peace* (Princeton, N.J.: Princeton University Press).

Pentzlin, Heinz (1980), *Hjalmar Schacht: Leben und Wirken einer umstrittenen Persönlichkeit* (Berlin: Ullstein).

Perkins, Edwin J. (1975), *Financing Anglo-American Trade: The House of Brown, 1800–1880* (Cambridge, Mass.: Harvard University Press).

Perrot, Marguerite (1955), *La Monnaie et l'opinion publique en France et en Angleterre, 1924–36* (Paris: Colin).

Pessen, Edward (1980), Wealth in America before 1865, in W. D. Rubenstein (ed.), *Wealth and the Wealthy in the Modern World,* pp. 167–88.

Pfleiderer, Otto (1979), Two types of inflation, two types of currency reform: the German currency miracles of 1923 and 1948, *Zeitschrift für die gesamte Staatswissenschaft,* vol. 135, pp. 352–64.

Philips, C. H. (1940 [1961]), *The East India Company, 1784–1834* (Manchester: Manchester University Press).

Phillippe, Raymond (1931), *Le Drâme financier de 1924–1928* (Paris: Gallimard).

Pigou, A. C. (1948), *Aspects of British Economic History, 1918–25* (London: Macmillan).

Pike, Ruth (1972), *Aristocrats and Traders: Sevillian Society in the Sixteenth Century* (Ithaca: Cornell University Press).

Pinner, Felix (1937), *Die grossen Weltkrisen, im Lichte des Strukturwandels der kapitalistischen Wirtschaft* (Zurich: Max Neihans Verlag).

Pitts, Jesse R. (1963), Continuity and change in bourgeois France, in Stanley Hoffmann et al., *In Search of France,* pp. 235–404.

Platt, D.C.M. (1984), *Foreign Finance in Continental Europe and the USA, 1815–1870: Quantities, Origins, Functions and Distribution* (London: Allen & Unwin).

Plessis, Alain (1982), *La Banque de France et ses deux cents actionnaires sous le Second Empire* (Geneva: Droz).

Plessis, Alain (1985a), *Les Régents et gouveneurs de la Banque de France sous le Second Empire* (Geneva: Droz).

Plessis, Alain (1985b), *La Politique de la Banque de France de 1851 à 1870* (Geneva: Droz).

Pohl, Manfred (1986), *Hamburger Bankengeschichte* (Mainz: v. Hase & Koehler Verlag).

Poidevin, R. (1977), Placements et investissements français en Allemagne, 1898–1914, in Maurice Lévy-Leboyer (ed.), *La Position internationale de la France,* pp. 217–36.

Pollard, Sidney (1964), Fixed capital in the industrial revolution in Britain, *Journal of Economic History,* vol. 24, pp. 299–314.

Pollard, Sidney (1965), *The Genesis of Modern Management: A Study in the Industrial Revolution* (Cambridge, Mass.: Harvard University Press).

Pollard, Sidney (1974), *European Economic Integration, 1815–1970* (New York: Harcourt Brace Jovanovich).

Porteous, J. Douglas (1977), *Canal Ports: The Urban Achievement of the Canal Age* (New York: Academic Press).

Pose, Alfred (1942), *La Monnaie et ses institutions* (Paris: Presses Universitaires de France).

Postan, M. M. (1973), *Medieval Trade and Finance* (Cambridge: Cambridge University Press). Original dates of essays in this collection are cited in the text.

Posthuma, S. (1963), The international monetary system, in Banca Nazionale del Lavoro, *Quarterly Review,* vol. 66, pp. 239–61.

Posthumus, N. W. (1928 [1969]), The tulip mania in Holland in the years 1636 and 1637, in Warren C. Scoville and J. Clayburn LaForce (eds.), *The Economic Development of Western Europe,* vol. 2, pp. 139–49.

Powell, Ellis T. (1915 [1966]), *The Evolution of the Money Market (1385–1915): An Historical and Analytical Study of the Rise and Development of Finance as a Central, Coordinated Force* (reprinted New York: A. M. Kelley).

Pressburger, Fritz Georg (1969), Die Krise der Osterreischen Creditanstalt, *Revenue internationale de l'histoire de la banque,* vol. 2, pp. 83–118.

Pressnell, L. S. (1956), *Country Banking in the Industrial Revolution* (Oxford: Clarendon Press).

Pressnell, L. S. (1960*a*), The rate of interest in the eighteenth century, in L. S. Pressnell (ed.), *Studies in the Industrial Revolution Presented to T. S. Ashton*, pp. 178–214.

Pressnell, L. S. (ed.) (1960*b*), *Studies in the Industrial Revolution Presented to T. S. Ashton* (London: Athlone Press).

Pressnell, L. S. (1978), 1925: the burden of sterling, *Economic History Review*, 2d ser., vol. 31, pp. 67–88.

Prestwich, Michael (1979), Italian merchants in late thirteenth and early fourteenth century England, in Center for Medieval and Renaissance Studies, *The Dawn of Modern Banking*, pp. 77–104.

Prochnow, Herbert V. (ed.) (1970), *The Eurodollar Market* (Chicago, Ill.: Rand McNally).

Radcliffe Committee, *see* Committee on the Working of the Monetary System.

Radford, R. A. (1945), The economic organization of a prisoner of war camp, *Economica*, vol. 12, pp. 189–201.

Ramon, Gabriel (1929), *Histoire de la Banque de France d'après les sources originales* (Paris: Grasset).

Rappard, William E. (1914), *La Révolution industrielle et les origines de la protection légale du travail en Suisse* (Berne: Stämfli).

Redlich, Fritz (1948), Jacques Laffitte and the beginnings of investment banking in France, *Bulletin of the Business Historical Society*, vol. 22, pp. 137–60.

Redlich, Fritz (1967), Two nineteenth-century financiers and autobiographers: a comparative study in creative destruction and business failure, *Economy and History*, vol. 10, pp. 37–126

Reed, M. C. (ed.) (1969), *Railways in the Victorian Economy: Studies in Finance and Economic Growth* (Newton Abbot: David & Charles).

Reed, M. C. (ed.) (1975), *Investment in Railways in Britain: A Study in the Development of the Capital Market* (London: Oxford University Press).

Reid, M. (1982), *The Secondary Banking Crisis of 1973–5* (London: Macmillan).

Report of the Second Committee of Experts, see Dawes Plan.

Richardo, David (1817 [1933]), *The Principles of Political Economy and Taxation*, Everyman's Library (London: Dent).

Rich, E. E., and Wilson, C. H. (1977), *The Cambridge History of Europe*, Vol. 5: *The Economic Organization of Early Modern Europe* (Cambridge: Cambridge University Press).

Richards, J. F. (1983), Outflows of precious metals from early Islamic India, in Richards, (ed.), *Precious Metals in the Later Medieval and Early Modern Worlds* (Durham, N.C.: Carolina Academic Press).

Richards, R. D. (1934), The first fifty years of the Bank of England, 1694–1744, in J. G. van Dillen (ed.), *History of the Principal Public Banks*, pp. 201–72.

Richards, R. D. (1965), *The Early History of Banking in England* (London: Frank Cass).

Richter, Rudolph (ed.) (1979), Currency and economic reform: West Germany after World War II, *Zeitschrift für die gesamte Staatswissenschaft*, vol. 135.

Rieke, Wolfgang (1989), Panel discussion: The prospects for a European central bank, in Marcello de Cecco and Alberto Giovanni (eds.), *A European Central Bank*, pp. 343–47.

Riesser, Jacob (1911), *The Great German Banks and Their Concentration, in Connection with the Economic Development of Germany*, translation of 3d ed., completely revised and enlarged (Washington, D. C.: United States Government Printing Office for the National Monetary Commission).

Riley, James C. (1980), *International Government Finance and the Amsterdam Capital Market, 1740–1815* (Cambridge: Cambridge University Press).

Robbins, Lionel C. (1939), *The Economic Causes of War* (London: J. Case).

Robert-Coutelle, Emile (n.d., but after 1876), *Le Crédit Foncier de France devant les chambres* (Paris: Amyot).

Rolfe, Sidney E., and Burtle, James L. (1973), *The Great Wheel: The World Monetary System* (New York: Quadrangle Books).

Roover, Raymond de (1942 [1953]), The commercial revolution of the thirteenth century, in F. C. Lane and J. C. Riersma (eds.), *Enterprise and Secular Change*, pp. 80–85.

Roover, Raymond de (1949), *Gresham on Foreign Exchange: An Essay on Early English Mercantilism* (Cambridge, Mass.: Harvard University Press).

Roover, Raymond de (1966), *The Rise and Fall of the Medici Bank, 1397–1494* (New York: Norton).

Rosa, Luigi de (1968), *Iniziative e capitale straniero nell' industria metalmeccanica del Mezzogiorno, 1840–1940* (Naples: Giannini).

Rosa, Luigi de (1980), *Capitali et banche (1896–1906)* (Naples: Edicione del Banco di Napoli).

Rosenbaum, Eduard (1962), *M. M. Warburg & Co., Merchant Bankers of Hamburg: A Survey of the First 140 Years, 1798–1938,* reprinted from *Yearbook VII* (London: Leo Baeck Institute).

Rosenbaum, Eduard, and Sherman, A. J. (1976 [1979]), *M. M. Warburg & Co., 1798–1938, Merchant Bankers of Hamburg* (New York: Holmes & Meier).

Rosenberg, Hans (1934), *Die Weltwirtschaftskrise von 1857–1859* (Stuttgart/Berlin: Verlag von W. Kohlhammer).

Ross, Duncan M. (1990), The clearing banks and industry—new perspectives on the interwar years, in J. J. van Helten and Y. Cassis (eds.), *Capitalism in a Mature Economy,* pp. 52–60.

Rostow, W. W. (1948), *British Economy of the Nineteenth Century* (London: Oxford University Press).

Rostow, W. W. (1960), *The Stages of Economic Growth* (Cambridge: Cambridge University Press).

Rostow, W. W. (1978), *The World Economy: Theory and Prospect* (London: Macmillan).

Rostow, W. W. (1980), *Why the Poor Get Richer and the Rich Slow Down: Essays in the Marshallian Long Period* (Austin, Tex.: University of Texas Press).

Rubenstein, W. D. (1977), Wealth, elites and the class structure of modern Britain, *Past and Present,* no. 76, pp. 99–126.

Rubenstein, W. D. (ed.) (1980), *Wealth and the Wealthy in the Modern World* (New York: St. Martin's Press).

Rubenstein, W. D. (1981), *Men of Property: The Very Wealthy in Britain Since the Industrial Revolution* (London: Croom Helm).

Rudé, George (1971), *Hanoverian London, 1714–1808* (Berkeley, Calif.: University of California Press).

Rudolph, Richard L. (1976), *Banking and Industrialization in Austria-Hungary: The Role of Banks in the Industrialization of the Czech Crown Lands* (Cambridge: Cambridge University Press).

Rueff, Jacques (1959 [1991]), Introduction to Emile Moreau, *The Golden Franc,* pp. 1–10.

Rueff, Jacques, and Hirsch, Fred (1965), The role and rule of gold: an argument, *Princeton Essays in International Finance,* no. 47 (Princeton, N.J.: Princeton University Press).

Rundell, W., Jr. (1964), *Black Market Money* (Baton Rouge, La.: Louisiana University Press).

Rupieper, Hermann J. (1979), *The Cuno Government and Reparations, 1922–23: Politics and Economics* (The Hague: Martinus Nijhoff).

Salin, Pascal (1980), *European Monetary Unity: For Whose Benefit?* (Ipswich, Mass.: Ipswich Press).

Salter, Sir Arthur (1967), *Slave of the Lamp* (London: Weidenfeld & Nicolson).

Samuelsson, Kurt (1955), International payments and credit movements by Swedish merchant-houses, 1730–1815, *Scandinavian Economic History Review,* vol. 3, pp. 163–202.

Samuelsson, Kurt (1968), *From Great Power to Welfare State: 300 Years of Swedish Social Development* (London: Allen & Unwin).

Sandberg, Lars G. (1978), Banking and economic growth in Sweden before World War II, *Journal of Economic History,* vol. 38, pp. 650–80.

Sandberg, Lars G. (1979), The case of the impoverished sophisticate: human capital and Swedish economic growth before World War I, *Journal of Economic History,* vol. 39, pp. 22–41.

Sanza, E. Lorenzo (1980), *Commercio de España con America en la epoca de de Felipe II,* 2 vols. (Valladolid, Spain).

Sardá Dexeus, Juan (1948), *La politica monetaria y la fluctiones de la economia española en el siglio XIX* (Madrid: Conseijo di Investigationes Cientificas).

Sargent, Thomas J., and Wallace, Neil (1973), Rational expectations and the dynamics of hyperinflation, *International Economic Review,* vol. 14, pp. 328–50.

Sauermann, Heinz (1979), On the economic and financial rehabilitation of Western Germany (1945–1949), *Zeitschrift für die gesamte Staatswissenschaft,* vol. 135, pp. 301–31.

Saul, S. B. (1969 [1972]), *The Myth of the Great Depression* (London: Macmillan).

Sauvy, Alfred (Vol. 1, 1965; Vol. 2, 1967), *Histoire économique de la France entre les deux guerres,* Vol. 1: *1918–31;* Vol. 2: *1931–1939* (Paris: Fayard).

Sayers, R. S. (1936), *Bank of England Operations, 1890–1914* (London: P. S. King).

Sayers, R. S. (1950), The springs of technical progress in Britain, 1919–1939, *Economic Journal,* vol. 60, pp. 275–91.

Sayers, R. S. (1957), *Lloyds Bank in the History of English Banking* (Oxford: Clarendon Press).

Sayers, R. S. (1968), *Gilletts in the London Money Market, 1867–1967* (Oxford: Clarendon Press).

Sayers, R. S. (1976), *The Bank of England, 1891–1944,* 3 vols (Cambridge: Cambridge University Press).

Sayers, R. S. (1978), introduction to *The Collected Works of Walter Bagehot*, ed. Norman St. John-Stevas, vol. 9, pp. 27–43.

Schacht, Hjalmar H. G. (1931), *The End of Reparations* (London: Cape).

Schacht, Hjalmar H. G. (1937), Germany's colonial demands, *Foreign Affairs*, vol. 14, pp. 223–34.

Schiemann, Jürgen (1980), *Die deutsche Währung in der Weltwirtschaftskrise 1929–1933. Währungspolitik und Abwertungskontroverse unter den Bedingungen der Reparationen* (Berne: Verlag Paul Haupt).

Schrecker, Ellen (1978), *The Hired Money: The French Debt to the United States* (New York: Arno Press).

Schubert, Auriel (1991), *The Credit-Anstalt Crisis of 1931* (Cambridge: Cambridge University Press).

Schubert, Eric S. (1988), Innovations, debts and bubbles: international integration of financial markets in Western Europe, 1680–1720, *Journal of Economic History*, vol. 58, no. 2 (June), pp. 299–306.

Schuker, Stephen A. (1976), *The End of French Predominance in Europe: The Financial Crisis of 1924 and the Adoption of the Dawes Plan* (Chapel Hill, N.C.: University of North Carolina Press).

Schuker, Stephen A. (1980), review of *The Collected Writings of John Maynard Keynes*, vols. 17 and 18, *Journal of Economic Literature* vol. 18, pp. 124–26.

Schuker, Stephen A. (1988), *American "Reparations" to Germany, 1919–33: Implications for the Third-World Debt Crisis*, Princeton Studies in International Finance, no. 61 (July) (Princeton, N.J.: International Finance Section).

Schumpeter, Joseph A. (1954), *History of Economic Analysis*, ed. from manuscript by Elizabeth Boody Schumpeter (London: Allen & Unwin).

Schwartz, Anna J. (1981), Understanding 1929–33, in Karl Brunner (ed.), *The Great Depression Revisited*, pp. 5–48.

Scott, William Robert (1911), *The Constitution and Finance of English, Scottish and Irish Joint-Stock Companies to 1720*, 3 vols. (Cambridge: Cambridge University Press).

Scoville, Warren C., and LaForce, J. Clayburn (eds.) (1969), *The Economic Development of Western Europe*, 5 vols. (Lexington, Mass.: D. C. Heath).

Sédillot, René (1953), *Le Franc: Histoire d'une monnaie des origines à nos jours* (Paris: Sirey).

Segré Report, *see* European Economic Community.

Seidenzahl, Fritz (1960 [1966]), Eine Denkschrift David Hansemanns vom Jahre 1856—Eine Beitrag zur Entstehungsgeschichte der deutschen Aktienbanken, *Tradition*, vol. 5, reprinted in Karl Erich Born (ed.), *Moderne deutsche Wirtschaftsgeschichte*, pp. 214–24.

Selgin George (1988), *The Theory of Free Banking* (Totowa, N.J.: Rowman and Littlefield).

Shannon, H. A. (1932), The first five thousand limited companies and their duration, *Economic History Review*, 2d ser., vol. 2, pp. 396–424.

Shannon, H. A. (1933 [1954]), The limited liability companies of 1866–1883, in E. M. Carus-Wilson (ed.), *Essays in Economic History*, vol. 1, pp. 380–405.

Shaw, Edward S. (1973), *Financial Deepening in Economic Development* (New York: Oxford University Press).

Shaw, William A. (1895), *The History of Currency, 1252–1894* (London: Wilson & Milne).

Shepherd, Henry L. (1936 [1978]), *The Monetary Experience of Belgium, 1914–1936* (reprinted New York: Arno Press).

Sheppard, Francis (1971), *London, 1808–1870, the Infernal Wen* (Berkeley, Calif.: University of California Press).

Sherwig, John M. (1969), *Guineas and Gunpowder: British Foreign Aid in the Wars with France, 1793–1815* (Cambridge, Mass.: Harvard University Press).

Sieveking, Heinrich (1934), Die Hamburger Bank, in J. C. van Dillen (ed.), *History of the Principal Public Banks*, pp. 125–63.

Silva, Jose-Gentil da (1969), *Banque et crédit en Italie au XVIIe siècle*, Vol. 1: *Les Foires de change et la dépréciation monétaire;* Vol. 2: *Sources et cours de changes* (Paris: Editions Klincksieck).

Simon, Maron J. (1971), *The Panama Affair* (New York: Scribner's).

Skidelsky, Robert (1967), *Politicians and the Slump: The Labour Government of 1929–1931* (London: Macmillan).

Slicher van Bath, H. H. (1960 [1963]), *An Agrarian History of Western Europe, 500–1850* (London: Arnold).

Smart, William (1911 [1964]), *Economic Annals of the Nineteenth Century*, Vol. 1: *1801–1820;* Vol. 2: *1821–1830* (reprinted New York: A. M. Kelley).

Smiles, Samuel (1865), *Lives of Bolton and Watt* (London: Murray).

Smith, Adam (1776 [1937]), *An Inquiry into the Nature and Causes of the Wealth of Nations*, ed. E. Cannan (New York: Modern Library).

Smout, T. C. (ed.) (1979), *The Search for Wealth and Stability: Essays in Economic and Social History Presented to M. W. Flinn* (London: Macmillan).

Söderlund, E. F. (1952), *Swedish Timber Exports, 1850–1950* (Uppsala: Almqvist & Wiksell).

Southard, Frank A., Jr. (1946 [1978]), *The Finances of European Liberation, with Special Reference to Italy* (reprinted New York: Arno Press).

Spielhagen, Friederich (1977), *Storm Flood* (New York: German Publications Society).

Spooner, Frank C. (1972), *The International Economy and Monetary Movements in France, 1493–1725* (Cambridge, Mass.: Harvard University Press).

Spooner, Frank C. (1983), *Risks at Sea: Amsterdam Insurance and Maritime Europe, 1766–1780* (Cambridge: Cambridge University Press).

Spring, David (1951), The English landed estate in the age of coal and iron, 1830–1880, *Journal of Economic History*, vol. 11, pp. 3–24.

Spring, David (1974), English landowners and nineteenth-century industrialization, in J. T. Ward and R. G. Wilson (eds.), *Land and Industry*, pp. 16–62.

Spring, David (ed.) (1977), *European Landed Elites in the Nineteenth Century* (Baltimore, Md: Johns Hopkins University Press).

Sraffa, Piero (1922), The bank crisis in Italy, *Economic Journal*, vol. 32, pp. 178–97.

Staley, Eugene (1935), *War and the Private Investor: A Study in the Relations of International Politics and International Private Investment* (New York: Doubleday).

Stead, Christina (1938), *House of All Nations* (New York: Knopf).

Steinherr, Alfred (1990), Financial integration, internationalization, deregulation and market integration in Europe: Why does it all happen now? in Donald E. Fair and Christian deBoissieu (eds.), *Financial Institutions in Europe*, pp. 49–64.

Stern, Fritz (1977*a*), *Gold and Iron: Bismarck, Bleichröder and the Building of the German Empire* (London: Allen & Unwin).

Stern, Fritz (1977*b*), Prussia, in David Spring (ed.)., *European Landed Elites in the Nineteenth Century*, pp. 45–67.

Stiefel, Dieter (1986), Austrian banks at the zenith of power and influence, *German Yearbook on Business History, 1985* (Berlin: Springer Verlag), pp. 79–95.

Stolper, Gustav, Hauser, Karl, and Borchardt, Knut (1964), *Deutsche Wirtschaft seit 1870* (Tübingen: J.C.B. Mohr [Paul Siebeck]).

Stolper, Wolfgang F. (1966), *Planning Without Facts: Lessons in Resource Allocation from Nigeria's Development* (Cambridge, Mass.: Harvard University Press).

Stone, Lawrence (1956), *An Elizabethan: Sir Horatio Palavicino* (Oxford: Clarendon Press).

Stone, Lawrence (1967), *The Crisis of the Aristocracy, 1558–1641*, abridged ed. (London: Oxford University Press).

Stone, Lawrence (1977), *The Family, Sex and Marriage in England, 1600–1800* (London: Weidenfeld & Nicolson).

Strange, Susan (1971), *Sterling and British Policy: A Political Study of an International Currency in Decline* (London: Oxford University Press).

Stringher, B., and Volpi, G. (1927), *The Financial Reconstruction of Italy* (New York: Italian Historical Society).

Stucken, Rudolph (1953 [1964]), *Deutsche Geld- und Kreditpolitik, 1914 bis 1963,* 3rd ed. (Tübingen: J.C.B. Mohr [Paul Siebeck]).

Sturmthal, Adolf (1943), *The Tragedy of European Labour, 1918–1939* (London: Gollancz).

Supple, Barry (1959), *Commercial Crisis and Change in England, 1600–1642: A Study in the Instability of the Mercantile Economy* (Cambridge: Cambridge University Press).

Supple, Barry (1970), *The Royal Exchange Assurance: A History of British Insurance, 1720–1970* (Cambridge: Cambridge University Press).

Sutherland, Lucy Stuart (1933), *A London Merchant, 1695–1774* (London: Oxford University Press).

Sutherland, Lucy Stuart (1952), *The East-India Company in Eighteenth-Century Politics* (Oxford: Clarendon Press).

Sylla, Richard (1980), Discussion of Michael D. Bordo and Anna J. Schwartz, "Money and prices in the nineteenth century," *Journal of Economic History*, vol. 40, pp. 70–72.

Taussig, Frank W. (1927), *International Trade* (New York: Macmillan).

Tavlas, George S. (1991), On the international use of currencies: the case of the Deutsche Mark, *Essays in International Finance*, no. 181 (March) (Princeton, N.J.: International Finance Section).

Tavlas, George S., and Ozeki, Yuzura (1992), The internationalization of currencies: An appraisal of the Japanese yen, *International Monetary Fund Occasional Paper No. 90* (January).

Tawney R. H. (1925), introduction to Thomas Wilson, *A Discourse on Usury* (1572).

Tawney, R. H. (1958), *Business and Politics Under James I: Lionel Cranfield as Merchant and Minister* (Cambridge: Cambridge University Press).

Taylor, Audrey M. (1964), *Gilletts, Bankers at Banbury and Oxford: A Study in Local Economic History* (Oxford: Clarendon Press).

Temin, Peter (1976), *Did Monetary Forces Cause the Great Depression?* (New York: Norton).

Temin, Peter (1989), *Lessons from the Great Depression* (Cambridge, Mass.: MIT Press).

Tenenbaum, J. Kipp (1980), Free to choose? a letter to the *New York Review of Books* (20 November).

Thiers, Louis Adolphe (1894), *History of the Consulate and the Empire in France under Napoleon*, 12 vols. (Philadelphia, Pa.: Lippincott).

Thiers, Louis Adolphe (1904), *Notes et souvenirs de M. Thiers, 1870–1873* (Paris: Calmann-Lévy).

Thirlwall, A. P. (ed.) (1976), *Keynes and International Monetary Relations* (London: Macmillan).

Thobie, J. (1977), Placements et investissements français dans l'empire ottoman, 1881–1914, in Maurice Lévy-Leboyer (ed.), *La Position internationale de la France*, pp. 285–95.

Thomas, Brinley (1936), *Monetary Policy and Crises: A Study of Swedish Experience* (London: Routledge).

Thomas, Brinley (1958 [1973]), *Migration and Economic Growth: A Study of Great Britain and the Atlantic Economy* (Cambridge: Cambridge University Press).

Thomas, W. A. (1973), *The Provincial Stock Exchanges* (London: Frank Cass).

Thomas, W. A. (1978), *The Finance of British Industry, 1918–1976* (London: Methuen).

Thorbecke, Erik (1960), *The Tendency Toward Regionalism in International Trade, 1928–1956* (The Hague: Martinus Nijhoff).

Thorner, Daniel (1950), *Investment in Empire: British Railway and Shipping Enterprise in India, 1825–1849* (Philadelphia, Pa.: University of Pennsylvania Press).

Thornton, Henry (1802 [1962]), *An Enquiry into the Nature and Effect of the Paper Credit of Great Britain together with the Evidence*, ed. with an introduction by F. A. Hayek (London: Frank Cass; reprint of London: Allen & Unwin, 1939).

Thornton, Henry (1811 [1962]), two speeches by Henry Thornton in app. 2 of ed. of *Paper Credit* cited above.

Tilly, Richard H. (1966), *Financial Institutions and Industrialization in the Rhineland, 1815–1870* (Madison, Wis.: University of Wisconsin Press).

Tilly, Richard H. (1967), Germany, 1815–1870, in Rondo Cameron et al., *Banking in the Early Stages of Industrialization*, pp. 151–82.

Tilly, Richard H. (1978), Capital formation in Germany in the nineteenth century, paper presented to the 7th International Economic History Congress, Edinburgh, August.

Tinbergen, Jan (1954), *International Economic Integration*, 2d revised ed. (Amsterdam: Elsevier).

Tolliday, Steven (1987), *Business, Banking and Politics: The Case of British Steel, 1918–1939* (Cambridge, Mass.: Harvard University Press).

Toniolo, Gianni (ed.) (1978), *Industrie e banca nella grande crisi 1929–1934* (Milan: Etas Libri).

Toniolo, Gianni (1980), *L'economia dell' Italia fascista* (Rome: Laterza).

Toniolo, Gianni (ed.) (1988), *Central Bank Independence in Historical Perspective* (New York: Walter deGruyter).

Toniolo, Gianni (1989), Discussion of Valeria Sannucci, The establishment of a central bank: Italy in the 19th century, in Marcello de Cecco and Alberto Giovanni (eds.), *A European Central Bank*, pp. 285–89.

Tooke, Thomas, and Newmarch, William (1838 [1928]), *A History of Prices and of the State of Circulation from 1792 to 1856*, 6 vols. reproduced from the original with an introduction by T. E. Gregory (New York: Adelphi).

Tortella, Gabriel (1969), Banking and industry in Spain, 1829–74, *Journal of Economic History*, vol. 29, pp. 163–66.

Tortella, Gabriel (1972), Spain, 1829–1874, in Rondo Cameron (ed.), *Banking and Economic Development*, pp. 91–121.

Triffin, Robert (1957), *Europe and the Money Muddle* (New Haven, Conn.: Yale University Press).

Triffin, Robert (1958), *Gold and the Dollar Crisis* (New Haven, Conn.: Yale University Press).

Truman, Harry S. (1955), *Memoirs*, Vol. 1, *Year of Decision* (New York: Doubleday).

Tuchman, Barbara W. (1978), *A Distant Mirror: The Calamitous 14th Century* (New York: Knopf).

Udovitch, Abraham L. (1979), Bankers without banks: commerce, banking and society in the

Islamic world of the middle ages, Center for Medieval and Renaissance Studies, *The Dawn of Modern Banking,* pp. 255–74.

United States Senate (1879 [1978]), *International Monetary Conference of 1878, Proceedings and Exhibits* (reprinted New York: Arno Press).

Upton, Anthony F. (1961), *Sir Arthur Ingram: A Study of the Origins of an English Landed Family* (London: Oxford University Press).

Usher, A. P. (1943), *The Early History of Deposit Banking in Mediterranean Europe* (Cambridge, Mass.: Harvard University Press).

Vagts, Alfred (1958), M. M. Warburg & Co., Ein Bankhaus in der deutschen Weltpolitik, 1905–1933, *Vierteljahrschrift für Sozial- und Wirtschaftsgeschichte,* vol. 45, pp. 280–83.

Van der Wee, Herman (1963), *The Growth of the Antwerp Market and the European Economy (Fourteenth–Sixteenth Centuries),* 3 vols. (The Hague: Martinus Nijhoff).

Van der Wee, Herman (ed.) (1972), *The Great Depression Revisited: Essays on the Economies of the Thirties* (The Hague: Martinus Nijhoff).

Van der Wee, Herman (1977), Money, credit and banking systems, in E. E. Rich and C. H. Wilson (eds.), *The Cambridge History of Europe,* vol. 5, pp. 290–392.

Van der Wee, Herman (1978), La Dette publique au XVIIIe siècle, *Actes du 9e Colloque International, Spa,* pp. 13–21.

Van de Wee, Herman (ed.) (1991), *La banque en Occident* (Antwerp: Fonds Mercator).

Van der Wee, Herman, and Tavernier, K. (1975), *La Banque Nationale de Belgique et l'histoire monétaire entre les deux guerres mondiales* (Brussels: National Bank of Belgium).

Van Dillen, *see* Dillen, van.

Van Dormael, Armand (1978), *Bretton Woods: Birth of a Monetary System* (New York: Holmes & Meier).

Van Helten, Jean-Jacques (1990), Mining shares, manias and speculation: British investment in overseas mining, 1880–1913, in J. J. Van Helten and Y. Cassis (eds.), *Capitalism in a Mature Economy,* pp. 159–85.

Van Helten, J. J., and Cassis, Y. (eds.) (1990), *Capitalism in a Mature Economy: Financial Institutions, Capital Exports and British Industry, 1870–1939* (Aldershot: Edward Elgar).

Van Klaveren, *see* Klaveren, van.

Vaubel, Roland (1977), Free currency competition, *Weltwirtschaftliches Archiv,* vol. 113, pp. 435–59.

Vaubel, Roland (1979), A Europe-wide parallel currency, in Samuel I. Katz (ed.), *US–European Monetary Relations,* pp. 156–83.

Vergeot, J. B. (1918), *Le Crédit comme stimulant et régulateur de l'industrie: la conception saint-simonienne, ses réalizations, son application au problème bancaire d'après-guerre* (Paris: Jouve).

Vincens Vives, Jaime (1969), *An Economic History of Spain* (Princeton, N.J.: Princeton University Press).

Vilar, Pierre (1969 [1976]), *A History of Gold and Money, 1450–1920* (London: New Left Books).

Viner, Jacob (1924), *Canada's Balance of International Indebtedness, 1900–1913* (Cambridge, Mass.: Harvard University Press).

Viner, Jacob (1937), *Studies in the Theory of International Trade* (New York: Harper).

Viner, Jacob (1952), *International Economics* (Glencoe, Ill.: Free Press).

Vleck, George W. van (1943), *The Panic of 1857: An Analytical Study* (New York: Columbia University Press).

Walch, Jean (1975), *Michel Chevalier, économiste, saint-simonien, 1806–1879* (Paris: Vrin).

Wallerstein, Immanuel (1980), *The Modern World System II: Mercantilism and the Consolidation of the European World-Economy, 1600–1750* (New York: Academic Press).

Walter, Norbert (1990), Frankfurt financial centre challenged by 1992, in Donald E. Fair and Christian de Boissieu (eds.), *Financial Institutions in Europe,* pp. 145–57.

Wandel, Eckhard (1979), Historical development prior to the German currency reform of 1948, *Zeitschrift für die gesamte Staatswissenschaft,* vol. 135, pp. 320–31.

Wanniski, Jude (1977), *The Way the World Works* (New York: Basic Books).

Ward, A. W., Prothero, G. W., and Leathes, Stanley (eds.) (1906), *The Cambridge Modern History,* vol. 4 (Cambridge: Cambridge University Press).

Ward, J. R. (1974), *The Finance of Canal Building in the Eighteenth Century* (London: Oxford University Press).

Ward, J. T., and Wilson, R. G. (eds.) (1974), *Land and Industry: The Landed Estate and the Industrial Revolution* (Newton Abbot: David & Charles).

Weber, Eugen (1976), *From Peasants into Frenchmen: The Modernization of Rural France, 1870–1914* (Stanford, Calif.: Stanford University Press).

Wedgwood, C. V. (1938), *The Thirty Years War* (London: Cape).

Wehler, H. U. (ed.) (1970), *Imperialismus* (Cologne/Berlin: Kiepenheuer & Witsch).

Wendt, Bernd-Jürgen (1981), 'Südosteuropa in der nationalsozialistischen Grossraumwirtschaft: Eine Antwort an Alan S. Milward,' in Gerhard Hirschfeld and Lothar Kettennacker (eds.), *Der "Führerstaat,"* pp. 414–26.

Werner Report, *see* European Economic Community.

Whale, F. Barrett (1930 [1968]), *Joint-Stock Banking in Germany: A Study of the German Credit Banks before and after the War* (reprinted New York: A. M. Kelley).

White, Eugene N. (ed.) (1990), *Crashes and Panics: The Lessons from History* (Homewood, Ill.: Dow-Jones-Irwin).

White, Harry D. (1933), *The French International Accounts, 1880–1913* (Cambridge, Mass.: Harvard University Press).

White, Lawrence H. (1984), *Free Banking in Britain: Theory, Experience and Debate, 1800–1845* (New York: Cambridge University Press).

Wicksell, Knut (1935), *Lectures on Political Economy,* Vol. 2: *Money* (New York: Macmillan).

Wilkins, Mira (1970), *The Emergence of Multinational Enterprise* (Cambridge, Mass.: Harvard University Press).

Williams, David (1963), London and the 1931 financial crisis, *Economic History Review,* 2d ser., vol. 15, pp. 513–28.

Williams, E. N. (1970), *The Ancient Regime in Europe: Government and Society in the Major States, 1648–1879* (New York: Harper & Row).

Williams, John H. (1947 [1978]), *Postwar Monetary Plans and Other Essays* (reprinted New York: Arno Press).

Williams, John H. (1952), An economist's confessions, *American Economic Review,* vol. 42, pp. 3–28.

Williamson, Jeffry G. (1978), review of Charles P. Kindleberger, *Economic Response, Journal of Economic History,* vol. 38, pp. 788–89.

Williamson, John (1971), *Karl Helfferich, 1872–1924: Economist, Financier, Politician* (Princeton, N.J.: Princeton University Press).

Wilson, Charles (1941), *Anglo-Dutch Commerce and Finance in the Eighteenth Century* (Cambridge: Cambridge University Press).

Wilson, Charles (1949 [1953]), Treasure and trade balances: the mercantilist problem, in F. C. Lane and J. C. Riersma (eds.), *Enterprise and Secular Change,* pp. 337–49.

Wilson, Charles (1968), *The Dutch Republic and Civilization of the Seventeenth Century* (New York: McGraw-Hill).

Wilson, Charles (1976), *The Transformation of Europe, 1558–1648* (Berkeley, Calif.: University of California Press).

Wilson, Thomas (1572 [1925]), *A Discourse upon Usury,* with a historical introduction by R. H. Tawney (New York: Harcourt Brace).

Winkler, Max (1933), *Foreign Bonds, an Autopsy: A Study of Defaults and Repudiations of Government Obligations* (Philadelphia, Pa.: Roland Swain).

Wirth, Max (1858 [1890]), *Geschichte der Handelskrisen* (Frankfurt, J. D. Sauerländer's Verlag).

Wirth, Max (1893), The crisis of 1890, *Journal of Political Economy,* vol. 1, pp. 214–35.

Wiskemann, Erwin (1929), *Hamburg und die Welthandelspolitik von den Anfängen bis zur Gegenwart* (Hamburg: Friederichsen, de Gruyter).

Withers, Hartley (1933), *National Provincial Bank, 1833–1933* (London; privately printed).

Wolowski, Louis (1864), *La Question des banques* (Paris: Guillaumin).

Wolowksi, Louis (1869), *La Question monétaire,* 2d ed. (Paris: Guillaumin).

Wood, Elmer (1939), *English Theories of Central Banking Control, 1819–1858, With Some Account of Contemporary Procedure* (Cambridge, Mass.: Harvard University Press).

Wood, Gundy & Company (1979), *Financing in the Eurobond Market* (November), quoted by Michele Fratianni in The dollar and the ECU (unpublished paper, February 1980).

Woodham-Smith, Cecil (1962), *The Great Hunger* (New York: Harper & Row).

Woodruff, William (1966), *The Impact of Western Man: A Study of Europe's Role in the World Economy, 1750–1960* (London: Macmillan).

Woytinsky, W. S. (1961), *Stormy Passage: A Personal History Through Two Russian Revolutions in Democracy and Freedom, 1905 to 1960* (New York: Vanguard Press).

Wright, H.R.C. (1955), *Free Trade and Protection in the Netherlands, 1816–39. A Study of the First Benelux* (Cambridge: Cambridge University Press).

Young, Arthur (1790 [1969]), *Travels in France during the Years 1787, 1788 and 1789* (Garden City, N.Y.: Doubleday/Anchor).

Youngson, A. J. (1960), *The British Economy, 1920–1957* (London: Allen & Unwin).

Zamagni, Vera (1980), The rich in a late industrializer: the case of Italy 1800–1945, in W. D. Rubenstein (ed.), *Wealth and the Wealthy in the Modern World*, pp. 123–66.

Zola, Emile (1890, reprinted n.d.), *L'Argent* (Paris: Le Livre de Poche).

Zucker, Stanley (1975), *Ludwig Bamberger, German Liberal Politician and Social Critic, 1823–1899* (Pittsburgh, Pa.: University of Pittsburgh Press).

Index